The Editor

JOYCE E. CHAPLIN is the James Duncan Phillips Professor of Early American History at Harvard University. She has taught at five different universities on two continents and an island, and in a maritime studies program in the middle of the Atlantic Ocean. She is the author of *An Anxious Pursuit: Agricultural Innovation and Modernity in the Lower South, 1730–1815* (1993), *Subject Matter: Technology, the Body, and Science on the Anglo-American Frontier, 1500–1676* (2001), *The First Scientific American: Benjamin Franklin and the Pursuit of Genius* (2006), and *Benjamin Franklin's Political Arithmetic: A Materialist View of Humanity* (2009).

W. W. NORTON & COMPANY, INC.
Also Publishes

ENGLISH RENAISSANCE DRAMA: A NORTON ANTHOLOGY
edited by David Bevington et al.

THE NORTON ANTHOLOGY OF AFRICAN AMERICAN LITERATURE
edited by Henry Louis Gates Jr. and Nellie Y. McKay et al.

THE NORTON ANTHOLOGY OF AMERICAN LITERATURE
edited by Nina Baym et al.

THE NORTON ANTHOLOGY OF CHILDREN'S LITERATURE
edited by Jack Zipes et al.

THE NORTON ANTHOLOGY OF DRAMA
edited by J. Ellen Gainor, Stanton B. Garner Jr., and Martin Puchner

THE NORTON ANTHOLOGY OF ENGLISH LITERATURE
edited by M. H. Abrams and Stephen Greenblatt et al.

THE NORTON ANTHOLOGY OF LITERATURE BY WOMEN
edited by Sandra M. Gilbert and Susan Gubar

THE NORTON ANTHOLOGY OF MODERN AND CONTEMPORARY POETRY
edited by Jahan Ramazani, Richard Ellmann, and Robert O'Clair

THE NORTON ANTHOLOGY OF POETRY
edited by Margaret Ferguson, Mary Jo Salter, and Jon Stallworthy

THE NORTON ANTHOLOGY OF SHORT FICTION
edited by R. V. Cassill and Richard Bausch

THE NORTON ANTHOLOGY OF THEORY AND CRITICISM
edited by Vincent B. Leitch et al.

THE NORTON ANTHOLOGY OF WORLD LITERATURE
edited by Sarah Lawall et al.

THE NORTON FACSIMILE OF THE FIRST FOLIO OF SHAKESPEARE
prepared by Charlton Hinman

THE NORTON INTRODUCTION TO LITERATURE
edited by Alison Booth and Kelly J. Mays

THE NORTON READER
edited by Linda H. Peterson and John C. Brereton

THE NORTON SAMPLER
edited by Thomas Cooley

THE NORTON SHAKESPEARE, BASED ON THE OXFORD EDITION
edited by Stephen Greenblatt et al.

For a complete list of Norton Critical Editions, visit
www.wwnorton.com/college/English/nce_home.htm

A NORTON CRITICAL EDITION

BENJAMIN FRANKLIN'S
AUTOBIOGRAPHY

AN AUTHORITATIVE TEXT
CONTEXTS
CRITICISM

Edited by

Joyce E. Chaplin
HARVARD UNIVERSITY

W · W · NORTON & COMPANY · *New York* · *London*

W. W. Norton & Company has been independent since its founding in 1923, when William Warder Norton and Mary D. Herter Norton first published lectures delivered at the People's Institute, the adult education division of New York City's Cooper Union. The firm soon expanded its program beyond the Institute, publishing books by celebrated academics from America and abroad. By midcentury, the two major pillars of Norton's publishing program—trade books and college texts—were firmly established. In the 1950s, the Norton family transferred control of the company to its employees, and today—with a staff of four hundred and a comparable number of trade, college, and professional titles published each year—W. W. Norton & Company stands as the largest and oldest publishing house owned wholly by its employees.

The text of this book is composed in Fairfield Medium
with the display set in Bernhard Modern.
Composition by Westchester.
Manufacturing by Courier.
Production manager: Sean Mintus.

Library of Congress Cataloging-in-Publication Data
Franklin, Benjamin, 1706–1790.
   [Autobiography]
   Benjamin Franklin's autobiography : an authoritative text, contexts, criticism / edited by Joyce E. Chaplin.—1st ed.
       p. cm.—(A Norton critical edition)
   Includes bibliographical references and index.
   ISBN 978-0-393-93561-5 (pbk.)
   1. Franklin, Benjamin, 1706–1790.   2. Statesmen—United States—Biography.   I. Chaplin, Joyce E.   II. TItle
   E302.6.F7A2 2012
   973.3092—dc23
   [B]   2011052085

W. W. Norton & Company, Inc., 500 Fifth Avenue, New York,
NY 10110-0017
wwnorton.com
W. W. Norton & Company Ltd., Castle House, 75/76 Wells Street,
London W1T 3QT

1 2 3 4 5 6 7 8 9 0

IN MEMORIAM

J. A. Leo Lemay (1935–2008)

Paul M. Zall (1922–2009)

Contents

Criticism

Illustrations

Introduction

In the thrilling days when it first became possible for anyone to be a celebrity, Benjamin Franklin was one. He wrote his memoirs (the word *autobiography* was not used until 1797) in complete confidence that his fame would survive him. It has, not least because of the *Autobiography*, an early celebrity memoir and the only lasting best-seller written in North America before the nineteenth century. But the story of Franklin's life is not as straightforward as it might seem. The *Autobiography* was intended to be a full narrative of his life, though it was never completed—it is the world's most widely read unfinished work. Though usually regarded as a quintessentially Anglo-American text, it was first published abroad, in Paris, and in a foreign language, French. Franklin's status as a man of science was the foundation of his fame at the time, the reason there would be any audience for his memoirs, yet the memoirs barely discuss his scientific pursuits. Above all, the readers today who cherish the homespun details of Franklin's early life usually do so without comprehending his later status as a dazzling international icon, a decidedly un-homespun status that was crucial both to his portrayal of himself and to his first readers' response to his memoirs.

Composition

Franklin wrote his memoirs during a critical moment of transition in what scholars now call life-writing, the first-person exposition of a life. Specifically, he had at his disposal both Christian traditions of self-abnegation and post-Renaissance examinations of a constantly evolving persona. Yet he wrote just a bit too early to consider shaping the story of his life according to even newer ideas of a unique and authentic inner self, and we do not know whether he even thought of himself in those terms.

In the societies of western Europe, the oldest genre in the tradition of life-writing is the religious confession, the criticism of the self as a means to spiritual redemption. Many Christian saints' lives, whether autobiographical or biographical, used this classic spiritual narrative, intended to show believers the value of an exemplary life and to make them imitate it. Franklin surely knew of St. Augustine's famous *Confessions*, and possibly of Jean-Jacques Rousseau's *Confessions*, which both cited and rejected the genre. And he had heard or read many New England puritan elegies to individuals who had led exemplary Christian lives—Protestant variations on the longer tradition of spiritual confessions. In his own memoirs, Franklin's emphasis on his religious upbringing in Boston, his reflections on his own errors (or *errata*), and his "bold and arduous Project of arriving at moral Perfection" all show his indebtedness to the spiritual tradition in life-writing.[1]

In his constant references to secular literature, and in his ironic, near-comic admission of his flaws, however, Franklin took a strategic step away from the Christian genre of confession. He distanced himself from conventional piety even as he praised that quality in other people—and recommended it, in theory. He balanced these religious remnants with the secular traditions of self-improvement that had characterized life-writing since the Renaissance. The creation and presentation of a polished persona were goals of early modern conduct manuals, guides that were usually written to advise young aristocrats and monarchs-to-be who would inherit power and needed to learn how to project authority in the correct way. Niccolò Machiavelli famously subverted this mirror-for-princes genre in *The Prince* (printed in 1532), which recommended cunning and the naked use of force where more traditional conduct manuals advocated mercy and justice.[2]

The ideal of princely self-improvement trickled down to the rest of society. Soon, self-help guides were produced to assist the middle class, whose numbers were greatly increasing. The guides told people how to polish themselves, in order to resemble the ruling orders, by acquiring a battery of graceful habits and expensive consumer goods: polite table manners, proper ways of speaking in public, fashionable dancing, wide reading, the acquisition of foreign languages, and appropriate dress and house furnishings. The development of guides to good living ran parallel to a general profusion, by the fourteenth and fifteenth centuries, of first-person narratives. Indeed, while life-writing continued to be dominated by the stories of elite or exemplary persons, literate members of the artisanal classes—men, usually, though sometimes women—increasingly kept diaries or other written explanations of themselves.[3]

1. Sacvan Bercovitch, *The Puritan Origins of the American Self* (New Haven: Yale UP, 1960); Daniel B. Shea, *Spiritual Autobiography in Early America* (Princeton: Princeton UP, 1968); Ruth A. Banes, "The Exemplary Self: Autobiography in Eighteenth-Century America," *Biography* 5 (1982): 226–39.
2. Felix Gilbert, "The Humanist Concept of the Prince and the Prince of Machiavelli," *Journal of Modern History* 11 (1939): 449–83.
3. Norbert Elias, *The Civilizing Process*, trans. Edmund Jephcott (Oxford: Blackwell, 1994); Stephen J. Greenblatt, *Renaissance Self-Fashioning: From More to Shakespeare*

This project of self-fashioning crossed the Atlantic with European colonists. Franklin was not unique in his enthusiasm for the genre of self-help literature, which was imported, read, and reprinted widely throughout the British colonies. Like many of his contemporaries, including George Washington, he drafted a program of self-improvement. He went further than others by writing self-help literature for publication, both in the form of sincere recommendations ("The Way to Wealth") and as parodies ("How to Make Oneself a Disagreeable Companion"). He responded to some friends' request that he complete and publish an essay called "The Art of Virtue" with a decision instead to incorporate his moral program into his life story.[4]

Franklin wrote his memoirs in four sections at four different times during the last quarter of his life. He composed on large sheets of paper, folio sized, folded in half to form pages that measured about 10 by 15 inches, roughly the dimensions of a laptop computer. He divided each page lengthwise and composed an initial draft on one half, leaving the other side blank so he could make notes to himself to add or alter material later.

Most of the pages—200 of the 230—include alterations of some kind, either made shortly after Franklin composed the original text or when he had moved on to later events and reconsidered his original composition. The page with the densest alterations is the very first, as Franklin, an accomplished writer, struggled to craft just the right start to his story. He began with an overview of the Franklin family history. That must have seemed too removed from his true subject, himself, because he added in the margin several personal comments: his progress "from the Poverty and Obscurity in which I was born and bred, to a State of Affluence and some Degree of Reputation," his belief that he "should have no Objection to a Repetition of the same Life from its Beginning" so long as he could correct its errors, and his disarming admission that writing his memoirs would gratify his "*Vanity*." He made decisions on how to shape the story as he went. For example, all but one of his famous "errata," the major mistakes of his youth, were at first marginal additions, afterthoughts that he inserted later into the narrative flow. Those little confessions add greatly to the story, preventing it from being merely a self-congratulatory story of Franklin's rise and rise.

Franklin's reasons for writing his memoirs changed over the nearly nineteen years in which he composed them. He wrote the first of the four sections (eighty-seven manuscript pages) in the summer of

---

(Chicago: U of Chicago P, 1980); James Amelang, *The Flight of Icarus: Artisan Autobiography in Early Modern Europe* (Stanford: Stanford UP, 1998).

4. Richard L. Bushman, *The Refinement of America: Persons, Houses, Cities* (New York: Knopf, 1992), 30–99.

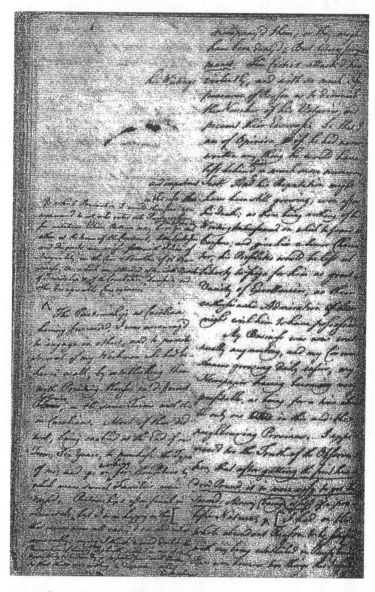

A page from the manuscript of the *Autobiography*.

1771, during a two-week visit to his friend Jonathan Shipley, Bishop of St. Asaph, in England. Franklin addressed this opening piece to his only surviving (and illegitimate) son, William Franklin, but by the time he wrote the next section he had broken with William, who had remained loyal to Great Britain while his father sided with the American Revolutionaries. Friends urged Franklin to continue his memoirs. When he resumed writing, he intended his life story for a wider audience, the rising generation of independent Americans. Franklin was at that point in France, and, released from his duties as American commissioner to that country in 1785—once the United States had achieved its independence from Great Britain—he was finally able to write part two of his memoirs, a total of twelve pages, including his delightful list of the thirteen virtues he tried to pursue. ("6. INDUSTRY. Lose no Time . . . 12. CHASTITY. Rarely use Venery but for Health or Offspring; Never to Dulness.") Public service distracted Franklin yet again when he returned to Philadelphia in 1785 and was swept into politics, as head of the government of Pennsylvania and as a Pennsylvania representative at the Federal Constitutional Convention in 1787.

In 1788, Franklin retired from public office for good and made time to write part three of his narrative, 119 pages. His rapidly declining health interrupted, however, and he was able to compose only a very short part four before his death in 1790. He was too weak even to grasp a pen himself, and probably dictated these final seven pages to his grandson until he was unable to continue. The narrative simply ends in the middle of 1758. Fortunately, Franklin had sketched an outline for the entire work, probably when he began writing the first part, so we have good evidence of what he had wanted to include, at least down through his departure for France in 1776.

Ambition

The *Autobiography* is only the most obvious evidence of Franklin's desire to shape and record his life in very particular ways. Born a younger son of a Boston artisan—his father made candles and bars of soap from animal fat—Franklin could not have expected to inherit any property, and always knew he would have to make his own way in the world. He had much to do to become successful, but he aimed even higher: he wanted to be famous.

At the time, the two acknowledged means to fame, for a man, were sword and pen, and Franklin seems to have considered those options in that order. In the memoirs of his youth, he is candid about his reading of Plutarch's *Lives* of the famous men of antiquity, many of whom were military leaders. His uncle, Benjamin Franklin the elder, warned him against the soldier's life, and his father nixed his plans to become a sailor, which, especially in times of war, was at least as dangerous. But his family essentially handed him a pen (and ink) when he was apprenticed to his brother, James, a printer, with whom young Benjamin inaugurated his writing career under the alias "Silence Dogood." Franklin also read the plentiful self-help and self-improvement literature of the day, including Daniel Defoe's *Essay upon Projects* (1697) and Thomas Tryon's *Way to Health* (1691).

Franklin was so confident of his future fame that, from an astonishingly early age, he maintained an archive on himself. He destroyed evidence of actions and thoughts that would not be flattering to him, as with a pamphlet he published at age twenty yet regretted later, and as with examples of his way of making decisions. He recommended this "prudential algebra" to others (see pp. 259–60), but evidently worried that it might reveal too much about himself; only one example survives. Meanwhile, Franklin saved letters and other manuscripts that documented his activities, especially his wide correspondence with friends who, over time, increased in number and prominence. Franklin had hoped to consult these documents when he began his autobiography, in order to verify certain facts and to provide quotations. When the British carried off a big trunk full of his papers during the War for Independence, Franklin lamented the difficulty of recalling the densely occurring and interconnecting events and people from his early life without those documents.

As a printer, Franklin had been trained to compose (and to publish) only writings for which he expected an audience, preferably a paying one. It is unlikely that he put aside this impulse when he began his memoirs, although he may have been sincere in his initial expectation that his son and other members of his family would be the primary audience for his reminiscences. Either way, he intended his text to help others improve themselves, as he had done. He was, by 1771, when he began his memoirs, one of the most famous American colonists of his generation, and he would be, by 1784, when he resumed writing, the most famous and instantly recognizable American of the era.

Reputation

The key to Franklin's fame was his work in natural science, especially the experiments that outlined the first convincing theory of electricity. Before he conducted those experiments, Franklin was modestly successful. Indeed, he was probably the most wealthy and prominent member of his extended family. Most of Franklin's male relatives remained artisans who worked skilled trades, though some of them were farmers, and several were tied to the sea as sailors, sea captains, and whalers.

Certainly, Franklin had come a long way since he had entered Philadelphia, in 1723, as a seventeen-year-old runaway printer's apprentice, with an "awkward ridiculous Appearance" that (he claimed) his future wife saw on that day, forgave, but never forgot. By the late 1740s, he had established himself as Philadelphia's premier printer, with a network of associates and clients throughout the mid-Atlantic colonies, in Georgia, and in parts of the Caribbean. He had also become a political figure, serving appointed positions as clerk to the Pennsylvania Assembly and postmaster of Philadelphia, and in elected office, as a member of the Philadelphia Common Council. He was able to retire in financial comfort, giving over the daily management of his printing house to his active partner, David Hall. Franklin's retirement meant that he could claim the status of gentleman, someone who owned property and did not have to work with his hands. Had that been the limit of his accomplishments—noteworthy, perhaps, but not outstanding—Franklin might have been consigned to the ranks of B-grade American provincials like Cadwallader Colden, Gouverneur Morris, and Henry Laurens, sturdy figures who were, at best, local heroes. Franklin knew it. Although widely known in the mid-Atlantic for his pieces in his newspaper, the *Pennsylvania Gazette*, and for his famous (and lucrative) almanac *Poor Richard*, he wanted a wider audience and even teased the faithful readers of *Poor Richard* that they were not enough for him.

Only after Franklin published his *Experiments and Observations on Electricity* in 1751 did his career and reputation soar. In that work, Franklin convincingly explained electricity, which had stumped earlier investigators: electrical charges did not come and go depending on how they were generated, rather, electricity always existed in the forms of negative and positive charges that, in equilibrium, constituted the material force ordinarily labeled as "electricity." As author of this theory, Franklin was quickly acknowledged as the foremost scientific experimenter of his generation, a self-educated colonial who had followed in the illustrious tradition of Robert Boyle and Isaac Newton to investigate the physical properties of nature. This gave Franklin a crucial boost and prevented his life ascent from stalling. Later in 1751, for example, he won election to the Pennsylvania Assembly; the next year, he was appointed deputy postmaster general of North America. In 1752, he also received honorary degrees from Harvard and Yale and was awarded the Copley Medal of the Royal Society of London, Britain's premier scientific organization. Subsequent honors followed, as well as political positions—colonial agent based in London, American commissioner based in

Paris—that would not have gone to a mere chandler's son and retired printer.[5]

Franklin's *Experiments and Observations on Electricity* became his first international best-seller; science gave him the large and important audience he had always wanted. That was possible because science was not yet a specialized field of interest with specialized practitioners; in fact, the word *scientist*, connoting a professional who earned a living from science, did not exist until the 1820s. Earlier, science and technology had been of broad public interest to everyone—nuns, sailors, and reigning monarchs, among others— and scientific literacy was an accomplishment expected of all genteel people. Indeed, there was no clear boundary between science and other forms of literary endeavor. Works on science and the natural world were supposed to be accessible to a general reading public, and were prized if written gracefully and with wit. Franklin's scientific prose was regarded as a model of lucid expressiveness. Within his lifetime, *Experiments and Observations* went through five editions in English and several more in foreign languages. French translations were especially important in promoting Franklin as Newton's heir; an expanded French edition of 1773 was instrumental in consolidating Franklin's reputation in Europe and in preparing the way for his diplomatic work in France during the American Revolution.

After he achieved international fame as a man of science, Franklin discovered that people found it charming that he could write also as a provincial American. To conclude his association with *Poor Richard*, Franklin wrote a kind of farewell. This was "The Speech of Father Abraham," a fictional village elder with near-encyclopedic knowledge of the many aphorisms that had appeared in Franklin's almanac over the years. The speech appeared as the preface to *Poor Richard Improved* for 1758 and was thereafter published on its own, both in English as "The Way to Wealth" and in French as *La Science du Bonhomme Richard*, as well as in other languages. It too became a best-seller, appearing in 145 editions before 1800. Coming on the heels of the *Experiments and Observations*, "The Way to Wealth" augmented Franklin's reputation as the American wonder who had rocketed to public attention in the 1750s.

Franklin might easily have become a forgotten historical figure, of specialized interest now to historians of science and scholars of American literature, but his status as an American Founder, and especially his diplomatic mission to France, consolidated and propelled his fame into a larger sphere of influence. It was widely remarked at the time that Franklin's scientific and political accom-

5. Joyce E. Chaplin, *The First Scientific American: Benjamin Franklin and the Pursuit of Genius* (New York: Perseus Books, 2006).

plishments reinforced each other, hence the famous epigram that he had snatched lightning from the sky and the scepter from the tyrant. It is useful, in this regard, to compare Franklin to George Washington: they were the two best-known American Founders, instantly recognizable to people throughout Europe and the Americas, yet they had begun at very different social levels. Only Franklin's fame as the theorist of electricity could have raised him to the level of Washington, who had been born a gentleman and had inherited property.

And it was wonderful for Franklin, who had wanted to achieve fame—to establish a reputation that would survive death—to have also become a celebrity, famous in his own lifetime. Cults of celebrity had begun at the end of the seventeenth century—Isaac Newton had enjoyed one—though they were rare. They became more common during the eighteenth century, with authors, military heroes, suddenly wealthy persons, men of science, ladies of fashion, and a great many others attracting acolytes and complete strangers who wanted to see, hear, and even touch them. Although a small cult had formed around Franklin in Britain, true celebrity engulfed him when he went to France in 1776. So abundant were the French prints and knickknacks that bore his image that he bragged to his daughter that his face was as recognizable as that of the moon. At a 1778 dinner party Franklin hosted in France to celebrate the Fourth of July, the guests stole silverware and other table items as souvenirs of the event and mementos of the great man. The celebrations of Franklin's fame made others jealous, not least a younger and resentful John Adams, one of Franklin's fellow commissioners in France.[6]

If Franklin's memoirs became, while he wrote them, a celebrity's life story, the point of the book was to reveal the author's humble beginnings, to show how the younger son of a Boston workingman had become famous on both sides of the Atlantic. It made for an excellent story, yet contemporaries understood that story very differently than we do now. In Franklin's day, everyone knew that his fame came from his electrical experiments. When he was alive, his most consequential piece of writing was his *Experiments and Observations on Electricity* and his autobiography was virtually unknown, because unpublished. The situation is reversed today, when almost no one reads the *Experiments and Observations*, and a great many read the *Autobiography*. Science was the elephant in the room then; the elephant has long since vanished. It is as if Albert Einstein were now remembered for the charming stories of his childhood and youth,

6. Fred Inglis, *A Short History of Celebrity* (Princeton: Princeton UP, 2010), 37–73; Leonard W. Labaree et al., eds., *The Papers of Benjamin Franklin*, 40 vols. to date (New Haven: Yale UP, 1959–), hereafter referred to as *Papers*, 29.613; *Papers* 30.44.

without any clear memory of what he had done to become so famous in the first place.

Franklin himself contributed to this misapprehension by barely outlining his scientific work in his memoirs. He was proud enough of his experiments to mention them in passing but, probably because he did not want to be regarded as too vain, his account is brief. The original manuscript shows that Franklin found it difficult to find the best places to discuss his scientific work. As he outlined his activities for the 1750s, for example, the years when he did his key electrical experiments, he wrote a note reminding himself to insert a discussion of electricity in between his roles as a frontier negotiator and as a founder of the Pennsylvania Hospital. But he crossed out the suggestion and decided to put the experiments later in the narrative, which has given readers ever since the misleading sense that Franklin's expanded role in Pennsylvania and colonial affairs preceded his scientific work, when in fact the reverse was true.

Publication

When Franklin died, he bequeathed the manuscript of his memoirs to the older of his two grandsons, William Temple Franklin, the illegitimate son of his estranged son William. Having taken the boy from his loyalist father, the grandfather had done his best to finish Temple's education and to launch him in life. He tried to make a good marriage for him in France and to get a good position for him in the U.S. government, neither of which worked out. The manuscript was yet another attempt to give the young man something of value which, when printed, might afford him a small income. But Franklin had asked his other grandson, Benjamin Franklin Bache, to make two copies of the first three parts of the memoirs to send to friends in England and France for their criticism and thoughts for revision. Although Temple inherited the fullest text, and the implied right to publish it, he made a strategic error by telling the French recipient of one of the two copies, Louis-Guillaume Le Veillard, of his intention to publish the memoirs along with several other of his grandfather's works.

Before Temple could do so, a French translation of the first part of his grandfather's autobiography appeared in Paris in 1791. Le Veillard denied that he had given his copy to anyone and the publisher never identified his source, who is still unknown. The publisher acknowledged that the affair was at least slightly nefarious by giving his work the title *Mémoires de la vie privée de Benjamin Franklin*. A *vie privée* or private life was, by 1791, only beginning to lose its originally scurrilous reputation as the breathless account of personal details that a famous person would not wish the public to know, or even invented details that he or she would nevertheless find it difficult to refute, rather similar to today's tabloid exposé of a celebrity. Before and during the French Revolution, many prominent individuals, including members of the royal family, had suffered the publication of many a *vie privée* that was propaganda intended to reveal the personal vice and systemic corruption of the old order. Some of these, which appeared around the time of Franklin's memoirs, were so defamatory that their true printers did not put their names on the title pages, instead attributing them to the press of none other than Benjamin Franklin! A clever ploy—Franklin was of course famous as a printer, and was known to have run a small press at his residence in France, where he published materials for the American republic that had removed itself from a monarchical system of government, as France had just done.[7]

The pirated *vie privée* was a far cry from the full and respectful edition of his grandfather's memoirs that Temple Franklin had hoped to publish. Worse, two English editions of the partial autobiography appeared in 1793, each one translated from the leaked French edition; by this point, Franklin's original prose was hardly recognizable. In the meantime, mistakenly believing that his own version of the manuscript might have more errors than either of the two copies, Temple offered it to Le Veillard in exchange for the Frenchman's copy, not realizing that his original included seven precious final pages that no other version contained. Temple published a six-volume edition of his grandfather's papers, including the Le Veillard version of the memoirs, in London, between 1817 and 1818. That edition of Franklin's memoirs had several flaws, notably the absence of the final section. Also, Temple had smoothed over some of his grandfather's plain, direct expressions with language that would have seemed to nineteenth-century readers more refined. Yet this *Memoirs of the Life and Writings of Benjamin Franklin*, however compromised and delayed, was for several generations the standard edition, much reprinted and read as Franklin's definitive "memoirs" or "life," first called an "autobiography" in the 1840s. Franklin's original manuscript resurfaced in 1867, but not until 1981 did an accurate edition based on it appear.[8]

Even more significant, Temple (and his competitors) had transformed the way in which the reading public would encounter and understand Benjamin Franklin. If the famous American had once presented himself to an international audience through collections of his writings (compiled by himself) that emphasized his work in

---

7. Robert Darnton, *The Devil in the Holy Water, or the Art of Slander from Louis XIV to Napoleon* (Philadelphia: U of Pennsylvania P, 2010), 422–38.
8. Christopher Hunter, "From Print to Print: The First Complete Edition of Benjamin Franklin's *Autobiography*," *Papers of the Bibliographical Society of America* (*PBSA*), 101 (2007): 481–505.

science, he was now presented in collections (compiled by others) that emphasized the man and his personal character, over and above the science. Franklin the philosopher of nature would gradually be eclipsed by Franklin the self-made man, and it is the latter version that has dominated both popular and scholarly discussions of Franklin since the early nineteenth century.

Reception

Such was Franklin's towering reputation that early responses to his *Autobiography* were largely positive. Enemies of the American movement for independence were occasionally critical, but demand for new works from the hand of Franklin had clearly survived his death. Readers marveled anew that someone of such humble beginnings, born so far from the European metropole, had become such a formidable intellect, and such a formidable critic of the empire that had bred him. The narrative was prized as historical evidence of a recent and important era, the preface to the American Revolution, though the memoirs were also noted for the plain and occasionally humorous style that was quintessentially that of "Poor Richard."

Yet by the time Franklin's memoirs were published, they were regarded as a record of an older generation and a passing era. His indebtedness to medieval and early modern forms of life-writing, invested in older definitions of the self, meant that he was unable to absorb or contribute to the new style of autobiography that was emerging toward the end of his life. Rather generally included under the label of Romanticism, this newer form of self-expression did not emphasize the rational examination of the soul in terms of virtue and vice, nor trace the improvement of a person through acquisition of good habits and good manners, nor present exemplary lives for others to emulate. Instead, the new form of life-writing explored different emotional states, especially the extremes—love, rage, wonder, terror—and presented a self that was distinctive, authentic only to itself and impossible for others to imitate. The exemplary figure was no longer a saint, political or military leader, or man of affairs, but the artist, the person most deeply engaged in imaginative reconstruction of the human experience. Rousseau's *Confessions* (1781–98) was a notable shift in this direction, and fictional narratives, including Goethe's *Sorrows of Young Werther* (1774) and Wordsworth's *Lyrical Ballads* (1798), reinforced the trend toward individual self-expression.[9]

9. Jay Paul, *Being in the Text: Self-Representation from Wordsworth to Roland Barthes* (Ithaca: Cornell UP, 1984); Charles J. Rzepka, *The Self as Mind: Vision and Identity in Wordsworth, Coleridge and Keats* (Cambridge: Harvard UP, 1986).

All of this meant that Franklin, a man of science who had explored nature's order through his senses, rather than imagining a natural order based on his sentiments, had fallen out of fashion. His notation of events and descriptions of his actions seemed shallow and cold; his unwillingness to discuss his interior mental or emotional states frustrated at least two generations of readers accustomed to another idea of the human self.[1]

And yet Franklin's memoirs were regarded as useful for working men and women who wished to better themselves. Throughout the industrializing West, and eventually in parts of the world that sought to emulate the West, Franklin's program of moral, economic, and educational self-discipline was exemplary. Sometimes, working people voluntarily embraced Franklin as a model; more often, he was foisted on them by people who thought that Romantic self-fulfillment was a luxury above a worker's station. His guide to self-improvement was considered useful precisely because it was old-fashioned. It is doubtful, however, that Franklin had intended his guide only to interest readers toward the bottom of society; certainly, the well-born friends who encouraged him to write his memoirs had thought that even aristocrats might emulate his virtues.

Today, Franklin interests people for still other reasons. Since the 1940s, scholars have worked to recover his reputation in science, to reestablish him as a progenitor of American scientists as well as of Americans who write literature. The romantic idea of an authentic and unique self has been replaced by theories of the human personality as the product of cultural context and as a performance to an external audience. Franklin's calculated shaping of his public persona is now regarded as something other than insincere, and his *Autobiography* has been set usefully in relation to other texts through which he persuaded people about himself, his life, and his historical era.

The story has not ended. *Benjamin Franklin's Autobiography*, never completed, never published in the author's lifetime, never called by him an autobiography, endures because it is so capacious and protean. It is dense with observation and detail. It covers childhood, youth, adulthood, and, in its elderly author's self-conscious moments of recollection, old age. It refers to almost every decade of an entire century, and a century's worth of monumental social, economic, and political changes all around the Atlantic world. It was composed by a master writer who chose his anecdotes carefully, injected the story with wit and drama, and makes us see him thinking about how to entertain us, even as he does so. Greater knowledge of what Franklin might have included in his memoirs

---

1. Hence D. H. Lawrence's scathing critique of the "dummy" or tame Franklin; see pp. 327–37 of this Norton Critical Edition.

only deepens our knowledge of the text and its author. Indeed, the story is tantalizingly open-ended because it is unfinished. The text ends with "never put into Execution"; the outline ends with "&c." Both are open invitations to read and reread the never-ending life of the celebrated Benjamin Franklin. Either of the inconclusive conclusions is more dramatic than "The End," so much more so that one wonders: Did he do it on purpose?

JOYCE E. CHAPLIN

Acknowledgments

My greatest debt is to J. A. Leo Lemay and Paul M. Zall, who not only prepared the first Norton Critical Edition of *Benjamin Franklin's Autobiography*, but even more important published *The Autobiography of Benjamin Franklin: A Genetic Text* (Knoxville: U of Tennessee P, 1981). That text was the first edition of Franklin's memoirs produced from the holograph manuscript held at the Henry E. Huntington Library and Art Gallery; it uses Franklin's original spelling and punctuation, and shows all of his emendations and alterations. Lemay and Zall pointed out that all editions of the *Autobiography* previous to the genetic text and their Norton edition had been prepared from earlier, published versions, and had therefore perpetuated many errors. Their work set a new standard in Franklin scholarship: subsequent reliable editions of the *Autobiography* have been prepared from the holograph manuscript.

I also owe thanks to the Huntington Library for allowing me the incomparable privilege of consulting Franklin's holograph manuscript in order to prepare this new edition. The J. Pierpont Morgan Library has permitted publication of the outline of the *Autobiography* (pp. 195–98), the American Antiquarian Society for Benjamin Franklin the Elder's poems on his nephew (p. 12), and the American Philosophical Society for Franklin's wagon advertisement (p. 128).

The ongoing project, *The Papers of Benjamin Franklin* (New Haven: Yale U P, 1959–), ed. Leonard W. Labaree et al., 40 volumes to date, was essential to the preparation of this work. I am particularly grateful to Kate Ohno, who quickly and cheerfully answered several last-minute questions. Jennifer van der Grinten did the translation from the Japanese and Ricardo Raul Salazar-Rey from the Spanish. David Armitage and Werner Sollors offered invaluable advice on the introduction. John Huffman was a blessedly sharp-eyed proofreader. Finally, at Norton, I wish to thank Carol Bemis and Rivka Genesen.

Notes on the Text

In Franklin's day, spelling had not been standardized, nor had rules for punctuation. In consequence, the original draft of his *Autobiography* contains many spelling variations that would have been perfectly legible to educated people of the time: *waggon* for *wagon*, *compleat* for *complete*, and *pannick* for *panic*, for example. It was typical practice to capitalize all nouns (*House, Club, Book*), though Franklin was not always consistent. He also abbreviated many words and names (as with *surpriz'd*) and gave minimal punctuation. Obviously, he would have corrected and standardized all these expressions once the text was printed, but that was not done during his lifetime. The Norton Critical Edition makes these corrections and standardizations without drawing attention to them. It also includes all of Franklin's later emendations, whether within the main text or added to it later, and omits whatever he himself struck out.

By making these changes silently, this edition is a clear text, one prepared without textual symbols that would make reading difficult. In addition, paragraph divisions are added to long sections that Franklin would doubtless have broken up, and the text is divided into the four parts that correspond to Franklin's four intervals of composition. A number of other emendations are silently made. The edition retains the eighteenth-century flavor of the original by capitalizing nouns and giving some now-outdated spellings.

For the most part, the text is based on J. A. Leo Lemay and Paul M. Zall's *The Autobiography of Benjamin Franklin: A Genetic Text* (1981), which preserves all of Franklin's original spelling and punctuation and uses textual symbols to indicate his emendations, corrections, and insertions. Readers who are interested in Franklin's original composition should consult the *Genetic Text*.

Franklin had wanted to insert six relevant documents into the *Autobiography*, though they were not written into the original manuscript. These additions were: notes on the family name of Franklin, poems that his uncle Benjamin Franklin wrote for him, an October 9, 1729, editorial on Massachusetts politics, letters from his friends Abel Jones and Benjamin Vaughan urging him to complete the *Autobiography*, the Golden Verses of Pythagoras, and documents concerning the wagons of provisions meant for Braddock's army. This edition includes all six supplements, one of them newly rediscovered, as well as Franklin's outline for the *Autobiography*.

The Text of the
AUTOBIOGRAPHY

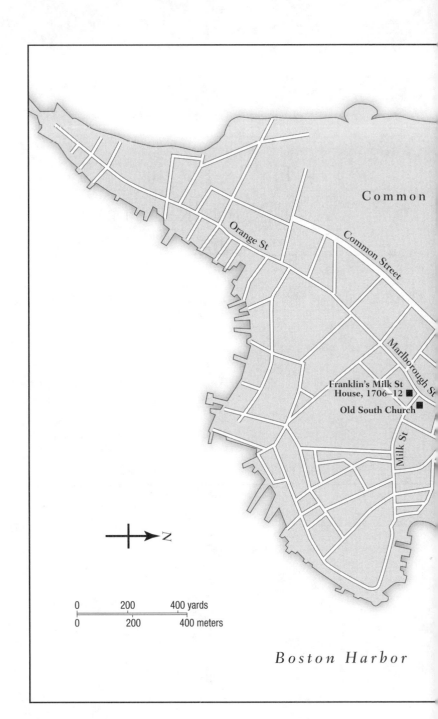

Common

Orange St

Common Street

Marlborough St

Franklin's Milk St
House, 1706–12 ■

Old South Church ■

Milk St

→N

0	200	400 yards
0	200	400 meters

Boston Harbor

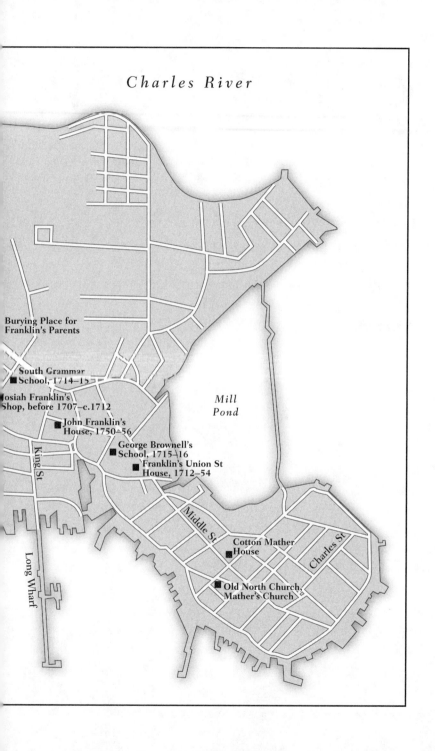

Charles River

Burying Place for
Franklin's Parents

South Grammar
■ School, 1714–15

Josiah Franklin's
Shop, before 1707–c.1712

■ John Franklin's
House, 1750–56

George Brownell's
■ School, 1715–16

■ Franklin's Union St
House, 1712–54

Mill
Pond

King St

Long Wharf

Middle St

Cotton Mather
■ House

■ Old North Church,
Mather's Church

Charles St

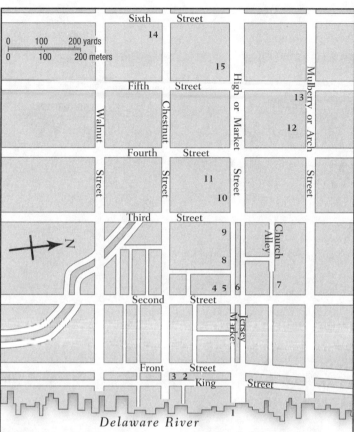

Delaware River

1. Market Street Wharf, where Franklin landed, 1723

2. Crooked Billet Tavern, where Franklin spent his first night in Philadelphia

3. Thomas Denham's shop, where Franklin was a clerk, 1726–27

4. Printing office of Andrew Bradford, 1724–38, and William Bradford, 1742–43.

5. Friends' Meeting House, where Franklin fell asleep on his first day in Philadelphia

6. Court House, built c. 1709

7. Christ Church, where Deborah Franklin worshiped

8. First Presbyterian Church, which Franklin sometimes attended

9. Indian King Tavern, where the Junto and the Free Masons sometimes met

10. John Read's residence, where Franklin said Deborah first looked him over, concluding he made "a most awkward ridiculous Appearance." Samuel Keimer's printing office was next door, 1723–26

11. Franklin Court, site of Franklin's last residence, completed 1765

12. New Building, erected for the Rev. George Whitefield in 1740, renovated (1749–50), on Franklin's initiative, to serve as the Philadelphia Academy, now the University of Pennsylvania

13. Christ Church Burial Ground, graves of Franklin, members of his family, and several friends and associates

14. State House (Independence Hall), occupied 1753. Original location for the Library Company and some of Franklin's electrical experiments

15. Pennsylvania Hospital, 1752–56

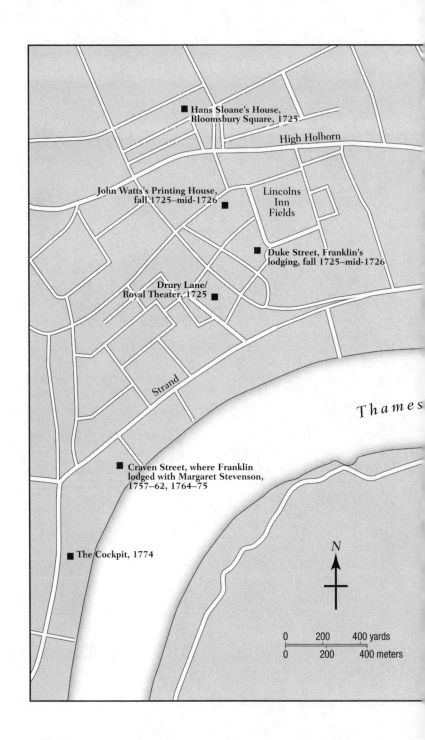

Hans Sloane's House,
Bloomsbury Square, 1725

High Holborn

John Watts's Printing House,
fall 1725–mid-1726

Lincolns
Inn
Fields

Duke Street, Franklin's
lodging, fall 1725–mid-1726

Drury Lane/
Royal Theater, 1725

Strand

Thames

Craven Street, where Franklin
lodged with Margaret Stevenson,
1757–62, 1764–75

The Cockpit, 1774

N

0   200   400 yards
0   200   400 meters

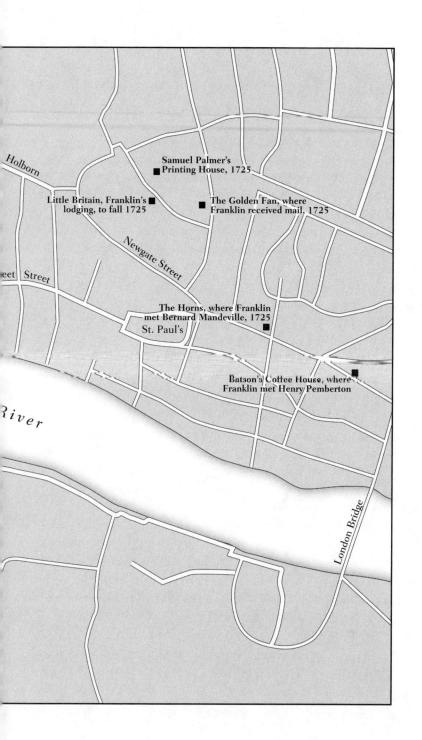

Holborn

Samuel Palmer's
Printing House, 1725

Little Britain, Franklin's
lodging, to fall 1725

The Golden Fan, where
Franklin received mail, 1725

Newgate Street

eet Street

The Horns, where Franklin
met Bernard Mandeville, 1725

St. Paul's

Batson's Coffee House, where
Franklin met Henry Pemberton

River

London Bridge

[Part One]

Dear Son,[2]

I have ever had a Pleasure in obtaining any little Anecdotes of my Ancestors. You may remember the Enquiries I made among the Remains of my Relations when you were with me in England; and the Journey I took for that purpose.[3] Now imagining it may be equally agreeable to you to know the Circumstances of *my* Life, many of which you are yet unacquainted with; and expecting a Week's uninterrupted Leisure in my present Country Retirement, I sit down to write them for you. To which I have besides some other Inducements. Having emerg'd from the Poverty and Obscurity in which I was born and bred, to a State of Affluence and some Degree of Reputation in the World, and having gone so far thro' Life with a considerable Share of Felicity, the conducting Means I made use of, which, with the Blessing of God, so well succeeded, my Posterity may like to know, as they may find some of them suitable to their own Situations, and therefore fit to be imitated. That Felicity, when I reflected on it, has induc'd me sometimes to say, that were it offer'd to my Choice, I should have no Objection to a Repetition of the same Life from its Beginning, only asking the Advantage Authors have in a second Edition to correct some Faults of the first. So would I if I might, besides correcting the Faults, change some sinister Accidents and Events of it for others more favorable, but tho' this were denied, I should still accept the Offer. However, since such a Repetition is not to be expected, the Thing most like living one's Life over again, seems to be a *Recollection* of that Life; and to make that Recollection as durable as possible, the putting it down in Writing. Hereby, too, I shall indulge the Inclination so natural in old Men, to be talking of themselves and their own past Actions, and I shall indulge it, without being troublesome to others who thro' respect to Age might think

1. Rural estate of Jonathan Shipley, Bishop of St. Asaph, six miles from Winchester, fifty miles south of London, where Franklin summered and wrote Part One of his *Autobiography*, July 30–August 13, 1771.
2. William Franklin was in 1771 the forty-year-old governor of New Jersey.
3. In July 1758, Benjamin Franklin and William Franklin visited the Franklin ancestral homes at Ecton and Banbury in Northamptonshire (*Papers* 8.114–21).

themselves oblig'd to give me a Hearing, since this may be read or not as any one pleases. And lastly, (I may as well confess it, since my Denial of it will be believ'd by no body) perhaps I shall a good deal gratify my own *Vanity.* Indeed I scarce ever heard or saw the introductory Words, *Without Vanity I may say,* etc. but some vain thing immediately follow'd. Most People dislike Vanity in others whatever Share they have of it themselves, but I give it fair Quarter wherever I meet with it, being persuaded that it is often productive of Good to the Possessor and to others that are within his Sphere of Action: And therefore in many Cases it would not be quite absurd if a Man were to thank God for his Vanity among the other Comforts of Life.

And now I speak of thanking God, I desire with all Humility to acknowledge, that I owe the mention'd Happiness of my past Life to his kind Providence, which led me to the Means I us'd and gave them Success. My Belief of This, induces me to *hope,* tho' I must not *presume,* that the same Goodness will still be exercis'd towards me in continuing that Happiness, or in enabling me to bear a fatal Reverso,[4] which I may experience as others have done, the Complexion of my future Fortune being known to him only: and in whose Power it is to bless to us even our Afflictions.

The Notes[5] one of my Uncles (who had the same kind of Curiosity in collecting Family Anecdotes) once put into my Hands, furnish'd me with several Particulars, relating to our Ancestors. From those Notes I learned that the Family had liv'd in the same Village, Ecton[6] in Northamptonshire, for 300 Years, and how much longer he knew not, (perhaps from the Time when the Name *Franklin* that before was the Name of an Order of People, was assum'd by them for a Surname, when others took Surnames all over the Kingdom)* on a Freehold of

* As a proof that FRANKLIN was anciently the common name of an order or rank in England, see Judge Fortescue, *De laudibus Legum Angliae,* written about the year 1412, in which is the following passage, to show that good juries might easily be formed in any part of England.

"Regio etiam illa, ita respersa refertaque est *possessoribus terrarum* et agrorum, quod in ea, villula tam parva reperiri non poterit, in qua non est *miles, armiger,* vel pater-familias, qualis ibidem *Franklin* vulgariter nuncupatur, magnis ditatus possessionibus, nec non libere tenentes et alii *valeci* plurimi, suis patrimoniis sufficientes ad faciendum juratam, in forma praenotata."

"Moreover, the same country is so filled and replenished with landed menne, that therein so small a Thorpe cannot be found

werein dweleth not a knight, an esquire, or such a householder, as is there commonly called a *Franklin,* enriched with great possessions; and also other freeholders and many yeomen able for their livelihoods to make a jury in form aforementioned."
—(*Old Translation.*)

Chaucer too calls his Country Gentleman, a *Franklin,* and after describing his good house-keeping thus characterises him:

"This worthy Franklin bore a purse of silk,
Fix'd to his girdle, white as morning milk.
Knight of the Shire, first Justice at th'
Assize, To help the poor, the doubtful to
advise. In all employments, generous, just,
he proved; Renown'd for courtesy, by all
beloved."

[Franklin's note, reprinted from
Lemay-Zall, *Genetic Text,* 175–77.]

4. Back-handed stroke used in swordplay.
5. Uncle Benjamin Franklin's "A short account of the Family of Thomas Franklin of Ecton in Northamptonshire. 21 June 1717" is at the Yale University Library.
6. Five miles northeast of Northampton, fifty miles northwest of London.

about 30 Acres, aided by the Smith's Business which had continued in the Family till his Time, the eldest Son being always bred to that Business. A Custom which he and my Father both followed as to their eldest Sons. When I search'd the Register at Ecton, I found an Account of their Births, Marriages and Burials, from the Year 1555 only, there being no Register kept in that Parish at any time preceding. By that Register I perceiv'd that I was the youngest Son of the youngest Son for 5 Generations back. My Grandfather Thomas, who was born in 1598, lived at Ecton till he grew too old to follow Business longer, when he went to live with his Son John, a Dyer at Banbury in Oxfordshire, with whom my Father serv'd an Apprenticeship. There my Grandfather died and lies buried. We saw his Gravestone in 1758. His eldest Son Thomas liv'd in the House at Ecton, and left it with the Land to his only Child, a Daughter, who with her Husband, one Fisher of Wellingborough, sold it to Mr. Isted, now Lord of the Manor there.

My Grandfather had 4 Sons that grew up, viz. Thomas, John, Benjamin and Josiah. I will give you what Account I can of them at this distance from my Papers, and if those are not lost in my Absence, you will among them find many more Particulars. Thomas was bred a Smith under his Father, but being ingenious, and encourag'd in Learning (as all his Brothers likewise were,) by an Esquire Palmer then the principal Gentleman in that Parish, he qualified himself for the Business of Scrivener,[7] became a considerable Man in the County Affairs, was a chief Mover of all public Spirited Undertakings for the County or Town of Northampton and his own Village, of which many Instances were told us at Ecton, and he was much taken Notice of and patroniz'd by the then Lord Halifax. He died in 1702, Jan. 6, old Stile,[8] just 4 Years to a Day before I was born. The Account we receiv'd of his Life and Character from some old People at Ecton, I remember struck you as something extraordinary from its Similarity to what you knew of mine. Had he died on the same Day, you said one might have suppos'd a Transmigration.

John was bred a Dyer, I believe of Woollens. Benjamin was bred a Silk Dyer, serving an Apprenticeship at London. He was an ingenious Man. I remember him well, for when I was a Boy he came over to my Father in Boston, and lived in the House with us some Years. He lived to a great Age. His Grandson Samuel Franklin now lives in Boston. He left behind him two Quarto[9] Volumes, Manuscript of

---

7. Professional penman.
8. Until September, 1752, England used the Julian calendar, in which the new year began on March 25. Since the Julian calendar did not have leap years, it had lost time, so the English skipped eleven days (September 3 to 13, 1752) when they adopted the Gregorian calendar. Franklin's birthday is reckoned January 6, 1705/6, "old style" or January 17, 1706, "new style."
9. In folio books, the sheet of paper is folded once, making four pages measuring about 15 in.×9.8 in.; in octavo, the sheet is folded twice, making eight pages (each about 9.8×7.5); and in quarto, the sheet is folded three times, making sixteen pages (each about 7.5×4.72).

his own Poetry, consisting of little occasional Pieces address'd to his Friends and Relations, of which the following sent to me, is a Specimen.* He had form'd a Shorthand of his own, which he taught me, but never practicing it I have now forgot it. I was nam'd after this Uncle, there being a particular Affection between him and my Father. He was very pious, a great Attender of Sermons of the best Preachers, which he took down in his Shorthand and had with him many Volumes of them. He was also much of a Politician, too much perhaps for his Station. There fell lately into my Hands in London a Collection he had made of all the principal Pamphlets relating to Public Affairs from 1641 to 1717. Many of the Volumes are wanting, as appears by the Numbering, but there still remains 8 Volumes Folio, and 24 in Quarto and Octavo. A Dealer in old Books met with them, and knowing me by my sometimes buying of him, he brought them to me. It seems my Uncle must have left them here when he went to America, which was above 50 Years since. There are many of his Notes in the Margins:[1]

This obscure Family of ours was early in the Reformation, and continu'd Protestants thro' the Reign of Queen Mary,[2] when they were sometimes in Danger of Trouble on Account of their Zeal against Popery. They had got an English Bible, and to conceal and secure it, it was fastened open with Tapes under and within the Frame of a Joint Stool. When my Great Great Grandfather read in it to his Family, he turn'd up the Joint Stool upon his Knees, turning over the Leaves then under the Tapes. One of the Children stood at

* Sent to My Name upon a Report of his
    Inclinnation to Martial affaires
                7 July 1710
Beleeve me Ben. It is a Dangerous Trade.
The Sword has Many Marr'd as well as
    Made;
By it doe many fall Not Many Rise;
Makes Many poor, few Rich and fewer Wise;
Fills Towns with Ruin, fields with blood
                            beside;   5
Tis Sloths Maintainer, And the Shield of
    pride;
Fair Citties Rich to Day, in plenty flow,
War fills with want. Tomorrow, & with woe.
Ruin'd Estates. The Nurse of Vice, broke
    limbs
                            & scarss
Are the Effects of Desolating Warrs.   10

    Sent to B. F. in N. E. 15 July 1710
B   e to thy parents an Obedient Son
E   ach Day let Duty constantly be Done
N   ever give Way to sloth or lust or pride

J   f free you'd be from Thousand Ills beside
A   bove all Ills be sure Avoide the shelfe 5
M   ans Danger lyes in Satan sin and selfe
I   n vertue Learning Wisdome progress
    Make
N   ere shrink at Suffering for thy saviours
    sake

F   raud and all Falshood in thy Dealings
    Flee
R   eligious Always in thy station be   10
A   dore the Maker of thy Inward part
N   ow's the Accepted time, Give him thy
    Heart

K   eep a Good Consceince 'tis a constant
    Frind
L   ike Judge and Witness This Thy Acts
    Attend
I   n Heart with bended knee Alone Adore 15
N   one but the Three in One Forevermore.
                [Franklin's note, reprinted
                from Papers 1.4–5.]

1. Franklin bought these books in early July 1771, but the penmanship was not his uncle's. See Edwin Wolf II, "The Reconstruction of Benjamin Franklin's Library," in Papers of the Bibliographical Society of America 56 (1962): 1–16.
2. Mary (r. 1553–58), the older sister of Elizabeth I, tried to reestablish Catholicism in England.

the Door to give Notice if he saw the Apparitor coming, who was an Officer of the Spiritual Court. In that Case the Stool was turn'd down again upon its feet, when the Bible remain'd conceal'd under it as before. This Anecdote I had from my Uncle Benjamin.[3] The Family continu'd all of the Church of England till about the End of Charles the Second's Reign,[4] when some of the Ministers that had been outed for Nonconformity, holding Conventicles[5] in Northamptonshire, Benjamin and Josiah adher'd to them, and so continu'd all their Lives. The rest of the Family remain'd with the Episcopal Church.

Josiah, my Father, married young, and carried his Wife with three Children unto New England, about 1682.[6] The Conventicles having been forbidden by Law, and frequently disturbed, induced some considerable Men of his Acquaintance to remove to that Country, and he was prevail'd with to accompany them thither, where they expected to enjoy their Mode of Religion with Freedom. By the same Wife he had 4 Children more born there, and by a second Wife ten more, in all 17, of which I remember 13 sitting at one time[7] at his Table, who all grew up to be Men and Women, and married. I was the youngest Son and the youngest Child but two, and was born in Boston, New England.

My Mother the second Wife was Abiah Folger, a Daughter of Peter Folger, one of the first Settlers of New England, of whom honorable mention is made by Cotton Mather, in his Church History of that Country, (entitled Magnalia Christi Americana) as a *godly learned Englishman*,[8] if I remember the Words rightly. I have heard that he wrote sundry small occasional Pieces, but only one of them was printed which I saw now many Years since. It was written in 1675, in the homespun Verse of that Time and People, and address'd to those then concern'd in the Government there. It was in favor of Liberty of Conscience, and in behalf of the Baptists, Quakers, and other Sectaries, that had been under Persecution; ascribing the Indian Wars and other Distresses that had befallen the Country to that Persecution, as so many Judgments of God, to punish so heinous an Offence; and exhorting a Repeal of those uncharitable Laws. The whole appear'd to me as written with a good deal of Decent Plainness and manly Freedom. The six last concluding Lines I remember, tho' I have forgotten the two first of the Stanza, but the Purport

---

3. Actually, Franklin's father, May 26, 1739 (*Papers* 2.230).
4. From 1660 to 1685, Parliament severely restricted dissenters who would not conform to the Church of England.
5. Private meetings for worship, outlawed in 1664.
6. October 1683.
7. At a dinner circa 1715 (*Papers* 9.18).
8. "An Able Godly Englishman" (*Magnalia*, London, 1702. Book VI, chapter vi, section 2, 54).

of them was that his Censures proceeded from *Goodwill*, and therefore he would be known as the Author,[9]

> because to be a Libeller, (says he)
>   I hate it with my Heart.
> From *Sherburne Town where now I dwell,
>   My Name I do put here,
> Without Offence, your real Friend,
>   It is Peter Folgier.

My elder Brothers were all put Apprentices to different Trades. I
was put to the Grammar School at Eight Years of Age, my Father
intending to devote me as the Tithe[1] of his Sons to the Service of the
Church. My early Readiness in learning to read (which must have
been very early, as I do not remember when I could not read) and
the Opinion of all his Friends that I should certainly make a good
Scholar, encourag'd him in this Purpose of his. My Uncle Benjamin
too approv'd of it, and propos'd to give me all his Shorthand Volumes of Sermons, I suppose as a Stock to set up with, if I would
learn his Character.[2] I continu'd however at the Grammar School
not quite one Year, tho' in that time I had risen gradually from the
Middle of the Class of that Year to be the Head of it, and farther was
remov'd into the next Class above it, in order to go with that into the
third at the End of the Year. But my Father in the meantime, from a
View of the Expense of a College Education which, having so large
a Family, he could not well afford, and the mean Living many so
educated were afterwards able to obtain, Reasons that he gave to his
Friends in my Hearing, altered his first Intention, took me from the
Grammar School, and sent me to a School for Writing and Arithmetic kept by a then famous Man, Mr. George Brownell, very successful in his Profession generally, and that by mild encouraging
Methods. Under him I acquired fair Writing pretty soon, but I fail'd
in the Arithmetic, and made no Progress in it.

At Ten Years old, I was taken home to assist my Father in his Business, which was that of a Tallow Chandler and Soap-Boiler.[3] A Business he was not bred to, but had assumed on his Arrival in New
England and on finding his Dying Trade would not maintain his
Family, being in little Request. Accordingly I was employed in cutting Wick for the Candles, filling the Dipping Mold, and the Molds
for cast Candles, attending the Shop, going of Errands, etc. I dislik'd

---

* "In the Island of Nantucket." [Franklin's note.]

---

9. Though dated April 23, 1676, Folger's *A Looking Glass for the Times* was not printed
   until 1725; reprinted, 1763.
1. Tenth part of annual income. Benjamin Franklin was the tenth son.
2. Shorthand symbols.
3. Manufactured candles and soap from animal fats.

the Trade and had a strong Inclination for the Sea; but my Father
declar'd against it; however, living near the Water, I was much in
and about it, learned early to swim well, and to manage Boats, and
when in a Boat or Canoe with other Boys I was commonly allow'd to
govern, especially in any case of Difficulty; and upon other Occasions I was generally a Leader among the Boys, and sometimes led
them into Scrapes, of which I will mention one Instance, as it shows
an early projecting public Spirit, tho' not then justly conducted.
There was a Salt Marsh that bounded part of the Mill Pond, on the
Edge of which at Highwater, we us'd to stand to fish for Minnows.
By much Trampling, we had made it a mere Quagmire. My Proposal
was to build a Wharf there fit for us to stand upon, and I show'd my
Comrades a large Heap of Stones which were intended for a new
House near the Marsh, and which would very well suit our Purpose.
Accordingly in the Evening when the Workmen were gone, I assem-
bled a Number of my Playfellows, and working with them diligently
like so many Emmets,[4] sometimes two or three to a Stone, we brought
them all away and built our little Wharf. The next Morning the
Workmen were surpris'd at Missing the Stones; which were found
in our Wharf; Enquiry was made after the Removers; we were discovered and complain'd of; several of us were corrected by our
Fathers; and tho' I pleaded the Usefulness of the Work, mine
convinc'd me that nothing was useful which was not honest.

I think you may like to know something of his Person and Character. He had an excellent Constitution of Body, was of middle Stature,
but well set and very strong. He was ingenious, could draw prettily,
was skill'd a little in Music and had a clear pleasing Voice, so that
when he play'd Psalm Tunes on his Violin and sung withal as he
some times did in an Evening after the Business of the Day was over,
it was extremely agreeable to hear. He had a mechanical Genius
too, and on occasion was very handy in the Use of other Tradesmen's
Tools. But his great Excellence lay in a sound Understanding, and
solid Judgment in prudential Matters, both in private and public
Affairs. In the latter indeed he was never employed, the numerous
Family he had to educate and the Straitness of his Circumstances,
keeping him close to his Trade, but I remember well his being frequently visited by leading People, who consulted him for his Opinion
on Affairs of the Town or of the Church[5] he belong'd to and show'd a
good deal of Respect for his Judgment and Advice. He was also much
consulted by private Persons about their Affairs when any Difficulty
occur'd, and frequently chosen an Arbitrator between contending
Parties. At his Table he lik'd to have as often as he could, some

4. Ants.
5. Boston's Old South Church.

sensible Friend or Neighbor, to converse with, and always took care to start some ingenious or useful Topic for Discourse, which might tend to improve the Minds of his Children. By this means he turn'd our Attention to what was good, just, and prudent in the Conduct of Life; and little or no Notice was ever taken of what related to the Victuals on the Table, whether it was well or ill drest, in or out of season, of good or bad flavor, preferable or inferior to this or that other thing of the kind; so that I was brought up in such a perfect Inattention to those Matters as to be quite Indifferent what kind of Food was set before me; and so unobservant of it, that to this Day, if I am ask'd I can scarce tell, a few Hours after Dinner, what I din'd upon. This has been a Convenience to me in travelling, where my Companions have been sometimes very unhappy for want of a suitable Gratification of their more delicate because better instructed Tastes and Appetites.

My Mother had likewise an excellent Constitution. She suckled all her 10 Children. I never knew either my Father or Mother to have any Sickness but that of which they died, he at 89 and she at 85 Years of age. They lie buried together at Boston, where I some Years since[6] plac'd a Marble stone over their Grave with this Inscription:

Josiah Franklin
And Abiah his Wife
Lie here interred.
They lived lovingly together in Wedlock
Fifty-five Years.
Without an Estate or any gainful Employment,
By constant Labour and Industry,
With God's Blessing,
They maintained a large Family
Comfortably;
And brought up thirteen Children,
And seven Grandchildren
Reputably.
From this Instance, Reader,
Be encouraged to Diligence in thy Calling,
And distrust not Providence.
He was a pious and prudent Man,
She a discreet and virtuous Woman.
Their youngest Son,
In filial Regard to their Memory,
Places this Stone.
J.F. born 1655—Died 1744. Ætat 89
A.F. born 1667—died 1752——85.

6. About 1753–54 (*Papers* 7.229–30).

By my rambling Digressions I perceive myself to be grown old. I us'd to write more methodically. But one does not dress for private Company as for a public Ball. 'Tis perhaps only Negligence.[7]

To return. I continu'd thus employ'd in my Father's Business for two Years, that is till I was 12 Years old; and my Brother John, who was bred to that Business having left my Father, married and set up for himself at Rhode Island, there was all Appearance that I was destin'd to supply his Place and be a Tallow Chandler. But my Dislike to the Trade continuing, my Father was under Apprehensions that if he did not find one for me more agreeable, I should break away and get to Sea, as his Son Josiah had done to his great Vexation. He therefore sometimes took me to walk with him, and see Joiners, Bricklayers, Turners, Braziers, etc. at their Work, that he might observe my Inclination, and endeavour to fix it on some Trade or other on Land. It has ever since been a Pleasure to me to see good Workmen handle their Tools; and it has been useful to me, having learned so much by it, as to be able to do little Jobs myself in my House, when a Workman could not readily be got; and to construct little Machines for my Experiments while the Intention of making the Experiment was fresh and warm in my Mind. My Father at last fix'd upon the Cutler's Trade, and my Uncle Benjamin's Son Samuel who was bred to that Business in London being about that time establish'd in Boston, I was sent to be with him some time on liking. But his Expectations of a Fee with me displeasing my Father, I was taken home again.

From a Child I was fond of Reading, and all the little Money that came into my Hands was ever laid out in Books. Pleas'd with the Pilgrim's Progress, my first Collection was of John Bunyan's Works, in separate little Volumes.[8] I afterwards sold them to enable me to buy R. Burton's Historical Collections;[9] they were small Chapmen's Books and cheap, 40 or 50 in all. My Father's little Library consisted chiefly of Books in polemic Divinity, most of which I read, and have since often regretted, that at a time when I had such a Thirst for Knowledge, more proper Books had not fallen in my Way, since it was now resolv'd I should not be a Clergyman. Plutarch's Lives there was, in which I read abundantly, and I still think that time spent to great Advantage.[1] There was also a Book of Defoe's called

---

7. This short paragraph begins atop Franklin's manuscript page 9. Carl Van Doren suggested that Franklin composed eight pages on the first day, then on the next day drew up the outline before writing this paragraph. Franklin probably added the long columnar insertion to the opening paragraph at this time.

8. Probably *Grace Abounding* (1666), *Life & Death of Mr. Badman* (1680), and *Holy War* (1682), all available in cheap, one-shilling editions.

9. "R. Burton" was Nathaniel Crouch, who published countless chapbooks, small enough to be carried by chapmen, or pedlars, yet averaging 230 pages of small type and selling for a shilling.

1. Franklin probably read John Dryden's translation (1683–86).

an Essay on Projects[2] and another of Dr. Mather's call'd Essays to
do Good,[3] which perhaps gave me a Turn of Thinking that had an
Influence on some of the principal future Events of my Life.

This Bookish Inclination at length determin'd my Father to make
me a Printer, tho' he had already one Son, (James) of that Profession. In 1717 my Brother James return'd from England with a Press
and Letters to set up his Business in Boston. I lik'd it much better
than that of my Father, but still had a Hankering for the Sea. To
prevent the apprehended Effect of such an Inclination, my Father
was impatient to have me bound to my Brother. I stood out some
time, but at last was persuaded and signed the Indentures,[4] when
I was yet but 12 Years old. I was to serve as an Apprentice till I was
21 Years of Age, only I was to be allow'd Journeyman's Wages during the last Year. In a little time I made great Proficiency in the
Business, and became a useful Hand to my Brother. I now had
Access to better Books. An Acquaintance with the Apprentices of
Booksellers enabled me sometimes to borrow a small one, which I
was careful to return soon and clean. Often I sat up in my Room
reading the greatest Part of the Night, when the Book was borrow'd
in the Evening and to be return'd early in the Morning lest it should
be miss'd or wanted. And after some time an ingenious Tradesman*
who had a pretty Collection of Books, and who frequented our
Printing-House, took Notice of me, invited me to his Library, and
very kindly lent me such Books as I chose to read. I now took a
Fancy to Poetry, and made some little Pieces. My Brother, thinking
it might turn to account encourag'd me, and put me on composing
two occasional Ballads. One was called the *Light House Tragedy*,
and contain'd an Account of the drowning of Capt. Worthilake
with his Two Daughters;[5] the other was a Sailor Song on the Taking
of *Teach* or Blackbeard the Pirate.[6] They were wretched Stuff, in
the Grubstreet Ballad Style,[7] and when they were printed he sent me
about the Town to sell them. The first sold wonderfully, the Event

---

* "Mr. Matthew Adams." [Franklin's note.]

2. Franklin twice quoted Defoe's book in his "Silence Dogood" essays, and followed its
   precepts in such civic improvements as hospitals and insurance companies (*Papers*
   1.20, 32–36).
3. The running title of Cotton Mather's *Bonifacius* (1710), spoofed by "Silence Dogood,"
   but inspiration for such improvement programs as the Junto. Franklin inserted this
   reference to Mather at a later date (1789?), echoing his letter of May 12, 1784, to
   Mather's son. (See Albert H. Smyth, *The Writings of Benjamin Franklin*, 10 vols. [New
   York: Macmillan, 1905–07], 9.208.) The books Franklin mentions were only some out
   of a very large number that he had read.
4. A typical apprentice contracted for seven years' board, room, and training.
5. George Worthylake, keeper of Boston Harbor light, drowned with his wife and daughter (not two daughters) on November 3, 1718 (*Papers* 1.6).
6. Edward Teach, alias Blackbeard, was killed off the Carolina coast on November 22, 1718.
   The *Boston News Letter* account of March 2, 1719, possibly inspired Franklin's ballad.
7. Doggerel. Franklin's ballads are probably lost (*Papers* 1.6–7).

being recent, having made a great Noise. This flatter'd my Vanity. But my Father discourag'd me, by ridiculing my Performances, and telling me Verse-makers were generally Beggars; so I escap'd being a Poet, most probably a very bad one. But as Prose Writing has been of great Use to me in the Course of my Life, and was a principal Means of my Advancement, I shall tell you how in such a Situation I acquir'd what little Ability I have in that Way.

There was another Bookish Lad in the Town, John Collins by Name, with whom I was intimately acquainted. We sometimes disputed, and very fond we were of Argument, and very desirous of confuting one another. Which disputatious Turn, by the way, is apt to become a very bad Habit, making People often extremely disagreeable in Company, by the Contradiction that is necessary to bring it into Practice, and thence, besides souring and spoiling the Conversation, is productive of Disgusts and perhaps Enmities where you may have occasion for Friendship. I had caught it by reading my Father's Books of Dispute about Religion. Persons of good Sense, I have since observ'd, seldom fall into it, except Lawyers, University Men, and Men of all Sorts that have been bred at Edinburgh.[8] A Question was once some how or other started between Collins and me, of the Propriety of educating the Female Sex in Learning, and their Abilities for Study. He was of Opinion that it was improper; and that they were naturally unequal to it. I took the contrary Side, perhaps a little for Dispute sake.[9] He was naturally more eloquent, had a ready Plenty of Words, and sometimes as I thought bore me down more by his Fluency than by the Strength of his Reasons. As we parted without settling the Point, and were not to see one another again for some time, I sat down to put my Arguments in Writing, which I copied fair and sent to him. He answer'd and I replied. Three or four Letters of a Side had pass'd, when my Father happen'd to find my Papers, and read them. Without entering into the Discussion, he took occasion to talk to me about the Manner of my Writing, observ'd that tho' I had the Advantage of my Antagonist in correct Spelling and pointing[1] (which I ow'd to the Printing House) I fell far short in elegance of Expression, in Method and in Perspicuity, of which he convinc'd me by several Instances. I saw the Justice of his Remarks, and thence grew more attentive to the *Manner* in Writing, and determin'd to endeavour at Improvement.

About this time I met with an odd Volume of the Spectator.[2] I had never before seen any of them. I bought it, read it over and over,

---

8. A joke possibly at the expense of Benjamin Franklin's Scottish friends.
9. The fifth Dogood essay (May 28, 1722) discusses the subject (*Papers* 1.18–21).
1. Punctuation.
2. Franklin's Silence Dogood essay series was indebted to Addison and Steele's influential *Spectator*, a weekly paper which appeared 1711–12 and 1714 (*Papers* 1.9, 44).

and was much delighted with it. I thought the Writing excellent, and wish'd if possible to imitate it. With that View, I took some of the Papers, and making short Hints of the Sentiment in each Sentence, laid them by a few Days, and then without looking at the Book, tried to complete the Papers again, by expressing each hinted Sentiment at length and as fully as it had been express'd before, in any suitable Words that should come to hand.[3]

Then I compar'd my Spectator with the Original, discover'd some of my Faults and corrected them. But I found I wanted a Stock of Words or a Readiness in recollecting and using them, which I thought I should have acquir'd before that time, if I had gone on making Verses, since the continual Occasion for Words of the same Import but of different Length, to suit the Measure, or of different Sound for the Rhyme, would have laid me under a constant Necessity of searching for Variety, and also have tended to fix that Variety in my Mind, and make me Master of it. Therefore I took some of the Tales and turn'd them into Verse: And after a time, when I had pretty well forgotten the Prose, turn'd them back again. I also sometimes jumbled my Collections of Hints into Confusion, and after some Weeks, endeavour'd to reduce them into the best Order, before I began to form the full Sentences, and complete the Paper. This was to teach me Method in the Arrangement of Thoughts. By comparing my Work afterwards with the original, I discover'd many faults and amended them; but I sometimes had the Pleasure of Fancying that in certain Particulars of small Import, I had been lucky enough to improve the Method or the Language and this encourag'd me to think I might possibly in time come to be a tolerable English Writer, of which I was extremely ambitious.

My Time for these Exercises and for Reading, was at Night after Work, or before Work began in the Morning; or on Sundays, when I contrived to be in the Printing-House alone, evading as much as I could the common Attendance on public Worship, which my Father used to exact of me when I was under his Care: And which indeed I still thought a Duty; tho' I could not, as it seemed to me, afford the Time to practice it.

When about 16 Years of Age, I happen'd to meet with a Book written by one Tryon,[4] recommending a Vegetable Diet. I determined to go into it. My Brother being yet unmarried, did not keep House, but boarded himself and his Apprentices in another Family. My refusing to eat Flesh occasioned an Inconveniency, and I was frequently chid for my singularity. I made myself acquainted with Tryon's Manner

---

3. Franklin proposed this method in his "Ideas of the English School" in 1751 (*Papers* 4.107).

4. Thomas Tryon's celebrated self-help medical book, *The Way to Health, Wealth, and Happiness* (1682–98), may also have inspired the title of Franklin's much later *Way to Wealth*.

of preparing some of his Dishes, such as Boiling Potatoes or Rice, making Hasty Pudding, and a few others, and then propos'd to my Brother, that if he would give me Weekly half the Money he paid for my Board, I would board myself. He instantly agreed to it, and I presently found that I could save half what he paid me. This was an additional Fund for buying Books: But I had another Advantage in it. My Brother and the rest going from the Printing-House to their Meals, I remain'd there alone, and dispatching presently my light Repast, (which often was no more than a Biscuit or a Slice of Bread, a Handful of Raisins or a Tart from the Pastry Cook's, and a Glass of Water) had the rest of the Time till their Return, for Study, in which I made the greater Progress from that greater Clearness of Head and quicker Apprehension which usually attend Temperance in Eating and Drinking. And now it was that being on some Occasion made asham'd of my Ignorance in Figures, which I had twice fail'd in learning when at School, I took Cocker's Book of Arithmetic, and went thro' the whole by myself with great Ease. I also read Seller's and Sturmy's Books of Navigation,[5] and became acquainted with the little Geometry they contain, but never proceeded far in that Science. And I read about this Time Locke on Human Understanding[6] and the Art of Thinking by Messrs. du Port Royal.[7]

While I was intent on improving my Language, I met with an English Grammar (I think it was Greenwood's)[8] at the End of which there were two little Sketches of the Arts of Rhetoric and Logic, the latter finishing with a Specimen of a Dispute in the Socratic Method. And soon after I procur'd Xenophon's Memorable Things of Socrates,[9] wherein there are many Instances of the same Method. I was charm'd with it, adopted it, dropped my abrupt Contradiction and positive Argumentation, and put on the humble Enquirer and Doubter. And being then, from reading Shaftesbury and Collins,[1] become a real Doubter in many Points of our Religious Doctrine, I found this Method safest for myself and very embarassing to those against whom I used it, therefore I took a Delight in it, practic'd it continually and grew very artful and expert in drawing People even of superior Knowledge into Concessions the Consequences of which

5. Edward Cocker's *Arithmetic* (1677), John Seller's *Practical Navigation* (1669), and Samuel Sturmy's *Mariner's Magazine* (1669) ran through multiple editions before 1700.
6. John Locke's *Essay Concerning Human Understanding* (1690), a fundamental work on philosophy for the eighteenth century, had five revised, expanded versions through 1706.
7. Jansenist monks set up a school at Port Royal, France, applying Cartesian inductive methods to education and emphasizing vernacular over classical languages.
8. Actually the second edition of "John Brightland" [Charles Gildon], *A Grammar of the English Tongue* (London: John Brightland, 1712), which added "The Arts of Poetry, Rhetoric, Logic, etc.," not in the first (1711) edition.
9. Translated by Edward Bysshe (1712).
1. Anthony Ashley Cooper, Third Earl of Shaftesbury, *Characteristics of Men, Manners, Opinions, Times*, 3 vols. (1711); and, among the several deistic works by Anthony Collins, perhaps *A Discourse of Free Thinking* (1713).

they did not foresee, entangling them in Difficulties out of which they could not extricate themselves, and so obtaining Victories that neither myself nor my Cause always deserved. I continu'd this Method some few Years, but gradually left it, retaining only the Habit of expressing myself in Terms of modest Diffidence, never using when I advance any thing that may possibly be disputed, the Words, *Certainly, undoubtedly*, or any others that give the Air of Positiveness to an Opinion; but rather say, *I conceive*, or *I apprehend* a Thing to be so or so, *It appears to me*, or *I should think it so or so for such and such Reasons*, or *I imagine* it to be so, or *it is so if I am not mistaken*. This Habit I believe has been of great Advantage to me, when I have had occasion to inculcate my Opinions and persuade Men into Measures that I have been from time to time engag'd in promoting. And as the chief Ends of Conversation are to *inform*, or to be *informed*, to *please* or to *persuade*, I wish well-meaning sensible Men would not lessen their Power of doing Good by a Positive assuming Manner that seldom fails to disgust, tends to create Opposition, and to defeat every one of those Purposes for which Speech was given us, to wit, giving or receiving Information, or Pleasure: For If you would *inform*, a positive dogmatical Manner in advancing your Sentiments, may provoke Contradiction and prevent a candid Attention. If you wish Information and Improvement from the Knowledge of others and yet at the same time express yourself as firmly fix'd in your present Opinions, modest sensible Men, who do not love Disputation, will probably leave you undisturb'd in the Possession of your Error; and by such a Manner you can seldom hope to recommend yourself in *pleasing* your Hearers, or to persuade those whose Concurrence you desire. Pope says, judiciously,

> *Men should be taught as if you taught them not,*
> *And things unknown propos'd as things forgot,*

farther recommending it to us,

> *To speak tho' sure, with seeming Diffidence.*[2]

And he might have coupl'd with this Line that which he has coupled with another, I think less properly,

> *For want of Modesty is want of Sense.*

If you ask why *less properly*, I must repeat the Lines;

> "Immodest Words admit of *no* Defence;
> *For* Want of Modesty is Want of Sense."[3]

---

2. Perhaps quoted from memory. In *Essay on Criticism* (1711), ll. 574–75 and 567, the second word is "must" and the third line begins with "And" rather than "To."

3. Again, evidently from memory. Wentworth Dillon, Earl of Roscommon, *Essay on Translated Verse* (1684), 114. The second line reads "Decency" instead of "Modesty."

Now is not *Want of Sense*, (where a Man is so unfortunate as to want it) some Apology for his *Want of Modesty*? and would not the Lines stand more justly thus?

> Immodest Words admit *but this* Defence,
> That Want of Modesty is Want of Sense.

This however I should submit to better Judgments.

My Brother had in 1720 or 21, begun to print a Newspaper. It was the second that appear'd in America,[4] and was called *The New England Courant*. The only one before it, was *the Boston News Letter*. I remember his being dissuaded by some of his Friends from the Undertaking, as not likely to succeed, one Newspaper being in their Judgment enough for America. At this time 1771 there are not less than five and twenty. He went on however with the Undertaking, and after having work'd in composing the Types and printing off the Sheets I was employ'd to carry the Papers thro' the Streets to the Customers. He had some ingenious Men among his Friends who amus'd themselves by writing little Pieces for this Paper, which gain'd it Credit, and made it more in Demand; and these Gentlemen[5] often visited us. Hearing their Conversations, and their Accounts of the Approbation their Papers were receiv'd with, I was excited to try my Hand among them. But being still a Boy, and suspecting that my Brother would object to printing any Thing of mine in his Paper If he knew it to be mine, I contriv'd to disguise my Hand, and writing an anonymous Paper I put it in at Night under the Door of the Printing-House.

It was found in the Morning and communicated to his Writing Friends when they call'd in as Usual. They read it, commented on it in my Hearing, and I had the exquisite Pleasure, of finding it met with their Approbation, and that in their different Guesses at the Author none were named but Men of some Character among us for Learning and Ingenuity. I suppose now that I was rather lucky in my Judges: And that perhaps they were not really so very good ones as I then esteem'd them. Encourag'd however by this, I wrote and convey'd in the same Way to the Press several more Papers,[6] which were equally approv'd, and I kept my Secret till my small Fund of Sense for such Performances was pretty well exhausted, and then I discovered[7] it; when I began to be considered a little more by my Brothers' Acquaintance, and in a manner that did not quite please

---

4. Three newspapers had preceded the *Courant*: the *Boston News-Letter* (April 24, 1704), the *Boston Gazette* (December 21, 1719), first printed by James Franklin, and, in Philadelphia, the *American Weekly Mercury* (December 22, 1719).
5. James Franklin's "Couranteers" included Matthew Adams, John Checkley, Dr. William Douglas, Thomas Fleet, and Nathaniel Gardner.
6. Fourteen "letters" from "Silence Dogood" (April 12–October 8, 1722) made up the earliest essay series in America (*Papers* 1.9–45).
7. Revealed.

him, as he thought, probably with reason, that it tended to make me too vain. And perhaps this might be one Occasion of the Differences that we began to have about this Time. Tho' a Brother, he considered himself as my Master, and me as his Apprentice; and accordingly expected the same Services from me as he would from another; while I thought he demean'd me too much in some he requir'd of me, who from a Brother expected more Indulgence. Our Disputes were often brought before our Father, and I fancy I was either generally in the right, or else a better Pleader, because the Judgment was generally in my favor: But my Brother was passionate and had often beaten me, which I took extremely amiss;* and thinking my Apprenticeship very tedious, I was continually wishing for some Opportunity of shortening it, which at length offered in a manner unexpected.*

One of the Pieces in our Newspaper, on some political Point which I have now forgotten, gave Offence to the Assembly. He was taken up, censur'd and imprison'd for a Month by the Speaker's Warrant, I suppose because he would not discover his Author.[8] I too was taken up and examin'd before the Council; but tho' I did not give them any Satisfaction, they contented themselves with admonishing me, and dismiss'd me; considering me perhaps as an Apprentice who was bound to keep his Master's Secrets. During my Brother's Confinement, which I resented a good deal, notwithstanding our private Differences, I had the Management of the Paper, and I made bold to give our Rulers some Rubs in it,[9] which my Brother took very kindly, while others began to consider me in an unfavorable Light, as a young Genius that had a Turn for Libelling and Satire. My Brother's Discharge was accompanied with an Order of the House, (a very odd one) *that James Franklin should no longer print the Paper called the New England Courant.*[1] There was a Consultation held in our Printing-House among his Friends what he should do in this Case. Some propos'd to evade the Order by changing the Name of the Paper; but my Brother seeing Inconveniences in that, it was finally concluded on as a better Way, to let it be printed for the future under the Name of *Benjamin Franklin.* And to avoid the Censure of the Assembly that might fall on him, as still printing it by his Apprentice,

---

* "I fancy his harsh and tyrannical Treatment of me, might be a means of impressing me with that Aversion to arbitrary Power that has stuck to me thro' my whole life." [Franklin's note.]

---

8. The *Courant* for June 11, 1722, suggested that local authorities had colluded with pirates raiding off Boston Harbor. James Franklin was promptly jailed from June 12 until July 7.
9. The Dogood letter of July 23, 1722, overtly satirized ex-governor Joseph Dudley, but covertly critiqued the Mathers and Chief Justice Samuel Sewall (*Papers* 1.30–32).
1. When the *Courant* for January 14, 1723, hinted at hypocrites in local government, James Franklin was ordered to submit to censorship or cease publishing. The *Courant* carried Benjamin Franklin's name as printer from February 11, 1723, until the paper failed in 1727.

the Contrivance was, that my old Indenture should be return'd to me with a full Discharge on the Back of it, to be shown on Occasion; but to secure to him the Benefit of my Service I was to sign new Indentures for the Remainder of the Term, which were to be kept private. A very flimsy Scheme it was, but however it was immediately executed, and the Paper went on accordingly under my Name for several Months. At length a fresh Difference arising between my Brother and me, I took upon me to assert my Freedom, presuming that he would not venture to produce the new Indentures. It was not fair in me to take this Advantage, and this I therefore reckon one of the first Errata of my Life:[2] But the Unfairness of it weigh'd little with me, when under the Impressions of Resentment, for the Blows his Passion too often urg'd him to bestow upon me. Tho' he was otherwise not an ill-natur'd Man: Perhaps I was too saucy and provoking.

When he found I would leave him, he took care to prevent my getting Employment in any other Printing-House of the Town, by going round and speaking to every Master, who accordingly refus'd to give me Work. I then thought of going to New York as the nearest Place where there was a Printer: and I was the rather inclin'd to leave Boston, when I reflected that I had already made myself a little obnoxious to the governing Party; and from the arbitrary Proceedings of the Assembly in my Brother's Case it was likely I might if I stay'd soon bring myself into Scrapes; and farther that my indiscreet Disputations about Religion began to make me pointed at with Horror by good People, as an Infidel or Atheist; I determin'd on the Point: but my Father now siding with my Brother, I was sensible that if I attempted to go openly, Means would be used to prevent me. My Friend Collins therefore undertook to manage a little for me. He agreed with the Captain of a New York Sloop for my Passage, under the Notion of my being a young Acquaintance of his that had got a naughty Girl with Child, whose Friends would compel me to marry her, and therefore I could not appear or come away publicly. So I sold some of my Books to raise a little Money, was taken on board privately, and as we had a fair Wind, in three Days I found myself in New York near 300 Miles from home, a Boy of but 17, without the least Recommendation to or Knowledge of any Person in the Place, and with very little Money in my Pocket.

My Inclinations for the Sea, were by this time worn out, or I might now have gratified them. But having a Trade, and supposing myself a pretty good Workman, I offer'd my Service to the Printer of the Place, old Mr. William Bradford. He could give me no Employment, having little to do, and Help enough already: But, says he, my

---

2. *Erratum* is Latin for "error" and a printer's term for misset type to be corrected in a future edition. Franklin's note on his "Errata" was a later insertion.

Son at Philadelphia has lately lost his principal Hand, Aquila Rose, by Death. If you go thither I believe he may employ you. Philadelphia was 100 Miles farther. I set out, however, in a Boat for Amboy;[3] leaving my Chest and Things to follow me round by Sea. In crossing the Bay we met with a Squall that tore our rotten Sails to pieces, prevented our getting into the Kill,[4] and drove us upon Long Island. In our Way a drunken Dutchman, who was a Passenger too, fell overboard; when he was sinking I reach'd thro' the Water to his shock Pate[5] and drew him up so that we got him in again. His Ducking sober'd him a little, and he went to sleep, taking first out of his Pocket a Book which he desir'd I would dry for him. It prov'd to be my old favorite Author Bunyan's Pilgrim's Progress in Dutch, finely printed on good Paper with copper Cuts,[6] a Dress better than I had ever seen it wear in its own Language. I have since found that it has been translated into most of the Languages of Europe, and suppose it has been more generally read than any other Book except perhaps the Bible. Honest John was the first that I know of who mix'd Narration and Dialogue, a Method of Writing very engaging to the Reader, who in the most interesting Parts finds himself as it were brought into the Company, and present at the Discourse. Defoe in his Cruso, his Moll Flanders, Religious Courtship, Family Instructor, and other Pieces, has imitated it with Success. And Richardson has done the same in his Pamela, etc.[7]

When we drew near the Island we found it was at a Place where there could be no Landing, there being a great Surf on the stony Beach. So we dropped Anchor and swung round towards the Shore. Some People came down to the Water Edge and hallow'd to us, as we did to them. But the Wind was so high and the Surf so loud, that we could not hear so as to understand each other. There were Canoes on the Shore, and we made Signs and hallow'd that they should fetch us, but they either did not understand us, or thought it impracticable. So they went away, and Night coming on, we had no Remedy but to wait till the Wind should abate, and in the mean time the Boatman and I concluded to sleep if we could, and so crowded into the Scuttle with the Dutchman who was still wet, and the Spray beating over the Head of our Boat, leak'd thro' to us, so that we were soon almost as wet as he. In this Manner we lay all Night with very

3. Perth Amboy, then capital of East Jersey, just across Arthur Kill from Staten Island, New York.
4. Dutch for "channel," this is the Kill van Kull, a channel northwest of Staten Island, New York Harbor.
5. Shaggy head.
6. The first Dutch edition (1682) had eleven small copperplate engravings.
7. *Robinson Crusoe* (1719), *Moll Flanders* (1722), *Religious Courtship* (1722), and *Family Instructor* (1715). Samuel Richardson's *Pamela* (1740) became the first novel printed in America when Franklin reprinted it from the fourth London edition in 1742 and 1743. It sold poorly.

little Rest. But the Wind abating the next Day, we made a Shift
to reach Amboy before Night, having been 30 Hours on the Water
without Victuals, or any Drink but a Bottle of filthy Rum: The Water
we sail'd on being salt.

In the Evening I found myself very feverish, and went ill to Bed.
But having read somewhere that cold Water drank plentifully was
good for a Fever, I follow'd the Prescription, sweat plentifully most
of the Night, my Fever left me, and in the Morning crossing the
Ferry, proceeded on my Journey, on foot, having 50 Miles to Burlington, where I was told I should find Boats that would carry me the
rest of the Way to Philadelphia.

It rain'd very hard all the Day, I was thoroughly soak'd, and by
Noon a good deal tir'd, so I stopped at a poor Inn, where I stayed all
Night, beginning now to wish I had never left home. I cut so miser-
able a Figure too, that I found by the Questions ask'd me I was sus-
pected to be some runaway Servant, and in danger of being taken up
on that Suspicion. However I proceeded the next Day, and got in the
Evening to an Inn within 8 or 10 Miles of Burlington, kept by one
Dr. Browne.[8]

He entered into Conversation with me while I took some Refresh-
ment, and finding I had read a little, became very sociable and
friendly. Our Acquaintance continu'd as long as he liv'd. He had
been, I imagine, an itinerant Doctor, for there was no Town in
England, or Country in Europe, of which he could not give a very
particular Account. He had some Letters, and was ingenious, but
much of an Unbeliever, and wickedly undertook some Years after to
travesty the Bible in doggerel Verse as Cotton had done Virgil.[9] By
this means he set many of the Facts in a very ridiculous Light, and
might have hurt weak minds if his Work had been publish'd: but
it never was. At his House I lay that Night, and the next Morning
reach'd Burlington.—But had the Mortification to find that the
regular Boats were gone a little before my coming, and no other
expected to go till Tuesday, this being Saturday. Wherefore I return'd
to an old Woman in the Town of whom I had bought Gingerbread to
eat on the Water, and ask'd her Advice; she invited me to lodge at
her House till a Passage by Water should offer; and being tired with
my foot Travelling, I accepted the Invitation. She understanding
I was a Printer, would have had me stay at that Town and follow my
Business, being ignorant of the Stock necessary to begin with. She

---

8. Dr. John Browne's inn (later called Washington House) was located at the northwest
   intersection of Main (or Farnsworth Street) and Crosswick Street, Bordentown, New
   Jersey. See Charles S. Boyer, *Old Inns and Taverns in West Jersey* (Camden, N.J.: 1962),
   39, map facing 38.
9. Charles Cotton, *Scarronides* (1664–65) travestied the first and fourth books of Virgil's
   Aeneid: "I sing the Man (read it who list, / A Trojan true as ever pist)."

was very hospitable, gave me a Dinner of Ox Cheek with great
Goodwill, accepting only of a Pot of Ale in return. And I thought
myself fix'd till Tuesday should come. However walking in the Evening by the Side of the River a Boat came by, which I found was
going towards Philadelphia, with several People in her. They took
me in, and as there was no Wind, we row'd all the Way; and about
Midnight not having yet seen the City, some of the Company were
confident we must have pass'd it, and would row no farther, the others knew not where we were, so we put towards the Shore, got into a
Creek, landed near an old Fence with the Rails of which we made
a Fire, the Night being cold, in October, and there we remain'd till
Daylight. Then one of the Company knew the Place to be Cooper's
Creek a little above Philadelphia,[1] which we saw as soon as we got
out of the Creek, and arriv'd there about 8 or 9 o'Clock, on the Sunday morning,[2] and landed at the Market Street Wharf.[3]

I have been the more particular in this Description of my Journey,
and shall be so of my first Entry into that City, that you may in your
Mind compare such unlikely Beginning with the Figure I have since
made there.[4] I was in my working Dress, my best Clothes being to
come round by Sea. I was dirty from my Journey; my Pockets were
stuff'd out with Shirts and Stockings; I knew no Soul, nor where to
look for Lodging. I was fatigu'd with Travelling, Rowing and Want
of Rest. I was very hungry, and my whole Stock of Cash consisted of
a Dutch Dollar and about a Shilling in Copper. The latter I gave the
People of the Boat for my Passage, who at first refus'd it on Account
of my Rowing; but I insisted on their taking it, a Man being sometimes more generous when he has but a little Money than when he
has plenty, perhaps thro' Fear of being thought to have but little.
Then I walk'd up the Street, gazing about, till near the Market
House I met a Boy with Bread. I had made many a Meal on Bread,
and inquiring where he got it, I went immediately to the Baker's he
directed me to in Second Street; and ask'd for Biscuit, intending such
as we had in Boston, but they it seems were not made in Philadelphia,
then I ask'd for a three-penny Loaf, and was told they had none such:
so not considering or knowing the Difference of Money and the
greater Cheapness nor the Names of his Bread, I bad him give me
three pennyworth of any sort. He gave me accordingly three great
Puffy Rolls. I was surpris'd at the Quantity, but took it, and having
no Room in my Pockets, walk'd off, with a Roll under each Arm,

---

1. Site of present Camden, New Jersey, across the Delaware River from Philadelphia.
2. Franklin arrived in Philadelphia on Sunday morning, October 6, 1723.
3. No. 1 in the map of Philadelphia. Other places mentioned are also located on the map.
4. When Franklin left Philadelphia for England on November 7, 1764, 300 people accompanied him to Chester, where he was honored by cannon salute and by a song that
   adapted "God Save the King" (*Papers* 11.447–48).

and eating the other. Thus I went up Market Street as far as Fourth
Street, passing by the Door of Mr. Read, my future Wife's Father,
when she standing at the Door saw me, and thought I made as
I certainly did a most awkward ridiculous Appearance. Then I turn'd
and went down Chestnut Street and part of Walnut Street, eating
my Roll all the Way, and coming round found myself again at Market Street Wharf, near the Boat I came in, to which I went for a
Draught of the River Water, and being fill'd with one of my Rolls,
gave the other two to a Woman and her Child that came down
the River in the Boat with us and were waiting to go farther. Thus
refresh'd I walk'd again up the Street, which by this time had many
clean dress'd People in it who were all walking the same Way; I join'd
them, and thereby was led into the great Meeting House of the
Quakers[5] near the Market. I sat down among them, and after looking
round a while and hearing nothing said, being very drowsy thro'
Labour and want of Rest the preceding Night, I fell fast asleep, and
continu'd so till the Meeting broke up, when one was kind enough to
rouse me. This was therefore the first House I was in or slept in, in
Philadelphia.

Walking again down towards the River, and looking in the Faces of
People, I met a young Quaker Man whose Countenance I lik'd, and
accosting him requested he would tell me where a Stranger could get
Lodging. We were then near the Sign of the Three Mariners. Here,
says he, is one Place that entertains Strangers, but it is not a reputable House; if thee wilt walk with me, I'll show thee a better. He
brought me to the Crooked Billet in Water Street. Here I got a Dinner. And while I was eating it, several sly Questions were ask'd me,
as it seem'd to be suspected from my youth and Appearance, that
I might be some Runaway. After Dinner my Sleepiness return'd: and
being shown to a Bed, I lay down without undressing, and slept till
Six in the Evening; was call'd to Supper; went to Bed again very early
and slept soundly till the next Morning. Then I made myself as tidy
as I could, and went to Andrew Bradford the Printer's. I found in the
Shop the old Man his Father, whom I had seen at New York, and
who travelling on horse back had got to Philadelphia before me. He
introduc'd me to his Son, who receiv'd me civilly, gave me a Breakfast, but told me he did not at present want a Hand, being lately supplied with one. But there was another Printer in town lately set up,
one Keimer, who perhaps might employ me; if not, I should be welcome to lodge at his House, and he would give me a little Work to do
now and then till fuller Business should offer.

---

5. Quakers are members of the Religious Society of Friends. "Quaker" was originally a
   derogatory description of their ecstatic trembling.

The old Gentleman said, he would go with me to the new Printer: And when we found him, Neighbor, says Bradford, I have brought to see you a young Man of your Business, perhaps you may want such a One. He ask'd me a few Questions, put a Composing Stick[6] in my Hand to see how I work'd, and then said he would employ me soon, tho' he had just then nothing for me to do. And taking old Bradford whom he had never seen before, to be one of the Towns-people that had a Goodwill for him, enter'd into a Conversation on his present Undertaking and Prospects; while Bradford not discovering that he was the other Printer's Father; on Keimer's Saying he expected soon to get the greatest Part of the Business into his own Hands, drew him on by artful Questions and starting little Doubts, to explain all his Views, what Interest he relied on, and in what manner he intended to proceed. I who stood by and heard all, saw immediately that one of them was a crafty old Sophister, and the other a mere Novice. Bradford left me with Keimer, who was greatly surpris'd when I told him who the old Man was.

Keimer's Printing-House I found, consisted of an old shatter'd Press and one small worn-out Fount of English,[7] which he was then using himself, composing in it an Elegy on Aquila Rose before-mentioned, an ingenious young Man of excellent Character much respected in the Town, Clerk of the Assembly, and a pretty Poet. Keimer made Verses, too, but very indifferently. He could not be said to write them, for his Manner was to compose them in the Types directly out of his Head; so there being no Copy, but one Pair of Cases,[8] and the Elegy likely to require all the Letter, no one could help him. I endeavour'd to put his Press (which he had not yet us'd, and of which he understood nothing) into Order fit to be work'd with; and promising to come and print off his Elegy as soon as he should have got it ready, I return'd to Bradford's who gave me a little Job to do for the present, and there I lodged and dieted. A few Days after Keimer sent for me to print off the Elegy.[9] And now he had got another Pair of Cases, and a Pamphlet[1] to reprint, on which he set me to work.

---

6. Compositors set type on a narrow, adjustable tray (or "stick") held in one hand.
7. A font, or complete set of letters and numbers, of the size called "English," was one size larger than pica and thus too large for newspapers or most books.
8. Two shallow trays divided into small partitions or boxes that held the types. The upper section held capitals, and the lower one lowercase letters—hence the terms upper-case and lowercase.
9. Printed on a single leaf, *An Elegy on the much Lamented Death of the Ingenious and Well-Beloved Aquila Rose . . .* appeared in 1723. See Charles Evans, *American Bibliography: A Chronological Dictionary of All Books, Pamphlets, and Periodical Publications Printed in the United States of America from the Genesis of Printing in 1639 Down to and Including the Year 1800*, 14 vols. (Chicago: Worcester, 1903–59), 2436.
1. The third edition of Thomas Chalkley, *Letter to a Friend in Ireland* (1723), perhaps commissioned by Philadelphia followers of this Quaker leader (Evans, *American Bibliography*, 2416).

These two Printers I found poorly qualified for their Business. Bradford had not been bred to it, and was very illiterate; and Keimer tho' something of a Scholar, was a mere Compositor, knowing nothing of Presswork.[2] He had been one of the French Prophets and could act their enthusiastic Agitations.[3] At this time he did not profess any particular Religion, but something of all on occasion; was very ignorant of the World, and had, as I afterwards found, a good deal of the Knave in his Composition. He did not like my Lodging at Bradford's while I work'd with him. He had a House indeed, but without Furniture, so he could not lodge me: But he got me a Lodging at Mr. Read's before-mentioned, who was the Owner of his House. And my Chest and Clothes being come by this time, I made rather a more respectable Appearance in the Eyes of Miss Read, than I had done when she first happen'd to see me eating my Roll in the Street.

I began now to have some Acquaintance among the young People of the Town, that were Lovers of Reading with whom I spent my Evenings very pleasantly and gaining Money by my Industry and Frugality, I lived very agreeably, forgetting Boston as much as I could, and not desiring that any there should know where I resided except my Friend Collins who was in my Secret, and kept it when I wrote to him. At length an Incident happened that sent me back again much sooner than I had intended.

I had a Brother-in-law, Robert Holmes,[4] Master of a Sloop that traded between Boston and Delaware. He being at New Castle 40 Miles below Philadelphia, heard there of me, and wrote me a Letter, mentioning the Concern of my Friends in Boston at my abrupt Departure, assuring me of their Goodwill to me, and that everything would be accommodated to my Mind if I would return, to which he exhorted me very earnestly. I wrote an Answer to his Letter, thank'd him for his Advice, but stated my Reasons for quitting Boston fully, and in such a Light as to convince him I was not so wrong as he had apprehended. Sir William Keith Governor of the Province, was then at New Castle, and Captain Homes happening to be in Company with him when my Letter came to hand, spoke to him of me, and show'd him the Letter. The Governor read it, and seem'd surpris'd when he was told my Age. He said I appear'd a young Man of promising Parts, and therefore should be encouraged: The Printers at Philadelphia were wretched ones, and if I would set up there, he made no doubt I should succeed; for his Part, he would

---

2. The compositor set the type. Printing it off was called "presswork."
3. In 1701, the French Prophets (or Camisards) were a London sect preaching doomsday, speaking in tongues, and swooning into fits. Outlawed in 1709, the sect dissolved. Descriptions of its ecstatic style were recycled in the 1740s as propaganda against the emotionalism of the Great Awakening.
4. Robert Homes.

procure me the public Business, and do me every other Service in his Power. This my Brother-in-Law afterwards told me in Boston. But I knew as yet nothing of it; when one Day Keimer and I being at Work together near the Window, we saw the Governor and another Gentleman (which prov'd to be Colonel French, of New Castle) finely dress'd, come directly across the Street to our House, and heard them at the Door.[5]

Keimer ran down immediately, thinking it a Visit to him. But the Governor enquir'd for me, came up, and with a Condescension and Politeness I had been quite unus'd to, made me many Compliments, desired to be acquainted with me, blam'd me kindly for not having made myself known to him when I first came to the Place, and would have me away with him to the Tavern where he was going with Colonel French to taste as he said some excellent Madeira. I was not a little surpris'd, and Keimer star'd like a Pig poison'd. I went however with the Governor and Colonel French, to a Tavern the Corner of Third Street, and over the Madeira he propos'd my Setting up my Business, laid before me the Probabilities of Success, and both he and Colonel French assur'd me I should have their Interest and Influence in procuring the Public-Business of both Governments. On my doubting whether my Father would assist me in it, Sir William said he would give me a Letter to him, in which he would state the Advantages, and he did not doubt of prevailing with him. So it was concluded I should return to Boston in the first Vessel with the Governor's Letter recommending me to my Father.

In the meantime the Intention was to be kept secret, and I went on working with Keimer as usual, the Governor sending for me now and then to dine with him, a very great Honor I thought it, and conversing with me in the most affable, familiar, and friendly manner imaginable. About the End of April 1724, a little Vessel offer'd for Boston. I took Leave of Keimer as going to see my Friends. The Governor gave me an ample Letter, saying many flattering things of me to my Father, and strongly recommending the Project of my setting up at Philadelphia, as a Thing that must make my Fortune. We struck on a Shoal in going down the Bay and sprung a Leak, we had a blustring time at Sea, and were oblig'd to pump almost continually, at which I took my Turn. We arriv'd safe however at Boston in about a Fortnight. I had been absent Seven Months and my Friends had heard nothing of me, for my Brother Homes was not yet return'd; and had not written about me. My unexpected Appearance surpris'd the Family; all were however very glad to see me and made me Welcome, except my Brother.

5. Keith was governor of both Pennsylvania and Delaware, where New Castle was capital. Colonel French was the Speaker of the Delaware assembly.

I went to see him at his Printing-House: I was better dress'd than ever while in his Service, having a genteel new Suit from Head to foot, a Watch, and my Pockets lin'd with near Five Pounds Sterling in Silver. He receiv'd me not very frankly, look'd me all over, and turn'd to his Work again. The Journeymen were inquisitive where I had been, what sort of a Country it was, and how I lik'd it? I prais'd it much, and the happy Life I led in it; expressing strongly my Intention of returning to it; and one of them asking what kind of Money we had there, I produe'd a handful of Silver and spread it before them, which was a kind of Raree-Show[6] they had not been us'd to, Paper being the Money of Boston.[7] Then I took an Opportunity of letting them see my Watch: and lastly, (my Brother still grum and sullen) I gave them a Piece of Eight to drink and took my Leave. This Visit of mine offended him extremely. For when my Mother some time after spoke to him of a Reconciliation, and of her Wishes to see us on good Terms together, and that we might live for the future as Brothers, he said, I had insulted him in such a Manner before his People that he could never forget or forgive it. In this however he was mistaken.

My Father receiv'd the Governor's Letter with some apparent Surprise; but said little of it to me for some Days; when Captain Homes returning, he show'd it to him, ask'd if he knew Keith, and what kind of a Man he was: Adding his Opinion that he must be of small Discretion, to think of setting a Boy up in Business who wanted yet 3 Years of being at Man's Estate. Homes said what he could in favor of the Project; but my Father was clear in the Impropriety of it; and at last gave a flat Denial to it. Then he wrote a civil Letter to Sir William thanking him for the Patronage he had so kindly offered me, but declining to assist me as yet in Setting up, I being in his Opinion too young to be trusted with the Management of a Business so important; and for which the Preparation must be so expensive.

My Friend and Companion Collins, who was a Clerk at the Post-Office, pleas'd with the Account I gave him of my new Country, determin'd to go thither also: And while I waited for my Father's Determination, he set out before me by Land to Rhode Island, leaving his Books which were a pretty Collection of Mathematics and Natural Philosophy, to come with mine and me to New York where he propos'd to wait for me. My Father, tho' he did not approve Sir William's Proposition, was yet pleas'd that I had been able to obtain so advantageous a Character from a Person of such Note where I had resided, and that I had been so industrious and careful as to equip

---

6. A sidewalk peepshow or puppet show, usually carried in a box.
7. Silver coins, rare in the colonies, were especially so in Boston, where they were fixed at a low value. Speculators bought them up to sell in other colonies, at higher prices.

myself so handsomely in so short a time: therefore seeing no Prospect of an Accommodation between my Brother and me, he gave his Consent to my Returning again to Philadelphia, advis'd me to behave respectfully to the People there, endeavour to obtain the general Esteem, and avoid lampooning and libelling to which he thought I had too much Inclination; telling me, that by steady Industry and a prudent Parsimony, I might save enough by the time I was One and Twenty to set me up, and that if I came near the Matter he would help me out with the Rest. This was all I could obtain, except some small Gifts as Tokens of his and my Mother's Love, when I embark'd again for New York, now with their Approbation and their Blessing.

The Sloop putting in at Newport, Rhode Island, I visited my Brother John, who had been married and settled there some Years. He received me very affectionately, for he always lov'd me. A Friend of his, one Vernon, having some Money due to him in Pennsylvania, about 35 Pounds Currency, desired I would receive it for him, and keep it till I had his Directions what to remit it in. Accordingly he gave me an Order. This afterwards occasion'd me a good deal of Uneasiness. At Newport we took in a Number of Passengers for New York: Among which were two young Women, Companions, and a grave, sensible Matron-like Quaker-Woman with her Attendants. I had shown an obliging Readiness to do her some little Services which impress'd her I suppose with a degree of Goodwill towards me. Therefore when she saw a daily growing Familiarity between me and the two Young Women, which they appear'd to encourage, she took me aside and said, Young Man, I am concern'd for thee, as thou has no Friend with thee, and seems not to know much of the World, or of the Snares Youth is expos'd to; depend upon it those are very bad Women, I can see it in all their Actions, and if thee art not upon thy Guard, they will draw thee into some Danger: they are Strangers to thee, and I advise thee in a friendly Concern for thy Welfare, to have no Acquaintance with them. As I seem'd at first not to think so ill of them as she did, she mention'd some Things she had observ'd and heard that had escap'd my Notice; but now convinc'd me she was right. I thank'd her for her kind Advice, and promis'd to follow it. When we arriv'd at New York, they told me where they liv'd, and invited me to come and see them: but I avoided it. And it was well I did: For the next Day, the Captain miss'd a Silver Spoon and some other Things that had been taken out of his Cabin, and knowing that these were a Couple of Strumpets, he got a Warrant to search their Lodgings, found the stolen Goods, and had the Thieves punish'd. So tho' we had escap'd a sunken Rock which we scrap'd upon in the Passage, I thought this Escape of rather more Importance to me.

At New York I found my Friend Collins, who had arriv'd there some Time before me. We had been intimate from Children, and had read the same Books together. But he had the Advantage of more time for Reading, and Studying and a wonderful Genius for Mathematical Learning in which he far outstripped me. While I liv'd in Boston most of my Hours of Leisure for Conversation were spent with him, and he continu'd a sober as well as an industrious Lad; was much respected for his Learning by several of the Clergy and other Gentlemen, and seem'd to promise making a good Figure in Life: but during my Absence he had acquir'd a Habit of Sotting with Brandy; and I found by his own Account and what I heard from others, that he had been drunk every day since his Arrival at New York, and behav'd very oddly. He had gam'd too and lost his Money, so that I was oblig'd to discharge his Lodgings, and defray his Expences to and at Philadelphia: Which prov'd extremely inconvenient to me. The then Governor of New York, Burnet, Son of Bishop Burnet, hearing from the Captain that a young Man, one of his Passengers, had a great many Books, desired he would bring me to see him. I waited upon him accordingly, and should have taken Collins with me but that he was not sober. The Governor treated me with great Civility, show'd me his Library, which was a very large one, and we had a good deal of Conversation about Books and Authors. This was the second Governor who had done me the Honor to take Notice of me, which to a poor Boy like me was very pleasing.

We proceeded to Philadelphia. I received on the Way Vernon's Money, without which we could hardly have finish'd our Journey. Collins wish'd to be employ'd in some Counting House; but whether they discover'd his Dramming by his Breath, or by his Behaviour, tho' he had some Recommendations, he met with no Success in any Application, and continu'd Lodging and Boarding at the same House with me and at my Expense. Knowing I had that Money of Vernon's he was continually borrowing of me, still promising Repayment as soon as he should be in Business. At length he had got so much of it, that I was distress'd to think what I should do, in case of being call'd on to remit it. His Drinking continu'd, about which we sometimes quarrel'd, for when a little intoxicated he was very fractious. Once in a Boat on the Delaware with some other young Men, he refused to row in his Turn: I will be row'd home, says he. We will not row you, says I. You must, says he, or stay all Night on the Water, just as you please. The others said, Let us row; What signifies it? But my Mind being soured with his other Conduct, I continu'd to refuse. So he swore he would make me row, or throw me overboard; and coming along stepping on the Thwarts towards me, when he came up and struck at me, I clapped my Hand under his Crotch, and rising, pitch'd him head-foremost into the River. I knew he was a good Swimmer, and so was under little Concern about him; but before he could get round to lay hold of the Boat, we had with a few Strokes

pull'd her out of his Reach. And ever when he drew near the Boat,
we ask'd if he would row, striking a few Strokes to slide her away
from him. He was ready to die with Vexation, and obstinately would
not promise to row; however seeing him at last beginning to tire, we
lifted him in; and brought him home dripping wet in the Evening.
We hardly exchang'd a civil Word afterwards; and a West India Captain who had a Commission to procure a Tutor for the Sons of a
Gentleman at Barbados, happening to meet with him, agreed to
carry him thither. He left me then, promising to remit me the first
Money he should receive in order to discharge the Debt. But I never
heard of him after.

The Breaking into this Money of Vernon's was one of the first
great Errata[8] of my Life. And this Affair show'd that my Father was
not much out in his Judgment when he suppos'd me too Young to
manage Business of Importance. But Sir William, on reading his
Letter, said he was too prudent. There was great Difference in Persons, and Discretion did not always accompany Years, nor was Youth
always without it. And since he will not set you up, says he, I will do
it myself. Give me an Inventory of the Things necessary to be had
from England, and I will send for them. You shall repay me when you
are able; I am resolv'd to have a good Printer here, and I am sure you
must succeed. This was spoken with such an Appearance of Cordial-
ity, that I had not the least doubt of his meaning what he said. I had
hitherto kept the Proposition of my Setting up a Secret in Philadelphia, and I still kept it. Had it been known that I depended on the
Governor, probably some Friend that knew him better would have
advis'd me not to rely on him, as I afterwards heard it as his known
Character to be liberal of Promises which he never meant to keep.
Yet unsolicited as he was by me, how could I think his generous
Offers insincere? I believ'd him one of the best Men in the World.

I presented him an Inventory of a little Printing House, amounting by my Computation to about 100 Pounds Sterling. He lik'd it,
but ask'd me if my being on the Spot in England to choose the Types
and see that everything was good of the kind, might not be of some
Advantage. Then, says he, when there, you may make Acquaintances and establish Correspondences in the Bookselling, and Stationery Way. I agreed that this might be advantageous. Then says
he, get yourself ready to go with Annis;[9] which was the annual Ship,
and the only one at that Time usually passing between London and
Philadelphia. But it would be some Months before Annis sail'd, so
I continu'd working with Keimer, fretting about the Money Collins

---

8. This mention of "errata" was also added after Franklin's original Composition.
9. Thomas Annis, captain of the annual mail packet, the *London Hope*.

had got from me, and in daily Apprehensions of being call'd upon by Vernon, which however did not happen for some Years after.

I believe I have omitted mentioning that in my first Voyage from Boston, being becalm'd off Block Island, our People set about catching Cod and haul'd up a great many. Hitherto I had stuck to my Resolution of not eating animal Food; and on this Occasion, I consider'd with my Master Tryon, the taking every Fish as a kind of unprovok'd Murder, since none of them had or ever could do us any Injury that might justify the Slaughter.[1] All this seem'd very reasonable. But I had formerly been a great Lover of Fish, and when this came hot out of the Frying Pan, it smelt admirably well. I balanc'd some time between Principle and Inclination: till I recollected, that when the Fish were opened, I saw smaller Fish taken out of their Stomachs: Then, thought I, if you eat one another, I don't see why we mayn't eat you. So I din'd upon Cod very heartily and continu'd to eat with other People, returning only now and then occasionally to a vegetable Diet. So convenient a thing it is to be a *reasonable Creature*, since it enables one to find or make a Reason for everything one has a mind to do.

Keimer and I liv'd on a pretty good familiar Footing and agreed tolerably well: for he suspected nothing of my Setting up. He retain'd a great deal of his old Enthusiasms, and lov'd an Argumentation. We therefore had many Disputations. I us'd to work him so with my Socratic Method, and had trapann'd[2] him so often by Questions apparently so distant from any Point we had in hand, and yet by degrees led to the Point, and brought him into Difficulties and Contradictions, that at last he grew ridiculously cautious, and would hardly answer me the most common Question, without asking first, *What do you intend to infer from that?* However it gave him so high an Opinion of my Abilities in the Confuting Way, that he seriously propos'd my being his Colleague in a Project he had of setting up a new Sect. He was to preach the Doctrines, and I was to confound all Opponents. When he came to explain with me upon the Doctrines, I found several Conundrums which I objected to, unless I might have my Way a little too, and introduce some of mine. Keimer wore his Beard at full Length, because somewhere in the Mosaic Law it is said, *thou shalt not mar the Corners of thy Beard.*[3] He likewise kept the seventh-day Sabbath; and these two Points were Essentials with him. I dislik'd both, but agreed to admit them upon Condition of his adopting the Doctrine of using no animal Food. I doubt, says he, my

---

1. "Flesh and Fish cannot be eaten without Violence, and doing that which a man would not be done unto" (Thomas Tryon, *Way to Health* [1683], 343).
2. Snared.
3. Leviticus 19.27 reads, "Ye shall not round the corners of your heads, neither shalt thou mar the corners of thy beard."

Constitution will not bear that. I assur'd him it would, and that he would be the better for it. He was usually a great Glutton, and I promis'd myself some Diversion in half-starving him. He agreed to try the Practice if I would keep him Company. I did so and we held it for three Months. We had our Victuals dress'd and brought to us regularly by a Woman in the Neighborhood, who had from me a List of 40 Dishes to be prepar'd for us at different times, in all which there was neither Fish Flesh nor Fowl, and the Whim suited me the better at this time from the Cheapness of it, not costing us above 18 Pence Sterling each, per Week. I have since kept several Lents most strictly, leaving the common Diet for that, and that for the common, abruptly, without the least Inconvenience: So that I think there is little in the Advice of making those Changes by easy Gradations. I went on pleasantly, but Poor Keimer suffer'd grievously, tir'd of the Project, long'd for the Flesh Pots of Egypt,[4] and order'd a roast Pig; He invited me and two Women Friends to dine with him, but it being brought too soon upon table, he could not resist the Temptation, and ate it all up before we came.

I had made some Courtship during this time to Miss Read. I had a great Respect and Affection for her, and had some Reason to believe she had the same for me: but as I was about to take a long Voyage, and we were both very young, only a little above 18, it was thought most prudent by her Mother to prevent our going too far at present, as a Marriage if it was to take place would be more convenient after my Return, when I should be as I expected set up in my Business. Perhaps too she thought my Expectations not so well founded as I imagined them to be.

My chief Acquaintances at this time were, Charles Osborne, Joseph Watson, and James Ralph; All Lovers of Reading. The two first were Clerks to an eminent Scrivener or Conveyancer in the Town, Charles Brockden; the other was Clerk to a Merchant. Watson was a pious sensible young Man, of great Integrity. The others rather more lax in their Principles of Religion, particularly Ralph, who as well as Collins had been unsettled by me, for which they both made me suffer. Osborne was sensible, candid, frank, sincere, and affectionate to his Friends; but in literary Matters too fond of Criticizing. Ralph, was ingenious, genteel in his Manners, and extremely eloquent; I think I never knew a prettier Talker. Both of them great Admirers of Poetry, and began to try their Hands in little Pieces. Many pleasant Walks we four had together, on Sundays into the Woods near Skuylkill, where we read to one another and conferr'd on what we read. Ralph was inclin'd to pursue the Study of Poetry, not doubting but he might

---

4. Forbidden by Moses to eat animal flesh in the wilderness, the Israelites yearned for the stew-pots of meat they had left behind in Egypt (Exodus 16.2–3).

become eminent in it and make his Fortune by it, alledging that the best Poets must when they first began to write, make as many Faults as he did. Osborne dissuaded him, assur'd him he had no Genius for Poetry, and advis'd him to think of nothing beyond the Business he was bred to; that in the mercantile way tho' he had no Stock, he might by his Diligence and Punctuality recommend himself to Employment as a Factor, and in time acquire wherewith to trade on his own Account. I approv'd the amusing oneself with Poetry now and then, so far as to improve one's Language, but no farther. On this it was propos'd that we should each of us at our next Meeting produce a Piece of our own Composing, in order to improve by our mutual Observations, Criticisms and Corrections. As Language and Expression was what we had in View, we excluded all Considerations of Invention, by agreeing that the Task should be a Version of the 18th Psalm, which describes the Descent of a Deity. When the Time of our Meeting drew nigh, Ralph call'd on me first, and let me know his Piece was ready. I told him I had been busy, and having little Inclination had done nothing. He then show'd me his Piece for my Opinion; and I much approv'd it, as it appear'd to me to have great Merit. Now, says he, Osborne never will allow the least Merit in any thing of mine, but makes 1000 Criticisms out of mere Envy. He is not so jealous of you. I wish therefore you would take this Piece, and produce it as yours. I will pretend not to have had time, and so produce nothing. We shall then see what he will say to it. It was agreed, and I immediately transcrib'd it that it might appear in my own hand. We met.

Watson's Performance was read: there were some Beauties in it: but many Defects. Osborne's was read: It was much better. Ralph did it Justice, remark'd some Faults, but applauded the Beauties. He himself had nothing to produce. I was backward, seem'd desirous of being excus'd, had not had sufficient Time to correct; etc. but no Excuse could be admitted, produce I must. It was read and repeated; Watson and Osborne gave up the Contest; and join'd in applauding it immoderately. Ralph only made some Criticisms and propos'd some Amendments, but I defended my Text. Osborne was against Ralph, and told him he was no better a Critic than Poet; so he dropped the Argument. As they two went home together, Osborne express'd himself still more strongly in favor of what he thought my Production, having restrain'd himself before as he said, lest I should think it Flattery. But who would have imagin'd, says he, that Franklin had been capable of such a Performance; such Painting, such Force! such Fire! He has even improv'd the Original! In his common Conversation, he seems to have no Choice of Words; he hesitates and blunders; and yet, good God, how he writes!

When we next met, Ralph discover'd the Trick we had played him, and Osborne was a little laughed at. This Transaction fix'd Ralph in his Resolution of becoming a Poet. I did all I could to dissuade him from it, but he continu'd scribbling Verses, till *Pope* cur'd him.[5] He became however a pretty good Prose Writer. More of him hereafter. But as I may not have occasion again to mention the other two, I shall just remark here, that Watson died in my Arms a few Years after, much lamented, being the best of our Set. Osborne went to the West Indies, where he became an eminent Lawyer and made Money, but died young. He and I had made a serious Agreement, that the one who happen'd first to die, should if possible make a friendly Visit to the other, and acquaint him how he found things in that separate State. But he never fulfill'd his Promise.

The Governor, seeming to like my Company, had me frequently to his House; and his Setting me up was always mention'd as a fix'd thing. I was to take with me Letters recommendatory to a Number of his Friends, besides the Letter of Credit to furnish me with the necessary Money for purchasing the Press and Types, Paper, etc. For these Letters I was appointed to call at different times, when they were to be ready, but a future time was still named. Thus we went on till the Ship whose Departure too had been several times postponed was on the Point of sailing. Then when I call'd to take my Leave and receive the Letters, his Secretary, Dr. Bard, came out to me and said the Governor was extremely busy, in writing, but would be down at New Castle before the Ship, and there the Letters would be delivered to me.

Ralph, tho' married and having one Child, had determined to accompany me in this Voyage. It was thought he intended to estab- lish a Correspondence, and obtain Goods to sell on Commission. But I found afterwards, that thro' some Discontent with his Wife's Rela- tions, he purposed to leave her on their Hands, and never return again. Having taken leave of my Friends, and interchang'd some Promises with Miss Read, I left Philadelphia in the Ship, which anchor'd at New Castle. The Governor was there. But when I went to his Lodging, the Secretary came to me from him with the civillest Message in the World, that he could not then see me being engag'd in Business of the utmost Importance, but should send the Letters to me on board, wish'd me heartily a good Voyage and a speedy Return, etc. I return'd on board, a little puzzled, but still not doubting.

Mr. Andrew Hamilton, a famous Lawyer of Philadelphia, had taken Passage in the same Ship for himself and Son: and with Mr. Denham

5. Ralph attacked Pope in his poem *Sawney* (1728). Pope alluded to Ralph's *Night* (also 1728) in the second edition of the *Dunciad* (1728): "Silence, ye Wolves! while Ralph to Cynthia howls, / And makes Night hideous—Answer him ye Owls!" (Book 3, 11.159–60). And in the 1742 *Dunciad*, Pope introduced Ralph into the first Book: "And see! The very Gazeteers give o'er, / Ev'n Ralph repents . . ." (1.21516). See James Sutherland, ed., *The Dunciad* (London: Methuen, 1953), 165, 285.

a Quaker Merchant, and Messrs. Onion and Russel Masters of an Iron Work in Maryland, had engag'd the Great Cabin; so that Ralph and I were forc'd to take up with a Berth in the Steerage: And none on board knowing us, were considered as ordinary Persons. But Mr. Hamilton and his Son (it was James, since Governor) return'd from New Castle to Philadelphia, the Father being recall'd by a great Fee to plead for a seized Ship.[6] And just before we sail'd Colonel French coming on board, and showing me great Respect, I was more taken Notice of, and with my Friend Ralph invited by the other Gentlemen to come into the Cabin, there being now Room. Accordingly we remov'd thither.

Understanding that Colonel French had brought on board the Governor's Dispatches, I ask'd the Captain for those Letters that were to be under my Care. He said all were put into the Bag together; and he could not then come at them; but before we landed in England, I should have an Opportunity of picking them out. So I was satisfied for the present, and we proceeded on our Voyage. We had a sociable Company in the Cabin, and lived uncommonly well, having the Addition of all Mr. Hamilton's Stores, who had laid in plentifully. In this Passage Mr. Denham contracted a Friendship for me that continued during his Life. The Voyage was otherwise not a pleasant one, as we had a great deal of bad Weather.

When we came into the Channel, the Captain kept his Word with me, and gave me an Opportunity of examining the Bag for the Governor's Letters. I found none upon which my Name was put, as under my Care; I pick'd out 6 or 7 that by the Handwriting I thought might be the promis'd Letters, especially as one of them was directed to Basket the King's Printer, and another to some Stationer. We arriv'd in London the 24th of December, 1724. I waited upon the Stationer who came first in my Way, delivering the Letter as from Governor Keith. I don't know such a Person, says he: but opening the Letter, O, this is from Riddlesden; I have lately found him to be a complete Rascal, and I will have nothing to do with him, nor receive any Letters from him. So putting the Letter into my Hand, he turn'd on his Heel and left me to serve some Customer. I was surprised to find these were not the Governor's Letters. And after recollecting and comparing Circumstances, I began to doubt his Sincerity. I found my Friend Denham, and opened the whole Affair to him. He let me into Keith's Character, told me there was not the least Probability that he had written any Letters for me, that no one who knew him had the smallest Dependence on him, and he laughed at the Notion of the Governor's giving me a Letter of Credit, having

6. The *American Weekly Mercury* (November 5, 1724) reported Hamilton had set out on November 2, but had been recalled for a fee of £300.

as he said no Credit to give. On my expressing some Concern about what I should do: He advis'd me to endeavour getting some Employment in the Way of my Business. Among the Printers here, says he, you will improve yourself; and when you return to America, you will set up to greater Advantage.

We both of us happen'd to know, as well as the Stationer, that Riddlesden the Attorney, was a very Knave. He had half ruin'd Miss Read's Father by drawing him in to be bound for him. By his Letter it appear'd, there was a secret Scheme on foot to the Prejudice of Hamilton, (Suppos'd to be then coming over with us,) and that Keith was concern'd in it with Riddlesden. Denham, who was a Friend of Hamilton's, thought he ought to be acquainted with it. So when he arriv'd in England, which was soon after, partly from Resentment and Ill-Will to Keith and Riddlesden, and partly from Goodwill to him: I waited on him, and gave him the Letter. He thank'd me cordially, the Information being of Importance to him. And from that time he became my Friend, greatly to my Advantage afterwards on many Occasions.

But what shall we think of a Governor's playing such pitiful Tricks, and imposing so grossly on a poor ignorant Boy! It was a Habit he had acquired. He wish'd to please everybody; and having little to give, he gave Expectations. He was otherwise an ingenious sensible Man, a pretty good Writer, and a good Governor for the People, tho' not for his Constituents the Proprietaries, whose Instructions he sometimes disregarded. Several of our best Laws were of his Planning, and pass'd during his Administration.

Ralph and I were inseparable Companions. We took Lodgings together in Little Britain[7] at 3 shillings 6 pence per Week, as much as we could then afford. He found some Relations, but they were poor and unable to assist him. He now let me know his Intentions of remaining in London, and that he never meant to return to Philadelphia. He had brought no Money with him, the whole he could muster having been expended in paying his Passage. I had 15 Pistoles. So he borrowed occasionally of me, to subsist while he was looking out for Business. He first endeavoured to get into the Playhouse, believing himself qualified for an Actor; but Wilkes,[8] to whom he applied, advis'd him candidly not to think of that Employment, as it was impossible he should succeed in it. Then he propos'd to Roberts, a Publisher in Paternoster Row, to write for him a Weekly Paper like the Spectator, on certain Conditions, which Roberts did not approve. Then he endeavour'd to get Employment as a Hackney

7. Neighborhood in mid-London, north of St. Paul's, that takes its name from a small alley, noted in Franklin's day for its slaughterhouses, printing houses, and booksellers.
8. Robert Wilks.

Writer to copy for the Stationers and Lawyers about the Temple:[9] but could find no Vacancy.

I immediately got into Work at Palmer's, then a famous Printing-House in Bartholomew Close;[1] and here I continu'd near a Year. I was pretty diligent; but spent with Ralph a good deal of my Earnings in going to Plays and other Places of Amusement.[2] We had together consum'd all my Pistoles, and now just rubb'd on from hand to mouth. He seem'd quite to forget his Wife and Child, and I by degrees my Engagements with Miss Read, to whom I never wrote more than one Letter, and that was to let her know I was not likely soon to return. This was another of the great Errata of my Life, which I should wish to correct if I were to live it over again. In fact, by our Expenses, I was constantly kept unable to pay my Passage.

At Palmer's I was employ'd in Composing for the second Edition of Wollaston's Religion of Nature.[3] Some of his Reasonings not appearing to me well-founded, I wrote a little metaphysical Piece, in which I made Remarks on them. It was entitled, A *Dissertation on Liberty and Necessity, Pleasure and Pain.* I inscrib'd it to my Friend Ralph. I printed a small Number. It occasion'd my being more consider'd by Mr. Palmer, as a young Man of some Ingenuity, tho' he seriously expostulated with me upon the Principles of my Pamphlet which to him appear'd abominable. My printing this Pamphlet was another Erratum.[4]

While I lodg'd in Little Britain I made an Acquaintance with one Wilcox a Bookseller, whose Shop was at the next Door. He had an immense Collection of second-hand Books. Circulating Libraries were not then in Use; but we agreed that on certain reasonable Terms which I have now forgotten, I might take, read and return any of his Books. This I esteem'd a great Advantage, and I made as much Use of it as I could.

My Pamphlet by some means falling into the Hands of one Lyons, a Surgeon, Author of a Book entitled *The Infallibility of Human Judgment*, it occasioned an Acquaintance between us; he took great Notice of me, call'd on me often, to converse on these Subjects, carried me to the Horns a pale Ale-House in [blank] Lane, Cheapside,[5]

9. One of the Inns of Court, where lawyers were trained.
1. Just off Little Britain, the remains of an ancient monastery attached to the church of St. Bartholomew the Great. Palmer's shop occupied the top floor at 54 Bartholomew Close, and the type foundry of Thomas and John James was evidently downstairs.
2. Four years later, Ralph published *The Touch-stone* (1729), a guide to London places of amusement.
3. Franklin set the type for the third edition of William Wollaston's *Religion of Nature Delineated* (London: Samuel Palmer, 1725) in January or February, for it was advertised for sale by the end of February 1725 (*Monthly Catalogue* for February 1724/25, 21).
4. *Papers* 1.58–71. Franklin nevertheless reused parts of his pamphlet in later writings.
5. Possibly a "Horns Tavern" in Gutter Lane, Cheapside. See Bryant Lillywhite, *London Signs: A Reference Book of London Signs from Earliest Times to About the Mid-Nineteenth Century* (London: Allen and Unwin, 1972), nos. 8911 and 8885.

and introduc'd me to Dr. Mandeville, Author of the Fable of the
Bees[6] who had a Club there, of which he was the Soul, being a
most facetious entertaining Companion. Lyons too introduc'd me
to Dr. Pemberton, at Batson's Coffee House,[7] who promis'd to give
me an Opportunity some time or other of seeing Sir Isaac Newton,
of which I was extremely desirous; but this never happened.

I had brought over a few Curiosities among which the principal
was a Purse made of the Asbestos, which purifies by Fire. Sir Hans
Sloane heard of it,[8] came to see me, and invited me to his House in
Bloomsbury Square; where he show'd me all his Curiosities, and
persuaded me to let him add that to the Number, for which he paid
me handsomely.

In our House there lodg'd a young Woman, a Millener, who I think
had a Shop in the Cloisters.[9] She had been genteelly bred, was sensible and lively, and of most pleasing Conversation. Ralph read Plays
to her in the Evenings, they grew intimate, she took another Lodging, and he follow'd her. They liv'd together some time, but he being
still out of Business, and her Income not sufficient to maintain them
with her Child, he took a Resolution of going from London, to try for
a Country School, which he thought himself well qualified to undertake, as he wrote an excellent Hand, and was a Master of Arithmetic
and Accounts. This however he deem'd a Business below him, and
confident of future better Fortune when he should be unwilling to
have it known that he once was so meanly employ'd, he chang'd his
Name, and did me the Honor to assume mine. For I soon after had
a Letter from him, acquainting me, that he was settled in a small
Village in Berkshire, I think it was, where he taught reading and
writing to 10 or a dozen Boys at 6 pence each per Week, recommending Mrs. T. to my Care, and desiring me to write to him directing
for Mr. Franklin Schoolmaster at such a Place. He continu'd to
write frequently, sending me large Specimens of an Epic Poem,[1]
which he was then composing, and desiring my Remarks and Corrections. These I gave him from time to time, but endeavour'd rather
to discourage his Proceeding. One of Young's Satires was then just
publish'd. I copied and sent him a great Part of it, which set in a
strong Light the Folly of pursuing the Muses with any Hope of

---

6. Published in 1714, it expanded an earlier poem, *The Grumbling Hive* (1705). Just before
   Franklin's arrival in London, the grand jury had declared the book "a public nuisance."
7. A rendezvous for physicians at No. 17, Cornhill, "against the Royal Exchange." See Bryant Lillywhite, *London Coffee Houses: A Reference Book* (London: Allen and Unwin,
   1963), no. 90.
8. In truth, Franklin himself in a letter of June 2, 1725, offered to show or sell these curiosities (*Papers* 1.54).
9. The ancient monastic cloisters of St. Bartholomew's had been converted to commercial
   use, including a tavern.
1. Perhaps Ralph's *Sawney*, "an heroic poem."

Advancement by them.[2] All was in vain. Sheets of the Poem continu'd
to come by every Post. In the mean time Mrs. T. having on his
Account lost her Friends and Business, was often in Distresses, and
us'd to send for me, and borrow what I could spare to help her out
of them. I grew fond of her Company, and being at this time under
no Religious Restraints, and presuming on my Importance to her, I
attempted Familiarities, (another Erratum),[3] which she repuls'd with
a proper Resentment, and acquainted him with my Behaviour. This
made a Breach between us, and when he return'd again to London,
he let me know he thought I had cancel'd all the Obligations he had
been under to me. So I found I was never to expect his Repaying me
what I lent to him or advanc'd for him. This was however not then of
much Consequence, as he was totally unable. And in the Loss of his
Friendship I found myself reliev'd from a Burden. I now began to
think of getting a little Money beforehand; and expecting better
Work, I left Palmer's to work at Watts's near Lincoln's Inn Fields,[4] a
still greater Printing-House.[5] Here I continu'd all the rest of my Stay
in London.

At my first Admission into this Printing-House, I took to working
at Press, imagining I felt a Want of the Bodily Exercise I had been
us'd to in America, where Presswork is mix'd with Composing. I
drank only Water; the other Workmen, near 50 in Number, were
great Guzzlers of Beer. On occasion I carried up and down Stairs a
large Form of Types in each hand, when others carried but one in
both Hands. They wonder'd to see from this and several Instances
that the Water-American as they call'd me was *stronger* than themselves who drunk *strong* Beer. We had an Alehouse Boy who attended
always in the House to supply the Workmen. My Companion at the
Press drank every day a Pint before Breakfast, a Pint at Breakfast
with his Bread and Cheese; a Pint between Breakfast and Dinner; a
Pint at Dinner; a Pint in the Afternoon about Six o'clock, and
another when he had done his Day's Work. I thought it a detestable
Custom. But it was necessary, he suppos'd, to drink *strong* Beer that
he might be *strong* to labour. I endeavour'd to convince him that the
Bodily Strength afforded by Beer could only be in proportion to the
Grain or Flour of the Barley dissolved in the Water of which it was
made; that there was more Flour in a Penny-worth of Bread, and
therefore if he would eat that with a Pint of Water, it would give him
more Strength than a Quart of Beer. He drank on however, and had

---

2. Satires i–iv of Edward Young's *The Universal Passion* appeared in 1725. Satire ii
   declared that "Fame and Fortune both are made of Prose."
3. Again, an addition to the text.
4. The largest park in mid-London.
5. Palmer had two apprentices, whereas Watts had fifteen. See Ellie Howe, *The London
   Compositor* (London: Bibliographical Society, 1947), 37.

4 or 5 Shillings to pay out of his Wages every Saturday Night for that muddling Liquor; an Expense I was free from. And thus these poor Devils keep themselves always under.

Watts after some Weeks desiring to have me in the Composing-Room, I left the Pressmen. A new *Bienvenu*[6] or Sum for Drink, being 5 Shillings, was demanded of me by the Compositors. I thought it an Imposition, as I had paid below. The Master thought so too, and forbad my Paying it. I stood out two or three Weeks, was accordingly considered as an Excommunicate, and had so many little Pieces of private Mischief done me, by mixing my Sorts, transposing my Pages, breaking my Matter,[7] etc. etc. if I were ever so little out of the Room, and all ascrib'd to the Chapel Ghost, which they said ever haunted those not regularly admitted, that notwithstanding the Master's Protection, I found myself oblig'd to comply and pay the Money; convinc'd of the Folly of being on ill Terms with those one is to live with continually. I was now on a fair Footing with them, and soon acquir'd considerable Influence. I propos'd some reasonable Alterations in their Chapel* Laws, and carried them against all Opposition. From my Example a great Part of them, left their muddling Breakfast of Beer and Bread and Cheese, finding they could with me be supplied from a neighboring House with a large Porringer of hot Water-gruel, sprinkled with Pepper, crumb'd with Bread, and a Bit of Butter in it, for the Price of a Pint of Beer, viz, three halfpence. This was a more comfortable as well as cheaper Breakfast, and kept their Heads clearer. Those who continu'd sotting with Beer all day, were often, by not paying, out of Credit at the Alehouse, and us'd to make Interest with me to get Beer, *their Light*, as they phras'd it, *being out*. I watch'd the Pay table on Saturday Night, and collected what I stood engag'd for them, having to pay some times near Thirty Shillings a Week on their Accounts. This, and my being esteem'd a pretty good Riggite, that is a jocular verbal Satirist, supported my Consequence in the Society. My constant Attendance, (I never making a St. Monday),[8] recommended me to the Master; and my uncommon Quickness at Composing, occasion'd my being put upon all Work of Dispatch, which was generally better paid. So I went on now very agreeably.

---

* "A Printing House is always called a Chappel by the Workmen.—" [Franklin's note.] The word referred both to the shop as a place of work and to the workmen as a self-governing group who set local customs, practices, and fines.

---

6. The traditional initiation fee was five shillings for those who had not yet finished their apprenticeship.
7. They put the types in the wrong boxes, mixed up the pages of the manuscript he was setting in type, and broke up the columns of type he had already set.
8. Taking Monday off to nurse a hangover from Sunday carousing.

My Lodging in Little Britain being too remote, I found another in
Duke Street opposite to the Romish Chapel.[9] It was two pair of
Stairs backwards at an Italian Warehouse. A Widow Lady kept the
House; she had a Daughter and a Maid Servant, and a Journeyman
who attended the Warehouse, but lodg'd abroad. After sending to
enquire my Character at the House where I last lodg'd, she agreed
to take me in at the same Rate, 3 Shillings 6 Pence per Week,
cheaper as she said from the Protection she expected in having a
Man lodge in the House. She was a Widow, an elderly Woman, had
been bred a Protestant, being a Clergyman's Daughter, but was converted to the Catholic Religion by her Husband, whose Memory she
much revered, had lived much among People of Distinction, and
knew a 1000 Anecdotes of them as far back as the Times of Charles
the second.[1] She was lame in her Knees with the Gout, and therefore seldom stirr'd out of her Room, so sometimes wanted Company;
and hers was so highly amusing to me that I was sure to spend an
Evening with her whenever she desired it. Our Supper was only half
an Anchovy each, on a very little Strip of Bread and Butter, and half
a Pint of Ale between us. But the Entertainment was in her Conversation. My always keeping good Hours, and giving little Trouble
in the Family, made her unwilling to part with me; so that when
I talk'd of a Lodging I had heard of, nearer my Business, for 2 Shillings a Week, which, intent as I now was on saving Money, made
some Difference; she bid me not think of it, for she would abate me
two Shillings a Week for the future, so I remain'd with her at 1 Shilling 6 Pence as long as I stayed in London.

In a Garret of her House there lived a Maiden Lady of 70 in the
most retired Manner, of whom my Landlady gave me this Account,
that she was a Roman Catholic, had been sent abroad when young
and lodg'd in a Nunnery with an Intent of becoming a Nun: but the
Country not agreeing with her, she return'd to England, where there
being no Nunnery, she had vow'd to lead the Life of a Nun as near
as might be done in those Circumstances: Accordingly She had
given all her Estate to charitable Uses, reserving only Twelve Pounds
a Year to live on, and out of this Sum she still gave a great deal in
Charity, living herself on Watergruel only, and using no Fire but
to boil it. She had lived many Years in that Garret, being permitted
to remain there gratis by successive catholic Tenants of the House
below, as they deem'd it a Blessing to have her there. A Priest visited
her, to confess her every Day. I have ask'd her, says my Landlady,
how she, as she liv'd, could possibly find so much Employment for a

---

9. Now Sardinia Street. About one mile closer than Little Britain, it was only two blocks
   south of Watts's shop on Wild Court.
1. Forty to sixty-five years earlier, i.e., 1660–85.

Confessor? O, says she, it is impossible to avoid *vain Thoughts.* I was permitted once to visit her: She was cheerful and polite, and convers'd pleasantly. The Room was clean, but had no other Furniture than a Mattress, a Table with a Crucifix and Book, a Stool, which she gave me to sit on, and a Picture over the Chimney of St. *Veronica,* displaying her Handkerchief with the miraculous Figure of Christ's bleeding Face on it, which she explain'd to me with great Seriousness. She look'd pale, but was never sick, and I give it as another Instance on how small an Income Life and Health may be supported.

At Watts's Printing-House I contracted an Acquaintance with an ingenious young Man, one Wygate, who having wealthy Relations, had been better educated than most Printers, was a tolerable Latinist, spoke French, and lov'd Reading. I taught him, and a Friend of his, to swim at twice going into the River, and they soon became good Swimmers. They introduced me to some Gentlemen from the Country who went to Chelsea by Water to see the College[2] and Don Saltero's Curiosities.[3] In our Return, at the Request of the Company, whose Curiosity Wygate had excited, I stripped and leaped into the River, and swam from near Chelsea to Blackfriars,[4] performing on the Way many Feats of Activity both upon and under Water, that surpris'd and pleas'd those to whom they were Novelties. I had from a Child been ever delighted with this Exercise, had studied and practic'd all Thevenot's Motions and Positions,[5] added some of my own, aiming at the graceful and easy, as well as the Useful. All these I took this Occasion of exhibiting to the Company, and was much flatter'd by their Admiration. And Wygate, who was desirous of becoming a Master, grew more and more attach'd to me on that account, as well as from the Similarity of our Studies. He at length propos'd to me travelling all over Europe together, supporting ourselves every where by working at our Business. I was once inclin'd to it. But mentioning it to my good Friend Mr. Denham, with whom I often spent an Hour when I had Leisure, he dissuaded me from it; advising me to think only of returning to Pennsylvania, which he was now about to do.

I must record one Trait of this good Man's Character. He had formerly been in Business at Bristol, but fail'd in Debt to a Number of

---

2. On the site of a former college, Chelsea Hospital, later a home for old soldiers, designed by Christopher Wren, had noted "physic" gardens and an avenue of elms running down to the river.
3. A former barber of Sir Hans Sloane who gave him cast-off curios, James Salter (dubbed Don Saltero by the *Tatler,* no. 34, June 28, 1709), kept a coffeehouse with such marvels as Job's tears, pieces of the Holy Cross, and "Pontius Pilate's wife's chambermaid's sister's hat" (Lillywhite, *London Coffee Houses,* no. 352).
4. Well over three miles.
5. World traveler and librarian to the king of France, Melchisédec Thévenot wrote *L'Art de Nager* (1696; trans. as *The Art of Swimming,* 1699), a small, sixty-page book with thirty-nine plates demonstrating various strokes and positions.

People, compounded and went to America. There, by a close Application to Business as a Merchant, he acquir'd a plentiful Fortune in a few Years. Returning to England in the Ship with me, He invited his old Creditors to an Entertainment, at which he thank'd them for the easy Composition they had favor'd him with, and when they expected nothing but the Treat, every Man at the first Remove found under his Plate an Order on a Banker for the full Amount of the unpaid Remainder with Interest.

He now told me he was about to return to Philadelphia, and should carry over a great Quantity of Goods in order to open a Store there: He propos'd to take me over as his Clerk, to keep his Books (in which he would instruct me), copy his Letters, and attend the Store. He added, that as soon as I should be acquainted with mercantile Business he would promote me by sending me with a Cargo of Flour and Bread etc. to the West Indies, and procure me Commissions from others; which would be profitable, and if I manag'd well, would establish me handsomely. The Thing pleas'd me, for I was grown tired of London, remember'd with Pleasure the happy Months I had spent in Pennsylvania, and wish'd again to see it. Therefore I immediately agreed, on the Terms of Fifty Pounds a Year, Pennsylvania Money; less indeed than my then Gettings as a Compositor, but affording a better Prospect.

I now took Leave of Printing, as I thought for ever, and was daily employ'd in my new Business; going about with Mr. Denham among the Tradesmen, to purchase various Articles, and see them pack'd up, doing Errands, calling upon Workmen to dispatch, etc. and when all was on board, I had a few Days' Leisure. On one of these Days I was to my Surprise sent for by a great Man I knew only by Name, a Sir William Wyndham and I waited upon him. He had heard by some means or other of my Swimming from Chelsey to Blackfriars, and of my teaching Wygate and another young Man to swim in a few Hours. He had two Sons about to set out on their Travels; he wish'd to have them first taught Swimming; and propos'd to gratify me handsomely if I would teach them. They were not yet come to Town and my Stay was uncertain, so I could not undertake it. But from this Incident I thought it likely, that if I were to remain in England and open a Swimming School, I might get a good deal of Money. And it struck me so strongly, that had the Overture been sooner made me, probably I should not so soon have returned to America. After Many Years, you and I had something of more Importance to do with one of these Sons of Sir William Wyndham, become Earl of Egremont, which I shall mention in its Place.[6]

6. Franklin initially planned his *Autobiography* to cover his life up to 1771. But, since this son of William Wyndham did not become secretary of state for the colonies until 1761, and since the *Autobiography* breaks off at 1757, he does not appear again.

Thus I spent about 18 Months in London. Most Part of the Time, I work'd hard at my Business, and spent but little upon myself except in seeing Plays, and in Books. My Friend Ralph had kept me poor. He owed me about 27 Pounds; which I was now never likely to receive; a great Sum out of my small Earnings. I lov'd him notwithstanding, for he had many amiable Qualities. Tho' I had by no means improv'd my Fortune, I had pick'd up some very ingenious Acquaintance whose Conversation was of great Advantage to me, and I had read considerably.

We sail'd from Gravesend on the 23d of July 1726. For The Incidents of the Voyage, I refer you to my Journal, where you will find them all minutely related. Perhaps the most important Part of that Journal is the *Plan*[7] to be found in it which I formed at Sea for regulating my future Conduct in Life. It is the more remarkable, as being form'd when I was so young, and yet being pretty faithfully adhered to quite thro' to old Age. We landed in Philadelphia the 11th of October, where I found sundry Alterations. Keith was no longer Governor, being superseded by Major Gordon: I met him walking the Streets as a common Citizen.[8] He seem'd a little asham'd at seeing me, but pass'd without saying anything. I should have been as much asham'd at seeing Miss Read, had not her Friends despairing with Reason of my Return, after the Receipt of my Letter, persuaded her to marry another, one Rogers, a Potter, which was done in my Absence.[9] With him however she was never happy, and soon parted from him, refusing to cohabit with him, or bear his Name, It being now said that he had another Wife. He was a worthless Fellow tho' an excellent Workman which was the Temptation to her Friends. He got into Debt, and ran away in 1727 or 28, went to the West Indies, and died there. Keimer had got a better House, a Shop well supplied with Stationery, plenty of new Types, a number of Hands tho' none good, and seem'd to have a great deal of Business.

Mr. Denham took a Store in Water Street, where we open'd our Goods. I attended the Business diligently, studied Accounts, and grew in a little Time expert at selling. We lodg'd and boarded together, he counsell'd me as a Father, having a sincere Regard for me: I respected and lov'd him: and we might have gone on together very happily: But in the Beginning of February 1726/7 when I had just pass'd my 21st Year, we both were taken ill.[1] My Distemper was

7. The full journal as well as the preamble and the outline of the *Plan* survive (*Papers* 1.72–99; extracts appear in the Contexts section of this Norton Critical Edition).
8. Removed in June 1726, Keith was now popular leader of the anti-proprietor party.
9. Deborah Read married John Rogers in Christ Church, Philadelphia, on August 5, 1725. See *Pa. Archives*, 2d Ser., 8.221. Rogers absconded in December 1727.
1. Events are compressed here; Franklin probably worked for Denham from October 1726 until August 1727, and was ill during March and April 1727. He evidently went back to work for Keimer in the fall of 1727; Denham died July 4, 1728.

a Pleurisy, which very nearly carried me off: I suffered a good deal, gave up the Point in my own mind, and was rather disappointed when I found myself recovering; regretting in some degree that I must now sometime or other have all that disagreeable Work to do over again. I forget what his Distemper was. It held him a long time, and at length carried him off. He left me a small Legacy in a nuncupative Will,[2] as a Token of his Kindness for me, and he left me once more to the wide World. For the Store was taken into the Care of his Executors, and my Employment under him ended: My Brother-in-law Homes, being now at Philadelphia, advis'd my Return to my Business. And Keimer tempted me with an Offer of large Wages by the Year to come and take the Management of his Printing-House that he might better attend his Stationer's Shop. I had heard a bad Character of him in London, from his Wife and her Friends, and was not fond of having any more to do with him. I tried for farther Employment as a Merchant's Clerk; but not readily meeting with any, I clos'd again with Keimer.

I found in *his* House these Hands; Hugh Meredith a Welsh-Pennsylvanian, 30 Years of Age, bred to Country Work: honest, sensible, had a great deal of solid Observation, was something of a Reader, but given to drink: Stephen Potts, a young Country Man of full Age, bred to the Same, of uncommon natural Parts, and great Wit and Humor, but a little idle. These he had agreed with at extreme low Wages, per Week, to be rais'd a Shilling every 3 Months, as they would deserve by improving in their Business, and the Expectation of these high Wages to come on hereafter was what he had drawn them in with. Meredith was to work at Press, Potts at Bookbinding, which he by Agreement, was to teach them, tho' he knew neither one nor t'other. John——a wild Irishman brought up to no Business, whose Service for 4 Years Keimer had purchas'd[3] from the Captain of a Ship. He too was to be made a Pressman. George Webb, an Oxford Scholar, whose Time for 4 Years he had likewise bought, intending him for a Compositor: of whom more presently. And David Harry, a Country Boy, whom he had taken Apprentice. I soon perceiv'd that the Intention of engaging me at Wages so much higher than he had been us'd to give,[4] was to have these raw cheap Hands form'd thro' me, and as soon as I had instructed them, then, they being all articled to him, he should be able to do without me. I went on however, very cheerfully; put his Printing-House in Order, which had been in great Confusion, and brought his Hands by degrees to mind their Business and to do it better.

2. The oral will was heard by three witnesses, December 29, 1726, and approved September 1, 1729. It forgave Franklin's debt of £10 owed Denham for the return fare from London.
3. Paid his passage in return for four years labor as an indentured servant.
4. Originally Franklin wrote "80 Pounds a Year."

It was an odd Thing to find an Oxford Scholar in the Situation of a bought Servant. He was not more than 18 Years of Age, and gave me this Account of himself; that he was born in Gloucester, educated at a Grammar School there, had been distinguish'd among the Scholars for some apparent Superiority in performing his Part when they exhibited Plays; belong'd to the Witty Club there, and had written some Pieces in Prose and Verse which were printed in the Gloucester Newspapers. Thence he was sent to Oxford; there he continu'd about a Year, but not well-satisfied, wishing of all things to see London and become a Player. At length receiving his Quarterly Allowance of 15 Guineas, instead of discharging his Debts, he walk'd out of Town, hid his Gown in a Furz Bush, and footed it to London, where having no Friend to advise him, he fell into bad Company, soon spent his Guineas, found no means of being introduc'd among the Players, grew necessitous, pawn'd his Clothes and wanted Bread. Walking the Street very hungry, and not knowing what to do with himself, a Crimp's Bill[5] was put into his Hand, offering immediate Entertainment and Encouragement to such as would bind themselves to serve in America. He went directly, sign'd the Indentures, was put into the Ship and came over; never writing a Line to acquaint his Friends what was become of him. He was lively, witty, good-natur'd and a pleasant Companion, but idle, thoughtless and imprudent to the last Degree.

John the Irishman soon ran away. With the rest I began to live very agreeably; for they all respected me, the more as they found Keimer incapable of instructing them, and that from me they learned something daily. We never work'd on a Saturday, that being Keimer's Sabbath. So I had two Days for Reading. My Acquaintance with ingenious People in the Town increased. Keimer himself treated me with great Civility and apparent Regard; and nothing now made me uneasy but my Debt to Vernon, which I was yet unable to pay, being hitherto but a poor Economist. He however kindly made no Demand of it.

Our Printing-House often wanted Sorts,[6] and there was no Letter Founder in America. I had seen Types cast at James's in London, but without much Attention to the Manner: However I now contriv'd a Mold, made use of the Letters we had as Puncheons, struck the Matrices in Lead,[7] and thus supplied in a pretty tolerable way all Deficiencies. I also engrav'd several Things on occasion. I made the Ink, I was Warehouse-man and everything, in short quite a Factotum.

But however serviceable I might be, I found that my Services became every Day of less Importance, as the other Hands improv'd

---

5. Advertisement by a recruiter of seamen and emigrant laborers.
6. Duplicate types.
7. Franklin thus made the first types in North America.

in the Business. And when Keimer paid my second Quarter's Wages, he let me know that he felt them too heavy, and thought I should make an Abatement. He grew by degrees less civil, put on more of the Master, frequently found Fault, was captious and seem'd ready for an Out-breaking. I went on nevertheless with a good deal of Patience, thinking that his encumber'd Circumstances were partly the Cause. At length a Trifle snapped our Connection. For a great Noise happening near the Courthouse, I put my Head out of the Window to see what was the Matter.[8] Keimer being in the Street look'd up and saw me, call'd out to me in a loud Voice and angry Tone to mind my Business, adding some reproachful Words, that nettled me the more for their Publicity, all the Neighbors who were looking out on the same Occasion being Witnesses how I was treated. He came up immediately into the Printing-House, continu'd the Quarrel, high Words pass'd on both Sides, he gave me the Quarter's Warning we had stipulated, expressing a Wish that he had not been oblig'd to so long a Warning: I told him his Wish was unnecessary for I would leave him that Instant; and so taking my Hat walk'd out of Doors; desiring Meredith whom I saw below to take care of some Things I left, and bring them to my Lodging.

Meredith came accordingly in the Evening, when we talk'd my Affair over. He had conceiv'd a great Regard for me, and was very unwilling that I should leave the House while he remain'd in it. He dissuaded me from returning to my native Country[9] which I began to think of. He reminded me that Keimer was in debt for all he possess'd, that his Creditors began to be uneasy, that he kept his Shop miserably, sold often without Profit for ready Money, and often trusted without keeping Account. That he must therefore fail; which would make a Vacancy I might profit of. I objected my Want of Money. He then let me know, that his Father had a high Opinion of me, and from some Discourse that had pass'd between them, he was sure would advance Money to set us up, if I would enter into Partnership with him. My Time, says he, will be out with Keimer in the Spring. By that time we may have our Press and Types in from London: I am sensible I am no Workman. If you like it, Your Skill in the Business shall be set against the Stock I furnish; and we will share the Profits equally.—The Proposal was agreeable, and I consented. His Father was in Town, and approv'd of it, the more as he saw I had great Influence with his Son, had prevail'd on him to abstain long from Dram-drinking, and he hop'd might break him of that wretched Habit entirely, when we came to be so closely connected. I gave an Inventory to the Father, who carried it to a Merchant; the Things were sent for; the Secret was to be kept till they should arrive, and in the

8. If this was Election Day, it must have been Monday, October 2, 1727.
9. Boston.

mean time I was to get Work if I could at the other Printing-House. But I found no Vacancy there, and so remain'd idle a few Days, when Keimer, on a Prospect of being employ'd to print some Paper-money, in New Jersey, which would require Cuts and various Types that I only could supply, and apprehending Bradford might engage me and get the Job from him, sent me a very civil Message, that old Friends should not part for a few Words, the Effect of sudden Passion, and wishing me to return. Meredith persuaded me to comply, as it would give more Opportunity for his Improvement under my daily Instructions. So I return'd, and we went on more smoothly than for some time before. The New Jersey Job was obtain'd. I contriv'd a Copper-Plate Press for it, the first that had been seen in the Country. I cut several Ornaments and Checks for the Bills. We went together to Burlington,[1] where I executed the Whole to Satisfaction, and he received so large a Sum for the Work, as to be enabled thereby to keep his Head much longer above Water.

At Burlington I made an Acquaintance with many principal People of the Province. Several of them had been appointed by the Assembly a Committee to attend the Press, and take Care that no more Bills were printed than the Law directed. They were therefore by Turns constantly with us, and generally he who attended brought with him a Friend or two for Company. My Mind having been much more improv'd by Reading than Keimer's, I suppose it was for that Reason my Conversation seem'd to be more valu'd. They had me to their Houses, introduc'd me to their Friends and show'd me much Civility, while he, tho' the Master, was a little neglected. In truth he was an odd Fish, ignorant of common Life, fond of rudely opposing receiv'd Opinions, slovenly to extreme dirtiness, enthusiastic in some Points of Religion, and a little Knavish withal. We continu'd there near 3 Months, and by that time I could reckon among my acquired Friends, Judge Allen, Samuel Bustill, the Secretary of the Province, Isaac Pearson, Joseph Cooper and several of the Smiths, Members of Assembly, and Isaac Decow the Surveyor General. The latter was a shrewd sagacious old Man, who told me that he began for himself when young by wheeling Clay for the Brickmakers, learned to write after he was of Age, carried the Chain for Surveyors, who taught him Surveying, and he had now by his Industry acquir'd a good Estate; and says he, I foresee, that you will soon work this Man out of his Business and make a Fortune in it at Philadelphia. He had not then the least Intimation of my Intention to set up there or anywhere. These Friends were afterwards of great Use to me, as I occasionally was to some of them. They all continued their Regard for me as long as they lived.

---

1. In spring 1728. While Keimer's press was at Burlington, Franklin and he printed the *Acts and Laws of . . . New Jersey* (Burlington: Keimer, 1725): Evans, 3071.

Before I enter upon my public Appearance in Business, it may be well to let you know the then State of my Mind, with regard to my Principles and Morals, that you may see how far those influenc'd the future Events of my Life. My Parents had early given me religious Impressions, and brought me through my Childhood piously in the Dissenting Way. But I was scarce 15 when, after doubting by turns of several Points as I found them disputed in the different Books I read, I began to doubt of Revelation itself. Some Books against Deism[2] fell into my Hands; they were said to be the Substance of Sermons preached at Boyle's Lectures.[3] It happened that they wrought an Effect on me quite contrary to what was intended by them: For the Arguments of the Deists which were quoted to be refuted, appeared to me much Stronger than the Refutations. In short I soon became a thorough Deist. My Arguments perverted some others, particularly Collins and Ralph: but each of them having afterwards wrong'd me greatly without the least Compunction, and recollecting Keith's Conduct towards me, (who was another Freethinker) and my own towards Vernon and Miss Read which at Times gave me great Trouble, I began to suspect that this Doctrine tho' it might be true, was not very useful.[4] My London Pamphlet, which had for its Motto those Lines of Dryden

> ———Whatever is, is right
> Tho' purblind Man Sees but a Part of
> The Chain, the nearest Link,
> His Eyes not carrying to the equal Beam,
> That poizes all, above.[5]

And from the Attributes of God, his infinite Wisdom, Goodness and Power concluded that nothing could possibly be wrong in the World, and that Vice and Virtue were empty Distinctions, no such Things existing: appear'd now not so clever a Performance as I once thought it; and I doubted whether some Error had not insinuated itself unperceiv'd into my Argument, so as to infect all that follow'd, as is common in metaphysical Reasonings. I grew convinc'd that *Truth*, *Sincerity* and *Integrity* in Dealings between Man and Man, were of the utmost Importance to the Felicity of Life, and I form'd

2. Perhaps these were the sermons of 1705 by Samuel Clarke, *Discourse Concerning . . . Natural Religion, and . . . Christian Revelation* (1706). Clarke quotes the arguments of four kinds of deists in order to refute them.
3. Chemical experimenter Robert Boyle (1627–1691) endowed £50 for preaching eight sermons a year against "notorious Infidels," excluding controversies among Christians themselves. A list of "The Boyle Lectures 1692–1714" is given in Margaret C. Jacob, *The Newtonians and the English Revolution 1689–1720* (Ithaca: Cornell UP, 1976), 273–74.
4. A well-known eighteenth-century intellectual debate. John Shebbeare (1709–1788), British polemicist, argued that utility is truth; see *Letters on the English Nation* (London, 1755), no. 9.
5. This quotation is actually from Pope's *Essay on Man* (1.284). Franklin's slip of memory is understandable, since a line in Dryden's *Oedipus* (3.i.244–48) reads: "Whatever is, is in its Causes just."

written Resolutions, (which still remain in my Journal Book) to practice them ever while I lived. Revelation had indeed no weight with
me as such; but I entertain'd an Opinion, that tho' certain Actions
might not be bad *because* they were forbidden by it, or good *because*
it commanded them; yet probably those Actions might be forbidden
because they were had for us, or commanded *because* they were beneficial to us, in their own Natures, all the Circumstances of things
considered. And this Persuasion, with the kind hand of Providence,
or some guardian Angel, or accidental favorable Circumstances
and Situations, or all together, preserved me (thro' this dangerous
Time of Youth and the hazardous Situations I was sometimes in
among Strangers, remote from the Eye and Advice of my Father)
without any *willful* gross Immorality or Injustice that might have
been expected from my Want of Religion. I say *willful*, because the
Instances I have mentioned, had something of *Necessity* in them,
from my Youth, Inexperience, and the Knavery of others. I had therefore a tolerable Character to begin the World with, I valued it properly, and determin'd to preserve it.

We had not been long return'd to Philadelphia, before the New
Types arriv'd from London. We settled with Keimer, and left him by
his Consent before he heard of it. We found a House to hire near
the Market, and took it.[6] To lessen the Rent, (which was then but
24 Pounds a Year tho' I have since known it let for 70) We took in
Thomas Godfrey a Glazier, and his Family, who were to pay a considerable Part of it to us, and we to board with them. We had scarce
opened our Letters and put our Press in Order, before George House,
an Acquaintance of mine, brought a Countryman to us; whom he
had met in the Street enquiring for a Printer. All our Cash was now
expended in the Variety of Particulars we had been obliged to procure, and this Countryman's Five Shillings, being our First Fruits
and coming so seasonably, gave me more Pleasure than any Crown[7]
I have since earn'd; and from the Gratitude I felt towards House, has
made me often more ready than perhaps I should otherwise have
been to assist young Beginners.

There are Croakers in every Country always boding its Ruin. Such
a one then lived in Philadelphia, a Person of Note, an elderly Man,
with a wise Look and very grave Manner of Speaking. His Name was
Samuel Mickle. This Gentleman, a Stranger to me, stopped one Day
at my Door, and ask'd me if I was the young Man who had lately
opened a new Printing-House: Being answer'd in the Affirmative; He
said he was sorry for me; because it was an expensive Undertaking,

---

6. Rented from a local pewterer, it was a narrow, brick house, three stories high, on Market Street below Second Street, at present 139 Market Street.
7. A crown was worth five shillings, and there were twenty shillings in a pound. If Franklin was paying £24 each year to rent a house, a crown represented one-eighth of one
month's rent.

and the Expense would be lost, for Philadelphia was a sinking Place, the People already half Bankrupts or near being so; all Appearances of the contrary such as new Buildings and the Rise of Rents, being to his certain Knowledge fallacious, for they were in fact among the Things that would soon ruin us.[8] And he gave me such a Detail of Misfortunes now existing or that were soon to exist, that he left me half-melancholy. Had I known him before I engag'd in this Business, probably I never should have done it. This Man continu'd to live in this decaying Place, and to declaim in the same Strain, refusing for many Years to buy a House there, because all was going to Destruction, and at last I had the Pleasure of seeing him give five times as much for one as he might have bought it for when he first began his Croaking.

I should have mention'd before, that in the Autumn of the preceding Year, I had form'd most of my ingenious Acquaintance into a Club, for mutual Improvement, which we call'd the Junto.[9] We met on Friday Evenings. The Rules I drew up, requir'd that every Member in his Turn should produce one or more Queries[1] on any Point of Morals, Politics or Natural Philosophy, to be discuss'd by the Company, and once in three Months produce and read an Essay of his own Writing on any Subject he pleased. Our Debates were to be under the Direction of a President, and to be conducted in the sincere Spirit of Enquiry after Truth, without fondness for Dispute, or Desire of Victory; and to prevent Warmth, all expressions of Positiveness in Opinion, or of direct Contradiction, were after some time made contraband and prohibited under small pecuniary Penalties. The first Members were, Joseph Breintnall, a Copier of Deeds for the Scriveners; a good-natur'd friendly middle-ag'd Man, a great Lover of Poetry, reading all he could meet with, and writing some that was tolerable; very ingenious in many little Nicknackeries, and of sensible Conversation. Thomas Godfrey, a self-taught Mathematician, great in his Way, and afterwards Inventor of what is now call'd Hadley's Quadrant:[2] But he knew little out of his way, and was not a pleasing Companion, as like most Great Mathematicians I have met with, he expected unusual Precision in everything said, or was forever denying or distinguishing upon Trifles, to the Disturbance of all Conversation. He soon left us. Nicholas Scull, a Surveyor, afterwards Surveyor-General, Who lov'd Books, and sometimes made a

8. Franklin opened the new printing house in spring 1728, just after the city suffered a depression (October 1727 to January 1728) and severe devaluation of Pennsylvania money.
9. From the Spanish *junta*, or fraternity. Clubs were a characteristic feature of eighteenth-century society; Franklin's immediate inspiration may have been a proposal for neighborhood associations in Cotton Mather's *Religious Societies* (Boston, 1724).
1. Examples are in *Papers* 1.255–64.
2. He perfected a quadrant in November 1730, but James Hadley, an Englishman working independently, had constructed a model in May 1730. The Royal Society gave Hadley priority but awarded Godfrey £200.

few Verses. William Parsons, bred a Shoemaker, but loving Reading, had acquir'd a considerable Share of Mathematics, which he first studied with a View to Astrology that he afterwards laughed at. He also became Surveyor General. William Maugridge, a Joiner, and a most exquisite Mechanic, and a solid sensible Man. Hugh Meredith, Stephen Potts, and George Webb, I have Characteris'd before. Robert Grace, a young Gentleman of some Fortune, generous, lively and witty, a Lover of Punning and of his Friends. And William Coleman, then a Merchant's Clerk, about my Age, who had the coolest clearest Head, the best Heart, and the exactest Morals, of almost any Man I ever met with. He became afterwards a Merchant of great Note, and one of our Provincial Judges: Our Friendship continued without Interruption to his Death, upwards of 40 Years. And the Club continu'd almost as long and was the best School of Philosophy, Morals and Politics that then existed in the Province; for our Queries which were read the Week preceding their Discussion, put us on reading with Attention upon the several Subjects, that we might speak more to the purpose: and here too we acquired better Habits of Conversation, everything being studied in our Rules which might prevent our disgusting each other. From hence the long Continuance of the Club, which I shall have frequent Occasion to speak farther of hereafter; But my giving this Account of it here, is to show something of the Interest I had, everyone of these exerting themselves in recommending Business to us.

Breintnall particularly procur'd us from the Quakers, the Printing 40 Sheets[3] of their History, the rest being to be done by Keimer: and upon this we work'd exceeding hard, for the Price was low. It was a Folio, Pro Patria Size, in Pica with Long Primer Notes. I compos'd of it a Sheet a Day, and Meredith work'd it off at Press. It was often 11 at Night and sometimes later, before I had finish'd my Distribution[4] for the next day's Work: For the little Jobs sent in by our other Friends now and then put us back. But so determin'd I was to continue doing a Sheet a Day of the Folio, that one Night when having impos'd my Forms, I thought my Day's Work over, one of them by accident was broken and two Pages reduc'd to Pie,[5] I immediately distributed and compos'd it over again before I went to bed. And this Industry visible to our Neighbors began to give us Character and Credit; particularly I was told, that mention being made of the new Printing Office at the Merchants' Every-night-Club, the general Opinion was that it must

---

3. Keimer printed the first 532 pages, Franklin the remaining 178 plus title page, of William Sewel, *History of the . . . Quakers*, 3rd ed. (Philadelphia: Samuel Keimer, 1728). Keimer received £300 for the edition of 500 copies, and probably paid Franklin a proportionate share.
4. After printing, he redistributed the letters back into their cases, ready for the next day's composing.
5. A jumbled pile of type.

fail, there being already two Printers in the Place, Keimer and Bradford; but Doctor Baird (whom you and I saw many Years[6] after at his native Place, St. Andrews in Scotland) gave a contrary Opinion; for the Industry of that Franklin, says he, is superior to anything I ever saw of the kind: I see him still at work when I go home from Club; and he is at Work again before his Neighbors are out of bed. This struck the rest, and we soon after had Offers from one of them to supply us with Stationery. But as yet we did not choose to engage in Shop Business.

I mention this Industry the more particularly and the more freely, tho' it seems to be talking in my own Praise, that those of my Posterity who shall read it, may know the Use of that Virtue, when they see its Effects in my Favor throughout this Relation.

George Webb, who had found a Friend that lent him wherewith to purchase his Time of Keimer, now came to offer himself as a Journeyman to us. We could not then employ him, but I foolishly let him know, as a Secret, that I soon intended to begin a Newspaper, and might then have Work for him. My Hopes of Success as I told him were founded on this, that the then only Newspaper, printed by Bradford was a paltry thing, wretchedly manag'd, no way entertaining; and yet was profitable to him. I therefore thought a good Paper could scarcely fail of good Encouragement. I requested Webb not to mention it, but he told it to Keimer, who immediately, to be before hand with me, published Proposals[7] for Printing one himself, on which Webb was to be employ'd. I resented this, and to counteract them, as I could not yet begin our Paper, I wrote several Pieces of Entertainment for Bradford's Paper,[8] under the Title of the Busy Body which Breintnall continu'd some Months.[9] By this means the Attention of the Public was fix'd on that Paper, and Keimer's Proposals which we burlesqu'd and ridicul'd, were disregarded. He began his Paper however, and after carrying it on three Quarters of a Year, with at most only 90 Subscribers, he offer'd it to me for a Trifle, and I having been ready some time to go on with it, took it in hand directly, and it prov'd in a few Years extremely profitable to me.[1]

6. In early October 1759 (*Papers* 8.431).
7. Dated October 1, 1728, Keimer's proposal promised publication of the *Universal Instructor in All Arts & Sciences: and Pennsylvania Gazette* about "the latter end of November," but the first issue was dated December 24, 1728.
8. *American Weekly Mercury.*
9. Periodically from February 4, 1728, through September 25, 1729.
1. In no. 39, September 25, 1729, Keimer announced that he had sold the paper to Franklin, who issued no. 40 for October 2 (*Papers* 1.157–61). After 1730, Franklin made an estimated £750 (Pennsylvania money) a year from the paper, with a circulation of about 1,500 copies weekly. His total income from printing was about £800 a year. See Lawrence C. Wroth, "Benjamin Franklin: The Printer at Work," *Journal of the Franklin Institute* 234 (1942): 163–64.

I perceive that I am apt to speak in the singular Number, though our Partnership still continu'd. The Reason may be, that in fact the whole Management of the Business lay upon me. Meredith was no Compositor, a poor Pressman, and seldom sober. My Friends lamented my Connection with him, but I was to make the best of it.

Our first Papers made a quite different Appearance from any before in the Province, a better Type and better printed: but some spirited Remarks* of my Writing on the Dispute then going on between Governor Burnet and the Massachusetts Assembly, struck the principal People, occasion'd the Paper and the Manager of it to be much talk'd of, and in a few Weeks brought them all to be our

---

* [Franklin wrote, "Insert these Remarks in a Note." Here follows his editorial from the *Pennsylvania Gazette*, October 9, 1729, 3:]

His Excellency Governor *Burnet* died unexpectedly about two Days after the Date of this Reply to his last Message: And it was thought the Dispute would have ended with him, or at least have lain dormant till the Arrival of a new Governor from *England*, who possibly might, or might not be inclin'd to enter too rigorously into the Measures of his Predecessor. But our last Advices by the Post acquaint us, that his Honour the Lieutenant Governor (on whom the Government immediately devolves upon the Death or Absence of the Commander in Chief) has vigorously renew'd the Struggle on his own Account; of which the Particulars will be seen in our Next.

Perhaps some of our Readers may not fully understand the Original or Ground of this warm Contest between the Governour and Assembly.—It seems, that People have for these Hundred Years past, enjoyed the Privilege of Rewarding the Governour for the Time being, according to *their Sense* of his Merit and Services; and few or none of their Governors have hitherto complain'd, or had Reason to complain, of a too scanty Allowance. But the late Gov. *Burnet* brought with him Instructions to demand a *settled Salary* of 1000 £. *per Annum*, Sterling, on him and all his Successors, and the Assembly were required to fix it immediately. He insisted on it strenuously to the last, and they as constantly refused it. It appears by their Votes and Proceedings, that they thought it an Imposition, contrary to their own Charter, and to *Magna Charta*; and they judg'd that by the Dictates of Reason there should be a mutual Dependence between the *Governor* and the *Governed*, and that to make any Governour independent on his People, would be dangerous, and destructive of their Liberties, and the ready Way to establish Tyranny: They thought likewise, that the Province was

not the less dependent on the Crown of *Great-Britain*, by the Governour's depending immediately on them and his own good Conduct for an ample Support, because all Acts and Laws which he might be induc'd to pass, must nevertheless be constantly sent Home for Approbation in Order to continue in Force. Many other Reasons were given and Arguments us'd in the Course of the Controversy, needless to particularize here, because all the material Papers relating to it, have been inserted already in our Public News.

Much deserved Praise has the deceas'd Governor received, for his steady Integrity in adhering to his Instructions, notwithstanding the great Difficulty and Opposition he met with, and the strong Temptations offer'd from time to time to induce him to give up the Point.—And yet perhaps something is due to the *Assembly* (as the Love and Zeal of that Country for the present Establishment is too well known to suffer any Suspicion of Want of Loyalty) who continue thus resolutely to Abide by what *they Think* their Right, and that of the People they represent, maugre all the Arts and Menaces of a Governour fam'd for his Cunning and Politicks, back'd with Instructions from Home, and powerfully aided by the great Advantage such an Officer always has of engaging the principal Men of a Place in his Party, by conferring where he pleases so many Posts of Profit and Honour. Their happy Mother Country will perhaps observe with Pleasure, that tho' her gallant Cocks and matchless Dogs abate their native Fire and Intrepidity when transported to a Foreign Clime (as the common Notion is) yet her SONS in the remotest Part of the Earth, and even to the third and fourth Descent, still retain that ardent Spirit of Liberty, and that undaunted Courage in the Defence of it, which has in every Age so gloriously distinguished BRITONS and ENGLISHMEN from all the Rest of Mankind. [Text taken from *Papers* 1.159–61.]

Subscribers. Their Example was follow'd by many, and our Number went on growing continually. This was one of the first good Effects of my having learned a little to scribble. Another was, that the leading Men, seeing a Newspaper now in the hands of one who could also handle a Pen, thought it convenient to oblige and encourage me. Bradford still printed the Votes and Laws and other Public Business. He had printed an Address of the House to the Governor in a coarse blundering manner; We reprinted it elegantly and correctly, and sent one to every Member.[2] They were sensible of the Difference, it strengthen'd the Hands of our Friends in the House, and they voted us their Printers for the Year ensuing.[3]

Among my Friends in the House I must not forget Mr. Hamilton before-mentioned, who was then returned from England and had a Seat in it.[4] He interested himself for me strongly in that Instance, as he did in many others afterwards, continuing his Patronage till his Death.* Mr. Vernon about this time put me in mind of the Debt I ow'd him: but did not press me. I wrote him an ingenuous Letter of Acknowledgments, crav'd his Forbearance a little longer which he allow'd me, and as soon as I was able I paid the Principal with Interest and many Thanks. So that *Erratum* was in some degree corrected.

But now another Difficulty came upon me, which I had never the least Reason to expect. Mr. Meredith's Father, who was to have paid for our Printing-House according to the Expectations given me, was able to advance only one Hundred Pounds, Currency, which had been paid, and a Hundred more was due to the Merchant; who grew impatient and su'd us all. We gave Bail, but saw that if the Money could not be rais'd in time, the Suit must come to a Judgment and Execution, and our hopeful Prospects must with us be ruined, as the Press and Letters must be sold for Payment, perhaps at half-Price. In this Distress two true Friends whose Kindness I have never forgotten nor ever shall forget while I can remember anything, came to me separately unknown to each other, and without any Application from me, offering each of them to advance me all the Money

---

* I got his Son once 500£.[5]

---

2. The address of March 29, 1729, asked the Governor to implement the riot act against "great Numbers of dissolute and disorderly Persons" who had been disturbing the peace. Franklin's separate reprint has not been found, but he later reprinted it as part of Pennsylvania's *Votes and Proceedings* (1754); (*Pennsylvania Archives*, 8th ser., 3: 1939–40; Miller, nos. 9, 596).
3. Franklin served as the colony's official printer from January 1730, until September 1766.
4. Elected Speaker of the Pennsylvania assembly, October 14, 1729, Hamilton held the same post in Delaware's assembly.
5. In February 1754, Governor James Hamilton was feuding with the Pennsylvania assembly but—conceivably through Franklin's influence—the legislators nevertheless voted him his salary of £500 (*Pa. Archives*, 8th ser., 5.3635).

that should be necessary to enable me to take the whole Business upon myself if that should be practicable, but they did not like my continuing the Partnership with Meredith, who as they said was often seen drunk in the Streets, and playing at low Games in Ale-houses, much to our Discredit. These two Friends were *William Coleman* and *Robert Grace.*

I told them I could not propose a Separation while any Prospect remain'd of the Merediths fulfilling their Part of our Agreement. Because I thought myself under great Obligations to them for what they had done and would do if they could. But if they finally fail'd in their Performance, and our Partnership must be dissolv'd, I should then think myself at Liberty to accept the Assistance of my Friends. Thus the matter rested for some time. When I said to my Partner, perhaps your Father is dissatisfied at the Part you have undertaken in this Affair of ours, and is unwilling to advance for you and me what he would for you alone: If that is the Case, tell me, and I will resign the whole to you and go about my Business. No—says he, my Father has really been disappointed and is really unable; and I am unwilling to distress him farther. I see this is a Business I am not fit for. I was bred a Farmer, and it was a Folly in me to come to Town and put myself at 30 Years of Age an Apprentice to learn a new Trade. Many of our Welsh People are going to settle in North Carolina where Land is cheap: I am inclin'd to go with them, and follow my old Employment. You may find Friends to assist you. If you will take the Debts of the Company upon you, return to my Father the hundred Pound he has advanc'd, pay my little personal Debts, and give me Thirty Pounds and a new Saddle, I will relinquish the Partnership and leave the whole in your Hands. I agreed to this Proposal. It was drawn up in Writing, sign'd and seal'd immediately.[6] I gave him what he demanded and he went soon after to Carolina; from whence he sent me next Year two long Letters, containing the best Account that had been given of that Country, the Climate, Soil, Husbandry, etc. for in those Matters he was very judicious. I printed them in the Papers, and they gave great Satisfaction to the Public.[7]

As soon as he was gone, I recurr'd to my two Friends; and because I would not give an unkind Preference to either, I took half what each had offered and I wanted, of one, and half of the other; paid off the Company Debts, and went on with the Business in my own Name, advertising that the Partnership was dissolved. I think this was in or about the Year 1729.

About this Time there was a Cry among the People for more Paper-Money, only 15,000 Pounds being extant in the Province and

6. July 14, 1730 (*Papers* 1.175).
7. In the *Pennsylvania Gazette*, May 6 and 13, 1731, posing as a correspondent "lately" a resident of North Carolina.

that soon to be sunk.[8] The wealthy Inhabitants oppos'd any Addition, being against all Paper Currency, from an Apprehension that it would depreciate as it had done in New England to the Prejudice of all Creditors. We had discuss'd this Point in our Junto, where I was on the Side of an Addition, being persuaded that the first small Sum struck in 1723 had done much good, by increasing the Trade, Employment, and Number of Inhabitants in the Province, since I now saw all the old Houses inhabited, and many new ones building, where as I remember'd well, that when I first walk'd about the Streets of Philadelphia, eating my Roll, I saw most of the Houses in Walnut Street between Second and Front Streets with Bills on their Doors, to be let; and many likewise in Chestnut Street, and other Streets; which made me then think the Inhabitants of the City were one after another deserting it. Our Debates possess'd me so fully of the Subject, that I wrote and printed an anonymous Pamphlet on it, entitled, *The Nature and Necessity of a Paper Currency*.[9] It was well receiv'd by the common People in general; but the Rich Men dislik'd it; for it increas'd and strengthen'd the Clamor for more Money; and they happening to have no Writers among them that were able to answer it, their Opposition slacken'd, and the Point was carried by a Majority in the House. My Friends there, who conceiv'd I had been of some Service, thought fit to reward me, by employing me in printing the Money, a very profitable Job, and a great Help to me.[1] This was another Advantage gain'd by my being able to write. The Utility of this Currency became by Time and Experience so evident, as never afterwards to be much disputed, so that it grew soon to 55,000 Pounds, and in 1739 to 80,000 Pounds, since which it arose during War to upwards of 350,000 Pounds—Trade, Building and Inhabitants all the while increasing. Tho' I now think there are Limits beyond which the Quantity may be hurtful.

I soon after obtain'd, thro' my Friend Hamilton, the Printing of the New Castle Paper Money, another profitable Job,[2] as I then thought it; small Things appearing great to those in small Circumstances. And these to me were really great Advantages, as they were great Encouragements. He procured me also the Printing of the

---

8. In 1723, paper money had become so scarce that the assembly issued £45,000 secured by real estate mortgages. When the mortgages were paid off, the bills would be "sunk," i.e., destroyed. But by 1726, the value of the bills had declined so much that they were recalled, even though only about £5000 had been sunk, and the assembly voted new currency based on new mortgage loans. In May 1729, the assembly would vote another issue of £30,000.
9. Dated April 3, 1729 (*Papers* 1.139–57).
1. Andrew Bradford printed the Pennsylvania money voted in May 1729; but Franklin may have printed the corresponding Delaware issue. Franklin did print Pennsylvania's additional £40,000 (for which he earned £100), voted February 6, 1731.
2. Delaware's assembly voted an issue of £12,000 in 1729, another in 1735, and £6,000 in 1739.

Laws and Votes of that Government[3] which continu'd in my Hands as long as I follow'd the Business.

I now open'd a little Stationer's Shop. I had in it Blanks of all Sorts the correctest that ever appear'd among us, being assisted in that by my Friend Breintnall; I had also Paper, Parchment, Chapmen's Books, etc. One Whitmarsh a Compositor I had known in London, an excellent Workman now came to me and work'd with me constantly and diligently, and I took an Apprentice the Son of Aquila Rose.[4] I began now gradually to pay off the Debt I was under for the Printing-House. In order to secure my Credit and Character as a Tradesman, I took care not only to be in *Reality* Industrious and frugal, but to avoid all *Appearances* of the Contrary. I dressed plainly; I was seen at no Places of idle Diversion; I never went out a-fishing or shooting; a Book, indeed, sometimes debauch'd me from my Work; but that was seldom, snug, and gave no Scandal: and to show that I was not above my Business, I sometimes brought home the Paper I purchas'd at the Stores, thro' the Streets on a Wheelbarrow. Thus being esteem'd an industrious thriving young Man, and paying duly for what I bought, the Merchants who imported Stationery solicited my Custom, others propos'd supplying me with Books, and I went on swimmingly. In the mean time Keimer's Credit and Business declining daily, he was at last forc'd to sell his Printing-House to satisfy his Creditors. He went to Barbados, and there lived some Years, in very poor Circumstances.

His Apprentice David Harry, whom I had instructed while I work'd with him, set up in his Place at Philadelphia, having bought his Materials. I was at first apprehensive of a powerful Rival in Harry, as his Friends were very able, and had a good deal of Interest. I therefore propos'd a Partnership to him; which he, fortunately for me, rejected with Scorn. He was very proud, dress'd like a Gentleman, liv'd expensively, took much Diversion and Pleasure abroad, ran in debt, and neglected his Business, upon which all Business left him; and finding nothing to do, he follow'd Keimer to Barbados; taking the Printing-House with him. There this Apprentice employ'd his former Master as a Journeyman. They quarrel'd often. Harry went continually behind-hand, and at length was forc'd to sell his Types, and return to his Country Work[5] in Pennsylvania. The Person that bought them employ'd Keimer to use them, but in a few years he died. There remain'd now no Competitor with me at Philadelphia, but the old one, Bradford, who was rich and easy, did a little Printing now and then by straggling Hands, but was not very anxious about

---

3. Franklin first printed the Delaware laws in 1734.
4. Thomas Whitmarsh joined him before April 1730, about the same time that Joseph Rose became apprentice.
5. Farming.

the Business. However, as he kept the Post Office, it was imagined he had better Opportunities of obtaining News, his Paper was thought a better Distributer of Advertisements than mine, and therefore had many more, which was a profitable thing to him and a Disadvantage to me. For tho' I did indeed receive and send Papers by the Post, yet the public Opinion was otherwise; for what I did send was by Bribing the Riders who took them privately: Bradford being unkind enough to forbid it: which occasion'd some Resentment on my Part; and I thought so meanly of him for it, that when I afterwards came into his Situation,[6] I took care never to imitate it.

I had hitherto continu'd to board with Godfrey who lived in Part of my House with his Wife and Children, and had one Side of the Shop for his Glazier's Business, tho' he work'd little, being always absorb'd in his Mathematics. Mrs. Godfrey projected a Match for me with a Relation's Daughter, took Opportunities of bringing us often together, till a serious Courtship on my Part ensu'd, the Girl being in herself very deserving. The old Folks encourag'd me by continual Invitations to Supper, and by leaving us together, till at length it was time to explain. Mrs. Godfrey manag'd our little Treaty. I let her know that I expected as much Money with their Daughter as would pay off my Remaining Debt for the Printing-House, which I believe was not then above a Hundred Pounds. She brought me Word they had no such Sum to spare. I said they might mortgage their House in the Loan Office.[7] The Answer to this after some Days was, that they did not approve the Match; that on Enquiry of Bradford they had been inform'd the Printing Business was not a profitable one, the Types would soon be worn out and more wanted, that S. Keimer and D. Harry had fail'd one after the other, and I should probably soon follow them; and therefore I was forbidden the House, and the Daughter shut up.

Whether this was a real Change of Sentiment, or only Artifice, on a Supposition of our being too far engag'd in Affection to retract, and therefore that we should steal a Marriage, which would leave them at Liberty to give or withhold what they pleas'd, I know not: But I suspected the latter, resented it, and went no more. Mrs. Godfrey brought me afterwards some more favorable Accounts of their Disposition, and would have drawn me on again: But I declared absolutely my Resolution to have nothing more to do with that Family.[8] This was resented by the Godfreys, we differ'd, and they removed, leaving me the whole House,[9] and I resolved to take no more Inmates. But

6. Franklin replaced Bradford as postmaster of Philadelphia in October 1737.
7. The office that disbursed paper money as loans secured by real estate.
8. Still smarting at the family's "artifice" several years later, Franklin recounted the story in his "Anthony Afterwit" newspaper skit (*Papers* 1.237–40).
9. The Godfreys lived with Franklin from May 1728 to mid-April 1730.

this Affair having turn'd my Thoughts to Marriage, I look'd round me, and made Overtures of Acquaintance in other Places; but soon found that the Business of a Printer being generally thought a poor one, I was not to expect Money with a Wife unless with such a one, as I should not otherwise think agreeable. In the mean time, that hard-to-be-govern'd Passion of Youth, had hurried me frequently into Intrigues with low Women that fell in my Way, which were attended with some Expense and great Inconvenience, besides a continual Risk to my Health by a Distemper which of all Things I dreaded, tho' by great good Luck I escaped it.

A friendly Correspondence as Neighbors and old Acquaintances, had continued between me and Mrs. Read's Family who all had a Regard for me from the time of my first Lodging in their House.[1] I was often invited there and consulted in their Affairs, wherein I sometimes was of Service. I pitied poor Miss Read's unfortunate Situation, who was generally dejected, seldom cheerful, and avoided Company. I consider'd my Giddiness and Inconstancy when in London as in a great degree the Cause of her Unhappiness; tho' the Mother was good enough to think the Fault more her own than mine, as she had prevented our Marrying before I went thither, and persuaded the other Match in my Absence. Our mutual Affection was revived, but there were now great Objections to our Union. That Match was indeed look'd upon as invalid, a preceding Wife being said to be living in England; but this could not easily be prov'd,[2] because of the Distance, etc. And tho' there was a Report of his Death, it was not certain. Then, tho' it should be true, he had left many Debts which his Successor might be call'd upon to pay. We ventured however, over all these Difficulties, and I took her to Wife Sept. 1, 1730. None of the Inconveniencies happened that we had apprehended, she prov'd a good and faithful Helpmate, assisted me much by attending the Shop, we throve together, and have ever mutually endeavour'd to make each other happy. Thus I corrected that great *Erratum* as well as I could.

About this Time our Club meeting, not at a Tavern, but in a little Room of Mr. Grace's set apart for that Purpose; a Proposition was made by me, that since our Books were often referr'd to in our Disquisitions upon the Queries, it might be convenient to us to have them all together where we met, that upon Occasion they might be consulted; and by thus clubbing our Books to a common Library, we should, while we lik'd to keep them together, have each of us the

---

1. Franklin lived with the Reads from 1723 to 1724.
2. Without proof of Rogers's bigamy, Deborah's marriage could not be annulled. If she and Franklin had officially married, they would have become liable to a charge of bigamy and could have been sentenced to thirty-nine lashes, plus life imprisonment at hard labor. Common-law marriage was a good choice.

Advantage of using the Books of all the other Members, which would be nearly as beneficial as if each owned the whole. It was lik'd and agreed to, and we fill'd one End of the Room with such Books as we could best spare. The Number was not so great as we expected; and tho' they had been of great Use, yet some Inconveniencies occurring for want of due Care of them, the Collection after about a Year was separated, and each took his Books home again.

And now I set on foot my first Project of a public Nature, that for a Subscription Library.[3] I drew up the Proposals, got them put into Form by our great Scrivener Brockden, and by the help of my Friends in the Junto, procur'd Fifty Subscribers of 40 Shillings each to begin with and 10 Shillings a Year for 50 Years, the Term our Company was to continue. We afterwards obtain'd a Charter, the Company being increas'd to 100. This was the Mother of all the North American Subscription Libraries now so numerous. It is become a great thing itself, and continually increasing. These Libraries have improv'd the general Conversation of the Americans, made the common Tradesmen and Farmers as intelligent as most Gentlemen from other Countries, and perhaps have contributed in some degree to the Stand so generally made throughout the Colonies in Defense of their Privileges.*

Memo.

Thus far was written with the Intention express'd in the Beginning and therefore contains several little family Anecdotes of no Importance to others. What follows was written many Years after in compliance with the Advice contain'd in these Letters, and accordingly intended for the Public. The Affairs of the Revolution occasion'd the Interruption.

---

* "My Manner of acting to engage People in this and future Undertakings." [Franklin's note. When he stopped writing in 1771, Franklin added this reminder to himself for his next topic.]

---

3. The Library Company of Philadelphia was America's first circulating library. The "Instrument of Association" was dated July 1, 1731, and the charter March 25, 1742 (*Papers* 1.208–10, 2.345–48).

[Part Two]

LETTER FROM MR. ABEL JAMES, WITH NOTES ON MY LIFE, (RECEIVED IN PARIS.)[1]

My dear and honored Friend.

I have often been desirous of writing to thee, but could not be reconciled to the thought that the Letter might fall into the Hands of the British, lest some Printer or busy Body should publish some Part of the Contents and give our Friends Pain and myself Censure.

Some Time since there fell into my Hands to my great Joy about 23 Sheets in thy own handwriting containing an Account of the Parentage and Life of thyself, directed to thy Son ending in the Year 1730 with which there were Notes likewise in thy writing, a Copy of which I enclose in Hopes it may be a means if thou continuedst it up to a later period, that the first and latter part may be put together; and if it is not yet continued, I hope thou wilt not delay it. Life is uncertain as the Preacher tells us, and what will the World say if kind, humane and benevolent Ben Franklin should leave his Friends and the World deprived of so pleasing and profitable a Work, a Work which would be useful and entertaining not only to a few, but to millions.

The Influence Writings under that Class have on the Minds of Youth is very great, and has no where appeared so plain as in our public Friends' Journals. It almost insensibly leads the Youth into the Resolution of endeavouring to become as good and as eminent as the Journalist. Should thine for Instance when published, and I think it could not fail of it, lead the Youth to equal the Industry and Temperance of thy early Youth, what a Blessing with that Class would such a Work be. I know of no Character living nor many of them put together, who has so much in his Power as Thyself to promote a greater Spirit of Industry and early Attention to Business, Frugality and Temperance with the American Youth. Not that I think the Work would have no other Merit and Use in the World, far

---

1. James probably wrote this letter in spring or summer 1782. The enclosed "Notes" were Franklin's topics (in effect, an outline) for the *Autobiography*.

69

from it, but the first is of such vast Importance, that I know nothing that can equal it.

The foregoing letter and the minutes accompanying it being shown to a friend, I received from him the following:

LETTER FROM MR. BENJAMIN VAUGHAN[2]

[*MY DEAREST SIR,*   *Paris, January 31, 1783.*]
When I had read over your sheets of minutes of the principal incidents of your life, recovered for you by your Quaker acquaintance; I told you I would send you a letter expressing my reasons why I thought it would be useful to complete and publish it as he desired. Various concerns have for some time past prevented this letter being written, and I do not know whether it was worth any expectation: happening to be at leisure however at present, I shall by writing at least interest and instruct myself; but as the terms I am inclined to use may tend to offend a person of your manners, I shall only tell you how I would address any other person, who was as good and as great as yourself, but less diffident. I would say to him, Sir, I *solicit* the history of your life from the following motives.

Your history is so remarkable, that if you do not give it, somebody else will certainly give it; and perhaps so as nearly to do as much harm, as your own management of the thing might do good.

It will moreover present a table of the internal circumstances of your country, which will very much tend to invite to it settlers of virtuous and manly minds. And considering the eagerness with which such information is sought by them, and the extent of your reputation, I do not know of a more efficacious advertisement than your Biography would give.

All that has happened to you is also connected with the detail of the manners and situation of *a rising* people; and in this respect I do not think that the writings of Caesar and Tacitus can be more interesting to a true judge of human nature and society.

But these, Sir, are small reasons in my opinion, compared with the chance which your life will give for the forming of future great men; and in conjunction with your *Art of Virtue,* (which you design to publish)[3] of improving the features of pri-

---

2. Text from Lemay-Zall, *Genetic Text*, 184–85. Note from William Temple Franklin, *Memoirs of the Life and Writings of Benjamin Franklin*, 3 vols. (London: H. Colburn, 1817–18), I.59–63. (Hereafter referred to as WTF, *Memoirs.*)
3. Vaughan refers to Franklin's long-projected plan to write "a little Work for the Benefit of Youth, to be call'd *The Art of Virtue*" (Franklin to Lord Kames, May 3, 1760; *Papers*

vate character, and consequently of aiding all happiness both
public and domestic.

The two works I allude to, Sir, will in particular give a noble
rule and example of *self-education*. School and other education
constantly proceed upon false principles, and show a clumsy
apparatus pointed at a false mark; but your apparatus is simple,
and the mark a true one; and while parents and young persons
are left destitute of other just means of estimating and becoming prepared for a reasonable course in life, your discovery that
the thing is in many a man's private power, will be invaluable!

Influence upon the private character late in life, is not only
an influence late in life, but a weak influence. It is in *youth*
that we plant our chief habits and prejudices; it is in youth that
we take our party as to profession, pursuits, and matrimony. In
youth therefore the turn is given; in youth the education even
of the next generation is given; in youth the private and public
character is determined; and the term of life extending from
youth to age, life ought to begin well from youth; and more
especially *before* we take our party as to our principal objects.

But your Biography will not merely teach self-education, but
the education of *a wise man*; and the wisest man will receive
lights and improve his progress, by seeing detailed the conduct
of another wise man. And why are weaker men to be deprived
of such helps, when we see our race has been blundering on in
the dark, almost without a guide in this particular, from the
farthest trace of time. Show then, Sir, how much is to be done,
both to sons and fathers; and invite all wise men to become like
yourself; and other men to become wise.

When we see how cruel statesmen and warriors can be to the
humble race, and how absurd distinguished men can be to their
acquaintance, it will be instructive to observe the instances multiply of pacific acquiescing manners; and to find how compatible
it is to be great and *domestic*; enviable and yet *good-humored*.

The little private incidents which you will also have to relate,
will have considerable use, as we want above all things, *rules of
prudence in ordinary affairs*; and it will be curious to see how
you have acted in these. It will be so far a sort of key to life, and
explain many things that all men ought to have once explained
to them, to give them a chance of becoming wise by foresight.

The nearest thing to having experience of one's own, is to
have other people's affairs brought before us in a shape that is
interesting; this is sure to happen from your pen. Your affairs
and management will have an air of simplicity or importance that will not fail to strike; and I am convinced you have

---

9.104). Except for its beginning, Part Two of the *Autobiography* presents Franklin's Art
of Virtue, perhaps partially because of Vaughan's reminder.

conducted them with as much originality as if you had been conducting discussions in politics or philosophy; and what more worthy of experiments and system, (its importance and its errors considered) than human life!

Some men have been virtuous blindly, others have speculated fantastically, and others have been shrewd to bad purposes; but you, Sir, I am sure, will give under your hand, nothing but what is at the same moment, wise, practical, and good.

Your account of yourself (for I suppose the parallel I am drawing for Dr. Franklin, will hold not only in point of character but of private history), will show that you are ashamed of no origin; a thing the more important, as you prove how little necessary all origin is to happiness, virtue, or greatness.

As no end likewise happens without a means, so we shall find, Sir, that even you yourself framed a plan by which you became considerable; but at the same time we may see that though the event is flattering, the means are as simple as wisdom could make them; that is, depending upon nature, virtue, thought, and habit.

Another thing demonstrated will be the propriety of every man's waiting for his time for appearing upon the stage of the world. Our sensations being very much fixed to the moment, we are apt to forget that more moments are to follow the first, and consequently that man should arrange his conduct so as to suit the *whole* of a life. Your attribution appears to have been applied to your *life*, and the passing moments of it have been enlivened with content and enjoyment, instead of being tormented with foolish impatience or regrets. Such a conduct is easy for those who make virtue and themselves their standard, and who try to keep themselves in countenance by examples of other truly great men, of whom patience is so often the characteristic.

Your Quaker correspondent, Sir (for here again I will suppose the subject of my letter resembling Dr. Franklin,) praised your frugality, diligence, and temperance, which he considered as a pattern for all youth: but it is singular that he should have forgotten your modesty, and your disinterestedness, without which you never could have waited for your advancement, or found your situation in the mean time comfortable; which is a strong lesson to show the poverty of glory, and the importance of regulating our minds.

If this correspondent had known the nature of your reputation as well as I do, he would have said; your former writings and measures would secure attention to your Biography, and Art of Virtue; and your Biography and Art of Virtue, in return, would secure attention to them. This is an advantage attendant upon a various character, and which brings all that belongs to it into greater play; and it is the more useful, as perhaps more persons are at a loss for the *means* of improving their minds and characters, than they are for the time or the inclination to do it.

But there is one concluding reflection, Sir, that will show the use of your life as a mere piece of biography. This style of writing seems a little gone out of vogue, and yet it is a very useful one; and your specimen of it may be particularly serviceable, as it will make a subject of comparison with the lives of various public cut-throats and intriguers, and with absurd monastic self-tormentors, or vain literary triflers. If it encourages more writings of the same kind with your own, and induces more men to spend lives fit to be written; it will be worth all Plutarch's Lives put together.

But being tired of figuring to myself a character of which every feature suits only one man in the world, without giving him the praise of it; I shall end my letter, my dear Dr. Franklin, with a personal application to your proper self.

I am earnestly desirous then, my dear Sir, that you should let the world into the traits of your genuine character, as civil broils may otherwise tend to disguise or traduce it. Considering your great age, the caution of your character, and your peculiar style of thinking, it is not likely that any one besides yourself can be sufficiently master of the facts of your life, or the intentions of your mind.

Besides all this, the immense revolution of the present period, will necessarily turn our attention towards the author of it; and when virtuous principles have been pretended in it, it will be highly important to show that such have really influenced; and, as your own character will be the principal one to receive a scrutiny, it is proper (even for its effects upon your vast and rising country, as well as upon England and upon Europe), that it should stand respectable and eternal. For the furtherance of human happiness, I have always maintained that it is necessary to prove that man is not even at present a vicious and detestable animal; and still more to prove that good management may greatly amend him; and it is for much the same reason, that I am anxious to see the opinion established, that there are fair characters existing among the individuals of the race; for the moment that all men, without exception, shall be conceived abandoned, good people will cease efforts deemed to be hopeless, and perhaps think of taking their share in the scramble of life, or at least of making it comfortable principally for themselves.

Take then, my dear Sir, this work most speedily into hand: show yourself good as you are good, temperate as you are temperate; and above all things, prove yourself as one who from your infancy have loved justice, liberty, and concord, in a way that has made it natural and consistent for you to have acted, as we have seen you act in the last seventeen years of your life.

Let Englishmen be made not only to respect, but even to love you. When they think well of individuals in your native country, they will go nearer to thinking well of your country; and when your countrymen see themselves well thought of by Englishmen, they will go nearer to thinking well of England. Extend your views even further; do not stop at those who speak the English tongue, but after having settled so many points in nature and politics, think of bettering the whole race of men.

As I have not read any part of the life in question, but know only the character that lived it, I write somewhat at hazard. I am sure however, that the life, and the treatise I allude to (on the *Art of Virtue*), will necessarily fulfil the chief of my expectations; and still more so if you take up the measure of suiting these performances to the several views above stated. Should they even prove unsuccessful in all that a sanguine admirer of yours hopes from them, you will at least have framed pieces to interest the human mind; and whoever gives a feeling of pleasure that is innocent to man, has added so much to the fair side of a life otherwise too much darkened by anxiety, and too much injured by pain.

In the hope therefore that you will listen to the prayer addressed to you in this letter, I beg to subscribe myself, my dearest Sir, etc. etc.

Signed   BENJ. VAUGHAN.

Continuation of the Account of my Life.
Begun at Passy, 1784.[4]

It is some time since I receiv'd the above Letters, but I have been too busy till now to think of complying with the Request they contain. It might too be much better done if I were at home among my Papers, which would aid my Memory, and help to ascertain Dates. But my Return being uncertain, and having just now a little Leisure, I will endeavour to recollect and write what I can; if I live to get home, it may there be corrected and improv'd.

Not having any Copy here of what is already written, I know not whether an Account is given of the means I used to establish the Philadelphia public Library, which from a small Beginning is now become so considerable, though I remember to have come down to near the Time of that Transaction, 1730. I will therefore begin here, with an Account of it, which may be struck out if found to have been already given.

---

4. Franklin wrote Part Two of the *Autobiography* at his French residence, the Hotel de Valentenois in Passy, which was then a Paris suburb. The peace treaty with Britain was signed on September 3, 1783, but Franklin remained in France until July 1785.

At the time I establish'd myself in Pennsylvania, there was not a good Bookseller's Shop in any of the Colonies to the Southward of Boston. In New York and Philadelphia the Printers were indeed Stationers, they sold only Paper, etc., Almanacs, Ballads, and a few common School Books. Those who lov'd Reading were oblig'd to send for their Books from England. The Members of the Junto had each a few. We had left the Alehouse where we first met, and hired a Room to hold our Club in. I propos'd that we should all of us bring our Books to that Room, where they would not only be ready to consult in our Conferences, but become a common Benefit, each of us being at Liberty to borrow such as he wish'd to read at home. This was accordingly done, and for some time contented us. Finding the Advantage of this little Collection, I propos'd to render the Benefit from Books more common by commencing a Public Subscription Library. I drew a Sketch of the Plan and Rules that would be necessary, and got a skillful Conveyancer Mr. Charles Brockden to put the whole in Form of Articles of Agreement to be subscribed, by which each Subscriber engag'd to pay a certain Sum down for the first Purchase of Books and an annual Contribution for increasing them. So few were the Readers at that time in Philadelphia, and the Majority of us so poor, that I was not able with great Industry to find more than Fifty Persons, mostly young Tradesmen, willing to pay down for this purpose Forty shillings each, and Ten Shillings per Annum. On this little Fund we began. The Books were imported.[5] The Library was open one Day in the Week for lending them to the Subscribers, on their Promissory Notes to pay Double the Value if not duly returned. The Institution soon manifested its Utility, was imitated by other Towns and in other Provinces, the Libraries were augmented by Donations, Reading became fashionable, and our People having no public Amusements to divert their Attention from Study became better acquainted with Books, and in a few Years were observ'd by Strangers to be better instructed and more intelligent than People of the same Rank generally are in other Countries.

When we were about to sign the above-mentioned Articles, which were to be binding on us, our Heirs, etc. for fifty Years, Mr. Brockden, the Scrivener, said to us, "You are young Men, but it is scarce probable that any of you will live to see the Expiration of the Term fix'd in this Instrument." A Number of us, however, are yet living: But the Instrument was after a few Years rendered null by a Charter that incorporated and gave Perpetuity to the Company.

5. See Edwin Wolf II, "The First Books and Printed Catalogues of the Library Company," in the *Pennsylvania Magazine of History and Biography* 78 (1954): 45–70. This article lists the books received, as well as the additional ones ordered (p. 46, n. 5).

The Objections, and Reluctances I met with in Soliciting the Subscriptions, made me soon feel the Impropriety of presenting oneself as the Proposer of any useful Project that might be suppos'd to raise one's Reputation in the smallest degree above that of one's Neighbors, when one has need of their Assistance to accomplish that Project. I therefore put myself as much as I could out of sight, and stated it as a Scheme of *a Number of Friends*, who had requested me to go about and propose it to such as they thought Lovers of Reading. In this way my Affair went on more smoothly, and I ever after practic'd it on such Occasions; and from my frequent Successes, can heartily recommend it. The present little Sacrifice of your Vanity will afterwards be amply repaid. If it remains a while uncertain to whom the Merit belongs, someone more vain than yourself will be encourag'd to claim it, and then even Envy will be dispos'd to do you Justice, by plucking those assum'd Feathers, and restoring them to their right Owner.

This Library afforded me the Means of Improvement by constant Study, for which I set apart an Hour or two each Day; and thus repair'd in some Degree the Loss of the Learned Education my Father once intended for me. Reading was the only Amusement I allow'd myself. I spent no time in Taverns, Games, or Frolics of any kind. And my Industry in my Business continu'd as indefatigable as it was necessary. I was in debt for my Printing-House, I had a young Family coming on to be educated, and I had to contend with for Business two Printers who were establish'd in the Place before me. My Circumstances however grew daily easier: my original Habits of Frugality continuing. And My Father having among his Instructions to me when a Boy, frequently repeated a Proverb of Solomon, *"Seest thou a Man diligent in his Calling, he shall stand before Kings, he shall not stand before mean Men."*[6] I from thence consider'd Industry as a Means of obtaining Wealth and Distinction, which encourag'd me: tho' I did not think that I should ever literally stand before Kings, which however has since happened; for I have stood before five, and even had the honor of sitting down with one, the King of Denmark, to Dinner.[7]

We have an English Proverb that says,

> He that would thrive
> Must ask his Wife,

---

6. Proverbs 22.29, though "Calling" replaces the scriptural "Business."
7. Louis XV and Louis XVI of France, George II and George III of England, and Christian VI of Denmark. Franklin's letter of October 5, 1768, includes a sketch of the seating arrangement (*Papers* 15.224–27).

it was lucky for me that I had one as much dispos'd to Industry and Frugality as myself. She assisted me cheerfully in my Business, folding and stitching Pamphlets, tending Shop, purchasing old Linen Rags for the Paper-makers, etc., etc. We kept no idle Servants, our Table was plain and simple, our Furniture of the cheapest. For instance my Breakfast was a long time Bread and Milk, (no Tea,) and I ate it out of a twopenny earthen Porringer with a Pewter Spoon. But mark how Luxury will enter Families, and make a Progress, in Spite of Principle. Being Call'd one Morning to Breakfast, I found it in a China Bowl with a Spoon of Silver. They had been bought for me without my Knowledge by my Wife, and had cost her the enormous Sum of three and twenty Shillings, for which she had no other Excuse or Apology to make, but that she thought *her* Husband deserv'd a Silver Spoon and China Bowl as well as any of his Neighbors. This was the first Appearance of Plate and China in our House, which afterwards in a Course of Years as our Wealth increas'd, augmented gradually to several Hundred Pounds in Value.

I had been religiously educated as a Presbyterian;[8] and tho' some of the Dogmas of that Persuasion, such as the Eternal Decrees of God, Election, Reprobation, etc. appear'd to me unintelligible, others doubtful, and I early absented myself from the Public Assemblies of the Sect, Sunday being my Studying Day, I never was without some religious Principles; I never doubted, for instance, the Existence of the Deity, that he made the World, and govern'd it by his Providence; that the most acceptable Service of God was the doing Good to Man; that our Souls are immortal; and that all Crime will be punished and Virtue rewarded either here or hereafter; these I esteem'd the Essentials of every Religion, and being to be found in all the Religions we had in our Country I respected them all, tho' with different degrees of Respect as I found them more or less mix'd with other Articles which without any Tendency to inspire, promote or confirm Morality, serv'd principally to divide us and make us unfriendly to one another. This Respect to all, with an Opinion that the worst had some good Effects, induc'd me to avoid all Discourse that might tend to lessen the good Opinion another might have of his own Religion; and as our Province increas'd in People and new Places of worship were continually wanted, and generally erected by voluntary Contribution, my Mite for such purpose, whatever might be the Sect, was never refused.

---

8. Presbyterianism was at a midpoint between Congregational and Anglican faiths. Franklin's parents were pillars of Boston's Old South Church, which was Congregational. Franklin's wife, Deborah, belonged to Philadelphia's Anglican Christ Church. Both children, Sarah and Francis Folger, were baptized at Christ Church. Franklin paid for three seats there and supported it generously, and he is buried there beside Deborah.

Tho' I seldom attended any Public Worship, I had still an Opinion of its Propriety, and of its Utility when rightly conducted, and I regularly paid my annual Subscription for the Support of the only Presbyterian Minister[9] or Meeting we had in Philadelphia. He us'd to visit me sometimes as a Friend, and admonish me to attend his Administrations, and I was now and then prevail'd on to do so, once for five Sundays successively. Had he been, *in my Opinion,* a good Preacher perhaps I might have continued, notwithstanding the occasion I had for the Sunday's Leisure in my Course of Study: But his Discourses were chiefly either polemic Arguments, or Explications of the peculiar Doctrines of our Sect, and were all to me very dry, uninteresting and unedifying, since not a single moral Principle was inculcated or enforc'd, their Aim seeming to be rather to make us Presbyterians than good Citizens. At length he took for his Text that Verse of the 4th Chapter of Philippians, *Finally, Brethren, Whatsoever Things are true, honest, just, pure, lovely, or of good report, if there be any virtue, or any praise, think on these Things;*[1] and I imagin'd in a Sermon on such a Text, we could not miss of having some Morality: But he confin'd himself to five Points only as meant by the Apostle, viz. 1. Keeping holy the Sabbath Day. 2. Being diligent in Reading the Holy Scriptures. 3. Attending duly the Public Worship. 4. Partaking of the Sacrament. 5. Paying a due Respect to God's Ministers.—These might be all good Things, but as they were not the kind of good Things that I expected from that Text, I despaired of ever meeting with them from any other, was disgusted, and attended his Preaching no more. I had some Years before compos'd a little Liturgy or Form of Prayer for my own private Use, viz. in 1728, entitled, *Articles of Belief and Acts of Religion.*[2] I return'd to the Use of this, and went no more to the public Assemblies. My Conduct might be blameable, but I leave it without attempting farther to excuse it, my present purpose being to relate Facts, and not to make Apologies for them.

It was about this time that I conceiv'd the bold and arduous Project of arriving at moral Perfection. I wish'd to live without committing any Fault at anytime; I would conquer all that either Natural Inclination, Custom, or Company might lead me into. As I knew, or thought I knew, what was right and wrong, I did not see why I might not *always* do the one and avoid the other. But I soon found I had undertaken a Task of more Difficulty than I had imagined:

---

9. Jedediah Andrews.
1. The same paraphrase of Philippians 4.8 is in James Foster, "Sermon XI," *Sermons* (1743), 250.
2. Dated November 20, 1728 (*Papers* 1.101–9).

While my Care was employ'd in guarding against one Fault, I was often surpris'd by another. Habit took the Advantage of Inattention. Inclination was sometimes too strong for Reason. I concluded at length, that the mere speculative Conviction that it was our Interest to be completely virtuous, was not sufficient to prevent our Slipping, and that the contrary Habits must be broken and good Ones acquired and established, before we can have any Dependence on a steady uniform Rectitude of Conduct. For this purpose I therefore contriv'd the following Method.

In the various Enumerations of the moral Virtues I had met with in my Reading, I found the Catalogue more or less numerous, as different Writers included more or fewer Ideas under the same Name.[3] Temperance, for Example, was by some confin'd to Eating and Drinking, while by others it was extended to mean the moderating every other Pleasure, Appetite, Inclination or Passion, bodily or mental, even to our Avarice and Ambition. I propos'd to myself, for the sake of Clearness, to use rather more Names with fewer Ideas annex'd to each, than a few Names with more Ideas; and I included after Thirteen Names of Virtues all that at that time occurr'd to me as necessary or desirable, and annex'd to each a short Precept, which fully express'd the Extent I gave to its Meaning.

These Names of Virtues with their Precepts were

1. TEMPERANCE.
Eat not to Dulness. Drink not to Elevation.
2. SILENCE.
Speak not but what may benefit others or your self. Avoiding trifling Conversation.
3. ORDER.
Let all your Things have their Places. Let each Part of your Business have its Time.
4. RESOLUTION.
Resolve to perform what you ought. Perform without fail what you resolve.
5. FRUGALITY.
Make no Expense but to do good to others or yourself: i.e. Waste nothing.
6. INDUSTRY.
Lose no Time. Be always employ'd in something useful. Cut off all unnecessary Actions.

---

3. About 1737, Franklin had voiced this complaint to James Logan, who was then writing a book "on Moral Good or Virtue" (*Papers* 2.185).

7. SINCERITY.

Use no hurtful Deceit. Think innocently and justly; and, if you speak; speak accordingly.

8. JUSTICE.

Wrong none, by doing Injuries or omitting the Benefits that are your Duty.

9. MODERATION.

Avoid Extremes. Forbear resenting Injuries so much as you think they deserve.

10. CLEANLINESS.

Tolerate no Uncleanness in Body, Clothes or Habitation.

11. TRANQUILITY.

Be not disturbed at Trifles, or at Accidents common or unavoidable.

12. CHASTITY.

Rarely use Venery but for Health or Offspring; Never to Dulness, Weakness, or the Injury of your own or another's Peace or Reputation.

13. HUMILITY.

Imitate Jesus and Socrates.

My intention being to acquire the *Habitude* of all these Virtues, I judg'd it would be well not to distract my Attention by attempting the whole at once, but to fix it on one of them at a time, and when I should be Master of that, then to proceed to another, and so on till I should have gone thro' the thirteen. And as the previous Acquisition of some might facilitate the Acquisition of certain others, I arrang'd them with that View as they stand above. *Temperance* first, as it tends to procure that Coolness and Clearness of Head, which is so necessary where constant Vigilance was to be kept up, and Guard maintained, against the unremitting Attraction of ancient Habits, and the Force of perpetual Temptations. This being acquir'd and establish'd, *Silence* would be more easy, and my Desire being to gain Knowledge at the same time that I improv'd in Virtue, and considering that in Conversation it was obtain'd rather by the Use of the Ears than of the Tongue, and therefore wishing to break a Habit I was getting into of Prattling, Punning and Joking, which only made me acceptable to trifling Company, I gave *Silence* the second Place. This, and the next, *Order*, I expected would allow me more Time for attending to my Project and my Studies; RESOLUTION once become habitual, would keep me firm in my Endeavours to obtain all the subsequent Virtues; *Frugality* and *Industry*, by freeing me from my remaining Debt, and producing Affluence and Independence would make more easy the Practice of *Sincerity* and *Justice*, etc. etc. Conceiving then that agreeable to the Advice of Pythagoras in his

Golden Verses,* daily Examination would be necessary, I contriv'd the following Method for conducting that Examination.

I made a little Book in which I allotted a Page for each of the Virtues. I rul'd each Page with red Ink so as to have seven Columns, one for each Day of the Week, marking each Column with a Letter for the Day. I cross'd these Columns with thirteen red Lines, marking the Beginning of each Line with the first Letter of one of the Virtues, on which Line and in its proper Column I might mark by a little black Spot every Fault I found upon Examination, to have been committed respecting that Virtue upon that Day.

I determined to give a Week's strict Attention to each of the Virtues successively. Thus in the first Week my great Guard was to avoid every the least Offence against Temperance, leaving the other Virtues to their ordinary Chance, only marking every Evening the Faults of the Day. Thus if in the first Week I could keep my first Line marked T clear of Spots, I suppos'd the Habit of that Virtue so much strengthen'd and its opposite weaken'd, that I might venture extending my Attention to include the next, and for the following Week keep both Lines clear of Spots. Proceeding thus to the last, I could go thro' a Course complete in Thirteen Weeks, and four Courses in a Year. And like him who having a Garden to weed, does not attempt to eradicate all the bad Herbs at once, which would exceed his Reach and his Strength, but works on one of the Beds at a time, and having accomplish'd the first proceeds to a second; so I should have, (I hoped) the encouraging Pleasure of seeing on my Pages the Progress I made in Virtue, by clearing successively my Lines of their Spots, till in the End by a Number of Courses, I should be happy in viewing a clean Book after a thirteen Weeks' daily Examination.

This my little Book had for its Motto these Lines from *Addison's Cato*,

> *Here will I hold: If there is a Pow'r above us,*
> *(And that there is, all Nature cries aloud*

---

* [Franklin wrote: "Insert those Lines that direct it in a Note." Here follow the lines from Nicholas Rowe's translation which Franklin used in his "Letter from Father Abraham," *The New England Magazine of Knowledge and Pleasure*, no. 1 (August 1758). 22:]

Let not the stealing God of Sleep surprize,
Nor creep in Slumbers on thy weary Eyes,
Ere ev'ry Action of the former Day,
Strictly thou dost, and righteously survey.
With Rev'rence at thy own Tribunal stand.
And answer justly to thy own Demand.

Where have I been? In what have I transgrest?
What Good or Ill has this Day's Life exprest?
Where have I fail'd in what I ought to do?
In what to GOD, to Man, or to myself I owe?
Inquire severe whate'er from first to last,
From Morning's Dawn till Ev'nings Gloom has past.

If Evil were thy Deeds, repenting mourn,
And let thy Soul with strong Remorse be torn:
If Good, the Good with Peace of Mind repay,
And to thy secret Self with Pleasure say,
Rejoice, my Heart, for all went well to Day.

	S	M	T	W	T	F	S
TEMPERANCE.							
Eat not to Dulness. *Drink not to Elevation.*							
T							
S	● ●	●		●		●	
O	●	●	●		●	●	●
R			●			●	
F		●			●		
I			●				
S							
J							
M							
Cl.							
T							
Ch							
H							

82

> *Thro' all her Works) he must delight in Virtue,*
> *And that which he delights in must be happy.*[4]

Another from *Cicero.*

> *O Vitæ Philosophia Dux! O Virtutum indagatrix, expultrixque*
> *vitiorum! Unus dies bene, et ex preceptis tuis actus, peccanti*
> *immortalitati est anteponendus.*[5]

Another from the Proverbs of Solomon speaking of Wisdom or
Virtue;

> Length of Days is in her right hand, and in her Left Hand
> Riches and Honors; Her Ways are Ways of Pleasantness, and
> all her Paths are Peace.
>
> III, 16, 17

And conceiving God to be the Fountain of Wisdom, I thought it
right and necessary to solicit his Assistance for obtaining it; to this
End I form'd the following little Prayer, which was prefix'd to my
Tables of Examination, for daily Use.

> *O Powerful Goodness! bountiful Father! merciful Guide!*
> *Increase in me that Wisdom which discovers my truest Interests;*
> *Strengthen my Resolutions to perform what that Wisdom dic-*
> *tates. Accept my kind Offices to thy other Children, as the only*
> *Return in my Power for thy continual Favors to me.*[6]

I us'd also sometimes a little Prayer which I took from *Thomson's*
Poems, viz.

> *Father of Light and Life, thou Good supreme,*
> *O teach me what is good, teach me thy self!*
> *Save me from Folly, Vanity and Vice,*
> *From every low Pursuit, and fill my Soul*
> *With Knowledge, conscious Peace, and Virtue pure,*
> *Sacred, substantial, neverfading Bliss!*[7]

The Precept of *Order* requiring that *every Part of my Business*
should have its allotted Time, one Page in my little Book contain'd
the following Scheme of Employment for the Twenty-four Hours of
a natural Day.

---

4. Addison's *Cato* (1713) V.i.15–18, which Franklin also used as epigraph for his "Articles
of Belief and Acts of Religion" (*Papers* 1.101).
5. *Tusculum Disputations* V.2.5, with several lines omitted. Cicero claimed that virtue
alone, without divine assistance, could make a happy life.
6. This prayer was evidently intended for Franklin's "Articles of Belief and Acts of Religion" (*Papers* 1.101–9). Franklin does not mention other parts of this youthful writing
that were radically unorthodox, including his belief in multiple inhabited worlds, each
with its own creator-deity.
7. James Thomson's *Winter* (1726).

I enter'd upon the Execution of this Plan for Self-examination, and continu'd it with occasional Intermissions for some time. I was surpris'd to find myself so much fuller of Faults than I had imagined, but I had the Satisfaction of seeing them diminish. To avoid the Trouble of renewing now and then my little Book, which by scraping out the Marks on the Paper of old Faults to make room for new Ones in a new Course, became full of Holes; I transferr'd my Tables and Precepts to the Ivory Leaves of a Memorandum Book, on which the Lines were drawn with red Ink that made a durable Stain, and on those Lines I mark'd my Faults with a black Lead Pencil, which Marks I could easily wipe out with a wet Sponge. After a while I went thro' one Course only in a Year, and afterwards only one in several Years; till at length I omitted them entirely, being employ'd in Voyages and Business abroad with a Multiplicity of Affairs, that interfered. But I always carried my little Book with me.

My Scheme of ORDER, gave me the most Trouble, and I found, that tho' it might be practicable where a Man's Business was such as to leave him the Disposition of his Time, that of a Journeyman Printer for instance, it was not possible to be exactly observ'd by a Master, who must mix with the World, and often receive People of Business at their own Hours. *Order* too, with regard to Places for Things, Papers, etc. I found extremely difficult to acquire. I had not been early accustomed to it, and having an exceeding good Memory, I was not so sensible of the Inconvenience attending Want of Method. This Article therefore cost me so much painful Attention and my Faults in it vex'd me so much, and I made so little Progress in Amendment, and had such frequent Relapses, that I was almost ready to give up the Attempt, and content myself with a faulty Character in that respect. Like the Man who in buying an Axe of a Smith my Neighbor, desired to have the whole of its Surface as bright as the Edge; the Smith consented to grind it bright for him if he would turn the Wheel. He turn'd while the Smith press'd the broad Face of the Axe hard and heavily on the Stone, which made the Turning of it very fatiguing. The Man came every now and then from the Wheel to see how the Work went on; and at length would take his Axe as it was without farther Grinding. No, says the Smith, Turn on, turn on; we shall have it bright by and by; as yet 'tis only speckled. Yes, says the Man; but—*I think I like a speckled Axe best.*—And I believe this may have been the Case with many who having for want of some such Means as I employ'd found the Difficulty of obtaining good, and breaking bad Habits, in other Points of Vice and Virtue, have given up the Struggle, and concluded that *a speckled Axe was best.* For something that pretended to be Reason was every now and then suggesting to me, that such extreme Nicety as

The Morning Question, What Good shall I do this Day?	5	Rise, wash, and address *Powerful Goodness;* contrive Day's Business and take the Resolution of the Day; prosecute the present Study: and breakfast? —
	6	
	7	
	8	
	9	Work.
	10	
	11	
	12	Read, or overlook my Accounts, and dine.
	1	
	2	Work.
	3	
	4	
	5	
	6	Put Things in their Places, Supper, Musick, or Diversion, or Conversation,
	7	
	8	
Evening Question, What Good have I done to day?	9	Examination of the Day.
	10	Sleep.—
	11	
	12	
	1	
	2	
	3	
	4	

I exacted of myself might be a kind of Foppery in Morals, which if it were known would make me ridiculous; that a perfect Character might be attended with the Inconvenience of being envied and hated; and that a benevolent Man should allow a few Faults in himself, to keep his Friends in Countenance.

In Truth I found myself incorrigible with respect to *Order*; and now I am grown old, and my Memory bad, I feel very sensibly the want of it. But on the whole, tho' I never arrived at the Perfection I had been so ambitious of obtaining, but fell far short of it, yet I was by the Endeavour made a better and a happier Man than I otherwise should have been, if I had not attempted it; As those who aim at perfect Writing by imitating the engraved Copies, tho' they never reach the wish'd for Excellence of those Copies, their Hand is mended by the Endeavour, and is tolerable while it continues fair and legible.[8]

And it may be well my Posterity should be informed, that to this little Artifice, with the Blessing of God, their Ancestor ow'd the constant Felicity of his Life down to his 79th Year in which this is written. What Reverses may attend the Remainder is in the Hand of Providence: But if they arrive, the Reflection on past Happiness enjoy'd ought to help his Bearing them with more Resignation. To *Temperance* he ascribes his long-continu'd Health, and what is still left to him of a good Constitution. To *Industry* and *Frugality* the early Easiness of his Circumstances, and Acquisition of his Fortune, with all that Knowledge which enabled him to be an useful Citizen, and obtain'd for him some Degree of Reputation among the Learned. To *Sincerity* and *Justice* the Confidence of his Country, and the honorable Employs it conferr'd upon him. And to the joint Influence of the whole Mass of the Virtues, even in their imperfect State he was able to acquire them, all that Evenness of Temper, and that Cheerfulness in Conversation which makes his Company still sought for, and agreeable even to his younger Acquaintance. I hope therefore that some of my Descendants may follow the Example and reap the Benefit.

It will be remark'd that, tho' my Scheme was not wholly without Religion there was in it no Mark of any of the distinguishing Tenets of any particular Sect. I had purposely avoided them; for being fully persuaded of the Utility and Excellency of my Method, and that it might be serviceable to People in all Religions, and intending some time or other to publish it, I would not have anything in it that should prejudice anyone of any Sect against it. I purposed writing a little Comment on each Virtue, in which I would have shown the Advan-

---

8. Models in penmanship books. Franklin here echoes the simile in *The Advancement of Learning*, book 7, chapter 1, paragraph 1, where Francis Bacon discusses the "science" of virtue or "moral knowledge."

tages of possessing it,* and the Mischiefs attending its opposite Vice; and I should have called my Book the ART *of Virtue*, because it would have shown the *Means and Manner* of obtaining Virtue; which would have distinguish'd it from the mere Exhortation to be good, that does not instruct and indicate the Means; but is like the Apostle's Man of verbal Charity, who only, without showing to the Naked and the Hungry *how* or where they might get Clothes or Victuals, exhorted them to be fed and clothed. *James* II, 15, 16.[9]

But it so happened that my Intention of writing and publishing this Comment was never fulfilled. I did indeed, from time to time put down short Hints of the Sentiments, Reasonings, etc. to be made use of in it; some of which I have still by me: But the necessary close Attention to private Business in the earlier part of Life, and public Business since, have occasioned my postponing it. For it being connected in my Mind with a *great and extensive Project* that required the whole Man to execute, and which an unforeseen Succession of Employs prevented my attending to, it has hitherto remain'd unfinish'd.

In this Piece it was my Design to explain and enforce this Doctrine, that vicious Actions are not hurtful because they are forbidden, but forbidden because they are hurtful, the Nature of Man alone consider'd: That it was therefore every one's Interest to be virtuous, who wish'd to be happy even in this World.[1] And I should from this Circumstance (there being always in the World a Number of rich Merchants, Nobility, States and Princes, who have need of honest Instruments for the Management of their Affairs, and such being so rare) have endeavoured to convince young Persons, that no Qualities were so likely to make a poor Man's Fortune as those of Probity and Integrity.

My List of Virtues contain'd at first but twelve: But a Quaker Friend having kindly inform'd me that I was generally thought proud; that my Pride show'd itself frequently in Conversation; that I was not content with being in the right when discussing any Point, but was overbearing and rather insolent; of which he convinc'd me by mentioning several Instances; I determined endeavouring to cure myself if I could of this Vice or Folly among the rest, and I added *Humility* to my List, giving an extensive Meaning to the Word. I cannot boast of much Success in acquiring the *Reality* of this Virtue; but

---

* "Nothing so likely to make a Man's Fortune as Virtue." [Franklin's memo.]

---

9. "If a brother or sister be naked, and destitute of daily food, and one of you say unto them, Depart in peace, be ye warmed and filled; notwithstanding ye give them not those things which are needful to the body; what doth it profit?"

1. Franklin articulated this doctrine as early as 1739: "Sin is not hurtful because it is forbidden but it is forbidden because it's hurtful" (*Poor Richard*, Oct. 1739; *Papers* 2.224).

I had a good deal with regard to the *Appearance* of it. I made it a Rule
to forbear all direct Contradiction to the Sentiments of others, and
all positive Assertion of my own. I even forbid myself, agreeable to
the old Laws of our Junto, the Use of every Word or Expression in the
Language that imported a fix'd Opinion; such as *certainly, undoubtedly,* etc. and I adopted instead of them, I *conceive,* I *apprehend,* or
I *imagine* a thing to be so or so, or it so appears to me at present.
When another asserted something that I thought an Error, I denied
myself the Pleasure of contradicting him abruptly, and of showing
immediately some Absurdity in his Proposition; and in answering
I began by observing that in certain Cases or Circumstances his
Opinion would be right, but that in the present case there *appear'd*
or *seem'd* to me some Difference, etc. I soon found the Advantage of
this Change in my Manners. The Conversations I engag'd in went
on more pleasantly. The modest way in which I propos'd my Opinions, procur'd them a readier Reception and less Contradiction; I
had less Mortification when I was found to be in the wrong, and
I more easily prevail'd with others to give up their Mistakes and
join with me when I happen'd to be in the right. And this Mode,
which I at first put on, with some violence to natural Inclination,
became at length so easy and so habitual to me, that perhaps for
these Fifty Years past no one has ever heard a dogmatical Expression escape me. And to this Habit (after my Character of Integrity)
I think it principally owing, that I had early so much Weight with my
Fellow Citizens, when I proposed new Institutions, or Alterations in
the old; and so much Influence in public Councils when I became a
Member. For I was but a bad Speaker, never eloquent, subject to
much Hesitation in my choice of Words, hardly correct in Language, and yet I generally carried my Points.

   In reality there is perhaps no one of our natural Passions so hard
to subdue as *Pride.* Disguise it, struggle with it, beat it down, stifle
it, mortify it as much as one pleases, it is still alive, and will every
now and then peep out and show itself. You will see it perhaps often
in this History. For even if I could conceive that I had completely
overcome it, I should probably be proud of my Humility.

               Thus far written at Passy, 1784.

[Part Three]

*I am now about to write at home, August 1788, but cannot have
the help expected from my Papers, many of them being lost in the
War.[1] I have however found the following.*

Having mentioned *a great and extensive Project* which I had
conceiv'd, it seems proper that some Account should be here given
of that Project and its Object. Its first Rise in my Mind appears in
the following little Paper, accidentally preserv'd, viz.

OBSERVATIONS on my Reading History in Library, May 9, 1731.
"That the great Affairs of the World, the Wars, Revolutions, etc.
are carried on and effected by Parties.

"That the View of these Parties is their present general Interest,
or what they take to be such.

"That the different Views of these different Parties, occasion all
Confusion.

"That while a Party is carrying on a general Design, each Man
has his particular private Interest in View.

"That as soon as a Party has gain'd its general Point, each
Member becomes intent upon his particular Interest, which thwart-
ing others, breaks that Party into Divisions, and occasions more
Confusion.

"That few in Public Affairs act from a mere View of the Good of
their Country, whatever they may pretend; and tho' their Actings
bring real Good to their Country, yet Men primarily consider'd that
their own and their Country's Interest was united, and did not act
from a Principle of Benevolence.

"That fewer still in public Affairs act with a View to the Good of
Mankind.

"There seems to me at present to be great Occasion for raising
an united Party for Virtue, by forming the Virtuous and good Men
of all Nations into a regular Body, to be govern'd by suitable good
and wise Rules, which good and wise Men may probably be more

---

1. Left for safekeeping with Joseph Galloway in Philadelphia, Franklin's papers were pil-
laged by British troops in 1778.

unanimous in their Obedience to, than common People are to common Laws.

"I at present think, that whoever attempts this aright, and is well qualified, cannot fail of pleasing God, and of meeting with Success.

B.F.

Revolving this Project in my Mind, as to be undertaken hereafter when my Circumstances should afford me the necessary Leisure, I put down from time to time on Pieces of Paper such Thoughts as occur'd to me respecting it. Most of these are lost; but I find one purporting to be the Substance of an intended Creed, containing as I thought the Essentials of every known Religion, and being free of everything that might shock the Professors of any Religion. It is express'd in these Words, viz.

"That there is one God who made all things.

"That he governs the World by his Providence.

"That he ought to be worshipped by Adoration, Prayer and Thanksgiving.

"But that the most acceptable Service of God is doing Good to Man.[2]

"That the Soul is immortal.

"And that God will certainly reward Virtue and punish Vice either here or hereafter."

My Ideas at that time were, that the Sect should be begun and spread at first among young and single Men only; that each Person to be initiated should not only declare his Assent to such Creed, but should have exercis'd himself with the Thirteen Weeks' Examination and Practice of the Virtues as in the before-mention'd Model; that the Existence of such a Society should be kept a Secret till it was become considerable, to prevent Solicitations for the Admission of improper Persons; but that the Members should each of them search among his Acquaintance for ingenuous well-disposed Youths, to whom with prudent Caution the Scheme should be gradually communicated: That the Members should engage to afford their Advice, Assistance and Support to each other in promoting one another's Interest, Business and Advancement in Life: That for Distinction we should be call'd the Society of the *Free and Easy;* Free, as being by the general Practice and Habit of the Virtues, free from the Dominion of Vice, and particularly by the Practice of Industry and Frugality, free from Debt, which exposes a Man to Confinement and a Species of Slavery to his Creditors. This is as much as I can now recollect of the Project, except that I communicated it in part to two young Men, who adopted it with some Enthusiasm. But my then narrow

---

2. The version in Franklin's *Proposals Relating to the Education of Youth* (1749) has "*Doing Good to Men* is the *only* Service of God in our Power" (*Papers* 3.419).

Circumstances, and the Necessity I was under of sticking close to my Business, occasion'd my Postponing the farther Prosecution of it at that time, and my multifarious Occupations public and private induc'd me to continue postponing, so that it has been omitted till I have no longer Strength or Activity left sufficient for such an Enterprise: Tho I am still of Opinion that it was a practicable Scheme, and might have been very useful, by forming a great Number of good Citizens: And I was not discourag'd by the seeming Magnitude of the Undertaking, as I have always thought that one Man of tolerable Abilities may work great Changes, and accomplish great Affairs among Mankind, if he first forms a good Plan, and, cutting off all Amusements or other Employments that would divert his Attention, makes the Execution of that same Plan his sole Study and Business.

In 1732 I first published my Almanac, under the Name of *Richard Saunders;*[3] it was continu'd by me about 25 Years, commonly call'd *Poor Richard's* Almanac.[4] I endeavour'd to make it both entertaining and useful, and it accordingly came to be in such Demand that I reap'd considerable Profit from it, vending annually near ten Thousand.[5] And observing that it was generally read, scarce any Neighborhood in the Province being without it, I consider'd it as a proper Vehicle for conveying Instruction among the common People, who bought scarce any other Books. I therefore filled all the little Spaces that occur'd between the Remarkable Days in the Calendar, with Proverbial Sentences, chiefly such as inculcated Industry and Frugality, as the Means of procuring Wealth and thereby securing Virtue, it being more difficult for a Man in Want to act always honestly, as (to use here one of those Proverbs) *it is hard for an empty Sack to stand upright.*[6] These Proverbs, which contained the Wisdom of many Ages and Nations, I assembled[7] and form'd into a connected

---

3. Name of a real London almanac maker (1613?–1687?) whose *Apollo Anglicanae, or English Apollo* was a best seller from 1664. It was continued after his death by a Richard Saunder (no "s"), a mathematician. See Donald Wing, *Short-Title Catalogue of Books Printed in England, Scotland, Ireland, Wales, and British America . . . 1641–1700*, 3 vols. (New York: Index Society, 1945–51), A2325–2370, and the Huntington Library Collection.

4. The title combined the Saunders name with the title of another successful London almanac, *Poor Robin* (1661–1776), a comic parody of both astrological and astronomical almanacs. James Franklin's *Rhode Island Almanac* (1728–41) had also used the pseudonym "Poor Robin."

5. During 1748–60, Philadelphia's population rose from 17,000 to 24,000, and Franklin's almanac sold slightly more than 10,000 a year, at fourpence apiece. Franklin's total profit was roughly £5,000 (Wroth, "Benjamin Franklin," 163, 173).

6. In 1740, "An empty Bag cannot stand upright"; in 1750, "An empty Sack can hardly stand upright"; and in 1758, " 'Tis hard for an empty Bag to stand upright" (*Papers* 2.248, 3.446, 7.348).

7. About two-thirds of the proverbs have been traced to some half-dozen earlier collections, but Franklin often refashioned them for brevity or comic effect; e.g., "A penny saved by wise provision availeth two" becomes "A penny saved is a penny earned" (*Papers* 1.281–82). See Frances M. Barbour, *A Concordance to the Sayings in Franklin's Poor Richard* (Detroit: Gale Research Co., 1974).

Discourse prefix'd to the Almanac of 1757, as the Harangue of a wise old Man to the People attending an Auction.[8] The bringing all these scatter'd Counsels thus into a Focus, enabled them to make greater Impression. The Piece being universally approved was copied in all the Newspapers of the Continent, reprinted in Britain on a Broadside to be stuck up in Houses, two Translations were made of it in French, and great Numbers bought by the Clergy and Gentry to distribute gratis among their poor Parishioners and Tenants. In Pennsylvania, as it discouraged useless Expense in foreign Superfluities, some thought it had its share of Influence in producing that growing Plenty of Money which was observable for several Years after its Publication.

I consider'd my Newspaper[9] also as another Means of communicating Instruction, and in that View frequently reprinted in it Extracts from the Spectator and other moral Writers, and sometimes publish'd little Pieces of my own which had been first compos'd for Reading in our Junto. Of these are a Socratic Dialogue tending to prove, that, whatever might be his Parts and Abilities, a vicious Man could not properly be called a Man of Sense. And a Discourse on Self-denial, showing that Virtue was not Secure, till its Practice became a Habitude, and was free from the Opposition of contrary Inclinations. These may be found in the Papers about the beginning of 1735.[1] In the Conduct of my Newspaper I carefully excluded all Libelling and Personal Abuse, which is of late Years become so disgraceful to our Country. Whenever I was solicited to insert anything of that kind, and the Writers pleaded as they generally did, the Liberty of the Press, and that a Newspaper was like a Stage Coach in which any one who would pay had a Right to a Place, my Answer was, that I would print the Piece separately if desired, and the Author might have as many Copies as he pleased to distribute himself, but that I would not take upon me to spread his Detraction, and that having contracted with my Subscribers to furnish them with what might be either useful or entertaining, I could not fill their Papers with private Altercation in which they had no Concern without doing them manifest Injustice.[2] Now many of our

8. Composed in 1757 for the 1758 *Poor Richard*, the prefatory "Harangue," later called "The Way to Wealth," was Franklin's most widely reprinted work—at least 145 editions before 1800 (*Papers* 7.340–50).
9. With weekly circulation averaging about 1500 copies, the *Pennsylvania Gazette* accounted for about sixty-one percent of Franklin's business, 1748–65 (Wroth, "Benjamin Franklin," 163, 173).
1. *Pennsylvania Gazette* for February 11 and 18, 1735. See also Franklin's 1731 "Apology for Printer" (*Papers* 2.194–99).
2. In the *Pennsylvania Gazette* for June 10, 1731, Franklin wrote of having displeased many men "for refusing absolutely to print any of their Party or Personal Reflections" (*Papers* 1.196). On December 24, 1782, he wrote Francis Hopkinson: "If People will print their Abuses of one another, let them do it in little Pamphlets, and distribute them where they think proper" (*Papers* 38.491).

Printers make no scruple of gratifying the Malice of Individuals by false Accusations of the fairest Characters among ourselves, augmenting Animosity even to the producing of Duels, and are moreover so indiscrete as to print scurrilous Reflections on the Government of neighboring States, and even on the Conduct of our best national Allies, which may be attended with the most pernicious Consequences. These Things I mention as a Caution to young Printers, and that they may be encouraged not to pollute their Presses and disgrace their Profession by such infamous Practices, but refuse steadily; as they may see by my Example, that such a Course of Conduct will not on the whole be injurious to their Interests.

In 1733, I sent one of my Journeymen to Charleston South Carolina where a Printer was wanting.[3] I furnish'd him with a Press and Letters, on an Agreement of Partnership, by which I was to receive One Third of the Profits of the Business, paying One Third of the Expense. He was a Man of Learning and honest, but ignorant in Matters of Account; and tho' he sometimes made me Remittances, I could get no Account from him, nor any satisfactory State of our Partnership while he lived. On his Decease, the Business was continued by his Widow, who being born and bred in Holland, where as I have been inform'd the Knowledge of Accounts makes a Part of Female Education, she not only sent me as clear a State as she could find of the Transactions past, but continu'd to account with the greatest Regularity and Exactitude every Quarter afterwards; and manag'd the Business with such Success that she not only brought up reputably a Family of Children, but at the Expiration of the Term was able to purchase of me the Printing-House and establish her Son in it. I mention this Affair chiefly for the Sake of recommending that Branch of Education for our young Females, as likely to be of more Use to them and their Children in Case of Widowhood than either Music or Dancing, by preserving them from Losses by Imposition of crafty Men, and enabling them to continue perhaps a profitable mercantile House with establish'd Correspondence till a Son is grown up fit to undertake and go on with it, to the lasting Advantage and enriching of the Family.

About the Year 1734, there arrived among us from Ireland, a young Presbyterian Preacher named Hemphill, who delivered with a good Voice, and apparently extempore, most excellent Discourses, which drew together considerable Numbers of different Persuasions, who join'd in admiring them. Among the rest I became one of his constant Hearers, his Sermons pleasing me as they had little of

---

3. Franklin had sponsored Thomas Whitmarsh (d. 1733) in South Carolina in 1731, and in November 1733 sent Louis Timothée to succeed him. Elizabeth Timothée succeeded her husband at his death in 1738 (*Papers* 1.205–8, 339–42).

the dogmatical kind, but inculcated strongly the Practice of Virtue, or what in the religious Style are called Good Works. Those however, of our Congregation, who considered themselves as orthodox Presbyterians, disapprov'd his Doctrine, and were join'd by most of the old Clergy, who arraign'd him of Heterodoxy before the Synod, in order to have him silenc'd. I became his zealous Partisan, and contributed all I could to raise a Party in his Favor; and we combated for him a while with some Hopes of Success. There was much Scribbling pro and con upon the Occasion; and finding that tho' an elegant Preacher he was but a poor Writer, I lent him my Pen and wrote for him two or three Pamphlets, and one Piece in the Gazette of April 1735. Those Pamphlets, as is generally the Case with controversial Writings, tho' eagerly read at the time, were soon out of Vogue, and I question whether a single Copy of them now exists.[4]

During the Contest an unlucky Occurrence hurt his Cause exceedingly. One of our Adversaries having heard him preach a Sermon that was much admired, thought he had somewhere read that Sermon before, or at least a part of it. On Search he found that Part quoted at length in one of the British Reviews, from a Discourse of Dr. Forster's.[5] This Detection gave many of our Party Disgust, who accordingly abandoned his Cause, and occasion'd our more speedy Discomfiture in the Synod. I stuck by him, however, as I rather approv'd his giving us good Sermons compos'd by others, than bad ones of his own Manufacture; tho' the latter was the Practice of our common Teachers. He afterwards acknowledg'd to me that none of those he preach'd were his own; adding that his Memory was such as enabled him to retain and repeat any Sermon after one Reading only. On our Defeat he left us, in search elsewhere of better Fortune, and I quitted the Congregation, never joining it after, tho' I continu'd many Years my Subscription for the Support of its Ministers.

I had begun in 1733 to study Languages. I soon made myself so much a Master of the French as to be able to read the Books with Ease. I then undertook the Italian. An Acquaintance who was also learning it, us'd often to tempt me to play Chess with him. Finding this took up too much of the Time I had to spare for Study, I at length refus'd to play anymore, unless on this Condition, that the Victor in every Game, should have a Right to impose a Task, either in Parts of the Grammar to be got by heart, or in Translation, etc., which Tasks the Vanquish'd was to perform upon Honor before our

---

4. The *Gazette* piece appeared on April 10, 1735. At least two copies of each of Franklin's three pamphlets are extant. See C. William Milter, *Benjamin Franklin's Philadelphia Printing* (Philadelphia: American Philosophical Society, 1974), nos. 101, 102, and 105 [2nd ed., 106] (*Papers* 2.27–33, 37–126).
5. James Foster, a leading liberal preacher. The Synod found Hemphill guilty of preaching "Unsound and Dangerous" doctrine (*Papers* 2.37).

next Meeting. As we play'd pretty equally we thus beat one another into that Language. I afterwards with a little Pains-taking acquir'd as much of the Spanish as to read their Books also.

I have already mention'd that I had only one Year's Instruction in a Latin School, and that when very young, after which I neglected that Language entirely.—But when I had attained an Acquaintance with the French, Italian and Spanish, I was surpris'd to find, on looking over a Latin Testament, that I understood so much more of that Language than I had imagined; which encouraged me to apply myself again to the Study of it, and I met with the more Success, as those preceding Languages had greatly smooth'd my Way. From these Circumstances I have thought, that there is some Inconsistency in our common Mode of Teaching Languages. We are told that it is proper to begin first with the Latin, and having acquir'd that, it will be more easy to attain those modern Languages which are deriv'd from it; and yet we do not begin with the Greek in order more easily to acquire the Latin. It is true, that if you can clamber and get to the Top of a Staircase without using the Steps, you will more easily gain them in descending: but certainly if you begin with the lowest you will with more Ease ascend to the Top. And I would therefore offer it to the Consideration of those who superintend the Educating of our Youth, whether, since many of those who begin with the Latin, quit the same after spending some Years, without having made any great Proficiency, and what they have learned becomes almost useless, so that their time has been lost, it would not have been better to have begun them with the French, proceeding to the Italian etc., for tho' after spending the same time they should quit the Study of Languages, and never arrive at the Latin, they would however have acquir'd another Tongue or two that being in modern Use might be serviceable to them in common Life.

After ten Years' Absence from Boston, and having become more easy in my Circumstances, I made a Journey[6] thither to visit my Relations, which I could not sooner well afford. In returning I call'd at Newport, to see my Brother then settled there with his Printing-House. Our former Differences were forgotten, and our Meeting was very cordial and affectionate. He was fast declining in his Health, and requested of me that in case of his Death which he apprehended not far distant, I would take home his Son, then but 10 Years of Age, and bring him up[7] to the Printing Business. This I accordingly perform'd, sending him a few Years to School before I took him into the Office. His Mother carried on the Business till he was grown up,

---

6. Of "near seven Weeks" in September and early October 1733 (*Papers* 1.346).
7. After James died, February 4, 1735, his son came to live with Benjamin Franklin while attending school, then served as an apprentice, 1740–47.

when I assisted him with an Assortment of new Types, those of his Father being in a Manner worn out.—Thus it was that I made my Brother ample Amends for the Service I had depriv'd him of by leaving him so early.

In 1736 I lost one of my Sons, a fine Boy of 4 Years old, by the Smallpox taken in the common way. I long regretted bitterly and still regret that I had not given it to him by Inoculation.[8] This I mention for the Sake of Parents, who omit that Operation on the Supposition that they should never forgive themselves if a Child died under it; my Example showing that the Regret may be the same either way, and that therefore the safer should be chosen.

Our Club, the Junto, was found so useful, and afforded such Satisfaction to the Members, that several were desirous of introducing their Friends, which could not well be done without exceeding what we had settled as a convenient Number, viz. Twelve. We had from the Beginning made it a Rule to keep our Institution a Secret, which was pretty well observ'd. The Intention was, to avoid Applications of improper Persons for Admittance, some of whom perhaps we might find it difficult to refuse. I was one of those who were against any Addition to our Number, but instead of it made in Writing a Proposal, that every Member separately should endeavour to form a subordinate Club, with the same Rules respecting Queries, etc. and without informing them of the Connection with the Junto. The Advantages propos'd were the Improvement of so many more young Citizens by the Use of our Institutions; Our better Acquaintance with the general Sentiments of the Inhabitants on any Occasion, as the Junto-Member might propose what Queries we should desire, and was to report to Junto what pass'd in his separate Club; the Promotion of our particular Interests in Business by more extensive Recommendations; and the Increase of our Influence in public Affairs and our Power of doing Good by spreading thro' the several Clubs the Sentiments of the Junto. The Project was approv'd, and every Member undertook to form his Club: but they did not all succeed. Five or six only were completed, which were call'd by different Names, as the Vine, the Union, the Band, etc. They were useful to themselves, and afforded us a good deal of Amusement, Information, and Instruction, besides answering in some considerable Degree our Views of influencing the public Opinion on particular Occasions, of which I shall give some Instances in course of time as they happened.

My first Promotion was my being chosen in 1736 Clerk of the General Assembly. The Choice was made that Year without Opposition;[9]

8. After Francis Folger Franklin died in November 1736, Benjamin Franklin printed a notice in his paper denying that the child had died from inoculation (*Papers* 2.154).
9. Franklin was selected on October 15, 1736, after the former clerk was defeated for the position (*Pa. Archives*, 8th ser., 3.2373).

but the Year following when I was again propos'd (the Choice, like
that of the Members being annual) a new Member made a long
Speech against me in order to favor some other Candidate.[1] I was
however chosen; which was the more agreeable to me, as besides the
Pay for immediate Service as Clerk, the Place gave me a better
Opportunity of keeping up an Interest among the Members, which
secur'd to me the Business of Printing the Votes, Laws, Paper Money,
and other occasional Jobs for the Public, that on the whole were
very profitable.[2] I therefore did not like the Opposition of this new
Member, who was a Gentleman of Fortune, and Education, with
Talents that were likely to give him in time great Influence in the
House, which indeed afterwards happened. I did not however aim at
gaining his Favor by paying any servile Respect to him, but after
some time took this other Method. Having heard that he had in his
Library a certain very scarce and curious Book, I wrote a Note to
him expressing my Desire of perusing that Book, and requesting he
would do me the Favor of lending it to me for a few Days. He sent it
immediately; and I return'd it in about a Week, with another Note
expressing strongly my Sense of the Favor. When we next met in the
House he spoke to me, (which he had never done before) and with
great Civility. And he ever afterwards manifested a Readiness to
serve me on all Occasions, so that we became great Friends, and our
Friendship continu'd to his Death. This is another Instance of the
Truth of an old Maxim I had learned, which says, *He that has once
done you a Kindness will be more ready to do you another, than he
whom you yourself have obliged.* And it shows how much more profitable it is prudently to remove, than to resent, return and continue
inimical Proceedings.

In 1737, Colonel Spotswood, late Governor of Virginia, and then
Postmaster General, being dissatisfied with the Conduct of his
Deputy at Philadelphia, respecting some Negligence in rendering,
and Inexactitude of his Accounts, took from him the Commission
and offered it to me.[3] I accepted it readily, and found it of great
Advantage; for tho' the Salary was small, it facilitated the Correspondence that improv'd my Newspaper, increas'd the Number
demanded, as well as the Advertisements to be inserted, so that it
came to afford me a very considerable Income. My old Competitor's

1. Evidently Isaac Norris (1701–1766), a new member fitting Franklin's description. The
   Norris family disliked Franklin both because he advocated a paper currency and because
   Franklin's newspaper supported Andrew Hamilton.
2. Franklin's combined salary as clerk and printer for the assembly grew from £24.9.6 in
   1736–37 to £113.2.0 in 1739–40 (*Pa. Archives*, 8th ser., 3.2402, 2662).
3. For the last three of his nine years as postmaster, Bradford did not submit accounts,
   and was thus succeeded in October 1737 by Franklin, who held office until he was
   made deputy postmaster for North America in 1753 (*Papers* 2.180, 235).

Newspaper declin'd proportionably,[4] and I was satisfied without
retaliating his Refusal, while Postmaster, to permit my Papers
being carried by the Riders.[5] Thus He suffer'd greatly from his
Neglect in due Accounting; and I mention it as a Lesson to those
young Men who may be employ'd in managing Affairs for others
that they should always render Accounts and make Remittances
with great Clearness and Punctuality. The Character of observing
Such a Conduct is the most powerful of all Recommendations to
new Employments and Increase of Business.

I began now to turn my Thoughts a little to public Affairs, beginning however with small Matters. The City Watch was one of the
first Things that I conceiv'd to want Regulation. It was managed
by the Constables of the respective Wards in Turn. The Constable
warn'd a Number of Housekeepers to attend him for the Night.
Those who chose never to attend paid him Six Shillings a Year to be
excus'd, which was suppos'd to be for hiring Substitutes; but was in
Reality much more than was necessary for that purpose, and made
the Constableship a Place of Profit. And the Constable for a little
Drink often got such Ragamuffins about him as a Watch, that reputable Housekeepers did not choose to mix with. Walking the Rounds
too was often neglected, and most of the Night spent in Tippling.
I thereupon wrote a Paper to be read in Junto, representing these
Irregularities, but insisting more particularly on the Inequality of
this Six Shilling Tax of the Constables, respecting the Circumstances of those who paid it, since a poor Widow Housekeeper, all
whose Property to be guarded by the Watch did not perhaps exceed
the Value of Fifty Pounds, paid as much as the wealthiest Merchant
who had Thousands of Pounds worth of Goods in his Stores. On the
whole I proposed as a more effectual Watch, the Hiring of proper
Men to serve constantly in that Business; and as a more equitable
Way of supporting the Charge, the levying a Tax that should be
proportion'd to Property. This Idea being approv'd by the Junto, was
communicated to the other Clubs, but as arising in each of them.
And tho' the Plan was not immediately carried into Execution,[6] yet
by preparing the Minds of People for the Change, it paved the Way
for the Law obtain'd a few Years after, when the Members of our
Clubs were grown into more Influence.

4. Although Bradford neglected his paper for ventures in real estate and mining, it did not
   decline appreciably from his loss of the post office.
5. Evidently Franklin complained of Bradford's unfair business practice to Alexander
   Spotswood, deputy postmaster general for North America, for Franklin advertised on
   January 23, 1735, that "By the Indulgence" of Spotswood, he was "allow'd to send the
   Gazettes by the Post" (Papers 2.131). In 1739, however, because of Bradford's still delinquent post office accounts, Spotswood forbade Franklin to allow Bradford's papers to
   be carried by the post (Papers 2.235–6, 275–81).
6. Though first proposed about 1735, the plan was not adopted until 1752 (Papers
   4.327–32).

About this time I wrote a Paper, (first to be read in Junto but it was afterwards publish'd)[7] on the different Accidents and Carelessnesses by which Houses were set on fire, with Cautions against them, and Means proposed of avoiding them. This was much spoken of as a useful Piece, and gave rise to a Project, which soon followed it, of forming a Company for the more ready Extinguishing of Fires, and mutual Assistance in Removing and Securing of Goods when in Danger. Associates in this Scheme were presently found amounting to Thirty. Our Articles of Agreement[8] oblig'd every Member to keep always in good Order and fit for Use, a certain Number of Leather Buckets, with strong Bags and Baskets (for packing and transporting of Goods), which were to be brought to every Fire; and we agreed to meet once a Month and spend a social Evening together, in discoursing, and communicating such Ideas as occur'd to us upon the Subject of Fires as might be useful in our Conduct on such Occasions. The Utility of this Institution soon appear'd, and many more desiring to be admitted than we thought convenient for one Company, they were advised to form another; which was accordingly done. And this went on, one new Company being formed after another, till they became so numerous as to include most of the Inhabitants who were Men of Property; and now at the time of my Writing this, tho' upwards of Fifty Years since its Establishment, that which I first formed, called the Union Fire Company, still subsists and flourishes, tho' the first Members are all deceas'd but myself and one who is older[9] by a Year than I am. The small Fines that have been paid by Members for Absence at the Monthly Meetings, have been applied to the Purchase of Fire Engines, Ladders, Firehooks, and other useful Implements for each Company, so that I question whether there is a City in the World better provided with the Means of putting a Stop to beginning Conflagrations; and in fact since these Institutions, the City has never lost by Fire more than one or two Houses at a time, and the Flames have often been extinguish'd before the House in which they began has been half-consumed.

In 1739 arriv'd among us from England the Rev. Mr. Whitefield, who had made himself remarkable there as an itinerant Preacher. He was at first permitted to preach in some of our Churches; but the Clergy taking a Dislike to him, soon refus'd him their Pulpits and he was oblig'd to preach in the Fields.[1] The Multitudes of all Sects and Denominations that attended his Sermons were enormous and

---

7. *Pennsylvania Gazette*, February 4, 1735 (*Papers* 2.12–15).
8. Dated December 7, 1736 (*Papers* 2.150–53).
9. Philip Syng, also a member of the original Junto and a founder of the Library Company.
1. During his second visit to America, 1739–40, many Anglican churches excluded Whitefield but most Presbyterian churches welcomed him. Preaching in the fields was his custom in England.

it was matter of Speculation to me who was one of the Number, to observe the extraordinary Influence of his Oratory on his Hearers, and how much they admir'd and respected him, notwithstanding his common Abuse of them, by assuring them they were naturally *half Beasts and half Devils*.[2] It was wonderful to see the Change soon made in the Manners of our Inhabitants; from being thoughtless or indifferent about Religion, it seem'd as if all the World were growing Religious; so that one could not walk thro' the Town in an Evening without Hearing Psalms sung in different Families of every Street.[3] And it being found inconvenient to assemble in the open Air, subject to its Inclemencies, the Building of a House to meet in was no sooner propos'd and Persons appointed to receive Contributions, but sufficient Sums were soon receiv'd to procure the Ground and erect the Building which was 100 feet long and 70 broad, about the Size of Westminster Hall, and the Work was carried on with such Spirit as to be finished in a much shorter time than could have been expected. Both House and Ground were vested in Trustees, expressly for the Use of any Preacher of any religious Persuasion who might desire to say something to the People of Philadelphia, the Design in building not being to accommodate any particular Sect, but the Inhabitants in general, so that even if the Mufti of Constantinople were to send a Missionary to preach Mahometanism to us, he would find a Pulpit at his Service.*

Mr. Whitefield, in leaving us, went preaching all the Way thro' the Colonies to Georgia. The Settlement of that Province had lately been begun; but instead of being made with hardy industrious Husbandmen accustomed to Labor, the only People fit for such an Enterprise, it was with Families of broken Shopkeepers and other insolvent Debtors, many of indolent and idle habits, taken out of the Jails, who being set down in the Woods, unqualified for clearing Land, and unable to endure the Hardships of a new Settlement, perished in Numbers, leaving many helpless Children unprovided for. The Sight of their miserable Situation inspired the benevolent Heart of Mr. Whitefield with the Idea of building an Orphan House there, in which they might be supported and educated. Returning northward he preach'd up this Charity, and made large Collections;—for his Eloquence had a wonderful Power over the Hearts and Purses of

---

* "This to come in hereafter, where I shall mention my Election as one of the Trustees." [Franklin's note. See p. 112.]

---

2. Preaching on the parable of the Pharisee and the Publican (Luke 18.9–14) Whitefield asked, "Would he ['this publican'] have been angry, if any one had told him, that, by nature, he was half a devil and half a beast?"
3. *Pennsylvania Gazette.* June 12, 1740: "Instead of idle Songs and Ballads, the People are every where entertaining themselves with Psalms, Hymns and Spiritual Songs" (*Papers* 2.288).

his Hearers, of which I myself was an Instance. I did not disapprove of the Design, but as Georgia was then destitute of Materials and Workmen, and it was propos'd to send them from Philadelphia at a great Expense, I thought it would have been better to have built the House here and brought the Children to it. This I advis'd, but he was resolute in his first Project, and rejected my Counsel, and I thereupon refus'd to contribute.

I happened soon after to attend one of his Sermons, in the Course of which I perceived he intended to finish with a Collection, and I silently resolved he should get nothing from me. I had in my Pocket a Handful of Copper Money, three or four silver Dollars, and five Pistoles in Gold. As he proceeded I began to soften, and concluded to give the Coppers. Another Stroke of his Oratory made me asham'd of that, and determin'd me to give the Silver; and he finish'd so admirably, that I emptied my Pocket wholly into the Collector's Dish, Gold and all. At this Sermon there was also one of our Club, who being of my Sentiments respecting the Building in Georgia, and suspecting a Collection might be intended, had by Precaution emptied his Pockets before he came from home; towards the Conclusion of the Discourse however, he felt a strong Desire to give, and apply'd to a Neighbor who stood near him to borrow some Money for the Purpose. The Application was unfortunately to perhaps the only Man in the Company who had the firmness not to be affected by the Preacher. His Answer was, *At any other time, Friend Hopkinson, I would lend to thee freely; but not now; for thee seems to be out of thy right Senses.*[4]

Some of Mr. Whitefield's Enemies affected to suppose that he would apply these Collections to his own private Emolument; but I, who was intimately acquainted with him, (being employ'd in printing his Sermons and Journals, etc.) never had the least Suspicion of his Integrity, but am to this day decidedly of Opinion that he was in all his Conduct, a perfectly *honest Man.* And methinks my Testimony in his Favor ought to have the more Weight, as we had no religious Connection. He us'd indeed sometimes to pray for my Conversion, but never had the Satisfaction of believing that his Prayers were heard. Ours was a mere civil Friendship, sincere on both Sides, and lasted to his Death.[5]

4. The sermon Franklin describes probably took place on Sunday, April 20, 1740. The *Pennsylvania Gazette* for April 24, 1740, describes the large sum of money Whitefield collected "on *Sunday* last . . . for the Orphans in *Georgia.*"
5. Franklin printed a number of Whitefield's books, as well as his journals, in 1739–41. (Miller, *Franklin's Philadelphia Printing*, nos. 180, 214–24, 269–70.) On November 26, 1740, Whitefield wrote to Franklin, "I do not despair of your seeing the reasonableness of Christianity. Apply to GOD; be willing to do the divine will, and you shall know it" (*Papers* 2.270).

The following Instance will show something of the Terms on which we stood. Upon one of his Arrivals from England at Boston, he wrote to me that he should come soon to Philadelphia, but knew not where he could lodge when there, as he understood his old kind Host Mr. Benezet[6] was remov'd to Germantown. My Answer was; You know my House, if you can make shift with its scanty Accommodations you will be most heartily welcome. He replied, that if I made that kind Offer for Christ's sake, I should not miss of a Reward.—And I return'd, *Don't let me be mistaken; it was not for Christ's sake, but for your sake.* One of our common Acquaintance jocosely remark'd, that knowing it to be the Custom of the Saints, when they receiv'd any favor, to shift the Burden of the Obligation from off their own Shoulders, and place it in Heaven, I had contriv'd to fix it on Earth.

The last time I saw Mr. Whitefield was in London,[7] when he consulted me about his Orphan House Concern, and his Purpose of appropriating it to the Establishment of a College.

He had a loud and clear Voice, and articulated his Words and Sentences so perfectly that he might be heard and understood at a great Distance, especially as his Auditors, however numerous, observ'd the most exact Silence. He preach'd one Evening from the Top of the Court House Steps, which are in the Middle of Market Street, and on the West Side of Second Street which crosses it at right angles. Both Streets were fill'd with his Hearers to a considerable Distance. Being among the hindmost in Market Street, I had the Curiosity to learn how far he could be heard, by retiring backwards down the Street towards the River, and I found his Voice distinct till I came near Front Street, when some Noise in that Street, obscur'd it. Imagining then a Semicircle, of which my Distance should be the Radius, and that it were fill'd with Auditors, to each of whom I allow'd two square feet, I computed that he might well be heard by more than Thirty Thousand. This reconcil'd me to the Newspaper Accounts of his having preach'd to 25,000 People[8] in the Fields, and to the ancient Histories of Generals haranguing whole Armies, of which I had sometimes doubted.[9]

By hearing him often I came to distinguish easily between Sermons newly compos'd, and those which he had often preach'd in the Course of his Travels. His Delivery of the latter was so improv'd by frequent Repetitions, that every Accent, every Emphasis, every Modulation of Voice, was so perfectly well turn'd and well plac'd,

6. John Stephen Benezet moved to Germantown in 1743, and Whitefield next came to Philadelphia in September 1745.
7. During the winter of 1767–68 (*Papers* 15.28).
8. Whitefield's own journal claims he preached to 30,000.
9. *Poor Richard* for January 1749, evidently inspired by Franklin's observation of the crowds attending Whitefield, comments that 45,000 auditors could "stand in a space . . . but 100 yards square" (*Papers* 3.336).

that without being interested in the Subject, one could not help being pleas'd with the Discourse, a Pleasure of much the same kind with that receiv'd from an excellent Piece of Music. This is an Advantage itinerant Preachers have over those who are stationary: as the latter cannot well improve their Delivery of a Sermon by so many Rehearsals.

His Writing and Printing from time to time gave great Advantage to his Enemies. Unguarded Expressions and even erroneous Opinions delivered in Preaching might have been afterwards explain'd, or qualified by supposing others that might have accompanied them; or they might have been denied; but *litera scripta manet*.[1] Critics attack'd his Writings violently, and with so much Appearance of Reason as to diminish the Number of his Votaries, and prevent their Increase: So that I am of Opinion, if he had never written anything he would have left behind him a much more numerous and important Sect. And his Reputation might in that case have been still growing, even after his Death; as there being nothing of his Writing on which to found a Censure; and give him a lower Character, his Proselytes would be left at Liberty to feign for him as great a Variety of Excellencies, as their enthusiastic Admiration might wish him to have possessed.

My Business was now continually augmenting, and my Circumstances growing daily easier, my Newspaper having become very profitable,[2] as being for a time almost the only one in this and the neighboring Provinces. I experienc'd too the Truth of the Observation, that *after getting the first hundred Pound, it is more easy to get the second:* Money itself being of a prolific Nature: The Partnership at Carolina having succeeded, I was encourag'd to engage in others, and to promote several of my Workmen[3] who had behaved well, by establishing them with Printing-Houses in different Colonies, on the same Terms with that in Carolina. Most of them did well, being enabled at the End of our Term, Six Years, to purchase the Types of me; and go on working for themselves, by which means several Families were raised. Partnerships often finish in Quarrels, but I was happy in this, that mine were all carried on and ended amicably; owing I think a good deal to the Precaution of having very explicitly settled in our Articles[4] everything to be done by or expected from each Partner, so that there was nothing to dispute, which Precaution

---

1. In full: "Vox audila perit, littera scripta manet": *The spoken word passes away, the written word remains.*
2. Franklin earned about £750 a year from his newspaper, 1748–65, when about twenty-five percent of its circulation went to out-of-town subscribers. Most of the paper's profits came from advertisements (Wroth, "Benjamin Franklin," 163).
3. Thomas Smith in Antigua (1748), Benjamin Mecom to succeed Smith (1752), and Samuel Holland in Lancaster, Pennsylvania (1753) (*Papers* 3.322n; 4.355–56; 4.506–7).
4. Franklin's contract with Holland is in *Papers* 4.506–7.

I would therefore recommend to all who enter into Partnerships, for whatever Esteem Partners may have for and Confidence in each other at the time of the Contract, little Jealousies and Disgusts may arise, with Ideas of Inequality in the Care and Burden of the Business, etc. which are attended often with Breach of Friendship and of the Connection, perhaps with Lawsuits and other disagreeable Consequences.

I had on the whole abundant Reason to be satisfied with my being established in Pennsylvania. There were however two things that I regretted: There being no Provision for Defense, nor for a complete Education of Youth. No Militia nor any College. I therefore in 1743, drew up a Proposal[5] for establishing an Academy; and at that time thinking the Rev. Mr. Peters, who was out of Employ, a fit Person to superintend such an Institution, I communicated the Project to him. But he having more profitable Views in the Service of the Proprietor, which succeeded, declin'd the Undertaking. And not knowing another at that time suitable for such a Trust, I let the Scheme lie a while dormant. I succeeded better the next Year, 1744, in proposing and establishing a Philosophical Society. The Paper[6] I wrote for that purpose will be found among my Writings when collected.

With respect to Defense, Spain having been several Years at War against Britain, and being at length join'd by France, which brought us into greater Danger,[7] and the laboured and long-continued Endeavours of our Governor Thomas to prevail with our Quaker Assembly to pass a Militia Law, and make other Provisions for the Security of the Province having proved abortive, I determined to try what might be done by a voluntary Association of the People. To promote this I first wrote and published a Pamphlet, entitled, PLAIN TRUTH,[8] in which I stated our defenseless Situation in strong Lights, with the Necessity of Union and Discipline for our Defense, and promis'd to propose in a few Days an Association to be generally signed for that purpose. The Pamphlet had a sudden and surprising Effect. I was call'd upon for the Instrument of Association: And having settled the Draft of it with a few Friends, I appointed a Meeting of the Citizens in the large Building before-mentioned.

The House was pretty full. I had prepared a Number of printed Copies, and provided Pens and Ink dispers'd all over the Room. I harangu'd them a little on the Subject, read the Paper and explain'd

---

5. Not extant.
6. *A Proposal for Promoting Useful Knowledge among the British Plantations in America* was dated May 14, 1743. The idea was botanist John Bartram's (*Papers* 2.380–83).
7. The war with Spain (the War of Jenkins' Ear) began 1737 and with France (King George's War) 1744. Enemy ships appeared in Delaware Bay, spring–summer 1747.
8. *Plain Truth; or, Serious Considerations on the Present State of the City of Philadelphia, and Province of Pennsylvania,* by "a Tradesman of Philadelphia" (November 17, 1747; *Papers* 3.188–204).

it, and then distributed the Copies which were eagerly signed, not the least Objection being made. When the Company separated, and the Papers were collected we found above Twelve hundred Hands; and other Copies being dispers'd in the Country the Subscribers amounted at length to upwards of Ten Thousand. These all furnish'd themselves as soon as they could with Arms; form'd themselves into Companies, and Regiments, chose their own Officers, and met every Week to be instructed in the manual Exercise, and other Parts of military Discipline. The Women, by Subscriptions among themselves, provided Silk Colors, which they presented to the Companies, painted with different Devices and Mottos which I supplied. The Officers of the Companies composing the Philadelphia Regiment, being met, chose me for their Colonel; but conceiving myself unfit, I declin'd that Station, and recommended Mr. Lawrence,[9] a fine Person and Man of Influence, who was accordingly appointed. I then propos'd a Lottery[1] to defray the Expense of Building a Battery below the Town, and furnishing it with Cannon. It filled expeditiously and the Battery was soon erected, the Merlons being fram'd of Logs and fill'd with Earth. We bought some old Cannon from Boston, but these not being sufficient, we wrote to England for more, soliciting at the same Time our Proprietaries for some Assistance, tho' without much Expectation of obtaining it.

Meanwhile Colonel Lawrence, William Allen, Abraham Taylor, Esquires, and myself were sent to New York by the Associators, commission'd to borrow some Cannon of Governor Clinton. He at first refus'd us peremptorily: but at a Dinner with his Council where there was great Drinking of Madeira Wine, as the Custom at that Place then was, he soften'd by degrees, and said he would lend us Six. After a few more Bumpers he advanc'd to Ten. And at length he very good-naturedly conceded Eighteen.[2] They were fine Cannon, 18 pounders, with their Carriages, which we soon transported and mounted on our Battery, where the Associators kept a nightly Guard while the War lasted: And among the rest I regularly took my Turn of Duty there as a common Soldier.

My Activity in these Operations was agreeable to the Governor and Council; they took me into Confidence, and I was consulted by them in every Measure wherein their Concurrence was thought useful to the Association. Calling in the Aid of Religion, I propos'd to them the Proclaiming a Fast, to promote Reformation, and implore the Blessing of Heaven on our Undertaking. They embrac'd the Motion, but as it was the first Fast ever thought of in the Province,

9. Thomas Lawrence was elected lieutenant colonel; Abraham Taylor, colonel.
1. Announced in the *Pennsylvania Gazette*, December 12, 1747 (*Papers* 3.223–24).
2. New York gave twelve 12-pounders and two 18-pounders. They arrived in April 1748 (*Papers* 3.222).

the Secretary had no Precedent from which to draw the Proclamation. My Education in New England, where a Fast is proclaim'd every Year, was here of some Advantage. I drew it in the accustomed Style, it was translated into German, printed in both Languages and divulg'd thro' the Province.[3] This gave the Clergy of the different Sects an Opportunity of Influencing their Congregations to join in the Association; and it would probably have been general among all but Quakers if the Peace had not soon interven'd.

It was thought by some of my Friends that by my Activity in these Affairs, I should offend that Sect, and thereby lose my Interest in the Assembly where they were a great Majority. A young Gentleman[4] who had likewise some Friends in the House, and wish'd to succeed me as their Clerk, acquainted me that it was decided to displace me at the next Election, and he therefore in goodwill advis'd me to resign, as more consistent with my Honor than being turn'd out. My Answer to him was, that I had read or heard of some Public Man, who made it a Rule never to ask for an Office, and never to refuse one when offer'd to him. I approve, says I, of his Rule, and will practice it with a small Addition; I shall never *ask*, never *refuse*, nor ever *resign* an Office.[5] If they will have my Office of Clerk to dispose of to another, they shall take it from me. I will not by giving it up, lose my Right of some time or other making Reprisals on my Adversaries. I heard however no more of this. I was chosen again, unanimously as usual, at the next Election. Possibly as they dislik'd my late Intimacy with the Members of Council, who had join'd the Governors in all the Disputes about military Preparations with which the House had long been harass'd, they might have been pleas'd if I would voluntarily have left them; but they did not care to displace me on Account merely of my Zeal for the Association; and they could not well give another Reason.

Indeed I had some Cause to believe, that the Defense of the Country was not disagreeable to any of them, provided they were not requir'd to assist in it. And I found that a much greater Number of them than I could have imagined, tho' against offensive War, were clearly for the defensive. Many Pamphlets *pro and con* were publish'd on the Subject, and some by good Quakers in favor of Defense,[6] which I believe convince'd most of their younger People. A Transaction in our Fire Company gave me some Insight into their prevailing

---

3. The proclamation of December 9, 1747, set January 7, 1748, as the fasting day (*Papers* 3.226–29).
4. James Read opposed Franklin as Clerk in 1747 (*Papers* 3.39n, 329–30).
5. Franklin repeats a letter of 1770, following rumors that critics were trying to remove him as deputy postmaster-general (*Papers* 17.314). In fact, he had actively sought that post, as well as his first post as assembly clerk.
6. Franklin offered to print such arguments either in his newspaper or as pamphlets at no charge (*Papers* 3.216).

Sentiments. It had been propos'd that we should encourage the Scheme for building a Battery by laying out the present Stock, then about Sixty Pounds, in Tickets of the Lottery. By our Rules no Money could be dispos'd of but at the next Meeting after the Proposal. The Company consisted of Thirty Members,[7] of which Twenty-two were Quakers, and Eight only of other Persuasions. We eight punctually attended the Meeting; but tho' we thought that some of the Quakers would join us, we were by no means sure of a Majority. Only one Quaker, Mr. James Morris, appear'd to oppose the Measure: He express'd much Sorrow that it had ever been propos'd, as he said *Friends* were all against it, and it would create such Discord as might break up the Company. We told him, that we saw no Reason for that; we were the Minority, and if *Friends* were against the Measure and outvoted us, we must and should, agreeable to the Usage of all Societies, submit.

When the Hour for Business arriv'd, it was mov'd to put the Vote. He allow'd we might then do it by the Rules, but as he could assure us that a Number of Members intended to be present for the purpose of opposing it, it would be but candid to allow a little time for their appearing. While we were disputing this, a Waiter came to tell me two Gentlemen below desir'd to speak with me. I went down, and found they were two of our Quaker Members. They told me there were eight of them assembled at a Tavern just by; that they were determin'd to come and vote with us if there should be occasion, which they hop'd would not be the Case; and desir'd we would not call for their Assistance if we could do without it, as their Voting for such a Measure might embroil them with their Elders and Friends. Being thus secure of a Majority, I went up, and after a little seeming Hesitation, agreed to a Delay of another Hour. This Mr. Morris allow'd to be extremely fair. Not one of his opposing Friends appear'd, at which he express'd great Surprise; and at the Expiration of the Hour, we carried the Resolution Eight to one; And as of the 22 Quakers, Eight were ready to vote with us and, Thirteen by their Absence manifested that they were not inclin'd to oppose the Measure, I afterwards estimated the Proportion of Quakers sincerely against Defense as one to twenty-one only. For these were all regular Members of that Society, and in good Reputation among them, and had due Notice of what was propos'd at that Meeting.

The honorable and learned Mr. Logan, who had always been of that Sect, was one who wrote an Address[8] to them, declaring his

---

7. Besides Franklin, three others were from the original Junto (*Papers* 2.376).
8. Franklin printed the four-page pamphlet, dated September 22, 1741: *To Robert Jordan, and other Friends of the Yearly Meeting.* James Logan withheld the total thirty copies from circulation, "For we are most unhappily divided and if I cannot heal I would do nothing to widen" (Miller, *Franklin's Philadelphia Printing*, no. 249).

Approbation of defensive War, and supporting his Opinion by many strong Arguments: He put into my Hands Sixty Pounds,[9] to be laid out in Lottery Tickets for the Battery, with Directions to apply what Prizes might be drawn wholly to that Service. He told me the following Anecdote of his old Master William Penn respecting Defense. He came over from England, when a young Man, with that Proprietary, and as his Secretary. It was War Time, and their Ship was chas'd by an armed Vessel suppos'd to be an Enemy. Their Captain prepar'd for Defense, but told William Penn and his Company of Quakers, that he did not expect their Assistance, and they might retire into the Cabin; which they did, except James Logan, who chose to stay upon Deck, and was quarter'd to a Gun. The suppos'd Enemy prov'd a Friend; so there was no Fighting. But when the Secretary went down to communicate the Intelligence, William Penn rebuk'd him severely for staying upon Deck and undertaking to assist in defending the Vessel, contrary to the Principles of *Friends*, especially as it had not been required by the Captain. This Reproof being before all the Company, piqu'd the Secretary, who answer'd, *I being thy Servant, why did thee not order me to come down: but thee was willing enough that I should stay and help to fight the Ship when thee thought there was Danger.*[1]

My being many Years in the Assembly, the Majority of which were constantly Quakers, gave me frequent Opportunities of seeing the Embarrassment given them by their Principle against War, whenever Application was made to them by Order of the Crown to grant Aids for military Purposes. They were unwilling to offend Government on the one hand, by a direct Refusal, and their Friends the Body of Quakers on the other, by a Compliance contrary to their Principles. Hence a Variety of Evasions to avoid Complying, and Modes of disguising the Compliance when it became unavoidable. The common Mode at last was to grant Money under the Phrase of its being *for the King's Use*, and never to enquire how it was applied. But if the Demand was not directly from the Crown, that Phrase was found not so proper, and some other was to be invented. As when Powder was wanting, (I think it was for the Garrison at Louisburg,) and the Government of New England solicited a Grant of some from Pennsylvania, which was much urg'd on the House by Governor Thomas, they could not grant Money to buy Powder, because that was an Ingredient of War, but they voted an Aid to New England, of Three Thousand Pounds, to be put into the hands of the Governor, and appropriated it for the Purchasing of Bread,

---

9. Actually £50 (*Papers* 3.220n, 247n).
1. This occurred in fall 1699. See Frederick B. Toiles, *James Logan and the Culture of Provincial America* (Boston: Little, Brown, 1957), 13–14.

Flour, Wheat, *or other Grain.* Some of the Council desirous of giving the House still farther Embarrassment, advis'd the Governor not
to accept Provision, as not being the Thing he had demanded. But
he replied, "I shall take the Money, for I understand very well their
Meaning; *Other Grain,* is Gunpowder;" which he accordingly
bought; and they never objected to it.*

It was in Allusion to this Fact, that when in our Fire Company we
feared the Success of our Proposal in favor of the Lottery, and I had
said to my friend Mr. Syng, one of our Members, if we fail, let us
move the Purchase of a Fire Engine with the Money; the Quakers
can have no Objection to that: and then if you nominate me, and
I you, as a Committee for that purpose, we will buy a great Gun,
which is certainly a *Fire-Engine:* I see, says he, you have improv'd
by being so long in the Assembly; your equivocal Project would be
just a Match for their Wheat *or other grain.*

These Embarrassments that the Quakers suffer'd from having
establish'd and publish'd it as one of their Principles, that no kind of
War was lawful, and which being once published, they could not
afterwards, however they might change their minds, easily get rid of,
reminds me of what I think a more prudent Conduct in another Sect
among us; that of the Dunkers.[2] I was acquainted with one of its
Founders, Michael Welfare, soon after it appear'd. He complain'd to
me that they were grievously calumniated by the Zealots of other
Persuasions, and charg'd with abominable Principles and Practices
to which they were utter Strangers. I told him this had always been
the case with new Sects; and that to put a Stop to such Abuse, I
imagin'd it might be well to publish the Articles of their Belief and
the Rules of their Discipline. He said that it had been propos'd
among them, but not agreed to, for this Reason; "When we were
first drawn together as a Society, says he, it had pleased God to
enlighten our Minds so far, as to see that some Doctrines which we
once esteemed Truths were Errors, and that others which we had
esteemed Errors were real Truths. From time to time he has been
pleased to afford us farther Light, and our Principles have been
improving, and our Errors diminishing. Now we are not sure that we
are arriv'd at the End of this Progression, and at the Perfection of
Spiritual or Theological Knowledge; and we fear that if we should
once print our Confession of Faith, we should feel ourselves as if
bound and confin'd by it, and perhaps be unwilling to receive farther

* "See the Votes." [Franklin's note. On July
24, 1745, the assembly voted £4000 "to
the King's Use . . . be laid out . . . in the
purchase of Bread, Beef, Pork, Flour, Wheat
or other Grain" (*Pa. Archives,* 8th ser.,
4.3042).]

2. So-called from the rite of baptizing through immersion ("Dunkards"), the sect settled
in Pennsylvania, 1729–33, and in the 1740s numbered about forty families at Ephrata.
They became the Church of the Brethren.

Improvement; and our Successors still more so, as conceiving what we their Elders and Founders had done, to be something sacred, never to be departed from."

This Modesty in a Sect is perhaps a singular Instance in the History of Mankind, every other Sect supposing itself in Possession of all Truth, and that those who differ are so far in the Wrong;[3] Like a Man travelling in foggy Weather: Those at some Distance before him on the Road he sees wrapped up in the Fog, as well as those behind him, and also the People in the Fields on each side; but near him all appears clear.—Tho' in truth he is as much in the Fog as any of them. To avoid this kind of Embarrassment the Quakers have of late Years been gradually declining the public Service in the Assembly and in the Magistracy.[4] Choosing rather to quit their Power than their Principle.

In Order of Time I should have mentioned before, that having in 1742 invented an open Stove, for the better warming of Rooms and at the same time saving Fuel,[5] as the fresh Air admitted was warmed in Entering, I made a Present of the Model to Mr. Robert Grace, one of my early Friends, who having an Iron Furnace, found the Casting of the Plates for these Stoves a profitable Thing, as they were growing in Demand. To promote that Demand I wrote and published a Pamphlet Entitled, *An Account of the New-Invented* PENNSYLVANIA FIRE PLACES: *Wherein their Construction and manner of Operation is particularly explained; their Advantages above every other Method of warming Rooms demonstrated; and all Objections that have been raised against the Use of them answered and obviated, etc.*[6] This Pamphlet had a good Effect. Governor Thomas was so pleas'd with the Construction of this Stove, as describ'd in it, that he offer'd to give me a Patent for the sole Vending of them for a Term of Years; but I declin'd it from a Principle which has ever weigh'd with me on such Occasions, viz. *That as we enjoy great Advantages from the Inventions of Others, we should be glad of an Opportunity to serve others by any Invention of ours, and this we should do freely and generously.* An Ironmonger in London, however, after assuming a good deal of my Pamphlet and working it up into his own, and making some small

3. At the Constitutional Convention, September 17, 1787, Franklin said: "Most men, indeed, as well as most sects in religion, think themselves in possession of all truth, and that wherever others differ from them, it is so far error" (Smyth, *Writings*, 9.607).
4. After June 15, 1756, twenty-three of thirty-five Quakers in the assembly resigned, partly from conscience though also because the British government sought to exclude all Quakers from the assembly but came to accept the resignations of the most conservative, or, as Franklin called them, "All the Stiffrumps" (*Papers* 6.456).
5. Franklin wrote that his common Room . . . is made twice as warm as it used to be, with a quarter of the Wood I formerly consum'd there" (*Papers* 2.437). He hoped that "by the Help of this saving Invention, our Wood may grow as fast as we consume it, and our Posterity may warm themselves at a moderate Rate" (*Papers* 2.422 and 441).
6. He printed his pamphlet in 1744 at the expense of Robert Grace, who was then manufacturing the stoves.

Changes in the Machine, which rather hurt its Operation, got a Patent for it there, and made as I was told a little Fortune by it.[7] And this is not the only Instance of Patents taken out for my Inventions[8] by others, tho' not always with the same success: which I never contested, as having no Desire of profiting by Patents myself, and hating Disputes. The Use of these Fireplaces in very many Houses both of this and the neighboring Colonies, has been and is a great Saving of Wood to the Inhabitants.

Peace being concluded, and the Association Business therefore at an End, I turn'd my Thoughts again to the Affair of establishing an Academy. The first Step I took was to associate in the Design a Number of active Friends, of whom the Junto furnished a good Part; the next was to write and publish a Pamphlet entitled, *Proposals relating to the Education of Youth in Pennsylvania.*[9] This I distributed among the principal Inhabitants gratis; and as soon as I could suppose their Minds a little prepared by the Perusal of it, I set on foot a Subscription for Opening and Supporting an Academy; it was to be paid in Quotas yearly for Five Years; by so dividing it I judg'd the Subscription might be larger, and I believe it was so, amounting to no less (if I remember right) than Five thousand Pounds.[1] In the Introduction to these Proposals, I stated their Publication not as an Act of mine, but of some *public-spirited Gentlemen,*[2] avoiding as much as I could, according to my usual Rule, the presenting myself to the Public as the Author of any Scheme for their Benefit.

The Subscribers, to carry the Project into immediate Execution chose out of their Number Twenty-four Trustees, and appointed Mr. Francis, then Attorney General, and myself, to draw up Constitutions for the Government of the Academy, which being done and signed, an House was hired, Masters engag'd and the Schools opened I think in the same Year 1749.[3] The Scholars increasing fast, the

---

7. Probably James Sharp, who took out his patent in 1781. See J. A. Woods, "James Sharp: Common Councillor of London," in A. Whiteman et al., *Statesmen, Scholars & Merchants* (Oxford: Clarendon Press, 1973), 280.
8. Franklin may have had in mind Joseph Jacob's patents (of July 13, 1769, and February 1, 1783) for wheel carriages (*Papers* 20.157), and for the application of copperplate engravings to tiles and other earthenware (*Papers* 20.459). Besides the stove and lightning rod, Franklin invented the glass armonica, the "long-arm" for taking down objects from high shelves, a chair that converts to a stepladder, a rocking chair with a fan that cools by the action of the rocker, a lamp with three wicks yielding the light of six candles, an umbrella-shaped ship's anchor, a laundry mangle, and bifocal glasses.
9. Franklin's thirty-two-page pamphlet, published in early fall 1749, featured an "English School" to rival the more conventional, classical curriculum. This feature, Franklin later claimed, attracted "most of the original Benefactors" (Smyth, *Writings*, 10.10), but was later subverted by the trustees (Miller, *Franklin's Philadelphia Printing*, no. 470; *Papers* 3.385–88 and 395–421).
1. Actually £2,000, to which Franklin contributed the annual sum of £10 (*Papers* 3.429).
2. ". . . to whom it has been privately communicated . . . they have directed a Number of Copies to be made by the Press, and properly distributed" (*Papers* 3.397).
3. In fact, January 1751, and even then the remodeling was incomplete, but by September there were "above 100 Scholars, and the Number daily encreasing" (*Papers* 4.194).

House was soon found too small, and we were looking out for a Piece of Ground properly situated, with Intention to build, when Providence threw into our way a large House ready built, which with a few Alterations might well serve our purpose, this was the Building before-mentioned erected by the Hearers of Mr. Whitefield, and was obtain'd for us in the following Manner.

It is to be noted, that the Contributions to this Building being made by People of different Sects, Care was taken in the Nomination of Trustees, in whom the Building and Ground was to be vested, that a Predominancy should not be given to any Sect, lest in time that Predominancy might be a means of appropriating the whole to the Use of such Sect, contrary to the original Intention; it was therefore that one of each Sect was appointed, viz. one Church-of-England-man, one Presbyterian, one Baptist, one Moravian, etc. Those in case of Vacancy by Death were to fill it by Election from among the Contributors. The Moravian happen'd not to please his Colleagues, and on his Death, they resolved to have no other of that Sect. The Difficulty then was, how to avoid having two of some other Sect, by means of the new Choice. Several Persons were named and for that Reason not agreed to. At length one mention'd me, with the Observation that I was merely an honest Man, and of no Sect at all; which prevail'd with them to choose me.

The Enthusiasm[4] which existed when the House was built, had long since abated, and its Trustees had not been able to procure fresh Contributions for paying the Ground Rent, and discharging some other Debts the Building had occasion'd, which embarrass'd them greatly. Being now a Member of both Sets of Trustees, that for the Building and that for the Academy, I had good Opportunity of negotiating with both, and brought them finally to an Agreement, by which the Trustees for the Building were to cede it to those of the Academy, the latter undertaking to discharge the Debt, to keep forever open in the Building a large Hall for occasional Preachers according to the original Intention, and maintain a Free School for the Instruction of poor Children. Writings were accordingly drawn, and on paying the Debts the Trustees of the Academy were put in Possession of the Premises, and by dividing the great and lofty Hall into Stories, and different Rooms above and below for the several Schools, and purchasing some additional Ground, the whole was soon made fit for our purpose, and the Scholars remov'd into the Building. The Care and Trouble of agreeing with the Workmen, purchasing Materials, and superintending the Work fell upon me, and I went thro' it the more cheerfully, as it did not then interfere

---

4. In the eighteenth century, the word *enthusiasm* implied a direct sense of divine will within.

with my private Business,[5] having the Year before taken a very able, industrious and honest Partner, Mr. David Hall, with whose Character I was well acquainted, as he had work'd for me four Years. He took off my Hands all Care of the Printing-Office, paying me punctually my Share of the Profits.[6] This Partnership continued Eighteen Years, successfully for us both.

The Trustees of the Academy after a while were incorporated by a Charter from the Governor; their Funds were increas'd by Contributions in Britain, and Grants of Land from the Proprietaries, to which the Assembly has since made considerable Addition, and thus was established the present University of Philadelphia.[7] I have been continued one of its Trustees from the Beginning, now near forty Years, and have had the very great Pleasure of seeing a Number of the Youth who have receiv'd their Education in it, distinguish'd by their improv'd Abilities, serviceable in public Stations, and Ornaments to their Country.

When I disengag'd myself as above-mentioned from private Business, I flatter'd myself that, by the sufficient tho' moderate Fortune I had acquir'd, I had secur'd Leisure during the rest of my Life, for Philosophical Studies[8] and Amusements; I purchas'd all Dr. Spencer's[9] Apparatus, who had come from England to lecture here; and I proceeded in my Electrical Experiments with great Alacrity; but the Public now considering me as a Man of Leisure, laid hold of me for their Purposes; every Part of our Civil Government, and almost at the same time, imposing some Duty upon me. The Governor put me into the Commission of the Peace; the Corporation of the City chose me of the Common Council, and soon after an Alderman; and the Citizens at large chose me a Burgess to represent them in Assembly.[1] This latter Station was the more agreeable to me, as I was at length tired with sitting there to hear Debates in which as Clerk I could take no part, and which were often so unentertaining, that I was induc'd to amuse myself with making magic Squares, or Circles, or anything to avoid Weariness.[2] And I conceiv'd my becoming a Member would

---

5. Though Franklin wrote, February 13, 1750: "In this Affair, as well as in other public Affairs I have been engag'd in, the Labouring Oar has lain and does lay very much upon me" (*Papers* 3.462).
6. About £350 a year. The partnership with Hall began on January 21, 1748 (*Papers* 3.263–67).
7. Chartered as an academy in 1743, as a college in 1755, and as the University of Pennsylvania, 1765. Franklin was ousted as head of the trustees in 1756, but served on the board until his death.
8. Scientific studies.
9. Archibald Spencer.
1. City Councilman, 1748; Justice of the Peace, 1749; Assemblyman, August 1751; and Alderman, October 1751.
2. In the squares, the sum of every row—horizontal, vertical, diagonal—is equal; in the circles, the sum of every concentric circle is equal (examples in *Papers* 4.397, 401).

enlarge my Power of doing Good. I would not however insinuate that my Ambition was not flatter'd by all these Promotions. It certainly was. For considering my low Beginning they were great Things to me. And they were still more pleasing, as being so many spontaneous Testimonies of the public's good Opinion, and by me entirely unsolicited.

The Office of Justice of the Peace I tried a little, by attending a few Courts, and sitting on the Bench to hear Causes. But finding that more knowledge of the Common Law than I possess'd, was necessary to act in that Station with Credit, I gradually withdrew from it, excusing myself by my being oblig'd to attend the higher Duties of a Legislator in the Assembly. My Election to this Trust was repeated every Year for Ten Years, without my ever asking any Elector for his Vote, or signifying either directly or indirectly any Desire of Being chosen. On taking my Seat in the House, my Son was appointed their Clerk.

The Year following, a Treaty being to be held with the Indians at Carlisle, the Governor sent a Message* to the House, proposing that they should nominate some of their Members to be join'd with some Members of Council as Commissioners for that purpose. The House nam'd the Speaker (Mr. Norris) and myself; and being commission'd we went to Carlisle, and met the Indians accordingly. As those People are extremely apt to get drunk, and when so are very quarrelsome and disorderly, we strictly forbad the selling any Liquor to them; and when they complain'd of this Restriction, we told them that if they would continue sober during the Treaty, we would give them Plenty of Rum when Business was over.[3] They promis'd this; and they kept their Promise—because they could get no Liquor—and the Treaty was conducted very orderly, and concluded to mutual Satisfaction. They then claim'd and receiv'd the Rum. This was in the Afternoon. They were near 100 Men, Women and Children, and were lodg'd in temporary Cabins built in the Form of a Square just without the Town. In the Evening, hearing a great Noise among them, the Commissioners walk'd out to see what was the Matter. We found they had made a great Bonfire in the Middle of the Square. They were all drunk, Men and Women, quarrelling and fighting. Their dark-color'd Bodies, half naked, seen only by the gloomy Light of the Bonfire, running after and beating one another with Firebrands, accompanied by their horrid Yellings, form'd a Scene the most resembling our

---

* "See the Votes to have this more correctly." [Franklin's memo. Fearing the encroaching French, some tribes asked the English to renew mutual defense treaties, asking for a conference at Carlisle, September 1753. Governor Hamilton quickly complied. He named Richard Peters; the assembly named Franklin and Isaac Norris (*Papers* 5.63–64).]

3. The order against liquor was on September 26, 1753; the conference lasted October 1–4, and the commissioners' report was made on November 1, 1753 (*Papers* 5.65, 84–107).

Ideas of Hell that could well be imagin'd. There was no appeasing the Tumult, and we retired to our Lodging. At Midnight a Number of them came thundering at our Door, demanding more Rum; of which we took no Notice. The next Day, sensible they had misbehav'd in giving us that Disturbance, they sent three of their old Counsellors to make their Apology. The Orator acknowledg'd the Fault, but laid it upon the Rum; and then endeavour'd to excuse the Rum, by saying, *"The great Spirit who made all things made everything for some Use, and whatever Use he design'd anything for, that Use it should always be put to; Now, when he made Rum, he said,* LET THIS BE FOR INDIANS TO GET DRUNK WITH. *And it must be so."*—And indeed if it be the Desire of Providence to extirpate these Savages in order to make room for Cultivators of the Earth, it seems not improbable that Rum may be the appointed Means. It has already annihilated all the Tribes who formerly inhabited the Seacoast.[4]

In 1751 Dr. Thomas Bond, a particular Friend of mine, conceiv'd the Idea of establishing a Hospital in Philadelphia for the Reception and Cure of poor sick Persons, whether Inhabitants of the Province or Strangers. A very beneficient Design, which has been ascrib'd to me, but was originally his. He was zealous and active in endeavouring to procure Subscriptions for it; but the Proposal being a Novelty in America, and at first not well understood, he met with small Success. At length he came to me, with the Compliment that he found there was no such thing as carrying a public-spirited Project through, without my being concern'd in it; "for, says he, I am often ask'd by those to whom I propose Subscribing, Have you consulted Franklin upon this Business? and what does he think of it? And when I tell them that I have not, (supposing it rather out of your Line,) they do not subscribe, but say they will consider of it." I enquir'd into the Nature, and probable Utility of his Scheme, and receiving from him a very satisfactory Explanation, I not only subscrib'd to it myself, but engag'd heartily in the Design of Procuring Subscriptions from others. Previous however to the Solicitation, I endeavoured to prepare the Minds of the People by writing on the Subject in the Newspapers,[5] which was my usual Custom in such Cases,

---

4. Franklin alludes to the stage theory of civilization, which held that increasingly less territory was necessary to support life in the four progressive "stages"—hunting, pastoral, agricultural, and manufacturing—of civilization. Franklin also refers ironically to the Puritan faith that God wisely oversees all human changes by "appointed Means." His theories about a rising colonial population and declining Indian population, articulated in his *Observations Concerning the Increase of Mankind*, influenced Thomas Malthus and the Victorian evolutionists Alfred Russel Wallace and Charles Darwin.

5. *Pennsylvania Gazette* for August 8 and 15, 1751; reprinted in Franklin's *Some Account of the Pennsylvania Hospital* (1754). The plan leaned heavily on Defoe's plan described in *Tour thro' . . . Great Britain* (3rd ed., 1742), extracts of which appear in Franklin's notes (*Papers* 4.147–54; 5.284–330).

but which he had omitted. The Subscriptions afterwards were more free and generous, but beginning to flag, I saw they would be insufficient without some Assistance from the Assembly, and therefore propos'd to petition for it, which was done.[6] The Country Members did not at first relish the Project. They objected that it could only be serviceable to the City, and therefore the Citizens should alone be at the Expense of it; and they doubted whether the Citizens themselves generally approv'd of it: My Allegation on the contrary, that it met with such Approbation as to leave no doubt of our being able to raise 2000 Pounds by voluntary Donations, they considered as a most extravagant Supposition, and utterly impossible. On this I form'd my Plan; and asking Leave to bring in a Bill, for incorporating the Contributors, according to the Prayers of their Petition, and granting them a blank Sum of Money, which Leave was obtain'd chiefly on the Consideration that the House could throw the Bill out if they did not like it, I drew it so as to make the important Clause a conditional One, viz. "And be it enacted by the Authority aforesaid That when the said Contributors shall have met and chosen their Managers and Treasurer, *and shall have raised by their Contributions a Capital Stock of 2000 Pounds Value*, (the yearly Interest of which is to be applied to the Accommodating of the Sick Poor in the said Hospital, free of Charge for Diet, Attendance, Advice and Medicines) and *shall make the same appear to the Satisfaction of the Speaker of the Assembly* for the time being; that *then* it shall and may be lawful for the said Speaker, and he is hereby required to sign an Order on the Provincial Treasurer for the Payment of Two Thousand Pounds in two yearly Payments, to the Treasurer of the said Hospital, to be applied to the Founding, Building and Finishing of the same."[7] This Condition carried the Bill through; for the Members who had oppos'd the Grant, and now conceiv'd they might have the Credit of being charitable without the Expense, agreed to its Passage; And then in soliciting Subscriptions among the People we urg'd the conditional Promise of the Law as an additional Motive to give, since every Man's Donation would be doubled. Thus the Clause work'd both ways. The Subscriptions accordingly soon exceeded the requisite Sum, and we claim'd and receiv'd the Public Gift, which enabled us to carry the Design into Execution. A convenient and handsome Building[8] was soon erected, the Institution has by constant Experience been found useful, and flourishes to this Day. And I do not remember any of my political Maneuvers, the Success of which gave me at the time more

---

6. The newspaper articles appeared six months after the petition (January 23. 1751), and even after Governor Hamilton signed the act of incorporation, May 11 (*Papers* 4.108–11).

7. Slight differences from a contemporary copy suggest that this was written from memory (*Papers* 5.289).

8. Erected in 1756 on 8th Street between Pine and Spruce (*Papers* 6.61–62).

Pleasure. Or that in after-thinking of it, I more easily excus'd myself for having made some Use of Cunning.

It was about this time that another Projector, the Revd. Gilbert Tennent, came to me, with a Request that I would assist him in procuring a Subscription for erecting a new Meetinghouse.[9] It was to be for the Use of a Congregation he had gathered among the Presbyterians who were originally Disciples of Mr. Whitefield. Unwilling to make myself disagreeable to my fellow Citizens, by too frequently soliciting their Contributions, I absolutely refus'd. He then desir'd I would furnish him with a List of the Names of Persons I knew by Experience to be generous and public-spirited. I thought it would be unbecoming in me, after their kind Compliance with my Solicitations, to mark them out to be worried by other Beggars, and therefore refus'd also to give such a List. He then desir'd I would at least give him my Advice. That I will readily do, said I; and, in the first Place, I advise you to apply to all those whom you know will give something; next to those whom you are uncertain whether they will give anything or not; and show them the List of those who have given: and lastly, do not neglect those who you are sure will give nothing; for in some of them you may be mistaken. He laugh'd, and thank'd me, and said he would take my Advice. He did so, for he ask'd of everybody, and he obtain'd a much larger Sum than he expected, with which he erected the capacious and very elegant Meetinghouse that stands in Arch Street.

Our City, tho' laid out with a beautiful Regularity, the Streets large, straight, and crossing each other at right Angles, had the Disgrace of suffering those Streets to remain long unpav'd, and in wet Weather the Wheels of heavy Carriages plough'd them into a Quagmire, so that it was difficult to cross them. And in dry Weather the Dust was offensive. I had liv'd near what was call'd the Jersey Market,[1] and saw with Pain the Inhabitants wading in Mud while purchasing their Provisions. A Strip of Ground down the middle of that Market was at length pav'd with Brick, so that being once in the Market they had firm Footing, but were often over Shoes in Dirt to get there. By talking and writing on the Subject, I was at length instrumental in getting the Street pav'd with Stone between the Market and the brick'd Foot-Pavement that was on each Side next the Houses. This for some time gave an easy Access to the Market, dry-shod. But the rest of the Street not being pav'd, whenever a Carriage came out of the Mud upon this Pavement, it shook off and left its Dirt on it, and it was soon cover'd with Mire, which was not

9. His Second Presbyterian Church was organized in 1743. The new building opened in 1752 at Arch (now Mulberry) and Third Streets.
1. The Jersey Market was in the middle of Market Street, between Front and Second.

remov'd, the City as yet having no Scavengers. After some Enquiry
I found a poor industrious Man, who was willing to undertake keeping the Pavement clean, by sweeping it twice a week and carrying
off the Dirt from before all the Neighbors' Doors, for the Sum of
Sixpence per Month, to be paid by each House. I then wrote and
printed a Paper,[2] setting forth the Advantages to the Neighborhood
that might be obtain'd by this small Expense; the greater Ease in
keeping our Houses clean, so much Dirt not being brought in by
People's Feet; the Benefit to the Shops by more Custom, as Buyers
could more easily get at them, and by not having in windy Weather
the Dust blown in upon their Goods, etc. etc. I sent one of these
Papers to each House, and in a Day or two went round to see who
would subscribe an Agreement to pay these Sixpences. It was unanimously sign'd, and for a time well executed. All the Inhabitants of
the City were delighted with the Cleanliness of the Pavement that
surrounded the Market; it being a Convenience to all; and this rais'd
a general Desire to have all the Streets paved; and made the People
more willing to submit to a Tax for that purpose.

After some time I drew a Bill for Paving the City, and brought it
into the Assembly. It was just before I went to England in 1757 and
did not pass till I was gone, and then with an Alteration in the Mode
of Assessment, which I thought not for the better, but with an additional Provision for lighting as well as Paving the Streets, which was
a great Improvement.[3] It was by a private Person, the late Mr. John
Clifton, his giving a Sample of the Utility of Lamps by placing one at
his Door, that the People were first impress'd with the Idea of enlight-
ening all the City. The Honor of this public Benefit has also been
ascrib'd to me, but it belongs truly to that Gentleman. I did but follow his Example; and have only some Merit to claim respecting the
Form of our Lamps as differing from the Globe Lamps we at first
were supplied with from London. Those we found inconvenient in
these respects; they admitted no Air below, the Smoke therefore did
not readily go out above, but circulated in the Globe, lodg'd on its
Inside, and soon obstructed the Light they were intended to afford;
giving, besides, the daily Trouble of wiping them clean: and an accidental Stroke on one of them would demolish it, and render it totally
useless. I therefore suggested the composing them of four flat Panes,
with a long Funnel above to draw up the Smoke, and Crevices admit-

---

2. No copy of this paper has been found. It appears in William J. Campbell, *The Collection of Franklin Imprints in the Museum of the Curtis Publishing Company* (Philadelphia: Curtis Publishing Co., 1918), no. 549.
3. Since 1718, householders paved the streets with gravel voluntarily. Ordinances requiring the practice were introduced in 1736, 1739, and March 3, 1758 (probably Franklin's petition), but did not pass until 1762 (*Pa. Archives*, 8th ser., 6.4743). An act of 1763
   extended earlier ordinances for lighting (1751, 1756) and paving (1762), with funds
   paid from a lottery as well as assessments.

ting Air below, to facilitate the Ascent of the Smoke.[4] By this means they were kept clean, and did not grow dark in a few Hours as the London Lamps do, but continu'd bright till Morning; and an accidental Stroke would generally break but a single Pane, easily repair'd. I have sometimes wonder'd that the Londoners did not, from the Effect Holes in the Bottom of the Globe Lamps us'd at Vauxhall,[5] have in keeping them clean, learn to have such Holes in their Street Lamps. But those Holes being made for another purpose, viz. to communicate Flame more suddenly to the Wick, by a little Flax hanging down thro' them, the other Use of letting in Air seems not to have been thought of.—And therefore, after the Lamps have been lit a few Hours, the Streets of London are very poorly illuminated.

The Mention of these Improvements puts me in mind of one I propos'd when in London, to Dr. Fothergill, who was among the best Men I have known, and a great Promoter of useful Projects. I had observ'd that the Streets when dry were never swept and the light Dust carried away, but it was suffer'd to accumulate till wet Weather reduc'd it to Mud, and then after lying some Days so deep on the Pavement that there was no Crossing but in Paths kept clean by poor People with Brooms, it was with great Labour rak'd together and thrown up into Carts open above, the Sides of which suffer'd some of the Slush at every Jolt on the Pavement to shake out and fall, sometimes to the Annoyance of Foot-Passengers. The Reason given for not sweeping the dusty Streets was, that the Dust would fly into the Windows of Shops and Houses. An accidental Occurrence had instructed me how much Sweeping might be done in a little Time. I found at my Door in Craven Street[6] one Morning a poor Woman sweeping my Pavement with a birch Broom.* She appeared very pale and feeble as just come out of a Fit of Sickness. I ask'd who employ'd her to sweep there. She said, "Nobody; but I am very poor and in Distress, and I sweeps before Gentlefolkeses Doors, and hopes they will give me something." I bid her sweep the whole Street clean and I would give her a Shilling. This was at 9 o'Clock. At 12 she came for the Shilling. From the Slowness I saw at first in her Working, I could scarce believe that the Work was done so soon, and sent my Servant to examine it, who reported that the whole Street was swept perfectly clean, and all the Dust plac'd in the Gutter which was in the Middle. And the next Rain wash'd it

---

* "The Happiness of Man consists in small Advantages occurring every Day—" "Sleep by Sunshine." [Franklin's marginal notes for future topics.]

---

4. Replicas are in Independence Square, Philadelphia.
5. Fashionable London amusement park where the lamps resembled Japanese lanterns (*Wits Magazine*, 1 [1784]: 200).
6. In 1757 to 1762 and 1764 to 1775, Franklin boarded in London with widow Margaret Stevenson at No. 7 Craven Street, later renumbered 36 (*Papers* 7. 245n).

quite away, so that the Pavement and even the Kennel[7] were perfectly clean. I then judg'd that if that feeble Woman could sweep such a Street in 3 Hours, a strong active Man might have done it in half the time. And here let me remark the Convenience of having but one Gutter in such a narrow Street, running down its Middle, instead of two, one on each Side near the Footway. For Where all the Rain that falls on a Street runs from the Sides and meets in the middle, it forms there a Current strong enough to wash away all the Mud it meets with: But when divided into two Channels, it is often too weak to cleanse either, and only makes the Mud it finds more fluid, so that the Wheels of Carriages and Feet of Horses throw and dash it up on the Foot Pavement which is thereby rendered foul and slippery, and sometimes splash it upon those who are walking. My Proposal communicated to the good Doctor, was as follows.

"For the more effectual cleaning and keeping clean the Streets of London and Westminister, it is proposed,

"That the several Watchmen be contracted with to have the Dust swept up in dry Seasons, and the Mud rak'd up at other Times, each in the several Streets and Lanes of his Round.

"That they be furnish'd with Brooms and other proper Instruments for these purposes, to be kept at their respective Stands, ready to furnish the poor People they may employ in the Service.

"That in the dry Summer Months the Dust be all swept up into Heaps at proper Distances, before the Shops and Windows of Houses are usually opened: when the Scavengers with close-covered Carts shall also carry it all away.

"That the Mud when rak'd up be not left in Heaps to be spread abroad again by the Wheels of Carriages and Trampling of Horses; but that the Scavengers be provided with Bodies of Carts, not plac'd high upon Wheels, but low upon Sliders; with Lattice Bottoms, which being cover'd with Straw, will retain the Mud thrown into them, and permit the Water to drain from it, whereby it will become much lighter, Water making the greatest Part of its Weight. These Bodies of Carts to be plac'd at convenient Distances, and the Mud brought to them in Wheelbarrows, they remaining where plac'd till the Mud is drain'd, and then Horses brought to draw them away."

I have since had Doubts of the Practicability of the latter Part of this Proposal, on Account of the Narrowness of some Streets, and the Difficulty of placing the Draining Sleds so as not to encumber too much the Passage: But I am still of Opinion that the former, requiring the Dust to be swept up and carried away before the Shops are open, is very practicable in the Summer, when the Days are long. For in walking thro' the Strand and Fleet Street one Morning at 7 o'Clock I observ'd there was not one shop open tho' it had

7. Channel, gutter.

been Daylight and the Sun up above three Hours. The Inhabitants of London choosing voluntarily to live much by Candle Light, and sleep by Sunshine; and yet often complain, a little absurdly, of the Duty on Candles and the high Price of Tallow.[8]

Some may think these trifling Matters not worth minding or relating. But when they consider, that tho' Dust blown into the Eyes of a single Person or into a single Shop on a windy Day, is but of small Importance, yet the great Number of the Instances in a populous City, and its frequent Repetitions give it Weight and Consequence; perhaps they will not censure very severely those who bestow some of [their] Attention to Affairs of this seemingly low Nature. Human Felicity is produc'd not so much by great Pieces of good Fortune that seldom happen, as by little Advantages that occur every Day. Thus if you teach a poor young Man to shave himself and keep his Razor in order, you may contribute more to the Happiness of his Life than in giving him a 1000 Guineas. The Money may be soon spent, and the Regret only remaining of having foolishly consum'd it. But in the other Case he escapes the frequent Vexation of waiting for Barbers, and of their sometimes, dirty Fingers, offensive Breaths and dull Razors. He shaves when most convenient to him, and enjoys daily the Pleasure of its being done with a good Instrument.[9]—With these Sentiments I have hazarded the few preceding Pages, hoping they may afford Hints which some time or other may be useful to a City I love, having lived many Years in it very happily, and perhaps to some of our Towns in America.

Having been for some time employed by the Postmaster General of America, as his Comptroller, in regulating the several Offices, and bringing the Officers to account, I was upon his Death in 1753 appointed jointly with Mr. William Hunter to succeed him by a Commission from the Postmaster General in England. The American Office had never hitherto paid anything to that of Britain. We were to have 600 Pounds a Year between us if we could make that Sum out of the Profits of the Office. To do this, a Variety of Improvements were necessary; some of these were inevitably at first expensive; so that in the first four Years the Office became above 900 Pounds in debt to us. But it soon after began to repay us, and before I was displac'd, by a Freak[1] of the Minister's, of which I shall speak hereafter, we had brought it to yield *three times* as much clear Revenue[2] to the Crown as the Post-Office of Ireland, Since that imprudent Transaction, they have receiv'd from it,—Not one Farthing.

---

8. Franklin's bagatelle ("An Economical Project") in *Journal de Paris*, April 26, 1784, jokingly calculated the expense of burning candles in the evening and proposed something like daylight saving time (Smyth, *Writings*, 9.183–89).
9. An echo of Franklin's letter, February 28, 1768, to Lord Kames (*Papers* 15.60–61).
1. Fancy; irrational preference. Franklin was fired on January 30, 1774, the day after his public humiliation in the Cockpit. (See 265–67 of this Norton Critical Edition.)
2. Almost £3000 a year.

The Business of the Post-Office occasion'd my taking a Journey this Year to New England, where the College of Cambridge of their own Motion, presented me with the Degree of Master of Arts. Yale College in Connecticut, had before made me a similar Compliment.[3] Thus without studying in any College I came to partake of their Honors. They were confer'd in Consideration of my Improvements and Discoveries in the electric Branch of Natural Philosophy.

In 1754, War with France being again apprehended, a Congress of Commissioners from the different Colonies, was by an Order of the Lords of Trade, to be assembled at Albany, there to confer with the Chiefs of the Six Nations,[4] concerning the Means of defending both their Country and ours. Governor Hamilton, having receiv'd this Order, acquainted the House with it, requesting they would furnish proper Presents for the Indians to be given on this Occasion; and naming the Speaker (Mr. Norris) and myself, to join Mr. Thomas Penn[5] and Mr. Secretary Peters, as Commissioners to act for Pennsylvania. The House approv'd the Nomination, and provided the Goods for the Present[6] tho' they did not much like treating out of the Province, and we met the other Commissioners and met at Albany about the Middle of June. In our Way thither, I projected and drew up a Plan[7] for the Union of all the Colonies, under one Government so far as might be necessary for Defense, and other important general Purposes. As we pass'd thro' New York, I had there shown my Project to Mr. James Alexander and Mr. Kennedy, two Gentlemen of great Knowledge in public Affairs, and being fortified by their Approbation I ventur'd to lay it before the Congress. It then appear'd that several of the Commissioners had form'd Plans of the same kind. A previous Question was first taken whether a Union should be established, which pass'd in the Affirmative unanimously. A Committee was then appointed, One Member from each Colony, to consider the several Plans and report. Mine happen'd to be prefer'd, and with a few Amendments was accordingly reported.

By this Plan, the general Government was to be administered by a President General appointed and supported by the Crown, and a Grand Council to be chosen by the Representatives of the People of the several Colonies met in their respective Assemblies. The Debates upon it in Congress went on daily hand in hand with the Indian

3. Actually Harvard's degree came on July 27 and Yale's on September 12, 1753 (*Papers*, 5.16–17, 58).
4. The Six Nations (or Iroquois Indians) were a confederacy (formed c. 1570) of Seneca, Cayuga, Onondaga, Oneida, Mohawk, and (after 1715) Tuscarora Indians. The colonists organized the Albany Congress because they feared that the Iroquois, exploited by New York traders, would defect to the French.
5. Not Thomas but John Penn, according to the commissions signed by Governor James Hamilton, May 13, 1754 (*Papers* 5.275–80).
6. Diplomacy required that presents be given to the Indians.
7. The complete plan, along with James Alexander's response, is in *Papers* 5.335–38.

Business. Many Objections and Difficulties were started, but at length they were all overcome, and the Plan was unanimously agreed to, and Copies ordered to be transmitted to the Board of Trade and to the Assemblies of the several Provinces. Its Fate was singular. The Assemblies did not adopt it, as they all thought there was too much *Prerogative* in it; and in England it was judg'd to have too much of the *Democratic:*[8] The Board of Trade therefore did not approve of it; nor recommend it for the Approbation of his Majesty; but another Scheme was form'd (suppos'd better to answer the same Purpose) whereby the Governors of the Provinces with some Members of their respective Councils were to meet and order the raising of Troops, building of Forts, etc. etc. to draw on the Treasury of Great Britain for the Expense, which was afterwards to be refunded by an Act of Parliament laying a Tax on America. My Plan, with my Reasons in support of it, is to be found among my political Papers that are printed.[9]

Being the Winter following in Boston, I had much Conversation with Governor Shirley upon both the Plans. Part of what pass'd between us on the Occasion may also be seen among those Papers.[1] The different and contrary Reasons of dislike to my Plan, makes me suspect that it was really the true Medium; and I am still of Opinion it would have been happy for both Sides the Water if it had been adopted. The Colonies so united would have been sufficiently strong to have defended themselves; there would then have been no need of Troops from England; of course the subsequent Pretense for Taxing America, and the bloody Contest it occasioned, would have been avoided. But such Mistakes are not new; History is full of the Errors of States and Princes.

> "Look round the habitable World, how few
>   Know their own Good, or knowing it pursue."[2]

Those who govern, having much Business on their hands, do not generally like to take the Trouble of considering and carrying into Execution new Projects. The best public Measures are therefore seldom *adopted from previous Wisdom*, but *forc'd by the Occasion*.

The Governor[3] of Pennsylvania in sending it down to the Assembly, express'd his Approbation of the Plan "as appearing to him to

---

8. The colonists also distrusted one another, and Britons worried about any potential transfer of power to America.
9. [Benjamin Vaughan, ed.,] *Political, Miscellaneous, and Philosophical Pieces* . . . (1779), 85–143.
1. Franklin's letters to Shirley, dated December 3, 4, and 22, 1754 (*Papers* 5.441–51), were widely reprinted, appearing first in the *London Chronicle*, February 8, 1766.
2. From Dryden's translation of Juvenal's "Satire X" (1693), ll. 1–2, showing the folly of pursuing wealth when virtue and health were enough for happiness.
3. James Hamilton.

be drawn up with great Clearness and Strength of Judgment, and therefore recommended it as well worthy their closest and most serious Attention."[4] The House however, by the Management of a certain Member,[5] took it up when I happen'd to be absent, which I thought not very fair, and reprobated it without paying any Attention to it at all, to my no small Mortification.

In my Journey to Boston this Year I met at New York with our new Governor, Mr. Morris, just arriv'd there from England, with whom I had been before intimately acquainted. He brought a Commission to supersede Mr. Hamilton, who, tir'd with the Disputes his Proprietary Instructions subjected him to, had resigned. Mr. Morris ask'd me, if I thought he must expect as uncomfortable an Administration.[6] I said, No; you may on the contrary have a very comfortable one, if you will only take care not to enter into any Dispute with the Assembly; "My dear Friend, says he, pleasantly, how can you advise my avoiding Disputes. You know I love Disputing; it is one of my greatest Pleasures: However, to show the Regard I have for your Counsel, I promise you I will if possible avoid them." He had some Reason for loving to dispute, being eloquent, an acute Sophister, and therefore generally successful in argumentative Conversation. He had been brought up to it from a Boy, his Father (as I have heard) accustoming his Children to dispute with one another for his Diversion while sitting at Table after Dinner. But I think the Practice was not wise, for in the Course of my Observation, these disputing, contradicting and confuting People are generally unfortunate in their Affairs. They get Victory sometimes, but they never get Good Will, which would be of more use to them. We parted, he going to Philadelphia, and I to Boston. In returning, I met at New York with the Votes of the Assembly,[7] by which it appear'd that notwithstanding his Promise to me, he and the House were already in high Contention, and it was a continual Battle between them, as long as he retain'd the Government.

---

4. Not quite. Governor Hamilton, on August 7, 1754, to the Assembly about both the "Representation of the present State of the Colonies" drawn up by the Albany commissioners and the "general Plan" for a union of the colonies "for their mutual Defense," addressed "And as both those Papers appear to me to contain Matters of the utmost Consequence to the Welfare of the Colonies in general, and to have been digested and drawn up with great Clearness and Strength of Judgment, I cannot but express my Approbation of them, and do, therefore, recommend them to you as well worthy of your closest and most serious Attention" (*Pa. Col. Records*, v. 6 [for 1754–1756]: 135).
5. Most likely Isaac Norris, Speaker of the Assembly. Franklin's plan would have diluted the assembly's control of finances. Thus Hamilton favored it and Norris opposed it. The House took it up on August 17, 1754 (*Papers* 5.376, 427n).
6. Franklin, on a postal inspection tour, missed two months of the legislative session, winter 1754–55, when Morris first tangled with the assembly.
7. Franklin was in New York in February 1755, on his way back to Philadelphia. Since the relevant *Votes and Proceedings of the House* were not printed until April 1755 (Miller, no. 595), Franklin probably saw the exchanges in the newspapers, perhaps those in the *Pennsylvania Gazette*, January 7 and 14, 1755.

I had my Share of it; for as soon as I got back to my Seat in the Assembly, I was put on every Committee for answering his Speeches and Messages, and by the Committees always desired to make the Drafts. Our Answers as well as his Messages were often tart, and sometimes indecently abusive.[8] And as he knew I wrote for the Assembly, one might have imagined that when we met we could hardly avoid cutting Throats. But he was so good-natur'd a Man, that no personal Difference between him and me was occasion'd by the Contest, and we often din'd together. One Afternoon in the height of this public Quarrel, we met in the Street. "Franklin, says he, you must go home with me and spend the Evening. I am to have some Company that you will like;" and taking me by the Arm he led me to his House. In gay Conversation over our Wine after Supper he told us Jokingly that he much admir'd the Idea of Sancho Panza, who when it was propos'd to give him a Government, requested it might be a Government of *Blacks*, as then, if he could not agree with his People he might sell them.[9] One of his Friends who sat next me, says, "Franklin, why do you continue to side with these damn'd Quakers? had not you better sell them? the Proprietor would give you a good Price." The Governor, says I, had not yet *black'd* them enough. He had indeed labour'd hard to blacken the Assembly in all his Messages, but they wip'd off his Coloring as fast as he laid it on, and plac'd it in return thick upon his own Face, so that finding he was likely to be negrified himself, he as well as Mr. Hamilton, grew tir'd of the Contest, and quitted the Government.*

These public Quarrels were all at bottom owing to the Proprietaries, our hereditary Governors; who when any Expense was to be incurr'd for the Defense of their Province, with incredible Meanness instructed their Deputies to pass no Act for levying the necessary Taxes, unless their vast Estates were in the same Act expressly excused; and they had even taken Bonds of those Deputies to observe such Instructions. The Assemblies for three Years[1] held out against this Injustice, Tho' constrain'd to bend at last. At length Captain Denny, who was Governor Morris's Successor, ventur'd to

---

* "My Acts in Morris's time—military etc." [Franklin's memo.]

---

8. When the Assembly replied to Governor Morris on May 17, 1755, it was probably Franklin who implicitly condemned him for his "Joy in Disputation" and called him an enemy to Pennsylvania (*Papers* 6. 49).

9. A distortion of Miguel de Cervantes's *Don Quixote,* Part One, Chapter 29, where Sancho, instead of requesting a government of blacks, grieves at the idea of governing blacks until realizing he can sell them. Franklin may also recall Chapter 31, where the subject is not obedience but the climate: "If the Air does not agree with me, I may transport my Black Slaves, make a Profit of them, and go live somewhere else" (trans. Peter Motleux, 2 vols. [1700–12], 1.381).

1. The conflict lasted 1751–59, but the assembly first tried to tax the proprietary estates in 1755.

disobey those Instructions; how that was brought about I shall show hereafter.*

But I am got forward too fast with my Story; there are still some Transactions to be mentioned that happened during the Administration of Governor Morris.

War being, in a manner, commenced with France, the Government of Massachusetts Bay projected an Attack upon Crown Point,[2] and sent Mr. Quincy to Pennsylvania, and Mr. Pownall, afterwards Governor Pownall, to New York to solicit Assistance. As I was in the Assembly, knew its Temper, and was Mr. Quincy's Countryman,[3] he applied to me for my Influence and Assistance. I dictated his Address to them which was well receiv'd. They voted an Aid of Ten Thousand Pounds, to be laid out in Provisions. But the Governor refusing his Assent to their Bill,[4] (which included this with other Sums granted for the Use of the Crown) unless a Clause were inserted exempting the Proprietary Estate from bearing any Part of the Tax that would be necessary, the Assembly, tho' very desirous of making their Grant to New England effectual, were at a Loss how to, accomplish it. Mr. Quincy laboured hard with the Governor to obtain his Assent, but he was obstinate. I then suggested a Method of doing the Business without the Governor, by Orders on the Trustees of the Loan-Office, which by Law the Assembly had the Right of Drawing. There was indeed little or no Money at that time in the Office, and therefore I propos'd that the Orders should be payable in a Year and to bear an Interest of Five percent. With these Orders I suppos'd the Provisions might easily be purchas'd. The Assembly with very little Hesitation adopted the Proposal. The Orders were immediately printed, and I was one of the Committee directed to sign and dispose of them. The Fund for Paying them was the Interest of all the Paper Currency then extant in the Province upon Loan, together with the Revenue arising from the Excise, which being known to be more than sufficient, they obtain'd instant Credit, and were not only receiv'd in Payment for the Provisions, but many money'd People who had Cash lying by them, vested it in those Orders, which they found advantageous, as they bore Interest while upon hand, and might on any Occasion be used as Money: So that they were eagerly all bought up, and in a few Weeks none of them were to be seen. Thus this important Affair was by my means completed. Mr. Quincy return'd Thanks to the Assembly in a handsome Memorial,[5] went home highly pleas'd

---

* "Lord Loudon etc." [Franklin's memo.]

2. A fort at Crown Point on Lake Champlain protected the southern approach to the St. Lawrence River.
3. A native of Massachusetts.
4. Although Morris supported Franklin's request, the assembly included it in an omnibus bill along with provisions for printing new money—which the Governor rejected.
5. Dated April 1, 1755 (*Papers* 6.3–5).

with the Success of his Embassy, and ever after bore for me the most cordial and affectionate Friendship.

The British Government not choosing to permit the Union of the Colonies, as propos'd at Albany, and to trust that Union with their Defense, lest they should thereby grow too military, and feel their own Strength, Suspicions and Jealousies at this time being entertain'd of them, sent over General Braddock with two Regiments of Regular English Troops for that purpose. He landed at Alexandria in Virginia, and thence march'd to Frederick Town in Maryland, where he halted for Carriages. Our Assembly apprehending, from some Information, that he had conceived violent Prejudices[6] against them, as averse to the Service, wish'd me to wait upon him, not as from them, but as Postmaster General, under the guise of proposing to settle with him the Mode of conducting with most Celerity and Certainty the Dispatches between him and the Governors of the several Provinces, with whom he must necessarily have continual Correspondence, and of which they propos'd to pay the Expense. My Son accompanied me on this Journey. We found the General at Frederick Town, waiting impatiently for the Return of those he had sent thro' the back Parts of Maryland and Virginia to collect Waggons. I stayed with him several Days, Din'd with him daily, and had full Opportunity of removing all his Prejudices, by the Information of what the Assembly had before his Arrival actually done and were still willing to do to facilitate his Operations.

When I was about to depart, the Returns of Waggons to be obtain'd were brought in, by which it appear'd that they amounted only to twenty-five, and not all of those were in serviceable Condition. The General and all the Officers were surpris'd, declar'd the Expedition was then at an End, being impossible, and exclaim'd against the Ministers for ignorantly landing them in a Country destitute of the Means of conveying their Stores, Baggage, etc. not less than 150 Waggons being necessary. I happen'd to say, I thought it was pity they had not been landed rather in Pennsylvania, as in that Country almost every Farmer had his Waggon. The General eagerly laid hold of my Words, and said, "Then you, Sir, who are a Man of Interest there, can probably procure them for us; and I beg you will undertake it." I ask'd what Terms were to be offer'd the Owners of the Waggons; and I was desir'd to put on Paper the Terms that appear'd to me necessary. This I did, and they were agreed to, and a Commission and Instructions accordingly prepar'd immediately. What those Terms were will appear in the Advertisement I publish'd as soon as I arriv'd at Lancaster, which being, from the great and

---

6. When Governor Morris warned him that the Quakers would not cooperate, Braddock threatened them (February 28, 1755) with "unpleasant Methods" if the assembly failed either to embargo French goods or to give his army decent postal service (*Papers* 6.13n, 54–55).

ADVERTISEMENT.

Lancaster, April 26, 1755.

WHEREAS 150 Waggons, with 4 Horses to each Waggon, and 1500 Saddle or Pack-Horses are wanted for the Service of his Majesty's Forces now about to rendezvous at *Will's* Creek; and his Excellency General *Braddock* hath been pleased to impower me to contract for the Hire of the same; I hereby give Notice, that I shall attend for that Purpose at *Lancaster* from this Time till next *Wednesday* Evening; and at *York* from next *Thursday* Morning till *Friday* Evening; where I shall be ready to agree for Waggons and Teams, or single Horses, on the following Terms, viz.

1st. That there shall be paid for each Waggon with 4 good Horses and a Driver, *Fifteen Shillings* per *Diem*: And for each able Horse with a Pack-Saddle or other Saddle and Furniture, *Two Shillings* per *Diem*. And for each able Horse without a Saddle, *Eighteen Pence* per *Diem.*

2dly, That the Pay commence from the Time of their joining the Forces at *Will's* Creek (which must be on or before the twentieth of *May* ensuing) and that a reasonable Allowance be made over and above for the Time necessary for their travelling to *Will's* Creek and home again after their Discharge.

3dly, Each Waggon and Team, and every Saddle or Pack Horse is to be valued by indifferent Persons, chosen between me and the Owner, and in Case of the Loss of any Waggon, Team or other Horse in the Service, the Price according to such Valuation, is to be allowed and paid.

4thly, Seven Days Pay is to be advanced and paid in hand by me to the Owner of each Waggon and Team, or Horse, at the Time of contracting, if required; and the Remainder to be paid by General *Braddock*, or by the Paymaster of the Army, at the Time of their Discharge, or from time to time as it shall be demanded.

5thly, No Drivers of Waggons, or Persons taking care of the hired Horses, are on any Account to be called upon to do the Duty of Soldiers, or be otherwise employ'd than in conducting or taking Care of their Carriages and Horses.

6thly, All Oats, Indian Corn or other Forage, that Waggons or Horses bring to the Camp more than is necessary for the Subsistence of the Horses, is to be taken for the Use of the Army, and a reasonable Price paid for it.

Note. My Son *William Franklin*, is impowered to enter into like Contracts with any Person in *Cumberland* County.   B. FRANKLIN.

To the Inhabitants of the Counties of Lancaster, York, and Cumberland.

Friends and Countrymen,

BEING occasionally at the Camp at *Frederic* a few Days since, I found the General and Officers of the Army extreamly exasperated, on Account of their not being supply'd with Horses and Carriages, which they had been expected from this Province as most able to furnish them; but thro' the Dissensions between our Governor and Assembly, Money had not been provided nor any Steps taken for that Purpose.

It was proposed to send an armed Force immediately into these Counties, to seize as many of the best Carriages and Horses as should be wanted, and compel as many Persons into the Service as would be necessary to drive and take care of them.

I apprehended that the Progress of a Body of Soldiers thro' these Counties on such an Occasion, especially considering the Temper they are in, and their Resentment against us, would be attended with many and great Inconveniencies to the Inhabitants; and therefore more willingly undertook the Trouble of trying first what might be done by fair and equitable Means.

The People of these back Counties have lately complained to the Assembly that a sufficient Currency was wanting; you have now an Opportunity of receiving and dividing among you a very considerable Sum; for if the Service of this Expedition should continue (as it's more than probable it will) for 120 Days, the Hire of these Waggons and Horses will amount to upwards of *Thirty thousand Pounds*, which will be paid you in Silver and Gold of the King's Money.

The Service will be light and easy, for the Army will scarce march above 12 Miles per Day, and the Waggons and Baggage Horses, as they carry those Things that are absolutely necessary to the Welfare of the Army, must march with the Army and no faster, and are, for the Army's sake, always plac'd where they can be most secure, whether on a March or in Camp.

If you are really, as I believe you are, good and loyal Subjects to His Majesty, you may now do a most acceptable Service, and make it easy to yourselves; for three or four of such as cannot separately spare from the Business of their Plantations a Waggon and four Horses and a Driver, may do it together, one furnishing the Waggon, another one or two Horses, and another the Driver, and divide the Pay proportionably between you. But if you do not this Service to your King and Country voluntarily, when such good Pay and reasonable Terms are offered you, your Loyalty will be strongly suspected; the King's Business must be done; so many brave Troops, come so far for your Defence, must not stand idle, thro' your backwardness to do what may be reasonably expected from you; Waggons and Horses must be had; violent Measures will probably be used; and you will be to seek for a Recompence where you can find it, and your Case perhaps be little pitied or regarded.

I have no particular Interest in this Affair; as (except the Satisfaction of endeavouring to do Good and prevent Mischief) I shall have only my Labour for my Pains. If this Method of obtaining the Waggons and Horses is not like to succeed, I am oblig'd to send Word to the General in fourteen Days; and I suppose Sir *John St. Clair* the Hussar, with a Body of Soldiers, will immediately enter the Province, for the Purpose aforesaid, of which I shall be sorry to hear, because I am,

    very sincerely and truly,

       your Friend and Well-wisher,

          B. FRANKLIN.

1957583b

The wagon broadside, printed by William Dunlap at Lancaster. Courtesy of the American Philosophical Society. Wills Creek, mentioned in the third line, flows into the Potomac River in western Maryland, at the site of present-day Cumberland.

sudden Effect[7] it produc'd, a Piece of some Curiosity, I shall insert at length, as follows.*

To the Inhabitants of the Counties of Lancaster, York, and Cumberland.

Friends and Countrymen,

BEING occasionally at the Camp at *Frederick* a few Days since, I found the General and Officers of the Army extremely exasperated, on Account of their not being supplied with Horses and Carriages, which had been expected from this Province as most able to furnish them; but thro' the Dissensions between our Governor and Assembly, Money had not been provided nor any Steps taken for that Purpose.

It was proposed to send an armed Force immediately into these Counties, to seize as many of the best Carriages and Horses as should be wanted, and compel as many Persons into the Service as would be necessary to drive and take care of them.

I apprehended that the Progress of a Body of Soldiers thro' these Counties on such an Occasion, especially considering the Temper they are in, and their Resentment against us, would be attended with many and great Inconveniences to the Inhabitants; and therefore more willingly undertook the Trouble of trying first what might be done by fair and equitable Means.

The People of these back Counties have lately complained to the Assembly that a sufficient Currency was wanting; you have now an Opportunity of receiving and dividing among you a very considerable Sum; for if the Service of this Expedition should continue (as it's more than probable it will) for 120 Days, the Hire of these Waggons and Horses will amount to upwards of *Thirty thousand Pounds,* which will be paid you in Silver and Gold of the King's Money.

The Service will be light and easy, for the Army will scarce march above 12 Miles per Day, and the Waggons and Baggage Horses, as they carry those Things that are absolutely necessary to the Welfare of the Army, must march with the Army and no faster, and are, for the Army's sake, always plac'd where they can be most secure, whether on a March or in Camp.

If you are really, as I believe you are, good and loyal Subjects to His Majesty, you may now do a most acceptable Service, and make

---

* "(Here insert it, from the Quire Book of Letters written during this Transaction)." [Franklin's note. In this Norton Critical Edition, pp. 166–68.]

7. Franklin secured more than 150 wagons and almost 300 horses within a week.

it easy to yourselves; for three or four of such as cannot separately spare from the Business of their Plantations a Waggon and four Horses and a Driver, may do it together, one furnishing the Waggon, another one or two Horses, and another the Driver, and divide the Pay proportionably between you. But if you do not this Service to your King and Country voluntarily, when such good Pay and reasonable Terms arc offered you, your Loyalty will be strongly suspected; the King's Business must be done; so many brave Troops, come so far for your Defense, must not stand idle, thro' your backwardness to do what may be reasonably expected from you; Waggons and Horses must be had; violent Measures will probably be used; and you will be to seek for a Recompense where you can find it, and your Case perhaps be little pitied or regarded.

I have no particular Interest in this Affair; as (except the Satisfaction of endeavouring to do Good and prevent Mischief) I shall have only my Labor, for my Pains. If this Method of obtaining the Waggons and Horses is not like to succeed, I am oblig'd to send Word to the General in fourteen Days; and I suppose Sir *John St. Clair* the Hussar, with a Body of Soldiers, will immediately enter the Province, for the Purpose aforesaid, of which I shall be sorry to hear, because *I am*,

very sincerely and truly
your Friend and Well-wisher,   B. FRANKLIN

I receiv'd of the General about 800 Pounds[8] to be disburs'd in Advance-money to the Waggon-Owners etc.: but that Sum being insufficient, I advanc'd upwards of 200 Pounds more, and in two Weeks, the 150 Waggons with 259 carrying Horses were on their March for the Camp. The Advertisement promised Payment according to the Valuation, in case any Waggon or Horse should be lost. The Owners however, alledging they did not know General Braddock, or what Dependance might be had on his Promise, insisted on my Bond for the Performance, which I accordingly gave them.

While I was at the Camp, supping one Evening with the Officers of Colonel Dunbar's Regiment, he represented to me his Concern for the Subalterns, who he said were generally not in Affluence, and could ill afford in this dear[9] Country to lay in the Stores that might be necessary in so long a March thro' a Wilderness where nothing was to be purchas'd. I commiserated their Case, and resolved to endeavour procuring them some Relief. I said nothing however to him of my Intention, but wrote the next Morning to the Committee of Assembly, who had the Disposition of some public Money, warmly recommending the Case of these Officers to their Consider-

8. £795.15.6 (*Papers* 6.17).
9. Expensive.

ation, and proposing that a Present should be sent them of Necessaries and Refreshments. My Son, who had had some Experience of a Camp Life, and of its Wants, drew up a List for me, which I enclos'd in my Letter. The Committee approv'd, and used such Diligence, that conducted by my Son, the Stores arrived at the Camp as soon as the Waggons.[1] They consisted of 20 Parcels, each containing

6 lb. Loaf Sugar

6 lb. good Muscovado[2] Ditto

1 lb. good Green Tea

1 lb. good Bohea[3] Ditto

6 lb. good ground Coffee

6 lb. Chocolate

½ Hundredweight[4] best white Biscuit

½ lb. Pepper

1 Quart best white Wine Vinegar

1 Gloucester Cheese

1 Keg containing 20 lb. good Butter

2 Doz. old Madeira Wine

2 Gallons Jamaica Spirits[5]

1 Bottle Flour of Mustard

2 well-cur'd Hams

½ Doz. dried Tongues

6 lb. Rice

6 lb. Raisins.

These 20 Parcels well pack'd were plac'd on as many Horses, each Parcel with the Horse, being intended as a Present for one Officer. They were very thankfully receiv'd, and the Kindness acknowledg'd by Letters to me from the Colonels of both Regiments in the most grateful Terms. The General too was highly satisfied with my Conduct in procuring him the Waggons, etc. and readily paid my Account of Disbursements; thanking me repeatedly and requesting my farther Assistance in sending Provisions after him. I undertook this also, and was busily employ'd in it till we heard of his Defeat, advancing, for the Service, of my own Money, upwards of 1000 Pounds Sterling,[6] of which I sent him an Account. It came to his Hands luckily for me a few Days before the Battle, and he return'd

---

1. Sixty wagons were ready to depart Philadelphia by May 30.
2. Brown sugar.
3. Black tea.
4. "C^wt."
5. Rum.
6. Expenses came to £1,005 even before Franklin advertised for wagons in Lancaster (*Papers* 6.18).

me immediately an Order on the Paymaster for the round Sum of 1000 Pounds, leaving the Remainder to the next Account. I consider this Payment as good Luck; having never been able to obtain that Remainder; of which more hereafter.

This General was I think a brave Man, and might probably have made a Figure as a good Officer in some European War, But he had too much self-confidence, too high an Opinion of the Validity of Regular Troops, and too mean a One of both Americans and Indians.[7] George Croghan, our Indian Interpreter, join'd him on his March with 100 of those People, who might have been of great Use to his Army as Guides, Scouts, etc. if he had treated them kindly; but he slighted and neglected them, and they gradually left him.

In Conversation with him one day, he was giving me some Account of his intended Progress. "After taking Fort Duquesne,[8] says he, I am to proceed to Niagara; and having taken that, to Frontenac,[9] if the Season will allow time; and I suppose it will; for Duquesne can hardly detain me above three or four Days; and then I see nothing that can obstruct my March to Niagara."—Having before revolv'd in my Mind the long Line his Army must make in their March, by a very narrow Road to be cut for them thro' the Woods and Bushes; and also what I had read of a former Defeat of 1500 French who invaded the Iroquois Country,[1] I had conceiv'd some Doubts, and some Fears for the Event of the Campaign. But I ventur'd only to say, To be sure, Sir, if you arrive well before Duquesne, with these fine Troops so well provided with Artillery, that Place, not yet completely fortified, and as we hear with no very strong Garrison, can probably make but a short Resistance. The only Danger I apprehend of Obstruction to your March, is from Ambuscades of Indians, who by constant Practice are dextrous in laying and executing them. And the slender Line near four Miles long, which your Army must make, may expose it to be attack'd by Surprise in its Flanks, and to be cut like a Thread into several Pieces, which from their Distance cannot come up in time to support each other.

He smil'd at my Ignorance, and replied, "These Savages may indeed be a formidable Enemy to your raw American Militia; but, upon the King's regular and disciplin'd Troops, Sir, it is impossible they should make any Impression." I was conscious of an Impropriety

---

7. Franklin replied to such criticisms in his thorough "Defense of the Americans," May 9, 1759 (*Papers* 8.340–56).
8. Now Pittsburgh.
9. Now Kingston, Ontario.
1. Perhaps Lahontan's exaggerated report of the ambush of Marquis de Brisay de Denonville by the Iroquois in 1687: "Had you but seen, Sir, what Disorder our Troops and Militia were in amidst the thick trees, you would have joyn'd with me, in thinking that several thousands of *Europeans* are no more than a sufficient number to make head against five hundred Barbarians" (*New Voyages to North America* [London, 1703], 1.76).

in my Disputing with a military Man in Matters of his Profession, and said no more.—The Enemy however did not take the Advantage of his Army which I apprehended its long Line of March expos'd it to, but let it advance without Interruption till within 9 Miles of the Place; and then when more in a Body, (for it had just pass'd a River, where the Front had halted till all were come over) and in a more open Part of the Woods than any it had pass'd, attack'd its advanc'd Guard, by a heavy Fire from behind Trees and Bushes; which was the first Intelligence the General had of an Enemy's being near him.[2] This Guard being disordered, the General hurried the Troops up to their Assistance, which was done in great Confusion thro' Waggons, Baggage and Cattle; and presently the Fire came upon their Flank; the Officers being on Horseback were more easily distinguish'd, pick'd out as Marks, and fell very fast; and the Soldiers were crowded together in a Huddle, having or hearing no Orders, and standing to be shot at till two-thirds of them were killed, and then being seiz'd with a Panic the whole fled with Precipitation, The Waggoners took each a Horse out of his Team, and scamper'd; their Example was immediately follow'd by others, so that all the Waggons, Provisions, Artillery and Stores were left to the Enemy.

The General being wounded was brought off with Difficulty, his Secretary Mr. Shirley[3] was killed by his Side, and out of 86 Officers 63 were killed or wounded, and 714 Men killed out of 1100. These 1100 had been picked Men, from the whole Army, the Rest had been left behind with Colonel Dunbar, who was to follow with the heavier Part of the Stores, Provisions and Baggage. The Fliers, not being pursu'd, arriv'd at Dunbar's Camp, and the Panic they brought with them instantly seiz'd him and all his People. And tho' he had now above 1000 Men, and the Enemy who had beaten Braddock did not at most exceed 400,[4] Indians and French together; instead of Proceeding and endeavouring to recover some of the lost Honor, he order'd all the Stores, Ammunitions, etc. to be destroy'd, that he might have more Horses to assist his Flight towards the Settlements, and less Lumber to remove. He was there met with Requests from the Governors of Virginia, Maryland and Pennsylvania, that he would post his Troops on the Frontiers so as to afford some Protection to the Inhabitants; but he continu'd his hasty March thro' all the Country, not thinking himself safe till he arriv'd at Philadelphia,

2. The British were not ambushed, Both sides were surprised. See Lawrence H. Gipson, *British Empire before the American Revolution*, 15 vols. (Caldwell, Id.: The Caxton Printers, 1936–70), 6.94–95.
3. William Shirley, Jr., son of Franklin's friend, Governor Shirley of Massachusetts.
4. Closer to 800, vs. the British 1459—of whom 977 were killed or wounded. Of the French and Indians, only twenty-five were killed and twenty-five wounded. See Douglas E. Leach, *Arms for Empire: A Military History of the British Colonies in North America, 1607–1763* (New York: Macmillian, 1973, 367; Gipson, 6.96).

where the Inhabitants could protect him.[5] This whole Transaction gave us Americans the first Suspicion that our exalted Ideas of the Prowess of British Regulars had not been well founded.

In their first March too, from their Landing till they got beyond the Settlements, they had plundered and stripped the Inhabitants, totally ruining some poor Families, besides insulting, abusing and confining the People if they remonstrated. This was enough to put us out of Conceit of such Defenders if we had really wanted any. How different was the Conduct of our French Friends in 1781, who during a March thro' the most inhabited Part of our Country, from Rhode Island to Virginia, near 700 Miles, occasion'd not the smallest Complaint, for the Loss of a Pig, a Chicken, or even an Apple!

Captain Orme, who was one of the General's Aides de Camp, and being grievously wounded was brought off with him, and continu'd with him to his Death, which happen'd in a few Days, told me, that he was totally silent, all the first Day, and at Night only said, *Who'd have thought it?* that he was silent again the following Days, only saying at last, *We shall better know how to deal with them another time*; and died a few Minutes after.

The Secretary's Papers with all the General's Orders, Instructions and Correspondence falling into the Enemy's Hands, they selected and translated into French a Number of the Articles, which they printed to prove the hostile Intentions of the British Court before the Declaration of War. Among these I saw some Letters of the General to the Ministry speaking highly of the great Service I had rendered the Army, and recommending me to their Notice. David Hume too, who was some Years after Secretary to Lord Harcourt when Minister in France, and afterwards to General Conway when Secretary of State, told me he had seen among the Papers in that Office Letters from Braddock highly recommending me. But the Expedition having been unfortunate, my Service it seems was not thought of much Value, for those Recommendations were never of any Use to me.[6]

As to Rewards from himself, I ask'd only one, which was, that he would give Orders to his Officers not to enlist any more of our bought servants,[7] and that he would discharge such as had been already enlisted. This he readily granted, and several were accord-

5. His troops spent a month at Philadelphia (August 29–October 1, 1755) on their way to New York.
6. Jacob Nicolas Moreau, *Mémoire Contenant le Précis des Faits* (Paris, 1756; trans. New York [2 eds.] and Philadelphia, 1757; London, 1759). Braddock's commendation, dated June 5, 1755, says that Franklin acted "with so much Goodness and Readiness, that it is almost the first Instance of Integrity, Address and Ability that I have seen in all these Provinces" (Philadelphia ed., 242; see also Evans, *Bibliography*, 7897). Lord "Harcourt" was actually Hertford.
7. Braddock's temporary successor, Governor (now General) Shirley, on September 19, 1755, ordered Dunbar "in the Strongest Manner" to avoid enlisting indentured servants, but a law permitted the practice the following year (*Papers* 6.190, 227n, 474–75).

ingly return'd to their Masters on my Application. Dunbar, when the Command devolv'd on him, was not so generous. He Being at Philadelphia on his Retreat, or rather Flight, I applied to him for the Discharge of the Servants of three poor Farmers of Lancaster County that he had enlisted, reminding him of the late General's Orders on that head. He promis'd me, that if the Masters would come to him at Trenton, where he should be in a few Days on his March to New York, he would there deliver their Men to them. They accordingly were at the Expense and Trouble of going to Trenton, and there he refus'd to perform his Promise, to their great Loss and Disappointment.

As soon as the Loss of the Waggons and Horses was generally known, all the Owners came upon me for the Valuation which I had given Bond to pay. Their Demands gave me a great deal of Trouble, my acquainting them that the Money was ready in the Paymaster's Hands, but that Orders for paying it must first be obtained from General Shirley, and my assuring them that I had applied to that General by Letter, but he being at a Distance an Answer could not soon be receiv'd, and they must have Patience; all this was not sufficient to satisfy, and some began to sue me. General Shirley at length reliev'd me from this terrible Situation, by appointing Commissioners to examine the Claims and ordering Payment.[8] They amounted to near twenty Thousand Pound, which to pay would have ruined me.

Before we had the News of this Defeat, the two Doctors Bond[9] came to me with a Subscription Paper, for raising Money to defray the Expense of a grand Firework, which it was intended to exhibit at a Rejoicing on receipt of the News of our Taking Fort Duquesne. I looked grave and said, "it would, I thought, be time enough to prepare for the Rejoicing when we knew we should have occasion to rejoice."—They seem'd surpris'd that I did not immediately comply with their Proposal. "Why, the D—l," says one of them, "you surely don't suppose that the Fort will not be taken?" "I don't know that it will not be taken; but I know that the Events of War are subject to great Uncertainty."—I gave them the Reasons of my doubting. The Subscription was dropped, and the Projectors thereby miss'd that Mortification they would have undergone if the Firework had been prepared. Dr. Bond on some other Occasions afterwards said, that he did not like Franklin's forebodings.

Governor Morris who had continually worried the Assembly with Message after Message before the Defeat of Braddock, to beat

8. As Commander-in-Chief, William Shirley asked Governor Morris to name the commission, and Franklin sent warrants to the paymaster on October 16, 1755. Nevertheless, Franklin continued to be annoyed by the unpaid account for decades (*Papers* 6.190; 19.73–74).
9. Thomas and Phineas Bond.

them into the making of Acts to raise Money for the Defense of the
Province without Taxing among others the Proprietary Estates, and
had rejected all their Bills for not having such an exempting Clause,
now redoubled his Attacks, with more hope of Success, the Danger
and Necessity being greater. The Assembly however continu'd firm,
believing they had Justice on their side, and that it would be giving up an essential Right, if they suffered the Governor to amend
their Money-Bills. In one of the last, indeed, which was for granting 50,000 Pounds, his propos'd Amendment was only of a single
Word; the Bill express'd that all Estates real and personal were to be
taxed, those of the Proprietaries *not* excepted. His Amendment was;
For *not* read *only*.[1] A small but very material Alteration! However,
when the News of this Disaster reach'd England, our Friends there
whom we had taken care to furnish with all the Assembly's Answers
to the Governor's Messages, rais'd a Clamour against the Proprietaries for their Meanness and Injustice in giving their Governor
such Instructions, some going so far as to say that by obstructing the
Defense of their Province, they forfeited their Right to it. They were
intimidated by this, and sent Orders to their Receiver General to
add 5000 Pounds of their Money to whatever Sum might be given by
the Assembly, for such Purpose.[2] This being notified to the House,
was accepted in Lieu of their Share of a general Tax, and a new Bill
was form'd with an exempting Clause which pass'd accordingly. By
this Act I was appointed one of the Commissioners for disposing of
the Money, 60,000 Pounds. I had been active[3] in modelling it, and
procuring its Passage: and had at the same time drawn a Bill for
establishing and disciplining a voluntary Militia, which I carried
thro' the House without much Difficulty, as Care was taken in it, to
leave the Quakers at their Liberty.[4]

To promote the Association necessary to form the Militia, I wrote
a Dialogue,* stating and answering all the Objections I could think
of to such a Militia, which was printed and had as I thought great

---

* "This Dialogue and the Militia Act, are
in the *Gentleman's Magazine* for February
and March 1756." [Franklin's note. The
"Dialogue between X, Y, and Z" appeared
first in the *Pennsylvania Gazette*, December
18, 1755, and was reprinted in the *Gentleman's Magazine*, 26 (March 1756), 122–26.
(*Papers* 6.266–73, 295–306.)]

---

1. Morris suggested this amendment on November 17, 1755. See the *Minutes of the Provincial Council of Pennsylvania*, 16 vols. (Philadelphia: J. Stevens & Co., 1838–53;
   hereafter referred to as *Pa. Col. Records*), 6.702.
2. On November 24, 1755, Governor Morris informed the assembly of the proprietors' gift
   of £5,000. The House accepted the sum in lieu of taxes on proprietary lands, and
   passed a tax bill of £55,000, exempting the proprietors' estates—only to learn that the
   £5,000 consisted mainly of uncollected bad debts (*Papers* 6.257n, 480–83).
3. Franklin served on the commission from December 1755 through December 1756,
   pending his mission to England.
4. Franklin's bill exempted conscientious objectors, made enlistment voluntary, and min-
   imized military discipline. The Ministry vetoed it on July 7, 1756 (*Papers* 6.266–73).

Effect. While the several Companies in the City and Country were forming and learning their Exercise, the Governor prevail'd with me to take Charge of our Northwestern Frontier,[5] which was infested by the Enemy, and provide for the Defense of the Inhabitants by raising Troops, and building a Line of Forts. I undertook this military Business, tho' I did not conceive myself well-qualified for it. He gave me a Commission with full Powers and a Parcel of blank Commissions for Officers to be given to whom I thought fit. I had but little Difficulty in raising Men, having soon 560 under my Command. My Son who had in the preceding War been an Officer in the Army rais'd against Canada,[6] was my Aide de Camp, and of great Use to me. The Indians had burned Gnadenhut, a Village settled by the Moravians,[7] and massacred the Inhabitants, but the Place was thought a good Situation for one of the Forts. In order to march thither, I assembled the Companies at Bethlehem, the chief Establishment of those People. I was surprised to find it in so good a Posture of Defense. The Destruction of Gnadenhut had made them apprehend Danger. The principal Buildings were defended by a Stockade: They had purchased a Quantity of Arms and Ammunition from New York, and had even plac'd Quantities of small Paving Stones between the Windows of their high Stone Houses, for their Women to throw down upon the Heads of any Indians that should attempt to force into them. The armed Brethren too, kept Watch, and reliev'd as methodically as in any Garrison Town. In Conversation with Bishop Spangenberg, I mention'd this my Surprise; for knowing they had obtain'd an Act of Parliament exempting them from military Duties in the Colonies, I had suppos'd they were conscientiously scrupulous of bearing Arms. He answer'd me, "That it was not one of their establish'd Principles; but that at the time of their obtaining that Act, it was thought to be a Principle with many of their People. On this Occasion, however, they to their Surprise found it adopted by but a few." It seems they were either deceiv'd in themselves, or deceiv'd the Parliament. But Common Sense aided by present Danger, will sometimes be too strong for whimsical Opinions.

It was the Beginning of January when we set out upon this Business of Building Forts. I sent one Detachment towards the Minisinks,

5. Franklin first went as one of a three-man commission (December 18–31, 1755), and was then named military and civilian commander January 5, 1756, just after the Governor learned of the latest attack on Gnadenhütten. (See page 139, note 4. For a chronology and map, see *Papers* 6.307–12.)
6. William Franklin was an ensign in a proposed expedition against Canada, 1746–47, during King George's War. He spent most of the time in bivouac at Albany (*Papers* 3.89).
7. The Church of the United Brethren, immigrants from Saxony in 1735, chose Bethlehem as their North American headquarters in 1744. Gnadenhütten, present-day Lehighton, Pennsylvania, had been burned November 24, 1755, and the new troops stationed there had been defeated on January 1, 1756 (*Papers* 6.340–52).

with Instructions to erect one for the Security of that upper Part of the Country; and another to the lower Part, with similar Instructions.[8] And I concluded to go myself with the rest of my Force to Gnadenhut,[9] where a Fort was thought more immediately necessary. The Moravians procur'd me five Waggons for our Tools, Stores, Baggage, etc. Just before we left Bethlehem, Eleven Farmers who had been driven from their Plantations by the Indians, came to me, requesting a supply of Fire Arms, that they might go back and fetch off their Cattle. I gave them each a Gun with suitable Ammunition. We had not march'd many Miles before it began to rain, and it continu'd raining all Day. There were no Habitations on the Road, to shelter us, till we arriv'd near Night, at the House of a German, where and in his Barn we were all huddled together as wet as Water could make us. It was well we were not attack'd in our March, for Our Arms were of the most ordinary Sort, and our Men could not keep their Gunlocks[1] dry. The Indians are dextrous in Contrivances for that purpose, which we had not. They met that Day the eleven poor Farmers above-mentioned and kill'd Ten of them. The one who escap'd inform'd that his and his Companions' Guns would not go off, the Priming being wet with the Rain.[2]

The next Day being fair, we continu'd our March and arriv'd at the desolated Gnadenhut. There was a Saw Mill near, round which were left several Piles of Boards, with which we soon hutted ourselves; an Operation the more necessary at that inclement Season, as we had no Tents. Our first Work was to bury more effectually the Dead we found there, who had been half interr'd by the Country People. The next Morning our Fort was plann'd and mark'd out, the Circumference measuring 455 feet, which would require as many Palisades to be made of Trees one with another of a Foot Diameter each. Our Axes, of which we had 70 were immediately set to work, to cut down Trees; and our Men being dextrous in the Use of them, great Dispatch was made. Seeing the Trees fall so fast, I had the Curiosity to look at my Watch when two Men began to cut at a Pine. In 6 Minutes they had it upon the Ground; and I found it of 14 Inches Diameter. Each Pine made three Palisades of 18 Feet long, pointed at one End. While these were preparing, our other Men, dug a Trench all round of three feet deep in which the Pali-

---

8. The area, named after Northern Delaware Indians, constituted northeastern Pennsylvania; Fort Norris was built here, fifteen miles northeast of Gnadenhütten, near present-day Kresgeville, Monroe Country. Franklin built Fort Allen—now Weissport, Carbon County—and the party sent to the "lower Part" built Fort Franklin, about fifteen miles southwest of Gnadenhütten, south of Snyders, Schuylkill County.
9. He had 500 men when he left Bethlehem.
1. Firing mechanisms that required priming gunpowder.
2. The farmers, led by Christian Bomper, were attacked on Saturday, January 17, Franklin's fiftieth birthday.

sades were to be planted, and our Waggons, the Body being taken off, and the fore and hind Wheels separated by taking out the Pin which united the two Parts of the Perch,[3] we had 10 Carriages with two Horses each, to bring the Palisades from the Woods to the Spot.[4] When they were set up, our Carpenters built a Stage of Boards all round within, about 6 Feet high, for the Men to stand on when to fire thro' the Loopholes. We had one swivel Gun which we mounted on one of the Angles; and fired it as soon as fix'd, to let the Indians know, if any were within hearing, that we had such Pieces. And thus our Fort, (if such a magnificent Name may be given to so miserable a Stockade) was finished in a Week, tho' it rain'd so hard every other Day that the Men could not work.

This gave me occasion to observe, that when Men are employ'd they are best contented. For on the Days they work'd they were good-natur'd and cheerful; and with the consciousness of having done a good Day's work they spent the Evenings jollily; but on the idle Days they were mutinous and quarrelsome, finding fault with their Pork, the Bread, etc. and in continual ill-humor: which put me in mind of a Sea-Captain, whose Rule it was to keep his Men constantly at Work; and when his Mate once told him that they had done every-thing, and there was nothing farther to employ them about; O, says he, *make them scour the Anchor.*

This kind of Fort, however contemptible, is a sufficient Defense against Indians who have no Cannon. Finding ourselves now posted securely, and having a Place to retreat to on Occasion, we ventur'd out in Parties to scour the adjacent Country. We met with no Indi-ans, but we found the Places on the neighboring Hills where they had lain to watch our Proceedings. There was an Art in their Con-trivance of these Places that seems worth mention. It being Winter, a Fire was necessary for them. But a common Fire on the Surface of the Ground would by its Light have discover'd their Position at a Distance. They had therefore dug Holes in the Ground about three feet Diameter, and somewhat deeper. We saw where they had with their Hatchets cut off the Charcoal from the Sides of burned Logs lying in the Woods. With these Coals they had made small Fires in

---

3. The driveshaft connecting the front and rear axles.
4. The *Pennsylvania Gazette*, January 29, 1756, quoted Franklin's dispatch: "We have been here [Gnadenhütten] since Sunday Afternoon. That Day [Jan. 18] we had only Time to get up some Shelter from the Weather and the Enemy. Yesterday [Jan. 19] all Day it rained, with so thick a Fog, that we could not see round us, so as either to chuse a Place for a Fort, or find Materials to build it. In the Night it cleared up, and this Morning [Jan. 20] we determined, marked out the Ground, and at Ten o'clock set the Men to work, and they have worked with such Spirit, that now, at Half past Three in the Afternoon, all the Logs for the Stockade are cut, to the Number of 450, being most of them more than a Foot in Diameter, and 15 Feel long. The Trench to set them in being three Feet deep, and two wide, is dug; 14 Pair of Wheels are drawing them together . . . The Fort will be about 125 Feet long, and 50 broad" (*Papers* 6.362–63; Franklin's sketch of fort, 367).

the Bottom of the Holes, and we observ'd among the Weeds and Grass the Prints of their Bodies made by their laying all round with their Legs hanging down in the Holes to keep their Feet warm, which with them is an essential Point. This kind of Fire, so manag'd, could not discover them either by its Light, Flame, Sparks or even Smoke. It appear'd that their Number was not great, and it seems they saw we were too many to be attack'd by them with Prospect of Advantage.

We had for our Chaplain a zealous Presbyterian Minister, Mr. Beatty, who complain'd to me that the Men did not generally attend his Prayers and Exhortations. When they enlisted, they were promis'd, besides Pay and Provisions, a Gill[5] of Rum a Day, which was punctually serv'd out to them, half in the Morning and the other half in the Evening, and I observ'd they were as punctual in attending to receive it. Upon which I said to Mr. Beatty, "It is perhaps below the Dignity of your Profession to act as Steward of the Rum. But if you were to deal it out, and only just after Prayers, you would have them all about you." He lik'd the Thought, undertook the Office, and with the help of a few hands to measure out the Liquor executed it to Satisfaction; and never were Prayers more generally and more punctually attended. So that I thought this Method preferable to the Punishments inflicted by some military Laws for Non-Attendance on Divine Service.

I had hardly finish'd this Business, and got my Fort well stor'd with Provisions, when I receiv'd a Letter from the Governor, acquainting me that he had called[6] the Assembly, and wish'd my Attendance there, if the Posture of Affairs on the Frontiers was such that my remaining there was no longer necessary. My Friends too of the Assembly pressing me by their Letters to be if possible at the Meeting, and my three intended Forts being now completed, and the Inhabitants contented to remain on their Farms under that Protection, I resolved to return. The more willingly as a New England Officer, Colonel Clapham,[7] experienc'd in Indian War, being on a Visit to our Establishment, consented to accept the Command. I gave him a Commission, and parading the Garrison had it read before them, and introduc'd him to them as an Officer who from his Skill in Military Affairs, was much more fit to command them than myself; and giving them a little Exhortation took my Leave. I was escorted as far as Bethlehem, where I rested a few Days, to recover from the Fatigue I had undergone. The first Night being in a good Bed, I could hardly

---

5. Quarter-pint.
6. The assembly would normally have met in March, but Morris capriciously called it for February.
7. William Clapham, a captain rather than colonel, had swindled the assembly out of £100 in anticipation of this appointment. He proved ineffectual and was dismissed.

sleep, it was so different from my hard Lodging on the Floor of our Hut at Gnaden, wrapped only in a Blanket or two.[8]

While at Bethlehem, I enquir'd a little into the Practices of the Moravians. Some of them had accompanied me, and all were very kind to me. I found they work'd for a common Stock, ate at common Tables, and slept in common Dormitories, great Numbers together. In the Dormitories I observ'd Loopholes at certain Distances all along just under the Ceiling, which I thought judiciously plac'd for Change of Air. I was at their Church, where I was entertain'd with good Music, the Organ being accompanied with Violins, Hautboys,[9] Flutes, Clarinets, etc. I understood that their Sermons were not usually preached to mix'd Congregations of Men, Women and Children, as is our common Practice; but that they assembled sometimes the married Men, at other times their Wives, then the Young Men, the young Women, and the little Children, each Division by itself. The Sermon I heard was to the latter, who came in and were plac'd in Rows on Benches, the Boys under the Conduct of a young Man their Tutor, and the Girls conducted by a young Woman. The Discourse seem'd well adapted to their Capacities, and was delivered in a pleasing familiar Manner, coaxing them as it were to be good. They behav'd very orderly, but look'd pale and unhealthy, which made me suspect they were kept too much within doors, or not allow'd sufficient Exercise. I enquir'd concerning the Moravian Marriages, whether the Report was true that they were by Lot? I was told that Lots were us'd only in particular Cases. That generally when a young Man found himself dispos'd to marry, he inform'd the Elders of his Class, who consulted the Elder Ladies that govern'd the young Women. As these Elders of the different Sexes were well acquainted with the Tempers and Dispositions of their respective Pupils, they could best judge what Matches were suitable, and their Judgments were generally acquiesc'd in. But if for example it should happen that two or three young Women were found to be *equally* proper for the young Man, the Lot was then recurr'd to. I objected, If the Matches are not made by the mutual Choice of the Parties, some of them may chance to be very unhappy. And so they may, answer'd my Informer,[1] if you let the Parties choose for themselves.— Which indeed I could not deny.

Being return'd to Philadelphia, I found the Association went on swimmingly, the Inhabitants that were not Quakers having pretty generally come into it, form'd themselves into Companies, and chosen their Captains, Lieutenants and Ensigns according to the new

8. On January 25, 1756, however, he said he slept "on deal feather beds, in warm blankets" (*Papers* 6.365). Franklin was probably recalling the march to Gnadenhütten.
9. Oboes.
1. Possibly, his host at Bethlehem, Timothy Horsfield.

Law.[2] Dr. B.[3] visited me, and gave me an Account of the Pains he had taken to spread a general good Liking to the Law, and ascrib'd much to those Endeavours. I had had the Vanity to ascribe all to my Dialogue; However, not knowing but that he might be in the right, I let him enjoy his Opinion, which I take to be generally the best way in such Cases.—The Officers meeting chose me[4] to be Colonel of the Regiment; which I this time accepted. I forget how many Companies we had, but We paraded about 1200 well-looking Men,[5] with a Company of Artillery who had been furnish'd with 6 brass Field Pieces, which they had become so expert in the Use of as to fire twelve times in a Minute. The first Time[6] I review'd my Regiment, they accompanied me to my House, and would salute me with some Rounds fired before my Door, which shook down and broke several Glasses of my Electrical Apparatus. And my new Honor prov'd not much less brittle; for all our Commissions were soon after broke by a Repeal of the Law in England.[7]

During the short time of my Colonelship, being about to set out on a Journey to Virginia, the Officers of my Regiment took it into their heads that it would be proper for them to escort me out of town as far as the Lower Ferry. Just as I was getting on Horseback, they came to my door, between 30 and 40, mounted, and all in their Uniforms. I had not been previously acquainted with the Project, or I should have prevented it, being naturally averse to the assuming of State on any Occasion, and I was a good deal chagrin'd at their Appearance, as I could not avoid their accompanying me. What made it worse, was, that as soon as we began to move, they drew their Swords, and rode with them naked all the way. Somebody wrote an Account of this to the Proprietor, and it gave him great Offense.[8] No such Honor had been paid him when in the Province; nor to any of his Governors; and he said it was only proper to Princes of the Blood Royal; which may be true for aught I know, who was, and still am, ignorant of the Etiquette, in such Cases. This silly Affair, however greatly increas'd his Rancour against me, which was before not a little, on

2. The militia elections of December 22–24 caused great excitement, even rioting, especially when Governor Morris refused to recognize the results.
3. WTF, *Memoirs* 1.121, has "Dr. Bond." Dr. Thomas Bond led reasoned reaction to the Governor's opposition (*Papers* 6.385).
4. Franklin was elected Colonel on February 12, and officially commissioned on February 24, 1756 (*Papers* 6.409–12).
5. The *Pennsylvania Gazette*, March 25, 1756, reported a parade on March 18 of "Upwards of 1000 able-bodied effective Men, besides Officers" (*Papers* 6.411n).
6. The first review was held on February 28.
7. October 1756 (*Papers* 6.411n).
8. March 19, 1756. Franklin said on November 5, 1756, that twenty officers and thirty men accompanied him about three miles to the ferry, and rode with swords drawn "to the End of the Street, which is about 200 Yards" (*Papers* 7.13). Richard Peters complained to Thomas Penn that the troops acted "as if he had been a member of the Royal Family or Majesty itself" (*Papers* 7.73).

account of my Conduct in the Assembly, respecting the Exemption of his Estate from Taxation, which I had always oppos'd very warmly, and not without severe Reflections on his Meanness and Injustice in contending for it. He accus'd me to the Ministry as being the great Obstacle to the King's Service, preventing by my Influence in the House the proper Forming of the Bills for raising Money; and he instanc'd this Parade with my Officers as a Proof of my having an Intention to take the Government of the Province out of his Hands by Force. He also applied to Sir Everard Fawkener, then Post Master General, to deprive me of my Office. But this had no other Effect, than to procure from Sir Everard a gentle Admonition.

Notwithstanding the continual Wrangle between the Governor and the House, in which I as a Member had so large a Share, there still subsisted a civil Intercourse between that Gentleman and myself, and we never had any personal Difference. I have sometimes since thought that his little or no Resentment against me for the Answers it was known I drew up to his Messages, might be the Effect of professional Habit, and that, being bred a Lawyer, he might consider us both as merely Advocates for contending Clients in a Suit, he for the Proprietaries and I for the Assembly. He would therefore sometimes call in a friendly way to advise with me on difficult Points, and sometimes, tho' not often, take my Advice. We acted in Concert to supply Braddock's Army with Provisions, and When the shocking News arriv'd of his Defeat, the Governor sent in haste for me, to consult with him on Measures for preventing the Desertion of the back Counties. I forget now the Advice I gave, but I think it was, that Dunbar should be written to and prevail'd with if possible to post his Troops on the Frontiers for their Protection, till by Reinforcements from the Colonies, he might be able to proceed on the Expedition.—[9] And after my Return from the Frontier, he would have had me undertake the Conduct of such an Expedition with Provincial Troops, for the Reduction of Fort Duquesne, Dunbar and his Men being otherwise employ'd; and he propos'd to commission me as General. I had not so good an Opinion of my military Abilities as he profess'd to have; and I believe his Professions must have exceeded his real Sentiments: but probably he might think that my Popularity would facilitate the Raising of the Men, and my Influence in Assembly the Grant of Money to pay them;—and that, perhaps, without taxing the Proprietary Estate. Finding me not so forward to engage as he expected, the Project was dropped: and he soon after left the Government, being superseded by Captain Denny.[1]

9. On July 28, 1755, the assembly asked the Governor to request Colonel Thomas Dunbar to post his troops on the frontier (*Papers* 6.111–12).
1. News of William Denny's appointment reached Philadelphia in mid July 1756.

Before I proceed in relating the Part I had in public Affairs under this new Governor's Administration, it may not be amiss here to give some Account of the Rise and Progress of my Philosophical Reputation.

In 1746 being at Boston, I met there with a Dr. Spencer,[2] who was lately arrived from Scotland, and show'd me some electric Experiments. They were imperfectly perform'd, as he was not very expert; but being on a Subject quite new to me, they equally surpris'd and pleas'd me. Soon after my Return to Philadelphia, our Library Company receiv'd from Mr. Peter Collinson, F.R.S.[3] of London a Present of a Glass Tube, with some Account of the Use of it in making such Experiments. I eagerly seiz'd the Opportunity of repeating what I had seen at Boston, and by much Practice acquir'd great Readiness in performing those also which we had an Account of from England, adding a Number of new Ones. I say much Practice, for my House was continually full for some time, with People who came to see these new Wonders.[4] To divide a little this Incumbrance among my Friends, I caused a Number of similar Tubes to be blown at our Glass-House, with which they furnish'd themselves, so that we had at length several Performers. Among these the principal was Mr. Kinnersley, an ingenious Neighbor, who being out of Business, I encouraged to undertake showing the Experiments for Money, and drew up for him two Lectures, in which the Experiments were rang'd in such Order and accompanied with Explanations, in such Method, as that the foregoing should assist in Comprehending the following. He procur'd an elegant Apparatus for the purpose, in which all the little Machines that I had roughly made for myself, were nicely form'd by Instrument-makers. His Lectures were well attended and gave great Satisfaction; and after some time he went thro' the Colonies exhibiting them in every capital Town, and pick'd up some Money. In the West India Islands indeed it was with Difficulty the Experiments could be made, from the general Moisture of the Air.[5]

Oblig'd as we were to Mr. Collinson for his Present of the Tube, etc., I thought it right he should be inform'd of our Success in

---

2. Franklin met Archibald Spencer in Boston in May and June 1743. When Franklin again visited Boston in November–December 1746, Spencer was settled in Virginia. See J. A. Leo Lemay's "Franklin's 'Dr. Spence': The Reverend Archibald Spencer (1698?–1760), M.D." in the *Maryland Historical Magazine* 59 (1964): 199–216, 200, and 204.
3. Fellow of the Royal Society of London.
4. A solid glass rod rubbed vigorously over cloth pads to produce electrical charges. Franklin thanked Collinson for his "kind present" on March 28, 1747 (*Papers* 3.118). Franklin did some experiments at home, and others at the State House (now Independence Hall), where the Library Co. met.
5. Ebenezer Kinnersley gave the first public lectures on the Franklinian theory of electricity, including the hypothesis of the electrical nature of lightning, in Annapolis, May 15, 1749.

using it, and wrote him several Letters containing Accounts of our Experiments.[6] He got them read in the Royal Society, where they were not at first thought worth so much Notice as to be printed in their Transactions. One Paper which I wrote for Mr. Kinnersley, on the Sameness of Lightning with Electricity, I sent to Dr. Mitchel, an Acquaintance of mine, and one of the Members also of that Society; who wrote me word that it had been read but was laughed at by the Connoisseurs:[7] The Papers however being shown to Dr. Fothergill, he thought them of too much value to be stifled, and advis'd the Printing of them. Mr. Collinson then gave them to *Cave* for publication in his Gentleman's Magazine; but he chose to print them separately in a Pamphlet,[8] and Dr. Fothergill wrote the Preface. *Cave* it seems judg'd rightly for his Profit; for by the Additions that arriv'd afterwards they swell'd to a Quarto Volume, which has had five Editions, and cost him nothing for Copy-money.[9]

It was however some time before those Papers were much taken Notice of in England. A Copy of them happening to fall into the Hands of the Count de Buffon, a Philosopher deservedly of great Reputation in France, and indeed all over Europe, he prevail'd with M. Dalibard to translate them into French; and they were printed at Paris.[1] The Publication offended the Abbé Nollet, Preceptor in Natural Philosophy to the Royal Family, and an able Experimenter, who had form'd and publish'd a Theory of Electricity, which then had the general *Vogue*. He could not at first believe that such a Work came from America, and said it must have been fabricated by his Enemies at Paris, to decry his System. Afterwards having been assur'd that there really existed such a Person as Franklin of Philadelphia, which he had doubted, he wrote and published a Volume of Letters,[2] chiefly address'd to me, defending his Theory, and denying the Verity of my Experiments and of the Positions deduc'd from them. I once purpos'd

6. The earlier ones are dated May 25 and July 28, 1747, and April 29, 1749 (*Papers* 3.126–35, 156–64, 352–76).
7. This letter is dated April 29, 1749. (See *Papers* 3.365, where the original addressee is mistakenly identified as Dr. John Mitchell.) Mitchell's letter is not extant, but one in the *Gentleman's Magazine* for June 1752 (22.263) states that the experts at first "ridiculed" Franklin's theory of the electrical nature of lightning. Other aspects of his theories won immediate acceptance. William Watson, England's foremost electrical scientist, reported on them in a paper read to the Royal Society on January 21, 1748.
8. *Experiments and Observations on Electricity, made at Philadelphia in America* (1751) appeared in April 1751. Edward Cave's *Gentleman's Magazine* printed notices of Franklin's work in January and May 1750 (20.34–35, 208; *Papers* 3.472–73; 4.126).
9. Payment to author; royalties.
1. *Expériences et observations . . .* (Paris, 1752; 2nd ed. 1756). Jacques Barbeu-Dubourg made a new translation for an expanded edition in 1773.
2. Abbé Nollet, "Conjectures sur les causes de l'électricité des corps," *Mémoires de l'Académie Royale des Sciences* (1745) 107–51. *Lettres sur l'électricité* (Paris, 1753). The ensuing controversy was again reported in the *Mémoires* for 1753 (429–46, 447–74, 475–514). In essence, Franklin was marshaled on one side in an ongoing French controversy pitting Cartesianism against Newtonianism.

answering the Abbé, and actually began the Answer.[3] But on Consideration that my Writings contain'd only a Description of Experiments, which any one might repeat and verify, and if not to be verified could not be defended; or of Observations, offer'd as Conjectures, and not delivered dogmatically, therefore not laying me under any Obligation to defend them; and reflecting that a Dispute between two Persons writing in different Languages might be lengthened greatly by mis-translations, and thence misconceptions of one another's Meaning, much of one of the Abbe's Letters being founded on an Error in the Translation;[4] I concluded to let my Papers shift for themselves; believing it was better to spend what time I could spare from public Business in making new Experiments, than in Disputing about those already made. I therefore never answer'd M. Nollet; and the Event gave me no Cause to repent my Silence; for my Friend M. le Roy of the Royal Academy of Sciences took up my Cause and refuted him,[5] my Book was translated into the Italian, German and Latin Languages,[6] and the Doctrine it contain'd was by degrees universally adopted by the Philosophers of Europe in preference to that of the Abbé, so that he liv'd to see himself the last of his Sect: except Mr. B——[7] his Elève and immediate Disciple.

What gave my Book the more sudden and general Celebrity, was the Success of one of its propos'd Experiments,[8] made by Messrs. Dalibard and Delor, at Marly, for drawing Lightning from the Clouds. This engag'd the public Attention everywhere. M. Delor, who had an Apparatus for experimental Philosophy, and lectur'd in that Branch of Science, undertook to repeat what he call'd the *Philadelphia Experiments*, and after they were performed before the King and Court, all the Curious of Paris flock'd to see them.[9] I will not

3. In January 1754, Franklin indirectly answered Nollet by including David Colden's "Remarks on the Abbé Nollet's Letters on Electricity" in the 1754 edition of his *Experiments and Observations* (*Papers* 5.135–44, 186).
4. Where the preface of Franklin's *Letters* said, "He exhibits to our consideration" the existence of electrical charges, Dalibard translated it to say that Franklin had "discovered" them (*Gentleman's Magazine* 26 [1756], 513–14).
5. Le Roy's "Mémoire sur l'électricité," in the *Histoire de l'Académie Royale des Sciences*, (1753): 447–74 and ibid. (1755): 22–27 (*Papers* 6.99n). Giambatista Beccaria of Italy also replied to Nollet (*Papers* 5.395n).
6. Carlo Giuseppe Campi, trans., *Scelta di lettere e di opuscoli del Signor Beniamino Franklin* (Milan, 1774); Johan Carl Wilcke, trans. *Des Herrn Benjamin Franklins Esq. Briefe von der Elektricität* (Leipzig, 1758). A Latin translation, evidently by Jan Ingenhousz, was made but not printed (*Papers* 1.127n.); Peter W. van der Pas, "The Latin Translation of Benjamin Franklin's Letters on Electricity," *Isis* 69 (1978), 82–85.
7. Mathurin-Jaques Brisson.
8. Using the tall, pointed rods on towers that Franklin had suggested to attract lightning, Dalibard and Delor verified the electrical nature of lightning on May 10 and 18, 1752. In June 1752, before learning of their experiment, Franklin achieved similar results in his famous kite experiment (*Papers* 4.302–10), thus demonstrating not only that lightning was electrical but also that electricity was a fundamental aspect of nature, not merely an amusing phenomenon of scientific demonstrations.
9. Playful and entertaining experiments included an attempted kiss "repuls'd by the Ladies Fire" and "A Leaf of the most weighty Metals, suspended in the Air."

swell this Narrative with an Account of that capital Experiment, nor of the infinite Pleasure I receiv'd in the Success of a similar one I made soon after with a Kite at Philadelphia, as both are to be found in the Histories of Electricity.[1] Dr. Wright, an English Physician then at Paris, wrote to a Friend who was of the Royal Society an Account of the high Esteem my Experiments were in among the Learned abroad, and of their Wonder that my Writings had been so little noticed in England. The Society on this resum'd the Consideration of the Letters that had been read to them, and the celebrated Dr. Watson drew up a summary Account of them, and of all I had afterwards sent to England on the Subject, which he accompanied with some Praise of the Writer.[2] This Summary was then printed in their Transactions: And some Members of the Society in London, particularly the very ingenious Mr. Canton, having verified the Experiment of procuring Lightning from the Clouds by a Pointed Rod,[3] and acquainting them with the Success, they soon made me more than Amends for the Slight with which they had before treated me. Without my having made any Application for that Honor, they chose me a Member, and voted that I should be excus'd the customary Payments, which would have amounted to twenty-five Guineas, and ever since have given me their Transactions gratis. They also presented me with the Gold Medal of Sir Godfrey Copley for the Year 1753,[4] the Delivery of which was accompanied by a very handsome Speech of the President Lord Macclesfield, wherein I was highly honored.[5]

Our new Governor, Captain Denny, brought over for me the beforementioned Medal from the Royal Society, which he presented to me at an Entertainment given him by the City. He accompanied it with very polite Expressions of his Esteem for me, having, as he said been long acquainted with my Character. After Dinner, when the Company as was customary at that time, were engag'd in Drinking, he took me aside into another Room, and acquainted me that

---

1. Joseph Priestley, *History and Present State of Electricity* (1767), reports the kite experiment, 179–81, evidently from Franklin's own statement. An earlier notice in the *Pennsylvania Gazette*, October 19, 1752, was reprinted in the London press (*Papers* 4.366–69).

2. Edward Wright's letter has not been found, but it was probably written after the successful French experiments in May 1752. Watson had actually followed the progress of Franklin's experiments with great interest and reported his observations in detail to the Royal Society (e.g., January 21, 1748, January 11, 1750, and June 6, 1751; see *Papers* 3.135n, 457–58; 4.136–42).

3. Canton succeeded in verifying Franklin's experiment on July 20, 1752. Besides Canton, John Bevis and Benjamin Wilson also made experiments in summer 1752 (*Papers* 4.390–92).

4. Franklin was elected a fellow of the Royal Society on April 29, 1756, three years after receiving the Copley Medal (*Papers* 6.375–76).

5. Actually, the medal and speech (made November 30, 1753) were given to Collinson for delivery to Franklin. Collinson sent them to Franklin by William Smith (future Provost of the Philadelphia Academy and political enemy of Franklin) in early 1754 (*Papers* 5.126–34, 334). Governor Denny did not come over until August 1756. Perhaps Denny delivered Franklin's diploma of membership in the Royal Society at an entertainment the City Corporation of New York held for Denny on August 22.

he had been advis'd by his Friends in England to cultivate a Friendship with me, as one who was capable of giving him the best Advice, and of contributing most effectually to the making his Administration easy. That he therefore desired of all things to have a good Understanding with me; and he begg'd me to be assur'd of his Readiness on all Occasions to render me every Service that might be in his Power. He said much to me also of the Proprietor's good Dispositions towards the Province, and of the Advantage it might be to us all, and to me in particular, if the Opposition that had been so long continu'd to his Measures, were dropped, and Harmony restor'd between him and the People, in effecting which it was thought no one could be more serviceable than myself, and I might depend on adequate Acknowledgements and Recompenses, etc. etc.

The Drinkers finding we did not return immediately to the Table, sent us a Decanter of Madeira, which the Governor made liberal Use of, and in proportion became more profuse of his Solicitations and Promises. My Answers were to this purpose, that my Circumstances, Thanks to God, were such as to make Proprietary Favors unnecessary to me; and that being a Member of the Assembly I could not possibly accept of any; that however I had no personal Enmity to the Proprietary, and that whenever the public Measures he propos'd should appear to be for the Good of the People, no one should espouse and forward them more zealously than myself, my past Opposition having been founded on this, that the Measures which had been urg'd were evidently intended to serve the Proprietary Interest with great Prejudice to that of the People. That I was much obliged to him (the Governor) for his Professions of Regard to me, and that he might rely on everything in my Power to make his Administration as easy to him as possible, hoping at the same time that he had not brought with him the same unfortunate Instructions[6] his Predecessor had been hamper'd with. On this he did not then explain himself. But when he afterwards came to do Business with the Assembly they appear'd again, the Disputes were renewed, and I was as active as ever in the Opposition, being the Penman first of the Request to have a Communication of the Instructions, and then of the Remarks upon them, which may be found in the Votes of the Time, and in the Historical Review I afterwards publish'd;[7] but between us person-

6. As proprietor, Thomas Penn gave detailed instructions to his governors. The assembly distinguished these from instructions issued by the British ministry, which they willingly obeyed. The basic question was who would control the money the assembly appropriated—Penn insisted on executive rather than legislative control.
7. The assembly requested Governor Denny's instructions on August 31, 1756, and made its long remarks on them on September 23, 1756 (*Papers* 6.496, 516). Richard Jackson wrote *Historical Review of the Constitution and Government of Pennsylvania* (1759), but it was based upon materials furnished by Franklin, who paid for its publication on behalf of the assembly (*Papers* 8.360–61).

ally no Enmity arose; we were often together, he was a Man of Letters, had seen much of the World, and was very entertaining and pleasing in Conversation. He gave me the first Information that my old Friend James Ralph was still alive, that he was esteem'd one of the best political Writers in England, had been employ'd in the Dispute between Prince Frederick[8] and the King, and had obtain'd a Pension of Three Hundred a Year; that his Reputation was indeed small as a Poet, *Pope* having damn'd his Poetry in the Dunciad, but his Prose was thought as good as any Man's.

The Assembly finally, finding the Proprietaries obstinately persisted in manacling their Deputies with Instructions inconsistent not only with the Privileges of the People, but with the Service of the Crown, resolv'd to petition the King against them, and appointed me their Agent to go over to England to present and support the Petition.[9] The House had sent up a Bill to the Governor granting a Sum of Sixty Thousand Pounds for the King's Use, (10,000 Pounds of which was subjected to the Orders of the then General Lord Loudon,) which the Governor absolutely refus'd to pass, in Compliance with his Instructions.[1] I had agreed with Captain Morris[2] of the Packet at New York for my Passage, and my Stores were put on board, when Lord Loudon arriv'd at Philadelphia, expressly, as he told me to endeavour an Accommodation between the Governor and Assembly, that his Majesty's Service might not be obstructed by their Dissensions: Accordingly he desir'd the Governor and myself to meet him[3] that he might hear what was to be said on both sides.

We met and discuss'd the Business. In behalf of the Assembly I urg'd all the Arguments that may be found in the public Papers of that Time, which were of my Writing, and are printed with the Minutes of the Assembly and the Governor pleaded his Instructions, the Bond he had given to observe them, and his Ruin if he disobey'd: Yet seem'd not unwilling to hazard himself if Lord Loudon would advise it. This his Lordship did not choose to do,[4] tho' I once thought I had nearly prevail'd with him to do it; but finally he rather chose to urge the Compliance of the Assembly; and he entreated me to use my

---

8. Frederic Louis, Prince of Wales (1707–51) and father of George III (1738–1820), feuded with his own father George II (1683–1760) for refusing to increase his allowance.
9. The assembly originally, on January 28, resolved to send "a Commission, or Commissioners," but settled on Franklin on February 3 because of his great scientific reputation abroad (*Papers* 7.109–11).
1. The quarrel between Governor Denny and the assembly took place September 13–16, 1756 (*Papers* 6.504–15).
2. William Morris captained the mail boat *Halifax*, which sailed from New York on March 15, 1757 (*Papers* 7.133n).
3. On February 20, 1757, Loudoun invited Franklin to a council of war with southern governors which met in Philadelphia, March 14 (*Papers* 7.133).
4. In fact, Loudoun initiated, and Denny passed the bill on March 21, 1757, much to Thomas Penn's disgust (*Papers* 7.152–53n). Because of the emergency, the assembly had already (February 3) exempted the proprietary estates from taxation (*Papers* 7.121–32).

Endeavours with them for that purpose; declaring he could spare none of the King's Troops for the Defense of our Frontiers, and that if we did not continue to provide for that Defense ourselves they must remain expos'd to the Enemy. I acquainted the House with what had pass'd, and (presenting them with a Set of Resolutions I had drawn up,[5] declaring our Rights, and that we did not relinquish our Claim to those Rights but only suspended the Exercise of them on this Occasion thro' *Force*, against which we protested) they at length agreed to drop that Bill and frame another[6] conformable to the Proprietary Instructions. This of course the Governor pass'd, and I was then at Liberty to proceed on my Voyage: but in the meantime the Packet had sail'd with my Sea-Stores, which was some Loss to me, and my only Recompense was his Lordship's Thanks for my Service, all the Credit of obtaining the Accommodation falling to his Share.

He set out for New York before me; and as the Time for dispatching the Packet Boats, was in his Disposition, and there were two then remaining there, one of which he said was to sail very soon, I requested to know the precise time, that I might not miss her by any Delay of mine. His Answer was, I have given out that she is to sail on Saturday next, but I may let you know *entre nous*, that if you are there by Monday morning you will be in time, but do not delay longer. By some Accidental Hindrance at a Ferry, it was Monday Noon before I arrived, and I was much afraid she might have sailed as the Wind was fair, but I was soon made easy by the Information that she was still in the Harbor, and would not move till the next Day.

One would imagine that I was now on the very point of Departing for Europe. I thought so; but I was not then so well acquainted with his Lordship's Character, of which *Indecision* was one of the Strongest Features. I shall give some Instances. It was about the Beginning of April that I came to New York, and I think it was near the End of June before we sail'd.[7] There were then two of the Packet Boats which had been long in Port, but were detain'd for the General's Letters, which were always to be ready tomorrow. Another Packet arriv'd, and she too was detain'd, and before we sail'd a fourth was expected. Ours was the first to be dispatch'd, as having been there longest. Passengers were engag'd in all, and some extremely impatient to be gone, and the Merchants uneasy about their Letters, and the Orders they had given for Insurance (it being War-time) and

5. January 26, 1757 (*Papers* 7.106–09).
6. March 21, 1757 (*Papers* 7.149–52).
7. Franklin left Philadelphia April 4, arrived at New York April 8, and boarded the *General Wall* June 5. The boat anchored off Sandy Hook until June 20, sailing with Loudoun's convoy on June 23 (*Papers* 7.174). Loudoun was awaiting reinforcements from England before obeying orders to attack Quebec.

for Fall Goods. But their Anxiety avail'd nothing; his Lordship's Letters were not ready. And yet whoever waited on him found him always at his Desk, Pen in hand, and concluded he must needs write abundantly.

Going myself one Morning to pay my Respects, I found in his Antechamber one Innis, a Messenger of Philadelphia, who had come from thence express, with a Packet from Governor Denny for the General. He deliver'd to me some Letters from my Friends there, which occasion'd my enquiring when he was to return and where he lodg'd, that I might send some Letters by him. He told me he was order'd to call tomorrow at nine for the General's Answer to the Governor, and should set off immediately. I put my Letters into his Hands the same Day. A Fortnight after I met him again in the same Place. So you are soon return'd, Innis! *Return'd*; No, I am not *gone* yet.—How so?—I have call'd here by Order every Morning these two Weeks past for his Lordship's Letter, and it is not yet ready.—Is it possible, when he is so great a Writer, for I see him constantly at his Scritoire. Yes, says Innis, but he is like St. George on the Signs, *always on horseback, and never rides on.*[8] This Observation of the Messenger was it seems well founded; for when in England, I understood that Mr. Pitt gave it as one Reason for Removing this General, and sending Amherst and Wolf, *that the Ministers never heard from him, and could not know what he was doing.*[9]

This daily Expectation of Sailing, and all the three Packets going down Sandy hook, to join the Fleet there, the Passengers thought it best to be on board, lest by a sudden Order the Ships should sail, and they be left behind. There if I remember right we were about Six Weeks, consuming our Sea Stores, and oblig'd to procure more. At length the Fleet sail'd, the General and all his Army on board, bound to Louisburg with Intent to besiege and take that Fortress; all the Packet Boats in Company, ordered to attend the General's Ship, ready to receive his Dispatches when those should be ready. We were out 5 Days before we got a Letter with Leave to part; and then our Ship quitted the Fleet and steered for England. The other two Packets he still detain'd, carried them with him to Halifax, where he stayed some time to exercise the Men in sham Attacks upon sham Forts, then alter'd his Mind as to besieging Louisburg, and return'd to New York with all his Troops, together with the two Packets above-mentioned and all their Passengers.[1] During his

8. The proverb was based on a common tavern sign that showed St. George on horseback, with a slain dragon beneath. See F. P. Wilson, ed., *The Oxford Dictionary of English Proverbs*, 3rd ed. (Oxford: Clarendon Press, 1970), 693–94.
9. The *London Gazetteer*, December 22, 1757: "Except a written scrap of paper, no advice has been received from him since June or July last."
1. They arrived in New York on September 1, 1757.

Absence the French and Savages had taken Fort George on the Frontier of that Province, and the Savages had massacred many of the Garrison after Capitulation.[2]

I saw afterwards in London, Captain Bonnell, who commanded one of those Packets. He told me, that when he had been detain'd a Month, he acquainted his Lordship that his Ship was grown foul, to a degree that must necessarily hinder her fast Sailing, a Point of consequence for a Packet Boat, and requested an Allowance of Time to heave her down and clean her Bottom. He was ask'd how long time that would require. He answer'd Three Days. The General replied, If you can do it in one Day, I give leave; otherwise not; for you must certainly sail the Day after tomorrow. So he never obtain'd leave tho' detain'd afterwards from day to day during full three Months. I saw also in London one of Bonnell's Passengers,[3] who was so enrag'd against his Lordship for deceiving and detaining him so long at New York, and then carrying him to Halifax, and back again, that he swore he would sue him for Damages. Whether he did or not I never heard; but as he represented the Injury to his Affairs it was very considerable.

On the whole I then wonder'd much, how such a Man came to be entrusted with so important a Business as the Conduct of a great Army: but having since seen more of the great World, and the means of obtaining and Motives for giving Places and Employments, my Wonder is diminished. General Shirley, on whom the Command of the Army devolved upon the Death of Braddock, would in my Opinion if continued in Place, have made a much better Campaign than that of Loudon in 1757, which was frivolous, expensive and disgraceful to our Nation beyond Conception: For tho' Shirley was not a bred Soldier, he was sensible and sagacious in himself, and attentive to good Advice from others, capable of forming judicious Plans, quick and active in carrying them into Execution. Loudon, instead of defending the Colonies with his great Army, left them totally expos'd while he paraded it idly at Halifax, by which means Fort George was lost;—besides he derang'd all our mercantile Operations, and distress'd our Trade by a long Embargo[4] on the Exportation of Provisions, on pretense of keeping Supplies from being obtain'd by the Enemy, but in Reality for beating down their Price in Favor of the Contractors, in whose Profits it was said, perhaps from Suspicion

---

2. The French had captured Fort William Henry on Lake George, August 9. General Amherst built a new fort, Fort George, near the site the following year.
3. Probably Major Charles Craven, Paymaster of the 51st Regiment, who had been detained in Bonnell's packet, the *Harriott*, from May to October, 1757. Loudoun refused to promote Craven to lieutenant colonel, questioned his accounts, and reprimanded him. See Stanley M. Pargellis, *Lord Loudoun in North America* (New Haven: Yale UP, 1933), 315 and 342.
4. From March 2 to June 27, to ensure sufficient supplies for the Louisburg campaign.

only, he had a Share. And when at length the Embargo was taken off, by neglecting to send Notice of it to Charlestown, the Carolina Fleet was detain'd near three Months longer, whereby their Bottoms were so much damag'd by the Worm,[5] that a great Part of them founder'd in the Passage home. Shirley was I believe sincerely glad of being reliev'd from so burdensome a Charge as the Conduct of an Army must be to a Man unacquainted with military Business. I was at the Entertainment given by the City of New York, to Lord Loudon on his taking upon him the Command. Shirley, tho' thereby superseded, was present also. There was a great Company of Officers, Citizens and Strangers, and some Chairs having been borrowed in the Neighborhood, there was one among them very low which fell to the Lot of Mr. Shirley. Perceiving it as I sat by him, I said, they have given you, Sir, too low a Seat.—No Matter, says he; Mr. Franklin, I find *a low Seat* the easiest!

While I was, as afore-mention'd, detain'd at New York, I receiv'd all the Accounts of the Provisions, etc. that I had furnish'd to Braddock, some of which Accounts could not sooner be obtain'd from the different Persons I had employ'd to assist in the Business. I presented them to Lord Loudon, desiring to be paid the Balance. He caus'd them to be regularly examin'd by the proper Officer, who, after comparing every Article with its Voucher, certified them to be right, and the Balance due, for which his Lordship promis'd to give me an Order on the Paymaster. This, however, was put off from time to time, and tho' I called often for it by Appointment, I did not get it. At length, just before my Departure, he told me he had on better Consideration concluded not to mix his Accounts with those of his Predecessors.[6] And you, says he, when in England, have only to exhibit your Accounts at the Treasury, and you will be paid immediately. I mention'd, but without Effect, the great and unexpected Expense I had been put to by being detain'd so long at New York, as a Reason for my desiring to be presently paid; and On my observing that it was not right I should be put to any farther Trouble or Delay in obtaining the Money I had advanc'd, as I charg'd no Commissions for my Service. O, Sir, says he, you must not think of persuading us that you are no Gainer. We understand better those Affairs, and know that every one concern'd in supplying the Army finds means in the doing it to fill his own Pockets. I assur'd him that was not my Case, and that I had not pocketed a Farthing: but he appear'd

5. Wormlike mollusk that bored through ships' planks.
6. Loudoun's journal records meeting Franklin on March 15, 19, 21, and 26, and April 9, 15, 25, 26, and 30. Loudoun's journal also says about Franklin's bill: "The state of his Accounts surprised me, being £17–2–6 a Load for Carrying each Load of Forrage from Philadelphia to the Camp—His Answer as to this was the Country gave near as much more to persuade the People to go—" (Loudon Papers, LO/1717, 2:166–67, Huntington Library, San Marino, Ca.).

clearly not to believe me; and indeed I have since learned that immense Fortunes are often made in such Employments.—As to my Balance,[7] I am not paid it to this Day, of which more hereafter.

Our Captain[8] of the Packet had boasted much before we sail'd, of the Swiftness of his Ship. Unfortunately when we came to Sea, she proved the dullest of 96 Sail,[9] to his no small Mortification. After many Conjectures respecting the Cause, when we were near another Ship almost as dull as ours, which however gain'd upon us, the Captain order'd all hands to come aft and stand as near the Ensign Staff as possible. We were, Passengers included, about forty Persons. While we stood there the Ship mended her Pace, and soon left our Neighbor far behind, which prov'd clearly what our Captain suspected, that she was loaded too much by the Head. The Casks of Water it seems had been all plac'd forward. These he therefore order'd to be remov'd farther aft; on which the Ship recover'd her Character, and prov'd the best Sailor in the Fleet.

The Captain said she had once gone at the Rate of 13 Knots, which is accounted 13 Miles per hour.[1] We had on board as a Passenger Captain Kennedy[2] of the Navy, who contended that it was impossible, that no Ship ever sailed so fast, and that there must have been some Error in the Division of the Log-Line, or some Mistake in heaving the Log. A Wager ensu'd between the two Captains, to be decided when there should be sufficient Wind. Kennedy thereupon examin'd rigorously the Log-line, and being satisfied with that, he determin'd to throw the Log himself. Accordingly some Days after when the Wind blew very fair and fresh, and the Captain of the Packet (Lutwidge) said he believ'd she then went at the Rate of 13 Knots, Kennedy made the Experiment, and own'd his Wager lost.

The above Fact I give for the sake of the following Observation. It has been remark'd as an Imperfection in the Art of Shipbuilding, that it can never be known 'till she is tried, whether a new Ship will or will not be a good Sailer; for that the Model of a good sailing Ship has been exactly follow'd in a new One, which has prov'd on the contrary remarkably dull. I apprehend this may be partly occasion'd by the different Opinions of Seamen respecting the Modes of lading, rigging and sailing of a Ship. Each has his System. And the same Vessel laden by the Judgment and Orders of one Captain shall sail better or worse than when by the Orders of another. Besides, it scarce ever happens that a Ship is form'd, fitted for the Sea, and

---

7. The balance owed to Franklin was only £17 12s. 6d.
8. Franklin paid Walter Lutwidge, master of the *General Wall*, 50 guineas on May 5, 1758—fare for himself, son, and two slaves (*Papers* 7.234n).
9. Loudoun's convoy had more than 100 ships (Gipson, *British Empire*, 7.102).
1. Nautical miles, or about seventeen land miles per hour.
2. Archibald Kennedy, Jr.

sail'd by the same Person. One Man builds the Hull, another rigs her, a third lades and sails her. No one of these has the Advantage of knowing all the Ideas and Experience of the others, and therefore cannot draw just Conclusions from a Combination of the whole. Even in the simple Operation of Sailing when at Sea, I have often observ'd different Judgments in the Officers who commanded the successive Watches, the Wind being the same. One would have the Sails trimm'd sharper or flatter than another, so that they seem'd to have no certain Rule to govern by. Yet I think a Set of Experiments might be instituted, first to determine the most proper Form of the Hull for swift sailing; next the best Dimensions and properest Place for the Masts; then the Form and Quantity of Sail, and their Position as the Winds may be; and lastly the Disposition of her Lading. This is the Age of Experiments; and such a Set accurately made and combin'd would be of great Use. I am therefore persuaded that ere long some ingenious Philosopher will undertake it—to whom I wish Success.

We were several times chas'd on our Passage,[3] but outsail'd everything, and in thirty Days had Sounding.[4] We had a good Observation,[5] and the Captain judg'd himself so near our Port, (Falmouth)[6] that if we made a good Run in the Night we might be off the Mouth of that Harbor in the Morning, and by running in the Night might escape the Notice of the Enemy's Privateers, who often cruis'd near the Entrance of the Channel. Accordingly all the Sail was set that we could possibly make, and the Wind being very fresh and fair, we went right before it, and made great Way. The Captain after his Observation, shap'd his Course as he thought so as to pass wide of the Scilly Isles,[7] but it seems there is sometimes a strong Indraft setting up St. George's Channel[8] which deceives Seamen, and caus'd the Loss of Sir Cloudsley Shovel's Squadron. This Indraft was probably the Cause of what happen'd to us. We had a Watchman plac'd in the Bow to whom they often call'd, *Look well out before, there*; and he as often answer'd *Aye, Aye!* But perhaps had his Eyes shut, and was half asleep at the time: they sometimes answering as is said mechanically: For he did not see a Light just before us, which had been hid by the Studding Sails from the Man at Helm and from the rest of the Watch; but by an accidental Yaw of the Ship was discover'd, and occasion'd a great Alarm, we being very near it, the

---

3. William Franklin also reported they were "several Times chac'd," apparently by French warships (*Papers* 7.244).
4. The lead line touched bottom, showing they were near shore.
5. Could determine their location from the position of the sun.
6. On the coast of Cornwall.
7. Group of islands and rocks twenty-five miles west of Land's End, southwestern tip of England.
8. Between Ireland and Wales.

light appearing to me as big as a Cart Wheel. It was Midnight, and Our Captain fast asleep. But Captain Kennedy jumping upon Deck, and seeing the Danger, ordered the Ship to wear round, all Sails standing. An Operation dangerous to the Masts, but it carried us clear, and we escap'd Shipwreck, for we were running right upon the Rocks on which the Lighthouse was erected. This Deliverance impress'd me strongly with the Utility of Lighthouses, and made me resolve to encourage the building more of them in America, if I should live to return there.[9]

In the Morning it was found by the Soundings, etc. that we were near our Port, but a thick Fog hid the Land from our Sight. About 9 o'Clock the Fog began to rise, and seem'd to be lifted up from the Water like the Curtain at a Playhouse, discovering underneath the Town of Falmouth, the Vessels in its Harbor, and the Fields that surrounded it. A most pleasing Spectacle to those who had been so long without any other Prospects, than the uniform View of a vacant Ocean! And it gave us the more Pleasure, as we were now freed from the Anxieties which the State of War occasion'd.

I set out immediately with my Son for London, and we only stopped a little by the Way to view Stonehenge on Salisbury Plain, and Lord Pembroke's House and Gardens, with his very curious Antiquities at Wilton.[1]

We arriv'd in London the 27th of July 1757.[2] [*Part Four*] As soon as I was settled in a Lodging Mr. Charles had provided for me,[3] I went to visit Dr. Fothergill, to whom I was strongly recommended, and whose Counsel respecting my Proceedings I was advis'd to obtain. He was against an immediate Complaint to Government, and thought the Proprietaries should first be personally applied to, who might possibly be induc'd by the Interposition and Persuasion of some private Friends to accommodate Matters amicably. I then waited on my old Friend and Correspondent Mr. Peter Collinson, who told me that John Hanbury, the great Virginia Merchant, had requested to be informed when I should arrive, that he might carry

---

9. At the time, Franklin wrote: "Were I a Roman Catholic, perhaps I should on this occasion vow to build a chapel to some saint; but as I am not, if I were to vow at all, it should be to build a *lighthouse*" (*Papers* 7.243).
1. Stonehenge is about ten miles north of Salisbury. Wilton House, where Sir Philip Sidney wrote his *Arcadia*, is famous for magnificent gardens, architecture, and art. The mansion of Sidney's day was destroyed in England's Civil War but rebuilt in the late seventeenth century.
2. Franklin arrived at Falmouth on July 17, 1757, and reached London on the evening of July 26 (*Papers* 7.243–45). This sentence concludes Part Three of the *Autobiography*, and was the last sentence in the ms. copies of the *Autobiography* that Franklin sent to Benjamin Vaughan and to Louis Le Veillard in November 1789, and therefore the last sentence in the *Autobiography* as printed by William Temple Franklin in 1818.
3. Franklin seems actually to have stayed with Peter Collinson his first night (July 26) in London, then at the Bear Inn for three nights (July 27–29), and, beginning on July 30, with Mrs. Margaret Stevenson on Craven Street.

me to Lord Granville's, who was then President of the Council,[4] and wish'd to see me as soon as possible. I agreed to go with him the next Morning. Accordingly Mr. Hanbury called for me and took me in his Carriage to that Nobleman's, who receiv'd me with great Civility; and after some Questions respecting the present State of Affairs in America, and Discourse thereupon, he said to me, "You Americans have wrong Ideas of the Nature of your Constitution; you contend that the King's Instructions to his Governors are not Laws, and think yourselves at Liberty to regard or disregard them at your own Discretion. But those Instructions are not like the Pocket Instructions given to a Minister going abroad, for regulating his Conduct in some trifling Point of Ceremony. They are first drawn up by Judges learned in the Laws; they are then considered, debated and perhaps amended in Council, after which they are signed by the King. They are then so far as relates to you, the *Law of the Land*; for THE KING IS THE LEGISLATOR OF THE COLONIES."[5]

I told his Lordship this was new Doctrine to me. I had always understood from our Charters, that our Laws were to be made by our Assemblies, to be presented indeed to the King for his Royal Assent, but that being once given the King could not repeal or alter them. And as the Assemblies could not make permanent Laws without his Assent, so neither could he make a Law for them without theirs. He assur'd me I was totally mistaken. I did not think so however. And his Lordship's Conversation having a little alarm'd me as to what might be the Sentiments of the Court concerning us, I wrote it down as soon as I return'd to my Lodgings.—[6] I recollected that about 20 Years before, a Clause in a Bill brought into Parliament by the Ministry, had propos'd to make the King's Instructions Laws in the Colonies; but the Clause was thrown out by the Commons, for which we ador'd them as our Friends and Friends of Liberty, till by their Conduct towards us in 1765, it seem'd that they had refus'd that Point of Sovereignty to the King, only that they might reserve it for themselves.[7]

After some Days, Dr. Fothergill having spoken to the Proprietaries, they agreed to a Meeting with me at Mr. J. Penn's[8] House in Spring Garden. The Conversation at first consisted of mutual Declarations

---

4. The Privy Council, or the King-in-Council, ruled the nation in the King's name.
5. For other versions, see Franklin's letters of March 19, 1759, January 13, 1772, and April 29, 1781 (*Papers* 8.293, 19.11).
6. Franklin evidently had the memo in January 1772, but it has disappeared (*Papers* 19.11).
7. The 1744 bill containing this clause died when Parliament adjourned for the summer. See Leo Francis Stock, ed., *Proceedings and Debates of the British Parliaments Respecting North America*, 5 vols. (Washington, D.C.: Carnegie Institution, 1924–41), 5.187. After repealing the Stamp Act in 1766, Parliament passed the Declaratory Act asserting the right to legislate for the colonies without their consent "in all cases whatsoever."
8. Not John Penn, but Thomas Penn. The interviews at Penn's house were on August 13 and 16 (*Papers* 7.250n, 291).

of Disposition to reasonable Accommodation; but I suppose each Party had its own Ideas of what should be meant by *reasonable*. We then went into Consideration of our several Points of Complaint which I enumerated. The Proprietaries justified their Conduct as well as they could, and I the Assembly's. We now appeared very wide, and so far from each other in our Opinions, as to discourage all Hope of Agreement. However, it was concluded that I should give them the Heads of our Complaints in Writing, and they promis'd then to consider them.—I did so soon after; but they put the Paper into the Hands of their Solicitor Ferdinando John Paris, who manag'd for them all their Law Business in their great Suit with the neighboring Proprietary of Maryland, Lord Baltimore, which had subsisted 70 Years,[9] and wrote for them all their Papers and Messages in their Dispute with the Assembly. He was a proud angry Man; and as I had occasionally in the Answers of the Assembly treated his Papers with some Severity, they being really weak in point of Argument, and haughty in Expression, he had conceiv'd a mortal Enmity to me,[1] which discovering itself whenever we met, I declin'd the Proprietary's Proposal that he and I should discuss the Heads of Complaint between our two selves, and refus'd treating with anyone but them. They then by his Advice put the Paper into the Hands of the Attorney and Solicitor General[2] for their Opinion and Counsel upon it, where it lay unanswered a Year wanting eight Days,[3] during which time I made frequent Demands of an Answer from the Proprietaries but without obtaining any other than that they had not yet receiv'd the Opinion of the Attorney and Solicitor General: What it was when they did receive it I never learned, for they did not communicate it to me, but sent a long Message to the Assembly drawn and signed by Paris reciting my Paper, complaining of its want of Formality[4] as a Rudeness on my part, and giving a flimsy Justification of their Conduct, adding that they should be willing to accommodate Matters, if the Assembly would send over *some Person of Candor* to treat with them for that purpose, intimating thereby that I was not such.[5]

9. The boundary dispute was settled by the Mason-Dixon line in 1767.
1. Governor Morris warned Paris to be wary of Franklin as having "nothing in view but to serve himself" (*Papers* 7.247n).
2. Franklin did not know that the "paper" sent to Charles Pratt, Attorney General, and Charles Yorke, Solicitor General, was a subverted version of his "Heads of Complaint." The officials had to give answers favoring the proprietors.
3. Yorke replied January 13, 1758, but Pratt delayed until November, thus preventing Penn's replying earlier (*Papers* 7.366).
4. Thomas Penn called Franklin's complaints "a loose Paper not address'd to any body" (*Papers* 7.251–52; cf. 8.184).
5. Although the proprietors did not send Franklin copies of the opinions of the Attorney and Solicitor General, they incorporated elements of these opinions in their answer to Franklin, dated November 27, 1758, which expressed the wish that the assembly would send over "some Persons of Candour" to treat with them (*Papers* 8.179–83). But the proprietors did not give him a copy of their message (November 28, 1758) to the assembly complaining of his "Disrespect" (*Papers* 8.184).

The want of Formality or Rudeness, was probably my not having address'd the Paper to them with their assum'd Titles of true and absolute Proprietaries of the Province of Pennsylvania, which I omitted as not thinking it necessary in a Paper the Intention of which was only to reduce to a Certainty by writing what in Conversation I had delivered *vivâ voce*. But during this Delay, the Assembly having prevail'd with Governor Denny to pass an Act[6] taxing the Proprietary Estate in common with the Estates of the People, which was the grand Point in Dispute, they omitted answering the Message.

When the Act however came over, the Proprietaries counsell'd by Paris[7] determin'd to oppose its receiving the Royal Assent. Accordingly they petition'd the King in Council, and a Hearing[8] was appointed, in which two Lawyers were employ'd by them against the Act, and two by me in Support of it. They alledg'd that the Act was intended to load the Proprietary Estate in order to spare those of the People, and that if it were suffer'd to continue in force, and the Proprietaries who were in Odium with the People, left to their Mercy in proportioning the Taxes, they would inevitably be ruined. We replied that the Act had no such Intention and would have no such Effect. That the Assessors were honest and discreet Men, under an Oath to assess fairly and equitably, and that any Advantage each of them might expect in lessening his own Tax by augmenting that of the Proprietaries was too trifling to induce them to perjure themselves. This is the purport of what I remember as urg'd by both Sides, except that we insisted strongly on the mischievous Consequences that must attend a Repeal; for that the Money, 100,000 Pounds, being printed and given to the King's Use, expended in his Service, and now spread among the People, the Repeal would strike it dead in their Hands to the Ruin of many, and the total Discouragement of future Grants, and the Selfishness of the Proprietors in soliciting such a general Catastrophe, merely from a groundless Fear of their Estate being taxed too highly, was insisted on in the strongest Terms.

On this Lord Mansfield, one of the Council rose, and beckoning to me, took me into the Clerk's Chamber, while the Lawyers were pleading, and ask'd me if I was really of Opinion that no Injury would be done the Proprietary Estate in the Execution of the Act. I said, Certainly. Then says he, you can have little Objection to enter into an Engagement to assure that Point. I answer'd None, at all. He then call'd in Paris, and after some Discourse his Lordship's

---

6. Denny signed on June 20, 1759 (*Papers* 8.419n).
7. Not Paris, who died on December 16, 1759, but Henry Wilmot (*Papers* 9.126).
8. Actually two hearings: Pratt and Yorke represented the proprietors, and William de Grey and Richard Jackson represented the assembly before the Board of Trade (May–June) which found in favor of the Penns. Franklin's lawyer, Francis Eyre, then appealed in the hearing described here (August, 27–28, 1760; *Papers* 8.396n.; 9.197).

Proposition was accepted on both Sides; a Paper to the purpose was drawn up by the Clerk of the Council, which I sign'd with Mr. Charles, who was also an Agent of the Province for their ordinary Affairs; when Lord Mansfield return'd to the Council Chamber where finally the Law was allowed to pass. Some Changes were however recommended and we also engag'd they should be made by a subsequent Law; but the Assembly did not think them necessary. For one Year's Tax having been levied by the Act before the Order of Council arrived, they appointed a Committee to examine the Proceedings of the Assessors, and On this Committee they put several particular Friends of the Proprietaries. After a full Enquiry they unanimously sign'd a Report that they found the Tax had been assess'd with perfect Equity.

The Assembly look'd on my entering into the first Part of the Engagement as an essential Service to the Province, since it secur'd the Credit of the Paper Money then spread over all the Country; and they gave me their Thanks in form when I return'd.[9] But the Proprietaries were enrag'd at Governor Denny for having pass'd the Act, and turn'd him out, with Threats of suing him for Breach of Instructions which he had given Bond to observe. He however having done it at the Instance of the General[1] and for his Majesty's Service, and having some powerful Interest at Court, despis'd the Threats, and they were never put in Execution

---

9. Franklin arrived in Philadelphia on November 1, 1762, and the Assembly voted him their thanks on February 19, 1763 (*Papers* 10.153n, 196–97, 238).
1. General Lord Jeffrey Amherst pressured the Governor and the assembly by threatening to remove his troops from the Pennsylvania frontier (*Papers* 8.326n).

"A Quire Book of Letters"[†]

The collection of letters to and from Franklin, which relate to the provisioning of Braddock's troops, has long been missing. It was rediscovered in the British Library by the historian Alan Houston in 2007, though with twelve missing pages. Although Franklin had entered a note in his manuscript where he wanted to insert the correspondence, it seems unlikely that he would have interrupted his narrative to have the reader peruse all forty-nine letters. More likely, he would have selected extracts from them, or perhaps had them all printed as a long running footnote below the narrative, or as an appendix, as they appear here.

All footnotes in this section are by Alan Houston, though edited to match others in this Norton Critical Edition, and are reprinted with his permission.

To John Ridout[1]

Dear Sir,[2]   Philadelphia Apr. 4. 1755.
I have been but a few Weeks returned from a Journey of six months.[3] About ten Days since I sent you Douglas's Summary in two Volumes unbound, which I brought you from Boston.[4] I hope they

[†] From Alan Houston, "Benjamin Franklin and the 'Wagon Affair' of 1755," *William and Mary Quarterly*, 3d ser., 66 (2009): 235–86. Reprinted by permission of the Omohundro Institute of Early American History and Culture.

1. In preparing these texts, I have adopted the following guidelines. Thomas Birch's manuscript presents the letters in rough chronological order. I have moved a handful of items so they appear in the order in which they were composed. * * * I give full citations for the two letters to Richard Partridge, interleaved here with the materials copied by Birch. All editorial insertions, including words added for textual clarity, are in brackets. All other material—including salutations, quotation marks, and asterisks—is in the original manuscript. The place and date of composition are set at the top. I have retained the original spelling, capitalization, and punctuation, except that every sentence now begins with a capital letter and ends with a period or other appropriate mark. I have expanded contractions and abbreviations, except in proper names; lowered superscripts; rendered ampersands as "and," except in the form "&c."; eliminated duplicated carryover words at the top of recto pages; spelled out the tailed "p" as "per"; and altered symbols of weights, measures, and monetary values to conform to modern usage.

2. John Ridout (1732–1797), English-born and Oxford-educated secretary to Governor Horatio Sharpe of Maryland.

3. Franklin traveled with fellow Deputy Postmaster for North America William Hunter (d. 1761) to Boston on postal business in September 1754; he returned to Philadelphia in late February 1755.

4. William Douglass, *A Summary, Historical and Political, of the first Planting, progressive Improvements, and present State of the* British Settlements in North-America . . . , 2 vols. (Boston, 1749–52). In 1766 Franklin recommended Douglass's *Summary* as "the most complete work on the British Colonies in North America." See "Gottfried Achenwall:

got safe to hand, for I did not know the person I sent them by. He was a short well-set Man, and I took him to be an Express from Annapolis, particularly as he presented your Compliments, and desired to know if I had any Commands for that place. I had not time to write by him, being just going to the Assembly.

Our House sent up a Bill last Week to the Governor granting £25,000 to the King's use, to be struck in bills of Credit, and sunk by the Excise in ten Years.[5] £5,000 of it was subjected to the Orders or Draughts of General Braddock; £5,000 to repay the money borrowed to purchase provisions for the Virginia Troops; £10,000 to New England, and £5,000 for clearing Roads, paying posts, Express &c. and with the General's Dispatches and other Expenses for the King's service. The Governor refusing to pass it, they have given £10,000 out of their Loan-Office Money to victual the New England Troops, about to make a diversion in favour of General Braddock, by attacking the French nearer home, and so obliging them to withdraw their troops from the Ohio, or at least prevent sending any reinforcements to them. This, they hope, that great Officer will take kindly of them, as it is all they have at present in their power; This £10,000 and the £5,000 borrowed before to buy the Wheat, and transport it to his army, exhausting their Treasury to the last farthing. They think he was rather too hasty in condemning them unheard in their dispute with their Governor; and think they could justify themselves to his satisfaction, if it were worth his while to attend to their State of the Case. But they suppose his time is employed in more important Affairs; and that he will by degrees receive more favourable sentiments of their Conduct.[6]

You are to have a grand Congress at Annapolis.[7] I pray God to bless your Counsels. When you have an opportunity be so good as to send the inclosed paper of Seeds to Major Barnes[8] with my

Some Observations on North America from Oral Information by Dr. Franklin," in Leonard Labaree, et al., *Papers of Benjamin Franklin* (New Haven: Yale Up, 1959), 13:346–77 (quotation, 13.348). Hereinafter *Papers.*

5. The bill, approved by the assembly on March 28, was intended to support Governor William Shirley's expedition against the French at Crown Point. Because the bill did not exempt the proprietors from taxes used to fund it, the governor refused his assent. On April 2 the House adopted an alternative scheme—proposed by Franklin, and not requiring the governor's approval—that funds be drawn on the Loan Office. See *Votes and Proceedings of the House . . .* (Philadelphia, 1755), 77–83; and above, pp. 126–27.

6. According to Franklin, Edward Braddock had "conceived violent Prejudices against" the assembly as "averse to the Service." See above, p. 127 (quotation). In March 1755, Braddock complained to imperial authorities that Pennsylvania, "tho' by far the richest and most populous Colony . . . has, as yet, contributed nothing" to the war effort. See Braddock to Sir Thomas Robinson, Mar. 18, 1755, British Library, Additional Manuscripts 32853, fol. 347.

7. The council was moved from Annapolis, Md., to Alexandria, Va., and convened on April 14. In addition to Edward Braddock and Augustus Keppel, the naval commander of North America, it included five colonial governors: James Delancey (New York), Robert Dinwiddie (Virginia), Robert Hunter Morris (Pennsylvania), Horatio Sharpe (Maryland), and William Shirley (Massachusetts). See BL Add. MSS 33029, fols. 174–76.

8. Abraham Barnes (ca. 1715–ca. 1778), Maryland assemblyman and delegate to the Albany Congress of 1754.

best respects. They are what he much wanted when here; and the fruit will, he thinks, be of great use to Mary Land, if propagated there.

My respectfull Compliments to Governor Sharpe;[9] and believe me to be with the greatest respect and esteem,

Dear Sir,

Your most humble Servant
B.F.

From Edward Braddock

[Frederick, Apr. 22, 1755]

By his Excellency Edward Braddock Esq, General and Commander in Chief of all his Majesty's Forces in North America.

To Benjamin Franklin Esq.

By virtue of the power and Authority to me given and granted [fol. 190l] by his Majesty, I do hereby empower you to contract and agree for one hundred and fifty Waggons with a team of four horses to each waggon, and for fifteen hundred horses, for the service of his Majesty's forces under my Command, or to appoint such persons under you for Transacting the said business, as shall be necessary, hereby empowering you to appoint two Waggon Masters to take care of the said Waggons and horses, and to conduct them to Fort Cumberland at Wills's Creek, there to receive my further Orders. And I promise to ratify and confirm such engagements, as you or such persons, as you shall appoint, shall enter into in consequence of the power hereby given you, and conformable to the instructions you shall herewith receive from me. Given at the Camp at Frederick this twenty second day of April 1755.

E. Braddock
   By his Excellency's Command
      W. Shirley
Benjamin Franklin Esq.

From Edward Braddock

[Frederick, Apr. 22, 1755]

Instructions to Benjamin Franklin Esq.

    1. You will with all convenient speed contract for one hundred and fifty waggons and 1500 horses to join the forces at Wills's Creek, and to proceed with the Army according to the orders they shall receive from me.

---

9. Horatio Sharpe (1718–1790), governor of Maryland from 1753 to 1769 and commander in chief of British forces in America prior to Edward Braddock's arrival in spring 1755.

2. You will settle the price of each Waggon at as low a rate as shall be practicable, not exceeding ten shillings sterling per day; as also the price of the horses, not allowing above two shillings sterling per day for each of them.

3. You will likewise provide saddles and furniture for each of the horses, or as many as can be met with.

4. You will fix upon two proper persons for wagon-masters, to take care of the said Waggons and horses, who shall receive from me such pay, as you shall promise them for their trouble, not exceeding five shillings sterling per day.

5. You will take care, that the Waggons and Teams, as also the horses, that shall be contracted for, be valued by two persons to be chosen by your self, or such persons, as shall be appointed by you and two more by the owners of the said Waggons and Horses; and are to inform the said Owners, that in case of the [loss of any of the] said Waggons and Horses or Teams, they shall be allowed the price of them, according to the said Valuation.

6. The pay of the Waggons and Horses you shall contract for is to commence from the time of their joining the Forces at Wills's Creek: and you are to make them such allowance for the time, that may be required for their going thither, as shall be reasonable.

7. You will take care, that every Waggon, which shall be hired for this service, is loaded with forage, and every horse with corn, for their own subsistence: and whatever they bring more than they use for that purpose, will be taken for the use of the Army, and a reasonable price paid for it.

8. You are in my name to assure the several persons hired for the service of the Waggons and Horses, that they shall on no account whatever be called up to do the Duty of Soldiers, or be otherwise employed than is necessary for conducting and taking care of their Carriages and Horses.

9. You will give orders to the persons, you shall appoint to transact the business intrusted to you, that they act conformable to these Instructions, who shall receive such allowance for their troubles, as you shall think reasonable.

E. Braddock.

Mem. The Terms to be proposed by the above Instructions were dictated by B.F.'s advice, as most likely to obtain what was wanted.

Pennsylvania Assembly Committee[1]

MINUTES OF THE COMMITTEE

April 24. 1755

Present Isaac Norris, Evan Morgan, Joseph Stretch, Joseph Fox, James Pemberton, William Callendar, and Joseph Trotter[2] The Secretary laid before us a Letter from Geo. Croghan and other Commissioners for laying out roads thro' this Province towards the Ohio,[3] which was read, as also a Letter from the Governor to this Committee in the following Words, viz.

[Here insert it][4]

1. The committee of the assembly appointed to disburse the £15,000 appropriated for defense on April 2. These minutes were evidently enclosed with Isaac Norris's letter of April 29 (see p. 172 of this Norton Critical Edition).
2. Isaac Norris (1701–1766), Philadelphia merchant and Quaker politician, was speaker of the House, 1750–1764. Evan Morgan (1709–1763) was a Philadelphia merchant and manager of the Pennsylvania Hospital. Joseph Stretch (n.d.) was director of the Library Company. Joseph Fox (1709–1779) was a Philadelphia landowner and carpenter. James Pemberton (1723–1809) was a Quaker merchant and politician. William Callender (b. 1703) and Joseph Trotter (d. 1778) were Philadelphia Quakers and politicians. Franklin was also a member of this committee.
3. On February 14 Quartermaster-General Sir John St. Clair wrote Governor Robert Hunter Morris, asking that two roads be built in Pennsylvania, one through the Cumber land Valley to Wills's Creek, the other to run westward from Shippensburg to the mouth of the Youghiogheny. George Croghan—an experienced Indian agent and fur trader— and four others were appointed by Morris to survey the latter route. See St. Clair to Morris, Feb. 14, 1755, in Samuel Hazard, *Minutes of the Provincial Council of Pennsylvania* . . . (Philadelphia, 1851–52), 6.300–1; Morris to Croghan et al., ibid., 6.318–19. The commission's letter of April 16, which included an account of St. Clair's storming "like a Lyon Rampant" and threatening to "oblige the Inhabitants" with "Fire and Sword," is in Geo. Croghan et al. to [Morris], Apr. 16, 1755, ibid., 6.368–69. For this outburst St. Clair "receiv'd from ye Gen'l, what is call'd, in ye Language of ye' Camp, a *Set Down*." See Franklin Thayer Tucker, "The Braddock Expedition" (Ph.D. diss., Harvard University, 1946), 199.
4. Brackets and note in original. The letter was printed as:

[Philadelphia, Apr. 24, 1755]

Gentlemen—By a Letter I have received this morning from the Commissioners for running out the Roads over the Hills, I find the Flower ordered to be provided for the Army has not been yet delivered at the Place agreed on, and the Retardation of the March with the Consequences that may thence ensue is ascribed by Sir John St. Clair to this Delay and the not clearing proper Roads.

I am indeed much surprised at the Flower's not having been delivered according to the Time fixed, and urge You to do all in your Power to expedite the Delivery of it. I think Orders should issue immediately by the Return of this express to have the Roads cleared with all possible Expedition at the Expence of the Province, and desire Supplies may be forthwith sent for that Purpose.

The Sasquehannah Indians expect a Present, which need not be great as they have no particular Business, and only come down to assure Us of the Continuance of their Friendship for Us. Pray give the necessary Orders that they may go out of Town and reach the Place of their Habitations before the Message arrives from the Six Nations and Col. Johnson, as mentioned in the Minutes, which the Secretary has my Orders to show you.

I am, Gentlemen, Your most humble Servant,

Rob't H. Morris

See Robert Hunter Morris to the Committee of Assembly, Apr. 24, 1755, in Hazard, *Minutes of Provincial Council of Pennsylvania* 6.374.

Evan Morgan likewise produced a Letter from John Smith of Carlisle, with a Copy of a Letter inclosed from one of the Commissioners for laying out the aforesaid Roads.

The Committee taking the several matters into their consideration were of Opinion, that some small present should be made to the Indians now here at the Expence of the Province; and that it may be necessary to dispatch them as soon as possible, to lessen the charge.

As the executive part of the Government neither does nor ought to be vested in the Assemblies of this province, we can only declare our Concern the Governor had not been pleased to pass our Bill, in which the clearing of roads and all the purposes recommended to us by the Crown had been provided for, according to our abilities.

Nevertheless, as we are willing to do every thing in our power for the King's service and welfare of this province, resolved, that the following Minute be signed by all the Members present, and sent to the Governor, viz.

"We are unanimously of Opinion, that the Assembly will very chearfully defray the reasonable Expenses arising upon the opening of such Roads, as may be judged necessary for the march of the King's Troops thro' the Province towards the Ohio.

"We are also of opinion, that some small present should be made to the Indians now here at the Expence of the Province; and that it may be necessary to dispatch them as soon as possible, to lessen the charge.

	Isaac Norris
	Evan Morgan
To Robert Hunter Morris Esq	Joseph Fox
Lieutenant Governor of Pennsylvania[5]	Joseph Stretch
	Joseph Trotter
	James Pemberton
	William Callender

Wagon Advertisement[6]

Advertisement of the Time as printed in one sheet with the following address:

To the Inhabitants of the Counties of Lancaster York and Cumberland.

---

5. Robert Hunter Morris's response, in a letter of instructions from Richard Peters dated April 25, is repr. in Peters to Commissioners, Apr. 25, 1755, ibid., 6.376–77.
6. This document is a copy of the famous "wagon advertisement," printed by William Dunlap in Lancaster. Thomas Birch's copy leaves out the first half of the broadside, which lays out the terms being offered, and begins with Franklin's letter of address. For the terms, see "Advertisement," Apr. 26, 1755, above, p. 128.

Lancaster Apr. 26 1755.

Friends and Countrymen,

Being occasionally at the Camp at Frederic a few days since, I found the General and officers of the Army extremely exasperated on account of their not being supplied with Horses and Carriages, which had been expected from this province as most able to furnish them; but, thro' the dissensions between our Governor and Assembly, Money hath not been provided nor any taken for that purpose.[7]

It was proposed to send an armed Force immediately into these Counties, to seize as many of the best Carriages and Horses as should be wanted, and compel as many Persons into the Service as would be necessary to Drive and take care of them.

I apprehended that the Progress of a Body of Soldiers thro' these Counties on such an Occasion, especially considering the Temper they are in, and their Resentment against us, would be attended with many and great Inconveniencies to the Inhabitants; and therefore more willingly undertook the Trouble of trying first what might be done by fair and equitable Means.

The People of these back Counties have lately complained to the Assembly that a sufficient Currency was wanting; you have now an Opportunity of receiving and dividing among you a very considerable Sum; for if the Service of this Expedition should continue (as it's more than probable it will) for 120 Days, the Hire of these Waggons and Horses will amount to upwards of *Thirty thousand Pounds*, which will be paid you in Silver and Gold of the King's Money.

The Service will be light and easy, for the Army will scarce march above 12 Miles per Day, and the Waggons and Baggage Horses, as they carry those Things that are absolutely necessary to the Welfare of the Army, must march with the Army and no faster, and are, for the Army's sake, always placed where they can be most secure, whether on a March or in Camp.

If you are really, as I believe you are, good and loyal Subjects to His Majesty, you may now do a most acceptable Service, and make it easy to yourselves; for three or four of such as cannot separately spare from the Business of their Plantations a Waggon and four Horses and a Driver, may do it together, one furnishing the Waggon, another one or two Horses, and another the Driver, and divide the Pay proportionably between you. But if you do not this Service to your King and Country voluntarily, when such good Pay and reasonable Terms are offered you, your Loyalty will be strongly suspected; the King's Business must be done; so many brave Troops, come so far for your Defence, must not stand idle, thro' your backwardness to do what may be reasonably expected from you; Waggons

---

7. The remainder of Thomas Birch's copy of the wagon advertisement is part of the twelve missing pages. Beginning here I supply a transcription from the printed broadside (see the figure on p. 128).

and Horses must be had; violent Measures will probably be used; and you will be to seek for a Recompence where you can find it, and your Case perhaps be little pitied or regarded.

I have no particular Interest in this Affair; as (except the Satisfaction of endeavouring to do Good and prevent Mischief) I shall have only my Labour for my Pains. If this Method of obtaining the Waggons and Horses is not like to succeed, I am oblig'd to send Word to the General in fourteen Days; and I suppose Sir *John St. Clair* the Hussar, with a Body of Soldiers, will immediately enter the Province, for the Purpose aforesaid, of which I shall be sorry to hear, because I *am*,

> *very sincerely and truly*
> *your Friend and Well-wisher,*   B. FRANKLIN

From John Smith[8]

Sir,   Carlisle 26 Apr. 1755.

According to promise I spoke to Wm. Buchanan about acting as Post-Master in Carlisle: and he tells me he is willing, if you will be so good as to give him directions how to act, which I suppose you will do.[9]

There is likewise a young Man here, that proposes to ride, if he knew the Encouragement, either from here to Philadelphia or to Winchester. But it is to be considered, that if one man rides either from here to Philadelphia or to Winchester once a week, that he must keep too [two] good horses at least, which will be attended with great Expence, and his Wages must be sufficient to defray it.

Our Country is siezed with a very great panic lest Sir John St. Clair should be as good as his Word in coming down and forcing them to clear and open the road towards the Ohio. I beg, if possi-

---

8. John Smith (1722–1794), a native of County Tyrone, Ireland, emigrated with his family to Lancaster in 1728. After moving to Carlisle in 1750, he climbed the local political ladder, from justice to assemblyman. In 1759 he resettled in Baltimore. See Charles G. Steffen, *From Gentlemen to Townsmen: The Gentry of Baltimore County, Maryland, 1660–1776* (Lexington: UP of Kentucky, 1993), 158–59; "Election Returns, Cumberland County—1756–1787," *Pennsylvania Archives*, ser. 6, 11.151–77, esp. 11.154–57.

9. In a hectoring letter of February 28, Edward Braddock called for postal service between Philadelphia and Winchester (near Cumberland, Md.) "for the forwarding yours and receiving my Dispatches." See Braddock to Governor Morris, Feb. 28, 1755, in Hazard, *Minutes of Provincial Council of Pennsylvania*, 6.307–8 (quotation, 6.307). Franklin presented a report and proposal to the assembly on April 9 and traveled to Winchester and Carlisle in mid-April. See *Votes and Proceedings of the House*, 70, 74–75, 87; Benjamin Franklin to Deborah Franklin, Apr. 13, 1755, in *Papers* 6.12. William Buchanan, Smith's business partner, may have come to Benjamin Franklin's attention during the Treaty of Carlisle, when he presented a letter concerning Indian affairs to the commissioners. See "Treaty of Carlisle," ibid., 5.84–107, esp. 5.90. In 1756 Buchanan, one of the commissary agents for Cumberland Co., was charged with profiteering. See "Provincial Commissioners: Orders for Payment," ibid., 6.392–96, esp. 6.395, 6.437–40, esp. 6.438, 440, 7.3–5, esp. 7.4, 7.25–28, esp. 7.28; "Provincial Commissioners to William Denny," Jan. 25, 1757, ibid., 7.102–5, esp. 7.102 n. 1.

ble, that something may be done by this Government immediately towards opening the road; for if Sir John should come and do, as he said, it would intirely ruin this Country.

I am,   Sir Your most obedient humble Servant
                                John Smith.

To Deborah Franklin

My dear Child,   Lancaster Apr. 26 1755.
    I wrote you last Saturday from Annapolis, from whence I set out soon after I took Leave of the Governor. Col. Tasker accompanied us 18 miles of the way to his Country seat Belair,[1] where we dined and lodged that night. The next morning we took Leave of the kind Colonel, and proceeded for Frederick in Maryland, where we understood the General would be in a day or two. About three in the afternoon we came to a Bed inn, where we found him just mounted after a Gate, intending, as we heard, 14 miles further to a house we had designed to lodge at. I did not then speak to him, but let him proceed, and concluded to stay at that inn, since the General and his attendants would certainly take up all the Lodgings at the other. However a good-natured Gentleman of a sweet Temper, tho' he had a sour name, Capt. Crab,[2] inviting us to his house about two miles further, we glad[ly] decamped, supped, and lodged with him very well. The next day about noon we reached Frederick, and after Dinner waited on the Secretary, Governor Shirley's son, and delivered some Letters for him, and some for the General. He not knowing us hardly treated us with common civility; so we left him, and, having got a lodging in the last Inn for our selves, (tho' we were obliged to send our horses two miles out of town, the stalls and pastures of the town being all full) we supped that night with Col. Dunbar and a great number of the Officers, who treated us with the greatest politeness, and had an opportunity of removing some violent prejudices they had entertained against Pennsylvania.[3] The next morning Mr Secretary came to our Lodging, made his apologies very gentilly and delivered the

1. Benjamin Tasker (1690–1768) was a naval officer and political leader in Maryland. Over the course of six decades, he was a member of the governor's council as well as the lower and upper houses of the Maryland legislature; he also served as mayor of Annapolis and governor of Maryland (1752–53). Belair, a Georgian plantation house located in present-day Bowie, Md., was built in 1745 by then-governor Samuel Ogle. Franklin's visit to Tasker's home was the occasion of his encounter with a whirlwind, charmingly recounted in a letter to Peter Collinson. See Franklin to Collinson, Aug. 25, 1755 (*Papers* 6.167–68).
2. Edward Braddock encamped at Owen's Ordinary (present-day Rockville, Md.) on April 20. Captain Henry Wright Crabb (1723–64) was a prominent local landowner and member of Maryland's lower house. See J. Hall Pleasants, ed., *Proceedings and Acts of the General Assembly of Maryland* (Baltimore: Maryland Historical Society, 1933–35), 50.28, 52.46, 140.
3. Thomas Dunbar (d. 1767), colonel of the 48th Regiment. One of Franklin's attempts to remove the officers' prejudices—by supplying provisions for the march—is referred to in letters on pp. 172, 174, and 177.

General's Compliments, inviting us to dinner; and we dined and breakfasted with him every day afterwards that we stayed in town.

Having settled the rest of the post to his satisfaction, we were about to take our Leave, when accounts came in from all parts of Virginia and Maryland, that the people, who had promised to collect horses and waggons for the Army, had failed in the performance; and it was impossible they could march without them.[4] Sir John St. Clair, who is a most violent Creature, said the damned people of Pennsylvania could furnish them, if they would; but they were Traiterous Frenchmen in their hearts, and would do nothing; for of all the flour they had promised, but two Waggons-load were yet arrived &c. &c.[5] and desired the General only to furnish him with a body of Troops, and he would scour the Country from one End to the other; and if they would not furnish Waggons and horses he would take them by force, and chastise the Resistors with Fire and Sword. I undertook the defence of our people; and the General seeming satisfied at length desired I would do the good office to my Country and the Army, to use my Endeavours to obtain Waggons &c. by fair means.

Thus you see, I am never to have leisure, but engage myself more and more in business, that does not properly belong to me.[6]

There is a great Court on tuesday, and another Court on thursday at York, which will soon give me an opportunity of knowing, whether I can succeed or not in this Affair.[7] I promised nothing but to do my endeavours, and to let the General know in a short time what might be depended on. And I hope to be at home in about ten or twelve days.

Inclosed you have my advertisement. I am furnished with a large quantity of Cash by the General to make good the terms proposed.[8]

The night after I left Frederic, I lodged miserably: but the next night got to Johnny Wright's[9] by a long and hard days journey,

4. Edward Braddock received less than "the tenth part of what" he had been promised by the governors of Maryland and Virginia. See Braddock to Robert Napier, June 8, 1755, in Stanley McCrory Pargellis, *Military Affairs in North America* (New York: D. Appleton-Century Co., 1936), 84–85 (quotation, 85), 92.

5. According to Sir John St. Clair, the lack of flour was an even greater drag on Edward Braddock's march than the lack of good roads. See Morris to Committee of Assembly, Apr. 24, 1755, in Hazard, *Minutes of Provincial Council of Pennsylvania*, 6.373–74.

6. Rhetorically, Franklin's beleaguered tone inverted relationships of power and knowledge between metropolitan center and colonial periphery. As Deborah Franklin explained to Peter Collinson, "My Husband is now in the Back Counties, contracting for some Waggons and Horses for the Army, which tho' so much out of his Way, he was obliged to undertake, for preventing some Inconveniencies that might have attended so many raw Hands sent us from Europe, who are not accustomed to necessary Affairs." See D. Franklin to Collinson, Apr. 30, 1755 (*Papers* 6.24).

7. Chief Justice William Allen was riding circuit at this time and scheduled to hold courts of oyer and terminer in Lancaster and York. See [William Smith], *A Brief View of the Conduct of Pennsylvania for the Year 1755 . . .* (London, 1756), 32; Franklin to Susanna Wright, Apr. 28, 1755 (*Papers* 6.23–24).

8. On April 23 Franklin received nearly £800 for expenses. See "Memorandum of Wagon Accounts," in *Papers* 6.13–22, esp. 6.13–19.

9. The Wright family ran "Wright's Ferry" across the Susquehanna River at Hempfield (present-day Columbia, Pa.). John Wright (1710–1759) represented York Co. in the assembly; his brother James (1714–1775), Lancaster Co. Their sister, Susanna Wright

where I was well accommodated, and yesterday I got here. I lodge at Debby's very comfortably, which is lucky for me, being indisposed with a Cold, and somewhat feverish.[1]

I received here your two agreable Letters, and Sally's.[2] My Love to her. I cannot now write to Brother John or Mr. Hunter.[3] Let them know how I am situated.

The Generall was on all occasions very obliging to me, and offered to make this service worth my while; but I refused to accept of a farthing.

I am glad you have seen my friend Governor Shirley.[4] My respects to Mr. Pownall, if you chance to see him.[5] Write to me by every Opportunity. I long to be with you, being, as ever,

Your loving Husband
B.F.

Billy is gone to Carlisle to settle a post-office there, and contract for Waggons &c. I am glad you sent my London Letters. Take especial Care to forward the inclosed Letters, particularly those to Ireland.

Pennsylvania Assembly Committee[6]

At a meeting of the Committee the 29th of April 1755

Present Isaac Norris, Evan Morgan, Joseph Fox, James Pemberton.

The Secretary having laid before us a Letter from General Braddock to the Governor, urging the necessity of laying out the road towards the Ohio for the Convenience of marching his forces:[7]

(1697–1784), a woman of extraordinary talents, was a Franklin family correspondent. See Whitfield J. Bell Jr., *Patriot-Improvers: Biographical Sketches of Members of the American Philosophical Society* (Philadelphia: The Society, 1999), 2.114–18.

1. Deborah Croker Dunlap (1732–1775), Deborah Franklin's niece and the wife of William Dunlap, the Lancaster printer of Franklin's wagon advertisement.
2. None of these letters has survived.
3. John Franklin (1690–1756), Benjamin's brother, was a Boston chandler and soapmaker. He was also the deputy postmaster of Boston. William Hunter (d. 1761) was a printer in Williamsburg, Va. He was joint postmaster general for the colonies with Benjamin Franklin.
4. Franklin's relationship to William Shirley (1694–1771), governor of Massachusetts, was complex. On the one hand, they fought over the Albany Plan of Union, which Franklin wrote and Shirley vigorously opposed. See "To Governor Shirley (December 1754) with a Preface (8 February 1766)," in *Papers* 5.443–47. On the other hand, they shared many concerns, including the growth of the British Empire in North America. At this very moment (see letter from Shirley on p. 187), Shirley was bringing into print Franklin's demographic treatise, "Observations concerning the Increase of Mankind." See Alan Craig Houston, *Benjamin Franklin and the Politics of Improvement* (New Haven: Yale UP, 2008), 136, 170–75.
5. Thomas Pownall (1722–1805), British colonial statesman and soldier, came to America in 1753 as private secretary to the governor of New York. At the June 1754 Albany Congress, Pownall and Franklin "created an Intimacy" that lasted until Franklin's death. See Pownall to Lord Halifax, July 23, 1754, in Beverly McAnear, ed., "Personal Accounts of the Albany Congress of 1754," *Mississippi Valley Historical Review* 39.4 (March 1953): 727–46, esp. 740–46 (quotation, 744).
6. These minutes were evidently enclosed with Isaac Norris's letter of April 29 (see pp. 172–73).
7. *Votes and Proceedings of the House*, 90.

It was unanimously agreed, that as the Governor hath ordered the said road to be immediately cleared, the sum of two hundred pounds shall be now paid to the Secretary towards defraying the Charge thereof.

It was also now moved, that a present of some Refreshments should be sent to Col. Dunbar's officers to be distributed amongst them; and that twenty horses should be sent to them from Lancaster County. It was now agreed, that the said twenty horses should be purchased for their use by James and John Wright to be conveyed thence to the Camp, nearly agre-able to a List now sent down from Lancaster by Benj. Franklin.[8]

From Isaac Norris[9]

[Apr. 29, 1755?][1]

before the Committee thy Letter dated from Lancaster the 26th instant, and we have not only entered in to the Engagement for clearing the Roads, as by the minute of the Committee inclosed, but have actually paid[2] two hundred pounds towards it. We have also unanimously agreed to supply the subaltern officers of Col. Dunbar's Regiment with the List and some additions of Rice, Raisins &c. which we have ordered to be purchased here, and shall find them with all Expedition made up in parcels to be divided without trouble. Pray tell my Friend Wright, that I have received his Letter of the 24th. but I presume you have altered your measures since and that he intends to send the Wheat he has got bolted to the Camp.[3]

I am extremely out of humour with the meanness of Cumberland County to purchase at high prices beyond their own agreement, and then put the Wheat into Mills, which cannot comply with their agreements, and to keep their Carriage till Necessity may engage

8. These "Refreshments," like the wagons, were intended to demonstrate the loyalty and ability of Pennsylvanians. As Franklin recalled, "While I was at the Camp [at Frederick], supping one Evening with the Officers of Col. Dunbar's Regiment, he represented to me his Concern for the Subalterns, who he said were generally not in Affluence, and could ill afford in this dear Country to lay in the Stores that might be necessary in so long a March thro' the Wilderness where nothing was to be purchas'd. I commisserated their Case, and resolved to endeavour procuring them some Relief." The list of supplies, drawn up by William Franklin, included sugar, tea, coffee, Madeira, rice, and raisins, as well as twenty horses. See above, pp. 130–31 (quotation, 130).
9. The opening to this letter is part of the twelve missing pages.
1. Isaac Norris evidently included the committee minutes of April 24 and April 29 in this letter (see the Pennsylvania Assembly Committee letters on pp. 165 and 171).
2. Marginal note: "it will be paid immediately."
3. Flour remained a bone of contention. On May 24 Edward Braddock complained to Robert Hunter Morris of the conduct of Daniel Cresap, a trader at Conegocheeg who "behaved in such a Manner in Relation to the Pennsylvania Flower that if he had been a French Commis[sioner] he could not have acted more for their Interest." James Wright delivered most of the flour by late June but was not paid until July. See [Braddock] to Morris, May 24, 1755, in Hazard, *Minutes of Provincial Council of Pennsylvania*, 6.400; Franklin to Wright, June 26, 1755, *Papers* 6.90–91, esp. 6: 90; Franklin to Wright, July 3, 1755, ibid., 6.101–2, esp. 6.102.

the Commissioners to give extravagant Wages. But we may consider this more at leisure.

The Bills we have are in so much demand, that the three thousand pounds is gone, mostly sold for money. I have therefore prevailed with my Brother to let James Johnson[4] go up with two Books to be signed: as it will be blank for the other Names the danger of miscarriage is not great, as we have taken the Numbers.

Please to make my respects acceptable at Hempfield to all there, and ask J. Wright what method he has taken up to purchase Wheat and Flour without money.

Thy assured Friend
Isaac Norris

From William Franklin

Honored Father,   Carlisle Apr: 29. 1755.

After your leaving Mr. Wright's, he and I went to all the Traders on the River-side, and amongst them they promised to furnish 250 horses, and that they would go down to Lancaster, and engage with you; which I hope they have done.

I can make no guess of what success I shall have in this Country, as almost all the Traders have either sold or engaged their horses to the Camp at Wills's Creek; and there are very few Waggons to be had, excepting those about Conegogee, who cannot possibly hear of our proposals time enough to be here, and contract with me. I would have sent an Express there with some advertisements, but not one horse could be hired in this town fit for the purpose. I have got Justice Smith and Mr. Alricks[5] to order the Constables of the neighbouring Townships to summon the people to meet together and consider the proposals on this day. I have likewise dispersed the advertisements to as many different parts of the County, as I possibly could: and I have the promise of several persons, that they will bring down their horses and waggons to me to morrow, and enter into Contracts for sending them to the Camp. Severall, who have horses nearer the Camp than to this place, have promised, that they will go there, and engage, as they cannot possibly bring them here, and then take them to the Camp in time. So that I have good reason to believe, that tho' I may not on account of the shortness of my stay contract with any great number, yet I shall be the means of sending many to the Camp as soon as they can possibly collect the horses together. No objection is made to the terms by any, that I have met with. The

---

4. Charles Norris (1712–66) was a Philadelphia merchant, treasurer of the Pennsylvania Hospital, and trustee of the General Loan Office; James Johnson was clerk of trustees of the General Loan Office.

5. John Smith and Harmanus Alrichs (1710–1772). The latter was one of the first settlers of Carlisle and a member of the assembly.

principall difficulty I meet with is contracting with some, who have
horses; and yet should they fail of complying with these contracts,
have not money to repay the advance-money or forfeiture; and their
horses being turned loose in the Woods would be hard to come at.
And there are some, that I must contract with, whose horses cannot
be got here in time to be valued before I go away. Therefore the Valuation must be left a blank till they come to Wills's Creek.

Mr. Wright being just going prevents my adding farther than that
I am,

Your very dutiful Son
W. Franklin.

P.S. By what I can find, the Camp will not be in any great Want of
either Wagons or Horses by the 20th of May, as a great many are
determined to go, and order them forthwith to Wills's Creek.

From William Dunlap[6]

W. Dunlap, Printer at Lancaster, to Mr. B.F.
May 1.

From Evan Morgan

May 1. Philadelphia
I think we were to blame in not writing to the General; for I have
heard, that both himself and his officers never till very lately understood, that the £5000 worth of provisions was a Gift of Pennsilvania, but thought, that the King was to pay for it.

This Waggoner brings up part of the present destined for Col.
Dunbar's officers.

We hear from Boston, that their forces are ready to go to the far
Expedition, but are detained for want of arms, which are daily
expected from England.[7]

To the Commanding Officer at Frederic[8]

Sir.   York May 2. 1755.
It is reported here, that the Regiment is marched from Frederic, and
that some officers only are left to receive the stores from Rock

---

6. William Dunlap (d. 1779), the Lancaster printer of Franklin's wagon advertisement.
   Birch copied only the heading for this letter.
7. Preparations were underway for northern campaigns against Crown Point, Fort Niagara, and Nova Scotia. The expedition against Fort Beauséjour in Nova Scotia, planned
   by William Shirley, relied on two New England battalions and a detachment of regulars
   from Halifax. The New Englanders were to have sailed as early as possible in spring
   1755 but were delayed in Boston by a lack of powder and small arms. See Lawrence
   Henry Gipson, *The British Empire before the American Revolution*, vol. 6, *The Great
   War for the Empire: The Years of Defeat, 1754–1757* (New York: Knopf, 1946), 226–28.
8. Thomas Dunbar's regiment left Frederick on April 29, reaching Wills's Creek on May 10;
   the identity of the commanding officer of the remaining troops is unknown. See Charles
   Hamilton, *Braddock's Defeat: The Journal of Captain Robert Chomley's Batman, the Journal of a British Officer; Halkett's Orderly Book* (Norman: U of Oklahoma P, 1959), 85 n. 24.

Creek, and get them forwarded to Wills's Creek; and that Waggons are expected from hence to assist in that service. I have engaged a number of Waggons here for the Army, but they will not pass thro' Frederic, unless directed so to do, having a shorter road by 30 miles. Therefore I write this, that if you have occasion for Waggons for the purpose above-mentioned, you may dispatch an Express to me at Lancaster where I shall be till the End of next Week, signifying the number you want; and I will direct so many to take their route thro' Frederic.

I am, Sir Your humble Servant
B. Franklin.

From John Harris Jr.[9]

May 2. Paxton

That an appointed meeting that Day the Inhabitants had agreed to furnish the English Camp with 5 Waggons, 4 Horses each team, and Drivers, to be at Wills's Creek on or before the 20th of May.

To William Shirley Jr.

Sir.   Lancaster May 5. 1755

I wrote to you on the 27th past, and inclosed you copies of my advertisements.

As soon as I got into this province from Frederic, I hastened the dispatch of the flour to Conegocheeg, and hope it will be all there, or near all, before the end of this Week.

At the Court of Oyer and Terminer here I got the Chief Justice[1] to recommend the affair of Waggons and Horses to the County from the Bench, and to send home the Constables of every township to convene the people, that they might have an opportunity of making up a number of Waggons and Horses in each town ship; and to morrow is appointed for the Contractors to appear here, and agree with me. In the mean time I attended the Court at York, and my son went to Cumberland. Between us we have engaged 79 Waggons, the owners of which have entered into Contracts under hand and seal and to morrow I expect to compleat the 150. I inclose you the form of the Contracts.[2]

I was obliged to give the Waggons time till the 20th of May: otherwise I found there could be no Expectation of getting near the Number.

9. John Harris Jr. (1716–1791) was an Indian trader and ferry keeper at Paxtang (present-day Harrisburg) on the Susquehanna.
1. William Allen (1704–1780), Philadelphia merchant and politician, was chief justice of the Pennsylvania Supreme Court from 1750 to 1774.
2. Harbanus Ashebriner's contract is reprinted in "From Harbanus Ashebriner: Contract for a Wagon and Horses," May 2, 1755, *Papers* 6.25–27, esp. 6.25–26.

I have received your favour of the 26th past. You may depend on having authentic Vouchers for every penny of the money put into my hands: but I find I shall want more; I suppose £200 for which I desire you will send me bills either on London or Virginia, by first opportunity, so I shall be obliged in the mean time to advance it.[3]

I have as yet engaged but 200 horses; for one Simons, a Jew, having informed the people, by direction of Mr. Walker,[4] as he says, that 2d per diem &c. will be given at Wills's Creek, the Indian Traders and others are, as I am told, making up gangs of horses, to send thither: so that you will however be supplied, tho' at a dearer rate. Yet I expect a number more from such, as cannot send them conveniently to Wills's Creek.

The Quakers by their influence on the Dutch have been very serviceable to me in procuring the Waggons, particularly the Wrights, two brothers of York and Lancaster Counties.

The people of York County, who have been very hearty in supplying all the Waggons in their power, complain grievously of the inlisting of their Servants, as an unequal Tax on them, and a very great Oppression.[5] If those Servants could possibly be spared, I should take it as a high favour, that they might be restored to their masters at my request, and think it a sufficient recompense for my trouble. But this I submit to the General's Goodness and Discretion. My respectfull Compliments to his Excellency, to Capt. Orme, Capt. Morris, &c.[6]

I am with great Esteem, Sir Your most humble Servant,
B.F.

P.S. The Waggons begin their march on Friday and Saturday next in two Divisions. Each Waggon will have 40 or 50 bushels of Oats, when they [go] from hence.

---

3. No bills arrived, and Franklin "advanc'd upwards of 200£" of his own money. See above, p. 130.
4. Joseph Simon (1712–1804), an Indian trader, merchant, and one of the largest landholders in Pennsylvania. Simon was a leader in Lancaster's small but vibrant Jewish community. See Oscar Reiss, *The Jews in Colonial America* (Jefferson, N.C.: McFarland & Co., 2004), 28. Richard Walker (1702–1791) was a militiaman, justice of the peace, and member of the assembly from Bucks Co.
5. Colonists were being recruited to fill out regiments intended for service in the campaigns against Crown Point, Fort Niagara, and Nova Scotia. The enlistment of indentured servants—costly to masters—was a point of controversy throughout this period. For actual enlistment, see Hamilton, *Braddock's Defeat*, 12 (Apr. 23, 1755). For the larger controversy, see Franklin's letters to William Shirley of May 8 and June 3 (pp. 177 and 183); Shirley to Franklin, Sept. 17, 1755, in *Papers* 6.190–91, esp. 6.190; "Pennsylvania Assembly: Reply to the Governor," ibid., 6.193–210, esp. 6.207; "Pennsylvania Assembly: Address to the Governor," ibid., 6.396–400; Franklin to Everard Fawkener, July 27, 1756, ibid., 6.472–76, esp. 6.474–75. In his *Autobiography*, Franklin recalled that the only reward for supplying wagons that he asked from Edward Braddock was "that he would give Orders to his Officers not to enlist any more of our bought Servants, and that he would discharge such as had been already enlisted." See above, p. 134.
6. Robert Orme (1725?–1790) and Roger Morris (1717–1794) were aides-de-camp to General Edward Braddock; both were wounded at the battle of the Monongahela.

To Thomas Dunbar

May 5.

Acquainting him with the present of the Committee of the Assembly to the subaltern Officers of the Army.

Dick Vernon's[7] pompous recruiting speech for Waggons was not used.

To William Shirley Jr.

[fol. 116v] Lancaster, May 7.

That he had this day completed the number of 150 Waggon; and could, he supposed, have engaged as many more, if wanted; but of horses he had only 259; but heard, that many were gone or going to be offered at Wills's Creek.

To William Shirley Jr.[8]

May 8. Lancaster

That his son would deliver with this the Contracts for 150 Waggons and 262 Horses.

"Tho' I have fallen short of the Number of Horses, I am in hopes you will have sufficient, as I hear many are to the Camp; the Owners from some reports expecting better Wages there, tho' all allow, that what I offered was fully sufficient; and had the time permitted, my applying to the other Counties, I am persuaded I could have got the whole."

Complains that a recruiting officer, Lieut. Culiny of Pepperel's[9] Regiment, begins to take away the people's bought servants. "Your Brother acted with honour and uprightness among us in that particular, as well as in every thing, and thereby gained so much esteem and respect that all sorts of people concurred to forward his Levies, and he got in a short time near 400 Men among us for your Father's regiment."[1]

---

7. Possibly the "R. Vernon" to whom Franklin advanced £2.9.6 as part of the wagon effort. See "Memorandum of Wagon Accounts," in *Papers* 6.13–22 (quotation, 6.18). No trace of Vernon's speech has survived.
8. This letter illustrates the combination of paraphrase and quotation. The reference in the first sentence—"his son," not "my son"—suggests that the paraphrase was composed by Birch.
9. William Pepperrell (1696–1759), merchant and soldier from Massachusetts who commanded the 51st Regiment. I have been unable to identify Culiny. Unlike William Shirley's 50th Regiment, which filled quickly, the 51st was "not half compleat" in early June. See Braddock to Napier, June 8, 1755, in Pargellis, *Military Affairs in North America*, 92 (quotation).
1. John Shirley (1725–1755) was an effective recruiting officer in Pennsylvania, raising more than two hundred men in the first three months of the year, earning a reputation for "great Prudence and good Sense." See Robert Hunter Morris to Edward Braddock, Mar. 12, 1755, in Hazard, *Minutes of Provincial Council of Pennsylvania*, 6.335–38 (quotation, 6.337).

To Edward Braddock

Sir.   Lancaster May 8 1755
  I have now executed, as far as I was able in so short a time, your
Excellency's Commission in procuring 150 Waggons and a number
of Horses for the service of the Troops under your Command. And
I must do this people the justice to say, that they have come into the
furnishing of these Necessaries with great readiness and alacrity,
many of them more from a sense of Duty, and a desire of rendering
some service to so good a King, than for the sake of the offered
Wages.
  The leading Men of all Sects and parties assisted me. The Chief
Justice of the Province and other Magistrates recommended the
affair strongly in their Courts; and the Quakers were very particularly hearty and serviceable, choosing by actions rather than Compliments, to demonstrate their Zeal for his Majesty's service.
  Please to accept my thanks for your Civilities to me and my Son
at Frederic, and most sincere wishes for your success and Welfare.
The Expedition you are now engaged in may in some respects seem
but a small one; but in its Consequences it will be of the greatest
importance to the British Nation.
  I have the honour to be with all possible respect
           Your Excellency's most obedient and most humble Servant
           B.F.

To Thomas Dunbar

                                                  May 8 Lancaster
"When it is considered, that not being so happy, as to obtain the Bill
sent up to the Governor for giving £25,000 to this Expedition, we
have nevertheless done all in our power by sending your army £5000
worth of flour, sending £10,000 in provisions to New England, to
enable those people to make a Diversion in your favour; voting a
large sum for cutting roads to facilitate the Carriage of Supplies to
you, when you shall have entered the Ohio Country; and withall
ordering a constant free post for your accommodation, which Grants
have now exhausted our stock till the Governor shall be pleased to
pass our bills, it is to be hoped, that a more favourable opinion of us
may in time obtain among you. For my part, I am persuaded, that
the more you know us, the better you will like us; and that during
your stay in America, you will not any where find a more friendly
and affectionate people than the Inhabitants of Pennsilvania.

From William Franklin[2]

[May 8–9, 1755?]

We had 40 Waggons appraised here on yesterday; but none of the Contracts were filled up till I came; and it took us up till Midnight before we could complete them. Never was such a Scene of Confusion, as we had during the whole time. There is not one, who is satisfied with the appraisement of his Waggons and Horses. Nothing but cursing and swearing at the appraisers, nay even threatening their lives. I had much ado to pacify them, they being almost all drunk. However, they have gone off this morning without giving me much disturbance.

To John Read[3]

May 9

His appointment of J.R. Waggon-master.

Instructions to Wagon Masters[4]

[May 9–10?, 1755]

Mr. B. Franklin's Instructions to the Waggon Masters.

From William Shirley Jr.

Fort Cumberland Wills's Creek

Sir, 10 May 1755.

We arrived here an hour ago. Before I left Winchester I received your Letter of May 5th but have not yet got that, which you sent by Capt. Rutherford's Men, and Mr. Leslie setting out immediately, have not time to inquire for it.[5]

You have done us great service in the Execution of the business you have kindly undertaken; and indeed without it, I do not see how the service could have been carried on, as the Expectations from Mary Land have come to nothing.

We have seen an advertisement very judiciously drawn up for the End proposed by it: but the last paragraph of it has greatly pleased

2. Undated; from location in the manuscript, probably May 8–9.
3. John Read, of York, was Deborah Franklin's brother. Edward Braddock's commission to Read, dated May 21, is in the Miscellaneous Benjamin Franklin Collections, B F85.x7b, American Philosophical Society. See also Read to B. Franklin, Oct. 8, 1755, in *Papers* 6.221–22.
4. Undated; from location in manuscript and dated appointment of John Read, probably May 9–10.
5. John Rutherford (d. 1758) was an officer in Sir Peter Halkett's brigade. Matthew Leslie, assistant deputy quartermaster general, was sent on May 10 to purchase "a large Quantity of Oats for the Service of the Forces." See Edward Braddock to Robert Hunter Morris, May 10, 1755, in Hazard, *Minutes of Provincial Council of Pennsylvania*, 6.383

and entertained your Friends here, as being a very proper ridicule and resentment of the ill Manners shown by the person described in it.[6]

From William Shirley Jr.

May 14 Fort Cumberland.
I have laid all your Letters before the General; who orders me to acquaint you, that he is greatly obliged to you for the great Care and ability, with which you have executed the business you undertook to him.

At your request he will with great pleasure discharge the Servants belonging to any persons, who have been serviceable to you, that may have inlisted in the Forces under his Command, or any others, for whom you may desire a discharge; and desires, that you would for that purpose send him their Names.

Since writing the above, the General having found upon inquiry, that all the great promises of the Provincial Contraction in these parts amount to no more than a supply of about 10 or 15 Waggons and 250 horses, has ordered me to beg the favour of you to assist him once more, if possible, by procuring 60 more Waggons with teams, and by completing the number of Horses you have already procured to 1500. For this purpose I inclose you another set of bills upon Col. Hunter[7] for £600 sterling.

William Shirley Jr. to Robert Hunter Morris[8]

[Wills's Creek, May 14, 1755]
Dear Morris,
This goes by an Express to Franklin of your province; who has been of the greatest service in procuring Horses and Waggons for the forces. He has already done much, but we are obliged to have recourse to him for further assistance, and doubt not you will help him, if he has any occasion for you.

I cannot but honour Franklin for the last clause of his advertisement.

6. William Shirley Jr. is referring to Franklin's thinly veiled threat, at the close of his wagon advertisement, that if wagons were not offered voluntarily then Braddock would send "Sir *John St. Clair* the Hussar, with a Body of Soldiers," to accomplish the task by force. See Wagon Advertisement on p. 167.
7. John Hunter (d. 1786), a merchant and colonel of the militia in Hampton, Va., was colonial agent for the London firm supplying Edward Braddock's troops.
8. The manuscript presents only those parts of this letter that relate to Franklin. The full text is in William Shirley [Jr.] to Robert Hunter Morris, 1755, in Hazard et al., *Pennsylvania Archives*, ser. 1, 2.310–11.

From William Franklin[9]

William's Ferry at the Mouth of
Conegocheeg May 15. 1755.

Account of a great Confusion among the Waggoners occasioned by a Dutch Quarter-master.

"'Tis scarcely to be believed what havock and oppression has been committed by the army in their march. Hardly a farmer in Frederic County has either Horse, Waggon or Servant to do the business of his plantation. Many are intirely ruined, being not able to plant their Corn, or do any thing for their subsistence. But what seems most extraordinary, is, that after they had pressed a considerable number of Waggons and Horses, they kept them standing at the Camp of this place for 7 or 8 days together under a Guard of soldiers, who would not suffer the Drivers to take the Horses out, or to go and get forage for them; so that many have died with hunger, after gnawing the tongues of the Waggon, to which they were fastened. The abuse they gave the people, at whose houses they stopped is scarce to be paralleled. They have not paid any of the Tavern-keepers much above one half of their bills, altho' no article in them is charged above the rate established by Law. And when they are shewn an authentic Copy of those rates, they grow immediately inraged, swearing that they are the Law during their stay in this Country; and that their Will and pleasure shall be the rule, by which the people shall square their Conduct.[1] Several of the Farmers, who made opposition to some of these outrageous doings have been sent for by a file of Musketeers, and kept along time confined, and otherwise mal-treated. To give you the many particulars of the like nature, which I [hear] almost every where, would be endless. However all those, who have given me these Informations, agree, that the General and others of the superior officers have acted in quite a different manner; and that it is by the subaltern officers chiefly they have been so scandalously insulted. Methinks, if any thing can add to the reproach of British Americans for giving reason to have these petty tyrants sent amongst us, it will be tamely submitting our selves to their arbitrary and unwarrantable insults. What must Posterity think of us, when history tells them, that such an infatuation prevailed in the Counsels of America, as to render it necessary for 1000 Men to be sent over to defend 3 or

9. The quotation mark at the start of the second paragraph of this letter is in the manuscript, indicating that the first summary sentence is by Birch, with the remainder copied from the original. There is no closing quotation mark in the manuscript.

1. Acts of Assembly provided that justices of the peace, in their quarter sessions, should set "reasonable prices" for taverns. For example, on Jan. 28, 1752, the justices of York Co. established the rate for one pint of Madeira at 1s. 6d, whereas one man's breakfast was 6d. See Hazard, *Minutes of Provincial Council of Pennsylvania*, 3.43; Peter Thompson, *Rum Punch & Revolution: Taverngoing & Public Life in Eighteenth Century Philadelphia* (Philadelphia: U of Pennsylvania P, 1999), 53–56; W. Walter Van Baman, *The Story of Yorktown: As Told by Conrad Shultz* (n.p., 2006), 179.

400,000 against one quarter of their number? But enough on this head: I can scarcely think of it with patience.[2]

From William Shirley Jr.[3]

[May 14–19, 1755?]
Very few Waggons or Horses having been provided for the Expedition, except by your self, the General had sent an Express to you, desiring your assistance in getting 60 more and 1500 or more Horses. The messenger was met by Mr. Franklin; and we find from him, that tho' they might easily be procured, it would be impossible to be done in time for our march.

The General has this day wrote to my Father, informing him of Lieut. Culiny's behaviour; and as he disapproves the practice of inlisting indented Servants, directing him particularly in this case to grant discharges to all such, in whose favour you shall make application, their masters first refunding the bounty-money, where any has been paid to them.

From William Franklin[4]

May 19. From the camp at Wills's Creek
That he arrived there well the morning of the day before.
"The General received me very graciously, invited Mr. Grace[5] and my self to dinner, and told me, that he had wrote over to England, that you had done him more real Service than all the persons in America put together. Mr. Orme and the other officers were also full of thanks to us for the services we had done them. Sir John also came, and waited upon me as soon as I arrived, and took me by the hand in a most courteous manner, and said, that he should write to England of the great service you had done the army.[6] I told him, that

---

2. As Franklin later recalled, "In their first March too, from their Landing till they got beyond the Settlements, they had plundered and stript the Inhabitants, totally ruining some poor Families, besides insulting, abusing and confining the People if they remonstrated.—This was enough to put us out of Conceit of such Defenders if we had really wanted any." See above, p. 134.
3. Franklin was in Philadelphia from May 12 until the middle of the summer. This letter must have been written after William Shirley Jr.'s letters of May 14 (see letters from Shirley on pp. 179–80) and was probably written before May 19, when Franklin and the assembly committee turned their attention to supplying forage for Edward Braddock's troops. See Robert Hunter Morris to the Assembly Committee, May 19, 1755, in *Papers* 6.50–51. Franklin presented it to the Committee of the Assembly on May 29. See "Pennsylvania Hospital Cornerstone Inscription," May 29, 1755, ibid., 6.61–65, esp. 6.64.
4. The quotation mark at the start of the second paragraph is in the manuscript, indicating that the first summary sentence is by Birch, with the remainder copied from the original.
5. Robert Grace (1709–1766), an original member of the Junto and proprietor of the Warwick Iron Works. In Lancaster on May 8, Franklin lent Grace £6 as part of the wagon affair. See "Memorandum of Wagon Accounts," in *Papers* 6.13–22, esp. 6.19.
6. Though he did not mention Benjamin Franklin by name, on June 13 Sir John St. Clair wrote Robert Napier that "we never cou'd have subsisted our little Army at Wills's Creek,

he would always find you ready to serve the army in general, or him in particular. By what I hear from all the Officers your advertisement afforded them a great deal of Diversion. Mr. Orme told me, that the General laughed for an hour together at it. And Sir John himself looked on it as a kind of Compliment, till he heard, that the officers made themselves merry with it; and even now he seems rather to be angry with them than you.

You cannot conceive what a prodigious Effect the present from the Committee has had in favour of our province. All the officers say, it is an extremely gentile one, and comes very *a propos*. Col. Dunbar says, it shall be published in the English News papers.[7] They say, that the other Provinces have promised them a great deal; but that Pennsilvania has done the most for them. They wish it had been their Lot to have come into Pennsilvania instead of Virginia, as they might then have furnished themselves with whatever they wanted much more readily and at much easier rates.

To William Shirley Jr.

20 May from Pensilvania. I am glad the advertisement afforded any Entertainment at the Camp. It answered its End tolerably among the people.

The Germans understood mighty well the word *Hussar*.

William Franklin to Sir John St. Clair

May 28. From the Mouth of the Conegogee Complains, that a large quantity of flour lay there exposed to the Weather.

From William Shirley Jr.

May 29. Wills's Creek That the General had wrote to him (Mr. F.) to desire his further assistance in enabling the General to lay in a magazine of flour for that place to serve for a second Convoy.

To William Shirley Jr.

June 3. Philadelphia Lieut. Culiny, before he went away, discharged those, he inlisted, or satisfied their Masters; and when I came to Philadelphia, I found

---

far less carried on our Expedition had not General Braddock contracted with the People in Pennsylvania for a Number of Waggons, which they have fulfilled." See St. Clair to Napier, June 13, 1755, in Pargellis, *Military Affairs in North America*, 93–95 (quotation, 93–94).

7. This promise appears to have remained unfulfilled.

the practice had not been so generally gone into by the other Officers, as was represented to me.

Pennsylvania Assembly Committee to John Lesher[8]

June 4.
Expressing their satisfaction in hearing, that there was so good a Disposition in the Inhabitants of Oley to the King's Service, as that it was proposed to furnish eight Waggons for the present occasion out of the Township.

N.B. The above was written to satisfy some of the foolish Germans, who said they would not furnish Waggons on the Governor's order, but would do it, if the Assembly or Committee approved of or desired it.

From John Hamilton[9]

June 9. From Wills's Creek
Our Regiment with the light Horse march with the General tomorrow. All the rest are gone before. We seem to be apprehensive of a worse Death than being shot, if not supported by the Pensilvanians. In short our whole Dependence for every necessary is upon them.

Thomas Penn to Richard Peters[1]

June 11. Extract of a Letter from Mr. Penn to Mr. Peters dated at London.

Your Letter of April 30th by Capt. Reeve gave the first intelligence of the Congress at Alexandria; and I immediately communicated it to my Lord Grenville and Sir Tho. Robinson, which last took it down in writing, and laid it yesterday before the Duke[2] and the Lords Justices, who were pleased to find, that we had ordered roads to be made, and that such a number of Horses and Waggons were likely to be got. This last service is looked upon as a very great

---

8. John Lesher (1711–1794), German-born ironmaster in Oley Township, Berks County, Pa.
9. The identity of Rev. John Hamilton remains obscure because there were two chaplains in Braddock's army. See Hamilton, *Braddock's Defeat*, 34. A modern authority identifies Hamilton as chaplain of the 48th Regiment and suggests that he was wounded at the Monongahela. See Archer Butler Hulbert, *Historic Highways of America*, vol. 4, *Braddock's Road and Three Relative Papers* (Cleveland, Ohio: A. H. Clark, 1903), 94 n. 33. Unfortunately, I have been unable to locate any contemporary references to substantiate this claim.
1. Thomas Penn (1702–1775) was the son of William Penn and proprietor of Pennsylvania; Richard Peters (1704?–1776) was an English-born clergyman and provincial secretary. An extract of a letter from Peters to Penn, dated May 14, 1755, was enclosed in a letter from Penn to Thomas Robinson, dated June 29, 1755. The extract described Franklin's success in supplying wagons and horses. See CO 5/15, fol. 282, National Archives.
2. Peter Reeve (d. 1780), ship captain and merchant, often carried letters to and from England; George Grenville (1712–1770), the future prime minister, was treasurer of the British navy in 1755; Thomas Robinson (1695–1770) was secretary of state; "the Duke" was Thomas Pelham-Holles, 1st Duke of Newcastle and prime minister.

one, and for which I shall send to Mr. Franklin my hearty thanks. I have not wrote to him, as I was to confer with Sir Everard Falkener[3] upon the Scheme for extending the posts. Pray tell Mr. Franklin this, and that he may be sure his service in furnishing the Waggons and Horses shall be properly represented.

To Edward Braddock[4]

12 June.

In answer to the General's Letter of 29 May, requesting Mr F. to procure a number of Waggons to carry up the flour given by the Province from Conegochee.

"By the time this reaches your hands, I apprehend you will your self have a better Opportunity at Wills's Creek of engaging Waggons in that service. For my Friends the Wrights of Susquehanna (who I had requested to assist Capt. Leslie) inform me, that they suppose near 60 Waggons were set out from these parts on or before the 8th instant with forage for the Camp; and we have here engaged and loaded all, that could possibly be secured in this Country, amounting to near sixty, fifty four of which are now in their way to Wills's Creek.[5]

To James Wright

June 19

The Governor harasses the House with message after message founded, as he says, on Letters and advices he has received, which however he will not lay before the House. A Bill is going up to give £15,000, ten of to General Braddock, and five for the Roads, Indian Expenses &c. I do not suppose it will pass.[6] The Governor spurs with both heels, but reins in with both hands.[7] At this rate no public service can be performed.

---

3. Everard Fawkener (1694–1758), British merchant, secretary to the Duke of Cumberland, and postmaster general.
4. This letter illustrates the combination of paraphrase and copy, with an open quotation mark signaling the transition. The reference in the first sentence—"Mr F."—suggests that the paraphrase was composed by Birch, not Franklin.
5. On May 10 Edward Braddock sent Matthew Leslie to Pennsylvania to purchase oats and other forage. On May 22 Franklin advertised for wagons; eight days later, sixty wagonloads were ready for delivery, though delays prevented their dispatch until June 8. See Braddock to Morris, May 10, 1755, in Hazard, *Minutes of Provincial Council of Pennsylvania*, 6.383; Morris to Braddock, June 3, 1755, ibid., 6.406–8; Morris to Braddock, June 4, 1755, ibid., 6. 408–10; Morris to Braddock, June 12, 1755, ibid., 6.415–16; "Advertisement for Wagons," in *Papers* 6.59; Morris to R. Peters, 1755, in Hazard et al., *Pennsylvania Archives*, ser. 1, 2.335; [Philadelphia] *Pennsylvania Gazette*, June 12, 1755, 2.
6. The bill was passed by the assembly on June 21 but, as predicted, it was denied by Robert Hunter Morris. See *Votes and Proceedings of the House*, 106–7, 111–12.
7. Franklin clearly liked this phrase; he used it in a letter to Peter Collinson written on June 26 and in a message from the assembly to Robert Hunter Morris on August 19. See Franklin to Collinson, June 26, 1755, in *Papers* 6.83–90, esp. 6.86; "Pennsylvania Assembly: Reply to the Governor," Aug., 19, 1755, ibid., 6.140–63, esp. 6.161.

From Edward Braddock

June 21. Bear Camp

The measures you propose taking for prevailing upon many of the Waggoners to engage in this service are extremely well judged, and I hope will have this Effect.

To Richard Partridge[8]

Sir,   Philadelphia. July 2. 1755.

By the last Ship, Capt. Shirley, I sent you, per Order of the Speaker, Copies of some Letters from the Officers of the Army to me, that you might have it in your Power to show the Ministry on any proper Occasion, that notwithstanding the Publick Reproaches thrown on this Province, as unwilling to assist the King's Forces, we had really been more serviceable to them, and had more of their Good Will than any of the neighbouring Provinces. But I would not, on any Account have those Letters printed.

As the Proprietor, it is suppos'd, has instructed the Governor to consent to no Money Bill by which any Money raised from the People may be disposed of by the Assembly without his Approbation, all our late Bills for giving Money to the Crown have been refused; and the Governor and Assembly are not likely soon to agree on any Bill of the kind, they being of Opinion, that as the Proprietors Estate is by our Laws exempted from Taxes, and so nothing is paid by him into the Publick Treasury, therefore he can have no natural or equitable Right to interfere in the Disposition of Money no part of which was ever his own; but the whole arising from the People, their Representatives, they think, are the only proper Persons to dispose of it. And indeed, it seems to have been very fortunate of late, that the Assembly had by Law some Money in their Power; for by that means near £20,000 has been and soon will be afforded to the present Expedition, which otherwise could not have been obtained, as Things are at present circumstanc'd. And besides, in a Constitution like ours, by which no Law can be pass'd without a Governor present in the Province, and so in Case of his Death or Absence no Money can be raised, it seems absolutely necessary that some should be always in the Hands and Disposal of the Assembly, to answer Emergencies. I suppose the Speaker and Mr. Callender write fully; I have only time to add that I am, very respectfully, Sir,

Your most obedient
Servant
B. Franklin

---

8. How White Papers, box 92, "Miscellaneous Letters," Bedfordshire and Luton Archives and Records Service, HW/92/13. Richard Partridge (1681–1759) was a New Hampshire–born merchant who lived in London as agent for colonial governments. He represented the assembly from 1740 to 1759.

To Edward Braddock

July 7. Philadelphia

The Waggons, that went from hence with forage to Wills's Creek returned well and satisfied. The Engagement I made to them in your name, that they should not be detained, having been punctually observed, we shall find less difficulty, I imagine, in procuring Waggons another time.[9]

I congratulate you on our good news from Halifax.[1] It gives us all great pleasure: but the News of your success on the Ohio will justly give us greater.

From William Shirley[2]

Dear Sir   Hudson's River July 10th 1755

I was determined not to go to Niagara without paying my Compliments to you before my departure.[3]

It gave me great pleasure to find in a Letter to me from General Braddock, that he was so sensible of the great service you had done for that part of the Expedition under his Command.[4]

No person can conceive the endless difficulties and disappointments in carrying a Provincial Expedition into Execution, when several Colonies are concerned, but those who experience it. I have gone thro' the whole Scene in that of Crown point, which hath often been a ground, and in danger of foundering; and I will not ensure it now.

I delivered the night before I left Boston to Dr. Clark his manuscript *Essay upon the importance of the Northern Colonies* &c. which he is now publishing. I wish I could have found time to correct it; but I had not a moment to do it in. Your treatise, which is to be annexed, hath been already printed off some time.[5]

---

9. "Protections and Passes will be given the Waggoners by Authority of the General, to prevent their being impressed, or detained after Delivery of their Loads." See the *Pennsylvania Gazette*, May 22, 1755, [4].
1. On June 16, in the first phase of the campaign against French forts in North America, British forces took control of Fort Beauséjour in Nova Scotia.
2. Governor of Massachusetts. Unbeknownst to Shirley, his son William Shirley Jr. had been killed in the battle on the Monongahela the previous day.
3. Shirley personally assumed command of the (ultimately unsuccessful) expedition against Fort Niagara in the summer and fall of 1755.
4. Edward Braddock sang Franklin's praises repeatedly. In a letter to Robert Napier, for example, he wrote that "Mr. Franklin undertook and perform'd his Engagements with the greatest readiness and punctuality." See Braddock to Napier, June 8, 1755, in Pargellis, *Military Affairs in North America*, 85 (quotation).
5. William Clarke (1709–1760), Boston physician and apparently dilatory political writer. In March 1754, at William Shirley's instigation, Clarke struck up a correspondence with Franklin over the need for colonial union. See Clarke to Franklin, Mar. 18, 1754, in *Papers* 5.250–52. In May Clarke asked Franklin to comment on the outlines of a pamphlet, which he thought nearly ready to print in February 1755. See Clarke to Franklin, May 6, 1754, ibid., 5.269–71. When finally issued in July, the pamphlet included Franklin's demographic treatise "Observations concerning the Increase of Mankind, Peopling of Countries, &c" as an appendix. See [Clarke], *Observations On the late and present Conduct of the French with Regard to their Encroachments upon the British Colonies in North America* . . . (Boston, 1755).

From John Hamilton

July 16.

From the Camp at Widow Barringers.[6]

Sir.   I intended before this to have sent you the particulars of that unfortunate action at Monongahela, but it is very difficult to know how it was. As far as I can comprehend it, I will let you know.

The 9th of July the General was within about nine miles of the French fort. He had seen no Enemy except a few Indians, who ran away at his approach. He had no Indians with him, that durst venture out; and, I believe, not the least intelligence. They were led by their Guides, or rather by Frazier,[7] one of them, twice cross the Monongahela, when, it is now said, they ought not to have passed it all: Some say, Frazier sold them; others, that he took them that way to carry the road thro' a plantation he had there. Col. Gage[8] with 200 Men and two Cannon took possession of the banks at Fraziers, and continued there untill the whole Army passed. After that they thought themselves secure. After they had marched about a mile the Front received a most smart fire without seeing any Enemy, on which the Generall ordered the Troops to march up to their Assistance, which was done in great Confusion thro' Waggons, Baggage, and Cattle. The Enemies then almost surrounded them: The Officers were all picked out, as marks, as you may judge from those of our Regiment. We had twenty five in the field, twenty of whom were killed or wounded; and every one of the rest had several shot thro' their cloathes, hats &c. This threw the soldiers into confusion, and after standing till two thirds of them were cut to pieces were siezed with so strong a panic, that nothing could recover them. Take it all together, there was never known so many killed in proportion to their number. Col. Dunbar was forty five miles from the Action. When the General came up, he ordered all the Canons, military stores, and provisions to be destroyed, by which Means he had horses to carry off the wounded.

6. John Hamilton was not with the main body of Thomas Dunbar's retreating troops, suggesting that this report is secondhand. Widow Barringer's is near present-day Winchester, Md. On this same day, Dunbar's forces were ninety miles away at Little Meadows, near present-day Grantsville, Md. See Hamilton, *Braddock's Defeat*, 33; George Washington to James Innes, July 17, 1755, in W. W. Abbot et al., eds., *The Papers of George Washington: Colonial Series* (Charlottesville: UP of Virginia, 1983), 1.334.

7. John Frazer was a blacksmith and gunsmith of uncertain nationality who operated a trading post at the mouth of Turtle Creek on the Monongahela, about ten miles from Fort Duquesne. Though the French had burned Frazer's cabin in 1753, he refused to leave. In early 1754 Frazer was made a lieutenant in the small company of Virginians sent to build a fort on the forks of the Ohio. When the French descended on the fort on April 14, Frazer refused to leave his store to defend the fort, leading Governor Robert Dinwiddie to call for his court-martial. Frazer was never tried, but doubts about his loyalty remained. See Paul E. Kopperman, *Braddock at the Monongahela* (Pittsburgh: U of Pittsburgh P, 1977), 31; Dinwiddie to George Washington, May 4, 1754, in Abbot et al., *Papers of George Washington*, 1.91–93; Dinwiddie to Washington, June 27, 1754, ibid., 1.150–51.

8. Thomas Gage (1720/1–1787), English army officer and future commander in chief for North America. As lieutenant colonel of the 44th Regiment, Gage commanded Edward Braddock's advance guard in the march.

This account is not in the military style, and very imperfect; but hope to see you, and discourse more. Inclosed is a List of the killed and wounded in the action, tho' I have done it in so great a hurry, that I fear you will scarcely understand it.

Col. Dunbar desires me to tell you, that it gives him infinite concern he could not write to you: but I can assure you he has been so plagued, that he has not time to write to his best Friends, and scarcely to eat his Meat. He desires his Compliments to you and [your] Son, as does

Your most humble and obedient Servant
John Hamilton

List
General Braddock died of his Wounds July 13.
Capt. Orme Roger}
Roger Morris}   aid de Camps wounded.
Geo. Washington, Esq.,   aid de Camp
William Shirley Esq.,   Secretary killed
Sr John St. Clair, Deputy
Quarter Master General,   wounded
Lieut. Matthew Leslie,
Assistant Quarter Master General,   wounded
Francis Halket Esq. Major of the Brigade[9]

according to the most exact returns we can as yet get, above seven hundred private Men were killed and wounded, exclusive of offi cers, Serjeants, Guides, Women, and other followers of the Camp.

From Robert Hunter Morris[1]

[July 21, 1755]

Sir.

If you can spare a few minutes, I shall be glad to have a word or two with you upon some intelligence I have received from the westward, which will make it necessary to take some step immediately to prevent the back Countries from being deserted. I am Sir Yours

Monday 11 o' Clock   Rob. H. Morris

9. William Shirley, the governor of Massachusetts, lost two children in 1755: his eldest son, William, died on the Monongahela, and his second son, John, died of fever during the Niagara campaign. Francis Halket was the son of Sir Peter Halket, commander of the rear guard (artillery and baggage) on July 9. Peter and Francis's brother James were both killed in the battle; their deaths are memorialized in a sketch by Benjamin West, "Discovering the bones of Sir Peter Halket."

1. Robert Hunter Morris received the first reports of Edward Braddock's defeat sometime between July 16, when he still spoke of offering "assistance," and July 20, when he wrote Governor Horatio Sharpe of "the first accounts of the defeat and death of the General, which I collected from frighted Waggoners who had left the army." See Morris to Sir Thos. Robinson, 1755, in Hazard et al., *Pennsylvania Archives*, ser. 1, 2.379; Morris to Sharpe, 1755, ibid., 2.382–83, esp. 2.382. Franklin first reported the defeat in the *Pennsylvania Gazette*, July 24, 1755, [2].

From James Read[2]

25 July. Reading

Dear Sir, The late accounts of the shamefull Defeat of our Army under General Braddock have given a shock to all this part of the Country. Our Inhabitants are apprehensive of being visited by the Indians: for we have vast barrens and hills to the north west of this town, extending to the Ends of the Province; so that we have but few Inhabitants near us on that side. I hope the Legislature will think seriously of our defenceless State, and enable us to put ourselves into a Condition to drive back our Enemies.

I am deeply grieved for our great Loss in the artillery. I think it irretrievable, and fear much that if his Excellency Major General Shirley should succeed in his attack on fort Niagara, yet it will be retaken by the Enemy with the artillery which we have furnished them with. They have a road lately cut from Fort Du Quesne thro' a fine level Country to Niagara.[3]

I think our Army was full of Reprobates, who never had any serious thought of what they were about; and our Officers were too confident of their own strength, and despised their Enemy.[4] Of the ill Consequences of such self-confidence and Contempt of Enemies you may read in the American Magazine for the Year 1746 p. 296 &c. I believe too we may justly say of them, that they were *mighty to drink Wine Men of strength to mingle strong drink.*[5]

2. James Read (1718–1793), a relative of Deborah Franklin, was a merchant, lawyer, and public official in Pennsylvania. By the fall of 1755, Read was serving as major of two "associated" (voluntary) companies in Reading, where conditions were unstable. As William Parsons reported in October, "our Roads are continually full of Travellers" as settlers from the frontier removed to Reading and residents of Reading moved closer to Philadelphia. See Read to Robert Hunter Morris, Oct. 27, 1755, in Hazard, *Minutes of Provincial Council of Pennsylvania*, 6.651 ("associated"); Parsons to R. Peters, Oct. 31, 1755, in Hazard et al., *Pennsylvania Archives*, ser. 1, 2.443–45 ("our Roads," 2.444). See also Horatio Sharpe to John Sharpe, Aug. 11, 1755, BL Add. MSS 32858, fols. 110–11.
3. In retreat Thomas Dunbar had ordered the destruction of the cannons, but two six-pounders were captured by the French. As feared these cannons were subsequently used by the French, when Louis-Joseph de Montcalm-Gozon led his successful attack on the British at Fort Oswego in August 1756. See Sargent, *History of an Expedition*, 257 n. 1.
4. Colonists frequently complained of British disdain for Indian warriors. See for example the report of Adam Stephens, a Virginia officer shot twice on the Monongahela (Stephens to John Hunter, July 18, 1755, BL Add. MSS 32857, fols. 216–17). Franklin had attempted to warn Edward Braddock of the unique dangers of colonial warfare in April, but as Braddock condescendingly replied, "These Savages may indeed be a formidable Enemy to your raw American Militia; but, upon the King's regular and disciplin'd Troops, Sir, it is impossible they should make any Impression." See above, p. 132.
5. For the conclusion to an article trumpeting the value of the fishery lost by France when Fort Louisbourg was captured by New England troops in June 1745, see Jeremy Gridly, ed., "A Computation of the Advantage of the French Fishery on the Banks of New-foundland, Acadia, Cape Breton, &c.—as it was carried on by the French, before the taking of Louisburg; by General Pepperrell," *American Magazine and Historical Chronicle* 3 (July 1746): 293–96, esp. 296. The passage in italics is from Isaiah 5.22.

Something surely is wanting to rouse the inhabitants of the Province out of their Lethargy. We have an open Enemy on our borders, and a popish intestine Enemy spread thro' all the Land.

From William Hunter

Dear Sir,   Williamsburg July 27 1755
**I cannot forbear mentioning what I wish I could forget, our shamefull Defeat at Ohio, which, if reports be true, can scarcely find its parallel in History.[6] It happened on the 9th and we had advice of it the 13th at night, but flattered ourselves it was false, till an Express this week has confirmed it. You will see the account published in the Gazette. The Governor says, but, I believe, without reason, that there are many damned Lies in it, which occasioned the postscript, of which no one here takes any notice. He wanted to publish much such an account as he did last Year of Washington's Defeat, and is therefore so frantic about this, that he threatens to nail up the office.[7] This, I believe, will occasion me some warm Work, for which I wish myself better in health.

The following additional Circumstances are here reported, and I am afraid, with too much foundation: that there were but four hundred of the Enemy, who being covered with wild pease breast-high, and falling down as soon as they had fired, lost scarce a man: That our artillery was fired but four rounds for want of ammunition. That at the first fire the Regulars fled, and being rallied in confusion fired directly on the Virginians, and killed more of them then the Enemy did; That the General would by no means permit a Man to take shelter and fight the Enemy in their own way, which would in all probability have prevented the sad Consequences: That they fled, or retired, as they call it, in such Confusion, that the wounded General and Colours had nearly fallen into the Enemy's hands: and That a great number of metal buttons have been extracted from our wounded, a convincing proof, that the Enemy had in a manner exhausted their ammunition: That when, in their retreat, they came in sight of Dunbar's detachment, great numbers deserted from him, and he immediately blew up the shells at least, if not the powder, expecting the Enemy to pursue them, and retiring in Confusion. There are many other reports, but the above, I believe, are nearly true.

---

6. Asterisks in original, suggesting that Thomas Birch did not copy the first part of this letter.
7. The original report of George Washington's defeat at Fort Necessity was in the [Williamsburg] *Virginia Gazette*, July 19, 1754, [2–3].

From Robert Orme

Dear Sir   [Fort Cumberland], 27 July

I am just able to acknowledge the receipt of your Letter, which came to my hands since I have been at this place ill of my Wounds.

The Manuscript you was so kind, as to send me, afforded me much Entertainment; and, I flatter myself, some knowledge. I implicitly agree with the author in his sentiments.[8]

Our affair of the 9th I would send you a particular account of, but my extreme Weakness and confinement to my Bed disables me. Governor Morris will, I am convinced, show you his Letter and List.[9] Our family suffered greatly: The Generall and Shirley killed, and Mr. Morris and my self very much wounded. The ball entered just above my knee, and went out near my Groin. But the surgeons tell me I shall do well. I purpose setting out for Philadelphia as soon as I am able; for I lost money and baggage, and am extremely destitute of every thing here. I will not fail waiting upon you as soon as I can limp to your Door.

Out of 86 Officers 63 were killed or wounded, and 714 men out of 1100 dead.

I beg you will present my Compliments to your son. I am sure you condole with us in great Loss. I am, Dear Sir,

> Your most humble and obedient Servant
> Robt. Orme

From James Innes[1]

Aug. 17. Fort Cumberland

Our Troops were no sooner off the field, and the Enemy in full possession of our artillery, then they instantly fell to work, burnt and destroyed our haubitzers and twelve pounders, not attempting to carry off any thing but our small two six pounders.

Depending upon our retreat was only in order to bring up Col. Dunbar, and attack them afresh, as they [sic] we had numbers sufficient, little dreaming, that they had got the Victory. And, I am afraid, all for despising and undervaluing our Enemies; what was not

---

8. Franklin's letter has not been found. The entertaining manuscript may have been either "A Parable against Persecution" or "A Parable on Brotherly Love," both of which are dated July 1755 by the editors of the *Papers of Benjamin Franklin*. See *Papers* 6.114–28.

9. Captain Robert Orme was recuperating at Fort Cumberland; his letter and list were sent to Robert Hunter Morris on July 18. See Orme to Morris, July 18, 1755, in Hazard, *Minutes of Provincial Council of Pennsylvania*, 6.487–89; "A List of the Officers who were present and of those killed and wounded in the Action on the Banks of the Monongahela the 9th Day of July, 1755," ibid., 6.489–92.

1. James Innes, a Virginia colonel, led the construction of Fort Cumberland in the winter of 1754 and acted as campmaster general at Wills's Creek until his appointment as governor of Fort Cumberland on June 2, 1755. See George Washington to William Fairfax, Aug. 11, 1754, in Abbot et al., *Papers of George Washington*, 1.183–88; Washington to Fairfax, June 7, 1755, ibid., 1.298–302.

thought worth spending a thought about in condescending to advise with those, who could have prevented the mischief.

To Richard Partridge[2]

Philadelphia. August 28. 1755.

You will receive by this Ship the Speeches and Messages that have passed between the Governor and Assembly in the late Sitting, which ended on Friday last, Also a Copy of the Bill for granting £50,000 to the King's Use which he refused to pass. It is expected that the Proceedings of the Assembly will be much misrepresented and therefore I am directed by the House, to State Matters clearly in their due light to you that you may be able to justify the Assembly so far as they are fairly and rightly justifiable——[3]

At the opening of the Sessions the Governor made a Speech to the House, acquainting them with the unhappy Situation of Publick Affairs by the Defeat of General Braddock, and recommending the Grant of a Supply for the Kings Service, withall cautioning them to avoid every Thing that ought revive any former dispute between him and them: The House accordingly voted a Supply of £50,000 for the Kings Use, to be raised by an equitable Tax on all Estates Real and Personal, which was thought a great Sum for this Province, tho' perhaps it may appear otherwise in England where 'tis said we have been invidiously represented as vastly Rich and able. In observance of the Governors Caution to avoid all former Disputes about extending the Excise Act, the House Chose to raise the Money by a Tax.

To avoid all Disputes about suspending Clauses, in Paper Money Acts, and the Royal Instruction enjoining such Clauses, they chose to make no Paper Money——

To avoid all Disputes about the Disposition of the Money arising by the Tax, and yet to Secure a right Application, they proposed by the Bill to put it into the Hands of Commissioners to be disposed of by them for the Kings Service, with the Consent and approbation of

---

2. CO 5/1274, fols. 82–83, National Archives. Franklin alludes to this letter in a missive to Peter Collinson, where the letter to Partridge is listed as "not found." See Franklin to Collinson, Aug. 27, 1755, in *Papers* 6.169–72 (quotation, 6.169 n. 5).
3. Edward Braddock's defeat heightened conflicts between the assembly and the governor over the proprietor's role in funding the colony's war efforts. On August 2 the assembly sent up a bill providing £50,000 for colonial defense; crucially, it proposed "that all Estates real and personal were to be taxed, those of the Proprietaries *not* excepted." Robert Hunter Morris proposed an amendment, substituting the word "only" for "not." As Franklin noted, it was "a small but very material Alteration!" (See above, p. 136.) Compounding the assembly's public relations problem was William Smith's book, which blamed the assembly for the colony's failure to stem the encroachments of the French on the Ohio. See [William Smith], *A Brief State of the Province of Pennsylvania . . .* , 2d ed. (London, 1755). The proceedings of the session, running July 23–August 22, are in *Votes and Proceedings of the House*, 113–57. The most important messages by the assembly are represented in "Pennsylvania Assembly: Reply to the Governor," in *Papers* 6.129–38, 140–66.

the Governor or of Commander in chief of the Kings Forces in North America.

But to obtain a Credit for imediate use as Collecting the Tax would require some Time they empowered the said Commissioners to draw orders on the Treasurer (not exceeding the Sum granted) payable out of the Tax as it should come into his hands which Orders it was presumed would have at least a short credit as orders on our Treasury have always been paid with punctuality and honor.

Lest the Issuing of these Orders should be considered as a making of Money To avoid all disputes on that head the Orders were not proposed a Legal Tender.

And to secure their Credit and give the Creditor a Compensation for the Credit he afforded, the Orders were to bear an Interest till paid at the Rate of 5 percent per annum.

To avoid all disputes concerning the Propriety of extending hither an Act of Parliament expressly made for other Colonies instead of taking more than 5 years for the Sinking these Orders, the House chose to have them sunk in Two years and so it was order'd in the Bill.

Thus all former Disputes and every thing that might seem to interfere with Royal Instructions, Old or new, or Acts of Parliament in Force, or not in Force here, and the like were carefully avoided by the House in the formation of their Bill.—And the Governor not being able to make any Objections to the passing of it on those accounts, was driven to the necessity of Saying—That he was restrained by the Proprietors—and accordingly refused his assent.

A True Copy of the Extract per Rd. Partridge.

The Outline of the *Autobiography*

It seems most likely that Franklin outlined his *Autobiography* just after he began to write it, probably on the morning of his second day at the Bishop of St. Asaph's, August 1, 1771. This is probable because the first eight pages of the *Autobiography* cover the Franklin family's history and Benjamin Franklin's childhood, which are not included in the outline. It might also be the case that, at the same time, Franklin added his reasons for writing his memoirs in the first place, which appear in the margin alongside his initial version of the manuscript.

The outline printed below is reproduced from a copy at the Pierpont Morgan Library. This is not in Franklin's own hand—the original has never been found—but was done by Henry Drinker (1734–1809, the business partner of Abel James), who added a heading in French that can be translated as "Very interesting writing by Benj. Franklin. First draft memorandum of his memoirs." To this outline, Franklin added several notes in red and black ink, to remind himself to cover or emphasize certain topics. After Franklin's death, Louis Guillaume Le Veillard, who also possessed a copy of the *Autobiography*, inked in another heading (in French): "Copy of a draft" and "The additions in red ink are in Franklin's hand."

For a full history of the outline, see Carl Van Doren's *Benjamin Franklin's Autobiographical Writings* (New York: Viking, 1945), 209–11, and Lemay and Zall's *Genetic Text*, pp. 196–211, which includes details of Franklin's corrections.

Copied'un [Autographe] Project très curieux de Bn. Franklin.—lere. Esquisse memorandum de ses mémoires. Les additions à l'encre rouge sont de la main de Franklin.

My writing. Mrs.. Dogoods Letters—Differences arise between my Brother and me (his temper and mine) their Cause in general. His News Paper. The Prosecution he suffered. My Examination. Vote of Assembly. His Manner of evading it. Whereby I became free. My Attempt to get employ with other Printers. He prevents me. Our frequent pleadings before our Father. The final Breach. My Inducements to quit Boston. Manner of coming to a Resolution. My leaving him & going to New York. (return to eating Flesh.) thence to Pennsylvania, The Journey, and its Events on the Bay, at Amboy, the

Road, meet with Dr. Brown. his Character, his great work. At Burlington. The Good Woman. On the River. My Arrival at Philada. . .
First Meal and first Sleep. Money left. Employment. Lodging. First
Acquaintance with my Afterwards Wife, with J. Ralph, with Keimer.
their Characters. Osborne. Watson. The Governor takes Notice of
me. the Occasion and Manner, his Character. Offers to set me up.
My return to Boston. Voyage and Accidents. Reception. My Father
dislikes the proposal. I return to New York and Philada. . . Governor
Burnet. J. Collins, the Money for Vernon. The Governors Deceit.
Collins not finding Employment goes to Barbados much in my Debt.
Ralph and I go to England. Disappointment of Governors Letters.
Col. French his Friend. Cornwallis's Letters. Cabbin. Denham.
Hamilton. Arrival in England. Get Employment. Ralph not. He is
an Expence to me. Adventures in England. Write a Pamphlet and
print 100. Schemes. Lyons. Dr. Pemberton. My Diligence and yet
poor thro Ralph. My Landlady, her Character. Wygate. Wilkes. Cib-
ber. Plays. Books I borrowed. Preachers I heard. Redmayne. At
Watts's— Temperance. Ghost. Conduct and Influence among the
Men, persuaded by Mr Denham to return with him to Philada. . &
be his Clerk. Our Voyage and Arrival. My resolutions in Writing. My
Sickness. His Death. Found D. R married. Go to work again with
Keimer. Terms. His ill Usage of me. My Resentment. Saying of
Decow. My Friends at Burlington. Agreement with H Meredith to set
up in Partnership. Do so. Success with the Assembly. Hamiltons
Friendship. Sewells History. Gazette. Paper Money. Webb. Writing
Busy Body. Breintnal. Godfrey. his Character. Suit against us. Offer
of my Friends Coleman and Grace. continue the Business and M.
goes to Carolina. Pamphlet on Paper Money. Gazette from Keimer.
Junto erected, its plan. Marry. Library erected. Manner of conduct-
ing the Project. Its plan and Utility. Children. Almanack. the Use
I made of it. Great Industry. Constant Study. Fathers Remark and
Advice upon Diligence. Carolina Partnership. Learn French and
German. Journey to Boston after 10 years. Affection of my Brother.
His Death and leaving me [p. 2] his Son. Art of Virtue. Occasion.
City Watch. amended. Post Office. Spotswood. Bradfords Behav-
iour. Clerk of Assembly. Lose one of my Sons. Project of subordi-
nate Junto's. Write occasionally in the papers. Success in Business.
Fire Companys. Engines. Go again to Boston in 1743. See Dr Spence.
Whitefield. My Connection with him. His Generosity to me. my
returns. Church Differences. My part in them. Propose a College.
not then prosecuted. Propose and establish a Philosophical Society.
War. Electricity. my first knowledge of it. Partnership with D Hall
&c. Dispute in Assembly upon Defence. Project for it. Plain Truth.
its Success. 10.000 Men raised and Disciplined. Lotteries. Battery
built. New Castle. My Influence in the Council. Colours, Devices

and Motto's.— Ladies. Military Watch. Quakers. chosen of the common council. Put in the Commission of the Peace. Logan fond of me. his Library. Appointed post Master General. Chosen Assembly Man. Commissioner to treat with Indians at Carlisle. and at Easton. Project and establish Academy. Pamphlet on it. Journey to Boston. At Albany. Plan of Union of the Colonies. Copy of it. Remarks upon it. It fails and how. (Journey to Boston in 1754.) Disputes about it in our Assembly. My part in them. New Governor. Disputes with him. His Character and Sayings to me. Chosen Alderman. Project of Hospital my Share in it. Its Success. Boxes. Made a Commissioner of the treasury My Commission to defend the Frontier Counties. Raise Men & build Forts. Militia Law of my drawing. Made Colonel. Parade of my Officers. Offence to Proprietor. Assistance to Boston Ambassadors— Journey with Shirley &c.. Meet with Braddock. Assistance to him. To the Officers of his Army. Furnish him with Forage. His Concessions to me and Character of me. Success of my Electrical Experiments. Medal sent me per Royal Society and Speech of President. Dennys Arrival & Courtship to me. his Character. My Service to the Army in the Affair of Quarters. Disputes about the Proprietors Taxes continued. Project for paving the City. I am sent to England. Negociation there. Canada delenda est. My Pamphlet. Its reception and Effect. Projects drawn from me concerning the Conquest. Acquaintance made and their Services to me Mrs,, S,,, Mr Small. Sir John P. Mr. Wood. Sargent Strahan and others. their Characters. Doctorate from St. Andrews [p. 3] Doctorate from Oxford. Journey to Scotland. Lord Leicester. Mr. Prat.— DeGrey. Jackson. State of Affairs in England. Delays. Event. Journey into Holland and Flanders. Agency from Maryland. Sons Appointment. My Return. Allowance and thanks. Journey to Boston. John Penn Governor. My Conduct, towards him. The Paxton Murders. My Pamphlet Rioters march to Philada . . . Governor retires to my House. My Conduct, towards him. The Paxton Murders. Sent out to the Insurgents—Turn them back. Little Thanks. Disputes revived. Resolutions against continuing under Proprietary Government. Another Pamphlet. Cool Thoughts. Sent again to England with Petition. Negociation there. Lord H. his Character. Agencies from New Jersey, Georgia, Massachusets. Journey into Germany 1766. Civilities received there. Gottingen Observations. Ditto into France in 1767. Ditto in 1769. Entertainment there at the Academy. Introduced to the King and the Mesdames. Mad. Victoria and Mrs. Lamagnon. Due de Chaulnes, M Beaumont. Le Roy. Dali[t]bard. Nollet. See Journals. Holland. Reprint my papers and add many. Books presented to me from many Authors. My Book translated into French. Lightning Kite. various Discoveries. My Manner of prosecuting that Study. King of Denmark invites me to Dinner. Recollect my Fathers Proverb. Stamp Act.

My Opposition to it. Recommendation of J. Hughes. Amendment of it. Examination in Parliament. Reputation it gave me. Caress'd by Ministry. Charles Townsends Act. Opposition to it. Stoves and Chimney plates. Armonica. Acquaintance with Ambassadors. Russian Intimation. Writing in Newspapers. Glasses from Germany. Grant of Land in Nova Scotia. Sicknesses. Letters to America returned hither. the Consequences. Insurance Office. My Character. Costs me nothing to be civil to inferiors, a good deal to be submissive to superiors &c &c..

Farce of perpetl. Motion

Writing for Jersey Assembly.   verte

[p. 4] Hutchinson's Letters. Temple. Suit in Chancery, Abuse before the Privy Council.—Lord Hillsborough's Character. & Conduct. Lord Dartmouth. Negotiation to prevent the War.—Return to America. Bishop of St. Asaph. Congress, Assembly. Committee of Safety. Chevaux de Frize.—Sent to Boston, to the Camp. To Canada, to Lord Howe.—To France, Treaty, &c

A Guide to People Mentioned in the *Autobiography*

More information on many of these individuals may be obtained from John A. Garraty and Mark C. Carnes, eds., *American National Biography* (New York: Oxford University Press, 1999) and H. C. G. Matthew and Brian Harrison, eds., *The Oxford Dictionary of National Biography* (Oxford: Oxford University Press, 2004). Others that appear only in the "Quire Book of Letters" are documented in its footnotes.

ADAMS, MATTHEW (?1694–1753), friend to the young Franklin; wrote for the *New-England Courant* and later the *New-England Weekly Journal* and the *Boston News-Letter*.

ALEXANDER, JAMES (1691–1756), New Yorker who approved of Franklin's Albany Plan. An aristocratic Scot who had fled to America as a Jacobite in 1715 and later held public offices in New York and New Jersey. Mathematician, intellectual, original member of the American Philosophical Society, and editor of John Peter Zenger's *New York Weekly Journal*.

ALLEN, JOHN (c. 1685–1750), member of the committee supervising Franklin's printing of money at Burlington in 1728; member of the New Jersey legislature (1722–27), treasurer of West Jersey (1722–50) and Superior Court judge after 1736.

ALLEN, WILLIAM (1704–1780), supported Franklin for postmaster-general in 1753 but became an enemy in the quarrel over proprietary privileges. Son-in-law of Andrew Hamilton and father-in-law of John Penn, he was chief justice (1750–74) but resigned when Pennsylvania moved toward Independence.

AMHERST, JEFFREY (1717–1797), succeeded Lord Loudoun as British commander-in-chief in North America. Defeated the French in a series of battles (1758–60) but proved inept at Indian relations.

ANDREWS, JEDEDIAH (1674–1747), Harvard-educated sole Presbyterian minister in Philadelphia before Samuel Hemphill became his assistant in September 1734. After having Hemphill excommunicated for "liberalism," Andrews was himself briefly suspended in 1744 for a "disgraceful act."

ANNIS, THOMAS, captain of the *London Hope*, the packet boat on which Franklin sailed to London, November 5, 1724.

BALTIMORE, CHARLES CALVERT, 5th BARON (1699–1751), proprietor of Maryland, where he resided 1732–33. Sued by the Penns in 1734 over a boundary dispute that was eventually settled by the Mason-Dixon survey of 1767. (Franklin printed the key documents in the suit.) Member of Parliament 1734–51.

BARD or BAIRD, PATRICK, politically powerful secretary of the province and clerk of the Council (1723–26, 1743); also health inspector for the port of Philadelphia (from 1720) and registrar of the Vice-Admiralty Court (1738).

BASKET OR BASKETT, JOHN (d. 1742), master of the Stationers Company (1714–15) and printer of the Oxford Bible (1716–17). Creditor of Sir William Keith and in February 1726 supported his retaining the governorship.

BEATTY, CHARLES CLINTON (c. 1715–1772), chaplain and participated in the successful campaign (1757) for Fort Duquesne.

BENEZET, JOHN STEPHEN (1683–1751), father of Franklin's friend, Quaker schoolmaster Anthony Benezet; John Stephen was a Huguenot merchant who moved to London in 1715 and returned to Philadelphia in 1731 as a Quaker. Became a Moravian in 1743 upon his retiring and moving to Germantown.

BENGER, ELLIOTT (d. 1753), deputy postmaster-general whom Franklin succeeded. He had purchased the office from his relative Alexander Spotswood, his predecessor, for the customary cost of £200, and earned about £150 a year.

BOND, THOMAS (1712–1784), Franklin's "particular Friend" and family physician. Along with brother PHINEAS (1717–1775), Thomas joined Franklin in founding Philadelphia's medical school, hospital, and American Philosophical Society.

BONNELL, JOHN DOD, captain of the packet *Harriott* on Loudoun's abortive Louisburg campaign; wounded there. Later commanded an East India packet.

BRADDOCK, EDWARD (1695–1755), named to command British forces in North America in 1755, he was the victim of ill-made plans based on bad advice. Said Franklin: "The General presum'd too much, and was too secure" (*Papers* 6.170).

BRADFORD, ANDREW (c. 1686–1742), sole printer in Philadelphia until the advent of Samuel Keimer (shortly before Franklin's arrival). Supported James Franklin's stand against the Massachusetts assembly in his *American Weekly Mercury* for February 26, 1723. Spirited competitor of Franklin, who succeeded him as local postmaster in 1737.

BRADFORD, WILLIAM (1663–1752), Franklin's early counselor in New York. Had apprenticed with London's principal Quaker printer and came to Philadelphia (1685) to be printer for the Quakers. But in 1692, he was accused of libel. Acquitted by a jury, he went to New York (1693) where he became that colony's official printer.

BREINTNALL, JOSEPH (d. 1746), Franklin's favorite in the Junto. Coauthor of the "Busy-Body" series and occasional poet, he shared Franklin's interest in science and corresponded with the Royal Society. When he drowned on March 16, 1746, some suspected suicide.

BRISSON, MATHURIN-JACQUES (1723–1806), translated Joseph Priestley's *History of Electricity* (1767) into French (1771), but added his own footnotes disparaging Franklin's theories. In 1785 he was convinced by Martin Van Marum of the correctness of Franklin's single-fluid theory of electricity.

BROCKDEN, CHARLES (1683–1769), Philadelphia's leading drafter of legal documents, and recorder of deeds and proprietary records. Franklin did much job printing for him during 1732–39. Grandfather of the novelist Charles Brockden Brown; successively an Anglican, a Quaker, a Whitefield "New Light," and a Moravian.

BROWNE, JOHN (1667–1737), physician-innkeeper of Burlington, had probably traveled in Europe in the course of medical training. Owned 230 acres near Burlington at his death. Franklin's obituary in the *Pennsylvania Gazette* (May 19, 1737) called Browne a "Gentleman of singular Skill in the Profession of Surgery."

BROWNELL, GEORGE (c. 1690–1738), Franklin's schoolmaster, settled in Boston from 1713, taught dancing and sewing as well as writing and ciphering. In 1718, opened the first licensed dancing school, which continued after his death.

BUFFON, GEORGES-LOUIS LECLERC, COMTE DE (1707–1788), suggested in 1751 that Franklin's electrical experiments be translated into French. Among the first to experiment with lightning rods; translated Newton; and devised a classification of animals. His thesis that America's extreme climates caused the degeneration of plants, animals, and men was answered at length by Jefferson's *Notes on the State of Virginia*.

BURNET, WILLIAM (1688–1729), son of Bishop Gilbert Burnet and godson of King William and Queen Mary, governed New York (1720–27) and Massachusetts (1728–29) as a steadfast champion of royal prerogatives. He occasioned Franklin's first editorial, October 1729, in the *Pennsylvania Gazette*.

BUSTILL, SAMUEL (d. 1742?), a Burlington Friend, leader in the assembly's struggles against governors of West Jersey, including its attempts to issue the new money that brought Franklin and Keimer there in 1728.

CANTON, JOHN (1718–1772), "very ingenious" London schoolmaster, was the first in England to repeat Franklin's electrical experiments. Continued to study electricity and later became Franklin's friend in the "Club of Honest Whigs," sharing his interests in science, rational religion, and liberalism.

CAVE, EDWARD (1691–1754), printer of Franklin's *Experiments & Observations* (1751). Published the influential *Gentleman's Magazine*.

CHARLES, ROBERT (d. 1770), joint Pennsylvania agent with Franklin (1757–61), had been secretary of the Provincial Council (1726–39), then emigrated to England and was named agent for New York (1748) and for Pennsylvania (1752).

CLAPHAM, WILLIAM (d. 1763), successor to Franklin at Fort Allen, later commanded Fort Augusta (1756–57). An ineffectual commander, rumored to be a drunkard.

CLIFTON, JOHN (d. 1759), Quaker apothecary, credited by Franklin with placing the first streetlight in Philadelphia.

CLINTON, GEORGE (c. 1686–1761), mercenary governor of New York (1743–53) who called the Albany conference in 1751. Father of Sir Henry Clinton, British commander during part of the Revolution.

COLEMAN, WILLIAM (1704–1769), helped subsidize Franklin's career in 1728 and remained a lifelong friend despite opposing him politically.

A merchant, he was also a Supreme Court justice (1758–69). When he went to London for cancer surgery in 1768, Franklin nursed him.

COLLINSON, PETER (1694–1768), early patron and London agent for the Library Company, merchant trading with America and correspondent with naturalists at home and abroad. Franklin wrote a memoir (February 8, 1770) testifying that his early work on electricity had been "encouraged by the friendly Reception he gave to the Letters I wrote to him upon it" (*Papers* 17.65–66).

CONWAY, HENRY SEYMOUR (1719–1795), field marshal and British secretary of state (1765–68), as well as cousin of Horace Walpole. Critic of Britain's war against the former colonies.

COOPER, JOSEPH (1691–1751), another New Jersey politician whom Franklin met at Burlington, assemblyman from Gloucester County, and, with Isaac Pearson, a Proprietary representative on the committee overseeing the new money.

COPLEY, GODFREY (c. 1654–1709). Franklin was first to receive the Copley medal as a choice of the president and council of the Royal Society. Previously it had been awarded by executors of the estate of Copley who, though not active in the study of natural science, had been a member of the Society and a close friend of Sir Hans Sloane.

CROGHAN, GEORGE (d. 1782), Irish immigrant trader and Indian expert, assisted Washington, Braddock, Forbes, and Bouquet in their western campaigns, and in 1756 was named Deputy Superintendent of Indian Affairs.

DALIBARD, THOMAS-FRANÇOIS (1703–1799), translator of Franklin's *Experiments & Observations* into French (February 1752), was first to prove Franklin's theory that lightning was electrical (May 10, 1752).

DECOW, ISAAC (d. 1750), Huguenot-Quaker scion of one of the pioneering families of New Jersey, proprietor of the province as well as clerk of the Council, treasurer, and surveyor-general.

DELOR (first name unknown), Dalibard's teacher at the Sorbonne, joined Dalibard in 1752 to test Franklin's theories on lightning; later (1753) translated into French a letter by Giambatista Beccaria answering Nollet's attacks on Franklin (1753).

DENHAM, THOMAS (d. 1728), Philadelphia merchant who left Bristol in 1715 after falling into "bad Company" and going bankrupt, but paid all debts seven years later. He lent Franklin passage money to return to Philadelphia in 1726 (he was half-owner of the ship) and forgave the debt in his will. Franklin worked for him in Philadelphia from October 1726 to March 1727/8; but by the time Denham died on July 4, 1728, Franklin had already begun his own business.

DENNY, WILLIAM (1709–1765), Pennsylvania's mercenary governor (1756–59), took bribes from the assembly to disobey the proprietors. Through these and other corrupt means he was able to retire to a life of ease in London.

DUNBAR, THOMAS (d. 1767), colonel who succeeded to Braddock's command in the field (1755); resigned after his much censured retreat and was appointed lieutenant-governor of Gibraltar.

EGREMONT, CHARLES WYNDHAM, 2D EARL OF (1710–1763), in 1761 succeeded William Pitt as the secretary of state in charge of colonial affairs. With George Grenville (his brother-in-law) and Lord Halifax, he headed the British government in 1763.

ENNIS, JAMES (c. 1709–1774), official courier for the government of Pennsylvania.

FAWKENER, EVERARD (1684–1758), London merchant, friend of Voltaire (who resided at his home when in England), and joint postmaster-general of Great Britain who appointed Franklin to his postmastership in 1753. His widow wed Franklin's friend Thomas Pownall.

FISHER, MARY FRANKLIN (1673–1758), Franklin's cousin in Wellingborough, England. She and her husband left their property to him and five cousins. Franklin generously divided his share between two of them, "ancient Women and poor" (*Papers* 8.414).

FOLGER, PETER (1617–1690), Franklin's maternal grandfather, Baptist and native of Norwich, England, emigrated in 1635. Married an indentured servant of Puritan leader Hugh Peter; settled on Nantucket (1664) as Indian interpreter and clerk of the court. He went to jail in 1676 rather than relinquish court records to an incoming administration.

FOSTER, JAMES (1697–1753), preacher from whom Samuel Hemphill copied sermons. A leading London Baptist "free-thinker" who, denying "mysteries in religion," urged every man to choose whatever religion seemed "most rational, and agreeable to the divine will."

FOTHERGILL, JOHN (1712–1780), Franklin's personal physician in London. He was also leader of the English Quakers and reported regularly to Pennsylvania on all matters affecting their sect. Physician to the highest government officers, he provided timely intelligence to Franklin.

FRANCIS, TENCH (d. 1758), appointed Pennsylvania's attorney-general (1741–55) only three years after his arrival from Maryland, prepared the draft of the Academy's charter, approved April 1752.

FRANKLIN, ABIAH FOLGER (1667–1752), Benjamin Franklin's mother, born on Nantucket, wed when twenty-two and her husband (a widower with six children under eleven) was thirty-five, then bore him ten children over the next twenty years. Widowed in 1745, she lived, said Benjamin, "a good life" with her daughter Jane Mecom (1712–1794) in Boston.

FRANKLIN, ANN SMITH (1696–1763), Franklin's sister-in-law at Newport, probably New England's first woman printer. When her husband James died (1735), she ran the business for thirteen years until James, Jr. returned from his apprenticeship with Franklin. With her son, she began *The Newport Mercury* in 1758 and continued it after his death in 1762.

FRANKLIN, BENJAMIN ("THE ELDER," 1650–1727), Franklin's favorite uncle, emigrated from London in 1715 after losing his wife and nine of ten children. Until his son Samuel could afford to take him in, he lived with Josiah.

FRANKLIN, DEBORAH READ ROGERS (c. 1707–1774), Franklin's wife of 44 years, whose birthplace and birthdate are unknown, second of seven children of carpenter and contractor John Read, who came to Philadelphia in 1711. She wed potter John Rogers in August 1725, but he fled to the West Indies in December 1727. Franklin explains in the *Autobiography* the two reasons for their common-law marriage on September 1, 1730. Because she dreaded the sea, Franklin was away from her for twenty-five of the fourty-four years of their marriage, yet their affection remained constant. After her death from a stroke, he said: "I have lately lost my old and faithful Companion; and I every day become more sensible of the greatness of the Loss; which cannot now be repair'd" (*Papers* 23.311).

FRANKLIN, FRANCIS FOLGER (1732–1736), Benjamin and Deborah Franklin's only son. He died of smallpox; Franklin greatly regretted the decision not to have him inoculated. "The DELIGHT of all that knew him," his gravestone announced.

FRANKLIN, JAMES (1697–1735), returning from London with a press and types in 1717, Franklin's brother set up shop and printed the *Boston Gazette* (December 1719–August 1720) and then his own *New-England Courant* (1721–26). After the *Courant* failed (1727), he moved to Newport, where he anticipated "Poor Richard's Almanac" with "Poor Robin's Almanac" (1728–35), became colony printer, and published the *Rhode-Island Gazette* (March 1732–September 1733). After his death, his son James, Jr. (c. 1730–1762) was apprenticed to Franklin.

FRANKLIN, JAMES, JR. (1730?–1762), Franklin's nephew, attended Philadelphia Academy with Franklin's son William before he was apprenticed to Franklin. He returned to Newport about 1748 and became his mother's partner circa 1754; they began the *Newport Mercury* in 1758.

FRANKLIN, JOHN (1690–1756), Franklin's favorite and eldest brother, followed his father's trade, making soap, moving to Newport in 1715 and there developing a clear, green soap stamped with a crown that helped support the family for many years. By 1744 he had returned to Boston, partner in a new glassworks; ten years later Franklin appointed him postmaster, an office he enjoyed till his death.

FRANKLIN, JOSIAH (1657–1745), Franklin's father, a silk-dyer on coming to Boston in 1683, settled nearly opposite the Old South Church where Franklin would be baptized. He was the "praecentor" or chant leader at Samuel Willard's South Church in Boston, and by 1708 belonged to a private religious worship group that included Chief Justice Samuel Sewall.

FRANKLIN, JOSIAH, JR. (1685–c. 1715), Franklin's half-brother who ran away to sea, spent about nine years in the East Indies, returned home for the memorable feast attended by thirteen Franklin children, and then was never heard of again.

FRANKLIN, THOMAS (fl. 1563–1573), Franklin's great-great-grandfather, started out as a tailor's apprentice, but his master "kept such a stingy house, that he left him" for a blacksmith and became a blacksmith himself.

FRANKLIN, THOMAS (1598–1682), Franklin's grandfather, also a blacksmith. He was once jailed a year and a day for writing libelous verse, but brought up his family in a religious way.

FRANKLIN, THOMAS (1673–1702), Franklin's uncle, whom he was said to resemble, had been bred a blacksmith but became a teacher, scrivener, tobacco merchant, clerk of county court and of the archdeacon. He devised a method of flood control, and, though some thought him a magician, all sorts of people sought his advice. He installed the chimes in Ecton church (England) and built an organ for himself.

FRANKLIN, WILLIAM (c. 1731–1813), Franklin's illegitimate son, mother unknown, was with Benjamin Franklin until 1762 when, having passed the bar and married an heiress, he was appointed Royal Governor of New Jersey. As Governor, he promoted agriculture and roads, managed Indian relations and tricky assembly relations, cautioned the Ministry against taxation without representation, and proposed a government-sponsored Continental Congress. He was probably the most successful Royal Governor in the colonies when Franklin wrote Part One of the autobiography in 1771—ostensibly for him. In 1773, Benjamin Franklin said he was "a thorough government man," and on September 7, 1774, wrote, "you, who are a thorough courtier, see everything with government eyes" (*Papers* 20.437). Remaining loyal, imprisoned with the outbreak of war then freed in an exchange of 1778, William Franklin became president of the Associated Loyalists in 1780 and sponsored guerrilla raids on Connecticut and New Jersey. After the British banned the raids, William lived in England on pension. In a postwar reconciliation, Benjamin Franklin wrote: "Our Opinions are not in our own Power; they are form'd and govern'd much by Circumstances, that are often as inexplicable as they are irresistible" (Smyth, *Writings*, 9.252). William's own illegitimate son WILLIAM TEMPLE FRANKLIN (1762–1823) succeeded him as Benjamin Franklin's companion and became Benjamin Franklin's (delinquent) literary heir.

FRENCH, JOHN (d. 1728), political henchman of Governor Keith at New Castle, Delaware, he held many offices: high sheriff, councilor in Indian affairs, commander of the fort, registrar of wills, speaker of the assembly, and also (when Franklin met him) justice of the Supreme Court (1722–28).

GODFREY, THOMAS (1704–1749), Franklin's lodger (1728–30), a brilliant self-taught mathematician. He supplemented his income from glazing (he did most of the glasswork on Independence Hall) with an almanac. Franklin printed *Godfrey's Almanac* in 1729, 1730, and 1731, but when Godfrey—angered by Franklin's satire in the *Pennsylvania Gazette* (July 10, 1732)—took his almanac to Andrew Bradford in late 1732, Franklin hastily prepared the first *Poor Richard's Almanac*. Godfrey independently invented Hadley's quadrant. His son was the poet Thomas Godfrey (1736–1763).

GORDON, PATRICK (1664–1736), army major who succeeded Keith as governor for ten uneventful years (1726–36). Gordon recommended Ferdinand John Paris as Pennsylvania's agent in London, thus launching a career culminating in the litigious contest of 1757.

GRACE, ROBERT (1709–1766), Franklin's early benefactor, who helped him finance his own business, was also his landlord for thirty-seven years. Philadelphian by birth, he inherited his grandfather's Irish estate at seventeen, and in 1740 married into a prosperous family of ironmasters. Franklin helped Grace when he was being pressed by creditors in 1748 (*Papers* 3.329–30), and designed the "Franklin stove" for Grace to manufacture. Grace studied mineralogy abroad for three years, then returned to manage the successful Warwick Furnace, Chester County (1745–65).

GRANVILLE, JOHN CARTERET, SECOND EARL OF (1690–1763), president of the powerful Privy Council (1751–63, that ruled on Franklin's case against the proprietors; his second wife (m. 1744) was Thomas Penn's sister-in-law.

HALIFAX, CHARLES MONTAGU, FIRST EARL OF (1661–1715), patron of Franklin's uncle Thomas, probably known to him as clerk of the Archbishop of Northampton, and president of the Royal Society (1695–98).

HALL, DAVID (1714–1772), Franklin's partner, a Scots printer working in London, came to Philadelphia in July 1744 at Franklin's invitation for a three-year trial prior to setting up under his sponsorship in the West Indies. At the end of the term, Franklin kept him as full partner in Philadelphia. On January 1, 1748, a week before he married into Deborah Franklin's family, he bought Franklin's stock for £700. He paid Franklin £500 a year from shop profits for the next eighteen years, plus a share of the profits from the *Pennsylvania Gazette* until 1772.

HAMILTON, ANDREW (c. 1676–1741), young Virginia lawyer left a sizeable fortune by his patron. Hamilton rose to be speaker of the Pennsylvania Assembly, and earned lasting fame (and created the sobriquet of "the Philadelphia Lawyer") for his defense of John Peter Zenger in the landmark censorship case. Franklin revered him as "the Poor Man's Friend," and defended "His free Manner of treating Religious Subjects": "If he could not subscribe to the Creed of any particular Church, it was not for want of considering them All" (*Papers* 2.238).

HAMILTON, JAMES (c. 1710–1783), son of Andrew Hamilton, worked with Franklin in the Masons and in founding the Library, the College, and the American Philosophical Society. Twice governor (1748–54, 1759–63), his administrations were marked by assembly quarrels. Franklin admired him as "a benevolent and upright . . . sensible Man" (*Papers* 3.283).

HANBURY, JOHN (1700–1758), wealthy merchant who welcomed Franklin to London in 1757; headed a large, influential Quaker family whose great fortune was based in the colonial tobacco trade.

HARRY, DAVID (1708–1760), resident of the "Welsh Barony" near Philadelphia, center of a large population of Welsh Quakers, he became the first printer in Barbados (1730). He sold out to Keimer in a year and moved to South Carolina for another seven years before returning to Philadelphia sometime before 1756.

HEMPHILL, SAMUEL, Irish Presbyterian minister, installed as Jedediah Andrew's assistant, September 23, 1734, who by April 1735 was charged with preaching subversive sermons, attracting a crowd of freethinkers, and plagiarizing. After April 26, 1735, when Hemphill was banned from the pulpit, Franklin began writing pamphlets in his defense (*Papers* 2.37–126).

HERTFORD, FRANCIS SEYMOUR CONWAY (1719–1794), served as privy councilor, ambassador to France, and lord lieutenant of Ireland.

HOMES, ROBERT (1694–d. before 1743), married to Franklin's sister Mary (1694–1731), he captained a ship plying between Boston and Philadelpha, and died at sea.

HOPKINSON, THOMAS (1709–1751), close friend of Franklin's in Junto activities; magistrate, with a reputation for honesty and integrity, brilliant wit, and bashfulness. First president of the American Philosophical Society. His humorist son, Francis (1737–1791), was an executor of Franklin's estate and was willed Franklin's scientific equipment.

HOUSE, GEORGE (d. 1754?), friend who sent Franklin his first customer in 1728, Quaker shoemaker, and an original member of Franklin's Union Fire Company. He later served on the common council and as overseer of the poor (1746).

HUME, DAVID (1711–1776), the great philosopher and historian, secretary to several leading British military and political figures. In 1762 he ranked Franklin as a "Philosopher, and . . . Great Man of Letters," but in 1771, angered at his politics, called him "a very factious man."

HUNTER, WILLIAM (d, 1761), joint deputy postmaster-general with Franklin, printer in Williamsburg, publisher of the *Virginia Gazette*. Franklin took charge of Hunters' illegitimate son's education— "for I loved his Father truly" (*Papers* 10.317).

ISTED, AMBROSE (1718–1781), owner of "Franklin House," Ecton, in which he lived when Franklin visited him in 1758. The manor house was also visited by the artist Hogarth and by Bishop Percy, who began work on his collection of ballads there.

JAMES, ABEL (1724–1790), for many years a political official of the Quakers' Friendly Association, he worked on Indian affairs with Franklin in the 1750s. As the Revolution approached, his mercantile business declined. He served as financial adviser and executor for distressed Quakers like Grace Galloway, among whose effects he recovered Franklin's manuscript of Part One of the *Autobiography*.

KEIMER, SAMUEL (c. 1688–1742), opened a school for slaves in Philadelphia (1722), but by Franklin's arrival (1723) had set up as a printer and, two years after, was hired to reprint Sewel's *History of the Quakers*. In 1728 he subcontracted 44½ sheets of the book to the new firm of Franklin and Meredith. In 1729, stung by the "Busy-Body" essays, he satirized Franklin as a combination of Diogenes and Don Quixote (*Pennsylvania Gazette*, March 13). After selling the newspaper to Franklin, he moved to Bridgetown, Barbados, where he started the first Caribbean newspaper in 1731.

KEITH, GEORGE (1638–1716), master (1689) of the Quaker school in Philadelphia, leader of Quakers opposed to being taxed to arm ships against pirates. Convicted of contempt of court for refusing to pay, he went into exile in England (1692), and later (1702–04) served as an Anglican minister in America.

KEITH, WILLIAM (1680–1749), descended from Scottish aristocrats, he was a popular customs inspector for the southern colonies when named governor (1716) at the request of Philadelphia merchants; they turned on him when he issued more paper money (1722). He formed his own political party and, after being fired (1726) by the proprietors as governor, was twice elected to the Assembly. At the height of his new power he fled from debt to England (1728), and consulted on colonial affairs until jailed for new debts (1734–35). He died in debtor's prison, November 18, 1749. A granddaughter, Elizabeth Graeme (Fergusson), was briefly engaged to William Franklin.

KENNEDY, ARCHIBALD (1685–1763), the "Mr. Kennedy" who approved Franklin's Albany Plan, receiver general of New York and a leading intellectual and political theorist of the pre-Revolutionary period. His pamphlet *The Importance of Gaining and Preserving the Friendship of the Indians* (1751) prefigured Franklin's plan and elicited a key letter (*Papers* 4.117–21) from Franklin on Indian affairs, colonial politics, and population.

KENNEDY, ARCHIBALD, JR. (d. 1794), son of the above, he (though a passenger) was the naval captain who dramatically prevented shipwreck off the Scilly Isles on Franklin's 1757 voyage. After acquiring extensive properties in New York and New Jersey, he (after the death of a cousin) became the 11th Earl of Cassillis (1792).

KINNERSLEY, EBENEZER (1711–1778), Franklin's chief collaborator on electrical experiments, a Baptist minister. Franklin's "Statement of Editorial Policy" (*Pennsylvania Gazette*, July 24, 1740) prefaced Kinnersley's letter opposing the Great Awakening's emotionalism Beginning in 1749, he lectured widely on the Franklinian theory of electricity (including the electrical nature of lightning). He headed the English School in Franklin's Academy (1753). When his superior, William Smith, Provost of the Academy and political enemy of Franklin, charged Franklin with taking credit for Kinnersley's experiments, Kinnersley refuted him in the *Gazette*, November 30, 1758, but the charge lingered.

LAWRENCE, THOMAS (1689–1754), Franklin's choice to lead the militia, was a native of New York who had become a partner, of Franklin's friend James Logan and served as a provincial councilor and trustee of the Academy.

LE ROY, JEAN-BAPTISTE (1720–1800), Franklin's friend, correspondent, and early scientific disciple. Elected to the French Academy of Sciences (1751) and shortly thereafter rebutted Nollet's attack on the Franklinian theory of electricity. Franklin met him in Paris in 1767.

LE VEILLARD, LOUIS-GUILLAUME (1733–1793), Franklin's next-door neighbor in Passy, urged him to complete his "Memoirs" and in November 1789 received a press-copy of the completed portion. William Temple Franklin exchanged the original, more complete manuscript for Le Veillard's copy, "as more convenient for the press." (The original remained in the Le Veillard family for over half a century.) Mayor of Passy, he was guillotined, June 1793.

Logan, James (1674–1751), book collector, classicist, and mathematicia, came to Philadelphia as William Penn's secretary in 1699 and then for fifty years looked after the proprietors' business and political interests. After 1710 his financial success enabled him to devote time to science, literature, and the classics. In 1730 he moved into a Philadelphia mansion, Stenton, where Franklin had free access to his 3,000-volume library and to his stimulating conversation.

Loudoun, John Campbell, Fourth Earl of (1705–1782), initially succeeded Braddock in 1756 as commander-in-chief, Franklin thought him "very well fitted" for the post (*Papers* 6.472), yet a year later concluded, "His Lordship has on all Occasions treated me with the greatest Goodness, but I find frequently that strong Prejudices are infus'd into his Mind against our Province" (*Papers* 7.228). After the Louisburg debacle (ordered by Sir William Pitt), he was recalled, but later regained his reputation.

Lutwidge, Walter (d. 1761), captain of the packet *General Wall*, who told Franklin on his 1757 trip to England that the cooks' greasy water accounted for the smooth wakes of two ships in the convoy, thus starting Franklin's interest in the surface tension of water (*Papers* 20.465). Lutwidge "was mortally wounded by a nine Pound shot" (March 20, 1761) in a battle with a French privateer.

Lyons, William, Franklin's early guide in London's intellectual circles, was a surgeon and author of *The Infallibility, Dignity, and Excellence of Humane Judgment* (London, 1719). Franklin treasured the copy of his own *Liberty and Necessity* (1725) that Lyons annotated.

Macclesfield, George Parker, Second Earl of (c. 1697–1764), the president of the Royal Society who presented Franklin the Copley Medal, was instrumental in having England change from the Julian ("Old Style") to the Gregorian ("New Style") calendar in 1752.

Mandeville, Bernard (c. 1670–1733), Dutch physician, Enlightenment philosopher, and important man-of-letters residing in London; was notorious for his satiric *Fable of the Bees; or Private Vices, Public Benefits* (1714), which popularized the view that only self-interest motivated humans. Mandeville epitomized avant-garde infamy when Franklin arrived in London in 1724.

MANSFIELD, WILLIAM MURRAY, BARON (1705–1793), Lord Chief Justice of the King's Bench (1756–88), worked out the compromise between Franklin and the proprietors in the interests of colonial defense and was moderate in everything but his insistence that Parliament had complete sovereignty over America.

MATHER, COTTON (1663–1728), assistant to and successor of his father Increase as pastor of the Second Church in Boston (1685–1728), he was the most visible American Puritan writer, politician, and promoter of his time. Compromised by his defense of the Salem witch trials, and losing official favor for asserting the power of the church over the state, he turned to and promoted such causes as inoculation against smallpox. Of his 450 books, at least three—*Bonifacius* ("Essays to Do Good") (1710), *Religious Societies* (1724), and *Manuductio ad Ministerium* (1726)—provided models for Franklin's Junto. Franklin wrote Mather's son Samuel about *Bonifacius*: "If I have been . . . a useful citizen, the public owes the advantage of it to that book" (Smyth, *Writings*, 9.208).

MAUGRIDGE, WILLIAM (d. 1766), Franklin's "solid, sensible" Junto friend was a ship-carpenter, and possibly Franklin's landlord in 1727–28. He left town in 1750 to take over the farm of relatives, parents of Daniel Boone. He twice mortgaged the farm through Franklin.

MEREDITH, HUGH (c. 1697–c. 1750), Franklin's partner, son of Simon Meredith, assemblyman from rural Chester County, withdrew from the printing business by April 1730, and moved to Cape Fear, North Carolina, which he described in the *Pennsylvania Gazette*, May 6 and 15, 1731. By 1738 he had returned to Pennsylvania and by 1742 became a leader of "the country party" in local politics. In 1750, after Franklin several times loaned him money, he dropped from view.

MICKLE, SAMUEL (1684–1765), a Quaker merchant, was the "croaker" who attempted to dishearten Franklin.

MITCHELL, JOHN (d. 1768), the friend who introduced Franklin's electrical theories to the Royal Society, was a naturalist, physician, and map-maker. Franklin used his map of "British and French Dominions in North America" (1755) to negotiate the peace in 1782–83. Franklin's last letter (to Thomas Jefferson, April 8, 1790) concerned the map, which continued to be cited in treaties and border adjustments down to 1932. Mitchell lived in Virginia (1725–46) before moving to London.

MORRIS, JAMES (1707–1751), the Quaker who protested Fire Company contributions to defense, belonged to a prominent Quaker family. An assemblyman, a trustee of the Loan Office, and a member of the Library Company.

MORRIS, ROBERT HUNTER (c. 1700–1764), governor of Pennsylvania (October 1754–August 1764), son of New Jersey governor Lewis Morris, who had named him Chief Justice of that province in 1730. Also, with Thomas Penn, a proprietor of New Jersey, and his reputation for being anti-Quaker and venal preceded him to Philadelphia. Replaced, he returned to his lifelong post as Chief Justice in New Jersey.

NEWTON, ISAAC (1642–1727), one of Franklin's heroes, this great scientist, best known for theorizing gravity, light, color, the motions of celestial bodies, and other physical laws, was president of the Royal Society from 1703 to 1727, succeeded by his friend Sir Hans Sloane.

NOLLET, JEAN-ANTOINE, ABBÉ (1700–1770), Franklin's antagonist in debates on electricity, was France's foremost experimenter in the field and director of the Academy of Sciences. His Cartesian two-fluid theory of electricity was widely accepted when Franklin introduced his Newtonian single-fluid theory. Nollet's *Lettres sur L'électricité* (1753) attacked Franklin's *Experiments and Observations* . . . (1751).

NORRIS, ISAAC (1701–1766), Franklin's companion at Carlisle and Albany, was his political ally against the proprietors. He was grandson of Thomas Lloyd (patriarch of Philadelphia's Quaker aristocracy), son of Isaac Norris (1671–1735, Quaker leader), son-in-law of the learned James Logan, and father-in-law of John Dickinson. Elected to the assembly in 1734, he already had served as common councilor of Philadelphia, and was an alderman (1730–42). If he were the "new member" whose opposition Franklin feared, Franklin was uncannily correct in his judgment. He led the Quaker majority in the Assembly (1734–66) and, as speaker (1750–64), worked closely with Franklin until they disagreed on petitioning for a royal provincial government. After James Logan's, his library was among Philadelphia's finest.

ONION, STEPHEN (d. 1754), fellow passenger on Franklin's first voyage to England, he and Thomas Russell had come to Maryland ca. 1722 for a syndicate of English investors in the Principio Iron Works. They returned to London (November 1724) to report their findings. Onion was named superintendent of the Works in 1726.

ORME, ROBERT (d. 1790), Braddock's aide-de-camp, wounded with his chief, then returned to England and resigned his captain's commission in 1756.

OSBORNE, CHARLES, Franklin's friend of his youth who became an eminent attorney in the West Indies, where he died young. He could be the subject of an obituary in the *Gentleman's Magazine* 19 (1749), 380: "——Osborne, Esq.: Barbadoes merchant worth 60,000 £ of the small pox."

PALMER, JOHN (1612–1679), Archdeacon of Northamptonshire (1665–79), employed Franklin's uncle Thomas as clerk. A son of the same name established "A School for Poor Children" (1752), and a granddaughter provided information about uncle Thomas to Franklin in 1758.

PALMER, SAMUEL (c. 1692–1732), Franklin's first employer in London, who had a shop in Bartholomew Close from about 1723. He wrote portions of a "very bad" *History of Printing*, published in *The Grub Street Journal*, and supervised a private press for the Royal Family in 1731, but went bankrupt.

PARIS, FERDINAND JOHN (d. 1759), Franklin's legal antagonist in London, had preceded him as agent in the 1730s and been the Penn family's adviser on colonial affairs since the 1720s. An expert on colonial law, he wrote instructions to the governors and replied to the assembly's messages. He died on December 16, 1759, only a few months after the hearing described in the final pages of Part Four.

PARSONS, WILLIAM (1701–1757), member of the original Junto, English-born shoemaker who became surveyor-general (1741–48). Member of the American Philosophical Society and librarian of the Library Company. Retiring because of ill health, he went to Easton as the proprietors' agent and there commanded the Northampton militia in Indian wars.

PEARSON, ISAAC (d. 1749), New Jersey assemblyman and "wet" Quaker (meaning a tippler), friend of Governor Lewis Morris who would have made him a judge in 1740 but wished to spare him public abuse. He had a large silversmith and clockmaking business in Burlington, New Jersey.

PEMBERTON, HENRY (1694–1771), the "Dr. Pemberton" Franklin met at Batson's, was a physician and member of the Royal Society. A friend of Newton's, he superintended publication of the *Principia*

(3rd ed., 1726) and also published a memoir, *A View of Sir Isaac Newton's Philosophy* (1728).

PENN, JOHN (1729–1795), friendly to Franklin and to Pennsylvania, this nephew of Thomas Penn lived in Philadelphia from 1752 to 1755; was governor from 1763 to 1771, and then from 1773 to 1776. He maneuvered to have delegates to the first Continental Congress elected by the assembly, thus giving them legitimacy. He remained in Philadelphia the rest of his life.

PENN, THOMAS (1702–1775), one of the three sons to whom William Penn willed Pennsylvania. The eldest son, John, died in 1746, willing his share to Thomas. The youngest, Richard, also left administration of the province up to Thomas. Thus Thomas made the policies which F. J. Paris conveyed as elaborate instructions to the governors (technically deputy governors). In 1754, Penn considered Franklin "as capable as any man in America to serve the Crown" (*Papers* 5.334n). But after the clash over taxes on proprietary lands, he refused to "have any conversation with [Franklin] on any pretence" (*Papers* 7.364n), while Franklin conceived "a more cordial and thorough Contempt for him than I ever before felt for any Man living—" (*Papers* 7.362).

PENN, WILLIAM (1644–1718), founder and proprietor of Pennsylvania who twice visited the province (1682–84, 1699–1701). His charter of 1701 was Pennsylvania's constitution until the Revolution. Franklin parodied his pamphlet on titles of honor, *No Cross, No Crown* (1669), in the *New England Courant* (February 18, 1723).

PETERS, RICHARD (c. 1704–1776), an early friend of Franklin's, was, as secretary of the Provincial Council (1743–62), the proprietors' chief correspondent. Peters headed the Academy's board of trustees. His friendship with Franklin ended when the latter attacked the proprietors. He left public service in 1762 and became pastor of Philadelphia's two Episcopal churches.

PITT, WILLIAM (1708–1778), a brilliant orator and savage opponent, was prime minister (1756–61), then made Earl of Chatham in 1766. He championed the American colonies and worked with Franklin in 1774–75 to avoid war. In 1761, Americans were said to "almost idolize him (*Papers* 9.403). He later called Franklin "an Honour not to the English Nation only but to Human Nature" (*Papers* 21.582).

POTTS, STEPHEN (1704–1758), a Quaker bookbinder, member of the original Junto, he was Franklin's lodger (1731–37) until becoming doorkeeper of the assembly. He later ran a tavern (1748–58). Franklin said he was "a Wit, that seldom acted wisely . . . in the midst of his Poverty, ever laughing!" (*Papers*, 8.159.)

POWNALL, THOMAS (1722–1805), Franklin's close friend and political ally abroad, was a professional administrator who came to New York as secretary to a governor who committed suicide, leaving him to travel the colonies. At Philadelphia, he began the alliance with Franklin that in 1756 alarmed the proprietors because of Pownall's influence in London and Franklin's in America (*Papers* 6.486n). After serving as secretary to Lord Loudoun (1756) and governor of Massachusetts (1757–60) he returned to England to write an influential book, *The Administration of the Colonies* (1764), and to defend the colonies as a Member of Parliament (1767–80). Also active in science.

PRATT, CHARLES, FIRST EARL CAMDEN (1714–1794), the "new" attorney general who studied Franklin's complaint against the proprietors in 1757, had previously received a retainer from the Pennsylvania assembly, but was not therefore barred from working on the new case. In 1759, Franklin found him inclined to favor the assembly, "tho' the Nature of his Office requires him to be something of a Prerogative Man" (*Papers* 8.294–95). In the House of Lords he championed the colonies.

QUINCY, JOSIAH (1710–1784), one of Massachusetts' richest merchants, a member of assembly, and later a patriot, he retired in 1750 to Braintree. He had an interest in John Franklin's glassworks, and Franklin also owned property near Quincy's, so they were not total strangers when Quincy solicited Franklin's assistance in 1755.

RALPH, JAMES (c. 1705–1762), stayed in London after Franklin left in 1726, writing poetry and plays, collaborating with Henry Fielding in political journalism, and becoming a skilled writer against the government, which in 1753 gave him a pension of £300 a year to stay out of politics. In 1757, at the request of the child Ralph had deserted thirty years earlier, Franklin located him in London, gave him editorial work, and, upon his death, bought books from his library to benefit his heirs.

READ, JAMES (1718–1793), husband of Deborah Franklin's second cousin, he was Benjamin Franklin's neighbor and rival bookseller. He unsuccessfully opposed Franklin as assembly clerk (1747), then moved to Reading, Pennsylvania, leaving debts Franklin tried to collect for London friends.

READ, JOHN (1677–1724), Franklin's father-in-law, came to Phila-delphia from Birmingham by 1711. As a carpenter and building contractor, he was well off; but before dying, he mortgaged his property (1724) and left his family in debt.

READ, SARAH WHITE (1675–1761), Franklin's mother-in-law, was born in Birmingham, wed John Read there in 1701, then bore him seven children, of whom only three survived to adulthood. As a widow, she shared Franklin's shop, selling medicines. At her death, Franklin consoled his wife: "Your Comfort will be, that no Care was wanting on your Part towards her," and "I cannot charge myself with having ever fail'd in one Instance of Duty and Respect for her" (*Papers* 10.69).

RIDDLESDEN, WILLIAM VANHAESDONCK (d. before 1733), interna-tional confidence man for whom John Read foolishly stood secu-rity, was transported to Maryland on October 27, 1720, for robbing a chapel. He fled to Philadelphia in 1721 where he bilked Read and others before fleeing the colonies. In France in 1722 he passed counterfeit English banknotes. Back in England, using an alias, he duped a wealthy woman into marriage and petitioned for lands in Maryland. He was unmasked and imprisoned (December 1723) but offered bail if he promised to transport him-self back to America for seven years. In 1724, he forged land grants for at least eleven thousand acres in Delaware and New Jersey.

ROBERTS, JAMES (1673?–1754), printer who rejected Ralph's offer to write a weekly paper for him; had an office in Warwick Lane and served as Master of the Stationers Company, 1729–31.

ROGERS, JOHN (d. 1745?), married (perhaps bigamously) on August 5, 1725, to Deborah Read, he fled his debtors in December 1727. If he is the John Rogers who died in Antigua, August 1745, then Franklin himself avoided the charge of bigamy by not officially marrying Deborah in 1730.

ROSE, AQUILA (c. 1695–1723), journeyman printer for Andrew Bradford, clerk of the assembly, and operator of a ferry. He died June 24, 1723. His son, Joseph, after apprenticeship with Franklin (1730), became foreman of his shop and printed Aquila Rose's *Poems on Several Occasions* (1740).

RUSSELL, THOMAS. *See* ONION, STEPHEN.

SCULL, NICHOLAS, II (1687–1761), one of the original Junto, surveyor and poet. He supervised the famous "Walking Purchase" of Indian lands that Franklin later called a fraud (*Papers* 9.222). Laid out Easton with William Parsons, succeeding him as surveyor-general (1748–61).

SHIPLEY, JONATHAN, BISHOP OF ST. ASAPH (1714–1788), one of Franklin's dearest English friends. His bishopric was perhaps lowest in the hierarchy, and he received no further advancement because of his fervent support of the American colonies.

SHIRLEY, WILLIAM (1694–1771), governor of Massachusetts (1741–57), he shared Franklin's hope for a colonial union and exchanged ideas with Franklin in letters of 1754, published for their bearing on the Stamp Act. In 1745 he led the successful expedition against Cape Breton, and in 1756 succeeded Braddock. Replaced as commander-in-chief by Lord Loudoun, he returned to London and later served as governor of the Bahamas (1759–67), before retiring to Roxbury, Massachusetts.

SHOVELL, CLOWDISLEY (1650–1707), hero of Queen Anne's fleet, went down with his flagship, the *Association*, and three other ships on the rocks of the Scilly Islands the night of October 22, 1707. Two other ships escaped to tell the tale. The incident prompted a contest for better ways to determine longitude at sea.

SLOANE, HANS (1660–1753), Irish-born botanist and physician to Queen Anne and George II, succeeded Newton as president of the Royal Society (1727–41). His museum and library were the nucleus of the British Museum—which still has the asbestos purse he purchased from Franklin in June 1725.

SPANGENBERG, AUGUSTUS GOTTLIEB (1704–1792), German-born Moravian Bishop whom Franklin met at Bethlehem, which Spangenberg had made the Moravian center for America in 1744. An internationally known expert on colonial missions, he introduced the mysticism of Jacob Boehme and William Law to America.

SPENCER, ARCHIBALD (c. 1698–1760), physician and popular lecturer on electricity whom Franklin met in Boston, June 1743, and probably the following year when he lectured in Philadelphia before settling in Fredericksburg, Virginia. Despite his infamy as a deist, he was ordained in 1749 and spent the rest of his life as an Anglican minister in Anne Arundel County, Maryland (1751–60).

SPOTSWOOD, ALEXANDER (1676–1740), an earlier deputy-postmaster (1730–40) for North America, also a military leader and acting governor of Virginia (1710–22).

SYNG, PHILIP (1703–1789), Irish-born silversmith and member of the original Junto, worked with Franklin on many civic enterprises and in his electrical experiments. Made the silver inkstand used for the signings of the Declaration of Independence and the Constitution.

TAYLOR, ABRAHAM (c. 1703–1772), one of Franklin's companions in seeking cannon from New York; merchant, deputy collector of customs, and provincial councilor as well as colonel of the militia.

TENNENT, GILBERT (1703–1764), Presbyterian preacher in New Brunswick, New Jersey (1726–43), he toured New England with Whitefield in 1740, then three years later gathered Whitefield's converts into a new Presbyterian congregation at Philadelphia.

THOMAS, GEORGE (c. 1695–1774), Antigua-born governor of Pennsylvania (1738–47) whose efforts at defense clashed with the Quaker-dominated assembly, though he managed Indian affairs ably. He later served as royal governor of the Leeward Islands (1753–66), and was knighted on his retirement.

TIMOTHÉE, ELIZABETH (d. 1757), wife of Louis Timothée (d. 1738), emigrating from Holland in 1731. Franklin employed Louis as journeyman printer and librarian of the Library Company (1732–33), then sent him as partner to South Carolina. At his death, Elizabeth continued the business, buying out Franklin's share in six years. She trained her son, Peter Timothy (an Americanization) (d. 1781), who took over the business in 1741. Peter Timothy's widow, Ann, succeeded him until their son, Benjamin Franklin Timothy, took over the press in 1792.

TRYON, THOMAS (1634–1703), English vegetarian, moralist, and author of many self-help books and pamphlets. The young Franklin read one of his books, probably Tryon's masterwork *The Way to Health* (1683, with many subsequent editions), and briefly became a vegetarian.

VAUGHAN, BENJAMIN (1751–1835), Franklin's independently wealthy disciple and editor. He studied law and medicine. Private secretary to Lord Shelburne, and his personal emissary to Franklin in the Paris peace talks (1782–83).

VERNON, SAMUEL (1683–1737), Rhode Island silversmith who entrusted Franklin to collect a debt. Franklin later appointed his son, THOMAS, postmaster of Newport (1754).

WATSON, JOSEPH (d. 1728?), poetical companion of Franklin's youth, a clerk of Charles Brockden's, later married Deborah Read's sister Frances.

WATSON, WILLIAM (1715–1787), summarized Franklin's electrical experiments for the Royal Society. He demonstrated that electricity was transmitted seemingly instantaneously through wires, water, earth, and a vacuum. Franklin repeated the experiments in Philadelphia in 1747.

WATTS, JOHN (c. 1678–1763), one of the most important London printers in the first half of the eighteenth century. Trained other eminent printers, such as William Strahan and Franklin's partner David Hall.

WEBB, GEORGE (1708–1736?), member of the original Junto who attended Oxford (1724–26) and may have taken a law degree at the Middle Temple in 1734. A female friend helped him buy his remaining time as an indentured servant from Keimer in 1728. Possibly the George Webb who printed for the Virginia assembly in 1728 and who became South Carolina's first printer in 1731. Franklin printed his poem *Batchelors-Hall* in 1731.

WELFARE (WOHLFAHRT), MICHAEL (1687–1741), "Brother Agonius," leader of the "Dunker," or Seventh Day Baptist, community at Ephrata. Franklin printed one of his sermons in 1737.

WHITEFIELD, GEORGE (1714–1770), Methodist minister and one inspiration for the "Great Awakening." He would return to America six times between 1739 and 1770, promoting evangelical religion and his Georgia orphanage. Franklin printed both sides of the controversies Whitefield ignited.

WHITMARSH, THOMAS (d. 1733), the "excellent Workman" Franklin brought from London to replace Meredith, came as a journeyman by April 1730. The next year Whitmarsh went to South Carolina as Franklin's partner and printed the *South Carolina Gazette* (1732–33).

WIGATE (WYGATE), JOHN, Franklin's fellow worker at Watts's printing shop in 1726. "Please to remember me affectionately to my old Friend Wigate," he wrote in 1744 (*Papers* 2.412n).

Wilcox, John (fl. 1721–1762), London bookseller who lent Franklin books when he lived next door in Little Britain. Possibly the John Wilcox who served as warden of the Stationer's Company in 1762.

Wilks, Robert (1665?–1732), Irish actor-manager of Drury Lane Theatre, to whom James Ralph applied for a job. One of three partners who dominated London theatrical life from 1710 to 1730.

Wolfe, James (1727–1759), commanded the campaign to capture Quebec, heroically dying on the Plains of Abraham in September 1759 at the climactic victory over Montcalm.

Wright, Edward (d. 1761), the Scottish "Dr. Wright" in Paris who reported Franklin's reputation. Fellow of the Royal Society who later wrote *Conjectures on the Course of Thunder* (Paris, 1756).

Wyndham, William (1687–1740), former Chancellor of the Exchequer (1713–14), Tory leader in Parliament during the exile of Henry St. John, Viscount Bolingbroke.

Yorke, Charles (1722–1770), solicitor-general at the time of Franklin's complaint against the proprietors. Became attorney-general in 1762 and lord chancellor in 1770.

CONTEXTS

Journal of a Voyage, 1726[†]

On his way from London to Philadelphia, the twenty-year-old Franklin kept a journal at sea. It is his first extensive memoir and good evidence of his ambitions for his writing and in natural science.

***

Friday, July 22, 1726

Yesterday in the afternoon we left London, and came to an anchor off Gravesend about eleven at night. I lay ashore all night, and this morning took a walk up to the Windmill Hill, whence I had an agreeable prospect of the country for above twenty miles round, and two or three reaches of the river with ships and boats sailing both up and down, and Tilbury Fort on the other side, which commands the river and passage to London. This Gravesend is a *cursed biting* place; the chief dependence of the people being the advantage they make of imposing upon strangers. If you buy any thing of them, and give half what they ask, you pay twice as much as the thing is worth. Thank God, we shall leave it to-morrow.

Saturday, July 23

This day we weighed anchor and fell down with the tide, there being little or no wind. In the afternoon we had a fresh gale, that brought us down to Margate, where we shall lie at anchor this night. Most of the passengers are very sick. Saw several Porpoises,[1] &c.

Sunday, July 24

This morning we weighed anchor, and, coming to the Downs, we set our pilot ashore at Deal and passed through. And now whilst I write this, sitting upon the quarter-deck, I have methinks one of the pleasantest scenes in the world before me. 'Tis a fine clear day, and we are going away before the wind with an easy pleasant gale. We have near fifteen sail of ships in sight, and I may say in company. On the left hand appears the coast of France at a distance, and on the right is the town and castle of Dover, with the green hills and chalky cliffs of England, to which we must now bid farewell. Albion, farewell!

* * *

---

† Leonard W. Labaree et al., eds., *The Papers of Benjamin Franklin*, 40 vols. to date (New Haven: Yale UP, 1959–), 1.72–73, 90–91, 93–95, and 98–99. Reprinted by permission of The Papers of Benjamin Franklin at the Yale University Library.
1. "Porpusses" in the transcript.

Friday, September 23

This morning we spied a sail to windward of us about two leagues. We shewed our jack upon the ensign-staff, and shortened sail for them till about noon, when she came up with us. She was a snow from Dublin,[2] bound to New York, having upwards of fifty servants on board, of both sexes; they all appeared upon deck, and seemed very much pleased at the sight of us. There is really something strangely cheering to the spirits in the meeting of a ship at sea, containing a society of creatures of the same species and in the same circumstances with ourselves, after we had been long separated and excommunicated as it were from the rest of mankind. My heart fluttered in my breast with joy when I saw so many human countenances, and I could scarce refrain from that kind of laughter which proceeds from some degree of inward pleasure. When we have been for a considerable time tossing on the vast waters, far from the sight of any land or ships, or any mortal creature but ourselves (except a few fish and sea birds) the whole world, for aught we know, may be under a second deluge, and we (like Noah and his company in the Ark) the only surviving remnant of the human race. The two Captains have mutually promised to keep each other company; but this I look upon to be only matter of course, for if ships are unequal in their sailing they seldom stay for one another, especially strangers. This afternoon the wind that has been so long contrary to us, came about to the eastward (and looks as if it would hold), to our no small satisfaction. I find our messmates in a better humour, and more pleased with their present condition than they have been since we came out; which I take to proceed from the contemplation of the miserable circumstances of the passengers on board our neighbour, and making the comparison. We reckon ourselves in a kind of paradise, when we consider how they live, confined and stifled up with such a lousy stinking rabble in this sultry latitude.

* * *

Wednesday, September 28

We had very variable winds and weather last night, accompanied with abundance of rain; and now the wind is come about westerly again, but we must bear it with patience. This afternoon we took up several branches of gulf weed (with which the sea is spread all over from the Western Isles to the coast of America); but one of these branches had something peculiar in it. In common with the rest it had a leaf about three quarters of an inch long, indented like a saw, and a small yellow berry filled with nothing but wind; besides which

2. The printed version calls this vessel the *Snow*.

it bore a fruit of the animal kind, very surprising to see. It was a small shell-fish like a heart, the stalk by which it proceeded from the branch being partly of a gristly kind. Upon this one branch of the weed there were near forty of these vegetable animals; the smallest of them near the end contained a substance somewhat like an oyster, but the larger were visibly animated, opening their shells every moment, and thrusting out a set of unformed claws, not unlike those of a crab; but the inner part was still a kind of soft jelly. Observing the weed more narrowly, I spied a very small crab crawling among it, about as big as the head of a ten-penny nail, and of a yellowish colour, like the weed itself. This gave me some reason to think that he was a native of the branch, that he had not long since been in the same condition with the rest of those little embrios that appeared in the shells, this being the method of their generation; and that consequently all the rest of this odd kind of fruit might be crabs in due time. To strengthen my conjecture, I have resolved to keep the weed in salt water, renewing it every day till we come on shore, by this experiment to see whether any more crabs will be produced or not in this manner. I remember that the last calm we had, we took notice of a large crab upon the surface of the sea, swimming from one branch of weed to another, which he seemed to prey upon; and I likewise recollect that at Boston, in New England, I have often seen small crabs with a shell like a snail's upon their backs, crawling about in the salt water; and likewise at Portsmouth in England. It is likely nature has provided this hard shell to secure them till their own proper shell has acquired a sufficient hardness, which once perfected, they quit their old habitation and venture abroad safe in their own strength. The various changes that silk-worms, butterflies, and several other insects go through, make such alterations and metamorphoses not improbable. This day the captain of the snow with one of his passengers came on board us; but the wind beginning to blow, they did not stay dinner, but returned to their own vessel.

Thursday, September 29

Upon shifting the water in which I had put the weed yesterday, I found another crab, much smaller than the former, who seemed to have newly left his habitation. But the weed begins to wither, and the rest of the embrios are dead. This new comer fully convinces me, that at least this sort of crabs are generated in this manner. The snow's Captain dined on board us this day. Little or no wind.

Friday, September 30

I sat up last night to observe an eclipse of the moon, which the calendar calculated for London informed us would happen at five o'clock in the morning, September 30. It began with us about eleven last night, and continued till near two this morning, darkening her body about six digits, or one half; the middle of it being about half an hour after twelve, by which we may discover that we are in a meridian of about four hours and half from London, or 67½ degrees of longitude, and consequently have not much above one hundred leagues to run. This is the second eclipse we have had within these fifteen days. We lost our consort in the night, but saw him again this morning near two leagues to windward. This afternoon we spoke with him again. We have had abundance of dolphins about us these three or four days; but we have not taken any more than one, they being shy of the bait. I took in some more gulf-weed to-day with the boat-hook, with shells upon it like that before mentioned, and three living perfect crabs, each less than the nail of my little finger. One of them had something particularly observable, to wit, a thin piece of the white shell which I before noticed as their covering while they remained in the condition of embrios, sticking close to his natural shell upon his back. This sufficiently confirms me in my opinion of the manner of their generation. I have put this remarkable crab with a piece of the gulf-weed, shells, &c. into a glass phial filled with salt water, (for want of spirits of wine) in hopes to preserve the curiosity till I come on shore. The wind is South-West.

* * *

Tuesday, October 11

This morning we weighed anchor with a gentle breeze, and passed by Newcastle, whence they hailed us and bade us welcome. 'Tis extreme fine weather. The sun enlivens our still limbs with his glorious rays of warmth and brightness. The sky looks gay, with here and there a silver cloud. The fresh breezes from the woods refresh us, the immediate prospect of liberty after so long and irksome confinement ravishes us. In short all things conspire to make this the most joyful day I ever knew. As we passed by Chester some of the company went on shore, impatient once more to tread on *terra firma,* and designing for Philadelphia by land. Four of us remained on board, not caring for the fatigue of travel when we knew the voyage had much weakened us. About eight at night, the wind failing us, we cast anchor at Redbank, six miles from Philadelphia, and thought we must be obliged to lie on board that night: but some young Philadelphians happening to be out upon their pleasure in a boat, they came on board, and offered to take us up with them: we accepted of their kind proposal, and about ten o'clock landed at Philadelphia, heartily congratulating each other upon our having happily completed so tedious and dangerous a voyage. Thank God!

Excerpts from Franklin's Letters
Mentioning the *Autobiography*

Franklin rarely mentioned his *Autobiography* until the last years of his life. Few references survive from the years before 1786. Of the most significant are the letters from Abel James and from Benjamin Vaughan that Franklin included as an introduction to Part Two of the *Autobiography*.

The following excerpts from his own letters constitute his most telling remarks about the *Autobiography*.

To Mathew Carey, August 10, 1786[1]

Sir:—The Memoirs you mention would be of little or no Use to your Scheme, as they contain only some Notes of my early Life, and finish in 1730. They were written to my Son, and intended only as Information to my Family. I have in hand a full Account of my Life which I propose to leave behind me; in the meantime I wish nothing of the kind may be publish'd, and shall be much oblig'd to the Proprietors of the Columbian Magazine if they will drop that Intention, for the present.

To the Duke de La Rochefoucauld, October 22, 1788[2]

* * *

Having now finish'd my Term of being President, and promising myself to engage no more in public Business, I hope to enjoy the small Remains of Life that are allow'd me, in the Repose I have so long wish'd for. I purpose to so employ it in compleating the personal History you mention. It is now brought down to my Fiftieth Year. What is to follow will be of more important Transactions: But it seems to me that what is done will be of more general Use to young Readers; as exemplifying strongly the Effect of prudent and imprudent Conduct in the Commencement of a Life of Business.

* * *

------

1. On August 9, 1786, Mathew Carey, publisher of the Philadelphia *Columbian Magazine*, had asked Franklin's permission to read over and possibly publish the memoirs that he heard Franklin had written some time ago. Franklin replied the next day with this letter. Smyth, *Writings*, 9.533–34.
2. The two Frenchmen closest to Franklin were Louis Le Veillard and the Duc de La Rochefoucauld. Both knew of his *Autobiography* and both urged Franklin to complete it. Smyth, *Writings*, 9.665.

To Benjamin Vaughan, October 24, 1788[3]

* * * I am recovering from a long-continued gout, and am diligently employed in writing the History of my Life, to the doing of which the persuasions contained in your letter of January 31st, 1783, have not a little contributed. I am now in the year 1756, just before I was sent to England. To shorten the work, as well as for other reasons, I omit all facts and transactions, that may not have a tendency to benefit the young reader, by showing him from my example, and my success in emerging from poverty, and acquiring some degree of wealth, power, and reputation, the advantages of certain modes of conduct which I observed, and of avoiding the errors which were prejudicial to me. If a writer can judge properly of his own work, I fancy, on reading over what is already done, that the book will be found entertaining, interesting, and useful, more so than I expected when I began it. If my present state of health continues, I hope to finish it this winter. When done, you shall have a manuscript copy of it, that I may obtain from your judgment and friendship such remarks, as may contribute to its improvement.

*   *   *

To Benjamin Vaughan, June 3, 1789[4]

My Dearest Friend,
I received your kind letter of March 4th, and wish I may be able to complete what you so earnestly desire, the Memoirs of my Life. But of late I am so interrupted by extreme pain, which obliges me to have recourse to opium, that, between the effects of both, I have but little time in which I can write any thing. My grandson, however, is copying what is done, which will be sent to you for your opinion by the next vessel; and not merely for your opinion, but for your advice; for I find it a difficult task to speak decently and properly of one's own conduct; and I feel the want of a judicious friend to encourage me in scratching out.

*   *   *

To Benjamin Vaughan, November 2, 1789[5]

* * * What is already done, I now send you, with an earnest request that you and my good friend Dr. Price would be so good as to take

3. One of Franklin's close English friends was his disciple Benjamin Vaughan, who published an edition of Franklin's writings in 1779. Smyth, *Writings*, 9.675–76.
4. Smyth, *Writings*, 10.32.
5. Smyth, *Writings*, 10.50.

the trouble of reading it, critically examining it, and giving me your candid opinion whether I had best publish or suppress it; and if the first, then what parts had better be expunged or altered. I shall rely upon your opinions, for I am now grown so old and feeble in mind, as well as body, that I cannot place any confidence in my own judgment. In the mean time, I desire and expect that you will not suffer any copy of it, or of any part of it, to be taken for any purpose whatever.

* * *

To M. Le Veillard, November 13, 1789[6]

Dear Friend:—This must be but a short Letter, for I have mislaid your last and must postpone answering them till I have found them; but to make you some Amends I send you what is done of the Memoirs, under this express Condition however, that you do not suffer any Copy to be taken of them, or of any Part of them, on any Account whatever, and that you will, with your excellent Friend the Duke de la Rochefoucault, read them over carefully, examine them critically, and send me your friendly, candid Opinion of the Parts you would advise me to correct or expunge; this in Case you should be of Opinion that they are generally proper to be published; and if you judge otherwise, that you would send me that Opinion as soon as possible, and prevent my taking farther Trouble in endeavouring to finish them.* * *

"Authentic Memoir of Dr. Franklyn"[†]

Alfred Owen Aldridge, in "The First Published Memoir of Franklin," *William and Mary Quarterly* 24 (1967): 624–28, identified this sketch as "the earliest known forerunner of the publication of Franklin's life story," and noted that it was "directly related" to the *Autobiography*. The sketch, which used Franklin's anecdotes, must have been written by someone (like Richard Price) who was a close friend and a sympathizer with the Americans. (By 1778, most Englishmen considered the American "patriots" as rebels or traitors.) This version of Franklin's early life focuses on his difficult journey to Philadelphia, the idea of self-improvement, and on the consequences of an older man's help to a young one—all major motifs in the *Autobiography*.

The Public have been already acquainted with the birth and parent-age of this great philosopher and statesman; and all Europe has lately

6. Smyth, *Writings*, 10.69–70.
† *London Chronicle*, October 1, 1778.

beheld, with astonishment, this venerable old man acting the part of a patriot, when perhaps he stands alone in the greatness of his cause and abilities. This memoir, therefore, only goes to show the accidental circumstance that first introduced him into life, and may well be reckoned in the catalogue of "great events from little causes."

Dr. Franklyn was bred a printer, and followed this profession for some time in Boston, but possessing too liberal a spirit at that time for the meridian of that city, he was obliged to quit it abruptly, and fly to Philadelphia. Being much narrowed in his circumstances, he was obliged to walk all the way to the last-mentioned place, where, being arrived just at the time that the congregation were going to morning service, young Franklyn mixed with the croud, and, perhaps partly for the benefit of getting a seat to sit down on, attended divine service.

Oppressed with too much fatigue, he had not been long there, when he fell asleep, and continued so, after the service was over, till the sexton, just going to lock the door, perceiving his situation, woke him. Franklyn on this immediately got up, *unknowing where to go, or what to do.*

At last a wealthy citizen of Philadelphia, seeing him a stranger, and perhaps seeing that perturbation of mind in his face which such a situation as his generally paints, he asked him, "Whether he was not a stranger? How long he had been in town, etc?" To these questions Franklyn gave such ingenious and modest answers, that the citizen asked him home to dinner with him; the consequence of which visit was, that liking his conversation, and above all, the openness of his manner, and the enterprise of his spirit, he made out an appointment for him in his own family, and there having the benefit of seeing and conversing with some of the principles of that city, he progressively laid the foundation of his present exalted situation.

Excerpts from Franklin's Writings and Correspondence on Ambition and Fame, Wealth, and Self-Improvement[†]

Amid the rich narrative of events that constituted his life, Franklin's *Autobiography* emphasizes three themes: ambition and the pursuit of fame, wealth (and its pitfalls), and self-improvement (or the pursuit of moral perfection). His other writings make clear his lifelong interest in these goals and his delight in achieving them.

Ambition and Fame

Despite cultivating a reputation for modesty, Franklin was clearly ambitious and admired famous individuals, both from the past and from his own time. At many points in his life, he reflected on the necessity of ambition. On his diplomatic mission in France, he rejoiced at having become so famous that his face "was as well known as that of the moon."

From Poor Richard Improved, *1750*[1]

Franklin reflects on the unlikelihood of his becoming famous as an almanac-maker.

To the READER.

The Hope of acquiring lasting FAME, is, with many Authors, a most powerful Motive to Writing. Some, tho' few, have succeeded; and others, tho' perhaps fewer, may succeed hereafter, and be as well known to Posterity by their Works, as the Antients are to us. We Philomaths, as ambitious of Fame as any other Writers whatever, after all our painful Watchings and laborious Calculations, have the constant Mortification to see our Works thrown by at the End of the Year, and

---

[†] Except where otherwise indicated, texts in this section are reprinted by permission of the Papers of Benjamin Franklin at the Yale University Library.

1. *Papers* 3.437.

treated as mere waste Paper. Our only Consolation is, that short-lived as they are, they out-live those of most of our Cotemporaries.

Yet, condemned to renew the Sisyphean Toil, we every Year heave another heavy Mass up the Muses Hill, which never can the Summit reach, and soon comes tumbling down again.

This, kind Reader, is my seventeenth Labour of the Kind. Thro' thy continued Good-will, they have procur'd me, if no *Bays*, at least *Pence*; and the latter is perhaps the better of the two; since 'tis not improbable that a Man may receive more solid Satisfaction from *Pudding*, while he is *living*, than from *Praise*, after he is *dead*.

From Poor Richard Improved, *January* 1758[2]

Franklin advises young people to be ambitious, but not unreasonably so.

On Ambition.

I know, young Friend, *Ambition* fills your Mind,
And in Life's Voyage is th'impelling Wind;
But at the Helm let sober Reason stand,
And steer the Bark with Heav'n-directed Hand:
So shall you safe *Ambition's* Gales receive,
And ride securely, tho' the Billows heave;
So shall you shun the giddy Hero's Fate,
And by her Influence be both good and great.

To Sarah (Franklin) Bache[3]

To his daughter in Philadelphia, Franklin reflects on his sudden celebrity in France.

Dear Sally,   Passy, June 3, 1779.

I have before me your letters of Oct. 22, and Jan. 17th:[4] they are the only ones I received from you in the course of eighteen months. If you knew how happy your letters make me, and considered how many miscarry, I think you would write oftener.

I am much obliged to the Miss Cliftons for the kind care they took of my house and furniture.[5] Present my thankful acknowledgments to them, and tell them I wish them all sorts of happiness.

The clay medallion of me you say you gave to Mr. Hopkinson was the first of the kind made in France.[6] A variety of others have been

2. *Papers* 7.350–51.
3. *Papers* 29.612–13, 615.
4. *Papers* 27.602–5; 28.390–92.
5. Anna Maria Clifton and her sister watched over Franklin's home during the British occupation of Philadelphia; see *Papers* 23.425–26n; 26.488; 27.602.
6. The medallion was one of those made by Jean-Baptiste Nini at Chaumont's faïence factory near Onzain. See *Papers* 24.23n; Charles Coleman Sellers, *Benjamin Franklin in Portraiture* (New Haven, YUP: 1962), 344–45.

made since of different sizes; some to be set in lids of snuff boxes, and some so small as to be worn in rings; and the numbers sold are incredible. These, with the pictures, busts,[7] and prints, (of which copies upon copies are spread every where) have made your father's face as well known as that of the moon, so that he durst not do any thing that would oblige him to run away, as his phiz would discover him wherever he should venture to show it. It is said by learned etymologists that the name *Doll*, for the images children play with, is derived from the word IDOL; from the number of *dolls* now made of him, he may be truly said, *in that sense*, to be *i-doll-ized* in this country.

* * *

If you happen again to see General Washington, assure him of my very great and sincere respect, and tell him that all the old Generals here amuse themselves in studying the accounts of his operations, and approve highly of his conduct.

Present my affectionate regards to all friends that enquire after me, particularly Mr. Duffield and family,[8] and write oftener, my dear child, to Your loving father,   B. FRANKLIN.

From Benjamin Vaughan, May 1785[9]

Franklin's friend urges him to consider how his memoirs will consolidate his reputation, and expresses envy over the older man's fame.

My dearest sir,

I send you some pamphlets &c. I wish devoutly I could add happy news to the little cargo. But this is not the country of wisdom. To a wise man like you I need say no more. I am sufficiently disposed to think that the West India intercourse is only held out upon, to serve as a concession at treating, that may save a dearer gift. Certainly we are not sulky; we are rather bigotted, hard, and like men who expected more return from your side; and a disappointment in this particular does not favor the growth of liberal principles.

* * *

The public business which I have, added to private domestics, nearly overcome me. But zeal and a willing mind supply strength. It however prevents my writing as, and when, I wish.

---

7. On June 1, William Temple Franklin wrote to his aunt that he was sending her as a present "the Bust of my best Friend your venerable Father." He also included directions for unpacking it (Franklin Papers, American Philosophical Society, Philadelphia). The bust, however, never arrived. After a long wait at Lorient it was put aboard the *Marquis de Lafayette*, which was later captured (William Temple Franklin to Sarah Bache, Sept. 14, 1781, Library of Congress).
8. Philadelphia friend Edward Duffield.
9. Reprinted by permission of the Benjamin Franklin Papers, American Philosophical Society.

Yet I hope to write to you once more before you commit yourself to the sea. In the mean time let me adjure you by every consideration that can affect the mind of a man of philanthropy and extensive views, to perfect your *life* and your *art of virtue*. In my opinion your being the author of the greatest revolutions in the world is a satisfaction not in the smallest degree comparable to that which you may anticipate, as likely to follow, from the latter work particularly, well treated by *you*. I *burn* for your *fame* and *ability* to do something of the kind myself. I *begin* to know more of my unhappy fellow creatures. My respect is not increased, but I feel a pity for them that is inexpressible, and that if I was sure of succeeding, would lead me almost to attempt *any* thing. I will not yet suffer myself to despair, but in the mean time I cannot but sigh. I know that man would *bear* happy condition, but he will not elect it, without infinite pains, and the revolutions of time will always be apt to undo the little that is well done. I know this, and I do not despair, probably because I am not wise, and have not been enough disappointed. I am, ever yours, and as much as man can be to man Your devoted, grateful and affectionate My best affection to your grandson, who I trust is recovered and vigorous. If he is not the Sea will restore him. God bless him

From Jane Mecom, July 21, 1786[1]

Franklin's youngest sister reminds him that not everyone has the opportunity to fulfill his or her ambitions, unlike such famous men of science as Robert Boyle, Samuel Clarke, Isaac Newton, and—presumably—Benjamin Franklin.

DEAR BROTHER   Boston
   you have given me Grat Pleasure in the short acount you have wrot concerning my Granson, for *you* not to Percive that he wants Either Advice or Reproff is a good charecter, but I percive you have some Exeptions to the Lose of your Advice & I flater my self I am won.

*   *   *

Dr [Richard] Price thinks Thousands of Boyles Clarks and Newtons have Probably been lost to the world, and lived and died in Ignorance and meanness, mearly for want of being Placed in favourable Situations, and Injoying Proper Advantages, very few we know is Able to beat thro all Impedements and Arive to any Grat Degre of superiority in Understanding

---

1. From Carl Van Doren, ed., *The Letters of Benjamin Franklin & Jane Mecom* (Princeton: Princeton UP, 1950), 274–75.

My Health is Tolarable, the Rest of the Famely as Usal, all Joyn in the most Affectionat Remembrance of you & yours with yr affectionit Sister

JANE MECOM

Wealth

To Cadwallader Colden, Philadelphia, September 29, 1748[2]

By 1740, just twelve years after opening his own printing shop in Philadelphia, Franklin had established himself as the most daring, innovative, skilled and successful printer in America. But he wanted more than financial success. On January 1, 1748, he formed a partnership with his shop foreman and retired before his forty-second birthday. He presented his reasons for retirement in a letter of September 29, 1748, to his friend Cadwallader Colden (1688–1776), philosopher, man of science and, later, Loyalist governor of New York.

Sir

I received your Favour of the 12th Inst. which gave me the greater Pleasure, as 'twas so long since I had heard from you. I congratulate you on your Return to your beloved Retirement: I too am taking the proper Measures for obtaining Leisure to enjoy Life and my Friends more than heretofore, having put my Printing house under the Care of my Partner David Hall, absolutely left off Bookselling, and remov'd to a more quiet Part of the Town, where I am settling my old Accounts and hope soon to be quite a Master of my own Time, and no longer (as the Song has it) *at every one's Call but my own*. If Health continues, I hope to be able in another Year to visit the most distant Friend I have, without Inconvenience. With the same Views I have refus'd engaging further in publick Affairs; The Share I had in the late Association, &c. having given me a little present Run of Popularity, there was a pretty general Intention of chusing me a Representative for the City at the next Election of Assemblymen; but I have desired all my Friends who spoke to me about it, to discourage it, declaring that I should not serve if chosen. Thus you see I am in a fair Way of having no other Tasks than such as I shall like to give my self, and of enjoying what I look upon as a great Happiness, Leisure to read, study, make Experiments, and converse at large with such ingenious and worthy Men as are pleas'd to honour me with their Friendship or Acquaintance, on such Points as may produce something for the common Benefit of Mankind, uninterrupted by the little Cares and Fatigues of Business. Among other Pleasures I promise my self, that of Corresponding more frequently and fully with Dr. Colden is none of the least; I shall only wish that what must be so agreable to me, may not prove troublesome to you.

* * *

To William Strahan, Philadelphia, June 2, 1750[3]

Franklin wrote to his friend Strahan—the successful London printer of Samuel Johnson, David Hume, Adam Smith, and Edward Gibbon, among others—of his disgust with "the Pursuit of Wealth to no End."

* * *

The Description you give of the Company and Manner of Living in Scotland, would almost tempt one to remove thither. Your Sentiments of the general Foible of Mankind, in the Pursuit of Wealth to no End, are express'd in a Manner that gave me great Pleasure in reading: They are extreamly just, at least they are perfectly agreable to mine. But London Citizens, they say, are ambitious of what they call *dying worth* a great Sum: The very Notion seems to me absurd; and just the same as if a Man should run in debt for 1000 Superfluities, to the End that when he should be stript of all, and imprison'd by his Creditors, it might be said, he *broke worth* a great Sum. I imagine that what we have above what we can use, is not properly *ours*, tho' we possess it; and that the rich Man who *must die*, was no more *worth* what he leaves, than the Debtor who *must pay*.

* * *

To Jane Mecom, London, December 30, 1770[4]

* * *

From the time that Franklin was appointed Joint Postmaster General of North America in 1755 until the Ministry took away the position in 1774, Franklin frequently outraged the Ministry because, although he held a patronage position, he did not always work for the Ministry's interests. On the other hand, some American patriots occasionally impugned his motives and his actions because he enjoyed official patronage. When his sister Jane Mecom expressed alarm about the latest rumor that he had been removed as Postmaster General, he explained his position to her and gave his "Rule" regarding the conflict of public and private interest.

3. *Papers* 3.479.
4. *Papers* 17.314–15.

As to the Rumour you mention (which was, as Josiah tells me, that I had been depriv'd of my Place in the Post Office on Account of a letter I wrote to Philadelphia) it might have this Foundation, that some of the Ministry had been displeas'd at my Writing such Letters, and there were really some Thoughts among them of shewing that Displeasure in that manner. But I had some Friends too, who unrequested by me advis'd the contrary. And my Enemies were forc'd to content themselves with abusing me plentifully in the Newspapers, and endeavouring to provoke me to resign. In this they are not likely to succeed, I being deficient in that Christian Virtue of Resignation. If they would have my Office, they must take it——I have heard of some great Man, whose Rule it was with regard to Offices, *Never to ask for them*, and *never to refuse them:* To which I have always added in my own Practice, *Never to resign them.* As I told my Friends, I rose to that office thro' a long Course of Service in the inferior Degrees of it: Before my time, thro' bad Management, it never produced the Salary annex'd to it; and when I receivd it, no Salary was to be allow'd if the office did not produce it. During the first four Years it was so far from defraying itself, that it became £950 Sterling in debt to me and my Collegue. I had been chiefly instrumental in bringing it to its present flourishing State, and therefore thought I had some kind of Right to it. I had hitherto executed the Duties of it faithfully, and to the perfect Satisfaction of my Superiors, which I thought was all that should be expected of me on that Account. As to the Letters complain'd of, it was true I did write them, and they were written in Compliance with another Duty, that to my Country. A Duty quite Distinct from that of Postmaster. My Conduct in this respect was exactly similar with that I held on a similar Occasion but a few Years ago, when the then Ministry were ready to hug me for the Assistance I afforded them in repealing a former Revenue Act. My Sentiments were still the same, that no such Acts should be made here for America; or, if made should as soon as possible be repealed; and I thought it should not be expected of me, to change my Political Opinions every time his Majesty thought fit to change his Ministers. This was my Language on the Occasion; and I have lately heard, that tho I was thought much to blame, it being understood that every Man who holds an Office should act with the Ministry whether agreable or not to his own Judgment, yet in consideration of the goodness of my private Character (as they are pleas'd to compliment me) the office was not to be taken from me. Possibly they may still change their Minds, and remove me; but no Apprehension of that sort, will, I trust, make the least Alteration in my Political Conduct. My rule in which I have always found Satisfaction, is, Never to turn asside in Publick Affairs thro' Views of private Interest; but to go strait forward in doing what appears to me right at the time, leaving the Consequences with

Providence. What in my younger Days enabled me more easily to walk upright, was, that I had a Trade; and that I could live upon a little; and thence (never having had views of making a Fortune) I was free from Avarice, and contented with the plentiful Supplies my business afforded me. And now it is still more easy for me to preserve my Freedom and Integrity, when I consider, that I am almost at the End of my Journey, and therefore need less to complete the Expence of it; and that what I now possess thro' the Blessing of God may with tolerable Oeconomy, be sufficient for me (great Misfortunes excepted) tho' I should add nothing more to it by any Office or Employment whatsoever.

* * *

To Thomas Cushing, London, June 10, 1771[5]

Since some Royal and Proprietary officials (in direct violation of their instructions from Britain) had passed popular measures in order to win high salaries from colonial assemblies, and since other officials were kept in comparative poverty by the colonial assemblies for not approving popular measures or for enforcing unpopular laws, the Crown reacted in the pre-Revolutionary era by paying Royal officials directly from Britain. The Boston patriots judged this action a threat to local self-rule. Franklin as the Massachusetts Assembly's Agent tried in vain to prevent the change, but in reporting his failure he philosophized about the nature of avarice.

* * *

I do not at present see the least likelihood of preventing the Grant of Salaries or Pensions from hence to the King's Officers in America, by any Application in Behalf of the People there. It is look'd on as a strange thing here to object to the King's paying his own Servants sent among us to do his Business; and they say we should seem to have much more Reason of Complaint if it were requir'd of us to pay them. And the more we urge the Impropriety of their not depending on us for their Support, the more Suspicion it breeds that we are desirous of influencing them to betray the Interests of their Master or of this Nation. Indeed if the Money is rais'd from us against our Wills, the Injustice becomes more evident than where it arises from hence. I do not think, however, that the Effect of these Salaries is likely to be so considerable, either in favour of Government here, or in our Prejudice, as may be generally apprehended. The Love of Money is not a Thing of certain Measure, so as that it may be easily filled and satisfied. Avarice is infinite, and where there is not good

Oeconomy, no Salary, however large, will prevent Necessity. He that has a fixed, and what others may think a competent Income, is often as much to be byassed by the Expectation of more, as if he had already none at all. If the Colonies should resolve on giving hand-some Presents to good Governors at or after their Departure, or to their Children after their Decease, I imagine it might produce even better Effects than our present annual Grants. But the Course prob-ably will soon be, that the Chief Governor to whom the Salary is given, will have Leave to reside in England, a Lieutenant or Deputy will be left to do the Business and live on the Perquisites, which not being thought quite sufficient, his receiving Presents yearly will be wink'd at thro' the Interest of his Principal, and thus things will get into the old Train, only this Inconvenience remaining, that while by our Folly in consuming the Duty-Articles, the fixed Salary is raised on ourselves without our Consent, we must pay double for the same Service. However, tho' it may be a hopeless Task while the Duties continue sufficient to pay the Salaries, I shall on all proper Occa-sions make Representations against this new Mode; and if by the Duties falling short, the Treasury here should be call'd on to pay those Salaries, it is possible they may come to be seen in another Light than at present, and dropt as unnecessary.

* * *

Benjamin Vaughan to Lord Shelburne, Dover, November 24, 1782[6]

Benjamin Vaughan, Lord Shelburne's private secretary, acted as Shel-burne's personal emissary in the Paris peace negotiations—perhaps because he was Franklin's friend and disciple. His letters to Shelburne record in detail his talks with the American peace commissioners, even when the discussions did not bear directly upon the peace negotia-tions. He thus reported Franklin's conversation concerning political equality among rich and poor, as well as Franklin's shrewd appraisal of the underlying economic reasons for past historical actions and his surprisingly modern view of the causes of poverty and oppression.

My lord,
  I think it necessary to inform your lordship in a few words, that Dr. Franklin's opinions about *parliaments* are, that people should not be rejected as electors because they are *at present* ignorant; or because their ignorance *arises* from their being excluded. He thinks that a statesman should meliorate his people; and I suppose would put this, among other reasons for extending the privilege of Election, that it

---

6. Reprinted by permission of the Benjamin Vaughan Papers, American Philosophical Society.

would meliorate them. When the act to lessen the number of voters, passed in Edward the 3d's time, it was followed by an act to reduce wages; & he thinks that probably one act was made with a view to the other. On the other hand when knowledge began to spread in England, it helped everything; for instance, the post office revenue increased beyond all conception, while the same revenue in Ireland continues still as contemptible, as to be worth only a few thousand pounds. He says, that with themselves in America, they find no inconvenience in every man's voting that is free; & that the qualifications of a representative are matters sufficiently well distinguished by them. He says that savages would do the same, taking their best men as they can find them, & others forming themselves in business under them.

Perhaps your lordship will think all this too theoretical. When I return, I hope to have the honor of communicating his *own* expressions. As an American, the Dr. would *choose* to give no opinion of a different cast; but I believe, by some more positions he added to it, that this is his own genuine opinion. He thinks that the lower people are as we see them, because oppressed; & then their situation in point of manners, becomes the reason for oppressing them. But he is full of the measure of raising the sentiments & habits of all, as a thing that is wanting to contribute to the real *sensible* happiness of *both* orders—the rich & the poor.

*   *   *

To Robert Morris, Passy, France, December 25, 1783[7]

In eighteenth-century fashion, Franklin related wealth to the origin of society and the basic rights of man. He reasoned that all wealth above whatever was necessary for the basic requirements of subsistence, clothing, and shelter was created by arbitrary conventions of society— and thus that such wealth should be at the disposal of society.

All Property, indeed, except the Savage's temporary Cabin, his Bow, his Matchcoat, and other little Acquisitions, absolutely necessary for his Subsistence, seems to me to be the Creature of public Convention. Hence the Public has the Right of Regulating Descents, and all other Conveyances of Property, and even of limiting the Quantity and the Users of it. All the Property that is necessary to a Man, for the Conservation of the Individual and the Propagation of the Species, is his natural Right, which none can justly deprive him of: But all Property superfluous to such purposes is the Property of the Publick, who, by their Laws, have created it, and who may therefore by other Laws dispose of it, whenever the Welfare of the Publick shall demand such Disposition. He that does not like civil Society on these Terms, let him retire and live among Savages. He can have no right to the benefits of Society, who will not pay his Club towards the Support of it.

* * *

To Benjamin Vaughan, Passy, France, July 26, 1784[8]

Luxury was a standard point of debate throughout the eighteenth century. Writers from the time of Joseph Addison's "A Letter from Italy" (1701) to Edward Gibbon's *Decline and Fall of the Roman Empire* (1776–88) generally attacked it, but at least one masterpiece of literary as well as intellectual history defended it—Bernard Mandeville's *Fable of the Bees* (1714–29). In America, the great Quaker stylist and humanitarian John Woolman (1720–72), in his *Journal* (1774) and in his classic essays, attacked "superfluities" just as Thoreau was later to do in *Walden* (1854) and as the economist Thorstein Veblen was to do in his *Theory of the Leisure Class* (1899). Franklin's complex attitudes toward luxury are set forth in his letter to Benjamin Vaughan; this is the conclusion.

* * *

One reflection more, and I will end this long, rambling Letter. Almost all the Parts of our Bodies require some Expence. The Feet demand Shoes; the Legs, Stockings; the rest of the Body, Clothing; and the Belly, a good deal of Victuals. *Our* Eyes, tho' exceedingly useful, ask, when reasonable, only the cheap Assistance of Spectacles, which could not much impair our Finances. But *the Eyes of other People* are the Eyes that ruin us. If all but myself were blind, I should want neither fine Clothes, fine Houses, nor fine Furniture.

Last Will and Testament, 1788, and Codicil, 1789[9]

Franklin's will makes clear that he had amassed a considerable fortune, including land, bank accounts, financial instruments, and even diamonds. The distribution of his property reveals his sense of the merits and demerits of his various family members, and the codicil shows his keen desire to maintain his public reputation long after his death.

FRANKLIN'S LAST WILL AND TESTAMENT

I, BENJAMIN FRANKLIN, of Philadelphia, printer, late Minister Plenipotentiary from the United States of America to the Court of

8. Smyth, *Writings*, 9.248. Reprinted by permission of the Benjamin Vaughan Papers, American Philosophical society.
9. Smyth, *Writings*, 10.493–510.

France, now President of the State of Pennsylvania, do make and declare my last will and testament as follows:—

To my son, *William Franklin*, late Governor of the Jerseys, I give and devise all the lands I hold or have a right to, in the province of Nova Scotia, to hold to him, his heirs, and assigns forever. I also give to him all my books and papers, which he has in his possession, and all debts standing against him on my account books, willing that no payment for, nor restitution of, the same be required of him, by my executors. The part he acted against me in the late war, which is of public notoriety, will account for my leaving him no more of an estate he endeavoured to deprive me of.

Having since my return from France demolished the three houses in Market Street, between Third and Fourth Streets, fronting my dwelling-house, and erected two new and larger ones on the ground, and having also erected another house on the lot which formerly was the passage to my dwelling, and also a printing-office between my dwelling and the front houses; now I do give and devise my said dwelling-house, wherein I now live, my said three new houses, my printing-office and the lots of ground thereto belonging; also my small lot and house in Sixth Street, which I bought of the widow Henmarsh; also my pasture-ground which I have in Hickory Lane, with the buildings thereon; also my house and lot on the north side of Market Street, now occupied by Mary Jacobs, together with two houses and lots behind the same, and fronting on Pewter-Platter Alley; also my lot of ground in Arch Street, opposite the church burying-ground, with the buildings thereon erected; also all my silver plate, pictures, and household goods, of every kind, now in my said dwelling-house, to my daughter, *Sarah Bache*, and to her husband, *Richard Bache*, to hold to them for and during their natural lives, and the life of the longest liver of them, and from and after the decease of the survivor of them, I do give, devise, and bequeath to all children already born, or to be born of my said daughter, and to their heirs and assigns forever, as tenants in common, and not as joint tenants.

And, if any or either of them shall happen to die under age, and without issue, the part and share of him, her, or them, so dying, shall go to and be equally divided among the survivors or survivor of them. But my intention is, that, if any or either of them should happen to die under age, leaving issue, such issue shall inherit the part and share that would have passed to his, her, or their parent, had he, she, or they been living.

And, as some of my said devisees may, at the death of the survivor of their father or mother, be of age, and others of them under age, so as that all of them may not be of capacity to make division, I in that case request and authorize the judges of the Supreme Court of Judicature of Pennsylvania for the time being, or any three of them, not personally interested, to appoint by writing, under their hands and seals, three honest, intelligent, impartial men to make the said division, and to assign and allot to each of my devisees their respective share, which division, so made and committed to writing under the hands and seals of the said three men, or of any two of them, and confirmed by the said judges, I do hereby declare shall be binding on, and conclusive between the said devisees.

All the lands near the Ohio, and the lots near the centre of Philadelphia, which I lately purchased of the State, I give to my son-in-law, Richard Bache, his heirs and assigns forever; I also give him the bond I have against him, of two thousand and one hundred and seventy-two pounds, five shillings, together with the interest that shall or may accrue thereon, and direct the same to be delivered up to him by my executors, cancelled, requesting that, in consideration thereof, he would immediately after my decease manumit and set free his negro man Bob. I leave to him, also, the money due to me from the State of Virginia for types. I also give to him the bond of William Goddard and his sister, and the counter bond of the late Robert Grace, and the bond and judgement of Francis Childs, if not recovered before my decease, or any other bonds, except the bond due from —— Killan, of Delaware State, which I give to my grandson, *Benjamin Franklin Bache*. I also discharge him, my said son-in-law, from all claim and rent of moneys due to me, on book account or otherwise. I also give him all my musical instruments.

The king of France's picture, set with four hundred and eight diamonds, I give to my daughter, *Sarah Bache*, requesting, however, that she would not form any of those diamonds into ornaments either for herself or daughters, and thereby introduce or countenance the expensive, vain, and useless fashion of wearing jewels in this country; and those immediately connected with the picture may be preserved with the same.[1]

I give and devise to my dear sister, *Jane Mecom*, a house and lot I have in Unity Street, Boston, now or late under the care of Mr. Jonathan Williams, to her and to her heirs and assigns for ever. I also give her the yearly sum of fifty pounds sterling, during life, to commence at my death, and to be paid to her annually out of the interests or dividends arising on twelve shares which I have since my arrival at Philadelphia purchased in the Bank of North America, and, at her decease, I give the said twelve shares in the bank to my daughter, *Sarah Bache*, and her husband, *Richard Bache*. But it is my express will and desire that, after the payment of the above fifty pounds sterling annually to my said sister, my said daughter be

---

1. Mrs. Bache sold the outer circle of diamonds and upon the proceeds she and her husband made the tour of Europe. [Albert H. Smyth's footnote.]

allowed to apply the residue of the interest or dividends on those shares to her sole and separate use, during the life of my said sister, and afterwards the whole of the interest or dividends thereof as her private pocket money.

I give the right I have to take up three thousand acres of land in the State of Georgia, granted to me by the government of that State, to my grandson, *William Temple Franklin*, his heirs and assigns for ever. I also give to my grandson, *William Temple Franklin*, the bond and judgement I have against him of four thousand pounds sterling, my right to the same to cease upon the day of his marriage; and if he dies unmarried, my will is, that the same be recovered and divided among my other grandchildren, the children of my daughter, *Sarah Bache*, in such manner and form as I have herein before given to them the other parts of my estate.

The philosophical instruments I have in Philadelphia I give to my ingenious friend, *Francis Hopkinson*.

To the children, grandchildren, and great-grandchildren of my brother, *Samuel Franklin*, that may be living at the time of my decease, I give fifty pounds sterling, to be equally divided among them. To the children, grandchildren, and great-grandchildren of my sister, *Anne Harris*, that may be living at the time of my decease, I give fifty pounds sterling, to be equally divided among them. To the children, grandchildren, and great-grandchildren of my brother, *James Franklin*, that may be living at the time of my decease, I give fifty pounds sterling, to be equally divided among them. To the children, grandchildren, and great-grandchildren of my sister, *Sarah Davenport*, that may be living at the time of my decease, I give fifty pounds sterling to be equally divided among them. To the children, grandchildren, and great-grandchildren of my sister, *Lydia Scott*, that may be living at the time of my decease, I give fifty pounds sterling, to be equally divided among them. To the children, grandchildren, and great-grandchildren of my sister, *Jane Mecom*, that may be living at the time of my decease, I give fifty pounds sterling, to be equally divided among them.

I give to my grandson, *Benjamin Franklin Bache*, all the types and printing materials, which I now have in Philadelphia, with the complete letter foundery, which, in the whole, I suppose to be worth near one thousand pounds; but if he should die under age, then I do order the same to be sold by my executors, the survivors or survivor of them, and the moneys thence arising to be equally divided among all the rest of my said daughter's children, or their representatives, each one on coming of age to take his or her share, and the children of such of them as may die under age to represent, and to take the share and proportion of, the parent so dying, each one to receive his or her part of such share as they come of age.

With regard to my books, those I had in France and those I left in Philadelphia, being now assembled together here, and a catalogue made of them, it is my intention to dispose of the same as follows: My "History of the Academy of Sciences," in sixty or seventy volumes quarto, I give to the *Philosophical Society of Philadelphia*, of which I have the honour to be President. My collection in folio of "Les Arts et les Métiers," I give to the *American Philosophical Society*, established in New England, of which I am a member. My quarto edition of the same, "Arts et Métiers," I give to the *Library Company of Philadelphia*. Such and so many of my books as I shall mark on the said catalogue with the name of my grandson, *Benjamin Franklin Bache*, I do hereby give to him; and such and so many of my books as I shall mark on the said catalogue with the name of my grandson, *William Bache*, I do hereby give to him; and such as shall be marked with the name of *Jonathan Williams*, I hereby give to my cousin of that name. The residue and remainder of all my books, manuscripts, and papers, I do give to my grandson, *William Temple Franklin*. My share in the Library Company of Philadelphia, I give to my grandson, *Benjamin Franklin Bache*, confiding that he will permit his brothers and sisters to share in the use of it.

I was born in Boston, New England, and owe my first instructions in literature to the free grammar-schools established there. I therefore give one hundred pounds sterling to my executors, to be by them, the survivors or survivor of them, paid over to the managers or directors of the free schools in my native town of Boston, to be by them, or by those person or persons, who shall have the superintendence and management of the said schools, put out to interest, and so continued at interest for ever, which interest annually shall be laid out in silver medals, and given as honourary rewards annually by the directors of the said free schools belonging to the said town, in such manner as to the discretion of the selectmen of the said town shall seem meet.

Out of the salary that may remain due to me as President of the State, I do give the sum of two thousand pounds to my executors, to be by them, the survivors or survivor of them, paid over to such person or persons as the legislature of this State by an act of Assembly shall appoint to receive the same in trust, to be employed for making the river Schuylkill navigable.

And what money of mine shall, at the time of my decease, remain in the hands of my bankers, Messrs. Ferdinand Grand and Son, at Paris, or Messrs. Smith, Wright, and Gray, of London, I will that, after my debts are paid and deducted, with the money legacies of this my will, the same be divided into four equal parts, two of which I give to my dear daughter, *Sarah Bache*, one to her son *Benjamin*, and one to my grandson, *William Temple Franklin*.

During the number of years I was in business as a stationer, printer, and postmaster, a great many small sums became due for books, advertisements, postage of letters, and other matters, which were not collected when, in 1757, I was sent by the Assembly to England as their agent, and by subsequent appointments continued there till 1775, when on my return, I was immediately engaged in the affairs of Congress, and sent to France in 1776, where I remained nine years, not returning till 1785: and the said debts, not being demanded in such a length of time, are become in a manner obsolete, yet are nevertheless justly due. These, as they are stated in my great folio ledger E, I bequeath to the *contributors to the Pennsylvania Hospital*, hoping that those debtors, and the descendants of such as are deceased, who now, as I find, make some difficulty of satisfying such antiquated demands as just debts, may, however, be induced to pay or give them as charity to that excellent institution. I am sensible that much must inevitably be lost, but I hope something considerable may be recovered. It is possible, too, that some of the parties charged may have existing old, unsettled accounts against me; in which case the managers of the said hospital will allow and deduct the amount, or pay the balance if they find it against me.

My debts and legacies being all satisfied and paid, the rest and residue of all my estate, real and personal, not herein expressly disposed of, I do give and bequeath to my son and daughter, *Richard* and *Sarah Bache*.

I request my friends, Henry Hill, Esquire, John Jay, Esquire, Francis Hopkinson, Esquire, and Mr. Edward Duffield, of Benfield, in Philadelphia County, to be the executors of this my last will and testament; and I hereby nominate and appoint them for that purpose.

I would have my body buried with as little expense or ceremony as may be. I revoke all former wills by me made, declaring this only to be my last.

[SEAL.] In witness thereof, I have hereunto set my hand and seal, this seventeenth day of July, in the year of our Lord one thousand seven hundred and eighty-eight.

B. FRANKLIN.

Signed, sealed, published, and declared by the above-named Benjamin Franklin, for and as his last will and testament, in the presence of us.

ABRAHAM SHOEMAKER,
JOHN JONES,
GEORGE MOORE.

CODICIL

I, Benjamin Franklin, in the foregoing or annexed last will and testament named, having further considered the same, do think proper to make and publish the following codicil or addition thereto.

It having long been a fixed political opinion of mine, that in a democratical state there ought to be no offices of profit, for the reasons I had given in an article of my drawing in our constitution, it was my intention when I accepted the office of President, to devote the appointed salary to some public uses. Accordingly, I had already, before I made my will in July last, given large sums of it to colleges, schools, building of churches, etc.; and in that will I bequeathed two thousand pounds more to the State for the purpose of making the Schuylkill navigable. But understanding since that such a sum will do but little towards accomplishing such a work, and that the project is not likely to be undertaken for many years to come, and having entertained another idea, that I hope may be more extensively useful, I do hereby revoke and annul that bequest, and direct that the certificates I have for what remains due to me of that salary be sold, towards raising the sum of two thousand pounds sterling, to be disposed of as I am now about to order.

It has been an opinion, that he who receives an estate from his ancestors is under some kind of obligation to transmit the same to their posterity. This obligation does not lie on me, who never inherited a shilling from any ancestor or relation. I shall, however, if it is not diminished by some accident before my death, leave a considerable estate among my descendants and relations. The above observation is made merely as some apology to my family for making bequests that do not appear to have any immediate relation to their advantage.

I was born in Boston, New England, and owe my first instructions in literature to the free grammar-schools established there. I have, therefore, already considered these schools in my will. But I am also under obligations to the State of Massachusetts for having, unasked, appointed me formerly their agent in England, with a handsome salary, which continued some years; and although I accidentally lost in their service, by transmitting Governor Hutchinson's letters, much more than the amount of what they gave me, I do not think that ought in the least to diminish my gratitude.

I have considered that, among artisans, good apprentices are most likely to make good citizens, and, having myself been bred to a manual art, printing, in my native town, and afterwards assisted to set up my business in Philadelphia by kind loans of money from two friends there, which was the foundation of my fortune, and of all the utility in life that may be ascribed to me, I wish to be useful even after my death, if possible, in forming and advancing other young men, that may be serviceable to their country in both these towns. To this end, I devote two thousand pounds sterling, of which I give one thousand thereof to the inhabitants of the town of Boston, in Massachusetts, and the other thousand to the inhabitants of the city of Philadelphia, in trust, to and for the uses, intents, and purposes hereinafter mentioned and declared.

The said sum of one thousand pounds sterling, if accepted by the inhabitants of the town of Boston, shall be managed under the direction of the selectmen, united with the ministers of the oldest Episcopalian, Congregational, and Presbyterian churches in that town, who are to let out the sum upon interest, at five per cent. per annum, to such young married artificers, under the age of twenty-five years, as have served an apprenticeship in the said town, and faithfully fulfilled the duties required in their indentures, so as to obtain a good moral character from at least two respectable citizens, who are willing to become their sureties, in a bond with the applicants, for the repayment of the moneys so lent, with interest, according to the terms hereinafter prescribed; all which bonds are to be taken for Spanish milled dollars, or the value thereof in current gold coin; and the managers shall keep a bound book or books, wherein shall be entered the names of those who shall apply for and receive the benefits of this institution, and of their sureties, together with the sums lent, the dates, and other necessary and proper records respecting the business and concerns of this institution. And as these loans are intended to assist young married artificers in setting up their business, they are to be proportioned by the discretion of the managers, so as not to exceed sixty pounds sterling to one person, nor to be less than fifteen pounds; and if the number of appliers so entitled should be so large as that the sum will not suffice to afford to each as much as might otherwise not be improper, the proportion to each shall be diminished so as to afford to every one some assistance. These aids may, therefore, be small at first, but, as the capital increases by the accumulated interest, they will be more ample. And in order to serve as many as possible in their turn, as well as to make the repayment of the principal borrowed more easy, each borrower shall be obliged to pay, with the yearly interest, one tenth part of the principal, which sums of principal and interest, so paid in, shall be again let out to fresh borrowers.

And, as it is presumed that there will always be found in Boston virtuous and benevolent citizens, willing to bestow a part of their time in doing good to the rising generation, by superintending and managing this institution gratis, it is hoped that no part of the money will at any time be dead, or be diverted to other purposes, but be continually augmenting by the interest; in which case there may, in time, be more than the occasions in Boston shall require, and then some may be spared to the neighbouring or other towns in the said State of Massachusetts, who may desire to have it; such towns engaging to pay punctually the interest and the portions of the principal, annually, to the inhabitants of the town of Boston.

If this plan is executed, and succeeds as projected without interruption for one hundred years, the sum will then be one hundred and thirty-one thousand pounds; of which I would have the managers of the donation to the town of Boston then lay out, at their discretion, one hundred thousand pounds in public works, which may be judged of most general utility to the inhabitants, such as fortifications, bridges, aqueducts, public buildings, baths, pavements, or whatever may make living in the town more convenient to its people, and render it more agreeable to strangers resorting thither for health or a temporary residence. The remaining thirty-one thousand pounds I would have continued to be let out on interest, in the manner above directed, for another hundred years, as I hope it will have been found that the institution has had a good effect on the conduct of youth, and been of service to many worthy characters and useful citizens. At the end of this second term, if no unfortunate accident has prevented the operation, the sum will be four millions and sixty one thousand pounds sterling, of which I leave one million sixty one thousand pounds to the disposition of the inhabitants of the town of Boston, and three millions to the disposition of the government of the state, not presuming to carry my views farther.

All the directions herein given, respecting the disposition and management of the donation to the inhabitants of Boston, I would have observed respecting that to the inhabitants of Philadelphia, only, as Philadelphia is incorporated, I request the corporation of that city to undertake the management agreeably to the said directions; and I do hereby vest them with full and ample powers for that purpose. And, having considered that the covering a ground plot with buildings and pavements, which carry off most of the rain and prevent its soaking into the Earth and renewing and purifying the Springs, whence the water of wells must gradually grow worse, and in time be unfit for use, as I find has happened in all old cities, I recommend that at the end of the first hundred years, if not done before, the corporation of the city Employ a part of the hundred thousand pounds in bringing, by pipes, the water of Wissahickon Creek into the town, so as to supply the inhabitants, which I apprehend may be done without great difficulty, the level of the creek being much above that of the city, and may be made higher by a dam. I also recommend making the Schuylkill completely navigable. At the end of the second hundred years, I would have the disposition of the four million and sixty one thousand pounds divided between the inhabitants of the city of Philadelphia and the government of Pennsylvania, in the same manner as herein directed with respect to that of the inhabitants of Boston and the government of Massachusetts.

It is my desire that this institution should take place and begin to operate within one year after my decease, for which purpose due notice should be publickly given previous to the expiration of that year, that those for whose benefit this establishment is intended may make their respective applications. And I hereby direct my executors, the survivors or survivor of them, within six months after my decease, to pay over the said sum of two thousand pounds sterling to such persons as shall be duly appointed by the Selectmen of Boston and the corporation of Philadelphia, to receive and take charge of their respective sums, of one thousand pounds each, for the purposes aforesaid.

Considering the accidents to which all human affairs and projects are subject in such a length of time, I have, perhaps, too much flattered myself with a vain fancy that these dispositions, if carried into execution, will be continued without interruption and have the effects proposed. I hope, however, that if the inhabitants of the two cities should not think fit to undertake the execution, they will, at least, accept the offer of these donations as a mark of my good will, a token of my gratitude, and a testimony of my earnest desire to be useful to them after my departure.

I wish, indeed, that they may both undertake to endeavour the execution of the project, because I think that, though unforeseen difficulties may arise, expedients will be found to remove them, and the scheme be found practicable. If one of them accepts the money, with the conditions, and the other refuses, my will then is, that both Sums be given to the inhabitants of the city accepting the whole, to be applied to the same purposes, and under the same regulations directed for the separate parts; and, if both refuse, the money of course remains in the mass of my Estate, and is to be disposed of therewith according to my will made the Seventeenth day of July, 1788.

I wish to be buried by the side of my wife, if it may be, and that a marble stone, to be made by Chambers, six feet long, four feet wide, plain, with only a small moulding round the upper edge, and this inscription:

Benjamin ⎫
And   ⎬ Franklin
Deborah ⎭

178–

to be placed over us both. My fine crab-tree walking-stick, with a gold head curiously wrought in the form of the cap of liberty, I give to my friend, and the friend of mankind, *General Washington*. If it were a Sceptre, he has merited it, and would become it. It was a present to me from that excellent woman, Madame de Forbach, the dowager Duchess of Deux-Ponts, connected with some verses which should go with it. I give my gold watch to my son-in-law, *Richard Bache*, and also the gold watch chain of the Thirteen United States, which I have not yet worn. My timepiece, that stands in my library, I give to my grandson *William Temple Franklin*. I give him also my Chinese gong. To my dear old friend, *Mrs. Mary Hewson*, I give one of my silver tankards marked for her use during her life, and after her decease I give it to her daughter *Eliza*. I give to her son, *William Hewson*, who is my godson, my new quarto Bible, Oxford edition, to be for his family Bible, and also the botanic description of the plants in the Emperor's garden at Vienna, in folio, with coloured cuts.

And to her son, *Thomas Hewson*, I give a set of *Spectators, Tatlers*, and *Guardians* handsomely bound.

There is an error in my will, where the bond of William Temple Franklin is mentioned as being four thousand pounds sterling, whereas it is but for three thousand five hundred pounds.

I give to my *executors*, to be divided equally among those that act, the sum of sixty pounds sterling, as some compensation for their trouble in the execution of my will; and I request my friend, *Mr. Duffield*, to accept moreover my French waywciser, a piece of clock-work in Brass, to be fixed to the wheel of any carriage, and that my friend, *Mr. Hill*, may also accept my silver cream pot, formerly given to me by the good Doctor Fothergill, with the motto, *Keep bright the Chain*.[2] My reflecting telescope, made by Short, which was formerly Mr. Canton's, I give to my friend, *Mr. David Rittenhouse*, for the use of his observatory.

My picture, drawn by Martin,[3] in 1767, I give to the *Supreme Executive Council of Pennsylvania*, if they shall be pleased to do me the honour of accepting it and placing it in their chamber. Since my will was made I have bought some more city lots, near the centre part of the estate of Joseph Dean. I would have them go with the other lots, disposed of in my will, and I do give the same to my Son-in-law, *Richard Bache*, to his heirs and assigns forever.

In addition to the annuity left to my sister in my will, of fifty pounds sterling during her life, I now add thereto ten pounds sterling more, in order to make the Sum sixty pounds. I give twenty guineas to my good friend and physician, *Dr. John Jones*.

With regard to the separate bequests made to my daughter *Sarah* in my will, my intention is, that the same shall be for her sole and

2. A motto of friendship that Fothergill adopted from diplomatic language that bound the British colonies to the Iroquois Six Nations.
3. David Martin (1737–1797), British painter.

separate use, notwithstanding her coverture, or whether she be covert or sole; and I do give my executors so much right and power therein as may be necessary to render my intention effectual in that respect only. This provision for my daughter is not made out of any disrespect I have for her husband.

And lastly, it is my desire that this, my present codicil, be annexed to, and considered as part of, my last will and testament to all intents and purposes.

In witness whereof, I have hereunto set my hand and Seal this twenty-third day of [SEAL.] June, Anno Domini one thousand Seven hundred and eighty nine.

B. FRANKLIN.

Signed, sealed, published, and declared by the above named Benjamin Franklin to be a codicil to his last will and testament, in the presence of us.

FRANCIS BAILEY,
THOMAS LANG,
ABRAHAM SHOEMAKER.

Self-Improvement

Franklin wrote numerous brief aphorisms on virtue in the Poor Richard almanacs, 1733–58; and, in order to help his nephew Benjamin Mecom, he wrote a version of the "Art of Virtue" ("A Letter from Father Abraham to his beloved Son"—*Papers* 8.123–31) for the initial issue of Mecom's *New England Magazine* (August 1758). Plans for self-improvement are commonplaces of ethical writing, and Franklin must have read numerous ones. Louis I. Bredvold, "The Invention of the Ethical Calculus" (in Richard Foster Jones, et al., *The Seventeenth Century* [Stanford: Stanford UP, 1951], 165–80) surveys some of Franklin's progenitors—and such plans for self-improvement continued to be written after Franklin's time. But what makes Franklin's scheme memorable is the interplay between the persona, the subject, and the audience.

Franklin's "project of arriving at moral Perfection" has been misunderstood for several reasons, including the meaning of *perfection*. We now think of *perfection* as a completed state, but in the eighteenth century, *perfect* did not necessarily mean an achieved condition, but could imply an approach to that condition. The words *perfecter* and *perfectest*, then in common use, give some idea of the comparative possibilities of the words *perfect* and *perfection*. Franklin frequently used them in this comparative manner. (In the quotations on perfection, the original italics have been ignored and italics have been supplied.)

Franklin's Epitaph, 1728[2]

The Body of
B. Franklin,
Printer;
Like the Cover of an old Book,
Its Contents torn out,
And stript of its Lettering and Gilding,
Lies here, Food for Worms.
But the Work shall not be wholly lost:
For it will, as he believ'd, appear once more,
In a new & *more perfect* Edition,
Corrected and amended
By the Author.
He was born Jan. 6. 1706
Died   17

Franklin's Junto Query on Human Perfection, 1732[3]

Qu. Can a Man arrive at *Perfection* in this Life as some Believe; or is it impossible as others believe?

A.   Perhaps they differ in the meaning of the Word *Perfection*.

I suppose the *Perfection* of any Thing to be only the greatest the Nature of that Thing is capable of;

Different Things have different *Degrees of Perfection;* and the same thing at different Times.

Thus an Horse is *more perfect* than an Oyster yet the Oyster may be a *perfect* Oyster as well as the Horse a *perfect* Horse.

And an Egg is not so *perfect* as a Chicken, nor a Chicken as a Hen; for the Hen has more Strength than the Chicken, and the C[hicken] more Life than the Egg: Yet it may be a *perfect* Egg, Chicken and Hen.

If they mean, a Man cannot in this Life be so *perfect* as an Angel, it is [written above: "may be"] true; for an Angel by being incorporeal is allow'd *some Perfections* we are at present incapable of, and less liable to *some Imperfections* that we are liable to.

If they mean a Man is not capable of being so *perfect* here as he is capable of being in Heaven, that may be true likewise. But that a Man is not capable of being so *perfect* here, as he is capable of being here; is not Sense; it is as if I should say, a Chicken in the State of a Chicken is not capable of being so *perfect* as a Chicken is capable of being in that State. In the above Sense if there may be a *perfect* Oyster, a *perfect* Horse, a *perfect* Ship, why not a *perfect* Man? that is as *perfect* as his present Nature and Circumstances admit?

2. *Papers* 1.111.
3. *Papers* 1.261–62.

Poor Richard on Self-Improvement, 1749[4]

Franklin adopted the following observation from Joseph Addison (*Spectator* no. 447, August 2, 1712), who, in turn, was reflecting Pythagoras.

It was wise counsel given to a young man, *Pitch upon that course of life which is most excellent, and Custom will make it the most delightful.* But many pitch on no course of life at all, nor form any scheme of living, by which to attain any valuable end; but wander perpetually from one thing to another.

Rules for Making Oneself a Disagreeable Companion, 1750[5]

In this comic piece, a fake self-help guide, Franklin shows how those who make no effort to improve themselves will appear foolish, even vicious, to others.

RULES, by the Observation of which, a Man of Wit and Learning may nevertheless make himself a *disagreeable* Companion.

Your Business is to *shine;* therefore you must by all means prevent the shining of others, for their Brightness may make yours the less distinguish'd. To this End,

1. If possible engross the whole Discourse; and when other Matter fails, talk much of your-self, your Education, your Knowledge, your Circumstances, your Successes in Business, your Victories in Disputes, your own wise Sayings and Observations on particular Occasions, &c. &c. &c.

2. If when you are out of Breath, one of the Company should seize the Opportunity of saying something; watch his Words, and, if possible, find somewhat either in his Sentiment or Expression, immediately to contradict and raise a Dispute upon. Rather than fail, criticise even his Grammar.

3. If another should be saying an indisputably good Thing; either give no Attention to it; or interrupt him; or draw away the Attention of others; or, if you can guess what he would be at, be quick and say it before him; or, if he gets it said, and you perceive the Company pleas'd with it, own it to be a good Thing, and withal remark that it had been said by Bacon, Locke, Bayle, or some other eminent Writer: thus you deprive him of the Reputation he might have gain'd by it, and gain some yourself, as you hereby show your great Reading and Memory.

---

4. *Papers* 3.341.
5. *Pennsylvania Gazette*, November 15, 1750, in *Papers* 4.73–74. William Franklin is the authority for assigning this piece to Benjamin Franklin. "He also wrote and published in one of his Papers 'Rules whereby a Man of Sense and Learning may make himself a disagreeable Companion,' which I should be glad to have." To Jonathan Williams, Jr., July 30, 1807, Indiana University Library.

4. When modest Men have been thus treated by you a few times, they will chuse ever after to be silent in your Company; then you may shine on without Fear of a Rival; rallying them at the same time for their Dullness, which will be to you a new Fund of Wit.

Thus you will be sure to please *yourself.* The polite Man aims at pleasing *others*, but you shall go beyond him even in that. A Man can be present only in one Company, but may at the same time be absent in twenty. He can please only where he *is*, you whereever you are *not*.

To Lord Kames, May 3, 1760[6]

Franklin's best description of his projected Art of Virtue is contained in a letter to Lord Kames.

* * * I purpose, likewise, a little Work for the Benefit of Youth, to be call'd *The Art of Virtue*. From the Title I think you will hardly conjecture what the Nature of such a Book may be. I must therefore explain it a little. Many People lead bad Lives that would gladly lead good ones, but know not *how* to make the Change. They have frequently *resolv'd* and *endeavour'd* it; but in vain, because their Endeavours have not been properly conducted. To exhort People to be good, to be just, to be temperate, &c. without shewing them *how* they shall *become* so, seems like the ineffectual Charity mention'd by the Apostle, which consisted in saying to the Hungry, the Cold, and the Naked, *be ye fed, be ye warmed, be ye clothed*, without shewing them how they should get Food, Fire or Clothing. Most People have naturally *some* Virtues, but none have naturally *all* the Virtues. To *acquire* those that are wanting, and *secure* what we acquire as well as those we have naturally, is the Subject of *an Art.* It is as properly an Art, as Painting, Navigation, or Architecture. If a Man would become a Painter, Navigator, or Architect, it is not enough that he is *advised* to be one, that he is *convinc'd* by the Arguments of his Adviser that it would be for his Advantage to be one, and that he *resolves* to be one, but he must also be taught the Principles of the Art, be shewn all the Methods of Working, and how to acquire the *Habits* of using properly all the Instruments; and thus regularly and gradually he arrives by Practice at some Perfection in the Art. If he does not proceed thus, he is apt to meet with Difficulties that discourage him, and make him drop the Pursuit. My *Art of Virtue* has also its Instruments, and teaches the Manner of Using them. Christians are directed to have *Faith in Christ*, as the effectual Means of obtaining the Change they desire. It may, when sufficiently strong, be effectual with many. A full Opinion that a Teacher is infinitely wise, good, and powerful,

6. *Papers* 9.104–5.

and that he will certainly reward and punish the Obedient and Dis-obedient, must give great Weight to his Precepts, and make them much more attended to by his Disciples. But all Men cannot have Faith in Christ; and many have it in so weak a Degree, that it does not produce the Effect. Our *Art of Virtue* may therefore be of great Service to those who have not Faith, and come in Aid of the weak Faith of others. Such as are naturally well-disposed, and have been carefully educated, so that good Habits have been early established, and bad ones prevented, have less Need of this Art; but all may be more or less benefited by it. It is, in short, to be adapted for universal Use. I imagine what I have now been writing will seem to savour of great Presumption; I must therefore speedily finish my little Piece, and communicate the Manuscript to you, that you may judge whether it is possible to make good such Pretensions. I shall at the same time hope for the Benefit of your Corrections.

* * *

To Abiah Franklin, Philadelphia, April 12, 1750[7]

In 1750, Franklin wrote his mother a letter of family news, joking about his expenses and telling her about the reputation he would prefer to have.

* * *

As to your Grandchildren, Will.[8] is now 19 Years of Age, a tall proper Youth, and much of a Beau.[9] He acquir'd a Habit of Idleness on the Expedition, but begins of late to apply himself to Business, and I hope will become an industrious Man. He imagin'd his Father had got enough for him: But I have assur'd him that I intend to spend what little I have, my self; if it please God that I live long enough: And as he by no means wants Sense, he can see by my going on, that I am like to be as good as my Word.

Sally[1] grows a fine Girl, and is extreamly industrious with her Needle, and delights in her book. She is of a most affectionate Tem-per, and perfectly Dutiful and obliging, to her Parents and to all. Perhaps I flatter my self too much; but I have Hopes that she will prove an ingenious sensible notable and worthy Woman, like her Aunt Jenney.[2] She goes now to the Dancing School.

For my own Part, at present I pass my time agreably enough. I enjoy (thro' Mercy) a tolerable Share of Health; I read a great deal, ride a little, do a little Business for my self, more for others; retire

---

7. *Papers* 3.474–75.
8. William Franklin, Benjamin Franklin's illegitimate son (see biographical sketch on p. 207).
9. Beau, i.e., a dandy and ladies' man.
1. Sarah Franklin (Bache), Benjamin and Deborah Franklin's daughter.
2. Jane (Franklin) Mecom, Benjamin Franklin's younger sister.

when I can, and go [into] Company when I please; so the Years roll round, and the last will come; when I would rather have it said, *He lived usefully*, than, *He died rich.*

* * *

To Joseph Priestley, September 19, 1772[3]

Franklin's "*Moral or Prudential Algebra*" attempts to measure values in order to have a rational basis for making decisions. It thus has affinities with the method and outlook of the "project for attaining moral Perfection." When Franklin recommended the system to his grandnephew Jonathan Williams on April 8, 1779, he concluded: "By the way, if you do not learn it [*Moral Algebra*], I apprehend you will never be married" (*Papers* 29.284). Only one example of Franklin's own use of prudential algebra survives, in a 1773 debate with himself over whether to leave London for Philadelphia. (He stayed.) He must have carefully destroyed all other examples of how he thought his way toward decisions, leaving only the decisions in view. (*Papers* 20.336–38.)

London Sept. 19. 1772

Dear Sir,

In the Affair of so much Importance to you, wherein you ask my Advice, I cannot for want of sufficient Premises, advise you *what* to determine, but if you please I will tell you *how*. When these difficult Cases occur, they are difficult chiefly because while we have them under Consideration all the Reasons *pro* and *con* are not present to the Mind at the same time; but sometimes one Set present themselves, and at other times another, the first being out of Sight. Hence the various Purposes or Inclinations that alternately prevail, and the Uncertainty that perplexes us. To get over this, my Way is, to divide half a Sheet of Paper by a Line into two Columns, writing over the one *Pro*, and over the other *Con*. Then during three or four Days Consideration I put down under the different Heads short Hints of the different Motives that at different Times occur to me for or against the Measure. When I have thus got them all together in one View, I endeavour to estimate their respective Weights; and where I find two, one on each side, that seem equal, I strike them both out: If I find a Reason *Pro* equal to some two Reasons *con*, I strike out the three. If I judge some two Reasons *con* equal to some three Reasons *pro*, I strike out the five; and thus proceeding I find at length where the Ballance lies; and if after a Day or two of farther Consideration nothing new that is of Importance occurs on either side, I come to a Determination accordingly. And tho' the Weight of Reasons cannot be taken with the Precision of Algebraic Quantities, yet when each is

3. *Papers* 19.299–300.

thus considered separately and comparatively, and the whole lies before me, I think I can judge better, and am less likely to make a rash Step; and in fact I have found great Advantage from this kind of Equation, in what may be called *Moral* or *Prudential Algebra*.

*　*　*

CRITICISM

Contemporary Opinions

Eighteenth-century opinions on Franklin were shaped by his activities as an author, man of science, and political figure. He was undoubtedly America's most famous writer, and would eventually have one of the most extensive and varied correspondences of any person in the eighteenth century. His work on electricity, and to a lesser extent on other problems in science, was crucial to his international fame. From the 1730s to the 1760s, he led the royal party against the proprietary party in Pennsylvania; in England and America during the pre-Revolutionary period, he personified American criticism of British imperialism; in America and France during the Revolution, he was the most famous American rebel; and in America after the Revolution, he was an outspoken Federalist.

IMMANUEL KANT

In his third essay on the devastating earthquake that struck Lisbon in 1755, the German philosopher Immanuel Kant described Franklin as "Prometheus der neuern Zeiten," a Prometheus of the modern age. By comparing the American electrical experimenter to the mythological Greek titan who had stolen fire from the gods, Kant cautioned humans not to defy the natural order of things, yet issued a backhanded compliment to the seemingly titanic Franklin. When translated into French, the idea of Franklin as "le prométhée moderne" would circulate throughout Europe. Mary Wollstonecraft Shelley would echo Kant's warning in the subtitle to her novel, *Frankenstein, or, the Modern Prometheus* (1818). Did Dr. Franken-stein imply Dr. Franklin-stein?

The Modern Prometheus†

The fire of the subterranean vaults has not yet calmed down. The concussions are still going on in frightened countries to which this evil was formerly unknown. The disorder in the atmosphere has changed the season in half the terrestrial globe. Some say, the

† Gabriele Rabel, trans. and ed., *Kant* (Oxford: Clarendon Press, 1963), 30. Reprinted by permission. From the German in Immanuel Kant, *Gesammelte Schriften . . .* (Berlin: George Reimer, 1900), 1.472.

263

earth has been moved nearer to the sun, others point once again at the comet, since Whiston[1] has taught even philosophers to be afraid of it. For a long time now, no suspicion has been thrown on the planets. The accusations against them have been filed away in the archives of obsolete chimeras, with fairies, sympathetic miracles, and the Blocksberg. Then Newton discovered a *real* force which even the remotest planets exert upon each other. We know exactly the amount of this force, and a scientist such as Professor Profe in Altona ought not to hold it responsible for occurrences which are so completely out of proportion.

Peirescius[2] saw in 1604 a rare conjunction of the three upper planets which happens only once in eight hundred years. But the earth remained quite calm and safe. There is such a thing as right *taste* in natural science, which knows how to distinguish the wild extravagances of unbridled curiosity from cautious judgements of reasonable credibility. From the Prometheus of recent times Mr. Franklin, who wanted to disarm the thunder, down to the man who wants to extinguish the fire in the workshop of Vulcanus, all these endeavours result in the humiliating reminder that Man never can be anything more than a man.

DAVID HUME

David Hume (1711–1776), the great English philosopher, evidently met Franklin (probably through their mutual friend William Strahan) in London in 1758–59. Although Hume was ambivalent toward the colonies, he found Franklin congenial but (as Franklin quickly perceived) too much an American patriot. Hume referred to Franklin's scientific papers, as well as some of his other writings, when he paid him the following great compliment.

To Franklin, Edinburgh, May 10, 1762[†]

* * *

I am very sorry, that you intend soon to leave our Hemisphere. America has sent us many good things, Gold, Silver, Sugar, Tobacco, Indigo &c: But you are the first Philosopher, and indeed the first Great Man of Letters for whom we are beholden to her: it is our own Fault, that we have not kept him: Whence it appears, that we do not

---

1. William Whiston (1667–1752), English astronomer.
2. Nicolas-Claude Fabri de Peiresc (1580–1637), French astronomer.
† Reprinted by permission of The Papers of Benjamin Franklin at the Yale University Library. *Papers* 10.81–82.

agree with Solomon,[1] that Wisdom is above Gold: For we take care
never to send back an ounce of the latter, which we once lay our
Fingers upon. * * *

FRANKLIN IN THE COCKPIT

In winter 1772, Franklin received a set of letters that Thomas Hutchinson, Royal Governor of Massachusetts, Andrew Oliver, Lieutenant
Governor, and others had written to Thomas Whateley in London.
Franklin stated that his never-named source had given him the letters to warn that the most blatant anti-American measures "Took their
Rise, not from Government here [in Britain], but were projected, proposed to administration solicited, and obtained by some of the most
respectable people among the Americans themselves, as necessary
Measures for the welfare of that Country" (*Papers* 21.419). Acting as
Agent of the Massachusetts House of Assembly, Franklin forwarded
the letters to Thomas Cushing, Speaker of the House, hoping that they
would reduce tensions between the colonies and Britain. But, when the
letters were published, tensions were instead inflamed. The radicals
in Boston claimed the letters were proof of a transatlantic conspiracy
against American liberties; the British found it outrageous that private
letters had been procured on the sly and exposed to public view.

After the letters were published, the Massachusetts House of Assembly petitioned for the removal of Governor Hutchinson and Lieutenant Govenor Oliver. When Franklin received a copy of the petition in
August, he forwarded it to Lord Darmouth with his belief that resentment against local American authorities would reduce resentment
against British ones (*Papers*, 20.373). On January 8, 1774, Franklin
learned that the Privy Council would hear the petition three days later,
in the "Cockpit." (The London location had previously been the site for
cockfights.) On the day of the hearing, the Attorney General, Alexander
Wedderburn (acting as counsel for Hutchinson and Oliver), demanded
to know how the letters had been obtained. That was a warning, and
Franklin duly engaged attorneys to represent him. The Privy Council
reconvened at the Cockpit on January 29, 1774. At that point, news had
reached London of the Boston Tea Party. Although Franklin did not
support the Tea Party rioters (and offered to pay for the damage they
had done, which would have ruined him), he was identified with the
Boston radicals. All of this meant that anti-American sentiments—and
anti-Franklin sentiments—had crested by the time Franklin appeared
before the Privy Council on January 29.

He was roundly attacked and would, after the hearing, be fired from
his position as Deputy Postmaster. The criticisms were in large part
deserved—an official of the postal system had abused his position in

1. Solomon, King of Israel, traditionally identified as author of proverbs, one of which
   Hume is paraphrasing (*Proverbs* 16:16).

order to expose private correspondence. But the public disgrace that followed was due as well to a widespread perception that Franklin had been too critical of the British ministry, especially in his brilliant hoaxes "An Edict by the King of Prussia" and "Rules by Which a Great Empire May be Reduced to a Small One," which had scored points against British officials.

This is the first notice of the Cockpit scene in Franklin's former newspaper, the *Pennsylvania Gazette*.

The *Pennsylvania Gazette* Report, 1774[†]

On Saturday last the Privy Council met to hear the arguments for and against the petition of the Assembly of Boston (which was some time since presented by their Agent Dr. Franklin) "praying that his Majesty would be pleased to remove the Governor, &c." Serjeant Glynn, and Mr. Dunning, were counsel for the petition, and urged very strongly the expediency and necessity of granting the prayer[1] of it. Mr. Solicitor General was employed on the other side, and instead of answering the learned arguments of his brethren, or refuting the allegations of the petition, contented himself with pronouncing a most severe *Phillipic* on the celebrated American Philosopher, in which he loaded him with all the licensed scurrility of the bar, and decked his harrangue with the choicest flowers of Billingsgate.[2] The Doctor seemed to receive the thunder of his eloquence with philosophic tranquility, and sovereign contempt, whilst the approving smiles of those at the board clearly shewed, that the coarsest language can be grateful to the politest ears.

The King of Prussia, in one of his epistles, calls Dr. Franklin "ce nouveau *Promethee*." Our correspondent says, that he could not help wishing (while the Solicitor General was pouring forth his tide of scurrility) that the American *Prometheus* could have called fire from Heaven to blast the unmannered railer.

Benjamin Vaughan's Account, 1779[‡]

Israel Mauduit, the agent for Hutchinson and Oliver, published Alexander Wedderburn's speech attacking Franklin but suppressed "the grosser parts of the abuse" because (according to Franklin) they were

---

† *Pennsylvania Gazette*, April 20, 1774, evidently reprinted from a London newspaper dated January 31.
1. The request of a complainant in a court of law.
2. Foul and abusive language.
‡ [Benjamin Vaughan, ed.], *Political, Miscellaneous and Philosophical Pieces* (London, 1779), 340–41.

"in their own eyes too foul to be seen on paper" (*Papers* 21.92–93). When Benjamin Vaughan published Franklin's *Political, Miscellaneous and Philosophical Pieces*, he mentioned that Mauduit "prudently omitted" Wedderburn's "most odious personal applications," but that he was now publishing them "as well as they could be collected" in order "to mark the politics of the times, and the nature of the censures passed in England upon Dr. Franklin's character."

'The letters could not have come to Dr. Franklin,' said Mr. Wedderburn, 'by fair means. The writers did not give them to him; nor yet did the deceased correspondent, who from our intimacy would otherwise have told me of it: Nothing then will acquit Dr. Franklin of the charge of obtaining them by fraudulent or corrupt means, for the most malignant of purposes; unless he stole them, from the person who stole them. This argument is irrefragable.'——

'I hope, my lords, you will mark [and brand] the man, for the honour of this country, of Europe, and of mankind. Private correspondence has hitherto been held sacred, in times of the greatest party rage, not only in politics but religion.'——'He has forfeited all the respect of societies and of men. Into what companies will he hereafter go with an unembarrassed face, or the honest intrepidity of virtue. Men will watch him with a jealous eye; they will hide their papers from him, and lock up their escritoires. He will henceforth esteem it a libel to be called *a man of letters; homo* trium[1] *literarum!*

'But he not only took away the letters from one brother; but kept himself concealed till he nearly occasioned the murder of the other. It is impossible to read his account, expressive of the coolest and most deliberate malice, without horror.' [*Here he read the letter above; Dr. Franklin being all the time present.*]——'Amidst these tragical events, of one person nearly murdered, of another answerable for the issue, of a worthy governor hurt in his dearest interests, the fate of America in suspense; here is a man, who with the utmost insensibility of remorse, stands up and avows himself the author of all. I can compare it only to Zanga in Dr. Young's *Revenge*.[2]

> "Know then 'twas—I:
> "I forged the letter, I disposed the picture;
> "I hated, I despised, and I destroy."

I ask, my Lords, whether the revengeful temper attributed, by poetic fiction only, to the bloody African; is not surpassed by the coolness and apathy of the wily American?'

1. I.e., FUR (or *thief*). [Vaughan's note.]
2. Act Vth. [*Vaughan's note.*] Edward Young's popular tragedy *The Revenge* (1721) was modeled on Shakespeare's *Othello*.

EDMUND BURKE

Edmund Burke (1729–1792), Whig leader in Parliament, found it extraordinary that the elderly Franklin (then sixty-nine, not "upwards of seventy") set off in 1775 on a dangerous ocean voyage to America in order to join a country on the verge of civil war.

To Count Patrick D'Arcy, October 5, 1775†

* * *

What say you to your friend and brother Philosopher Franklin, who at upwards of seventy years of age, quits the Study of the Laws of Nature, in order to give Laws to new Commonwealths; and has crossed the Atlantick ocean at that time of Life, not to seek repose, but to plunge into the midst of the most laborious and most arduous affairs that ever were. Few things more extraordinary have happened in the history of mankind. These rebels of ours are a singular sort of people—[1]

* * *

From the *New-Jersey Gazette*, December 31, 1777

This commentary by an anonymous submitter offers another image of an all-powerful, titanic Franklin, this time on the side of the American rebels.

INTELLIGENCE EXTRAORDINARY.

WE are well assured that Dr. Franklin, whose knowledge in philosophical sciences is universally allowed, and who has carried the powers of electricity to a greater length than any of his contemporaries, intends shortly to produce an *electrical machine*, of such wonderful force, that, instead of giving a slight stroke to the elbows of fifty or an hundred thousand men, who are joined hand in hand, it will give a violent shock even to nature herself, so as to disunite

---

† Thomas W. Copeland, ed., *The Correspondence of Edmund Burke*, 10 vols. (Cambridge: Cambridge UP, 1958–1978), 3.228. Reprinted by permission of Cambridge University Press.

1. When Burke wrote Franklin on August 15, 1781, he addressed him as "Doctor Franklin the Philosopher; my friend, and the lover of his Species." And on February 28, 1782, informing Franklin of the vote in Parliament that ended the war in America, he said: "*I congratulate you, as the friend of America, I trust, as not the enemy of England, I am sure, as the friend of mankind.*" Source: Copeland, *Correspondence*, 4.364–65. 419. [Copeland's note.]

kingdoms, join islands to continents, and render men of the same nation strangers and enemies to each other; and that, by a certain chymical preparation from oil, he will be able to smooth the waves of the sea in one part of the globe, and raise tempests and whirlwinds in another, so as to be universally acknowledged for the greatest physician, politician, mathematician, and philosopher, this day living.

PETER OLIVER

Peter Oliver (1713–1791), Loyalist and Chief Justice of the Massachusetts Superior Court, was particularly angry at Franklin because the Hutchinson letters that Franklin sent to the Boston patriot leaders included letters by Peter's brother Andrew Oliver (1706–1774), Lieutenant Governor of Massachusetts. The publication of the Hutchinson letters caused public demonstrations against Hutchinson and both Olivers. Peter Oliver's facts about Franklin are often wrong—for example, he confuses the young Franklin with his brother James Franklin—but his animosity is obviously sincere.

From Origins & Progress of the American Rebellion[†]

⚜   I   ⚜

There was one Person more who might, *now*, be termed, the *instar omnium*[1] of Rebellion. The Features of whose Soul were so minutely expressed in the Lines of his Countenance, that a Gentleman, whose Acumen was so great as to strike out a Character from a very slight View of a Face, was introduced to his Company many Years since; and upon his being asked his Opinion of the Man, he replied, "that he was calculated to set a whole Kingdom in a Flame." This was his Opinion of Dr. *Benjamin Franklin.*

This Narrative hath been frequently interrupted by the Description of Characters; but it seemed necessary to describe, when the Persons introduced theirselves upon the Stage. Let this suffice for Apology. It is now Dr. *Franklyn's Turn* to sit for his Portrait; & I shall endeavor to sketch the Outlines: perhaps I may catch a Feature or two as I go on with the Narrative.

Dr. *Benjamin Franklin* was a Native of *Boston* in the *Massachusetts Bay.* He was born in 1706, of very reputable Parents. His Father was a capital Tallow Chandler, & a worthy honest Man. His Brother

---

[†] Douglass Adair and John A. Schultz, eds., *Peter Oliver's Origin & Progress of the American Rebellion* (San Marino, Calif.: Huntington Library, 1961), 78–82. Reprinted by permission.

1. Image of all, archetype.

also was a Man held in very good esteem. The Doctor himself was what is called a *Printers Devil* but, by a Climax in Reputation, he reversed the Phrase, & taught us to read it backward, as Witches do the Lords Prayer. He worked at the Business of the Press untill he went to *England*, & continued in *London* for about two Years, to perfect himself in the Art, & black as the Art was before, he made it much blacker, by forcing the Press often to speak the Thing that was not. He published a Libel in *Boston*, for which he was obliged to quit. He fled to *Rhode Island*,[2] the Asylum for those who had done what they ought not to have done—from thence he went to *Philadelphia*, & settled in the printing Business. The *Philadelphia* News Paper was published by him; & the Almanacks of *Poor Richard*, which he annually struck off, were interlaced with many usefull Observations in Agriculture & other Sciences.

Dr. *Franklin* (pardon the Expression) was cursed with a full Share of Understanding; he was a Man of Genius, but of so unprincipled an Heart, that the Merit of all his political & philosophical Disquisitions can never atone for the Mischiefs which he plunged Society into, by the Perversion of his Genius. He had such an Insight into human Nature, that he insinuated himself into various publick Departments in the Province of *Pennsilvania*, & at last arrived to the Office of one of the Post Masters in *America*, a Place worth 4 or £500. Sterling per Year. He was now released from the necessary Cares for a moderate Support; & was at Leisure to indulge in what might first strike his Fancy. He invented a Fire Stove, to warm Rooms in the northern Climates, & at the same Time to save Fuel; he succeeded: but, at the same Time, they were so destructive of Health that they fell into Disuse. He also invented a Chamber Urn contrived to make the Flame descend instead of rising from the Fire: upon which a young Clergyman of a poetical Turn, made the following Lines,[3] vizt.

> Like a *Newton*, sublimely he soar'd
>   To a Summit before unattain'd,
> New Regions of Science explor'd,
>   And the Palm of Philosophy gain'd.

> ———

> With a Spark that he caught from the Skies
>   He display'd an unpararell'd Wonder,
> And we saw, with Delight & Surprize,
>   That his Rod would defend us from Thunder.

> ———

2. Oliver confuses Benjamin Franklin with his older brother James.
3. The poem by Jonathan Odell had appeared in the *Gentleman's Magazine* 47 (April 1777), 188. See A. Owen Aldridge, "Charles Brockden Brown's Poem on Benjamin Franklin," *American Literature* 38 (May 1966), 230–35.

Oh! had he been Wise to pursue
The Track for his Talents design'd,
What a Tribute of Praise had been due
To the Teacher & Friend of Mankind?

————

But, to covet political Fame
Was in him a degrading Ambition,
A Spark that from *Lucifer* came,
And kindled the Blaze of Sedition.

————

Let Candor then write on his Urn,
Here lies the renowned Inventor,
Whose Flame to the Skies ought to burn,
But, inverted, descends to the Centre.

————

Agreeable to the Hint given in the above Lines, the Doctor had made some new Experiments in Electricity, which drew the Attention of the Literate, as well as of the great Vulgar & the Small. The Eclat, which was spread from some new Phænomena he had discovered in this Science, introduced him into some of the first Company in *England*, whither he came, soon after he struck out these new Scenes. Men of Science gave their Attention, and others, of no ignoble Degree, gaped with a foolish Face of Praise; & it was this Circumstance, lucky for him, but unlucky for *Great Britain* & her Colonies, which gave such a Shock to Government, & brought on such Convulsions, as the english Constitution will not be cured of in one Century, if ever. By this Introduction, he grew into Importance with the Leaders of the Opposition in *England*. They found him to be usefull to them, in their Attempts, to subvert the Foundations of Government, & they caught at every Circumstance that Chance threw in their Way. They knew him to be as void of every Principle as theirselves, & each of them play'd into the others Hands. The Doctor play'd his Card well, & procured the Agency of some of the Colonies; & the lower House of *Massachusetts* Assembly chose him for theirs. I have seen Letters from him to the latter, inciting them to a Revolt, at the same Time when he enjoyed the above lucrative Office from the Crown; but he was so abandoned to an utter Insensibility of Virtue or Honor, that he would not stick at any Villainy to gratifye his Pride.

When the Stamp Act was on the Tapis, he encouraged the passing of it; & procured, for one of his Friends, the Appointment of a Stamp Master. He procured the Government of *New Jersies* for his Son; who hath behaved with a spirited Fidelity to his Sovereign to this Day. But his unnatural Treatment of this Son will fix upon him an indelible Reproach; for when the Son was about to imbark for his Government, he was in Arrears £100 Sterling, & could not leave *England* without discharging them. The Father refused to assist him, & a private Gentleman, out of Compassion, lent him the Mony—[4] and this Son afterwards was harrassed for his Loyalty & kept in a Gaol as a Prisoner in *Connecticut*, where he suffered greatly his self & where he lost his Lady, through Hardships. All this he underwent, whilst his humane Father had the Control of the Congress, & never attempted his Release. This fixes a Character which a Savage would blush at. Whilst he was in *England*, he travelled from one manufacturing Town to another, spreading Sedition as he went, & prognosticating the Independance of *America*; & notwithstanding all the Civilities he met with here, & the Bounties of the Crown, he afterwards boasted, in an intercepted Letter to his american Friends, of humbling *this huckstering Nation*, as he politely & gratefully termed them. Surely! his patriotick Friends in *England* must have Souls callous to every virtuous Feeling, to support a Man, whose every Exertion tends to the Ruin of his Country.

After the Destruction of Lieut. Govr. *Hutchinson's* House in 1765, Dr. *Franklin* maintained a familiar literary Correspondence with him, & condemned the Opposition of the Faction to him. Yet this very Man, a Traitor to his Friend as well as to his Country, set another abandoned Man to filch, from a Gentleman's File of Letters, left in his Custody by a deceased Brother, a Number of confidential ones wrote by Mr. *Hutchinson* to that Brother, which did Honor to the Writer; & had they been attended to by Government, would in all Probability have put a Stop to the present Rebellion. This base Theft brought on a Duel between the Thief & the Proprietor of the Letters. The Latter nearly lost his Life, being unacquainted with the Sword; but fought upon the false Principle of Honor, because he must fight; & carried off those Marks in his Back which Swordsmen pronounced of the murderous Kind. Upon a hearing of the State of this Transaction, before the King and Council, Dr. *Franklin*, with the Effrontery of that Countenance where Virtue could never raise a Blush, took the Theft upon himself; & was discarded by every Man who felt any Regard to Propriety of Character. It may, with strict Justice, be said of the Doctor, what *Churchill* says of his Hero in the Duellist,

> ———of Virtue,
> Not one dull, dim Spark in his Soul,
> Vice, glorious Vice, possess'd the whole;
> And in her Service truly warm,
> He was in Sin, most Uniform.

Pride is Dr. *Franklin's* ruling Passion, & from this Source may be traced all the Actions of his Life. He had a Contempt of Religion, of Mankind, & even of those whom he had duped; & had he viewed

4. A false story.

the Subject in a moral Light, he would have contemned hisself. Had *Churchill* drawn his Character, instead of saying, as he did of His Hero,

And shove his Savior from the Wall. He would have changed his Phrase into—*and shove his Savior, God & All.*

He is now caressed at that perfidious Court, where it would have been Thought; further Instructions were not necessary; untill this Adept in the Science of Perfidy appeared, like a blazing Meteor, & has taught them, that all their former Knowledge was but the first Rudiments of their Grammar; & has qualified them for *Professors* in that Art which they were too well acquainted with before. This Hatred to the english Nation is so rivetted that it is no Breach of Charity to suppose, that when he makes his Exit:

> Such, in those Moments as in all the past
> *Ye Gods! let Britain sink!* will be his last.

* * *

RICHARD PRICE

Richard Price (1723–1791), dissenting minister, chemical experimenter, and philosopher, was one of the two English friends whose opinion Franklin solicited during the process of composing the *Autobiography*. Price replied just a few days before he learned of Franklin's death.

Only a shorthand draft of Price's letter survives. Nevertheless, Price's comments on Franklin's humor and moral purpose reveal the reactions that Franklin must have expected from those contemporary intellectuals and friends to whose judgment he submitted the manuscripts— Benjamin Vaughan and Richard Price in England, and the Duc de La Rochefoucauld and Louis Le Veillard in France. Price's letter is the earliest reaction to the *Autobiography*, and his religious criticism anticipates the commonest eighteenth and nineteenth century strictures.

The letter has graciously been made available by Professor D. O. Thomas, whose wife Beryl Thomas deciphered the shorthand, and it is printed with the permission of Professor Bernard Peach.

To Franklin, May 1790[†]

(c. 30 May 1790)

My dear Friend,

I writ to you in March last and accompanied my letter with a discourse which I hope you have received. I cannot help taking the

---

† Shorthand notes on the back and margins of Franklin's holograph letter to Price of April 30, 1789. Reprinted by permission of the American Philosophical Society.

opportunity which Mr. Will[iam's] return to America offers me to write again a line to you to return you my best thanks for that account of your life which with your permission Mr. Vaughan has allowed me to peruse and which indeed I have read with particular pleasure and satisfaction. Mr. Vaughan will probably send you some remarks but none have occurred to me that I can think worth communicating to you. Your life has been so distinguished that your account of it must, were it made public, excite much curiosity and be read with *eagerness*, and it is agreeable to look forward to the good it must do. It is writ with an agreeable sense of *pleasantry* and many parts of it convey the most important instruction by showing in a striking example how talents when tied to industry, prudence and integrity may elevate us from obscurity to the first consequence and *eminence*. I cannot however help wishing that the qualities and talents which produced this eminence had been aided by a faith in Christianity and the animating hopes of a resurrection to an endless life with which it inspires. Had this been the case such talents and qualities would I fancy have (been) raised to still greater eminence. But indeed is it not wonderful[1] that the nonsense that has been mistaken for Christianity and the liberality generally encountered with the profession of it should render many wise and upright men averse to them. Nor do I think that such will suffer in any other way than by losing in this life a satisfaction and an additional spur to eminence for a character which they might have derived from their bright views of the government of the world and those boundless hopes which true religion communicates. But I am afraid I have reason to apologize for writing thus to you. I have no doubt of the equal happiness hereafter of all equally virtuous men and honest inquirers, whether they have or have not been attended with a feeling of difficulties, whatever their faith has been and I wish I was myself better than I am by the faith I profess. A faith, however, in most instances only a preponderance (greater or less) in favour of particular points.

I have heard with great concern of your ill-health and wish it may not prevent you from going on with the account of your life. Having been a witness to and actively concerned in bringing about two of the most important revolutions that ever took place in the world, it is extremely desirable that your health and your life may be preserved to see it down to the present time. I cannot express to you the satisfaction that the proceedings in France continue to give me. They seem a prelude to happier times than any this world has yet seen. And the last determination, the account of which is just arrived here—that the right of declaring peace and war shall belong to the nation and not to the King, and that they renounce for ever all

1. Astonishing.

offensive wars—exhibits an example to the world which may produce the time when the aspirations [?] of Kings and the intrigues of courts will be no longer capable of kindling the flame of war and delighting the rich.

I know what it is from my own experience how burdensome it is to have a multiplicity of letters to write. I would not therefore encumber you by desiring you to write to me. Should I by any means hear that you are tolerably well and going on with your important history and also that I retain a place in your favourable remembrance I shall be satisfied and happy. I continue to enjoy as much health as well as a man of a weak [?] constitution [at] my age can well expect. My spirits however often fail me and all business becomes more and more a burden to me. I am often thinking of withdrawing into some distant corner in order to spend the remainder of my life as much as possible in obscurity and quietness.

I am, my dear Friend, with the warmest affection and the greatest respect

Additional Note appended to the Draft

But indeed I cannot wonder that the liberality which (is) commonly encountered with regard (to) and the nonsense which is commonly mistaken for Christianity should render many wise and honest men averse to them

Nor do I think that such men will suffer in any other way than by a loss in this world of the satisfaction inspired (?) from the boundless hopes and bright views of the Divine Government. I have no doubt of the equal happiness hereafter of all equally honest and virtuous men

HONORÉ GABRIEL RIQUETI, COMTE DE MIRABEAU

By the time Franklin died, French radicals had removed King Louis XVI and instituted a National Assembly in place of royal power. Mirabeau (1749–1791) was a leading figure in this first stage of the French Revolution and, in his eulogy of Franklin, lionized the American as a fellow revolutionary. His words echoed the famous description of Franklin, attributed to Anne Robert-Jacques Turgot, Baron de Laune, that the philosopher-revolutionary had snatched lightning from heaven and the scepter from the tyrants (*Eripuit coelo fulmen, sceptrumque tyrannis*). The eulogy was quickly translated into English and circulated in British and American newspapers.

Eulogy for Franklin before the National Assembly of France, 1790†

On the 11th, M. Mirabeau rose, and thus addressed the Assembly, "Franklin is dead! the man who freed America, who enlightened Europe! that sage whom two worlds claim, held a distinguished rank among the human species.

"Courts have long in hypocrisy mourned, with idle pomp, the death of the great who have been useless to them. Nations ought only to mourn their benefactors. It belongs to the representatives of the people to appoint such mournings.

"The Congress has ordered a two months mourning.¹ Would it not be worthy of you to unite in an homage so sacred! The nations of antiquity would have raised altars to the man who could bring thunder into subjection, and humble the pride of tyrants.

"I propose that the Assembly should decree, that the Assembly wear mourning three days for the death of Benjamin Franklin."

The decree was accordingly passed, M. Mirabeau's speech ordered to be printed, and a letter of condolence to be written to the American Congress.

JOSÉ ANTONIO DE ALZATE Y RAMÍREZ

Spain had been an American ally in the War for Independence though it abhorred the revolutionists' politics, and, unlike France, avoided any immediate revolution either at home or in the Spanish colonies of Central and South America. When the Mexican man of letters Alzate (1737–1799) composed a eulogy for Franklin in 1790, he wisely avoided politics and emphasized Franklin's role in science.

A Brief Eulogy for Benjamin Franklin, 1790‡

The published news has revealed the death of the celebrated physicist Franklin,¹ who was born in Pennsylvania, one of the provinces

† *Scots Magazine*, June 1790.
1. Mirabeau's belief that the American Congress had instituted two months of mourning for Franklin was incorrect; the House of Representatives wore badges of mourning for a month, but the Senate did not.
‡ *Gazette of Literature* (Mexico), December 13, 1790.
1. Although the *Gazette* of Madrid assures us that he died at 84 years of age, I think that in this there is a mistake, because in one of his printed works three or four years ago, Franklin expresses himself thus: *I have been reading newspapers for seventy-two years.* Would he start reading at such a young age works that are not intelligible to children? The academies of Europe need to be diligent when composing his eulogy, and then we shall know the year of his birth and the circumstances of his life, which must be very particular, as was his genius. [*Alzate's note.*]

that compose the body of the colonies: his discoveries mark a memorable epoch in true physics, those which are useful to humanity. He
was not one of those physicists whose works bristle with laborious
calculations that push beginners away from the sanctuary of physics; experience, observation and examples were the sources from
which Franklin deduced his discoveries, and so the attacks of envy
and imitation have never reduced his merit. What physicist has made
more important discoveries? Has any other than he known how, as
if another Prometheus, to steal fire from the sky, subjecting it to the
power of men, in order to free them from the most fearsome and
powerful weapon that is lightning? He said, and experience has confirmed more and more, that an iron rod placed in the correct position will disarm nature of its fury: physicists of great renown have,
through observation, verified the discovery of our sage.

But oh the passions of men! What weaknesses!

Nollet, that physicist of the first-rank (who should have been supporting the progress of his favored discipline), controlled other,
lesser physicists, and used his authority to challenge Franklin's discoveries. Seeing that the rods are electrified during storms, he turned
to another explanation, and tried to show that the iron rods were not
capable of stripping the clouds of the matter that causes the storms,
and therefore we were as always surrounded by danger. Known facts
belied Nollet's assertion, so he turned to the use of a ruse (would
that it were not so common!); since he could not challenge the findings, he took recourse to the weapons of the weak [by relating misleading anecdotes of earlier "discoveries" of atmospheric electricity]:
he published that in a small Adriatic port an iron rod was placed to
which a guard would periodically touch his halberd [sword] to see
if there was a spark, and if there was, a bell was rung to warn the
fishermen that they should return to port because of an impending
storm. Also, neither Nollet nor his supporters missed a chance to
register the old story that under certain circumstances the tips of
the pikes of a Roman legion were observed to light up. But did anyone mention these phenomena before Franklin's discovery? Had
Nollet used them in his electrical experiments? There is not the
least evidence of this: however this is the way of men. They hear
that a discovery was made, they challenge it: when they can no longer resist the evidence, they say: this was said by so and so, in such
and such scholarly work it is indicated, etc., etc.

It is very easy to make progress once something has been invented:
once it was recognized that an iron rod became electrified during a
storm, it was very easy to push forward, and therefore place the rod
on a kite, raising it higher and making the electricity more visible:
Franklin did this, but they tried to deny him even this small advance,
and attempts were made to crown Mr. Romas with glory in order to
diminish Franklin's merit. An idea that fifty years ago would have

been taken as ridiculous, and whoever had proposed it would have
been treated as insane, will make men, as long as education is pur-
sued, as long as storms are studied, recognize he who gave them such
a simple way to avoid a violent death.

The great naturalist Pliny (who was more than the light and men-
dacious author of popular conception) said that sailors, to protect
themselves from the violence of the waves in a storm, would throw
some oil onto the sea. People generally believe that strong evils must
be treated with strong remedies—how could they be convinced that
a very small portion of oil could contain the fury of the sea? However our physicist [Franklin] has demonstrated the exactitude of
Pliny in this matter,[2] and because of this we have, not necessarily a
new discovery, but a useful practice, once ignored and now restored
by the immortal Franklin.

I would need a lot of paper and a more expansive field than the
narrow one offered me by this *Gazette* to give a faithful report of
Franklin's discoveries, and not even all of them, because I don't know
if all his works have arrived in New Spain. (I rely on the memories
I have of those that I have read in one or another work of literature.)
But even if we list his accomplishments in brief, mind you, it was he
who discovered the two species of electricity, positive and negative,
which, however impugned by his rival Nollet, explain many electrical phenomena: in his latter years he worked on maritime matters,
and his instructions should be read by anyone who must cross open
oceans, even if just for the rules he proposes in order to save oneself
from a shipwreck. He advises forming a sail [kite] with a handkerchief, for instance, so that the wind can carry a castaway to land,
freeing him from the necessity of finding the often insufficient
strength to swim to shore.[3]

Finally, navigation will have much to thank him for; because the
arts he proposed to produce safe and light ships are being realized.
In order to show this sage's characteristic way of philosophizing,

2. In January 1789, the town of Cuernavaca suffered from a very violent wind; at a nearby
   pool that extends one hundred and sixty *varas* in length, I proposed to experiment on
   the effects of oil on the waves, which appeared to be very high. I cannot remember
   without joy how a thimble's worth of oil, thrown over the area from which the wind was
   blowing, in a few seconds calmed that whole mass of waves, leaving the top of the pond
   as smooth as a mirror: not even the slightest movement in the water could be detected.
   It would be very easy to repeat this experiment in Mexico, in an irrigation ditch, or
   some other place where a stillness in the water can be verified, as in a river of some
   extent; for it is worth seeing how such a slight thing can cause effects of such magnitude to fade. How many possibilities this presents to the imagination! How much might
   be known and improved with small trouble and with little expense! When men in order
   to be happy devote themselves to observation, they may use and serve the world as a
   relief and not as an encumbrance! [*Alzate's note.*]
3. The [Duc de] Bouillon, in the *Journal* [*Encyclopedique*], communicates and praises
   a poetic epitaph that Franklin composed for a squirrel, which escaped its cage only to
   be devoured by a dog. However Father [Matías] Bocanegra had already published this
   allegory in his song that begins: *One afternoon in May.* [*Alzate's note.*]

which was always directed towards the good of man, I follow this eulogy with the translations of a few fragments, and will continue to do so in the future, because I can see that we lack more than a few fragments of Franklin's works in Spanish.

JOSÉ FRANCISCO CORREIA DA SERRA

This Portuguese man of science specialized in botany and had an extensive correspondence throughout Europe and the Americas. He was well-qualified to offer this appreciation of Franklin. Correia (1750–1823) lived in the United States from 1812 to 1820 and frequently visited Thomas Jefferson, who called him "perhaps the most learned man in the world."

Eulogy for Franklin to the Royal Academy of Sciences, Lisbon, 1791[†]

A notable difference lies between this and the other eulogies, which on behalf I have had the honour of pronouncing previously on behalf of this Society.

Benjamin Franklin, Philosopher and Legislator, like those of Greece, Governor of the State of Pensylvania and Director General of the Posts of United America, was born in Boston in New England in the year 1706.

The still little known character of the present Member, his so distant homeland and the circumstances of his life even more remote from us bring naturally to mind questions for reflection and discussion.

What connection can there be between this governor of Pensylvania and the Portuguese? How to explain our meeting together to praise his life with a solemnity lacking in the case of almost all our heroes? What event could create for us an obligation out of this honour which we bestow upon him? The name of Franklin is indeed famous, his discoveries are sublime and unusual, but had he not lived in the century of Queen Maria I, it would not have been in Portugal that his memory would thus be celebrated. The Portuguese nation had not yet understood the confederation nor the investigators of nature. In Portugal silence would have attended the death of Franklin as it had attended that of Newton. This century of peace and energetic gentleness brought into being our alliance, and it is to

† José Corrêa da Serra, *Elogio de Benjamin Franklin: Texto Original e versão en inglês* (Lisbon: Fundação o Luso-Americana para o Desenvolvimento, 1996), 33–47. Reprinted by permission.

it that we owe the advantages of our association, like those who in other nations may be seen as leaders of enlightenment and knowledge. This century now is ours and we are part of it.

> Hujus pacificis debemus moribus omnes
> Quod cuncti gens una simus

In the shade of the virtues of our sovereign, may the memory of Franklin become a natural thing for the Portuguese, and in honouring it let us honour in the happy reign which brought him to add to our advancement with the glory of his name.

To European eyes there can be no greater distance than that which lies between the first and the final occupations of the life of Doctor Franklin. His first employment was as maker of tallow candles. The famous Flechier, Esprit (1632–1710) French theologian and preacher also began in the same fashion, and when, after becoming one of the luminaries of the French Church, it came into the head of a courtier of Louis XIV to humiliate him for that very reason, he replied: "Not only do you remind me of this, but I recollect also that had your Excellency begun by making candles, you would still be making them".

Franklin spent little time in this trade, advancing to be a printer, a more liberal activity and one closer to that curiosity and that thirst for knowledge which dominated him. It would be a book interesting indeed which contained the story of his progress and his studies, the connection and interlocking of his ideas, and how an official printer working daily at his trade would suddenly emerge at the age of forty years in the first rank of Sages, from there onward increasing ever more in the glory of his name.

It is most likely that nature made the greatest change upon his enterprise, giving him a most lively comprehension, a direct method of thought and a sobriety, order and clarity of understanding, which might connect ideas in the same form and simplicity as that in which they appear in nature. All such qualities were what later caused him to acquire those lights which we imparted to us, and that knowledge most certainly provided him with the means to acquire the same.

The lack of classical studies in such a case is but an advantage. Full understanding of the robustness and regularity of the limbs could only be encumbered with those weapons so necessary for ordinary men, and his strength was better employed, entering the stadium as the athletes of Greece, just as they emerged from the hands of nature.

The occasion on which the world made his acquaintance was the curiousity aroused in Europe by certain phenomena of electricity. Since ancient times Thales the father of Greek philosophy had observed that amber when rubbed would attract fragments. During twenty four centuries the news of the singular behaviour was passed

from hand to hand, like some trifling bagatelle, capable only of occupying vacant minds, just as persons of importance ordinarily deem
the researches of nature. That Roman Consul whose fear was great
seeing lightning fall on his left side, and that Augur who sought to
attract the ray with a curved staff, both full of the importance of
their offices and knowledge, but laughed at the care with which Pliny
informs us of this phenomenon. Nature has no phenomenon which
is insignificant, and it is high time that this unfortunate error be
destroyed. For they are all parts of the same whole, all equal children
of that same wisdom which in creating regulated them. For a rational
man they are like Princes. However small they be, yet they always
belong to the sovereign family, deserving the greatest attention.

In the last century Gilbert, Otto de Guerike, Boyle and Hauks-
bee had devoted some time to the observation of this fact, and the
result was the discovery of many other materials apart from amber
possessing the same quality, which was transmitted from one body
to another according to certain laws, and which in darkness produced light. Little by little means were accumulated to observe
them, but the phenomena multiplied with greater speed than the
ideas to explain them. During this century Grey, Dufay, Nollet, and
Professor Cuneus followed these studies, and although the planting
of such observations was great, the hypotheses which destroyed
them were, as always happens, as many.

It was in these conditions that Pedro Collinson a wealthy English
Merchant, sent an electric apparatus as a present to some friends of
his in Philadelphia, who were also friends of the printer Franklin.
The latter began to inform himself as to the material and to make
experiments, and that which had produced so many conjectures and
so many books among the learned men of England, France, Holland, Germany and Italy, was explained in a manner which nature
has confirmed. He it was who saw that the electric fluid was not
produced, but accumulated or dispersed according to constant laws,
determining that subject more to attraction than to gravity the
impulses of the fluid reacted with variant affinity to various bodies,
and that in such bodies pointed forms attracted the fluid in preference to others. He understood the great influence which this fluid
had in meteors and other general phenomena of nature. He analysed the most terrible of these, the ray of lightning whose power
could penetrate with fear all human kind, and not content with
broadcasting his knowledge, he subjected it to human industry
through the invention of conductors.

Eripuit cœlo fulmen

The dignity and conceit of the mass of European sages felt
offended in receiving in a few familiar letters this lesson from a

printer of Philadelphia, and to our even greater astonishment, the English in whose language they were written, showed the highest disdain for their author and their contents. The Royal Society of London even refused to include them in their annals, which Mr. Collinson so justly sought to do. A veiled contempt and a manifest envy were likewise shown by those who with more ostentation than results, had distinguished themselves in these matters in the nations of the continent. One sage however whose books were the admiration of their time and are the delight of all men, Mr. de Buffon, translated them into French, and he it was who caused the principal experiments to be shown to the public against payment. All Paris hastened to see them and learned the name of their author. Those who had opposed fell silent and English began to honour the name of Franklin. Providence however had laid it down that another nation, inexistent as yet, and to whose birth he would come to contribute, would be that which would boast of his glory.

Even more surprising is that these secrets of nature were announced in his letters with a simplicity far removed from the form of any book. They are familiar letters telling of his experiments, and announce his ideas as if someone were performing some indifferent act which merely amused him. The most ingenious of the games depart from or follow the rarest of truths. A desire to turn everything to the utility of men can be seen in action in any place were it has been practised. And not only in matters of electricity did Doctor Franklin act in like manner. His moral works take the form of almanachs or very simple, unassuming tales. His discoveries in Physics, in music and the arts and his political ideas take the form of letters, not written to the public but to whom they are addressed. This author has not a single book, because for him the sciences were an occupation and a companion, not a profession. What the philosopher of Geneva wished to appear, Franklin was in reality, since activities more important than the composition of books occupied his time and his diligence.

The life of an American still under the English dominion was always mixed with public occupations. Judging in court as a member of the jury, being a justice of the peace for some years, voting in all elections are tributes which a Citizen pays to the State. Wherever greater talents and patriotic conduct distinguish someone, sooner or later he will represent some part of the state in its legislative assembly. At forty one years of age Dr. Franklin was chosen for this office and immediately he began to reveal the man he was. The influence of the land owners of Pensylvania was strong in the assembly, the principal orators were in the pay of others, and those questions which they sought to pass under the shade of their eloquence and intrigue highly pernicious for the country. The Philosopher did not compete with them in eloquence but his clear, strong and concise argument could destroy with few words the effect of long and studied speeches. He spoke but rarely, but an indirect argument, an irony, a story could open the eyes of all those whom the malice of the orators wished to deceive. In this as in many other things, like Socrates, but of better fortune, since the latter was condemned to death and the former was the idol of his citizens. A great difference exists, however, between Greece and Pensylvania, despite many reasons of similarity. The Greeks had the cult of reasoning and the peoples of Pensylvania the cult of beeing reasoned with.

The fruits of his support in the legislative body were the present University of Pensylvania, an educational establishment for ladies, a reform school, and the magnificent provisions which yet still exist for those who are ill and in poverty in Philadelphia and its surroundings. Beyond the simplicity and good sense which reign in each of these institutions, it is most important to note the attention of the legislator in endowing his institutes for a future size which lay already far ahead. There is an instinct in great men which reaches well beyond the present, and rarely does it deceive them.

The war of 1755 commenced. The then English Colonies took up arms, and Franklin raised a regiment of 1200 men, of which he was colonel. He marched with them against the enemy, and covered the frontier area during one campaign. At the end thereof his lack was felt in the legislative chamber. They called him and he was sent as agent and attorney of the colonies to England. The glory of his name was by now established and the courtesy and honour with which he was received were substantial, as indeed his residence at the court was honoured down to the peace of 1763 which returned him again to his own land.

It would be an invasion of the limits of history were I to explain to you the later actions of this Philosopher, his firmness with the English Government, the part he played as member of the American Congress at the time of independence of those states, his Embassy to France, the Treaty which he signed with the Ministers of the King of England as between equals, his return to his homeland and the triumphant reception which greeted him, his nomination as Chief Magistrate of Pensylvania, his speech at the Convention of which he was a member to approve the new American constitution. To go further would be to exceed the limits of an Academic Eulogy. Even if we may praise knowledge in general, it is not for us to treat all species of knowledge.

But one fact which my listeners will probably not anticipate after so wide a citation of honours, public business and political commissions is most surely the perseverance of Doctor Franklin in his office as a printer. When a Senator for Pensylvania he was a printer.

A printer he was when agent in England, when colonel, when ambassador in France, when member of Congress and Governor of Pensylvania. His grandson, heir to his name and to his property and today a printer in Philadelphia, took charge of the presses of his grandfather. In Paris he lived in closest friendship with the finest printers and conferred with them toward the perfection of this art, with the same dedication and zeal with which he sought to tame British Pride and establish the independence of a great, new Nation.

This printer phylosopher died last year, and the law demanded two months of mourning from the Americans, while the present Government of France required the same for several days. It was for certain neither dependency nor adulation which led to these provisions. It was those same sentiments which brought us to make him a member of this Society during his life, and which, following upon his death, guided us in designing this outline portrait of his deeds.

JOHN ADAMS

Despite his notable hostility toward Franklin, John Adams (1735–1826) wrote one of the most interesting and detailed appreciations of him. Adams was most critical of Franklin's diplomatic relations with the French, which he regarded as too partial to French opinion and policy. Adams was also jealous of the older American's fame and influence. But whatever his vanity and American provincialism, Adams always tried "To do justice to [Franklin's] merits."

On Franklin, May 15, 1811[†]

Mr. Jefferson has said that Dr. Franklin was an honor to human nature. And so, indeed, he was. Had he been an ordinary man, I should never have taken the trouble to expose the turpitude of his intrigues, or to vindicate my reputation against his vilifications and calumnies. But the temple of human nature has two great apartments: the intellectual and the moral. If there is not a mutual friendship and strict alliance between these, degradation to the whole building must be the consequence. There may be blots on the disk of the most refulgent luminary, almost sufficient to eclipse it. And it is of great importance to the rising generation in this country that they be put upon their guard against being dazzled by the surrounding blaze into an idolatry to the spots. If the affable archangel[1] understood the standard of merit, that

---

† Charles Francis Adams, ed., *The Works of John Adams* (Boston: Little, Brown, 1856), 1.659–64, reprinting from the newspaper the *Boston Patriot*, May 15, 1811.
1. In Milton's *Paradise Lost*. bk. 7. l. 41, Raphael is called the "affable archangel."

Great or bright infers not excellence,[2]
Franklin's moral character can neither be applauded nor condemned,
without discrimination and many limitations.

To all those talents and qualities for the foundation of a great
and lasting character, which were held up to the view of the whole
world by the university of Oxford, the Royal Society of London, and
the Royal Academy of Sciences in Paris, were added, it is believed,
more artificial modes of diffusing, celebrating, and exaggerating
his reputation, than were ever before or since practised in favor of
any individual.

His reputation was more universal than that of Leibnitz or Newton, Frederick or Voltaire, and his character more beloved and
esteemed than any or all of them. Newton had astonished perhaps
forty or fifty men in Europe; for not more than that number, probably, at any one time had read him and understood him by his discoveries and demonstrations. And these being held in admiration in
their respective countries as at the head of the philosophers, had
spread among scientific people a mysterious wonder at the genius of
this perhaps the greatest man that ever lived. But this fame was confined to men of letters. The common people knew little and cared
nothing about such a recluse philosopher. Leibnitz's name was more
confined still. Frederick was hated by more than half of Europe as
much as Louis the Fourteenth was, and as Napoleon is. Voltaire,
whose name was more universal than any of those before mentioned,
was considered as a vain, profligate wit, and not much esteemed or
beloved by anybody, though admired by all who knew his works. But
Franklin's fame was universal. His name was familiar to government
and people, to kings, courtiers, nobility, clergy, and philosophers, as
well as plebeians, to such a degree that there was scarcely a peasant
or a citizen, a *valet de chambre*, coachman or footman, a lady's chambermaid or a scullion in a kitchen, who was not familiar with it,
and who did not consider him as a friend to human kind. When
they spoke of him, they seemed to think he was to restore the golden
age. They seemed enraptured enough to exclaim
          Aspice, venturo lætentur ut omnia sæclo.[3]
To develop that complication of causes, which conspired to produce so singular a phenomenon, is far beyond my means or forces.
Perhaps it can never be done without a complete history of the
philosophy and politics of the eighteenth century. Such a work
would be one of the most important that ever was written; much
more interesting to this and future ages than the "Decline and Fall
of the Roman Empire," splendid and useful as that is. La Harpe

2. *Paradise Lost*, bk. 8. 11. 90–91.
3. "Behold, how all things exult in the age that is at hand!" Virgil, *Eclogue* 4, 1. 50.

promised a history of the philosophy of the eighteenth century; but he died and left us only a few fragments. Without going back to Lord Herbert, to Hobbes, to Mandeville, or to a host of more obscure infidels, both in England, France, and Germany, it is enough to say that four of the finest writers that Great Britain ever produced, Shaftesbury, Bolingbroke, Hume, and Gibbon, whose labors were translated into all languages, and three of the most eloquent writers that ever lived in France, whose works were also translated into all languages, Voltaire, Rousseau, and Raynal, seem to have made it the study of their lives and the object of their most strenuous exertions, to render mankind in Europe discontented with their situation in life, and with the state of society, both in religion and government. Princes and courtiers as well as citizens and country-men, clergy as well as laity, became infected. The King of Prussia, the Empress Catherine, were open and undisguised. The Emperor Joseph the Second was suspected, and even the excellent and amiable King of France grew impatient and uneasy under the fatiguing ceremonies of the Catholic church. All these and many more were professed admirers of Mr. Franklin. He was considered as a citizen of the world, a friend to all men and an enemy to none. His rigorous taciturnity was very favorable to this singular felicity. He conversed only with individuals, and freely only with confidential friends. In company he was totally silent.

When the association of Encyclopedists[4] was formed, Mr. Franklin was considered as a friend and zealous promoter of that great enterprise, which engaged all their praises. When the society of economists[5] was commencing, he became one of them, and was solemnly ordained a knight of the order by the laying on the hands of Dr. Quesnay, the father and founder of that sect. This effectually secured the affections and the panegyrics of that numerous society of men of letters. He had been educated a printer, and had practised his art in Boston, Philadelphia, and London for many years, where he not only learned the full power of the press to exalt and to spread a man's fame, but acquired the intimacy and the correspondence of many men of that profession, with all their editors and many of their correspondents. This whole tribe became enamoured and proud of Mr. Franklin as a member of their body, and were consequently always ready and eager to publish and embellish any panegyric upon him that they could procure. Throughout his whole life he courted and was courted by the printers, editors, and correspondents of reviews, magazines, journals, and pamphleteers, and those little busy med-

---

4. The French intellectuals (led by Denis Diderot) who wrote *L'Encyclopédie*, 35 vols. (1751–80).
5. The French physiocrats, economic theorists, including François Quesnay and Pierre-Samuel du Pont de Nemours.

dling scribblers that are always buzzing about the press in America, England, France, and Holland. These, together with some of the clerks in the Count de Vergennes's office of interpreters, (*bureau des interprètes,*) filled all the gazettes of Europe with incessant praises of Monsieur Franklin. If a collection could be made of all the Gazettes of Europe for the latter half of the eighteenth century, a greater number of panegyrical paragraphs upon "*le grand Franklin*" would appear, it is believed, than upon any other man that ever lived.

While he had the singular felicity to enjoy the entire esteem and affection of all the philosophers of every denomination, he was not less regarded by all the sects and denominations of Christians. The Catholics thought him almost a Catholic. The Church of England claimed him as one of them. The Presbyterians thought him half a Presbyterian, and the Friends believed him a wet Quaker.[6] The dissenting clergymen in England and America were among the most distinguished asserters and propagators of his renown. Indeed, all sects considered him, and I believe justly, a friend to unlimited toleration in matters of religion.

Nothing, perhaps, that ever occurred upon this earth was so well calculated to give any man an extensive and universal celebrity as the discovery of the efficacy of iron points and the invention of lightning-rods. The idea was one of the most sublime that ever entered a human imagination, that a mortal should disarm the clouds of heaven, and almost "snatch from his hand the sceptre and the rod." The ancients would have enrolled him with Bacchus and Ceres, Hercules and Minerva.[7] His *Paratonnères*[8] erected their heads in all parts of the world, on temples and palaces no less than on cottages of peasants and the habitations of ordinary citizens. These visible objects reminded all men of the name and character of their inventor; and, in the course of time, have not only tranquillized the minds, and dissipated the fears of the tender sex and their timorous children, but have almost annihilated that panic terror and superstitious horror which was once almost universal in violent storms of thunder and lightning. To condense all the rays of this glory to a focus, to sum it up in a single line, to impress it on every mind and transmit it to all posterity, a motto was devised for his picture, and soon became familiar to the memory of every schoolboy who understood a word of Latin:—

"Eripuit cœlo fulmen sceptrumque tyrannis."[9] * * *

---

6. One not strict in the observances of the sect.
7. According to the doctrine of euhemerism, the classical gods were people made divine because of their contributions to culture: Bacchus supposedly discovered how to make wine; Ceres first cultivated wheat; Hercules was an individual of great strength who performed incredible feats; and Minerva discovered how to make cloth.
8. Lightning rods.
9. Anne Robert-Jacques Turgot's famous epigram on Franklin: "he seized the lightning from the sky and the scepter from the tyrants."

The few who think and see the progress and tendency of things, have long foreseen that resistance in some shape or other must be resorted to, some time or other. They have not been able to see any resource but in the common people; indeed, in republicanism, and that republicanism must be democracy; because the whole power of the aristocracy, as of the monarchies, aided by the church, must be wielded against them. Hence the popularity of all insurrections against the ordinary authority of government during the last century. Hence the popularity of Pascal Paoli,[1] the Polish insurrections, the American Revolution, and the present struggle in Spain and Portugal. When, where, and in what manner all this will end, God only knows. To this cause Mr. Franklin owed much of his popularity. He was considered to be in his heart no friend to kings, nobles, or prelates. He was thought a profound legislator, and a friend of democracy. He was thought to be the magician who had excited the ignorant Americans to resistance. His mysterious wand had separated the Colonies from Great Britain. He had framed and established all the American constitutions of government, especially all the best of them, *i.e.* the most democratical. His plans and his example were to abolish monarchy, aristocracy, and hierarchy throughout the world. Such opinions as these were entertained by the Duke de la Rochefoucauld, M. Turgot, M. Condorcet, and a thousand other men of learning and eminence in France, England, Holland, and all the rest of Europe.

Mr. Franklin, however, after all, and notwithstanding all his faults and errors, was a great and eminent benefactor to his country and mankind.

＊　＊　＊

1. Pasquale di Paoli (1725–1807), Corsican patriot.

Nineteenth-Century Opinions

Over the course of the nineteenth century, Franklin's role as an American founder was taken for granted, but no longer analyzed, and his scientific work would cease to influence scientists directly. Perhaps because his political and scientific writings were of declining interest, the *Autobiography* drew new attention; Franklin's success story had both admirers and critics. Franklin's deism remained objectionable to many commentators, even though a few ministers, like the Reverend Edward Everett Hale, were nevertheless devoted Franklinists. The increasingly popular role of the self-made man in American culture, together with the characterization of American society as materialistic and pragmatic, led a number of people to seek the origins of these traits in Franklin—a position that could be supported by a selective reading of Franklin's best-known writings, *The Way to Wealth* and the *Autobiography*. Naturally the Romantics and later writers, English and American, revolted against the supposedly typical nineteenth-century philistine American and his supposed eighteenth-century progenitor. On the other hand, multivolume editions of Franklin's works by Jared Sparks (ten volumes, 1836–40) and John Bigelow (ten volumes, 1887–89) and the major biography by James Parton (two volumes, 1864) made the writings and the life of a complex, multifaceted, idealistic, and artful Franklin widely available.

FRANCIS, LORD JEFFREY

Francis, Lord Jeffrey (1773–1850), a founder of the *Edinburgh Review* (1802–1929), wrote a long appreciation of the writings and character of Franklin in a review of an unauthorized edition of Franklin's *Complete Works*, 3 vols. (London: Johnson, 1806). Although Jeffrey has some pet theories (he begins by blaming America for its "singular want of literary enterprize" and insists that Franklin was able to achieve greatness because of his lack of education), he also articulates several key ideas in Franklin criticism—Franklin's common sense, the artlessness of his scientific theories and speculations, an appreciation of how Franklin's writings are adapted to the audience, the comparisons to Swift, and an appreciation of his private correspondence.

289

From the Edinburgh Review, 1806[†]

*   *   *

This self-taught American is the most rational, perhaps, of all philosophers. He never loses sight of common sense in any of his speculations; and when his philosophy does not consist entirely in its fair and vigorous application, it is always regulated and controuled by it in its application and result. No individual, perhaps, ever possessed a juster understanding, or was so seldom obstructed in the use of it by indolence, enthusiasm, or authority. *   *   *

As a writer on morality and general literature, the merits of Dr Franklin cannot be estimated properly, without taking into consideration the peculiarities, that have been already alluded to, in his early history and situation. He never had the benefit of any academical instruction, nor of the society of men of letters;—his style was formed entirely by his own judgement and occasional reading; and most of his moral pieces were written while he was a tradesman, addressing himself to the tradesmen of his native city. We cannot expect, therefore, either that he should write with extraordinary elegance or grace; or that he should treat of the accomplishments, follies, and occupations of polite life. He had no great occasion, as a moralist, to expose the guilt and the folly of gaming or seduction; or to point a poignant and playful ridicule against the lighter immoralities of fashionable life. To the mechanics and traders of Boston and Philadelphia, such warnings were altogether unnecessary; and he endeavoured, therefore, with more appropriate eloquence, to impress upon them the importance of industry, sobriety, and economy, and to direct their wise and humble ambition to the attainment of useful knowledge and honourable independence. That morality, after all, is certainly the most valuable, which is adapted to the circumstances of the greater part of mankind; and that eloquence is the most meritorious, that is calculated to convince and persuade the multitude to virtue. Nothing can be more perfectly and beautifully adapted to its object, than most of Dr. Franklin's compositions of this sort. The tone of familiarity, of good-will, and homely jocularity—the plain and pointed illustrations—the short sentences, made up of short words—and the strong sense, clear information, and obvious conviction of the author himself, make most of his moral exhortations perfect models of popular eloquence; and afford the finest specimens of a style which has been but too little cultivated in a country, which numbers perhaps more than 100,000 readers among its tradesmen and artificers.

†   *Edinburgh Review* 8 (1806), 328, 340–41, 344.

*   *   *

His account of his own life, down to the year 1730, has been in the hands of the public since 1790. It is written with great simplicity and liveliness, though it contains too many trifling details and anecdotes of obscure individuals. It affords a striking example of the irresistible force with which talents and industry bear upwards in society, as well as an impressive illustration of the substantial wisdom and good policy of invariable integrity and candour. We should think it a very useful reading for all young persons of unsteady principle, who have their fortunes to make or to mend in the world. *   *   *

CHARLES BROCKDEN BROWN

When Charles Brockden Brown (1771–1810), early American novelist, reprinted Francis Jeffrey's review (excerpt immediately above) in his Philadelphia *Literary Magazine*, he prefaced it with a brief comment endorsing Jeffrey's evaluation.

From the *Literary Magazine*, 1806[†]

*   *   *

A just view of the character of Dr. Franklin has probably never been given by any of his countrymen. While living, the world was divided into passionate friends and rancorous enemies, and since his death a kind of political tincture still adheres to all our sentiments concerning him. Among his own countrymen, prejudice and passion, which used to be enlisted wholly on his side, has, in some respects, become hostile to him, and an impartial estimate of his merits can perhaps only be looked for among foreigners. The following portrait is taken from a foreign publication, and seems to be altogether dispassionate and equitable. *   *   *

JOHN KEATS

The English poet John Keats (1795–1821), in a letter to his brother and sister-in-law, reveals that he knows only the Poor Richard caricature of Franklin, which Keats uses to mock Americans generally.

[†] *Literary Magazine* 6 (November 1806), 367.

To George and Georgiana Keats,
October 14–31, 1818[†]

* * * Dilke,[1] whom you know to be a Godwin perfectibil[it]y Man,[2] pleases himself with the idea that America will be the country to take up the human intellect where england leaves off—I differ there with him greatly—A country like the united states whose greatest Men are Franklins and Washingtons will never do that—They are great Men doubtless but how are they to be compared to those our countrey men Milton and the two Sidneys—The one is a philosophical Quaker full of mean and thrifty maxims the other sold the very Charger who had taken him through all his Battles—Those American's are great but they are not sublime Man—the humanity of the United States can never reach the sublime.

* * *

HUMPHRY DAVY

Sir Humphry Davy (1778–1829), a noted British chemist, was most famous for his experiments isolating different elements through electrolysis. In his short history of scientific investigations of electricity, he credited the "Franklinian Theory" for identifying electricity's two states, positive and negative, and describing its tendency to seek equilibirum between the two. Davy also praised Franklin for his lucid explication of science. Scientists after Davy would also honor Franklin, but with a less precise sense of what the American had done.

Historical Sketch of Electrical Discovery[‡]

The foundations for this theory, were laid by the ingenuity and industry of our countryman, Dr. Watson; the construction of it is owing to the sagacity of Dr. Franklin. Dr. Watson ascertained that a communication with the ground, is necessary for the production of a continued stream of electricity by the machine; and hence he

---

† Hyder Edward Rollins, ed., *Letters of John Keats, 1814–1821*, 2 vols. (Cambridge: Harvard UP, 1958), 1.397–98. Copyright © 1958 by the President and Fellows of Harvard College. Reprinted by permission of the publisher.
1. Charles Wentworth Dilke (1789–1864), a close personal friend of Keats, later published many items about him in the *Athenaeum*.
2. William Godwin (1756–1836), English novelist and philosopher, advocated man's perfectibility.
‡ From John Davy, ed., *The Collected Works of Humphry Davy* (London: Smith, Elder and Co., 1840), VIII.263–65.

concluded that there is an afflux of electricity from the conducting bodies to the glass, and from the glass to the prime conductor. This idea was made known early in 1747; and towards the middle of the same year, Dr. Franklin transmitted his first letter on the subject to Mr. Collinson, containing an account of experiments and observations on electricity made at Philadelphia. In this letter, and in several subsequent letters, in a correspondence that continued till 1774, he brought forward those enlightened ideas of the subject, which have been so generally admired, under the name of the Franklinian Theory. Dr. Franklin proved that the conductor in contact with the rubber of the electrical machine had an opposite electricity from that of the great conductor; that the outside and the inside of the Leyden phial, were likewise in opposite states; and that an equilibrium was made by their mutual agency: and he referred all the phenomena to the redundancy or deficiency of a single fluid. The experiments adduced by Dr. Franklin in support of his hypothesis, were most ingeniously contrived and happily executed. A singular felicity of induction guided all his researches, and by very small means he established very grand truths. The style and manner of his publication are almost as worthy of admiration, as the doctrines it contains. He has endeavoured to remove all mystery and obscurity from the subject; he has written equally for the uninitiated and for the philosopher; and he has rendered his details amusing as well as perspicuous—elegant as well as simple. Science appears in his language in a dress wonderfully decorous, the best adapted to display her native loveliness. He has in no case exhibited that false dignity, by which philosophy is kept aloof from common applications, and he has sought rather to make her a useful inmate and servant in the common habitations of man, than to preserve her merely as an object of admiration in temples and palaces. * * *

* * *

EDGAR ALLAN POE

Renowned American author Edgar Allan Poe (1809–1899) wrote a *reductio ad absurdum* of Franklin's Art of Virtue. The parody applies Franklin's practical advice on conduct and achievement to the efforts of a scoundrel who prides himself on being a methodical businessman. Of course, the criticism, as Poe knew, did not explain the real Benjamin Franklin or even the *Autobiography*. It was typical, however, of a tendency within American society of the nineteenth (and twentieth) century, and it described numerous businessmen who imitated some aspects of Franklin and were proud to do so.

The Business Man†

Method is the soul of business.—OLD SAYING

I AM a business man. I am a methodical man. Method is *the* thing, after all. But there are no people I more heartily despise, than your eccentric fools who prate about method without understanding it; attending strictly to its letter, and violating its spirit. These fellows are always doing the most out-of-the-way things in what they call an orderly manner. Now here—I conceive—is a positive paradox. True method appertains to the ordinary and the obvious alone, and cannot be applied to the *outré*. What definite idea can a body attach to such expressions as "methodical Jack o'Dandy," or "a systematical Will o' the Wisp"?

My notions upon this head might not have been so clear as they are, but for a fortunate accident which happened to me when I was a very little boy. A good-hearted old Irish nurse (whom I shall not forget in my will) took me up one day by the heels, when I was making more noise than was necessary, and, swinging me round two or three times, d——d my eyes for "a skreeking little spalpeen,"[1] and then knocked my head into a cocked hat against the bed-post. This, I say, decided my fate, and made my fortune. A bump arose at once on my sinciput, and turned out to be as pretty an organ of *order* as one shall see on a summer's day. Hence that positive appetite for system and regularity which has made me the distinguished man of business that I am.

If there is anything on earth I hate, it is a genius. Your geniuses are all arrant asses—the greater the genius the greater the ass— and to this rule there is no exception whatever. Especially, you cannot make a man of business out of a genius, any more than money out of a Jew, or the best nutmegs out of pine-knots. The creatures are always going off at a tangent into some fantastic employment, or ridiculous speculation, entirely at variance with the "fitness of things," and having no business whatever to be considered as a business at all. Thus you may tell these characters immediately by the nature of their occupations. If you ever perceive a man setting up as a merchant, or a manufacturer; or going into the cotton or tobacco trade, or any of those eccentric pursuits; or getting to be a dry-goods dealer, or soap-boiler, or something of that kind; or pretending to be a lawyer, or a blacksmith, or a physician—anything out of the usual way—you may set him down at once as a genius, and then, according to the rule-of-three, he's an ass.

---

† *Broadway Journal* 2 (August 2, 1845), 49–52.
1. Rascal.

Now I am not in any respect a genius, but a regular business man. My Day-book and Ledger will evince this in a minute. They are well kept, though I say it myself; and, in my general habits of accuracy and punctuality, I am not to be beat by a clock. Moreover, my occupations have been always made to chime in with the ordinary habitudes of my fellow men. Not that I feel the least indebted, upon this score, to my exceedingly weak-minded parents, who, beyond doubt, would have made an arrant genius of me at last, if my guardian angel had not come, in good time, to the rescue. In biography the truth is everything, and in autobiography it is especially so—yet I scarcely hope to be believed when I state, however solemnly, that my poor father put me, when I was about fifteen years of age, into the counting-house of what he termed "a respectable hardware and commission merchant doing a capital bit of business!" A capital bit of fiddlestick! However, the consequence of this folly was, that in two or three days, I had to be sent home to my button-headed family in a high state of fever, and with a most violent and dangerous pain in the sinciput, all round about my organ of order. It was nearly a gone case with me then—just touch-and-go for six weeks—the physicians giving me up and all that sort of thing. But, although I suffered much, I was a thankful boy in the main. I was saved from being a "respectable hardware and commission merchant, doing a capital bit of business," and I felt grateful to the protuberance which had been the means of my salvation, as well as to the kind-hearted female who had originally put these means within my reach.

The most of boys run away from home at ten or twelve years of age, but I waited till I was sixteen. I don't know that I should have gone, even then, if I had not happened to hear my old mother talking about setting me up on my own hook in the grocery way. The *grocery* way!—only think of that! I resolved to be off forthwith, and try and establish myself in some *decent* occupation, without dancing attendance any longer upon the caprices of these eccentric old people, and running the risk of being made a genius of in the end. In this project I succeeded perfectly well at the first effort, and by the time I was farily eighteen, found myself doing an extensive and profitable business in the Tailor's Walking-Advertisement line.

I was enabled to discharge the onerous duties of this profession, only by that rigid adherence to system which formed the leading feature of my mind. A scrupulous *method* characterised my actions, as well as my accounts. In my case, it was method—not money—which made the man: at least all of him that was not made by the tailor whom I served. At nine, every morning, I called upon that individual for the clothes of the day. Ten o'clock found me in some fashionable promenade or other place of public amusement. The precise regularity with which I turned my handsome person about, so as to bring successively into view every portion of the suit upon my back, was the admiration of all the knowing men in the trade. Noon never passed without my bringing home a customer to the house of my employers, Messieurs Cut and Comeagain. I say this proudly, but with tears in my eyes—for the firm proved themselves the basest of ingrates. The little account about which we quarreled and finally parted, cannot, in any item, be thought overcharged, by gentlemen really conversant with the nature of the business. Upon this point, however, I feel a degree of proud satisfaction in permitting the reader to judge for himself. My bill ran thus:

Messrs. Cut and Comeagain, Merchant Tailors.
          To Peter Proffit, Walking Advertiser,   Drs.

July 10.	To promenade, as usual, and customer brought home,	$00 25
July 11.	To do. do. do.	25
July 12.	To one lie, second class; damaged black cloth sold for invisible green,	25
July 13.	To one lie, first class, extra quality and size; recommending milled sattinet as broadcloth,	75
July 20.	To purchasing bran new paper shirt collar or dickey, to set off gray Petersham,	2
Aug. 15.	To wearing double-padded bobtail frock, (thermometer 106 in the shade,)	25
Aug. 16.	Standing on one leg three hours, to show off new-style strapped pants, at 12½ cts. per leg, per hour	37½
Aug. 17.	To promenade, as usual, and large customer brought (fat man,)	50
Aug. 18.	To do. do. (medium size,)	25
Aug. 19.	To do. do. (small man and bad pay,)	6
		$2 96½

The item chiefly disputed in this bill was the very moderate charge of two pennies for the dickey. Upon my word of honor, this *was not* an unreasonable price for that dickey. It was one of the cleanest and prettiest little dickeys I ever saw; and I have good reason to believe that it effected the sale of three Petershams. The elder partner of the firm, however, would allow me only one penny of the charge, and took it upon himself to show in what manner four of the same sized conveniences could be got out of a sheet of foolscap. But it is needless to say that I stood upon the *principle* of the thing. Business is business, and should be done in a business way. There was no *system* whatever in swindling me out of a penny—a clear fraud of

fifty per cent.—no *method* in any respect. I left, at once, the employment of Messieurs Cut and Comeagain, and set up in the Eye-Sore
line by myself—one of the most lucrative, respectable, and independent of the ordinary occupations.

My strict integrity, economy, and rigorous business habits, here
again came into play. I found myself driving a flourishing trade, and
soon became a marked man upon 'Change. The truth is, I never
dabbled in flashy matters, but jogged on in the good old sober routine of the calling—a calling in which I should, no doubt, have
remained to the present hour, but for a little accident which happened to me in the prosecution of one of the usual business operations of the profession. Whenever a rich old hunks, or prodigal heir,
or bankrupt corporation, gets into the notion of putting up a palace,
there is no such thing in the world as stopping either of them, and
this every intelligent person knows. The fact in question is indeed
the basis of the Eye-Sore trade. As soon, therefore, as a building-
project is fairly afoot by one of these parties, we merchants secure
a nice corner of the lot in contemplation, or a prime little situation
just adjoining or right in front. This done, we wait until the palace
is half-way up, and then we pay some tasty architect to run us up an
ornamental mud hovel, right against it; or a Down-East or Dutch
Pagoda, or a pig-sty, or any ingenious little bit of fancy work, either
Esquimau, Kickapoo, or Hottentot. Of course, we can't afford to take
these structures down under a bonus of five hundred per cent. upon
the prime cost of our lot and plaster. *Can* we? I ask the question. I
ask it of business men. It would be irrational to suppose that we can.
And yet there was a rascally corporation which asked me to do this
very thing—this *very thing*! I did not reply to their absurd proposition, of course; but I felt it a duty to go that same night, and lamp-
black the whole of their palace. For this, the unreasonable villains
clapped me into jail; and the gentlemen of the Eye-Sore trade could
not well avoid cutting my connexion when I came out.

The Assault and Battery business, into which I was now forced to
adventure for a livelihood, was somewhat ill-adapted to the delicate
nature of my constitution; but I went to work in it with a good heart,
and found my account, here as heretofore, in those stern habits of
methodical accuracy which had been thumped into me by that
delightful old nurse—I would indeed be the basest of men not to
remember her well in my will. By observing, as I say, the strictest
system in all my dealings, and keeping a well regulated set of books,
I was enabled to get over many serious difficulties, and, in the end,
to establish myself very decently in the profession. The truth is, that
few individuals, in any line, did a snugger little business than I. I will
just copy a page or so out of my Day-Book; and this will save me the

necessity of blowing my own trumpet—a contemptible practice, of which no high-minded man will be guilty. Now, the Day-Book is a thing that don't lie.

"Jan. 1.—New Year's day. Met Snap in the street, groggy. Mem—he'll do. Met Gruff shortly afterwards, blind drunk. Mem—he'll answer, too. Enter both gentlemen in my Ledger, and opened a running account with each.

"Jan. 2.—Saw Snap at the Exchange, and went up and trod on his toe. Doubled his fist, and knocked me down. Good!—got up again. Some trifling difficulty with Bag, my attorney. I want the damages at a thousand, but he says that, for so simple a knockdown, we can't lay them at more than five hundred. Mem—must get rid of Bag—no *system* at all.

"Jan. 3.—Went to the theatre, to look for Gruff. Saw him sitting in a side box, in the second tier, between a fat lady and a lean one. Quizzed the whole party through an opera glass, till I saw the fat lady blush and whisper to G. Went round, then, into the box, and put my nose within reach of his hand. Wouldn't pull it—no go. Blew it, and tried again—no go. Sat down then, and winked at the lean lady, when I had the high satisfaction of finding him lift me up by the nape of the neck, and fling me over into the pit. Neck dislocated, and right leg capitally splintered. Went home in high glee, drank a bottle of champagne, and booked the young man for five thousand. Bag says it'll do.

"Feb. 15.—Compromised the case of Mr. Snap. Amount entered in Journal—fifty cents—which see.

"Feb. 16.—Cast by that villain, Gruff, who made me a present of five dollars. Costs of suit, four dollars and twenty five cents. Nett profit—see Journal—seventy-five cents."

Now, here is a clear gain, in a very brief period, of no less than one dollar and twenty five cents—this is in the mere cases of Snap and Gruff; and I solemnly assure the reader that these extracts are taken at random from my Day-Book.

It's an old saying, and a true one, however, that money is nothing in comparison with health. I found the exactions of the profession somewhat too much for my delicate state of body; and, discovering, at last, that I was knocked all out of shape, so that I didn't know very well what to make of the matter, and so that my friends, when they met me in the street, couldn't tell that I was Peter Proffit at all, it occurred to me that the best expedient I could adopt, was to alter my line of business. I turned my attention, therefore, to Mud-Dabbling, and continued it for some years.

The worst of this occupation, is, that too many people take a fancy to it, and the competition is in consequence excessive. Every ignoramus of a fellow who finds that he hasn't brains in sufficient quantity to make his way as a walking advertiser, or an eye-sore-prig, or a salt and batter man, thinks, of course, that he'll answer very well as a dabbler of mud. But there never was entertained a more erroneous idea than that it requires no brains to mud-dabble. Especially, there is nothing to be made in this way without *method*. I did only a retail business myself, but my old habits of *system* carried me swimmingly along. I selected my street-crossing, in the first place, with great deliberation, and I never put down a broom in any part of the town *but that*. I took care, too, to have a nice little puddle at hand, which I could get at in a minute. By these means I got to be well known as a man to be trusted; and this is one-half the battle, let me tell you, in trade. Nobody ever failed to pitch *me* a copper, and got over *my* crossing with a clean pair of pantaloons. And, as my business habits, in this respect, were sufficiently understood, I never met with any attempt at imposition. I wouldn't have put up with it, if I had. Never imposing upon any one myself, I suffered no one to play the possum with me. The frauds of the banks of course I couldn't help. Their suspension put me to ruinous inconvenience. These, however, are not individuals, but corporations; and corporations, it is very well known, have neither bodies to be kicked, nor souls to be damned.

I was making money at this business, when, in an evil moment, I was induced to merge it in the Cur-Spattering—a somewhat analogous, but, by no means, so respectable a profession. My location, to be sure, was an excellent one, being central, and I had capital blacking and brushes. My little dog, too, was quite fat and up to all varieties of snuff. He had been in the trade a long time, and, I may say, understood it. Our general routine was this:—Pompey, having rolled himself well in the mud, sat upon end at the shop door, until he observed a dandy approaching in bright boots. He then proceeded to meet him, and gave the Wellingtons a rub or two with his wool. Then the dandy swore very much, and looked about for a boot-black. There I was, full in his view, with blacking and brushes. It was only a minute's work, and then came a sixpence. This did moderately well for a time;—in fact, I was not avaricious, but my dog was. I allowed him a third of the profit, but he was advised to insist upon half. This I couldn't stand—so we quarreled and parted.

I next tried my hand at the Organ-Grinding for a while, and may say that I made out pretty well. It is a plain, straightforward business, and requires no particular abilities. You can get a music-mill for a mere song, and, to put it in order, you have but to open the works, and give them three or four smart raps with a hammer. It improves the tone of the thing, for business purposes, more than you can imagine. This done, you have only to stroll along, with the mill on your back, until you see tan-bark in the street, and a knocker wrapped up in buck skin. Then you stop and grind; looking as if you meant to stop and grind till doomsday. Presently a window opens, and somebody pitches you a sixpence, with a request to "Hush up and go on," &c. I am aware that some grinders have actually afforded to "go on" for this sum; but for my part, I found the necessary outlay of capital too great, to permit of my "going on" under a shilling.

At this occupation I did a good deal, but, somehow, I was not quite satisfied, and so finally abandoned it. The truth is, I labored under the disadvantage of having no monkey—and American streets are *so* muddy, and a Democratic rabble is *so* obtrusive, and so full of demnition mischievous little boys.

I was now out of employment for some months, but at length succeeded, by dint of great interest, in procuring a situation in the Sham-Post. The duties, here, are simple, and not altogether unprofitable. For example:—very early in the morning I had to make up my packet of sham letters. Upon the inside of each of these I had to scrawl a few lines—on any subject which occurred to me as sufficiently mysterious—signing all the epistles Tom Dobson, or Bobby Tompkins, or anything in that way. Having folded and sealed all, and stamped them with sham post-marks—New Orleans, Bengal, Botany Bay, or any other place a great way off—I set out, forthwith, upon my daily route, as if in a very great hurry. I always called at the big houses to deliver the letters, and receive the postage. Nobody hesitates at paying for a letter—especially for a double one—people are *such* fools—and it was no trouble to get round a corner before there was time to open the epistles. The worst of this profession was, that I had to walk so much and so fast; and so frequently to vary my route. Besides, I had serious scruples of conscience. I can't bear to hear innocent individuals abused—and the way the whole town took to cursing Tom Dobson and Bobby Tompkins, was really awful to hear. I washed my hands of the matter in disgust.

My eighth and last speculation has been in the Cat-Growing way. I have found this a most pleasant and lucrative business, and, really, no trouble at all. The country, it is well known, has become infested with cats—so much so of late, that a petition for relief, most numerously and respectably signed, was brought before the legislature at its last memorable session. The assembly, at this epoch, was unusually well-informed, and, having passed many other wise and wholesome enactments, it crowned all with the Cat-Act. In its original form, this law offered a premium for cat-*heads*, (four-pence a-piece) but the Senate succeeded in amending the main clause, so as to substitute the words "*tails*" for "heads." This amendment was so obviously proper, that the house concurred in it *nem. con.*

As soon as the Governor had signed the bill, I invested my whole estate in the purchase of Toms and Tabbies. At first, I could only afford to feed them upon mice (which are cheap) but they fulfilled the Scriptural injunction at so marvellous a rate, that I at length considered it my best policy to be liberal, and so indulged them in oysters and turtle. Their tails, at the legislative price, now bring me in a good income; for I have discovered a way, in which, by means of Macassar oil, I can force three crops in a year. It delights me to find, too, that the animals soon get accustomed to the thing, and would rather have the appendages cut off than otherwise. I consider myself, therefore, a made man, and am bargaining for a country seat on the Hudson.

LEIGH HUNT

Leigh Hunt (1784–1859), essayist, and friend of Byron, Keats, and Shelley, was the grandson of Isaac Hunt (1742?–1809), one of Franklin's political enemies in the 1770s. In his *Autobiography*, Hunt tells how as a youth he disliked his grandfather for inviting him to come to Philadelphia where "he would make a man of me." Hunt concluded that: "As a nation, I can not get it out of my head, that the Americans are Englishmen with the poetry and romance taken out of them; and that there is one great counter built along their coast from north to south, behind which they are all standing like so many linendrapers." His view of Franklin is of a piece with his view of America. The opening "Partly on the same account" refers to his dislike for his grandfather.

From Autobiography†

* * *

Partly on the same account, I acquired a dislike for my grandfather's friend Dr. Franklin, author of *Poor Richard's Almanack*: a heap, as it appeared to me, of "Scoundrel maxims."[1] I think I now appreciate Dr. Franklin as I ought; but although I can see the utility of such

† Leigh Hunt, *Autobiography* (New York: Harper, 1850), 1.130–32.
1. Thomson's phrase, in the *Castle of Indolence*, speaking of a miserly money-getter:

> "'A penny saved is a penny got;'
> Firm to this scoundrel maxim keepeth he,
> Ne of its rigor will he bate a jot,
> Till it hath quench'd his fire and banishèd his pot."

The reader will not imagine that I suppose all money-makers to be of this description. Very gallant spirits are to be found, among them, who only take to this mode of activity for want of a better, and are as generous in disbursing as they are vigorous in acquiring. You may always know the common run, as in other instances, by the soreness with which they feel attacks on the body corporate.

For the assertion that Dr. Franklin cut off his son with [only] a shilling, my only authority is family tradition. It is observable, however, that the friendliest of his biographers are not only forced to admit that he seemed a little too fond of money, but notice the mysterious secrecy in which his family history is involved. [*Leigh Hunt's note.*]

publications as his Almanack for a rising commercial state, and hold it useful as a memorandum to uncalculating persons like myself, who happen to live in an old one, I think it has no business either in commercial nations long established, or in others who do not found their happiness in that sort of power. Franklin, with all his abilities, is but at the head of those who think that man lives "by bread alone." He will commit none of the follies, none of the intolerances, the absence of which is necessary to the perfection of his system; and in setting his face against these, he discountenances a great number of things very inimical to higher speculations. But he was no more a fit representative of what human nature largely requires, and may reasonably hope to attain to, than negative represents positive, or the clearing away a ground in the back-settlements, and setting to work upon it, represents the work in its completion. Something of the pettiness and materiality of his first occupation always stuck to him. He took nothing for a truth or a matter-of-fact that he could not handle, as it were, like his types: and yet, like all men of this kind, he was liable, when put out of the ordinary pale of his calculations, to fall into the greatest errors, and substitute the integrity of his reputation for that of whatsoever he chose to do. From never doing wrong in little things, he conceived that he could do no wrong in great; and, in the most deliberate act of his life, he showed he had grievously mistaken himself. He was, I allow, one of the *cardinal* great men of his time. He was Prudence. But he was not what he took himself for—all the other Virtues besides; and, inasmuch as he was deficient in those, he was deficient even in his favorite one. He was not Temperance; for, in the teeth of his capital recommendations of that virtue, he did not scruple to get burly and big with the enjoyments that he cared for. He was not Justice; for he knew not how to see fair play between his own wisdom and that of a thousand wants and aspirations, of which he knew nothing: and he cut off his son with [only] a shilling, for differing with him in politics. Lastly, he was not Fortitude; for having few passions and no imagination, he knew not what it was to be severely tried; and if he had been there is every reason to conclude, from the way in which he treated his son, that his self-love would have been the part in which he felt the torture; that as his Justice was only arithmetic, so his Fortitude would have been nothing but stubbornness.

If Franklin had been the only great man of his time, he would merely have contributed to make the best of a bad system, and so hurt the world by prolonging it; but, luckily, there were the French and English philosophers besides, who saw farther than he did, and provided for higher wants. I feel grateful to him, for one, inasmuch as he extended the sphere of liberty, and helped to clear the earth of the weeds of sloth and ignorance, and the wild beasts of superstition; but when he comes to build final homes for us, I rejoice that wiser hands interfere. His line and rule are not every thing; they are not even a tenth part of it. Cocker's numbers are good; but those of Plato and Pythagoras have their merits too, or we should have been made of dry bones and tangents, and not had the fancies in our heads, and the hearts beating in our bosoms, that make us what we are. We should not even have known that Cocker's numbers were worth any thing; nor would Dr. Franklin himself have played on the harmonica, albeit he must have done it in a style very different from that of Milton or Cimarosa. Finally, the writer of this passage on the Doctor would not have ventured to give his opinion of so great a man in so explicit a manner. I should not have ventured to give it, had I not been backed by so many powerful interests of humanity, and had I not suffered in common, and more than in common, with the rest of the world, from a system which, under the guise of economy and social advantage, tends to double the love of wealth and the hostility of competition, to force the best things down to a level with the worst, and to reduce mankind to the simplest and most mechanical law of their nature, divested of its heart and soul—the law of being in motion. Most of the advantages of the present system of money-making, which may be called the great *lay* superstition of modern times, might be obtained by a fifth part of the labor, if more equally distributed. Yet all the advantages could not be so obtained; and the system is necessary as a portion of the movement of time and progress, and as the ultimate means of dispensing with its very self.

* * *

HERMAN MELVILLE

Herman Melville (1819–1891) evidently read much of Franklin, perhaps in Jared Sparks's edition, *The Works of Benjamin Franklin*, 10v. (Boston: Hilliard, Gray & Co., 1836–40). Melville refers to Franklin and his writings numerous times, and presents a detailed impression in his semi-historical novel *Israel Potter*.

From Israel Potter[†]

Chapter 8

WHICH HAS SOMETHING TO SAY ABOUT DR. FRANKLIN
AND THE LATIN QUARTER

THE first, both in point of time and merit, of American envoys was famous not less for the pastoral simplicity of his manners than for

---

[†] *Israel Potter: His Fifty Years of Exile* (1855).

the politic grace of his mind. Viewed from a certain point, there was a touch of primeval orientalness in Benjamin Franklin. Neither is there wanting something like his scriptural parallel. The history of the patriarch Jacob is interesting not less from the unselfish devotion which we are bound to ascribe to him, than from the deep worldly wisdom and polished Italian tact, gleaming under an air of Arcadian unaffectedness. The diplomatist and the shepherd are blended; a union not without warrant; the apostolic serpent and dove. A tanned Machiavelli in tents.

Doubtless, too, notwithstanding his eminence as lord of the moving manor, Jacob's raiment was of homespun; the economic envoy's plain coat and hose, who has not heard of ?

Franklin all over is of a piece. He dressed his person as his periods; neat, trim, nothing superfluous, nothing deficient. In some of his works his style is only surpassed by the unimprovable sentences of Hobbes of Malmesbury,[1] the paragon of perspicuity. The mental habits of Hobbes and Franklin in several points, especially in one of some moment, assimilated. Indeed, making due allowance for soil and era, history presents few trios more akin, upon the whole, than Jacob, Hobbes, and Franklin; three labyrinth-minded, but plainspoken Broadbrims,[2] at once politicians and philosophers; keen observers of the main chance; prudent courtiers; practical Magians in linsey-woolsey.

In keeping with his general habitudes, Doctor Franklin while at the French Court did not reside in the aristocratical faubourgs. He deemed his worsted hose and scientific tastes more adapted in a domestic way to the other side of the Seine, where the Latin Quarter, at once the haunt of erudition and economy, seemed peculiarly to invite the philosophical Poor Richard to its venerable retreats. * * *

In this congenial vicinity of the Latin Quarter, and in an ancient building something like those alluded to, at a point midway between the Palais des Beaux Arts and the College of the Sorbonne, the venerable American envoy pitched his tent when not passing his time at his country retreat at Passy. The frugality of his manner of life did not lose him the good opinion even of the voluptuaries of the showiest of capitals, whose very iron railings are not free from gilt. Franklin was not less a lady's man, than a man's man, a wise man, and an old man. Not only did he enjoy the homage of the choicest Parisian literati, but at the age of seventy-two he was the caressed favourite of the highest born beauties of the Court; who through blind fashion having been originally attracted to him as a famous savant, were

---

1. Thomas Hobbes (1588–1679), English philosopher, author of *Leviathan* (1651).
2. Although usually a description of Quakers, "Broadbrims" here suggests a combination of morality and worldliness.

permanently retained as his admirers by his Plato-like graciousness
of good humour. Having carefully weighed the world, Franklin
could act any part in it. By nature turned to knowledge, his mind
was often grave, but never serious. At times he had seriousness—
extreme seriousness—for others, but never for himself. Tranquillity
was to him instead of it. This philosophical levity of tranquillity, so
to speak, is shown in his easy variety of pursuits. Printer, postmaster, almanac maker, essayist, chemist, orator, tinker, statesman,
humorist, philosopher, parlour man, political economist, professor
of housewifery, ambassador, projector, maxim-monger, herb-doctor,
wit: Jack of all trades, master of each and mastered by none—the
type and genius of his land. Franklin was everything but a poet. But
since a soul with many qualities, forming of itself a sort of handy
index and pocket congress of all humanity, needs the contact of just
as many different men, or subjects, in order to the exhibition of its
totality; hence very little indeed of the sage's multifariousness will
be portrayed in a simple narrative like the present. This casual private intercourse with Israel but served to manifest him in his far
lesser lights; thrifty, domestic, dietarian, and, it may be, didactically
waggish. There was much benevolent irony, innocent mischievous-
ness, in the wise man. Seeking here to depict him in his less exalted
habitudes, the narrator feels more as if he were playing with one of
the sage's worsted hose, than, reverentially handling the honoured
hat which once oracularly sat upon his brow.

* * *

MARK TWAIN

As a newspaperman, printer, humorist, and writer, Twain knew he followed in an American tradition begun by Franklin. Although this is his
only sustained piece on Franklin, Twain shows by allusions throughout
his writings that he, too, had read widely in Franklin. As Alan Gribben
has shown in his monumental study *Mark Twain's Library*, 2 vols. (Boston: G. K. Hall, 1980), 241–43, Twain's attitude was strongly influenced
by the great admiration for Franklin of Orion Clemens, Twain's beloved
older brother, who even imitated the regimens Franklin imposed upon
himself until his early death. Although Twain reveals in the following
primarily humorous piece his exasperation at Poor Richard's proverbs
and at the example Franklin presents in the *Autobiography*, the criticism is ironic, partially because it recalls his beloved deceased brother,
partially because Twain appreciates Franklin both as a prototype of the
self-made man and as a great genius, and partially because Twain sees
himself as a latter-day Franklin.

The Late Benjamin Franklin[†]

[Never put off till to-morrow what you can do day after to-morrow just as well.—B.F.]

This party was one of those persons whom they call Philosophers. He was twins, being born simultaneously in two different houses in the city of Boston. These houses remain unto this day, and have signs upon them worded in accordance with the facts. The signs are considered well enough to have, though not necessary, because the inhabitants point out the two birth-places to the stranger anyhow, and sometimes as often as several times in the same day. The subject of this memoir was of a vicious disposition, and early prostituted his talents to the invention of maxims and aphorisms calculated to inflict suffering upon the rising generation of all subsequent ages. His simplest acts, also, were contrived with a view to their being held up for the emulation of boys forever—boys who might otherwise have been happy. It was in this spirit that he became the son of a soap-boiler; and probably for no other reason than that the efforts of all future boys who tried to be anything might be looked upon with suspicion unless they were the sons of soap-boilers. With a malevolence which is without parallel in history, he would work all day and then sit up nights and let on to be studying algebra by the light of a smouldering fire, so that all other boys might have to do that also or else have Benjamin Franklin thrown up to them. Not satisfied with these proceedings, he had a fashion of living wholly on bread and water, and studying astronomy at meal time—a thing which has brought affliction to millions of boys since, whose fathers had read Franklin's pernicious biography.

His maxims were full of animosity toward boys. Nowadays a boy cannot follow out a single natural instinct without tumbling over some of those everlasting aphorisms and hearing from Franklin on the spot. If he buys two cents' worth of peanuts, his father says, "Remember what Franklin has said, my son.—'A groat a day's a penny a year;'" and the comfort is all gone out of those peanuts. If he wants to spin his top when he is done work, his father quotes, "Procrastination is the thief of time." If he does a virtuous action, he never gets anything for it, because "Virtue is its own reward." And that boy is hounded to death and robbed of his natural rest, because Franklin said once in one of his inspired flights of malignity—

† *The Galaxy* 10 (July 1870), 138–40.

Early to bed and early to rise
Make a man healthy and wealthy and wise.

As if it were any object to a boy to be healthy and wealthy and wise on such terms. The sorrow that that maxim has cost me through my parents' experimenting on me with it, tongue cannot tell. The legitimate result is my present state of general debility, indigence, and mental aberration. My parents used to have me up before nine o'clock in the morning, sometimes, when I was a boy. If they had let me take my natural rest, where would I have been now? Keeping store, no doubt, and respected by all.

And what an adroit old adventurer the subject of this memoir was! In order to get a chance to fly his kite on Sunday, he used to hang a key on the string and let on to be fishing for lightning. And a guileless public would go home chirping about the "wisdom" and the "genius" of the hoary Sabbath-breaker. If anybody caught him playing "mumble-peg" by himself, after the age of sixty, he would immediately appear to be ciphering out how the grass grew—as if it was any of his business. My grandfather knew him well, and he says Franklin was always fixed—always ready. If a body, during his old age, happened on him unexpectedly when he was catching flies, or making mud pies, or sliding on a cellar door, he would immediately look wise, and rip out a maxim, and walk off with his nose in the air and his cap turned wrong side before, trying to appear absent-minded and eccentric. He was a hard lot.

He invented a stove that would smoke your head off in four hours by the clock. One can see the almost devilish satisfaction he took in it, by his giving it his name.

He was always proud of telling how he entered Philadelphia, for the first time, with nothing in the world but two shillings in his pocket and four rolls of bread under his arm. But really, when you come to examine it critically, it was nothing. Anybody could have done it.

To the subject of this memoir belongs the honor of recommending the army to go back to bows and arrows in place of bayonets and muskets. He observed, with his customary force, that the bayonet was very well, under some circumstances, but that he doubted whether it could be used with accuracy at long range.

Benjamin Franklin did a great many notable things for his country, and made her young name to be honored in many lands as the mother of such a son. It is not the idea of this memoir to ignore that or cover it up. No; the simple idea of it is to snub those pretentious maxims of his, which he worked up with a great show of originality out of truisms that had become wearisome platitudes as early as the dispersion from Babel; and also to snub his stove, and his military inspirations, his unseemly endeavor to make himself conspicuous when he entered Philadelphia, and his flying his kite and fooling away his time in all sorts of such ways, when he ought to have been foraging for soap-fat, or constructing candles. I merely desired to do away with somewhat of the prevalent calamitous idea among heads of families that Franklin *acquired* his great genius by working for nothing, studying by moonlight, and getting up in the night instead of waiting till morning like a Christian, and that this programme, rigidly inflicted, will make a Franklin of every father's fool. It is time these gentlemen were finding out that these execrable eccentricities of instinct and conduct are only the *evidences* of genius, not the *creators* of it. I wish I had been the father of my parents long enough to make them comprehend this truth, and thus prepare them to let their son have an easier time of it. When I was a child I had to boil soap, notwithstanding my father was wealthy, and I had to get up early and study geometry at breakfast, and peddle my own poetry, and do everything just as Franklin did, in the solemn hope that I would be a Franklin some day. And here I am.

EMPRESS SHŌKEN OF JAPAN

After the Meiji Restoration reinstated imperial rule over Japan in 1867, the emperor and empress advocated major changes to Japanese society, including a program of cultural westernization. The capitalist system of industrialized Western nations was their model. Franklin was regarded as a harbinger of Western enlightenment. After hearing a lecture by a Confucian tutor, who had translated the thirteen virtues of Franklin's *Autobiography* into Japanese (omitting "chastity"), the empress (1849–1914) composed this poem, which reflects Franklin's concerns for self-improvement and to use time wisely. The poem was set to music so it could be sung, typically at Japanese schools.

A Franklinian Poem, c. 1890[†]

Even a diamond, if left unpolished,
Emits not its precious splendor.
Likewise, education alone
Exposes humanity's true virtue.

---

† From Inoe Takeshi, ed., *Nihon shōkashū* (Tokyo: Iwanami shoten, 1958), 48–49. Trans. by Jennifer van der Grinten. Music image on p. 309 is reprinted by permission of Harvard College Library, Yenching Library.

Be as the hands of the clock,
  Incessant in their turning.
Strive to waste not a moment
  And nothing is impossible.

Water conforms to its vessel
Assuming myriad form and shape.
Man becomes righteous or corrupt
According to the company he keeps.

  So seek out those friends
Whose character surpasses your own.
  Together, harness your ambition
And progress down the path of learning.

FREDERICK JACKSON TURNER

The great American historian Frederick Jackson Turner began a review of an important book about Franklin with an appreciation of his reputation, image, and achievement.

From The Dial, May 1887[†]

* * *

Of late the question has been asked, Who was the first great American? If we accept as necessary conditions of this title that the recipient must be preëminently the representative of the leading tendencies of the nation, original as it is original, and that he must have won and held the admiration of the world, whom can we find to fulfil the requirements before Benjamin Franklin, and who has better satisfied them? His greatness lay in his ability to apply to the world a shrewd understanding that disclosed in the ordinary things about him potent forces for helpfulness. His life is the story of American common-sense in its highest form, applied to business, to politics, to science, to diplomacy, to religion, to philanthropy. Surely this self-made man, the apostle of the practical and the useful, is by the verdict of his own country and of Europe entitled to the distinction of being the first great American. Probably the three men who would find the choicest niches in an American Pantheon would be Franklin, Washington, and Lincoln. They achieved their success not so much by brilliancy of the higher intellectual powers as by their personal character. This is generally recognized in the case of Washington and of Lincoln, and it will be apparent in that of Franklin if we consider the leading incidents in his political services. There is truth in the remark of Condorcet[1] that he was really an envoy not to the ministers of France, but to her people. He was welcomed by them not alone as the wise and simple searcher of nature's secrets; it was the Poor Richard wearing his fur cap among the powdered wigs, the shrewd humorist, the liberal in religion, the plain republican, that became the idol of the gay society of the Ancient Régime. Of such a man in such an age one can scarcely gain too full a knowledge.

* * *

[†] *The Dial* 8 (May 1887), 7–8.
1. The Marquis de Condorcet (1743–1794), French philosopher, revolutionary, and Franklin's friend, gave a eulogy (November 13, 1790) on Franklin.

WILLIAM DEAN HOWELLS

Although Howells never wrote at length on Franklin, he reviewed several books about him, including Bigelow's edition of the *Autobiography* in 1868, and gave thoughtful opinions in snippets over the course of more than forty years. In 1888, reviewing John Bach McMaster's *Life of Franklin*, he delivered a balanced judgment.

From Editor's Study, April 1888[†]

* * * One cannot very well mention autobiography without mentioning Franklin, whose fragment in that sort remains the chief literary work of his life, and the perpetual pleasure of whoever likes to meet a man face to face in literature.* * *

Franklin, who was in many if not most respects the greatest American of his time, has come down to ours with more reality than any of his contemporaries, and this has by no means hurt him in the popular regard. It could not be shown by the most enthusiastic whitewasher that Franklin's personal conduct was exemplary, and Professor McMaster is not a whitewasher. He is not tempted to paint Franklin as a hero or a saint, and Franklin was assuredly neither. But he was a very great man, and the objects to which he dedicated himself with an unfailing mixture of motive were such as concerned the immediate comfort of men, and the advancement of knowledge in even greater degree than they promoted Franklin's own advantage. He tore the lightning from the clouds, and the sceptre from tyrants; he also invented the Franklin stove, and gave America her first postal system. He was a great natural philosopher, a patriotic statesman, a skilful diplomatist, a master of English prose; he was likewise the father of a natural son whose mother he abandoned to absolute oblivion; he was a rather blackguardly newspaper man, a pitiless business rival, a pretty selfish liberal politician, and at times (occasionally the wrong times) a trivial humorist. The sum of him was the intellectual giant who towers through history over his contemporaries, indifferent to fame, almost cynically incredulous of ideals and beliefs sacred to most of us, but instrumental in promoting the moral and material welfare of the race; a hater of folly, idleness, and unthrift; and finally, one of the most truthful men who ever lived. It would be hard to idolize him or to overvalue him.

---

† *Harper's* 76 (April 1888), 804–05.

Howells returned to Franklin in July of 1888, in an essay addressing Matthew Arnold's criticisms of America. Replying to Arnold's conclusion that America lacked men of "distinction," Howells claimed that this very lack of an aristocratic tradition was the hallmark of American democratic success. This thought took him to the creation of the American democracy—an evolving civilization which Howells hoped would continue to become more democratic.

From Editor's Study, July 1888[†]

* * * We spoke in a recent Study of the character of Franklin, and we think of him now as the most modern, the most American, among his contemporaries. Franklin had apparently none of the distinction which Mr. Arnold lately found lacking in us; he seems to have been a man who could no more impose upon the imagination of men used to abase themselves before birth, wealth, achievement, or mastery in any sort, as very many inferior men have done in all times, than Lincoln or Grant. But he was more modern, more American than any of his contemporaries in this, though some of them were of more democratic ideals than he. His simple and plebeian past made it impossible for a man of his common-sense to assume any superiority of bearing, and the unconscious hauteur which comes of aristocratic breeding, and expresses itself at its best in distinction, was equally impossible to him. * * *

When Howells was reviewing Mark Twain's latest book, *A Connecticut Yankee at the Court of King Arthur* in January, 1890, he remarked on the traditions of American humor.

From Editor's Study, January 1890[‡]

* * *

This kind of humor, the American kind, the kind employed in the service of democracy, of humanity, began with us a long time ago; in fact Franklin may be said to have torn it with the lightning from the skies. Some time, some such critic as Mr. T. S. Perry[1] (if we ever have another such) will study its evolution in the century of our literature and civilization; but no one need deny himself meanwhile

---

[†] *Harper's* 77 (July 1888), 316.
[‡] Harper's 80 (January 1890), 321.
1. Thomas Sergeant Perry (1845–1928), American intellectual, had recently written *English Literature of the Eighteenth Century* (1883).

the pleasure we feel in Mr. Clemens's book as its highest development. * * *

In October, 1905, Howells reviewed a new autobiography which, in
turn, led him to think of the origins and traditions of autobiography as
a genre.

From Editor's Easy Chair, October 1905[†]

* * *

Autobiography is almost as modern a thing in letters as music in the
arts, and it is perhaps still more modern in its development. * * *
   Why with the revival of learning this agreeable species of literature should have sprung up, and since flourished so vigorously, with
such richness of flower and fruit, in almost every modern language,
it would be curious to inquire, but such an inquiry would lead our
wandering steps too far. It seems to have risen from that nascent
sense of the importance of each to all which the antique world
apparently ignored; and perhaps the wonder should be that we have
not ourselves more abounded in it. Autobiography seems supremely
the Christian contribution to the forms of literaturing. As the special charge and care of the Almighty, every anxious soul has doubtless had the impulse to record its aspirations and experiences; and
many, we know, have done so, the weaker souls keeping to the narrative of their sins and sufferings, and the stronger souls involun-
tarily glancing, if only askance, at the manners and customs of the
provisional world they were born into. One of the most charming in
this involuntary humanness is the brief, too brief, autobiography of
the great Jonathan Edwards,[1] the mighty theologue who first gave
our poor American provinciality world-standing, and did for us in
one way almost as much as Franklin in another. Edwards's sketch of
his own life is very slight, and Franklin's is more lamentably slight.
Yet Franklin's is one of the greatest autobiographies in literature,
and towers over other autobiographies as Franklin towered over
other men. It is about as long as Goethe's autobiography,[2] and goes
about as far as that in the story of the author's life. If either had gone
farther, the record might have come to things of less real value to
the reader, to impersonal things, to the things that history is made
of; but in a region of literature rich in masterpieces they remain

---

† *Harper's* 119 (October 1905), 795–96.
1. Jonathan Edwards (1703–1758), American theologian whose "Personal Narrative" is a
   classic spiritual autobiography.
2. Goethe (1749–1832), the great German author of *Faust*, wrote an autobiography entitled *Dichtung und Wahrheit* (1831).

alike monumental, and exalt forever the memories of geniuses equally great; for the sage whose make was pure prose was not inferior to the sage whose make was of poetry and prose a good deal mixed.

* * *

Recent Opinions

In addition to numerous specialized studies, twentieth-century Franklin scholars brought out Smyth's edition of Franklin's writings (1907), the path-breaking biography by Carl Van Doren (1938), and the great edition of *The Papers of Benjamin Franklin* (in progress; 39 volumes to 2010). D. H. Lawrence, who seems to have read only the *Autobiography* and *The Way to Wealth*, published the classic attack on Franklin as a spiritual philistine in 1923. And, in opposition to the religious critics who have reviled Franklin, the renowned German sociologist Max Weber, in his influential Marxist interpretation, portrayed Franklin as a typical example of the Protestant ethic, although Weber continued one nineteenth-century criticism by finding that Franklin embodied American capitalism.

Although the old views persist, there have been a number of new and even brilliant historical and critical studies of Franklin's prolific achievements. The most noteworthy developments have been rediscovery of Franklin's place in the history of science and appreciation of his craft, not to mention his slipperiness, in his portrayals of himself, including in his *Autobiography*.

MAX WEBER

From The Protestant Ethic and the Spirit of Capitalism[†]

In the title of this study is used the somewhat pretentious phrase, the *spirit* of capitalism. What is to be understood by it? The attempt to give anything like a definition of it brings out certain difficulties which are in the very nature of this type of investigation.

If any object can be found to which this term can be applied with any understandable meaning, it can only be an historical individual, i.e. a complex of elements associated in historical reality which we unite into a conceptual whole from the standpoint of their cultural significance.

[†] *The Protestant Ethic and the Spirit of Capitalism*, trans. Talcott Parsons (London: G. Allen & Unwin, Ltd., 1930), 47–56, 192–98. Reprinted by permission. Except where otherwise specified, the notes are Weber's.

Such an historical concept, however, since it refers in its content to a phenomenon significant for its unique individuality, cannot be defined according to the formula *genus proximum, differentia specifica*,[1] but it must be gradually put together out of the individual parts which are taken from historical reality to make it up. Thus the final and definitive concept cannot stand at the beginning of the investigation, but must come at the end. We must, in other words, work out in the course of the discussion, as its most important result, the best conceptual formulation of what we here understand by the spirit of capitalism, that is the best from the point of view which interests us here. This point of view (the one of which we shall speak later) is, further, by no means the only possible one from which the historical phenomena we are investigating can be analysed. Other standpoints would, for this as for every historical phenomenon, yield other characteristics as the essential ones. The result is that it is by no means necessary to understand by the spirit of capitalism only what it will come to mean to *us* for the purposes of our analysis. This is a necessary result of the nature of historical concepts which attempt for their methodological purposes not to grasp historical reality in abstract general formulæ, but in concrete genetic sets of relations which are inevitably of a specifically unique and individual character.[2]

Thus, if we try to determine the object, the analysis and historical explanation of which we are attempting, it cannot be in the form of a conceptual definition, but at least in the beginning only a provisional description of what is here meant by the spirit of capitalism. Such a description is, however, indispensable in order clearly to understand the object of the investigation. For this purpose we turn to a document of that spirit which contains what we are looking for in almost classical purity, and at the same time has the advantage of being free from all direct relationship to religion, being thus, for our purposes, free of preconceptions.

"Remember, that *time* is money. He that can earn ten shillings a day by his labour, and goes abroad, or sits idle, one half of that day, though he spends but sixpence during his diversion or idleness,

---

1. Classified according to genus and species. [*Editor's note.*]
2. These passages represent a very brief summary of some aspects of Weber's methodological views. At about the same time that he wrote this essay he was engaged in a thorough criticism and revaluation of the methods of the Social Sciences, the result of which was a point of view in many ways different from the prevailing one, especially outside of Germany. In order thoroughly to understand the significance of this essay in its wider bearings on Weber's sociological work as a whole it is necessary to know what his methodological aims were. Most of his writings on this subject have been assembled since his death (in 1920) in the volume *Gesammelte Aufsäze zur Wissenschaftslehre*. A shorter exposition of the main position is contained in the opening chapters of *Wirtschaft und Gesellschaft, Grundriss der Sozialökonomik*, III.—TRANSLATOR'S NOTE.

ought not to reckon *that* the only expense; he has really spent, or rather thrown away, five shillings besides.

"Remember, that *credit* is money. If a man lets his money lie in my hands after it is due, he gives me the interest, or so much as I can make of it during that time. This amounts to a considerable sum where a man has good and large credit, and makes good use of it.

"Remember, that money is of the prolific, generating nature. Money can beget money, and its offspring can beget more, and so on. Five shillings turned is six, turned again it is seven and threepence, and so on, till it becomes a hundred pounds. The more there is of it, the more it produces every turning, so that the profits rise quicker and quicker. He that kills a breeding-sow, destroys all her offspring to the thousandth generation. He that murders a crown, destroys all that it might have produced, even scores of pounds."

"Remember this saying, *The good paymaster is lord of another man's purse*. He that is known to pay punctually and exactly to the time he promises, may at any time, and on any occasion, raise all the money his friends can spare. This is sometimes of great use. After industry and frugality, nothing contributes more to the raising of a young man in the world than punctuality and justice in all his dealings; therefore never keep borrowed money an hour beyond the time you promised, lest a disappointment shut up your friend's purse for ever.

"The most trifling actions that affect a man's credit are to be regarded. The sound of your hammer at five in the morning, or eight at night, heard by a creditor, makes him easy six months longer; but if he sees you at a billiard-table, or hears your voice at a tavern, when you should be at work, he sends for his money the next day; demands it, before he can receive it, in a lump.

"It shows, besides, that you are mindful of what you owe; it makes you appear a careful as well as an honest man, and that still increases your credit.

"Beware of thinking all your own that you possess, and of living accordingly. It is a mistake that many people who have credit fall into. To prevent this, keep an exact account for some time both of your expenses and your income. If you take the pains at first to mention particulars, it will have this good effect: you will discover how wonderfully small, trifling expenses mount up to large sums, and will discern what might have been, and may for the future be saved, without occasioning any great inconvenience."

"For six pounds a year you may have the use of one hundred pounds, provided you are a man of known prudence and honesty.

"He that spends a groat a day idly, spends idly above six pounds a year, which is the price for the use of one hundred pounds.

"He that wastes idly a groat's worth of his time per day, one day with another, wastes the privilege of using one hundred pounds each day.

"He that idly loses five shillings' worth of time, loses five shillings, and might as prudently throw five shillings into the sea.

"He that loses five shillings, not only loses that sum, but all the advantage that might be made by turning it in dealing, which by the time that a young man becomes old, will amount to a considerable sum of money."[3]

It is Benjamin Franklin who preaches to us in these sentences, the same which Ferdinand Kürnberger satirizes in his clever and malicious *Picture of American Culture*[4] as the supposed confession of faith of the Yankee. That it is the spirit of capitalism which here speaks in characteristic fashion, no one will doubt, however little we may wish to claim that everything which could be understood as pertaining to that spirit is contained in it. Let us pause a moment to consider this passage, the philosophy of which Kürnberger sums up in the words, "They make tallow out of cattle and money out of men". The peculiarity of this philosophy of avarice appears to be the ideal of the honest man of recognized credit, and above all the idea of a duty of the individual toward the increase of his capital, which is assumed as an end in itself. Truly what is here preached is not simply a means of making one's way in the world, but a peculiar ethic. The infraction of its rules is treated not as foolishness but as forgetfulness of duty. That is the essence of the matter. It is not mere business astuteness, that sort of thing is common enough, it is an ethos. *This* is the quality which interests us.

When Jacob Fugger, in speaking to a business associate who had retired and who wanted to persuade him to do the same, since he had made enough money and should let others have a chance, rejected that as pusillanimity and answered that "he (Fugger) thought otherwise, he wanted to make money as long as he could",[5] the spirit of his statement is evidently quite different from that of Franklin. What in the former case was an expression of commercial daring and a per-

---

3. The final passage is from *Necessary Hints to Those That Would Be Rich* (written 1736, Works, Sparks edition, II, 80), the rest from *Advice to a Young Tradesman* (written 1748, Sparks edition, II, 87 ff.). The italics in the text are Franklin's.

4. *Der Amerikamüde* (Frankfurt, 1855), well known to be an imaginative paraphrase of Lenau's impressions of America. As a work of art the book would to-day be somewhat difficult to enjoy, but it is incomparable as a document of the (now long since blurred-over) differences between the German and the American outlook, one may even say of the type of spiritual life which, in spite of everything, has remained common to all Germans, Catholic and Protestant alike, since the German mysticism of the Middle Ages, as against the Puritan capitalistic valuation of action.

5. Sombart has used this quotation as a motto for his section dealing with the genesis of capitalism (*Der moderne Kapitalismus*, first edition, 1, 193. See also 390).

sonal inclination morally neutral,[6] in the latter takes on the character of an ethically coloured maxim for the conduct of life. The concept spirit of capitalism is here used in this specific sense,[7] it is the spirit of modern capitalism. For that we are here dealing only with Western European and American capitalism is obvious from the way in which the problem was stated. Capitalism existed in China, India, Babylon, in the classic world, and in the Middle Ages. But in all these cases, as we shall see, this particular ethos was lacking.

Now, all Franklin's moral attitudes are coloured with utilitarianism. Honesty is useful, because it assures credit; so are punctuality, industry, frugality, and that is the reason they are virtues. A logical deduction from this would be that where, for instance, the appearance of honesty serves the same purpose, that would suffice, and an unnecessary surplus of this virtue would evidently appear to Franklin's eyes as unproductive waste. And as a matter of fact, the story in his autobiography of his conversion to those virtues,[8] or the discussion of the value of a strict maintenance of the appearance of modesty, the assiduous belittlement of one's own deserts in order to gain general recognition later,[9] confirms this impression. According to

6. Which quite obviously does not mean either that Jacob Fugger was a morally indifferent or an irreligious man, or that Benjamin Franklin's ethic is completely covered by the above quotations. It scarcely required Brentano's quotations (*Die Anfänge des modernen Kapitalismus*, 150 ff.) to protect this well known philanthropist from the misunderstanding which Brentano seems to attribute to me. The problem is just the reverse: how could such a philanthropist come to write these particular sentences (the especially characteristic form of which Brentano has neglected to reproduce) in the manner of a moralist?

7. This is the basis of our difference from Sombart in stating the problem. Its very considerable practical significance will become clear later. In anticipation, however, let it be remarked that Sombart has by no means neglected this ethical aspect of the capitalistic entrepreneur. But in his view of the problem it appears as a result of capitalism, whereas for our purposes we must assume the opposite as an hypothesis. A final position can only be taken up at the end of the investigation. For Sombart's view see *op. cit.*, 357, 380, etc. His reasoning here connects with the brilliant analysis given in Simmel's *Philosophie des Geldes* (final chapter). Of the polemics which he has brought forward against me in his *Bourgeois* I shall come to speak later. At this point any thorough discussion must be postponed.

8. "I grew convinced that truth, sincerity, and integrity in dealings between man and man were of the utmost importance to the felicity of life; and I formed written resolutions, which still remain in my journal book to practise them ever while I lived. Revelation had indeed no weight with me as such; but I entertained an opinion that, though certain actions might not be bad because they were forbidden by it, or good because it commanded them, yet probably these actions might be forbidden because they were bad for us, or commanded because they were beneficial to us in their own nature, all the circumstances of things considered." *Autobiography* (ed. F. W. Pine, Henry Holt, New York, 1916), 112. [See this edition, 55–56.]

9. "I therefore put myself as much as I could out of sight and started it"—that is the project of a library which he had initiated—"as a scheme of a *number of friends*, who had requested me to go about and propose it to such as they thought lovers of reading. In this way my affair went on smoothly, and I ever after practised it on such occasions; and from my frequent successes, can heartily recommend it. The present little sacrifice of your vanity will afterwards be amply repaid. If it remains awhile uncertain to whom the merit belongs, someone more vain than yourself will be encouraged to claim it, and then even envy will be disposed to do you justice by plucking those assumed feathers and restoring them to their right owner." *Autobiography*, 140. [See this edition, 76.]

Franklin, those virtues, like all others, are only in so far virtues as
they are actually useful to the individual, and the surrogate of mere
appearance is always sufficient when it accomplishes the end in view.
It is a conclusion which is inevitable for strict utilitarianism. The
impression of many Germans that the virtues professed by Ameri-
canism are pure hypocrisy seems to have been confirmed by this
striking case. But in fact the matter is not by any means so simple.
Benjamin Franklin's own character, as it appears in the really
unusual candidness of his autobiography, belies that suspicion. The
circumstance that he ascribes his recognition of the utility of virtue
to a divine revelation which was intended to lead him in the path of
righteousness, shows that something more than mere garnishing for
purely egocentric motives is involved.

In fact, the *summum bonum* of this ethic, the earning of more and
more money, combined with the strict avoidance of all spontaneous
enjoyment of life, is above all completely devoid of any eudæmonis-
tic, not to say hedonistic, admixture. It is thought of so purely as an
end in itself, that from the point of view of the happiness of, or utility
to, the single individual, it appears entirely transcendental and absolutely irrational.[1] Man is dominated by the making of money, by
acquisition as the ultimate purpose of his life. Economic acquisition
is no longer subordinated to man as the means for the satisfaction of
his material needs. This reversal of what we should call the natural
relationship, so irrational from a naïve point of view, is evidently as
definitely a leading principle of capitalism as it is foreign to all peoples not under capitalistic influence. At the same time it expresses
a type of feeling which is closely connected with certain religious
ideas. If we thus ask, *why* should "money be made out of men", Benjamin Franklin himself, although he was a colourless deist, answers
in his autobiography with a quotation from the Bible, which his strict
Calvinistic father drummed into him again and again in his youth:
"Seest thou a man diligent in his business? He shall stand before
kings" (Prov. xxii. 29). The earning of money within the modern eco-

---

1. Brentano (*op. cit.*, 125, 127, note 1) takes this remark as an occasion to criticize the later
discussion of "that rationalization and discipline" to which worldly asceticism [This
seemingly paradoxical term has been the best translation I could find for Weber's *inner-
weltliche Askese*, which means asceticism practised within the world as contrasted with
ausserweltliche Askese, which withdraws from the world (for instance into a monastery).
Their precise meaning will appear in the course of Weber's discussion. It is one of the
prime points of his essay that asceticism does not need to flee from the world to be
ascetic. I shall consistently employ the terms worldly and otherworldly to denote the
contrast between the two kinds of asceticism.—TRANSLATOR'S NOTE.] has subjected
men. That, he says, is a rationalization toward an irrational mode of life. He is, in fact,
quite correct. A thing is never irrational in itself, but only from a particular rational
point of view. For the unbeliever every religious way of life is irrational, for the hedonist
every ascetic standard, no matter whether, measured with respect to its particular basic
values, that opposing asceticism is a rationalization. If this essay makes any contribution at all, may it be to bring out the complexity of the only superficially simple concept
of the rational.

nomic order is, so long as it is done legally, the result and the expression of virtue and proficiency in a calling; and this virtue and proficiency are, as it is now not difficult to see, the real Alpha and Omega of Franklin's ethic, as expressed in the passages we have quoted, as well as in all his works without exception.[2]

And in truth this peculiar idea, so familiar to us to-day, but in reality so little a matter of course, of one's duty in a calling, is what is most characteristic of the social ethic of capitalistic culture, and is in a sense the fundamental basis of it. It is an obligation which the individual is supposed to feel and does feel towards the content of his professional[3] activity, no matter in what it consists, in particular no matter whether it appears on the surface as a utilization of his personal powers, or only of his material possessions (as capital).

Of course, this conception has not appeared only under capitalistic conditions. On the contrary, we shall later trace its origins back to a time previous to the advent of capitalism. Still less, naturally, do we maintain that a conscious acceptance of these ethical maxims on the part of the individuals, entrepreneurs or labourers, in modern capitalistic enterprises, is a condition of the further existence of present-day capitalism. The capitalistic economy of the present day is an immense cosmos into which the individual is born, and which presents itself to him, at least as an individual, as an unalterable order of things in which he must live. It forces the individual, in so far as he is involved in the system of market relationships, to conform to capitalistic rules of action. The manufacturer who in the long run acts counter to these norms, will just as inevitably be eliminated from the economic scene as the worker who cannot or will not adapt himself to them will be thrown into the streets without a job.

Thus the capitalism of to-day, which has come to dominate economic life, educates and selects the economic subjects which it needs through a process of economic survival of the fittest. But here one can easily see the limits of the concept of selection as a means of historical explanation. In order that a manner of life so well adapted to the peculiarities of capitalism could be selected at all, i.e. should come to dominate others, it had to originate somewhere, and not in isolated individuals alone, but as a way of life common to whole groups of men. This origin is what really needs explanation.

2. In reply to Brentano's (*Die Anfänge des modernen Kapitalismus*, 150 ff.) long and somewhat inaccurate apologia for Franklin, whose ethical qualities I am supposed to have misunderstood, I refer only to this statement, which should, in my opinion, have been sufficient to make that apologia superfluous.

3. The two terms profession and calling I have used in translation of the German *Beruf*, whichever seemed best to fit the particular context. Vocation does not carry the ethical connotation in which Weber is interested. It is especially to be remembered that profession in this sense is not contrasted with business, but it refers to a particular attitude toward one's occupation, no matter what that occupation may be. This should become abundantly clear from the whole of Weber's argument.—TRANSLATOR'S NOTE.

Concerning the doctrine of the more naïve historical materialism, that such ideas originate as a reflection or superstructure of economic situations, we shall speak more in detail below. At this point it will suffice for our purpose to call attention to the fact that without doubt, in the country of Benjamin Franklin's birth (Massachusetts), the spirit of capitalism (in the sense we have attached to it) was present before the capitalistic order. There were complaints of a peculiarly calculating sort of profitseeking in New England, as distinguished from other parts of America, as early as 1632. It is further undoubted that capitalism remained far less developed in some of the neighbouring colonies, the later Southern States of the United States of America, in spite of the fact that these latter were founded by large capitalists for business motives, while the New England colonies were founded by preachers and seminary graduates with the help of small bourgeois, craftsmen and yeomen, for religious reasons. In this case the causal relation is certainly the reverse of that suggested by the materialistic standpoint.

But the origin and history of such ideas is much more complex than the theorists of the superstructure suppose. The spirit of capitalism, in the sense in which we are using the term, had to fight its way to supremacy against a whole world of hostile forces. A state of mind such as that expressed in the passages we have quoted from Franklin, and which called forth the applause of a whole people, would both in ancient times and in the Middle Ages[4] have been pro-

---

4. I make use of this opportunity to insert a few anti-critical remarks in advance of the main argument. Sombart (*Bourgeois*) makes the untenable statement that this ethic of Franklin is a word-for-word repetition of some writings of that great and versatile genius of the Renaissance, Leon Battista Alberti, who besides theoretical treatises on Mathematics, Sculpture, Painting, Architecture, and Love (he was personally a woman-hater), wrote a work in four books on household management (*Della Famiglia*). (Unfortunately, I have not at the time of writing been able to procure the edition of Mancini, but only the older one of Bonucci.) The passage from Franklin is printed above word for word. Where then are corresponding passages to be found in Alberti's work, especially the maxim "time is money", which stands at the head, and the exhortations which follow it? The only passage which, so far as I know, bears the slightest resemblance to it is found towards the end of the first book of *Della Famiglia* (ed. Bonucci, II, 353), where Alberti speaks in very general terms of money as the *nervus rerum* of the household, which must hence be handled with special care, just as Cato spoke in *De Re Rustica*. To treat Alberti, who was very proud of his descent from one of the most distinguished cavalier families of Florence (*Nobilissimi Cavalieri, op. cit.*, 213, 228, 247, etc.), as a man of mongrel blood who was filled with envy for the noble families because his illegitimate birth, which was not in the least socially disqualifying, excluded him as a bourgeois from association with the nobility, is quite incorrect. It is true that the recommendation of large enterprises as alone worthy of a *nobileè onesta famiglia* and a *libero è nobile animo*, and as costing less labour is characteristic of Alberti (209; compare *Del governo della Famiglia*, IV, 55, as well as 116 in the edition for the Pandolfini). Hence the best thing is a putting-out business for wool and silk. Also an ordered and painstaking regulation of his household, i.e. the limiting of expenditure to income. This is the *santa masserizia*, which is thus primarily a principle of maintenance, a given standard of life, and not of acquisition (as no one should have understood better than Sombart). Similarly, in the discussion of the nature of money, his concern is with the management of consumption funds (money or *possenioni*), not with that of capital; all that is clear from the expression of it which is put into the mouth of Gianozzo. He recommends, as protec-

scribed as the lowest sort of avarice and as an attitude entirely lacking in self-respect. It is, in fact, still regularly thus looked upon by all those social groups which are least involved in or adapted to modern capitalistic conditions. This is not wholly because the instinct of acquisition was in those times unknown or undeveloped, as has often been said. Nor because the *auri sacra fames*, the greed for gold, was then, or now, less powerful outside of bourgeois capitalism than

tion against the uncertainty of *fortuna*, early habituation to continuous activity, which is also (73–74) alone healthy in the long run, *in cose magnifiche è ample*, and avoidance of laziness, which always endangers the maintenance of one's position in the world. Hence a careful study of a suitable trade in case of a change of fortune, but every *opera mercenaria* is unsuitable (op. cit., 1, 209). His idea of *tranquillita dell 'animo* and his strong tendency toward the Epicurean λάθε βιώσας (*vivere a sè stesso*, 262); especially his dislike of any office (258) as a source of unrest, of making enemies, and of becoming involved in dishonourable dealings; the ideal of life in a country villa; his nourishment of vanity through the thought of his ancestors; and his treatment of the honour of the family (which on that account should keep its fortune together in the Florentine manner and not divide it up) as a decisive standard and ideal—all these things would in the eyes of every Puritan have been sinful idolatry of the flesh, and in those of Benjamin Franklin the expression of incomprehensible aristocratic nonsense. Note, further, the very high opinion of literary things (for the *industria* is applied principally to literary and scientific work), which is really most worthy of a man's efforts. And the expression of the *masserizia*, in the sense of "rational conduct of the household" as the means of living independently of others and avoiding destitution, is in general put only in the mouth of the illiterate Gianozzo as of equal value. Thus the origin of this concept, which comes (see below) from monastic ethics, is traced back to an old priest (249).

Now compare all this with the ethic and manner of life of Benjamin Franklin, and especially of his Puritan ancestors; the works of the Renaissance *littérateur* addressing himself to the humanistic aristocracy, with Franklin's works addressed to the masses of the lower middle class (he especially mentions clerks) and with the tracts and sermons of the Puritans, in order to comprehend the depth of the difference. The economic rationalism of Alberti, everywhere supported by references to ancient authors, is most clearly related to the treatment of economic problems in the works of Xenophon (whom he did not know), of Cato, Varro, and Columella (all of whom he quotes), except that especially in Cato and Varro, *acquisition* as such stands in the foreground in a different way from that to be found in Alberti. Furthermore, the very occasional comments of Alberti on the use of the *fattori*, their division of labour and discipline, on the unreliability of the peasants, etc., really sound as if Cato's homely wisdom were taken from the field of the ancient slave-using household and applied to that of free labour in domestic industry and the metayer system. When Sombart (whose reference to the Stoic ethic is quite misleading) sees economic rationalism as "developed to its farthest conclusions" as early as Cato, he is, with a correct interpretation, not entirely wrong. It is possible to unite the *diligens pater familias* of the Romans with the ideal of the *massajo* of Alberti under the same category. It is above all characteristic for Cato that a landed estate is valued and judged as an object for the investment of consumption funds. The concept of *industria*, on the other hand, is differently coloured on account of Christian influence. And there is just the difference. In the conception of *industria*, which comes from monastic asceticism and which was developed by monastic writers, lies the seed of an *ethos* which was fully developed later in the Protestant worldly asceticism. Hence, as we shall often point out, the relationship of the two, which, however, is less close to the official Church doctrine of St. Thomas than to the Florentine and Siennese mendicant-moralists. In Cato and also in Alberti's own writings this *ethos* is lacking; for both it is a matter of worldly wisdom, not of ethic. In Franklin there is also a utilitarian strain. But the ethical quality of the sermon to young business men is impossible to mistake, and that is the characteristic thing. A lack of care in the handling of money means to him that one so to speak murders capital embryos, and hence it is an ethical defect.

An inner relationship of the two (Alberti and Franklin) exists in fact only in so far as Alberti, whom Sombart calls pious, but who actually, although he took the sacraments and held a Roman benefice, like so many humanists, did not himself (except for two quite colourless passages) in any way make use of religious motives as a justification of the manner of life he recommended, had not yet, Franklin on the other hand no longer,

within its peculiar sphere, as the illusions of modern romanticists
are wont to believe. The difference between the capitalistic and pre-
capitalistic spirits is not to be found at this point. The greed of the
Chinese Mandarin, the old Roman aristocrat, or the modern peasant, can stand up to any comparison. And the *auri sacra fames* of a
Neapolitan cab-driver or *barcaiuolo*,[5] and certainly of Asiatic representatives of similar trades, as well as of the craftsmen of southern

---

related his recommendation of economy to religious conceptions. Utilitarianism, in
Alberti's preference for wool and silk manufacture, also the mercantilist social utilitarianism "that many people should be given employment" (see Alberti, *op. cit.*, 292), is in
this field at least formally the sole justification for the one as for the other. Alberti's discussions of this subject form an excellent example of the sort of economic rationalism
which really existed as a reflection of economic conditions, in the work of authors interested purely in "the thing for its own sake" everywhere and at all times; in the Chinese
classicism and in Greece and Rome no less than in the Renaissance and the age of the
Enlightenment. There is no doubt that just as in ancient times with Cato, Varro, and
Columella, also here with Alberti and others of the same type, especially in the doctrine
of *industria*, a sort of economic rationality is highly developed. But how can anyone
believe that such a literary *theory* could develop into a revolutionary force at all comparable to the way in which a religious belief was able to set the sanctions of salvation and
damnation on the fulfillment of a particular (in this case methodically rationalized)
manner of life? What, as compared with it, a really religiously oriented rationalization of
conduct looks like, may be seen, outside of the Puritans of all denominations, in the
cases of the Jains, the Jews, certain ascetic sects of the Middle Ages, the Bohemian
Brothers (an offshoot of the Hussite movement), the Skoptsi and Stundists in Russia, and
numerous monastic orders, however much all these may differ from each other.

The essential point of the difference is (to anticipate) that an ethic based on religion
places certain psychological sanctions (not of an economic character) on the maintenance of the attitude prescribed by it, sanctions which, so long as the religious belief
remains alive, are highly effective, and which mere worldly wisdom like that of Alberti
does not have at its disposal. Only in so far as these sanctions work, and, above all, in
the direction in which they work, which is often very different from the doctrine of the
theologians, does such an ethic gain an independent influence on the conduct of life
and thus on the economic order. This is, to speak frankly, the point of this whole essay,
which I had not expected to find so completely overlooked.

Later on I shall come to speak of the theological moralists of the late Middle Ages,
who were relatively friendly to capital (especially Anthony of Florence and Bernhard of
Siena), and whom Sombart has also seriously misinterpreted. In any case Alberti did not
belong to that group. Only the concept of *industria* did he take from monastic lines of
thought, no matter through what intermediate links. Alberti, Pandolfini, and their kind
are representatives of that attitude which, in spite of all its outward obedience, was
inwardly already emancipated from the tradition of the Church. With all its resemblance to the current Christian ethic, it was to a large extent of the antique pagan
character, which Brentano thinks I have ignored in its significance for the development
of modern economic thought (and also modern economic policy). That I do not deal
with its influence here is quite true. It would be out of place in a study of the Protestant
ethic and the spirit of capitalism. But, as will appear in a different connection, far from
denying its significance, I have been and am for good reasons of the opinion that its
sphere and direction of influence were entirely different from those of the Protestant
ethic (of which the spiritual ancestry, of no small practical importance, lies in the sects
and in the ethics of Wyclif and Hus). It was not the mode of life of the rising bourgeoisie
which was influenced by this other attitude, but the policy of statesmen and princes;
and these two partly, but by no means always, convergent lines of development should
for purposes of analysis be kept perfectly distinct. So far as Franklin is concerned, his
tracts of advice to business men, at present used for school reading in America, belong
in fact to a category of works which have influenced practical life, far more than Alberti's large book, which hardly became known outside of learned circles. But I have
expressly denoted him as a man who stood beyond the direct influence of the Puritan
view of life, which had paled considerably in the meantime, just as the whole English
enlightenment, the relations of which to Puritanism have often been set forth.

5. Boatman. [*Editors' note.*]

European or Asiatic countries, is, as anyone can find out for himself, very much more intense, and especially more unscrupulous than that of, say, an Englishman in similar circumstances.[6]

* * *

D. H. LAWRENCE

Benjamin Franklin[†]

The Perfectibility of Man! Ah heaven, what a dreary theme! The perfectibility of the Ford car! The perfectibility of which man? I am many men. Which of them are you going to perfect? I am not a mechanical contrivance.

Education! Which of the various me's do you propose to educate, and which do you propose to suppress?

Anyhow, I defy you. I defy you, oh society, to educate me or to suppress me, according to your dummy standards.

The ideal man! And which is he, if you please? Benjamin Franklin or Abraham Lincoln? The ideal man! Roosevelt or Porfirio Díaz?

There are other men in me, besides this patient ass who sits here in a tweed jacket. What am I doing, playing the patient ass in a tweed jacket? Who am I talking to? Who are you, at the other end of this patience?

Who are you? How many selves have you? And which of these selves do you want to be?

Is Yale College going to educate the self that is in the dark of you, or Harvard College?

The ideal self! Oh, but I have a strange and fugitive self shut out and howling like a wolf or a coyote under the ideal windows. See his red eyes in the dark? This is the self who is coming into his own.

The perfectibility of man, dear God! When every man as long as he remains alive is in himself a multitude of conflicting men. Which of these do you choose to perfect, at the expense of every other?

---

6. Unfortunately Brentano (*op. cit.*) has thrown every kind of struggle for gain, whether peaceful or warlike, into one pot, and has then set up as the specific criterion of capitalistic (as contrasted, for instance, with feudal) profit-seeking, its acquisitiveness of *money* (instead of land). Any further differentiation, which alone could lead to a clear conception, he has not only refused to make, but has made against the concept of the spirit of (modern) capitalism which we have formed for our purposes, the (to me) incomprehensible objection that it already includes in its assumptions what is supposed to be proved.

† From: D. H. Lawrence, *Studies in Classic American Literature* (London: Martin Secker, 1924), 15–27. Reprinted by permission of Pollinger Limited and Frieda Lawrence Ravagli.

Old Daddy Franklin will tell you. He'll rig him up for you, the
pattern American. Oh, Franklin was the first down-right American.
He knew what he was about, the sharp little man. He set up the
first dummy American.

At the beginning of his career this cunning little Benjamin drew
up for himself a creed that should "satisfy the professors of every
religion, but shock none".

Now wasn't that a real American thing to do?

"That there is One God, who made all things."

(But Benjamin made Him.)

"That He governs the world by His Providence."

(Benjamin knowing all about Providence.)

*"That He ought to be worshipped with adoration, prayer, and
thanksgiving."*

(Which cost nothing.)

"But——" But me no buts, Benjamin, saith the Lord.

"But that the most acceptable service of God is doing good to men."

(God having no choice in the matter.)

"That the soul is immortal."

(You'll see why, in the next clause.)

*"And that God will certainly reward virtue and punish vice, either
here or hereafter."*

Now if Mr. Andrew Carnegie, or any other millionaire, had
wished to invent a God to suit his ends, he could not have done
better. Benjamin did it for him in the eighteenth century. God is
the supreme servant of men who want to get on, to *produce*. Providence. The provider. The heavenly storekeeper. The everlasting
Wanamaker.[1]

And this is all the God the grandsons of the Pilgrim Fathers had
left. Aloft on a pillar of dollars.

"That the soul is immortal."

The trite way Benjamin says it!

But man has a soul, though you can't locate it either in his purse
or his pocket-book or his heart or his stomach or his head. The
wholeness of a man is his soul. Not merely that nice little comfortable bit which Benjamin marks out.

It's a queer thing is a man's soul. It is the whole of him. Which
means it is the unknown him, as well as the known. It seems to me
just funny, professors and Benjamins fixing the functions of the soul.
Why, the soul of man is a vast forest, and all Benjamin intended
was a neat back garden. And we've all got to fit into his kitchen
garden scheme of things. Hail Columbia!

---

1. Wanamaker's was once the largest department store in Philadelphia, founded
in 1910 by the famous merchant and philanthropist John Wanamaker (1838–1922).

The soul of man is a dark forest. The Hercynian Wood[2] that scared the Romans so, and out of which came the white-skinned hordes of the next civilization.

Who knows what will come out of the soul of man? The soul of man is a dark vast forest, with wild life in it. Think of Benjamin fencing it off!

Oh, but Benjamin fenced a little tract that he called the soul of man, and proceeded to get it into cultivation. Providence, forsooth! And they think that bit of barbed wire is going to keep us in pound for ever? More fools they.

This is Benjamin's barbed wire fence. He made himself a list of virtues, which he trotted inside like a grey nag in a paddock.

1
TEMPERANCE

Eat not to fulness [sic]; drink not to elevation.

2
SILENCE

Speak not but what may benefit others or yourself; avoid trifling conversation.

3
ORDER

Let all your things have their places; let each part of your business have its time.

4
RESOLUTION

Resolve to perform what you ought; perform without fail what you resolve.

5
FRUGALITY

Make no expense but to do good to others or yourself—i.e., waste nothing.

6
INDUSTRY

Lose no time, be always employed in something useful; cut off all unnecessary action.

---

2. The classical name for the forests of middle Germany.

7
Sincerity

Use no hurtful deceit; think innocently and justly, and, if you speak, speak accordingly.

8
Justice

Wrong none by doing injuries, or omitting the benefits that are your duty.

9
Moderation

Avoid extremes, forbear resenting injuries as much as you think they deserve.

10
Cleanliness

Tolerate no uncleanliness in body, clothes, or habitation.

11
Tranquillity

Be not disturbed at trifles, or at accidents common or unavoidable.

12
Chastity

Rarely use venery but for health and offspring, never to dulness, weakness, or the injury of your own or another's peace or reputation.

13
Humility

Imitate Jesus and Socrates.

A Quaker friend told Franklin that he, Benjamin, was generally considered proud, so Benjamin put in the Humility touch as an afterthought. The amusing part is the sort of humility it displays. "Imitate Jesus and Socrates," and mind you don't outshine either of these two. One can just imagine Socrates and Alcibiades roaring in their cups over Philadelphian Benjamin, and Jesus looking at him a little puzzled, and murmuring: "Aren't you wise in your own conceit, Ben?"

"Henceforth be masterless," retorts Ben. "Be ye each one his own master unto himself, and don't let even the Lord put His spoke in." "Each man his own master" is but a puffing up of masterlessness.

Well, the first of Americans practised this enticing list with assiduity, setting a national example. He had the virtues in columns, and gave himself good and bad marks according as he thought his behaviour deserved. Pity these conduct charts are lost to us. He only remarks that Order was his stumbling block. He could not learn to be neat and tidy.

Isn't it nice to have nothing worse to confess?

He was a little model, was Benjamin. Doctor Franklin. Snuff-coloured little man! Immortal soul and all!

The immortal soul part was a sort of cheap insurance policy.

Benjamin had no concern, really, with the immortal soul. He was too busy with social man.

1. He swept and lighted the streets of young Philadelphia.

2. He invented electrical appliances.

3. He was the centre of a moralizing club in Philadelphia, and he wrote the moral humorisms of Poor Richard.

4. He was a member of all the important councils of Philadelphia, and then of the American colonies.

5. He won the cause of American Independence at the French Court, and was the economic father of the United States.

Now what more can you want of a man? And yet he is *infra dig.*,[3] even in Philadelphia.

I admire him. I admire his sturdy courage first of all, then his sagacity, then his glimpsing into the thunders of electricity, then his common-sense humour. All the qualities of a great man, and never more than a great citizen. Middle-sized, sturdy, snuff-coloured Doctor Franklin, one of the soundest citizens that ever trod or "used venery".

I do not like him.

And, by the way, I always thought books of Venery were about hunting deer.

There is a certain earnest naïveté about him. Like a child. And like a little old man. He has again become as a little child, always as wise as his grandfather, or wiser.

Perhaps, as I say, the most complete citizen that ever "used venery".

Printer, philosopher, scientist, author and patriot, impeccable husband and citizen, why isn't he an archetype?

Pioneer, Oh Pioneers! Benjamin was one of the greatest pioneers of the United States. Yet we just can't do with him.

What's wrong with him then? Or what's wrong with us?

I can remember, when I was a little boy, my father used to buy a scrubby yearly almanac with the sun and moon and stars on the cover. And it used to prophesy bloodshed and famine. But also crammed in corners it had little anecdotes and humorisms, with a moral tag. And I used to have my little priggish laugh at the woman

3. Beneath dignity.

who counted her chickens before they were hatched and so forth, and I was convinced that honesty was the best policy, also a little priggishly. The author of these bits was Poor Richard, and Poor Richard was Benjamin Franklin, writing in Philadelphia well over a hundred years before.

And probably I haven't got over those Poor Richard tags yet. I rankle still with them. They are thorns in young flesh.

Because, although I still believe that honesty is the best policy, I dislike policy altogether; though it is just as well not to count your chickens before they are hatched, it's still more hateful to count them with gloating when they *are* hatched. It has taken me many years and countless smarts to get out of that barbed wire moral enclosure that Poor Richard rigged up. Here am I now in tatters and scratched to ribbons, sitting in the middle of Benjamin's America looking at the barbed wire, and the fat sheep crawling under the fence to get fat outside, and the watchdogs yelling at the gate lest by chance anyone should get out by the proper exit. Oh America! Oh Benjamin! And I just utter a long loud curse against Benjamin and the American corral.

Moral America! Most moral Benjamin. Sound, satisfied Ben!

He had to go to the frontiers of his State to settle some disturbance among the Indians. On this occasion he writes:

"We found that they had made a great bonfire in the middle of the square; they were all drunk, men and women quarrelling and fighting. Their dark-coloured bodies, half-naked, seen only by the gloomy light of the bonfire, running after and beating one another with fire-brands, accompanied by their horrid yellings, formed a scene the most resembling our ideas of hell that could well be imagined. There was no appeasing the tumult, and we retired to our lodging. At midnight a number of them came thundering at our door, demanding more rum, of which we took no notice.

"The next day, sensible they had misbehaved in giving us that disturbance, they sent three of their counsellors to make their apology. The orator acknowledged the fault, but laid it upon the rum, and then endeavoured to excuse the rum by saying: The Great Spirit, who made all things, made everything for some use; and whatever he designed anything for, that use it should always be put to. Now, when he had made the rum, he said: "Let this be for the Indians to get drunk with." And it must be so.'

"And, indeed, if it be the design of Providence to extirpate these savages in order to make room for the cultivators of the earth, it seems not improbable that rum may be the appointed means. It has already annihilated all the tribes who formerly inhabited all the seacoast. . . ."

This, from the good doctor with such suave complacency, is a little disenchanting. Almost too good to be true.

But there you are! The barbed wire fence. "Extirpate these savages in order to make room for the cultivators of the earth." Oh, Benjamin Franklin! He even "used venery" as a cultivator of seed.

Cultivate the earth, ye gods! The Indians did that, as much as they needed. And they left off there. Who built Chicago? Who cultivated the earth until it spawned Pittsburgh, Pa?

The moral issue! Just look at it! Cultivation included. If it's a mere choice of Kultur or cultivation, I give it up.

Which brings us right back to our question, what's wrong with Benjamin, that we can't stand him? Or else, what's wrong with us, that we find fault with such a paragon?

Man is a moral animal. All right. I am a moral animal. And I'm going to remain such. I'm not going to be turned into a virtuous little automaton as Benjamin would have me. "This is good, that is bad. Turn the little handle and let the good tap flow," saith Benjamin, and all America with him. "But first of all extirpate those savages who are always turning on the bad tap."

I am a moral animal. But I am not a moral machine. I don't work with a little set of handles or levers. The Temperance-silence-order resolution- frugality- industry- sincerity- justice- moderation- cleanliness- tranquillity- chastity- humility keyboard is not going to get me going. I'm really not just an automatic piano with a moral Benjamin getting tunes out of me.

Here's my creed, against Benjamin's. This is what I believe:

> "That I am I."
> "That my soul is a dark forest."
> "That my known self will never be more than a little clearing in the forest."
> "That gods, strange gods, come forth from the forest into the clearing of my known self, and then go back."
> "That I must have the courage to let them come and go."
> "That I will never let mankind put anything over me, but that I will try always to recognize and submit to the gods in me and the gods in other men and women."

There is my creed. He who runs may read. He who prefers to crawl, or to go by gasoline, can call it rot.

Then for a "list". It is rather fun to play at Benjamin.

1
TEMPERANCE

Eat and carouse with Bacchus, or munch dry bread with Jesus, but don't sit down without one of the gods.

2
SILENCE

Be still when you have nothing to say; when genuine passion moves you, say what you've got to say, and say it hot.

3
ORDER

Know that you are responsible to the gods inside you and to the men in whom the gods are manifest. Recognize your superiors and your inferiors, according to the gods. This is the root of all order.

4
RESOLUTION

Resolve to abide by your own deepest promptings, and to sacrifice the smaller thing to the greater. Kill when you must, and be killed the same: the *must* coming from the gods inside you, or from the men in whom you recognize the Holy Ghost.

5
FRUGALITY

Demand nothing; accept what you see fit. Don't waste your pride or squander your emotion.

6
INDUSTRY

Lose no time with ideals; serve the Holy Ghost; never serve mankind.

7
SINCERITY

To be sincere is to remember that I am I, and that the other man is not me.

8
JUSTICE

The only justice is to follow the sincere intuition of the soul, angry or gentle. Anger is just, and pity is just, but judgment is never just.

9
MODERATION

Beware of absolutes. There are many gods.

10
CLEANLINESS

Don't be too clean. It impoverishes the blood.

11
TRANQUILLITY

The soul has many motions, many gods come and go. Try and find your deepest issue, in every confusion, and abide by that. Obey the man in whom you recognize the Holy Ghost; command when your honour comes to command.

12
CHASTITY

Never "use" venery at all. Follow your passional impulse, if it be answered in the other being; but never have any motive in mind, neither offspring nor health nor even pleasure, nor even service. Only know that "venery" is of the great gods. An offering-up of yourself to the very great gods, the dark ones, and nothing else.

13
HUMILITY

See all men and women according to the Holy Ghost that is within them. Never yield before the barren.

There's my list. I have been trying dimly to realize it for a long time, and only America and old Benjamin have at last goaded me into trying to formulate it.

And now I, at least, know why I can't stand Benjamin. He tries to take away my wholeness and my dark forest, my freedom. For how can any man be free, without an illimitable background? And Benjamin tries to shove me into a barbed wire paddock and make me grow potatoes or Chicagoes.

And how can I be free, without gods that come and go? But Benjamin won't let anything exist except my useful fellow men, and I'm sick of them; as for his Godhead, his Providence, He is Head of nothing except a vast heavenly store that keeps every imaginable line of goods, from victrolas to cat-o'-nine tails.

And how can any man be free without a soul of his own, that he believes in and won't sell at any price? But Benjamin doesn't let me have a soul of my own. He says I am nothing but a servant of mankind—galley-slave I call it—and if I don't get my wages here below—that is, if Mr. Pierpont Morgan or Mr. Nosey Hebrew or the grand United States Government, the great US, US or SOMEOFUS, manages to scoop in my bit, along with their lump—why, never mind, I shall get my wages HEREAFTER.

Oh Benjamin! Oh Binjum! You do NOT suck me in any longer.

And why, oh why should the snuff-coloured little trap have wanted to take us all in? Why did he do it?

Out of sheer human cussedness, in the first place. We do all like to get things inside a barbed wire corral. Especially our fellow men. We love to round them up inside the barbed wire enclosure of FREEDOM, and make 'em work. *"Work, you free jewel, WORK!"* shouts the liberator, cracking his whip. Benjamin, I will not work. I do not choose to be a free democrat. I am absolutely a servant of my own Holy Ghost.

Sheer cussedness! But there was as well the salt of a subtler purpose. Benjamin was just in his eyeholes—to use an English vulgarism, meaning he was just delighted—when he was at Paris judiciously milking money out of the French monarchy for the overthrow of all monarchy. If you want to ride your horse to somewhere you must put a bit in his mouth. And Benjamin wanted to ride his horse so that it would upset the whole apple-cart of the old masters. He wanted the whole European apple-cart upset. So he had to put a strong bit in the mouth of his ass.

"Henceforth be masterless."

That is, he had to break-in the human ass completely, so that much more might be broken, in the long run. For the moment it was the British Government that had to have a hole knocked in it. The first real hole it ever had: the breach of the American rebellion.

Benjamin, in his sagacity, knew that the breaking of the old world was a long process. In the depths of his own under-consciousness he hated England, he hated Europe, he hated the whole corpus of the European being. He wanted to be American. But you can't change your nature and mode of consciousness like changing your shoes. It is a gradual shedding. Years must go by, and centuries must elapse before you have finished. Like a son escaping from the domination of his parents. The escape is not just one rupture. It is a long and half-secret process.

So with the American. He was a European when he first went over the Atlantic. He is in the main a recreant European still. From Benjamin Franklin to Woodrow Wilson may be a long stride, but it is a stride along the same road. There is no new road. The same old road, become dreay and futile. Theoretic and materialistic.

Why then did Benjamin set up this dummy of a perfect citizen as a pattern to America? Of course, he did it in perfect good faith, as far as he knew. He thought it simply was the true ideal. But what we *think* we do is not very important. We never really know what we are doing. Either we are materialistic instruments, like Benjamin, or we move in the gesture of creation, from our deepest self, usually unconscious. We are only the actors, we are never wholly the authors of our own deeds or works. IT is the author, the unknown inside us or outside us. The best we can do is to try to hold ourselves in unison with the deeps which are inside us. And the worst we can do is to try to have things our own way, when we run counter to IT, and in the long run get our knuckles rapped for our presumption.

So Benjamin contriving money out of the Court of France. He was contriving the first steps of the overthrow of all Europe, France included. You can never have a new thing without breaking an old. Europe happens to be the old thing. America, unless the people in America assert themselves too much in opposition to the inner gods, should be the new thing. The new thing is the death of the old. But you can't cut the throat of an epoch. You've got to steal the life from it through several centuries.

And Benjamin worked for this both directly and indirectly. Directly, at the Court of France, making a small but very dangerous hole in the side of England, through which hole Europe has by now almost bled to death. And indirectly in Philadelphia, setting up this unlovely, snuff-coloured little ideal, or automaton, of a pattern American. The pattern American, this dry, moral, utilitarian little democrat, has done more to ruin the old Europe than any Russian nihilist. He has done it by slow attrition, like a son who has stayed at home and obeyed his parents, all the while silently hating their authority, and silently, in his soul, destroying not only their authority but their whole existence. For the American spiritually stayed at home in Europe. The spiritual home of America was, and still is, Europe. This is the galling bondage, in spite of several billions of heaped-up gold. Your heaps of gold are only so many muck-heaps, America, and will remain so till you become a reality to yourselves.

All this Americanizing and mechanizing has been for the purpose of overthrowing the past. And now look at America, tangled in her own barbed wire, and mastered by her own machines. Absolutely got down by her own barbed wire of shalt-nots, and shut up fast in her own "productive" machines like millions of squirrels running in millions of cages. It is just a farce.

Now is your chance, Europe. Now let Hell loose and get your own back, and paddle your own canoe on a new sea, while clever America lies on her muck-heaps of gold, strangled in her own barbed wire of shalt-not ideals and shalt-not moralisms. While she goes out to work like millions of squirrels in millions of cages. Production!

Let Hell loose, and get your own back, Europe!

W. SOMERSET MAUGHAM

In 1940, the British writer W. Somerset Maugham (1874–1965) wrote an essay on "The Classic Books of America" for *The Saturday Evening Post*, beginning with praise for Franklin's *Autobiography*. In context, the first sentence below says that autobiographies are rarely ranked among literary classics—but Franklin's is an exception.

The Classic Books of America[†]

* * * The histories of literature contain few autobiographies; they contain none more consistently entertaining than Benjamin Franklin's. It is written plainly, as befitted its author, but in pleasant easy English, for Franklin, as we know, had studied under good masters, and it is interesting not only for its narrative but for the vivid and credible portrait which the author has succeeded in painting of himself. I cannot understand why in America Franklin is often spoken of with depreciation. Fault is found with his character; his precepts are condemned as mean and his ideals as ignoble. It is obvious that he was not a romanticist. He was shrewd and industrious. He was a good business man. He wished the good of his fellowmen, but was too clear-sighted to be deceived by them, and he used their failings with pawky humour to achieve the ends, sometimes selfish, it is true, but as often altruistic, that he had in view. He liked the good things of life, but accepted hardship with serenity. He had courage and generosity. He was a good companion, a man of witty and caustic conversation, and he liked his liquor; he was fond of women, and being no prude, took his pleasure of them. He was a man of prodigious versatility. He led a happy and a useful life. He achieved great things for his country, his state and the city in which he dwelt. To my thinking he is as truly the typical American as Doctor Johnson is the typical Englishman, and when I ask myself why it is that his countrymen are apt to grudge him their sympathy, I can only think of one explanation. He was entirely devoid of hokum.

* * *

I. B. COHEN

Franklin and Science[‡]

I. Diplomat and Scientist

A great deal[1] has been written about Benjamin Franklin, his varied activities and many interests. That the greater part of the literature

---

† From Maugham's *Books and You* (New York: Doubleday, Doran & Co., 1940), 81–82. Reprinted by permission.
‡ From *Benjamin Franklin's Experiments: A New Edition of Franklin's Experiments and Observations on Electricity* (Cambridge, Mass.: Harvard UP, 1941), 3–12.
1. The chief collections of printed source materials used in this Introduction are (1) *The Writings of Benjamin Franklin*, ed. Albert H. Smyth (10 vols.; New York, 1905–07), referred to throughout the Introduction as "*Writings*," and (2) "The Cadwallader

concerning him should relate to the political aspects of his career is no occasion for surprise. The attitude of most writers is much like that of Erasmus Darwin, who wrote to Franklin:

> Whilst I am writing to the Philosopher & a friend, I can scarcely forget that I am also writing to the greatest Statesman of the present or perhaps any century, who spread the happy contagion of liberty among his countrymen; & . . . delivered them from the house of bondage and the scourge of oppression.[2]

Franklin, the great apostle of liberty, will be remembered as long as mankind is interested in democracy and freedom. Free American citizens will not forget Franklin's tremendous effort during the first years of their country's independence.

Among scientists, however, his reputation, other than political, has suffered a different fate. The practicing physicist is too much concerned with projecting his science into the future to be interested in the past. As a scientific discipline, the history of science is still in its adolescence and is looked upon with equal suspicion by the orthodox historian and the scientist. Small wonder that Franklin the scientist has become a shadowy figure and that the countless number of monographs and books about Franklin give no clear picture of his scientific temperament, genius, or achievement.

Most American historians willingly admit that Franklin's scientific career is a subject well worth investigating, since his political success on the Continent was conditioned to a large degree by the fame and reputation which he had acquired as a scientist. Furthermore, the most casual examination of his correspondence leaves no doubt concerning the status of science among his many interests. Science was, in the words of the eminent American historian, Carl Becker,

> one activity which Franklin pursued without outward prompting, from some compelling inner impulse; one activity from

Colden Papers," *Collections of the New York Historical Society* (1917–23, Colden Papers vols. I–VII; 1934–35, Colden Papers vols. VIII–IX), referred to throughout this Introduction as "*Colden Papers.*" Colden (1688–1776), New York's scientist-Lt. Governor, was one of Franklin's earliest and most consistent scientific correspondents. Cf. Alice Mapelsden Keys, *Cadwallader Colden—A Representative Eighteenth Century Official* (New York, 1906), especially 1–26, "A Colonial Savant."

The dates in Franklin's life present a problem since the English world changed its calendar in the middle period of his life. Although the Catholic world adopted the Gregorian calendar in 1582, the Protestant countries continued to use the Julian; England did not accept the Gregorian calendar until 1752. In the portion of the eighteenth century prior to 1752, there was a difference of 11 days in date between the two calendars. In order to have the dates in Franklin's life correspond to the dates of documents I have used the Julian dates for events prior to 1752 and Gregorian dates for events after 1752. The only danger in such a system would occur in cases where one would want to compare a date for a French event with a similar date for an English event. Fortunately, the first French event mentioned in this Introduction is May 1752, which is after the reform of the English calendar. Hence there is no confusion.

2. Quoted in Paul L. Ford, *The Many-Sided Franklin* (New York, 1898; reissued 1926), 387.

which he never wished to retire, to which he would willingly have devoted his life, to which he always gladly turned in every odd day or hour of leisure, even in the midst of the exacting duties and heavy responsibilities of his public career. Science was after all the one mistress to whom he gave himself without reserve and served neither from a sense of duty nor for any practical purpose.[3]

Franklin's active interest in science was not thoroughly aroused until he was forty years old. Before then he had been too busy earning a living to give himself up wholeheartedly to science, although his alert mind had always been occupied with scientific problems, as well as with means for furthering the state of scientific enterprise in the Colonies. When Franklin finally decided to retire from business, the decision was conditioned by a wish to devote all his energy to the investigation of electricity, a topic with which he had just become acquainted. But no sooner had he given himself to this study than a civic emergency arose.

The years 1747–1749 were fruitful years for Franklin's experiments. It was during these years that he laid the foundations of modern electrical science. But they were years not without their own turmoil. In 1747 rumors had reached Philadelphia that French privateers were plotting to sack the city. Although England had been at war with Spain since 1739 and with France since 1744, the city of Philadelphia had not been molested. Protected by their distance up the Delaware River from enemy ships ranging the coast, its citizenry had been lulled into false security and a belief that "this is not our war."

Then, in July of 1747, soon after Franklin had written to his English patron, Peter Collinson, telling him about the discoveries resulting from his first electrical experiments, a group of French and Spanish privateers plundered homes within twenty miles of Philadelphia and captured a ship coming from Antigua, murdering its captain. Philadelphia was unprepared for an emergency; it had no cannon, no ammunition, no militia. The Assembly, dominated by Quakers, refused to appropriate any money for purposes of war. With the very existence of the city threatened and its population apathetic, the situation was critical.

Benjamin Franklin, enjoying his newly found leisure, was in the midst of electrical experiments, but rose to the urgency of the moment and met with a group of friends to formulate some plan. They decided that Franklin, simply as a "Tradesman of Philadelphia," should write and publish a pamphlet in order to arouse the popula-

---

3. "Benjamin Franklin," *Dictionary of American Biography* ed. Allen Johnson, Dumas Malone, et al. (New York: Scribner, 1937).

tion to the dangers at hand. Thus was born his first political pamphlet, *Plain Truth*,[4] which was to have the desired effect. It united the merchants, the farmers, the liberal Quakers (who felt that they could support a "defensive" war), and defense plans were under way at once. Franklin called a meeting of the citizens, who formed an "Association" which raised the money necessary to buy cannons and organized a militia. And Franklin was the spearhead of this movement, though he refused office and served his turn of duty like anyone else. Fortunately, no war came, for the Peace of Aix-la-Chapelle in October of 1748 brought an end to possible hostilities.

By September it was certain that the danger of invasion had passed. Franklin wrote to his friend Cadwallader Colden in New York:

> I . . . am takeing the proper Measures for obtaining Leisure to enjoy Life & my Friends more than heretofore, having put my Printing house under the Care of my Partner David Hall, absolutely left off Bookselling, and remov'd to a more quiet Part of the Town where I am settling my old Acc^ts. and hope soon to be quite a Master of my own Time, and no longer (as the Song has it) *at every one's Call but my own*. . . . With the same Views I have refus'd engaging further in publick Affairs. The Share I had in the late Association, &c. having given me a little present Run of Popularity, there was a pretty general Intention of chusing me a Representative for the City at the next Election of Assemblymen; but I have desired all my Friends who Spoke to me about it, to discourage it, declaring that I should not Serve if chosen. Thus you see I am in a fair Way of having no other Tasks than such as I shall like to give my Self, and of enjoying what I look upon as a great Happiness, Leisure to read, study, make Experiments, and converse at large with such ingenious & worthy Men as are pleas'd to honour me with their Friendship or Acquaintance, on such Points as may produce something for the common Benefit of Mankind, uninterrupted by the little Cares & Fatigues of Business.[5]

Franklin seems to have believed it possible for him to slip back unnoticed into private life. "But his skill and zeal in recent affairs had made him too well known to be long an undisturbed philosopher. . . . Now he was, though not an official, a public man."[6] There were to be only a few precious years of uninterrupted scientific investigation, and then his country came to need his services more

4. Published November 14, 1747.
5. Benjamin Franklin to Cadwallader Colden, Philadelphia, Sept. 29, 1748. *Colden Papers*, vol. IV, 78–79.
6. Carl Van Doren, *Benjamin Franklin* (New York, 1938), 187. For full details of Franklin's part in the defense of Philadelphia, see 183–87.

and more. In the precarious years before the Revolution there was less and less time for science. During the Revolution itself, Franklin had to give himself almost entirely to political activity.

Franklin's letters show that he always wanted to be a scientist but felt that the nature of the troubled times did not permit it; there were other and more important things to be done. Something of his opinion can be found in a letter dating towards the end of his stay in Paris as agent for the Colonies during the Revolution. An unknown correspondent had written to him about some of his earlier discoveries in electricity. Franklin replied: ". . . It is many years since I was engaged in those pleasing studies, and my mind is at present too much occupied with other and more important affairs to permit my returning to them."[7] One month and a half later, he wrote to Sir Joseph Banks, the President of the Royal Society of London: "I hope soon to have more Leisure, and to spend a part of it in those Studies, that are much more agreeable to me than political Operations."[8]

At the conclusion of the Revolution, Banks had written to Franklin:

> General Washington has we are told Cincinnatus like return'd to cultivate his garden now the emancipated States have no farther occasion for his sword. How much more pleasant would it be for you to return to your more interesting more elevated and I will say more useful pursuit of Philosophy. The head of the Philosopher guides the hand of the farmer to a more abundant crop than nature or instinct or unguided reason could have produced. He leads the sailor. . . . Would I could see you abdicate the station of Legislator . . . and return to your Friends here & to those studies which rais'd you formerly to a hight less elevated perhaps but I am sure more satisfactory. . . . [9]

Franklin answered:

> Be assured that I long earnestly for a Return of those peaceful Times, when I could sit down in sweet Society with my English philosophic Friends, communicating to each other new Discoveries, and proposing Improvements of old ones; . . . . Much more happy should I be thus employ'd in your most desirable Company, than in that of all the Grandees of the Earth. . . . [1]

Throughout his long political and diplomatic career, Franklin never despaired of returning to the life of a private citizen. Till the

7. Letter dated Passy, June 14, 1783. *Writings*, vol. IX, 52.
8. Franklin to Banks, Passy, July 27, 1783. *Writings*, vol. IX, 74.
9. Unpublished letter in the University of Pennsylvania Library; Banks to Franklin, London, August 25, 1783.
1. Franklin to Banks, Passy, Sept. 9, 1782. *Writings*, vol. VIII, 592.

day he died he hoped to resume his work in experimental science. When he was eighty-one years of age, he believed that the period of his public service was over and made plans for returning to America and his experiments. To his friend Ingenhousz, he wrote:

> Rejoice with me, my dear Friend, that I am once more a Free-man: after Fifty Years Service in Public Affairs. And let me know soon if you will make me happy the little Remainder left me of my Life, by spending the Time with me in America.
>
> I have Instruments if the Enemy did not destroy them all, and we will make Plenty of Experiments together.[2]

Luckily for him, Ingenhousz did not accompany Franklin to America, for ahead there lay no leisure in which to perform experiments but rather the trying days of the Constitutional Convention.

It is thus perfectly clear that Franklin considered himself not so much a politician or diplomat as a scientist fulfilling his necessary obligations to the society of which he was a member. No man ever took his duty as patriot or citizen more seriously and very few have been able to execute that service with more zeal or greater efficiency. According to Franklin's standards, a scientist was simply a member of the community, just like everybody else. He was entitled to no special privileges, no exemptions. According to Franklin's credo, however, the needs of the community are always of greater importance than the pleasures and desires of a single individual. In time of national emergency, the pursuit of science, however interesting, is a luxury to be given its due "weight" and no more. As Franklin expressed this himself: "Had Newton been Pilot but of a single common Ship, the finest of his Discoveries would scarce have excus'd, or atton'd for his abandoning the Helm one Hour in Time of Danger; how much less if she carried the Fate of the Commonwealth."[3]

One of the most interesting documents in Franklin's political career, from the point of view of Franklin as scientist, is the "passport" which he issued for Captain Cook on March 10, 1779. Addressed "To all Captains and Commanders of armed Ships acting by Commission from the Congress of the United States of America, now in war with Great Britain," the "passport" reads:

> Gentlemen,
> A Ship having been fitted out from England before the Commencement of this War, to make Discoveries . . . in Unknown Seas, under the Conduct of that most celebrated Navigator and Discoverer Captain Cook; an Undertaking truly laudable in itself, as the Increase of Geographical Knowledge facilitates

2. Franklin to Ingenhousz, Passy, Apr. 29, 1785. *Writings*, vol. IX, 321.
3. Franklin to Colden, Philadelphia, Oct. 11, 1750. *Colden Papers*, vol. IV, 227.

the Communication between distant Nations, in the Exchange
of useful Products and Manufactures, and the Extension of
Arts, whereby the common Enjoyments of human Life are
multiply'd and augmented, and Science of other kinds increased
to the benefit of Mankind in general; this is . . . to recommend
to . . . you, that . . . in case the said Ship . . . should happen to
fall into your Hands, you would not consider her as an Enemy,
nor suffer any Plunder to be made of the Effects contain'd in
her, nor obstruct her immediate Return to England. . . . [4]

In recognition of his generosity in this matter, Franklin was presented with one of the gold medals struck in honor of Captain Cook.
The Admiralty Board also sent him a copy of the printed account of
Cook's voyage "accompanied with the elegant collection of plates,
and a very polite letter from Lord Howe, signifying that the present
was made with the king's express approbation."[5]

In the same spirit, Franklin and Jefferson proposed to Congress
that the "non-importation" considerations should not be applied to
books, and especially not to science.[6] When Franklin returned from
France to America, at the age of eighty, he began to keep a journal
as he had once done fifty-nine years earlier. His friends all hoped
that he would use the leisure time of the ocean voyage for completing his autobiography, but Franklin, convinced that his public life
was over, decided that he was finally free for his beloved science.
With the aid of Jonathan Williams, he took temperature soundings
at different depths, he noted the currents and the kind of weeds to
be found in the Gulf Stream, he devised numerous experiments
to improve the state of navigation. Of these last he wrote an account
to David Le Roy, the brother of his electrician friend. Once he has
started, he cannot stop, since, as he says, "the garrulity of the old
man has got hold of me, and, as I may never have another occasion
of writing on this subject, I think I may as well now, once for all,
empty my nautical budget."[7] But this was not all, for he wrote to
Ingenhousz on the "Causes and Cure of Smoky Chimneys" and gave
a very technical description of a new type of stove.

Historians lament the fact that Franklin did not use the time of
the voyage "more profitably" by completing the *Autobiography*, and
maybe they are right. But as one who is chiefly interested in Frank-

4. *Writings*, vol. VII, 242–43.
5. Note of Willam Temple Franklin, quoted by Smyth in *Writings*, vol. VII, 242. Cf. Benjamin Franklin's letter to Lord Howe (Passy, August 18, 1784) thanking him for the
books, *Writings*, vol. IX, 258. In 1789 the author of a book about Cook remarked that
although the French had generously offered Cook protection, "the narrow-souled
Americans did all they could to obstruct him." Cf. Franklin's open letter in reply to this
accusation, *Writings*, vol. X, 43–44.
6. *The Writings of Thomas Jefferson*, collected and edited by Paul L. Ford (New
York, 1899), vol. X, 118.
7. "Maritime Observations," *Writings*, vol. IX, 372–413.

lin as a scientist, I must say I am glad that he spent the voyage in the fashion that he did. For science was very dear to his heart, and in the evening of his life he was deprived of the privilege of scientific investigation. This voyage was his last opportunity, for no sooner had he arrived in America than he was chosen President of the Commonwealth of Pennsylvania. Since he personally contributed so much to history itself, he can be forgiven the refusal of the further gift to historians.

DAVID LEVIN

The Autobiography of Benjamin Franklin: The Puritan Experimenter in Life and Art[†]

It would be difficult to find a book that seems more widely understood, as a model of plain exposition of character, than *The Autobiography of Benjamin Franklin*. Everyone knows that this is the life of a self-made, self-educated man and that *Poor Richard's Almanac* was a best-seller. Everyone knows that the penniless sixteen-year-old boy who first walked down the streets of Philadelphia with his pockets bulging with shirts and stockings, and with two great puffy rolls under his arms, worked so diligently at his calling that for him the promise of Scripture was fulfilled, and he one day stood before kings. (He "stood before five," he wrote later, with characteristic precision, and sat down to dine with one.) We all know, too, that the Franklin stove and bifocals and the electrical experiments bear witness to Franklin's belief in life-long education, and that it was because of his ability to explain clearly and persuade painlessly—even delightfully— that his international reputation soared higher than his famous kite.

Too often, however, we forget a few simple truths about this great man and his greatest works. We forget the chief purposes for which he wrote his autobiography, and the social system that led him to conceive such aims. Remembering his plainness, his clarity, we overlook the subtlety of his expression, his humor, and his qualifying statements. Above all, we forget that he was a writer, that he had a habit of creating characters. And so he takes us in. Some of us forget that Poor Richard is just as clearly Franklin's creation as is Mrs. Silence Dogood, the fictitious character through whom young Benjamin had published in his brother's newspaper in Boston; many of us forget that *The Way to Wealth*, Franklin's brilliantly successful collection of economic proverbs, is a humorous *tale* narrated by Poor Richard, who at first makes fun of himself and then

† *Yale Review* 53 (Winter 1964), 258–75. Reprinted by permission.

reports the long speech made by another fictitious character named Father Abraham; and most of us overlook the crucial distinction, especially in the first half of Franklin's autobiography, between the *writer* of the book and the chief *character* he portrays.

Please understand that I do not mean to call Franklin's autobiography a work of fiction. I must insist, however, that we refuse to let its general fidelity to historical fact blind us to the author's function in creating the character who appears in the book. Franklin's first entry into Philadelphia may serve as an example. We are apt to consider the picture of that boy as a natural fact of history, as if no conceivable biographer could have omitted it. It merges in our experience with the myth that Horatio Alger exploited a century later, and with dozens of other pictures of successful men at the beginning of their careers: the country boy walking into the big city, the immigrant lad getting off the boat and stepping forth in search of his fortune. So grandly representative is this human experience that our current critical fashion would call it archetypal. But it was Franklin the writer who elected to describe this picture, and who made it memorable. He was not obliged to include it. He *chose* to make it represent an important moment in his life, and he chose to depict his young former self in particular detail. His dirty clothes, his bulging pockets, and the huge rolls constitute nearly the only details respecting his personal appearance in the entire book. He might have omitted them, and he might have ignored the whole incident.

If we try to imagine what our view of Franklin might have been had he not written his autobiography, we will recognize that the author's conception of himself has considerably more literary significance than one can find in a single descriptive passage. Though the honest autobiographer refuses to invent fictitious incidents, he *actually creates himself as a character.* He selects incidents and qualities for emphasis, and discards or suppresses others. He portrays himself in relation to some other character (whom he also "creates" in this book), but refrains from portraying himself in relation to some others whom he once knew. He decides on the meaning of his life and the purpose of his book, and he selects traits, incidents, and characters accordingly. Obviously he cannot record everything that happened unless he spews forth every feeling, impulse, twitch that ever entered his mind or affected his senses. Indeed, the very conception of a happening requires some selection, some ordering of experience, and a point of view from which to perceive that order. D. H. Lawrence did not understand Franklin's autobiography, but he saw that it recognized a kind of order, and a view of the self, which imposed a planned control on natural feelings. "The ideal self!" he cried scornfully in his critique of Franklin.

Oh, but I have a strange and fugitive self shut out and howling
like a wolf or a coyote under the ideal windows. See his red
eyes in the dark? This is the self who is coming into his own.

The perfectibility of man, dear God! When every man as
long as he remains alive is in himself a multitude of conflicting
men. Which of these do you choose to perfect, at the expense
of every other?

Old Daddy Franklin will tell you. He'll rig him up for you,
the pattern American. Oh, Franklin was the first downright
American.

As we shall see later on, this gross caricature of "the sharp little
man" reflects some imperfections in Franklin's ability to communicate with ages beyond his own, and as we shall see even sooner, it
reflects an inability or unwillingness in Lawrence and many others to
read carefully. For the moment, however, let us content ourselves
with two observations in support of Lawrence's limited perception.
First, Franklin's autobiography represents that kind of art in which
the author tries to understand himself, to evaluate himself, to see
himself, in a sense, from outside; it is a *portrayal* of the self rather
than simply an *expression* of current feeling or an outpouring of those
multiple selves that Lawrence celebrates. Old Daddy Franklin did
indeed know what he was about. But the second observation must
limit the praise in the first. The very terms in which Franklin expresses
his admirable self-awareness limit his communication in a way that
obscures the identity of the author. The technique of humor, and the
disarming candor about techniques of influence and persuasion—
these occasionally make us wonder which of several selves Benjamin
Franklin is.

Franklin's art is deceptive. At first there may seem to be none at
all. The book, written at four different times from 1771 to 1790, the
year Franklin died, is loosely constructed; it is almost conversational
in manner. It begins, indeed, as a letter to Franklin's son. It is epi-
sodic, anecdotal. Clearly, however, its narrative order includes two
major divisions: the first half of the book describes his education, as
he strives for a secure position in the world and for a firm character;
the second half concentrates on his career of *public* service, though
the account breaks off well before the American Revolution.

That simple pattern itself illustrates the most important fact about
Franklin's autobiography. He not only creates an attractive image of
himself but uses himself as a prototype of his age and his country.
There are three essential ways in which he establishes this story of
the self-made man securely in the broadest experience of his time. If
we examine them with some care, we may understand his purposes
and his achievement more clearly.

The first context is that of Puritanism, represented here by Franklin's admiration for John Bunyan's *Pilgrim's Progress* and Cotton Mather's *Essays To Do Good*. Although Franklin says that he was converted to Deism by some anti-Deistic tracts in his Presbyterian father's library, we cannot overestimate the importance of his Puritan heritage, and his own account gives it due credit. (I refer, of course, not to the gross distortion suggested by the word "puritanical," the joy-killing and fanatical, but to that firm tradition that required every Christian to venture into this world as a pilgrim, doing right for the glory of God.) It is to this tradition that we owe Franklin's great proverb "Leisure is time for doing something useful," his emphasis on diligence in one's calling, the moral preoccupation that colors his view of ordinary experience. We see the Puritan influence in his insistence on frugality, simplicity, and utility as standards of value; and we see it just as clearly in his acceptance of public duty, his constant effort to improve the community, his willingness at last to serve the local and international community without pay. When we remember that the Protestant ethic combines the profit motive with religious duty, we should remember that in Franklin's day (as in John Winthrop's before him) it also obliged one to use one's fortune, and one's own person, in public service.

The Puritan tradition, indeed, gave Franklin a more purely literary kind of model. By the time he was growing up there existed in both old and New England a fairly large body of personal literature that emphasized objective self-examination and the need to keep an objective record of divine Providence as it affected an individual life. One recorded one's daily life in order to evaluate one's conduct and also to find evidence of God's will in the pattern of events. It was the Puritan custom, moreover, to improve every opportunity to find moral instruction and signs of universal meaning in particular experience. Franklin himself describes and exemplifies this custom in an anecdote (not in the *Autobiography*, but in a letter) of a visit that he made in 1724 to the old Puritan minister Cotton Mather. As Franklin was leaving, he wrote later, Mather

> showed me a shorter way out of the house, through a narrow passage, which was crossed by a beam overhead. We were talking as I withdrew, he accompanying me behind, and I turning partly towards him when he said hastily, "STOOP, STOOP!" I did not understand him till I felt my head against the beam. He was a man that never missed any occasion of giving instruction, and upon this he said to me: "You are young, and have the world before you; STOOP as you go through it, and you will miss many hard thumps." This advice, thus beat into my head, has frequently been of use to me, and I often think of it when

I see pride mortified and misfortunes brought upon people by
carrying their heads too high.

One of the most successful devices that Franklin uses in his autobiography is this kind of symbolic anecdote, or parable; what brings
Franklin's practice closer to Puritan preaching than to the parables
in the Bible is his careful addition of a conclusion that drives home
the point—the application or use—for those who might otherwise
misunderstand it.

Before turning from Puritanism to a second quality of eighteenth-
century experience, we should pause for another minute over the
name of John Bunyan. For the first half of Franklin's autobiography, as Charles Sanford has said, represents a kind of pilgrim's
progress. As his pious contemporaries Jonathan Edwards and John
Woolman published accounts of their growth in Christian grace, so
Franklin, acknowledging the aid of Providence, narrates the progress of a chosen, or at least fortunate, and often undeserving young
man through a series of perils (including the valley of the shadow
of death) to a relatively safe moral haven, if not to the Heavenly
City. Others, we must remember, do not fare so well. A number of
his early associates fall into one pit or another, and although Franklin tries to show what he did to save himself, so that others might
profit by his example, he makes it perfectly clear that on several
occasions he was so foolish that he too would have gone down had
he not been preserved by Providence—or plain good luck.

It is this sense of the perils facing a young man in the free society
of the new capitalism that brings me to the second of my three
kinds of representativeness. Whether he was a Puritan or not, the
young indentured servant, the young apprentice, the young artisan
or farmer of Franklin's time had to walk a perilous way in the
world. And if, like a great many Americans, he was leaving his
childhood community as well as the restraints and comforts of his
childhood religious faith, when he came forth to make his way in
the world, he faced those dangers with very little help from outside
himself. He had precious little help in the experience of others, for
often his experience was new for the entire society. The mistakes
he made did not entitle him to the protection of bankruptcy laws
or of the less grand comforts of our welfare state. They sent him to
a debtor's prison, or subjected him to the permanent authority of a
creditor. Franklin described plain economic fact as well as moral
truth when he said, "It is hard for an empty sack to stand upright."

Thus one of Franklin's major purposes in the *Autobiography* was
to instruct the young, not only by good example but by warning.
Especially in his account of his youth, he presents himself repeatedly as the relatively innocent or ignorant young man in conflict

with those who would take advantage of him. Much of the sharp dealing that annoys D. H. Lawrence and others occurs in this kind of situation. Franklin's older brother, exploiting and sometimes beating the young apprentice, tries to circumvent a court ruling against his newspaper by freeing young Benjamin and making him nominal owner of the paper; Benjamin takes advantage of the opportunity by going off to Philadelphia to strike out on his own. Samuel Keimer uses Franklin to train other printers so that Franklin's services may then be dispensed with; but Franklin plans to set up his own shop, and when he does, he prospers as Keimer fails.

As in the fiction of Daniel Defoe, whom Franklin admired, and Samuel Richardson, whom he was among the first American printers to publish, Franklin's *Autobiography* indicates clearly that the relations between the sexes concealed some of the chief dangers to the young freeman's liberty. Luckily, he concedes, he escaped the worst consequences of occasional encounters with "low women"; but in a society that frankly recognized marriage as an economic contract he was almost entrapped by a clever pair of parents who seem to have counted on hoodwinking the young lad because he had to bargain for himself in a matter that required cooler heads. Franklin's account of the episode is priceless:

Mrs. Godfrey [his landlady] projected a match for me with a relation's daughter, took opportunities of bringing us often together, till a serious courtship on my part ensued, the girl being in herself very deserving. The old folks encouraged me by continued invitations to supper and by leaving us together, till at length it was time to explain. Mrs. Godfrey managed our little treaty. I let her know that I expected as much money with their daughter as would pay off my remaining debt for the printing house, which I believe was not then above a hundred pounds. She brought me word they had no such sum to spare. I said they might mortgage their house in the Loan Office. The answer to this after some days was that they did not approve the match; that on enquiry of Bradford [another printer] they had been informed the printing business was not a profitable one, the types would soon be worn out and more wanted; that Samuel Keimer and D. Harry had failed one after the other, and I should probably soon follow them; and therefore I was forbidden the house, and the daughter shut up. Whether this was a real change of sentiment or only artifice, on a supposition of our being too far engaged in affection to retract and therefore that we should steal a marriage, which would leave them at liberty to give or withhold what they pleased, I know not. But I suspected the motive, resented it, and went no more. Mrs. Godfrey brought me afterwards some more favourable accounts of their disposition and would have drawn me on again, but I declared absolutely my resolution to have nothing more to do with that family.

This anecdote is not among the most popular with modern readers. It should be noticed, however, that people who owned their house outright did not ordinarily leave their daughter alone with a young man until they had some assurance of his economic eligibility for marriage, and that these parents were not worried about Franklin's ability to provide for their daughter until he demanded the usual dowry. We should notice, too, that the young Franklin who is described in this anecdote seems at last to have obeyed his own feelings of resentment rather than the economic interest that might have been served by allowing the girl's parents to re-open negotiations.

But although he always prospers, the innocent young man is not infallibly wise. Although he is never so roguish as Moll Flanders, his confession appears to be remarkably candid. He concedes that he was greatly deceived by the Governor of Pennsylvania, who sent him as a very young man to England, along with supposed letters of recommendation and letters of credit that never arrived. (That, by the way, was probably the greatest peril of Franklin's young life, and he confesses that he walked into it despite his father's clear warning.) He admits freely to motives and perceptions that we, along with most of his contemporaries, prefer to conceal. He thanks heaven for vanity, "along with the other comforts of life," and admits that it is useful to cultivate not only the reality but the *appearance* of industry and humility. It was effective, he says, to carry his own paper stock through the streets in a wheelbarrow, so that people could see how hard he was willing to work. A book, he confesses, "sometimes debauch'd me from my work, but that was seldom, snug, and gave no scandal."

This apparent honesty leads us to the heart of the book. My third kind of representativeness, the most important of all, can be summed up in a single statement that appears near the end of the *Autobiography.* "This," Franklin wrote, "is an age of experiments." It *was* an age of experiments, an age of empirical enlightenment, when every freeman might, if wary and lucky, learn by experience and test for himself. Franklin's greatest achievement in this book is that of characterizing himself repeatedly as a man of inquiry. He creates for us a convincing image of the inquiring man, self-educated, testing for himself, in morality, in business, in religion, in science. On almost every page we see some evidence of his willingness to learn. He contrives to reveal the vast range of his interests—from the pure science of electricity, to the effect of lading on the speed of merchant ships, to street-lighting and street-cleaning, to the value of learning modern romance languages before trying to learn Latin—all these he contrives to reveal in anecdotes of questioning and discovery. And in anecdote after anecdote, the plain questioning of Benjamin Franklin in action applies an experimental test to theories and assumptions. As a young journeyman printer in England, he demonstrates to his fellow workmen that the customary beer is not necessary to the maintenance of strength; he drinks water, and carries more type than they can carry. Young Franklin and a friend agree that the one who dies first will prove the possibility of communicating from beyond the grave by getting in touch with the other who remains alive; but, Old Franklin the narrator reports, "he never fulfilled his promise." As a military commander at the start of the Seven Years' War with France, Franklin hears the zealous Presbyterian chaplain's complaint that the men do not attend religious services; he solves the problem by persuading the chaplain himself to serve out the men's daily rum ration just *after* prayers. ". . . and never," the narrator comments, "were prayers more generally and more punctually attended—so that I thought this method preferable to the punishments inflicted by some military laws for non-attendance on divine service."

Especially in the narrative of the early years, this wide-eyed freshness of perception is perfectly compatible with the young man's shrewdness, and it is nowhere more delightful than in his depiction of some of the other chief characters in the book. One of the most remarkable qualities in the book is the author's almost total lack of rancor. His brother James, Samuel Keimer, Governor Keith, and General Edward Braddock—all these people may be said to have injured him; yet he presents them all with the charitable curiosity of a man who was once interested in learning from his experience with them something about human nature. I refer here not to the kind of curiosity that can be so easily caricatured, the ingenious Yankee's humor that leads him to tell us how he measured reports of the distance at which the revivalist George Whitefield's voice might be heard. What I mean to admire is the humorous *discovery* of another person's strange faults. Consider the economy of this portrayal of Samuel Keimer, whose faults are balanced against those of the young Franklin:

> Keimer and I lived on a pretty good familiar footing and agreed tolerably well, for he suspected nothing of my setting up [for myself]. He retained a great deal of his old enthusiasm and loved argumentation. We therefore had many disputations. I used to work him so with my Socratic method and had trappaned him [that is, tricked him] so often by questions apparently so distant from any point we had in hand, and yet by degrees

leading to the point and bringing him into difficulties and contradictions, that at last he grew ridiculously cautious and would
hardly answer the most common question without asking first,
"What do you intend to infer by that?" However, it gave him so
high an opinion of my abilities in the confuting way that he seriously proposed my being his colleague in a project he had of
setting up a new sect. He was to preach the doctrines, and I
was to confound all opponents. When he came to explain with
me upon the doctrines, I found several conundrums which
I objected to, unless I might have my way a little, too, and introduce some of mine. Keimer wore his beard at full length,
because somewhere in the Mosaic Law it is said, "Thou shalt
not mar the corners of thy beard." He likewise kept the seventh
day Sabbath, and these two points were essentials with him. I
disliked both but agreed to admit them upon condition of his
adopting the doctrine of not using animal food. "I doubt," says
he, "my constitution will bear it." I assured him it would and
that he would be the better for it. He was usually a great glutton,
and I wished to give myself some diversion in half-starving him.
He consented to try the practice if I would keep him company;
I did so, and we held it for three months. Our provisions were
purchased, cooked, and brought to us regularly by a woman in
the neighbourhod who had from me a list of forty dishes to be
prepared for us at different times, in which there entered neither fish, flesh, nor fowl. This whim suited me better at this time
from the cheapness of it, not costing us above eighteen pence
sterling each per week. I have since kept several Lents most
strictly, leaving the common diet for that, and that for common,
without the least inconvenience, so that I think there is little in
the advice of making those changes by easy gradations. I went
on pleasantly, but poor Keimer suffered grievously, tired of the
project, longed for the flesh pots of Egypt, and ordered a roast
pig. He invited me and two women friends to dine with him, but
it being brought too soon upon table, he could not resist the
temptation and ate it all up before we came.

Franklin's acute awareness that Keimer is a ridiculously pretentious, affected character does not prevent him from expressing
some unsentimental sympathy for his former victim, or from hint-
ing broadly that he himself now disapproves of giving himself diversion at the expense of others—although he might relish the chance
to repeat the same experiment. We must remember, in reading this
anecdote, that Franklin has previously told us of his decision some
years later to abandon the Socratic method, because it had sometimes won him victories that neither he nor his cause deserved. And
we must notice that his rational skepticism, his testing by experience, extends even to reason itself.

In an age of reason Franklin was not afraid to admit the limits of reason nor did he hesitate in his autobiography to illustrate those limits by recounting an experience in which young Franklin himself is the only target of his humor. He used this device on several occasions, but one of them is astonishing in its brilliance, for it not only establishes the author's attitude toward himself but phrases the issue in the key terms of eighteenth-century psychology. The battle in young Franklin is a battle between principle and inclination. The anecdote appears immediately before the vegetarian experiment with Keimer. During a calm on his voyage back from Boston to Philadelphia, Franklin says,

> our crew employed themselves catching cod, and hauled up a great number. Till then I had stuck to my resolution to eat nothing that had had life; and on this occasion I considered . . . the taking every fish as a kind of unprovoked murder, since none of them had or ever could do us any injury that might justify this massacre. All this seemed very reasonable. But I had formerly been a great lover of fish, and when this came hot out of the frying pan, it smelled admirably well. I balanced some time between principle and inclination, till I recollected that when the fish were opened, I saw smaller fish taken out of their stomachs. "Then," thought I, "if you eat one another, I don't see why we mayn't eat you." So I dined upon cod very heartily and have since continued to eat as other people, returning only now and then occasionally to a vegetable diet. So convenient a thing it is to be a *reasonable creature*, since it enables one to find or make a reason for everything one has a mind to do.

Franklin gives us, then, the picture of a relatively innocent, unsophisticated, sometimes foolish young man who confounds or at least survives more sophisticated rivals. Consistently, the young man starts at the level of testing, and he often stumbles onto an important truth. We see his folly and his discoveries through the ironically humorous detachment of a candid old man, whose criticism of the young character's rivals is tempered by the same kind of affectionate tolerance that allows him to see the humor of his own mistakes. The wise old writer expects people to act selfishly, but retains his affection for them. He leads us always to consider major questions in terms of simple practical experience, as when he tells us that he soon gave up converting people to belief in Deism because the result seemed often to be that they thus became less virtuous than before. Deism, he said, might be true, but it did not seem to be very useful. Because he assumed that at best people will usually act according to their conception of their own true interest, because all his experience seemed to confirm this hypothesis, and because metaphysical reasoning often turned out to be erroneous, he concentrated on demonstrating the usefulness of virtue.

It is right here, just at the heart of his most impressive achievement as an autobiographer, that Franklin seems to have made his one great error in communication. Many people, first of all, simply misunderstand him; he did not take sufficient account of the carelessness of readers. Many are completely taken in by the deceptive picture. So effective has Franklin been in demonstrating the usefulness of virtue through repeated anecdotes from his own educational experience, so insistent on effectiveness as a test of what is good in his own life, that many readers simply believe he has no other basis for deciding what is good. They simply conclude that the man who would say, "Honesty is the best *policy*" will be *dis*honest if ever dishonesty becomes the best policy. Readers wonder what the man who tells them candidly that he profited by *appearing* to be humble hopes to gain by *appearing* to be candid.

If I were to follow Franklin and judge chiefly by the results, I would give up trying to clarify the misunderstanding, for I am sure that many readers will refuse to follow me beyond this point. Yet it seems to me important to understand Franklin's intention as clearly as possible, if only to measure properly the degree of his miscalculation or his inadequacy. Let us examine one other brief passage from the *Autobiography*, a statement describing Franklin's own effort to propagate a new set of religious beliefs, to establish a new sect which he proposed, characteristically, to call The Society of the Free and Easy. "In this piece [a book to be called *The Art of Virtue*] it was my design to explain and enforce this doctrine: That vicious actions are not hurtful because they are forbidden, but forbidden because they are hurtful, *the nature of man alone considered*; that it was therefore everyone's interest to be virtuous who wished to be happy *even in this world*."

I have stressed the qualifying phrases in this statement in order to emphasize the nature of Franklin's faith: *the nature of man alone considered*; everyone who wished to be happy *even in this world*. This doctrine of enlightened self-interest represents an important reversal—almost an exact reversal—of a sentence written by a sixteenth-century English Puritan named William Perkins, who in propounding the absolute sovereignty of God had declared: "A thing is not first of all reasonable and just, and then afterwards willed by God; it is first of all willed by God, and thereupon becomes reasonable and just." Yet Franklin's reversal does *not* say that discovering what is apparently to our interest is the only way of *defining* virtue. He, every bit as much as the Calvinist, believes that virtues must be defined by some absolute standard. Vicious actions, he says, *are forbidden*—by the benevolent authority of a wise God and by the universal assent, as he understood it, of wise men throughout history. But some actions *are* inherently vicious, whether or not they seem profitable.

Franklin's faith, then, professes that a true understanding of one's interest even in this world will lead one to virtue. Since the obvious existence of viciousness and folly in every society demonstrates that men do not yet practice the virtues on which most philosophers *have* agreed, finding a way to increase the practice of virtue—the number of virtuous actions—is a sufficiently valuable task to need no elaborate justification. And so the same Franklin who in the year of his death refused to dogmatize on the question of Jesus Christ's divinity because he expected soon to "have an opportunity of knowing the truth with less trouble," contented himself with questions of moral practice. His faith told him that the best way to serve God was to do good to one's fellow men, and he reasoned that just as all wise men preferred benevolent acts to flattery, so the infinitely wise God would not care very much to be flattered, but would prefer to have men *act* benevolently. He denied, however, that any man could ever *deserve* a heavenly, infinite reward for finite actions. He knew perfectly well the implications of his faith, but he saw no reason to worry very much about whether it was absolutely correct. For all his experience indicated that whether or not virtue and interest do coincide, no other argument but that of self-interest will persuade men to act virtuously, and even that argument will not always persuade them.

It is in this context that we must read Franklin's account of the thirteen-week course he gave himself in the Art of Virtue. D. H. Lawrence and other critics have overlooked the humorous self-criticism with which Franklin introduces the account. "It was about this time," Franklin says, "that I conceived the bold and arduous project of arriving at moral perfection. As I knew, or thought I knew, what was right and wrong, I did not see why I might not *always* do the one and avoid the other. But I soon found I had undertaken a task of more difficulty than I had imagined. While my attention was taken up and care employed against one fault, I was often surprized by another." Franklin, you will remember, listed the chief instrumental virtues under thirteen headings and at first devoted a week to concentrating especially on the habit of practicing one of the thirteen virtues. He made himself a chart, and in the daily period that he allotted to meditating the question "What good have I done today?" he entered a black mark for each action that could be considered a violation of the precepts. He worked to achieve a clear page. At thirteen weeks for each completed "course," he was able, he says, to go through four courses in a year. As he was surprised, at first, to find himself so full of faults, so he was pleased to find that he was able to decrease the number of his faulty actions. He endeavors to persuade us by pointing out that this improvement of conduct made him happier and helped him to prosper. But he makes perfectly clear the relative nature of his progress. He compares his method of attacking one problem at a time to weeding a garden, a task that is never really completed. He tells us not only that he later advanced to taking one course each year (with four weeks for each virtue), but also that he bought a book with ivory pages, so that he could erase the black marks at the end of one term and begin the course anew. The task was endless. Wondering about D. H. Lawrence's reading of Franklin, we may echo his own uncomprehending words: the perfectibility of man, indeed!

In trying to clarify Franklin's beliefs, I have not meant to absolve him of all responsibility for the widespread misunderstanding of his work. As I have already suggested, he invites difficulty by deliberately appearing to be more simple than he is, by choosing the role of the inquisitive, experimental freeman. By daring to reduce metaphysical questions to the terms of practical experience, he sometimes seems to dismiss them entirely, and he draws our attention away from the books that he has read. Thus, although he alludes to the most influential philosophical and psychological treatises of his age, and although he certainly read widely in every kind of learning that attracted his remarkably curious mind, he does not give this theoretical groundwork any important place in the narrative of his life. He mentions that he read John Locke at a certain point, and the Earl of Shaftesbury, and he says that this sort of education is extremely valuable. But in the narrative itself he is plain Benjamin Franklin, asking questions prompted by the situation. Even as he recounts, much later in the book, his successful correspondence with some of the leading scientists of England and the Continent, he underemphasizes his learning and portrays himself as a fortunate and plain, if skillful and talented, amateur.

This effect is reinforced by another quality of Franklin's literary skill, the device of humorous understatement. I have already cited one or two examples, as in his statement about answering the question of the divinity of Jesus. Similarly, he refers to the discovery that an effective preacher was plagiarizing famous English sermons as "an unlucky occurrence," and he says that he preferred good sermons by others to bad ones of the minister's own manufacture. He repeatedly notices ridiculous incongruity by putting an apt word in a startlingly subordinate place and thus shocking us into a fresh, irreverent look at a subject that we may well have regarded in a conventional way. So he says that for some time he had been regularly absent from Presbyterian church services, "Sunday being my studying day"; and he remarks that enormous multitudes of people admired and respected the revivalist George Whitefield, "notwithstanding his common abuse of them by assuring them they were naturally 'half beasts and half devils.'" This is the method that Henry Thoreau later used in *Walden* when he declared that the new railroads and highways, which were then called internal improvements, were all external and superficial; it is the method Samuel Clemens employed through his narrator Huckleberry Finn, who says that at mealtime the widow Douglas began by lowering her head and grumbling over the victuals, "though there warn't really anything the matter with them." The device is often delightfully effective in negative argument, in revealing ludicrous inconsistency. But because it depends on an appeal to simple self-reliance, and often to a hard-headed practicality, it is not conducive to the exposition of positive, complex theory. The particular form of Franklin's wit, his decision to portray himself as an inquisitive empiricist, the very success of his effort to exemplify moral values in accounts of practical experience, his doctrine of enlightened self-interest, and the fine simplicity of his exposition—all these combine to make him seem philosophically more naïve, and practically more materialistic, than he is.

Yet this is a great book, and despite the limitations implicit in his pedagogical method, the breadth and richness of Franklin's character do come through to the reasonably careful reader. One chief means, of course, is the urbane yet warm tone of the wise old narrator, who begins by conceding that one of his reasons for writing an autobiographical statement to his son is simply the desire of an old man to talk about himself. We should also notice that although his emotional life is clearly beyond the bounds of his narrative purpose, he expresses an unmistakable affection, even in retrospect, for his parents, his brother, and his wife. His judgment is nowhere firmer or more admirable than in his account of the self-satisfied young Benjamin's return to taunt brother James, his former master, with the signs of the Philadelphia journeyman's prosperity. His record of his wife's life-long usefulness to him is not in the least incompatible with genuine affection for her. And in one brief paragraph citing as an argument for smallpox vaccination the death of his own son, "a fine boy of four years old," he reveals that his serenity could be rippled by the memory of an old grief.

We must remember, finally, that Franklin was one of the most beloved men of his time. The first American who was called the father of his country, he had no reason to feel anxious about the quality of what our own public relations men would call his "image." He had retired at the age of 42 to devote the rest of his long life to public service and scientific study; he was known internationally as a faithful patriot who had for decades defended the popular cause in almost every political controversy; he had been a great success at the French court, and he was a member of the Royal Society in England. With these sides of his character known so well, he had no reason to expect that his instructive *Autobiography* would be taken as the complete record of his character, or of his range as a writer. The polished *Bagatelles* that he had written in France; the brilliant ironic essays that he had published in England during the years just before the Revolution; the state papers that he had written in all seriousness as an agent of the Congress—all these formed a part of his public character before he completed his work on the *Autobiography*. He could not foresee that, in a romantic age in which many writers believed capitalism and practical science were overwhelming the human spirit, a novelist like D. H. Lawrence would make him a symbol of acquisitive smugness; nor could he foresee that F. Scott Fitzgerald, lamenting in *The Great Gatsby* the betrayal of the great American dream, would couple Ben Franklin's kind of daily schedule with a Hopalong Cassidy book, and would imply that in the 1920's anyone who followed Franklin's advice would have to be a stock-waterer or a bootlegger.

What Franklin represented in his day, and what we should see in his greatest book, was something much more complex than this stereotype. He was deceptively simple, to be sure; but his life and his character testified to the promise of experience, the value of education, the possibility of uniting fruitful public service with simple self-reliance, the profitable conduct of a useful business enterprise, and the free pursuit of knowledge in both pure and practical science. His book remains an admirable work of art, and its author still speaks truth to us as an admirable representative of the Enlightenment.

MICHAEL WARNER

Franklin: The Representational Politics of the Man of Letters[†]

> He knew what he was about, the sharp little man.
> He set up the first dummy American.
> —D. H. *Lawrence*

Benjamin Franklin's career as a republican statesman centers on an inescapable difficulty: while the statesman's task is to embody legitimate power, the task of republicanism was to remove legitimacy from the hands of persons. In the new republican polity, as François Furet has remarked of the French context, "power would

---

† From Warner, *The Letters of the Republic: Publication and the Public Sphere in Eighteenth-Century America* (Cambridge, Mass.: Harvard UP, 1990), 74–96. Copyright © 1990 by the President and Fellows of Harvard College. Reprinted by permission of the publisher.

belong only to the people, that is, to nobody . . . The 'people' was
not a datum or a concept that reflected existing society. Rather, it
was the Revolution's claim to legitimacy, its very definition as it
were; for henceforth all power, all political endeavour revolved
around that founding principle, *which it was nonetheless impossible
to embody.*"[1] The republican statesman, therefore, is in some measure a contradiction in terms: he is the embodiment of that which,
by definition, cannot be embodied. How could such a contradiction
be mediated or disguised? In the case of Franklin the answer lies in
the involution of republicanism and print. To the extent that he
succeeded in appearing to embody representational legitimacy, he
did so by virtue of his career as a printer and man of letters.

In the epitaph he wrote for himself, Ben Franklin announces his
peculiar relation to print in a dramatic way:

> The Body of
> B. Franklin,
> Printer;
> Like the Cover of an old Book,
> Its Contents torn out,
> And stript of its Lettering and Gilding,
> Lies here, Food for Worms.
> But the Work shall not be wholly lost.
> For it will, as he believ'd, appear once more,
> In a new & more perfect Edition,
> Corrected and amended
> by the Author.[2]

This epitaph has a metaphoric excess that makes it difficult to
take literally. But that very excess *tempts* us to take it literally.
Franklin delivers the conceit with a bravura air that deflects attention from the ostensible subject (death and the hoped-for resurrection). He draws us instead into a fantasy of being-in-print. What
makes the trope compelling—too compelling—is that Franklin
wrote the epitaph not for a gravestone, but for a page. He composed
it at the age of twenty-two, continuing later in his life to produce
holographs of it which he left with hosts as mementos of his visits.[3]
In such circumstances the ostensible message of piety could only be
eclipsed in the pleasure of a fantasy about print, a fantasy that
Franklin trades from hand to hand as a mark of his wit. But the way

---

1. François Furet, *Interpreting the French Revolution* (Cambridge: Cambridge UP, 1981),
   48, 51; my emphasis.
2. Benjamin Franklin, "Epitaph," in Leonard W. Labaree et al., eds., *The Papers of Benjamin Franklin* (New Haven: Yale UP, 1959–), 1.111. Further references to Franklin's
   works will refer to this edition, except where otherwise noted, and will be made parenthetically.
3. On the textual history of the epitaph, see Lyman H. Butterfield, "B. Franklin's Epitaph," *New Colophon* 3 (1950): 9–30.

the epitaph presents him as a text that lies here (on the page?) holds our attention even more than it would need to in order to exhibit his cleverness. The metaphor has a suggestive power that exceeds the familiar logocentric distinction between accidental substance (body, book) and plenary meaning (spirit, text).

The epitaph is disturbing because it treats print and life in equivalent terms: to live is to be published. At first glance the gesture of the epitaph defies the termination of death; on closer inspection, it poses a grave question about what it means to live. Such implications are all the more striking in a document composed in 1728—the year in which Franklin set up shop as a partner in a printing house—since the epitaph may be said to announce not his death, but his intentions for his career.[4] Embarking on a new enterprise in printing, he describes himself all too literally as a man of letters.

Nor is this an isolated moment in Franklin's career. We need only recall his now infamous habit, in the *Autobiography*, of referring to his mistakes as "errata." In a more extended way that habit repeats the identification between Franklin's life and his printed work. The entire project of the autobiography repeats and develops the central themes and assumptions of the epitaph. At the outset of the work, which had no clear generic precedent to serve as a rationale, Franklin returns to the themes of the epitaph to explain what he is doing.

> I should have no Objection to a Repetition of the same Life from its Beginning, only asking the Advantage Authors have in a second Edition to correct some Faults of the first. So would I if I might, besides corr^g the Faults, change some sinister Accidents & Events of it for others more favourable, but tho' this were deny'd, I should still accept the Offer. However, since such a Repetition is not to be expected, the Thing most like living one's Life over again, seems to be a *Recollection* of that Life; and to make that Recollection as durable as possible, the putting it down in Writing.[5]

These introductory remarks are written at an early stage of the manuscript, when Franklin shows no clear intention to publish the work, considering it instead a private record for his son. Yet even here he is already describing it as a "second Edition." And already

---

4. Dating of the epitaph rests only on Franklin's later recollection. We do not know exactly when it first appeared, but the description of himself as "B. Franklin, Printer" suggests that he must already have been contemplating the establishment of his own printing house, even if he had not yet brought it about. On the events of Franklin's career, the best single source is still Carl Van Doren, *Benjamin Franklin* (New York: Viking, 1938).

5. *Autobiography*, in the Franklin volume of the Library of America, ed. J. A. Leo Lemay (New York, 1987), 1307. Further references to the *Autobiography* will be to this edition and will be made parenthetically.

the autobiographical posture of self-objectification (life becomes book) has its meaning in the analogous self-objectification that is the posture of modernity. One's life can be repeated in the form of a book because life is already understood to have some of the features of books: authorial design, durability, corrigibility, and exposure before a public. Those features of Franklin's self-relation can be traced to the cultural assumptions of a certain print discourse. For that reason, although Franklin has been (at least since Weber's *Protestant Ethic and the Spirit of Capitalism*) the exemplary figure of modernity, his exemplary modern subjectivity can be read as a very special cultural articulation of printing.

Franklin's practice of regarding himself as "B. Franklin, Printer" partakes of the general revaluation of print that we have seen in eighteenth-century America. When Franklin was a child print was a negligible phenomenon, and most colonies had no press at all. That was soon to change, and his career corresponds in striking detail to the path of the press's expansion. In 1718, at the age of twelve, he was apprenticed to his printer brother James in Boston—just as the currency debates in that city were heating up. In that year and the following, he wrote two broadside ballads, now lost, which he hawked in the streets. (They sold "wonderfully," according to his later memory.) After printing the *Boston Gazette* for several months in 1719 and 1720, the Franklin shop began producing the *New-England Courant* in 1721. By this time the younger brother, now fifteen, was at the center of the print explosion in Boston.

More important is that Franklin quickly displayed an understanding of the character of that development. The *Courant* was aggressively republican and Whiggish, and soon ran into trouble. When, in the paper's first summer, James Franklin was imprisoned and forbidden to publish, the paper began to appear under Benjamin's name. The younger Franklin, whose Dogood papers had already begun to appear, used that serial persona to reprint, on the front page, the essay on the liberty of the press from Trenchard and Gordon's *Cato's Letters*.[6] He was already promoting the republican principles that would be the metadiscourse of a specialized subsystem in print.

Franklin moved to Philadelphia just in time to become involved, as a printer and writer, in a similar transformation of the political. His was the press that competed with Andrew Bradford's in the 1730s, and he wrote for Bradford's *American Weekly Mercury* in the 1720s until he established his *Pennsylvania Gazette* as its rival.

---

6. *Cato's Letters* No. 15 appeared in the *London Journal* on February 4, 1720, and was largely reprinted as Silence Dogood No. 8 in the *New-England Courant* for July 9, 1722. Selections from *Cato's Letters*, including the reprinted essay, have been published as *The English Libertarian Heritage*, ed. David Jacobson (Indianapolis: Bobbs-Merrill, 1965).

He also followed closely the events of the Zenger controversy in New York, having known William Bradford from the time of his arrival in Philadelphia, and being a friend and ally of Andrew Hamilton. When two pamphlets were published attacking the arguments put forward by Andrew Hamilton in the Zenger case, Franklin printed James Alexander's replies in the *Pennsylvania Gazette*. He developed an elaborate network of printers—such as the Timothys of South Carolina—whom he supported in one kind of partnership or another; he also branched into related trades, such as papermaking and typecasting. He was both printer for the Assembly and clerk of the Assembly before becoming an assemblyman himself, and no one understood better than he the connection between public discourse and representative polity.

But the importance of print in Franklin's career is more than a matter of his having been involved in the local struggles through which the politics of print changed. He may be said to have embodied the written subject, to have lived within the structures of career and personality in a way that was profoundly shaped by the printed discourse of the public sphere, articulating a career for the subject of that discourse.

Franklin was the first American to fashion a career entirely of letters. All previous figures whom we sometimes describe as men of letters—the Mathers, Cotton, Edwards, Taylor—achieved their prominence in oral settings, usually as preachers. Only with Franklin was this not the case, and the differences were so determining as to make him a man of letters in an entirely different and more profound sense.[7] His career placed him in exactly those situations in which it had become possible to adjudicate political struggles by appeals to a neutral and rational ground of public representation, where citizens were called on to exercise civic virtue by placing the common good over personal interest. The print ideology of the public sphere, as we have seen, valorized the general above the personal and construed the opposition between the two in the republican terms of virtue and interest. It is at this point that Franklin becomes an especially illustrative case, as his career best exhibits the paradoxical embodiment of print ideology in the personal. In an anonymous broadside poem of 1756, for example, Franklin is praised as a perfect republican citizen because he is "Void of all partial, or all private

---

7. The novelty of Franklin's career is acknowledged by the period's other great man of letters, David Hume, who wrote to Franklin: "America has sent us many good things, gold, silver, sugar, tobacco, indigo, etc.; but you are the first philosopher, and indeed the first great man of letters, for whom we are beholden to her"; quoted in Van Doren, *Benjamin Franklin*, 290. On this subject generally, see Lewis Simpson, "The Printer as Man of Letters: Franklin and the Symbolism of the Third Realm," in J. A. Leo Lemay, ed., *The Oldest Revolutionary: Essays on Benjamin Franklin* (Philadelphia: U of Pennsylvania P, 1976), 3–20.

ends."[8] His virtue is predicated on his absorption into generality. If it is difficult to see what allowance is being made for Franklin's person when he is praised in such terms (or, for that matter, in the terms of the epitaph), my argument here will be that his career is preeminently that of the republican man of letters, the citizen of print.[9]

We may assume that Franklin was relatively deliberate in articulating the career of the man of letters, since he often remarks on the political agency of print and frequently allegorizes the problem of the subject who writes.[1] The epitaph is one example; more dramatic is the preface to the 1740 edition of *Poor Richard's Almanack*. Richard there inserts a document purportedly authored by his competitor, Titan Leeds. The trick is that Leeds is alleged by Richard to be dead, and the document has been written by the dead Leeds through Richard's own hand:

> You will wonder perhaps, how this Paper comes written on your Table. You must know that no separate Spirits are under any Confinement till after the final Settlement of all Accounts. In the mean time we wander where we please, visit our old Friends, observe their Actions, enter sometimes into their Imaginations, and give them Hints waking or sleeping that may be of Advantage to them. Finding you asleep, I entred your left Nostril, ascended into your Brain, found out where the Ends of those Nerves were that move your right Hand and Fingers, by the Help of which I am now writing unknown to you; but when

---

8. "Musing near a Cool Spring," in *Papers* 7.73.
9. My general understanding of the career of the man of letters relies on Jerome Christensen, *Practicing Enlightenment: Hume's Career as Man of Letters* (Madison: U of Wisconsin P, 1986), though Franklin's case requires that more centrality be accorded to republicanism. See especially Christensen's discussions of the career and generality in chapters 1 and 5.
1. Franklin's remarks on writing and print typically employ a contrast with spoken oratory in order to emphasize the republican advantages of print. In the 1749 *Proposals Relating to the Education of Youth in Pennsylvania*, for example, he writes: "History will show the wonderful Effects of ORATORY, in governing, turning, and leading great Bodies of Mankind, Armies, Cities, Nations . . . Modern Political Oratory being chiefly performed by the Pen and Press, its Advantages over the Antient in some Respects are to be shown; as that its Effects are more extensive, more lasting, &c." (*Papers* 3.412–13). Similarly, in 1782 Franklin would write to Richard Price, urging him to follow Franklin's own practice of press agitation: "The ancient Roman and Greek orators could only speak to the number of citizens capable of being assembled within the reach of their voice. Their *writings* had little effect, because the bulk of the people could not read. Now by the press we can speak to nations; and good books and well written pamphlets have great and general influence. The facility, with which the same truths may be repeatedly enforced by placing them daily in different lights in *newspapers*, which are everywhere read, gives a great chance of establishing them"; Franklin to Richard Price, June 13, 1782; in Albert H. Smyth, ed., *The Writings of Benjamin Franklin*, 10 vols. (New York: Macmillan, 1906), 8.457. This contrast between the general politics of print and the localized person of the orator often appears with great animus, as in the 1735 *Poor Richard's Almanac*: "Here comes the Orator! with his Flood of Words, and his Drop of Reason" (2.9). See also 3.448–49, 4.104, 6.276. On Franklin's extraordinary covert press campaigns, see Verner Crane, *Benjamin Franklin's Letters to the Press, 1758–1775* (Chapel Hill: U of North Carolina P, 1950).

you open your Eyes, you will see that the Hand written is mine,
tho' wrote with yours.   (*Papers* 2.246)

This extraordinary fantasy of ghostwriting dramatizes a discrepancy
between persons and texts. As in the epitaph of twelve years earlier,
the writing subject is necessarily cut off from the body. There is
considerable emphasis on the separation of the two, since the writing subject is an incorporeal agent acting not only separate from the
body but also to violate it. In the epitaph the writing body is decom-
posed; in the preface it is entered through the nose and handled like
a puppet. This gap between the person who writes and the person
who lives is focused in the play on "hand": "the Hand written is
mine, tho' wrote with yours." The pun is one of Franklin's ways of
marking the difference between the man *of letters* (the Hand written) and the *man* of letters (Richard's fleshy, manipulated hand).[2]

The same difference is marked by Poor Richard himself since he
is the pseudonymous screen for B. Franklin, Printer. Some years
earlier, the real Titan Leeds had accused Richard of nonexistence;
in the preface to the 1736 almanac, Richard had been forced to
defend his writing hand:

> They say in short, *That there is no such a Man as I am*; and have
> spread this Notion so thoroughly in the Country, that I have
> been frequently told it to my Face by those that don't know me.
> This is not civil Treatment, to endeavour to deprive me of my
> very Being, and reduce me to a Non-entity in the Opinion of
> the publick . . . [But] if there were no such Man as I am, how is
> it possible I should appear publickly to hundreds of People, as I
> have done for several Years past, in print? I need not, indeed,
> have taken any Notice of so idle a Report, if it had not been for
> the sake of my Printer, to whom my Enemies are pleased to
> ascribe my Productions; and who it seems is as unwilling to
> father my Offspring, as I am to lose the Credit of it.   (2.136)

Richard is an anti-Quixote, an imaginary man of discourse vainly
taking himself for real. As such he is the perfect screen for the
Printer who is so unwilling to father his offspring, preferring to have
them stray onto the page unaffiliated.[3] The games Franklin typically

2. I am indebted here to Jonathan Goldberg's *Writing Matter*, a provocative study of the
   investitures of the hand and writing in an earlier period. In particular, my earlier use
   of the phrase "being-in-print" responds to his discussion of Heidegger's "being-in-the-
   hand," and its relation to Western understandings of technology. That discussion
   shows by contrast the extent to which Franklin's fantasy of writing without (or inviola-
   tion of) the hand endangers the constitutively human in the Western tradition.
3. The image of castration implied in Franklin's struggle not to father offspring
   will reappear below in the Dogood papers; it also bears a strong resemblance to Hume's
   depiction of himself as incapacitated or castrated, which, as Jerome Christensen has
   argued, is for Hume a powerfully enabling strategy in shaping a career in letters
   (Christensen, *Practicing Enlightenment*, chapters 1 and 2).

plays with his personae often take this form: a fantasmatic self-splitting or self-objectification that results in a concealed or absent agent behind a manipulated surface. What stake does B. Franklin, Printer, have in this fantasy?

Ben Franklin was not out of childhood before he was struggling with the issue of personhood and written discourse. He seems to have been quite self-conscious about living after the model of print. In what I take to be a crucial passage of the *Autobiography*, for example, he narrates his discovery that thought could conform to the manipulation of objects—a discovery that foreshadows the 1740 image of Titan Leeds's ghost manipulating the hand of Poor Richard. Franklin has just mentioned that "Prose Writing has been of great Use to me in the Course of my Life, and was a principal Means of my Advancement," when he begins the anecdote as a way of explaining how writing came to be so important to him. In the anecdote, he is engaged in argument by correspondence with his bookish friend Collins, when his father points out to him that "in elegance of Expression, in Method, and in Perspecuity," Franklin is being bested by Collins. At this point he comes across a volume of the *Spectator*.

> I thought the Writing excellent, & wish'd if possible to imitate it. With that View, I took some of the Papers, & making short Hints of the Sentiment in each Sentence, laid them by a few Days, and then without looking at the Book, try'd to compleat the Papers again, by expressing each hinted Sentiment at length & as fully as it had been express'd before, in any suitable Words that should come to hand.
>
> Then I compar'd my *Spectator* with the Original, discovered some of my Faults & corrected them . . . I also sometimes jumbled my Collections of Hints into Confusion, and after some Weeks, endeavour'd to reduce them into the best Order, before I began to form the full Sentences & compleat the Paper. This was to teach me Method in the Arrangement of Thoughts.
>
> [above, p. 20]

It is worth thinking carefully about this passage, because it portrays in some detail the often-remarked connection between texts—whether written or printed—and ways of thinking. Franklin claims to learn a certain rationality ("Method in the Arrangement of Thoughts") directly from handling textual artifacts. Being a type compositor and press worker by day as well as a writer at night, he has a keen sense of the duplicability of letters; here he sees that feature of letters as expressive of something in the nature of thought and discourse, marking a distinction between form and content. But what is most important about this passage, and holds the key to the significance of any link between print and rationality for Franklin, is that his picture of printed artifacts is structured from the beginning by an instrumental objectification. He does not just confront or see the texts; he handles them. And he handles them not for pleasure or for violence but in a strictly instrumental way. As a result, the link between texts and thoughts amounts to modeling the act of thinking after the manipulation of objects.

This kind of rationality, with its literal patterning of intellection after an instrumental relation to discourse, is quite different from the abstract thought for which New England was famous. By characterizing thinking itself as manipulation of thought, it postulates a manipulating self that does not coincide with thought, that is not even immanent in it. It assumes this absent agent in just the same way that print, so conceived, postulates a generative agent not immanent in it. Franklin's ideal of method in the arrangement of thoughts therefore reintroduces, on another level, the basic problem that he dramatizes through the persona of Poor Richard. In rational thought, who is thinking?

Franklin is famous for the sort of calculating rationality that he depicts here. And his rationality is often understood to make him representative of his historical moment. But how could something like rationality be contextualized? We can begin to answer that question by noting that although rationality, in the special sense exemplified here by Franklin, has an intersubjective dimension, it is primarily conceived as a private self-relation. That is why it seems difficult to contextualize: it is a feature of the individual and is usually assumed to be distinct from "context." But it is just this private, individual nature of Franklin's rationality that makes it relevant to a certain historical context.

Method in the arrangement of thoughts is something that Franklin teaches *himself*. There are two parallel self-splittings in that notion: the first divides the arranging and methodical agent from the subject who has thoughts; the second divides the teacher of method from the thinker who learns it. These splittings allow Franklin to have an internally privative relation to himself: neither way of describing his action or his thinking can comprise his "self." He can carry out actions of which he is both subject and object, and in which neither God nor anyone else participates. So his reason seems to be pure individuality. At the same time, it requires a thorough and normative self-division. And the latter is the key to its contextualization. Franklin's internal relation to self is fundamentally negative and critical. By adopting such a paradoxically privative posture (who is thinking?), he could fit himself to the negativity of public discourse.[4]

4. The relation of reason to the self is a common theme in Franklin criticism. See, for example, Robert F. Sayre, *The Examined Self* (Princeton: Princeton UP, 1964). The best study of the subject, however, is Mitchell Robert Breitweiser's *Cotton Mather and Benjamin Franklin* (Cambridge: Cambridge UP, 1984). I entirely endorse Breitweiser's

His internalized, private understanding of rationality implies a set of properly social and public norms.

The remainder of the passage in the *Autobiography* clarifies what I mean. Franklin goes on to tell us that his rationalizing experiments with letters led him to the resolution of

> never using when I advance anything that may possibly be disputed, the Words, *Certainly, undoubtedly,* or any others that give the Air of Positiveness to an Opinion; but rather say, *I conceive,* or *I apprehend* a Thing to be so or so, *It appears to me,* or *I should think it so or so for such & such Reasons,* or *I imagine* it to be so, or *it is so* if *I am not mistaken.*—This Habit I believe has been of great Advantage to me, when I have had occasion to inculcate my Opinions & persuade Men into Measures that I have been from time to time engaged in promoting.—And as the chief Ends of Conversation are to *inform,* or to be *informed,* to *please* or to *persuade,* I wish well meaning sensible Men would not lessen their Power of doing Good by a Positive assuming Manner that seldom fails to disgust, tends to create Opposition, and to defeat every one of those Purposes for which Speech was given to us, to wit, giving or receiving Information, or Pleasure. [above, p. 22]

In this famous passage Franklin seems only to be recommending a rhetorical tactic. If you want to persuade, couch your language in modest and uncertain tones. But second thought discloses that the rhetorical tactic—or rather, the idea here presented of discourse *as* tactical—extends the object manipulation of literal intellection as a principle of social discourse. Just as the young Franklin arranged paper and type, and just as the good writer arranges words and expressions, and just as the rational thinker arranges thought, so also rational man arranges discourse.

The notion has a certain ambiguity. Franklin, like the "P.P." quoted in Chapter 2, repudiates *personal* authority in favor of a general authority based in a negative relation to one's own person. And that can be taken as a strongly universalizing claim to truth. At the same time, it is an inherently rhetorical principle; indeed, Franklin presents it as a theory of rhetoric. He claims that the rhetorical self-objectification he describes is eminently rational. But it is more than

---

emphasis on what he calls the "abstract blankness" of Franklin's character, which results in "a corollary reduction of the world to calculability" (258). Or rather, the relation between blankness and rationality must work both ways; as Breitweiser elsewhere says. Franklin's construction of reason is such that "behind the masks is the universal capacity to take on masks" (233). The main point of difference between this book and Breitweiser's lies not in any detail of interpretation, but in the general source of interest. Where Breitweiser regards the self as a subject in its own right, traceable from Mather directly to Franklin, I am trying to direct attention to the social practices and political structures of which self and reason are only related manifestations.

that. Rhetoric ceases to be duplicitous masking in Franklin's rationality because the negative self-relation of the instrumental rhetori-
cian just *is* the structure of rationality. Rhetoric is rational because
rationality is rhetorical.

It is not accidental that the particular tactic Franklin recommends
as the example of rationality in discourse is the gesture of self-
negation. "I conceive or apprehend a thing to be so or so"; "it appears
to me," or "I should think it so or so, for such and such reasons"; or "I
imagine it to be so"; or "it is so, if I am not mistaken"—these phrases
foreground the self only to eliminate it from discourse; thought has
validity not *because* it is vouched for by a self, but *despite* any relation
it might have to a self. The self from the beginning appears in its fal-
libility, its negligibility, its evanescence. Any form of "Positive" assertion disgusts. It is as though the personal is, for literal intellection
and rational society, a necessary postulation, nothing more.

I am not just willfully reading this problem out of the *Autobiography*; in his 1726 journal Franklin wrote,

> Man is a sociable being, and it is for aught I know one of the
> worst of punishments to be excluded from society . . . I have
> heard of a gentleman who underwent seven years close confine-
> ment, in the Bastile at Paris. He was a man of sense, he was a
> thinking man; but being deprived of all conversation, to what
> purpose should he think? for he was denied even the instru-
> ments of expressing his thoughts in writing . . . He was forced at
> last to have recourse to this invention: he daily scattered pieces
> of paper about the floor of his little room, and then employed
> himself in picking them up and sticking them in rows and fig-
> ures on the arm of his elbow-chair; and he used to tell his
> friends, after his release, that he verily believed if he had not
> taken this method he should have lost his senses.   (1.85–86)

The passage demonstrates that thought is unimaginable for Franklin without exchange or objects, that the personal is an insufficient
context for thinking. The mere asking of the question, "to what
purpose should he think?" implies an inseparability between thought
and instrumental reason. Remarkably, the narrative satisfactorily
substitutes for the act of thinking, as an example of the rational, the
act of sticking pieces of paper onto a chair. The substitution pre-
sumes an analogy, and the common thread is that both reasoning
and pinning scraps of paper are seen to conform to the same model
of objectification. Thus, where one would expect to find the self,
Franklin anticipates madness, and where one would expect to find
nothing personal at all, Franklin finds reason.

The thinness of the personal might seem to be a problem for the
civic vision of rationality. Since the virtuous citizen is one who

surveys society from a detached perspective, detecting corruption, as one Philadelphia paper put it, in its "obscure Lurking Holes," he stands for the authority of the social. But how can he assert the efficacy of virtue without being endowed also with the authority of utterance?[5] In the extreme of republican print ideology, this is a nonquestion. Social authority, like truth, holds validity not in persons, but despite them; it is located not in the virtuous citizen nor in God nor in the king, but in the light of day, in the supervision of publicity itself. Thus print—not speech—is the ideal and idealized guardian of civic liberty, as print discourse exposes corruption in its lurking holes but does so without occupying a lurking hole of its own. It represents a public vision from a nonparticular perspective, as though the whole system of object-exchange could see.

Franklin's earliest extant publications, the Dogood papers, attempt to enact the translation of print rationality into civic virtue. Written during the height of the factional conflict in Boston, they present themselves as conspicuously written (each one begins: "To the Author of the *New England Courant"*) and advertise themselves as public criticism and information. "I am naturally very jealous for the Rights and Liberties of my Country; and the least appearance of an Incroachment on those invaluable Priviledges, is apt to make my Blood boil exceedingly. I have likewise a natural Inclination to observe and reprove the Faults of others, at which I have an excellent Faculty. I speak this by Way of Warning to all such whose Offences shall come under my Cognizance, for I never intend to wrap my Talent in a Napkin" (1.13). Or again, "I have from my Youth been indefatigably studious to gain and treasure up in my Mind all useful and desireable Knowledge, especially such as tends to improve the Mind, and enlarge the Understanding: And as I have found it very beneficial to me, I am not without Hopes, that communicating my small Stock in this Manner, by Peace-meal to the Publick, may be at least in some Measure useful" (1.13). Mrs. Dogood, that is, will be publicly useful to the degree that she is rational. She validates the combination of her letters' writtenness and their claim to usefulness by appealing to the authoritative vision of print: "A true and natural Representation of any Enormity, is often the best Argument against it and Means of removing it, when the most severe Reprehensions alone, are found ineffectual" (1.39). The Dogood papers propose to be such true and natural representations of "the present reigning Vices of the Town" (1.21).

---

5. *The American Weekly Mercury*, April 25, 1734. Bradford, the printer, is drawing heavily on Trenchard and Gordon, and the ideas discussed here would have been a familiar way of relating republicanism and print for any reader of *Cato's Letters*.

In good republican form they oppose their own legible appeal to the corruption and dominating desire of arrogant men. "Among the many reigning Vices of the Town which may at any Time come under my Consideration and Reprehension, there is none which I am more inclin'd to expose than that of *Pride* . . . The proud Man aspires after Nothing less than an unlimited Superiority over his Fellow-Creatures. He has made himself a King in *Soliloquy*; fancies himself conquering the World; and the Inhabitants thereof consulting on proper Methods to acknowledge his Merit" (1.21). Mrs. Dogood's claim to have transcended pride (though she admits to having been proud before) is vouched for by her act of writing the letters, for they show her not to be "in Soliloquy." She incorporates into her text letters written to her as additional evidence that she is merged into the public discourse.

The subjects of the Dogood papers demonstrate the concatenation of ideas associated with print and civic virtue: liberty of the press (#8); the value of broad learning and the failure of restrictive and elitist institutions like Harvard to foster it (#4); the domination of women (#5); the pride of decorating the body in extravagant apparel (#6); the boundaries of reason in poetry (#7); religious hypocrisy as a mode of false power in social relations (#9); and so on. Because in each case they argue for the breadth of an undifferentiated social field against the restriction of the personal, the letters support in particular arguments their own claim to oppose true and natural representations against soliloquies. They are purely socializing texts. But what about their author, who has already admitted to having been proud as a girl, and who has moved from her country seat to Boston expressly for the purpose of airing her opinions? Would it not seem that the appearance of these letters *as* her opinions would vitiate their claim to be civic representations?

The fictional environment of the letters addresses these very questions. The letters are not of course by Mrs. Dogood at all, and the pretence that they are is the sixteen-year-old Ben Franklin's way of airing opinions without reference to himself. The fictionality of the Dogood papers validates their truth claims, but not because of any potency or value in fictionality per se. Mrs. Dogood's authorship is a ruse, the very transparency of which endorses neither authorship nor fictionality, but anonymity. These papers are those which, Franklin tells us in the *Autobiography*, he slipped under the door of his brother's printing shop at night for fear that they would be dismissed if his brother knew the author's identity. His fear that the contamination of the personal would occult the letters' value as civic representations takes remedy in the persona of the papers, but it also repeats itself thematically in the announcement of that persona. Following the model of *The Spectator*—which, as we saw in the previous chapter, had already been imitated by his brother—Franklin writes at the beginning of the first letter, "since it is observed, that the Generality of People, now a days, are unwilling either to commend or dispraise what they read, until they are in some measure informed who or what the Author of it is, whether he be *poor* or *rich, old* or *young*, a *Schollar* or a *Leather Apron Man*, &c. and give their Opinion of the Performance, according to the Knowledge which they have of the Author's Circumstances, it may not be amiss to begin with a short Account of my past Life and present Condition, that the Reader may not be at a Loss to judge whether or no my Lucubrations are worth his reading." Puritans would have found good reason to be unwilling to commend or dispraise an utterance without knowing something about the person making the utterance, since faith and status governed truth and value. Franklin invokes the still common assumption that the personal was the necessary guarantee of any statement only to defy that assumption with the screen of Mrs. Dogood's persona.

Mrs. Dogood's persona thematically repeats the same abnegation of the personal. Her "having no Relation on Earth" figures her literariness and the generality of her social function. This is especially true since she tells us that in lieu of relatives she has spent most of her youth "with the best of Company, *Books*." For Mrs. Dogood, then, the written quite literally constitutes the social. In the context of her writing's claims to police the social without the corruption of character, her name, Silence Dogood, takes on added importance as signifying not just a Puritan humility but a generality of person. It was thus supremely fitting—in relation both to the ostensible subjects of the Dogood papers and to the conditions of their production—that when Franklin ceased to supply them his brother entered the following advertisement in the newspaper: "If any Person or Persons will give a true Account of Mrs. Silence Dogood, whether Dead or alive, Married or unmarried, in Town or Countrey, that so, (if living) she may be spoke with, or Letters convey'd to her, they shall have Thanks for their Pains" (1.45).

Silence Dogood's silence, her final disappearance, makes narratively concrete what had been a condition of her virtue, as does her anonymous invisibility in her account of a moonlight walk through the streets of Boston:

> Here I found various Company to observe, and various Discourse to attend to. I met indeed with the common Fate of *Listeners*, (who *hear no good of themselves*,) but from a Consciousness of my Innocence, receiv'd it with a Satisfaction beyond what the Love of Flattery and the Daubings of a Parasite could produce. The Company who rally'd me were about Twenty in Number, of

both Sexes; and tho' the *Confusion of Tongues* (like that of Babel) which always happens among so many impetuous Talkers, render'd their Discourse not so intelligible as I could wish, I learnt thus much, That one of the Females pretended to know me, from Discourse she had heard at a certain House before the Publication of one of my Letters; adding, *That I was a Person of an ill Character, and kept a criminal Correspondence with a Gentleman who assisted me in Writing.* One of the Gallants clear'd me of this random Charge, by saying, *That tho' I wrote in the Character of a Woman, he knew me to be a Man; But,* continu'd he, *he has more need of endeavouring a Reformation in himself, than spending his Wit in satyrizing others.*   (1.41–42)

Roaming incognito through the town, observing "various Company," attending to "various Discourse," Silence narrativizes and personifies the civic vision of print, even as her narrative and her persona present themselves as part of that vision. Her ability to see without being seen is that of the republican reader, while at the same time she exemplifies the republican stoicism of publicness in the regime of supervision. Though assaulted by libels, she regards them with a "Satisfaction beyond what the Love of Flattery and the Daubings of a Parasite could produce." It is, therefore, appropriate that opposed to her printlike silent anonymity should be the gossip about her person, the "Confusion of Tongues" generated by "impetuous Talkers." The talkers surveyed by her text wish to locate her in their speech. The first who claims to know her has "heard," or claims to have heard, some "Discourse" about Silence "before the Publication of one of my Letters."

The woman's desire to corporealize Silence, to identify her, is so aggressive as to take the form of a sexual fantasy. Silence, she has heard, was "a Person of an ill Character, and kept a criminal Correspondence with a Gentleman who assisted [her] in Writing." Silence's reputation for criminal correspondence is an extraordinary detail; it depicts an obsessional need in the oral setting to posit a body for writing. The woman posits, moreover, not just any body for writing, but a corrupt body, as though writing were necessarily a degeneration. The identification of writing with illicit liaison also appears in the puns on "ill Character" and "criminal Correspondence," which, immediately preceding the phrase, "a Gentleman who assisted me in Writing," cumulatively suggest that the latter may itself be sexual slang on the order of "criminal Correspondence." Of course the joke is on the gossiper; since Silence has already noted that the gossip is taking place in mixed company, and since the subject of the letter as a whole is patterns of courtship, we are meant to see the woman's "random Charge" as a sexual maneuver exposed in the light of Silence's writing.

A gallant then remarks that he knows Silence to be a man writing "in the Character of a Woman." His comment, by reversing the genders, dismisses the sexual scenario—or, rather, confuses it in such a way as to convert that vivid erotics of correspondence into a muted suggestion of the autoerotic, the man writing in the character of the woman. That suggestion is further hinted at by the language in which she continues: "But he has more need of endeavouring a Reformation in himself, than spending his Wit in satyrizing others." In this case, however, a further complication arises in our knowledge that Silence is neither man nor woman, but a sixteen-year-old boy. Through an elaborate and witty scenario, Franklin suggests that to "satyrize" others and to satyrize himself can be consonant because, despite the care with which he has larded the passage with sexual innuendo, neither act has a corporal object. The sexual references are there because for Franklin writing is reproductive; they are confused into a bodiless autoeroticism because the reproduction of writing is general and continues without the corruptive body it associates with the oral. In one respect Franklin inhabits a major contradiction in print discourse. He has access to its voice only on the basis of a gendered body, with its *virtue* and its privilege of freehold, but as citizen-in-print he must negate even the particularity of gender that his citizenship requires. In another sense this is but the earliest version of what we have already witnessed in the 1736 preface to *Poor Richard's Almanac:* Franklin the printer, "unwilling to father [his] Offspring," diffuses his person in print behind the screen of another.

The most important point about the passage is that Franklin envisions writing as the scene of pure socialization, and even of a social erotic, paradoxically because it is freed from the localization of the personal, the bodily, the corruptible. It is not that he envisions the elimination of self, and least of all does he envision self-denial.[6] In one *Busy-body* essay he speaks strongly of "innate Worth and unshaken Integrity." But what he proposes is that innate worth and integrity be seen as such only when they are seen as reproducible. The paradox is that the personal is founded on and valued within the pure reproduction of the social, not, as is usually assumed, the other way around.

Equally illustrative of this paradox is the frame narrative of Franklin's best-known piece, "The Way to Wealth." Far from being the simple catalogue of capitalist maxims it is often taken for, the essay is a complicated ventriloquist act, projecting its aphorisms into

---

6. See, for example, "Self-Denial Not the Essence of Virtue" (1735), in which Franklin argues that "Self-denial is neither good nor bad, but as 'tis apply'd"—an argument that exhibits Franklin's habit of subdividing the self out of existence. The self that not only denies itself but further applies that denial is scarcely recognizable *as* a self.

repetitive screens of fictitious personae. They appear first as Poor Richard's. But the beginning of the essay offers one of Franklin's usual jokes about Richard's fictitiousness.

> I have heard that nothing gives an Author so great Pleasure, as to find his Works respectfully quoted by other learned Authors. This Pleasure I have seldom enjoyed; for tho' I have been, if I may say it without Vanity, an *eminent Author* of Almanacks annually now a full Quarter of a Century, my Brother Authors in the same Way, for what Reason I know not, have ever been very sparing in their Applauses; and no other Author has taken the least Notice of me, so that did not my Writings produce me some solid *Pudding*, the great Deficiency of *Praise* would have quite discouraged me.
>
> I concluded at length, that the People were the best Judges of my Merit; for they buy my Works; and besides, in my Rambles, where I am not personally known, I have frequently heard one or other of my Adages repeated, with, *as Poor Richard says*, at the End on't; this gave me some Satisfaction, as it showed not only that my Instructions were regarded, but discovered likewise some Respect for my Authority; and I own, that to encourage the Practice of remembering and repeating those wise Sentences, I have sometimes *quoted myself* with great Gravity.

Richard then narrates having overheard his maxims being delivered by the equally fictitious Father Abraham. The layered screens vividly detach the worth of the maxims from the "Authority" allegedly behind them. That kind of detached utterance can only be made by a rational subject, who internalizes its negativity. Richard's vain petulance about not being credited for his productions shows him not to be such a subject. But the internalized negativity of the rational author Franklin, the author unwilling to acknowledge his offspring—is parodically mirrored in the picture of Richard quoting himself. Richard's own productions return to him from another, even from "the People" in places where he is "not personally known." And in the same way, his words return to him from himself. Though his writing is in general circulation, he clings to the desire for acknowledgment as author. But the inverted quixotism of this desire is the counterpoint of the negativity being enacted by Franklin, here and at every point in his career, through the projection of his personae.

Franklin might seem to be mocking our notions of integrity. Yet I take him to be ironizing an *incomplete* rationality rather than the ideal of sincerity itself. He reconceives sincere worth and integrity as deriving from rational discourse. They are positive traits of character only insofar as they exhibit the *resources* of negativity. The point can be illustrated by the description of that man of worth and integrity in the *Busy-body*, who is introduced only as "Cato": "He appear'd in the plainest Country Garb; his Great Coat was coarse and looked old and thread-bare; his Linnen was homespun; his Beard perhaps of Seven Days Growth, his Shoes thick and heavy, and every Part of his Dress corresponding. Why was this Man receiv'd with such concurring Respect from every Person in the Room, even from those who had never known him or seen him before? It was not an exquisite Form of Person, or Grandeur of Dress that struck us with Admiration."[7] The answer will turn out to be virtue, here rendered visible by the very *disregard* that Cato has for his own person. And although Franklin was as fond of fine cloth as the next man, he too could adopt the Catonic costume when he needed to appear the man of virtue, especially in France.

Print ideology as formulated by Franklin and others, by incorporating the republican tradition of political thought, was to shape the course of American political behavior and American writing for the remainder of the century. But print ideology was also to shape lives and careers. It may be difficult to imagine how that could be. What would it mean, one might wonder, to live out the contradictory imperatives of self-repudiation and self-validation as Franklin describes them? Franklin explicitly imposed the structure of print rationality on his career from an early date, with regard both to rationality of character and to rationality of life progression. He wrote in his journal when he was twenty:

> Those who write of the art of poetry teach us that if we would write what may be worth the reading, we ought always, before we begin, to form a regular plan and design of our piece: otherwise, we shall be in danger of incongruity. I am apt to think it is the same as to life. I have never fixed a regular design in life; by which means it has been a confused variety of different scenes. I am now entering upon a new one: let me, therefore, make some resolutions, and form some scheme of action, that henceforth, I may live in all respects like a rational creature.[8]

Unfortunately the full plan is no longer extant. But we can see from this preamble that Franklin thought of his own life with the detachment with which one arranges objects, thus bringing career under the structure of rationality. Life, in his rationality, conforms exactly to the model of writing, even as Franklin writes the model of his life. The notorious perfection chart and self-examination scheme of the *Autobiography* are more than a printer's convenience; they represent a reconception of what it means to live—not just because Franklin did live in accordance with such rationalizing documents

---

7. *Busy-Body* No. 3, from the *American Weekly Mercury*, February 18, 1729, in *Writings*, 97.
8. "Plan of Conduct," in Franklin, *Papers* 1.99–100.

(as he says in the *Autobiography*, "I always carried my little Book with me" [84]), but because those documents for him exemplify reproducible generality: "tho' I never arrived at the Perfection I had been so ambitious of obtaining, but fell far short of it, yet I was by the Endeavour made a better and a happier Man than I otherwise should have been, if I had not attempted it; As those who aim at perfect Writing by imitating the engraved Copies, tho' they never reach the wish'd for Excellence of those Copies, their Hand is mended by the Endeavour, and is tolerable while it continues fair & legible" [86]. Franklin's famous ambition of perfection is formed on the model of print, on the submersion of the personal in a general reproduction.[9]

Life has become reified as the object of design; by comparison, the previously supposed immediacy of oral relations appears as "a confused variety of different scenes." But when one lives "in all respects like a rational creature," who is living? When one's life is thus objectified, must it not be a shadow screen for an "I" postulated behind it, designing? We seem to be in the presence of a crippling contradiction in the rational. But it is this very contradiction on which the rational founds itself, for by the paradoxical logic of literal intellection, though the "I" must be entirely occulted as the designing agent detached from any of the phenomena from which its existence is inferred, it is also seen as perfectly transparent, so that Franklin can speak of his plan as the condition necessary for "sincerity in every word and action—the most amiable excellence in a rational being." Not to be any particular man is not to be a "Partyman," and not to be a Partyman is to possess a character of integrity.

Franklin's career of public involvement was the articulation of what was implicit in his Plan of Conduct. For although that plan only announced the intention of designing his life the way one would design a piece of writing, in the social context of that announcement the analogy guaranteed for the career the same civic publicity that it allotted for writing; even private virtue was imagined in terms of civic visibility. It followed that the life most consistent with the model of writing would be the public life, but—and this is crucial—a public life uncontaminated by particular aspirations, party

9. It is because Franklin locates himself in generality that he is so difficult to locate. Hence Carl Becker's well-known remark in the *Dictionary of American Biography* that Franklin was never fully immersed in anything he did. (See the discussion of Becker's remark in Breitweiser, *Mather and Franklin*, 233, 258.) The same relation to self helps to account for Franklin's addiction to pseudonyms and fictional personae—exceptional even in his time. Crane counts forty-two different pseudonyms just in the period covered by his study. No one has counted the fictional personae, such as Alice Addertongue or the King of Prussia, but they abound. That perfection is associated with print for Franklin takes a less serious form in the 1738 *Poor Richard's Almanac,* where Bridget Saunders exclaims, "What a peasecods! cannot I have a little Fault or two, but all the Country must see it in print!" (2.191).

affiliations, dependencies on governments and ministers, influences of powerful men, and the like.

From the outside such rationality ironically bore a strong resemblance to the self-centered cunning of officeholders to which, as part of a print ideology, it was opposed. Franklin's political enemies make the point for us. They portrayed him as lecherous and greedy, but above all as "designing"; a common theme in anti-Franklin literature is the connection between his self-concealing designs and his manipulation of letters. A good example is a 1758 pamphlet allegorizing local politics in scriptural style. In the allegory Franklin is "Adonis the scribe": "And Adonis the scribe was a learned man, after the learning of the Jews; for he had read over the seven volums [sic] of the *Talmud,* containing the dreams and visions of those who hated truth; and from thence he learnt to say the things that *was not.*" Adonis, furthermore, is accused of imitating Jacobs, whom he loves as David loved Jonathan: "For *Adonis* the scribe took the dictionary of *Jacobs* the translator, and he interleaved it; and whatever he catched, in talking, or reading, or——sleeping, he popped it down, saying, Now are we as one, O my brother *Jacobs!* for my knowledge is as thy knowledge, and thy knowledge is as my knowledge."[1]

The pamphlet quite vividly depicts a Franklin whose real self is secret or void, concealed behind a screen of misleading texts. It can be seen as the flip side of the broadside quoted earlier, which praised Franklin for being "Void of all partial, or all private ends." Similarly, a 1764 broadside proclaimed:

> Yet tutor'd by the Flying Post
> The Gazettes, and the Post-Man,
> Each Fancies he can rule a host
> Or steer a Fleet with most Men.
> . . . . .
> Therefore the Prudent *Dutch* should Use
> All Female soft Perswasion,
> To draw F——n from raising News.
> To mind (his occupation)."[2]

---

1. *A Fragment of the Chronicles of Nathan Ben Saddi (Constantinople [Philadelphia],* 5707 [1758]). I have been unable to determine whom "Jacobs" designates in the Philadelphia scene; the available information on the pamphlet and its key seems to be limited to the notes in the Evans *Bibliography.* One would like to know, if for no other reason than the oddly homoerotic language of the satire against Franklin.

2. *An Answer to the Plot* (Philadelphia, 1764). The poem was a reply to a satire called *The* PLOT *by way of a* BURLESK, *To turn F——n out of the Assembly* (Philadelphia, 1764), and in at least some copies was printed on the verso of the latter. Both are election polemics in a year in which the election turned decisively on the interpretation of a printed text. Seeking to turn the German population against Franklin, his opponents uncovered an old publication in which he had referred to Germans as *"Palatine Boors."* They then publicized the remark among the German population. Franklin's allies leapt to his defense, in part by writing *The Plot,* which, addressing those who were using the

The broadside is typical of attacks on print ideology, as well as those on Franklin's person, for it fixes in two ways on Franklin's role as printer, publisher of the *Gazette*, and postmaster. First, it depicts Franklin's dissemination of print as part of a leveling tendency, and as effecting a false pretension on the part of the common people to belong to the realm of the public. Instead of being misled by the general nature of print, the broadside tells them, they should mind "their betters." Further, the broadside imposes a class stigma on Franklin's origin as a "leather-apron man," suggesting not only that print discourse encourages leveling but also that Franklin the printer (mere mechanic) manipulates that tendency in print in order to arrogate political power to himself.[3] "Post" and "Post-Man" share alike in the perversion of the public.

The strongest and most famous denunciation of Franklin came in 1774, in the so-called Cockpit confrontation with Alexander Wedderburn. Again, Franklin's manipulation of letters was the occasion. He had obtained by secret means some incriminating letters written by Thomas Hutchinson, then governor of Massachusetts. He had then sent them from London, where he was acting as agent for the Massachusetts Assembly, back to a group of influential men in the colonies, that they might know what Hutchinson had been writing in private about colonial affairs. Though the letters for the most part stated only what Hutchinson had already written publicly, the effect of their circulation was highly inflammatory, and eventually they were published. The colonials thus spread written evidence that their governor had privately advised such things as "There must be an abridgement of what are called English liberties." The publication of the letters exacerbated colonial discontent to the point that the Assembly addressed a petition to the royal government to remove Hutchinson from the governorship.[4]

Ironically, Franklin was the Assembly's agent at that time, so it fell to his lot to present the petition. Between the time of the letters' circulation and the hearing before the Privy Council, however,

remark to attack Franklin, says: "Your *Wisdoms* have mistook a Letter. / *Boar* may be Hogs but *Boor* is Peasant . . . *Go* home ye *Dunces* learn to spell."

3. The latter was a common theme in the election of 1764, when Franklin led the move to end proprietary government in Pennsylvania by appealing for a royal charter. At least one pamphlet accused him of wanting to be royal governor himself: *To the Freeholders and Electors of . . . Philadelphia* (Philadelphia, 1764). At the same time another pamphlet accused him of leveling, of trying to destroy "Every *necessary Subordination*"; *What Is Sauce for a Goose Is Also Sauce for a Gander* (Philadelphia, 1764). The theme of Franklin's lower-class origins appears both in the latter and in William Smith's *An Answer to Franklin's Remarks on a Late Protest* (Philadelphia, 1764). For background on the election, its polemics, and the extremes of Franklin's reputation, see J. Philip Gleason, "A Scurrilous Colonial Election and Franklin's Reputation," *William and Mary Quarterly* 18 (1961): 68–84.

4. The Hutchinson correspondence can be found in the Franklin *Papers*, 20:539–80. A good account of the whole affair is Bernard Bailyn's *The Ordeal of Thomas Hutchinson* (Cambridge, Mass.: Harvard UP, 1974), esp. chapter 7.

two other parties to the affair—both ignorant of Franklin's hand in it—engaged in a near-fatal duel about the responsibility over revealing and publishing the private correspondence. Franklin was forced to admit his role in order to avoid another duel. He justified his disclosure of the letters by arguing that they were public correspondence about public matters. Naturally the admission made him the focus of the anger of the ministry, who were already agitated by colonial intransigence.

Enter Alexander Wedderburn. Wedderburn was already on the upward trajectory of a career that would make him Lord Chancellor and an earl, though not too long before he had been dismissed from the Scottish bar for insulting the Lord President in the courtroom.[5] His skills in this case were to take Franklin as their object. His defense of Hutchinson's position as governor centered upon the argument that Hutchinson had been the victim of Franklin's unscrupulous schemes to incite rebellion. And Franklin, Wedderburn suggested, schemed in this manner primarily in order to have *himself* made governor. Wedderburn addressed a crowded and highly anticipated hearing before Privy Council; the audience included Burke, Priestley, and the young Bentham among its common ranks. In that charged setting, he heaped such invective on Franklin's head as to make the "Cockpit" fully deserving of its name.

> I hope, my Lords, you will mark (and brand) the man, for the honour of this country, of Europe, and of mankind. Private correspondence has hitherto been held sacred, in times of the greatest party rage, not only in politics but religion. He has forfeited all the respect of societies and of men. Into what companies will he hereafter go with an unembarrassed face, or the honest intrepidity of virtue. Men will watch him with a jealous eye; they will hide their papers from him, and lock up their escritoires. He will henceforth esteem it a libel to be called *a man of letters; homo* trium *literarum!*   (21.48–49)

Wedderburn's scapegoating constructs an agonistic force for the authoritative oral setting. The florid periods of his self-consciously oratorical denunciation enact what they describe, simply by constituting an exemplary orality backed by law—an orality that both stands in opposition to and disciplines the vagrancy of the literal.

The wit with which Wedderburn substitutes "thief" (Latin *fur,* hence "homo trium literarum," man of three letters)[6] for "man of letters" hangs on a reversal of the relation of man to letter. Whereas the

5. Wedderburn's role is described in Ronald Clark, *Benjamin Franklin* (New York: Random House, 1983).
6. The joke is from Plautus, *Aulularia:* "Tun, trium litterarum homo me vituperas? fur" ["You running me down, you? You five letter man, you! You T-H-I-E-F!"]; Loeb ed., trans. Paul Nixon (London: Heinemann, 1928), 268.

man of letters finds his identity, or loses it, in letters, the man of three letters suffers the imposition of writing that is exterior to his person. It is consistent with the fact of his own authoritative speech and with its opposition to Franklin's literate transgression that Wedderburn conjures an image of bodily disfiguration: "I hope, my Lords, you will mark (and brand) the man." The brand restricts the written to the body, thereby furnishing the furtive manipulator of texts with a localized identity. Since identity in official orality is a disciplinary category, the body is specifically the body of the outcast.[7] By such logic Wedderburn portrays Franklin as being henceforward unfit for company because of the embarrassment of his face. And it is in the service of the same subordination of the written to the oral that he depicts private correspondence, hidden papers, locked escritoires.[8]

The faceless designing of Franklin's literal manipulation can appear only as a contradictory combination of impassivity and evil purposes or, in Wedderburn's words, "the coolest and most deliberate malevolence":

> [Here] is a man, who with the utmost insensibility of remorse, stands up and avows himself the author of all. I can compare it only to Zanga in Dr. Young's *Revenge*.
> "Know then 'twas—I:
> I forged the letter, I dispos'd the picture;
> I hated, I despised, and I destroy."
> I ask, my Lords, whether the revengeful temper attributed to the bloody African, is not surpassed by the coolness and apathy of the wily American?   (21.49–50)

"It was a year of fine harangues," wrote Horace Walpole at the memory of Wedderburn's speech.[9] What is telling about the harangue is that the terms in which Franklin was most vitriolically condemned—his apathy, his wile—were the exact inversion, in a paradigm of imperial orality, of the virtues imagined by Franklin for

7. Compare another remark of Wedderburn: "This property [correspondence] is as sacred and precious to Gentlemen of integrity, as their family plate or jewels are" (21.51). The examples of plate and jewels are telling because of their contiguity with the body. Wedderburn has to insist on a metonymy between letters and the body, a metonymy contained by the juridical force of property relations. Franklin, while denying the force of the metonymy, exploited it, for it is the *same* metonymic bond of letters to the body that had been parodically foregrounded in the 1728 epitaph, or the 1740 preface to Poor Richard.

8. At the same time, a Chancery suit brought against Franklin by Whately over the affair charges with a sneer that in disseminating the letters Franklin was merely "carrying on the Trade of a Printer" (21.432). This theme of the silent manipulator of letters became something of a tradition among Franklin's enemies. Thomas Hutchinson reports with horror seeing Franklin "staring with his spectacles" during an embarrassing speech in Parliament on behalf of the Ministry. "The relation of this speech," Hutchinson wails, "is on its way to America" (letter to Israel Williams, Sept. 29, 1774, quoted in Bailyn, *Ordeal*, 322).

9. A. Francis Steuart, ed., *The Last Journals of Horace Walpole* (London: Bodley Head, 1908), 1.333.

rationality in a paradigm of print. His use of the material circulation of print in the service of oppositional republicanism (the morning after the hearing he told Priestley that, given another chance, he would have done everything in the same way), though exemplary of civic virtue in the ideology of print, was for the authority of orality the most heinous of crimes.

But if Franklin was being abused before the assembled peerage of the British Empire for his coolness, apathy, deliberate plotting, and wile, he did nothing to deny the charge. The *Public Advertiser* reports on February 2, 1774, that "The Doctor seemed to receive the thunder of his [Wedderburn's] Eloquence with philosophic Tranquility and sovereign Contempt." According to one witness, Franklin "stood *conspicuously erect,* without the smallest movement of any part of his body. The muscles of his face had been previously composed, so as to afford a placid tranquil expression of countenance, and he did not suffer the slightest alteration of it to appear during the continuance of the speech in which he was so harshly and improperly treated.—In short, to quote the words which he employed concerning himself on another occasion, he kept his 'countenance as immovable as if his features had been made of *wood.*'"[1] Declining to take the stand, Franklin endured Wedderburn's hour-long harangue impassively. He thus turned the tables on Wedderburn, implicitly proposing the very detachment for which he was being castigated as an exemption from that castigation. Like Silence amid the impetuous talkers, Franklin maintained secrecy and inscrutability because, when the imperial oral setting yielded to the specialized subsystem of public printing, those same qualities would be transformed into the integrity of a public virtue. "On this occasion it suited the Purposes of the Ministry to have me abused," he wrote. "And having myself been long engaged in Publick Business, this Treatment is not new to me, I am almost as used to it as they are themselves, and perhaps can bear it better . . . [W]hat I feel on my own account is half lost in what I feel for the publick."[2] The incident greatly recuperated Franklin's colonial reputation, which had suffered in the mid-1760s, and did much to inflame revolutionary sentiment.

It was not a mere flourish, then, when one writer recorded the Cockpit affair as follows:

> Sarcastic Sawney, swol'n with spite and prate
> On silent Franklin poured his venal hate.

1. Edward Bancroft, quoted in William Temple Franklin, ed., *Memoirs of the Life and Writings of Benjamin Franklin* (London, 1818), 1.358n.
2. Franklin to Jan Ingenhousz, March 18, 1774 (21.148), and to Thomas Cushing, February 15, 1774 (21.93).

> The calm philosopher, without reply,
> Withdrew, and gave his country liberty.[3]

The ethic of silence and withdrawal is a salient feature of the lived form of rationality, a transformation of agon within the structures of print discourse; and silent Franklin's withdrawal is in a very strong sense equivalent with the conferral of liberty. And if it be objected that his image as this sort of "calm philosopher" is a calculated one, we should remember that it is precisely the nature both of liberty and of calm philosophy to be a calculated image.

The extent of Franklin's willingness to pursue this paradox is stunning enough in the Cockpit affair, but even more so in its coda. On February 16, 1774, eighteen days after the confrontation with Wedderburn, the following letter appeared in the pages of *The Public Advertiser*:

> The Admirers of Dr. Franklin in England are much shocked at Mr. Wedderburne's calling him a Thief; but perhaps they will be less surprised at this Circumstance when they are informed, that his greatest Admirers on the Continent agree in entertaining the same Idea of him. As an Evidence of this, I send you a Copy of a poetical Stanza, which is engraved under his Portrait prefixed to the late French Translation of his Work, in two Volumes, Quarto.
>
> I shall also send you an Attempt of a Translation of them, that the English Reader may be able to judge of the Similarity between the Idea of Mr. Wedderburne and that of the French Philosopher, with whom all the Philosophers in Europe intirely concur. It will even be seen that Foreigners represent him as much more impudent and audacious in his Thefts than the English Orator (though he was under no Restraint from a Regard to Truth) has ventured to insinuate. I am, Sir, Your humble Servant,
>
> HOMO TRIUM LITERARUM
>
>> Il a ravi le feu des cieux,
>> Il fait fleurir les arts en des climats sauvages.
>> L'Amerique le place a la tete des sages,
>> La Grece l'auroit mis au nombre de ses Dieux.
>
> IN ENGLISH.
>
>> To steal from Heaven its sacred Fire he taught,
>> The Arts to thrive in savage Climes he brought:
>> In the New World the first of Men esteem'd;
>> Among the Greeks a God he had been deem'd.

---

3. Anon., recorded in Horace Walpole, *Last Journals,* 2.77.

The letter is anonymous, but the audacious wit by which the theft of letters is revalued as promethean suggests Franklin as the author. If he wrote the letter, it would be his only direct response to Wedderburn. But who else could have taken up the signature "Homo trium literarum"? Franklin's appropriation of the epithet is itself a theft and therefore ironically proves the truth of the epithet. "Ironically," because the same theft also warrants his revaluation of the epithet, exemplifying his ability to locate himself in letters, free of strictures, anonymous and first of men at once. The letter of "Homo trium literarum" thus resembles the epitaph with which we began in this chapter, since it too indulges with remarkable literalness a fantasy of being-in-print. And the vaguely postmodern tone of Franklin's super-irony here may be attributed to the very rigor of his modernity, to his at times untempered pursuit of print negativity.

For the same reason, if the character of the man of three letters appears here in the form of a joke, we must remember that the stakes are high. Some four years after the Wedderburn affair, Joseph-Siffred Duplessis would paint his famous portrait of Franklin, the frame of which would bear the bold, simple legend "vir." It might seem that only a poor pun unites the three-letter man of Duplessis' portrait to the man of three letters named by Wedderburn, but the logic that would justify such a pun has been provided by Franklin himself. In Franklin's career the virtuous citizen of the republic (*vir*) attests to his virtue by constituting himself in the generality of letters; if the designation of manipulator (*fur*) is made appropriate, so is the exemplary and general status that makes possible the designation of "vir" rather than "Franklin." The poet who claimed that the calm philosopher's withdrawal bestowed liberty upon his country had disclosed the central truth of Franklin as man of letters: his career is designed at every level to exploit the homology between print discourse and representative polity. He cashes in like no one else on the resource of negativity. The logic of his career is the logic of representation.

Its closest analogue may be the fictive speaking voice of the written constitution, that bizarre invention in which Franklin took a hand. "We, the People," like B. Franklin, Printer, Richard Saunders, Silence Dogood, and the Homo Trium Literarum, speaks only in print, and for precisely that reason speaks with the full authority of representative legitimacy. It is with the Constitution, therefore, at the climax of Franklin's career, that his lifelong effort to locate himself in the generality of republican letters finds its embodiment. In his well-known speech to the convention, Franklin submerges his own voice to the motion for unanimous passage, authorizing as his own the voice of the document, as publication comes literally to constitute the public in yet another pseudonymous text.

PETER STALLYBRASS

Benjamin Franklin: Printed Corrections and Erasable Writing[†]

The most famous of Franklin's ethical inventions didn't work: namely, his table of virtues, of which he drew the only two diagrams in his autobiography [82, 85]. And if the ethical project failed, so at first did the technology that Franklin invented for carrying it out: a "little Book" in which to record his lapses. He tells us in great detail how he made this book:

> I allotted a Page for each of the Virtues. I rul'd each Page with red Ink, so as to have seven Columns, one for each Day of the Week, marking each Column with a Letter for the Day. I cross'd these Columns with thirteen red Lines, marking the Beginning of each Line with the first Letter of one of the Virtues, on which Line and in its proper Column I might mark by a little black Spot every Fault I found upon Examination, to have been committed respecting that Virtue upon that Day. [81][1]

But before Franklin could mark up a new week's faults, he first had to erase the faults that he had noted down the previous week, and the constant erasures destroyed the notebooks that he had made. Although he does not tell us what he was writing with, it must have been a black-lead pencil, because at least graphite was simpler to erase than ink.

That does not mean that it was simple. A version of the modern erasers that we now use was first proposed in the 1752 *Proceedings* of the French Academy. In 1770, Joseph Priestley named the gum from which erasers were made "rubber," precisely because it was used to rub out writing. Erasers are still called "rubbers" in England, to the amusement of my American students. No such erasers existed when Franklin was using his tables in the 1740s. The commonest method of erasing graphite at that time was by rubbing bread back and forth over the paper, a method still in widespread use in the twentieth century.

Such a method was advocated in 1661 in *Every Man's Companion*, which, according to the title page, combined various printed

[†] From Proceedings of the American Philosophical Society, Vol. 150, No. 4 (December 2006), 553–567. Read April 27, 2006, during the Annual General Meeting celebrating the Franklin Tercentenary. Reprinted by permission of the American Philosophical Society.

1. Page numbers with no other information refer to this Norton Critical Edition. I am particularly grateful to James N. Green for help and advice at every stage of my work on this paper. Like every other Franklin scholar, I owe a particular debt to the Herculean labors of Leo Lemay.

materials not only with "A Paper-Book" but also with an erasable "Table-Book."[2] In fact, where the table-book should have been, there appeared instead the following instructions: "Having a black-Lead-Pencil, write therewith upon the white Paper (as with Ink) what you please; and when you would take it off again, (as from a Table-Book) take a piece of new bread, and rub upon the writing, and it will take it clean off, so that you may write any thing there again. Perhaps to some this may seem idle and ridiculous: but it may easily be experimented, to satisfaction. Keep a Black-Lead-Pencil in your Book, and it will always be ready for *Memorandums*."[3] What is really idle and ridiculous is that *Every Man's Companion* did not have the promised erasable table-book. Neither did it contain a pencil, which you had to buy separately. The instructions for erasing graphite, though, would have been necessary for many people in the seventeenth century. Graphite was first mentioned and depicted in 1565, but it was not in common use for writing until the later seventeenth century, which explains why these instructions are so specific. Bread certainly works as an eraser but not particularly well.

Franklin, however, appears to have been using a knife to *scrape* off his earlier writing, and that would have destroyed the paper much faster than bread. Franklin writes, "To avoid the Trouble of renewing now and then my little Book, which by scraping out the Marks on the Paper of old Faults to make room for new Ones in a new Course, became full of Holes: I transferr'd my Tables and Precepts to the Ivory Leaves of a Memorandum Book, on which the Lines were drawn with red Ink that made a durable Stain, and on those Lines I mark'd my Faults with a black Lead Pencil, which Marks I could easily wipe out with a wet Sponge. . . . I always carried my little Book with me" (84).[4] Ivory had the crucial advantage of being erasable, unlike the paper that Franklin was using, which "became full of Holes" through constant "scraping." Writings in pencil on ivory could easily be wiped off with a sponge. But where would Franklin have got hold of an ivory memorandum book and what was it like?

2. One should note that neither "paper-book" nor "table-book" refers here to a book in our sense of the word. They mean the blank leaves of ordinary and erasable paper that were bound together with the printed *Companion*.

3. *Every Man's Companion, or, An Useful Pocket-book, Containing I. an everlasting almanack, II. the moons age for ever, III. high-water at London-Bridge, IV. a table of interest at 6 per cent, V. the high-ways of England and Wales, VI. the fairs of England and Wales, VII. a paper-book, VIII. a table book, IX. a letter-case, or a comb case, with other useful things* (London: Printed for Francis Cossinet, 1661), Wing E3552, Bodleian Library, Oxford, MS Lister 19. With MS notes by Martin Lister of his journey to Paris and Montpellier in 1663–66. I am indebted to Andrew Honey of the Bodleian's Conservation Workshop for a detailed analysis of the only surviving copy of *Every Man's Companion*.

4. William Temple Franklin inherited his grandfather's ivory notebook, but it has not survived. See Benjamin Franklin, *Memoirs of the Life and Writings of Benjamin Franklin* (London: Printed for Henry Colburn, British and Foreign Public Library, 1818), 1.72n.

Franklin would have had no problem in finding such ivory note-books, since he sold them at his own shop. On 1 June 1738, Frank-lin advertised that he had "just imported" a variety of books and stationery that included "Wax, Wafers, Dutch Quills, Ivory-Leav'd Memorandum Books." He repeatedly advertised such notebooks over the years, including, on 20 May 1742, "curious large Ivory Books, and common ditto."[5] The "common ditto" are particularly interest-ing, since they show that ivory notebooks were not exotic novelties but the kind of stationery that you would expect to find in a major city in colonial America. In fact, Franklin could have bought his own ivory memorandum-book from his major rival, Andrew Brad-ford, who was advertising "Tablet-Books [and] Books with Ivory Leaves" in 1734/35, three years before Franklin was advertising them himself.[6]

Ivory memorandum-books had been used since the Middle Ages; an early fourteenth-century example, made from elephants' tusks, contains three leaves to write on in addition to the elaborately carved and painted covers.[7] The clerk of Chaucer's summoner writes upon "[a] peyre of tables al of yvory" with a "poyntel" or stylus.[8] This tech-nology, relatively common in the Middle Ages, virtually disap-peared from the early sixteenth century until the later seventeenth century, when it was revived again. In "Verses wrote in a Lady's Ivory Table-Book," Jonathan Swift describes the lady's ivory leaves as being "[s]crawl'd o'er with Trifles." And he emphasizes that the tables are erasable. A rival can "blot . . . out" what a previous lover has written with the simple aid of "Spittle and a Clout" and then "[c]lap his own Nonsense in the place."[9]

But these new kinds of ivory notebook are significantly different from those used in the Middle Ages. First, they are usually much smaller, with very thin leaves. Second, they are nearly always made like fans, held together by a single pin. Thomas Jefferson's fan-shaped ivory memorandum-book still retains his writing. Jefferson used these notebooks daily for recording the temperature and tak-ing quick notes that he would later transfer into a more permanent

5. *Pennsylvania Gazette*, 1 June 1738, and 20 May 1742.
6. Titan Leeds, *The American Almanack for . . . 1735* (Philadelphia: Andrew Bradford, [1734]).
7. *Writing Tablet with Scenes of the Passion*, ca. 1300–20, French or German, elephant ivory, polychromy, and gold. The Jack and Belle Linsky Collection, Metro-politan Museum of Art, 1982.60.399.
8. Geoffrey Chaucer, "The Somnour's Tale," in *The Complete Works of Geoffrey Chaucer*, ed. Walter W. Skeat (Oxford: Clarendon Press, 1894–97), 4.373. The *OED* defines a "pointel" as "a small pointed instrument," "a writing or graving instrument; a stylus, a pencil."
9. Jonathan Swift, "Verses wrote in a Lady's Ivory Table-Book," in *Miscellanies in Prose and Verse* (London, 1711), 351.

notebook.[1] The more elegant kinds were put to practical use as, for instance, dance cards. Ivory notebooks were also sold as erasable diaries, like a nineteenth-century copy, which, when fanned out, reveals the days of the week stamped on the leaves, Sunday excluded. Presumably, one gets one day of rest from note-taking. Such erasable notebooks were also widely used by writers, including Jane Austen, whose ivory memorandum book can still be seen at her house in Chawton, Hampshire.[2]

If Franklin stressed the erasability of his ivory memorandum book, its portability was equally significant: "I always carried my little Book with me." In fact, Franklin carried this little book with him long after he had given up on his table of virtues. He first used his ivory memorandum-book in Philadelphia sometime in the early 1730s, but he still had it with him in Paris in 1784 when he sat down to write about it in his autobiography more than fifty years later.[3] Given how small these notebooks were, they could be carried everywhere in a pocket and used to jot down notes as necessary. In Great Expectations, Dickens describes the last meeting between Miss Havisham and Pip. The old lady, wanting to write a note to Pip, "looked about the blighted room for the means of writing." Not finding any, "she took from her pocket a yellow set of ivory tablets" and wrote upon them "with a pencil in a case of tarnished gold that hung from her neck."[4] In other words, Miss Havisham, like Franklin, carries the means of writing about her person: ivory tablets in her pocket; a graphite pencil in a case suspended from a chain around her neck.

Franklin's use of an ivory memorandum book was related to his wider interest in the making of erasable surfaces. On 26 June 1755, he sent to a friend in London some sheets of paper made of asbestos, one of the materials with which papermakers were experimenting to make new kinds of erasable paper.[5] Although erasable paper or parchment had been used by apprentices in the Middle Ages, it was being produced on a much larger scale in the sixteenth century,

1. The ivory memorandum book in which Thomas Jefferson recorded daily notes in pencil can still be seen at Monticello. For an image of Jefferson's ivory notebook, see http://www.loc.gov/exhibits/jefferson/images/vc65.jpg. And for a description of how he used them, see http://www.loc.gov/exhibits/jefferson/jefflife.html. I am indebted to Ellen Dunlap for this information. See also Charles M. Harris, "Jefferson's Memorandum Books: Accounts, with Legal Records and Miscellany, 1767–1826," *Technology and Culture* 40.3 (July 1999): 662–64.
2. I am indebted to Nan Ridenhalgh for this information.
3. Pierre Cabanis, *Oeuvres Posthumes* (Paris: Bossanges Frères and Firmin Didot, 1825), 232.
4. Charles Dickens, *Great Expectations* (London: Chapman and Hall, 1861), 3.156–57.
5. See George Simpson Eddy, ed., *Account Books Kept by Benjamin Franklin: Ledger "D" 1739–1747* (New York: Columbia UP, 1929), 19–20. See also J. A. Leo Lemay, *The Life of Benjamin Franklin*, vol. 2, *Printer and Publisher, 1730–1747* (Philadelphia: U of Pennsylvania P, 2005), 466.

when it was usually sold bound with a printed almanac, as in the 1661 *Every Man's Pocket Book.*[6] The earliest surviving copy that I have found of these "writing tables" or "table-books," as they were called in England, was made in Antwerp in 1527. The title page of the printed almanac calls attention to the novelty of the technology by describing it in detail: "¶Item you may write here with a stylus of gold, silver, tin, copper, or brass, and you may erase [what you have written] with a wet finger. ¶And when you have worn out [the erasable surface], so that you cannot write on it any more, you can get it repaired by Jan Severszoon, parchment maker, for a little money, and you can then write on it as if it was new. . . . ¶Item if you get grease on it by erasing with your finger, you should use a clay sponge [*cleyspongie*] with a little flour, and the grease will come off."[7]

By an extraordinary coincidence, a copy of these tables, bound by the same binder, is depicted by the Antwerp painter Jan Gossaert in *The Merchant*, one of the best-preserved paintings of the sixteenth century.[8] The Folger Shakespeare Library recently acquired a similar erasable notebook, made in Germany in the late sixteenth century, which also uses the stylus with which one writes as a closing device for the wallet binding.[9] It is writing tables like these that Hamlet refers to when, having seen his father's ghost, he says:

> Remember thee?
> You, from the Table of my Memory
> Ile wipe away all triuiall fond Records. . . .

Hamlet imagines his memory as an erasable table-book that can be wiped clean. This virtual notebook of the mind, though, requires the supplement of the actual notebook that Hamlet now produces:

6. See Peter Stallybrass, Roger Chartier, Frank Mowery, and Heather Wolfe, "Hamlet's Tables and the Technologies of Writing in Renaissance England," *Shakespeare Quarterly* 55.4 (Winter 2004): 379–419. See also Roger Chartier, *Inscrire et Effacer: Culture Écrite et Littérature (XIe–XVIIIe Siècle)* (Paris: Seuil/Gallimard, 2005).

7. "Calengier: ¶ Item men mach hier in scriuen met priemen ghemaect van gout, of van siluer, of van ten, of van koeper, of van laettoen, ende met eene[n] natten vingher machment wt doen. ¶ Ende wanneer soe veroudt is, dattet niet meer scriuen en wil, soe salt den seluen Jan Seuers soon parkementmaker om een cleyn ghelt vermaeken, dattet so wel scriuen saloft nieuwe waer. ¶ Met vinste te koop in die vermaerde coopstadt van Antwerpen, op di Lombaerde veste: By Jan Seuers soon int gros, in die huyse van Jan Gasten boecke bijnder. ¶ Item of den wtwisschers vingher vet waer, soe salmen neme[n] een cleyspongie met wat weyten bloems, en daer salt veter mede wt gaen. ¶ Int iaer ons Heeren. 1527." New York Public Library, Spencer Collection, Netherlands, 1527, 94–143.

8. Jan Gossaert, *Portrait of a Merchant*, Washington, D.C., National Gallery of Art. There is an early copy of this painting in the John G. Johnson Collection, Philadelphia Museum of Art. See Max J. Friedländer, *Jan Gossart and Bernart van Orley*, trans. Heinz Norden, vol. 8 of *Early Netherlandish Painting* (New York: Praeger, 1972), plates 57 and 56. See also John Oliver Hand and Martha Wolff, *Early Netherlandish Painting* (Washington: National Gallery of Art, 1986), 103–07.

9. *Writing Tables*, German, ca. 1580, Folger Shakespeare Library, V.a.480.

My Tables, my Tables; meet it is I set it downe
That one may smile, and smile and be a villaine. . . .[1]

Such tables were being mass-produced in London by the end of the sixteenth century. *Writing Tables* like those made by Robert Triplet in 1604 could be bought for a shilling.[2] The erasable surface of these notebooks is made from a simple mixture of glue and gesso, and you can write on it with soft metal, graphite, or ink.[3] All are equally erasable with a damp sponge or cloth. The directions for wiping one's tables clean are included on the December page of Triplet's almanac: "To make cleane your Tables, when they are written on. Take a litle peece of a Spunge, or a Linnen cloath, being cleane without any soyle: wet it in water, and wring it hard, & wipe that you haue written very lightly, and it will out, and within one quarter of an howre you may wryte in the same place againe: put not your leaues together, whilest they be very wet with wyping."[4]

Andrew Bradford was selling similar kinds of notebook in Philadelphia in the early eighteenth century under the name of "Tablet-Books"; by that time the erasable paper itself was usually called "asses' skin."[5] In 1774, Nicholas Brooks, a Philadelphia shopkeeper, was advertising "the improved patent asses skin for writing upon with gold, silver, common metal, or blacklead pencil, [which] may be rubbed of[f] at pleasure."[6]

---

1. William Shakespeare, *The Tragedie of Hamlet* in *Mr. William Shakespeares Comedies, Histories & Tragedies* (London: Isaac Jaggard and Ed. Blount, 1623), 1.5.95–108. Act, scene, and line numbers are keyed to *The Riverside Shakespeare*, ed. G. Blakemore Evans (Boston: Houghton Mifflin, 1974).
2. Robert Triplet, *Writing Tables* (London: Stationers' Company, 1604), Folger STC24284. For the price of such tables, see the Account Books of Richard Stonley, Folger MS V.a.460, f. 78v and Folger MS V.a.495, f. 10. See also Folger MS V.a.334, f. 23v.
3. For one of the more practical recipes, see Alessio Piemontese, *The Secretes of the Reuerende Maister Alexis of Piemont*, trans. W. Warde (London: Thomas Wight, 1595), f. 87v: "To make white tables to write in with the pointe of a wire, such as come out of Germanie. Take plaster called *Gypsum*, cribled or sifted, and steepe it and temper it with Hartes glue, or other, and giue your Parchement leafe one touche with it, and when it is drie, scrape it, that it may bee euen and bright, and couer it againe with the saied plaster called *Gypsum*, and scrape it as before: then take Ceruse, well braied and sifted, and steepe it with the oile of Line seede sodden: annointe your Tables with this mixtion, and let it drie in the shadowe, the space of fiue or sixe daies. This doen, take a cloute or Linnen clothe weate in water, wherewith you shall sticke and make smoothe the saied Tables, but the clothe must firste be wroong harde, and the water pressed out, then leaue it the space of fifteene or xx. daies, vntill it be through drie, then applie it to your vse." See also John Martin, "Several Receipts for the Use of Mankind, 1696" ("Watford, Herford shair, MDCLXXXXVI"), Folger MS V.b.258, f. 10v. Sarah G. Pringle of Cinch, Easthampton, Massachusetts, has perfectly re-created various forms of the erasable surfaces that one finds in Renaissance notebooks and, with Peter Geraty of Praxis Bindery, has also made a copy of the kind of erasable notebook that Rembrandt used for sketching.
4. Triplet, *Writing Tables*.
5. There is no entry for this in the *OED*, although "asses' skin" notebooks were commonly sold by eighteenth-century stationers in Britain and North America.
6. *Pennsylvania Gazette*, 5 January 1774.

Like asses' skin, Franklin's ivory memorandum book not only provided a practical alternative to paper but also suggested a new model
for moral reformation. The language of erasure, correction, and revision was indeed central to Franklin's thinking until the end of his
life. But Franklin reveals the important differences between models
of reformation drawn from the radically different technologies of
correction employed in printing and in manuscript. From antiquity,
the human mind has been imagined as a writing surface: for Plato, it
was like a wax tablet; for Hamlet, an erasable notebook; for Locke, a
tabula rasa; for Freud, a "mystic writing pad" (a form of Etch A
Sketch).[7] In contrast to the tradition that, from Plato to Derrida,
took *writing* as its model, Franklin analyzed himself primarily in
terms of *printing*. In his epitaph, which he wrote when he was only
twenty-eight, he imagines his possible resurrection as a printed book:

> The Body of
> B Franklin Printer,
> (Like the Cover of an old Book
> Its Contents torn out
> And stript of its Lettering & Gilding)
> Lies here, Food for Worms.
> But the Work shall not be lost;
> For it will, (as he believ'd) appear once more,
> In a new and more elegant Edition
> Revised and corrected,
> By the Author.[8]

In his autobiography, Franklin's work as compositor "for the second
Edition of Wollaston's Religion of Nature" (43) is immediately preceded by his desire for a second edition of his own life. In a second
edition, he could correct or erase all his great "Errata" (43).

The *Autobiography* is indeed structured around Franklin's recollection of five "Errata," as he calls them, all of which he claims to
have put right as best he could. The breaking of his indentures with
his brother James is "the first errata of my life," which he partially

---

7. Plato, *Theaetetus* in *The Dialogues of Plato*, trans. and ed. J. Jowett, 2nd ed. (Oxford:
   Clarendon Press, 1875), 4.345–46; William Shakespeare, *The Tragedie of Hamlet* (1623),
   2.2.167–68; John Locke, *An Essay Concerning Human Understanding*, ed. Peter Nid-
   ditch (Oxford: Oxford UP, 1975), 104; Sigmund Freud, "Notes on a Mystic Writing Pad,"
   The Standard Edition, trans. and ed. James Strachey et al. (London: Hogarth Press and
   the Institute of Psychoanalysis, 1953–73), 29.227. See also Jocelyn Penny Small, *Wax
   Tablets of the Mind: Cognitive Studies of Memory and Literacy in Classical Antiquity* (London: Routledge, 1997); Mary Carruthers, *The Book of Memory: A Study of Memory in
   Medieval Culture* (Cambridge: Cambridge UP, 1990); Juliet Fleming, *Graffiti and the
   Writing Arts of Early Modern England* (Philadelphia: U of Pennsylvania P, 2000); and
   Jacques Derrida, "Freud and the Scene of Writing," in *Writing and Difference*, trans.
   Alan Bass (Chicago: U of Chicago P, 1978).
8. Quoted in L. H. Butterfield, "B. Franklin's Epitaph," *New Colophon* 3 (1950),
   fig. 2 and 12–14. Butterfield gives the most complete account of Franklin's epitaph.

corrects by taking on his brother's son as an apprentice after James's death. The second erratum is frittering away money that he had been given by a friend of his brother John to repay a debt. "The breaking into this money of Vernon's," Franklin writes, "was one of the first great errata of my life," but many years later Franklin "paid the principal with interest, and many thanks; so that erratum was in some degree corrected." His third erratum was the effective breaking of his engagement with Deborah Read by not responding to her letters when he was in England. But, he writes, "I took her to wife, September 1st, 1730" and "Thus I corrected that great erratum as well as I could." His fourth erratum was printing his free-thinking pamphlet, "A Dissertation on Liberty and Necessity, Pleasure and Pain," when he was an apprentice in England, an erratum that was only partly corrected by the small number of copies that he printed and by his attempts to recall them. The fifth and final erratum that he records also took place while he was an apprentice in London, when he attempted to seduce the mistress of his friend James Ralph. Franklin does not pretend that he was able to "correct" this error.

The correction of printed errata was central to Franklin's successful attempt to displace both of his rival printers in Philadelphia. His first rival was his former employer, Samuel Keimer, but Keimer knew "nothing of Presswork," according to Franklin, and so was easily displaced (31). Andrew Bradford, his other rival, posed a more serious problem, not least because he was employed to do the lucrative government printing for Pennsylvania. Franklin outmaneuvered Bradford by exposing the superior quality and accuracy of his own printing. As James Green writes, "In 1729 Franklin rather deviously finagled away the job of printing the Assembly's votes and laws by 'elegantly and correctly' reprinting a document that Bradford had printed in a 'coarse blundering manner.' . . . He sent one to every member of the Assembly. 'They were sensible of the Difference, it strengthen'd the Hands of our Friends in the House, and they voted us their Printers for the Year ensuing.'"[9] The "correct" printing that Franklin did for the government was supplemented by the accuracy of the blank forms that he now began to sell at his own stationer's shop. With the aid of his Junto friend Joseph Breintnall, "a Copier of Deeds for the Scriveners," Franklin was able to print legal forms "of all Sorts, the correctest that ever appear'd among us" (57, 64).

But Franklin also deliberately printed errata when it suited his purposes. Mocking the Massachusetts governor, Jonathan Belcher, Franklin published in his *Pennsylvania Gazette* the deliberate misprint that Belcher had "died," rather than "dined," at Pontack's, "a

9. James N. Green and Peter Stallybrass, *Benjamin Franklin, Printer and Writer* (New Castle, Del.: Oak Knoll, the Library Company of Philadelphia, and the British Library, 2006), 37.

noted Tavern and Eating-House in London for Gentlemen of Condition."[1] Capitalizing on his "misprint," Franklin went on to publish an "apology" on printers' errors. The essay gave Franklin the opportunity to bring together for satiric purposes some of the most famous biblical misprints, which had transformed "I am fearfully and wonderfully made" into "I am fearfully and wonderfully *mad*," "We shall all be changed in a moment" into "We shall all be *hanged* in a moment," and, most famously, "Thou shalt not commit Adultery" into "Thou *shalt* commit Adultery."[2] Here, even as Franklin attacked the colonial government, he employed the language of printers' errata and corrections that he would use throughout his life.

In fact, Franklin took justifiable pride in the accuracy of his printing, which required the catching and correcting of errata. The usual practices of correcting a printed text can be crudely divided up into the following:

1. Stop-press corrections, in which corrections are made during the printing of the text
2. The addition of a printed errata sheet at the beginning or end of a book
3. Manuscript corrections of the printed text, made either in the printing house (to all copies when possible) or by the reader
4. The correction of an earlier edition for a later "new and revised" edition

Franklin used all of these methods to correct both other people's texts and his own. When Benjamin Vaughan was working on his edition of Franklin's *Political, Miscellaneous, and Philosophical Pieces*, he consulted Franklin on every detail when Franklin was living in London.[3] And when Franklin returned to America, Vaughan sent him a copy of his edition for approval. Franklin responded on 9 November 1779, praising Vaughan for "the great Care & Pains you have taken in regulating & correcting the Edition of those Papers." But he nevertheless could not refrain from pointing out further errata: "I have noted some Faults of Impression that hurt the Sense, and some other little Matters, which you will find all in a Sheet under the title of Errata. You can best judge whether it may be worth while to add any of them to the Errata already printed, or whether it may not be as well to reserve the whole for Correction in another Edition, if such should ever be."[4] Vaughan proceeded to add eight pages of "Addenda & Corrigenda" to his edition. But it is clear that Franklin's

1. *Pennsylvania Gazette*, 19 February 1730.
2. *The Papers of Benjamin Franklin*, ed. Leonard W. Labaree et al. (New Haven: Yale UP, 1959–), 1.169.
3. Benjamin Franklin, *Political, Miscellaneous, and Philosophical Pieces* [ed. Benjamin Vaughan] (London: Printed for J. Johnson, 1779).
4. *The Papers of Benjamin Franklin*, 31:57–58.

own preference was for "another Edition," in which the eight pages of errata would have been incorporated into a corrected text.

I argued above that Franklin was unusual in primarily taking printing, rather than writing, as a model for correcting the errata of his own life. But it is worth noting that by the end of his life Franklin was beginning to use a new technology for "printing" manuscripts, thus partially overcoming any simple opposition between the two. The new technology not only eliminated the slow process of copying out a manuscript by hand, but also produced an exact copy of the original manuscript. "Press copies," as they were called, were the precursors of photocopies in that they allowed you to duplicate a text without recopying it.[5] They were made by dampening the original written page when the ink was still relatively fresh and pressing a thin sheet of paper onto it. ("Press" copies were so called not because of any relation to the printing-press but because of the pressure employed to make the copy.) Under pressure, the original manuscript leaves a reversed image of the text on the thin sheet. The paper made for the duplicate was so thin that when you turned the sheet over to unreverse the image, you could read the text (now on the other side of the sheet) through the paper. By the nineteenth century, press copies were being made on a large scale for keeping records of business correspondence.

Franklin's whole family, though, had already been experimenting with press copies in the 1780s. In 1781, Franklin's grandson, William Temple Franklin, wrote to Jonathan Williams:

> Your Copying Machine, in two Cases and a Ream of thin Paper, forming a Packet are . . . being sent you to Nantes. You had better be yourself at the unpacking of them; & you should open the large Flatt Box, where you will [find] a little Book which you should read before you continue to unpack. (As to the wetting Book & drying Book, which you will [hear] often mentioned, they have not sent us any over: I imagine they are a seperate Expence and are only sent when order'd. We have done however very well without them, by means of a Quire of Spungy Paper, called I believe, Papier Joseph, 3 of which we open, & lay in it the thin Paper which is to receive the Impression, then daub it over with the wet Brush, shut the Quire & press it with your hands which soaks up all the superfluous Moisture & leaves the thin paper for Use. This we call our Wetting Book): & we have a similar Quire which we call our drying Book, wherein we lay the Papers after they have received the

5. On the development of press copies, see Barbara Rhodes and William Wells Streeter, *Before Photocopying: The Art and History of Mechanical Copying, 1780–1938* (New Castle, Del.: Oak Knoll Press, 1999). I am deeply indebted to James Green for drawing my attention to the significance of press copies.

Impression, & put the weight upon it. If when you take them out of the drying Book, you do not [find] them smooth, you can soon make them so by putting them singly in a sheet of the same Spungy Paper, & passing them through your Press. Mr: Le Veillard will deliver to you among other Pacquets, one containing Ink Powder proper for Copying: But I [think] the common Ink does as well. The Proprieters say that it will not keep its Colour as well as theirs.[6]

Temple Franklin had already discovered what most modern historians of press copies are still unaware of: namely, that the makers' claims for "Ink Powder proper for Copying" were greatly exaggerated; "common ink does as well."

Benjamin Franklin himself used this new technology in 1789 to make two duplicates of parts two and three of his autobiography, which he sent to Louis Guillaume Le Veillard in France and Benjamin Vaughan in England in 1789.[7] He thus not only spared his other grandson, Benjamin Franklin Bache, the trouble of copying out these parts of the autobiography twice, but also eliminated the introduction of errors in the process of copying, a particular danger in this case since Bache was "a miserable copyist."[8]

But if press copies helped to overcome the introduction of new errata, they did not touch the problem of how to correct and revise the first draft of a manuscript. Here again, Franklin came up with an innovative solution when he sat down to write his autobiography. Before writing, he first folded each sheet of paper vertically, so as to create two columns, and he then wrote only in one of the columns, leaving the other column blank for later corrections, revisions, and additions [see p. xvi, above]. This made it easier, if not easy, for later copyists (and eventually, editors) to decipher a much-corrected manuscript, since the corrections and additions did not have to be squeezed in between lines or into narrow margins.

All of these attempted solutions to correct printed or manuscript texts, however, presume that there is a text that you want to preserve in the first place. That is, they are all in one way or another technologies of memory. But Franklin employed his ivory memorandum book for a radically different purpose: as a technology whose fulfillment would be total erasure and forgetfulness. For the table of virtue is in fact a record of failures. As those failures are corrected, the table should become progressively empty and finally blank, with

6. William Temple Franklin, Letter to Jonathan Williams Jr., 20 February 1781, Library of Congress, Franklin Papers 02/20/1781.
7. J. A. Leo Lemay and P. M. Zall, "Introduction," *The Autobiography of Benjamin Franklin: A Genetic Text* (Knoxville: University of Tennessee Press, 1981), xli–xlii and xlvi.
8. Ibid., xlii.

no more faults to remember and record. The virtues of this system of erasure as a writing technology suggested to Franklin a radical perfectionism of life.

But by making erasure and correction so easy, the ivory notebook revealed by contrast how interminable was the process of moral correction. And Franklin's "exceeding good Memory" posed a further problem. He remembered too much. Indeed, to record all of his faults would have meant his failure as a printer: "My Scheme of ORDER, gave me the most Trouble, and I found, that tho' it might be practicable where a Man's Business was such as to leave him the Disposition of his Time, that of a Journeyman Printer for instance, it was not possible to be exactly observ'd by a Master, who must mix with the World, and often receive People of Business at their own Hours" [84]. Franklin goes on to compare himself to a man who takes his axe to be sharpened and polished. Growing tired of the long wait to have his axe made as good as new, he takes it back, deciding that "*a speckled Axe was best*" (84; Franklin's emphasis).

The irony of Franklin's attempt at reformation is that it leads him to find good reasons for *not* reforming. He begins to think "that such extreme Nicety as I exacted of myself might be a kind of Foppery in Morals, which if it were known would make me ridiculous; that a perfect Character might be attended with the Inconvenience of being envied and hated; and that a benevolent Man should allow a few Faults in himself, to keep his Friends in Countenance" (84, 86). Franklin's ivory memorandum book conspicuously failed to provide him with a model for living or even for the writing of his autobiography. In the same passage that describes the technology for erasable writing that allowed him to wipe away all faults with the greatest of ease, Franklin deliberately introduces errata as the required "Faults" of a "benevolent Man."

Benjamin Franklin:
A Chronology

1706 Born January 17 (January 6, 1705, Old Style) in Boston to Josiah and Abiah Folger Franklin, Josiah's second wife.

1714–16 Attends Boston Grammar School (one year) and George Brownell's English school (one year); withdraws when his father can no longer afford school fees.

1718(?) Apprenticed to brother James, Boston printer; writes earliest work, a street ballad.

1721 James Franklin begins newspaper, the *New-England Courant*.

1722 Benjamin Franklin writes fourteen letters, under the alias Silence Dogood, printed in *New-England Courant*.

1723 While imprisoned by Massachusetts Assembly for printing challenges to local authorities, James prints his newspaper under Benjamin's name.

1723 Benjamin Franklin abandons his apprenticeship and flees to New York City in search of work; continues to Philadelphia, where he arrives on October 6 and is hired as journeyman printer to Samuel Keimer.

1724 Takes passage to London with James Ralph and Thomas Denham; works in printing offices of Palmer and Watts.

1725 Writes and prints *A Dissertation on Liberty and Necessity*.

1726 Departs London; keeps journal of ship's passage and outlines a "Plan of Conduct." Arrives in Philadelphia October 11; works for Denham as clerk.

1727 Nearly dies of pleurisy; Denham dies. Returns to work for Keimer. With friends, forms the Junto.

1728 Starts printing business with Hugh Meredith.

1729 Writes "Busy-Body" essays and pamphlet on paper currency; buys Keimer's failed *Pennsylvania Gazette*.

1730   Franklin and Meredith appointed printers to Pennsylvania Assembly; Franklin dissolves partnership with Meredith. Enters common-law marriage with Deborah Read Rogers. Possible year of birth of William Franklin, mother unknown.

1731   Writes "Apology for Printers." Joins Freemasons and becomes junior warden of St. John's Lodge. Forms Library Company of Philadelphia.

SECOND PART OF THE *AUTOBIOGRAPHY*

1732   Francis Folger Franklin born; first *Poor Richard: An Almanack* published (for 1733).

1733   Conceives of his "bold and arduous Project of arriving at moral Perfection."

THIRD PART OF THE *AUTOBIOGRAPHY*

1734   Elected Grand Master of Freemasons in Philadelphia.

1735   Controversy over the Reverend Samuel Hemphill.

1736   Appointed clerk of Pennsylvania Assembly. Son Francis dies. Forms Union Fire Company.

1737   Appointed postmaster at Philadelphia (serves until 1753).

1738   Scandal over mock Masonic initiation ritual.

1739   The Reverend George Whitefield's first visit to Philadelphia.

1741   Publishes *The General Magazine*.

1743   Publishes *Proposal for Promoting Useful Knowledge*, basis for the American Philosophical Society. Meets Archibald Spencer and witnesses his electrical experiments in Boston. Daughter Sarah born.

1744   Publishes *An Account of the New-Invented Pennsylvanian Fire-Places*.

1745   Receives instruments for and account of electrical experiments.

1747   Publishes *Plain Truth*; association formed for defense of Pennsylvania. Also publishes "The Speech of Miss Polly Baker" and reports on electrical experiments.

1748   Forms eighteen-year printing partnership with David Hall and retires from the business. Elected to Philadelphia Common Council.

1749   Appointed justice of the peace for Philadelphia, Provincial Grand Master of Masons of Pennsylvania. Publishes *Proposals Relating to the Education of Youth in Pensilvania*; elected president of trustees of Academy of

Philadelphia (later Academy and College of Philadelphia; now the University of Pennsylvania). Continues as president to 1756 and trustee to his death.

1750   Proposes experiment to identify lightning as electricity.

1751   *Experiments and Observations on Electricity* published in London. Pennsylvania Hospital chartered. Elected member of Assembly from Philadelphia; elected alderman of the city. Publishes *Observations Concerning the Increase of Mankind*.

1752   Fire insurance company founded. *Experiments and Observations* translated and published in Paris; Dalibard performs Franklin's lightning experiment. Franklin performs kite experiment in Philadelphia (reported in October).

1753   Receives honorary A.M. degree from Harvard and honorary M.A. degree from Yale. Publishes second edition (with new experiments) of *Experiments and Observations on Electricity*. Appointed deputy-postmaster general of North America (jointly with William Hunter). Invests in scheme to discover Northwest Passage. Awarded Copley Medal of Royal Society of London.

1754   Attends Albany Congress; proposes a Plan of Union. Publishes third edition of *Experiments and Observations on Electricity*.

1755   Supplies General Braddock with wagons and provisions during French and Indian War; supports proposal to tax Pennsylvania proprietors (Penn family). Elected president of Managers of Pennsylvania Hospital.

1756   Commands troops and builds forts on western frontier. Commissioned colonel of Philadelphia militia. Receives honorary M.A. from College of William and Mary; elected fellow of the Royal Society.

1757   Appointed Assembly agent in London. En route, observes effect of oil on water; writes "Speech of Father Abraham," the preface to *Poor Richard* for 1758, later known as "The Way to Wealth."

FOURTH PART OF THE *AUTOBIOGRAPHY*

1757   Lodges with Margaret Stevenson in Craven Street; commences business as colonial agent.

YEARS NOT COVERED IN THE *AUTOBIOGRAPHY*

1758   While in London, begins to associate with important and influential Britons. Invents damper for his improved fireplace. Tours England with son William.

1759   Tours Scotland; receives honorary L.L.D. from University of Saint Andrews, granted freedom of the cities of Edinburgh and Glasgow and the burgh of Saint Andrews; forms friendships with Scottish men of letters, including Kames and Hume.

1760   Publishes *The Interest of Great Britain Considered* (the "Canada Pamphlet"). Assembly agents win right to tax proprietary estates, though only under certain legal circumstances. Takes seat on Council of Royal Society (serves again in 1765, 1766, 1772). Tours England.

1761   Tours Flanders and Holland with Richard Jackson and son William; returns to see coronation procession of George III.

1762   Receives honorary D.C.L. degree from Oxford University (William receives honorary M.A.); describes his newly invented glass armonica. Sails from Portsmouth for Philadelphia (arrives November 1); son William marries Elizabeth Downes and is commissioned royal governor of New Jersey.

1763   Work begins on new house in Philadelphia. Tours Virginia, New Jersey, New York, and New England on post-office business. Seven Years' War ends with the Treaty of Paris.

1764   Publishes *A Narrative of the Late Massacres*, criticizing frontier attacks on Indians, and *Cool Thoughts*, recommending that king assume power over Pennsylvania in place of proprietors. Elected speaker of the Assembly but then defeated in reelection to Assembly (only electoral defeat in his public career). Appointed Assembly agent for England; sails in November and makes observations of Gulf Stream; arrives in London and resumes lodging at Craven Street.

1765   Confers with British ministry on proposed Stamp Act.

1766   Publishes newspaper pieces recommending repeal of Stamp Act. Questioned before House of Commons. (Stamp Act repealed; Declaratory Act passed.) Tours Germany with Sir John Pringle, Queen's physician; both men elected members of the Royal Society of Sciences at Göttingen.

1767   Publishes multiple pieces criticizing British ministers. Visits Paris with Pringle; meets French men of science (Dubourg, the Le Roys, Mirabeau, Quesnay) and Horace Walpole; presented to Louis XV. Daughter Sarah marries Richard Bache.

1768   Continues to publish newspaper pieces on colonial affairs. Appointed agent of Georgia Colony. Develops phonetic alphabet and spelling. Dines with King Christian VII of Denmark.

1769   Elected president of American Philosophical Society (reelected annually until his death). Publishes fourth edition of *Experiments and Observations on Electricity*. Organizes land company (Vandalia) for Ohio Valley. Tours France. Appointed agent of New Jersey House of Representatives.

1770   Appointed agent for Massachusetts House of Representatives.

1771   Acrimonious interview with Lord Hillsborough over his commission as agent for Massachusetts. Elected to Batavian Society of Experimental Science. Visits Twyford, home of Bishop Shipley; writes first part of the *Autobiography*. Tours Ireland and Scotland.

1772   Vandalia Land Company receives charter (but territory never conveyed). Tours northwest England. Publishes "The Sommersett Case and the Slave Trade." Elected to French Academy of Sciences (one of only eight foreign members); drafts Royal Society report for Board of Ordnance on protecting gunpowder magazines from lightning. Sends "Hutchinson letters" to the Massachusetts Committee of Correspondence.

1773   Warns ministry of likely colonial opposition to Tea Act; publishes "Rules by Which a Great Empire May be Reduced to a Small One" and "Edict by the King of Prussia." French translation of enlarged edition of his scientific writings published in Paris. Conducts experiments on oil spread upon water.

1774   Called before Privy Council Committee; roundly attacked by Solicitor General Wedderburn for role in "Hutchinson letters"; dismissed as deputy postmaster general. Publishes fifth and final edition of *Experiments and Observations*. Confers with Lord Chatham on American crisis; recommends Thomas Paine to friends in Philadelphia. Deborah Franklin dies.

1775   Returns to Philadelphia; on the way, writes "An Account of Negotiations in London" and makes further observations of the Gulf Stream. Chosen delegate to Second Continental Congress; serves on several committees; submits draft of Articles of Confederation; elected postmaster general.

1776   Visits Montreal on four-man mission to convince Francophone Canadians to support movement for independence. Son William removed from position as governor of New Jersey and placed under house arrest. Serves on committee to draft Declaration of Independence. Elected commissioner to France; sails in October, accompanied by two grandsons, William Temple Franklin (sixteen years old) and Benjamin Franklin Bache (seven); reaches Paris in December.

1777　　Celebrated in France; attends French Academy of Science; elected to Royal Medical Society. Settles in Passy between Paris and Versailles; sets up private press. Appointed commissioner to Spain.

1778　　After American victory at Saratoga, secures treaties of alliance and support from France; formally presented to Louis XVI; joined by John Adams as commissioner. Sponsors Voltaire's initiation into Masonic Lodge of the Nine Sisters; participates in Voltaire's Masonic funeral.

1779　　Receives appointment as sole minister plenipotentiary. Issues letters to warships to honor free passage of Captain James Cook's scientific expedition. Writes essay on aurora borealis; *Political, Miscellaneous, and Philosophical Pieces* published in London. Granted major French loan to the United States.

1780　　Voted medal from Royal Society for his letters regarding Captain Cook. Deterioration of health. Negotiates new French loan.

1781　　Among five men appointed by Congress to act as peace commissioners; Cornwallis surrenders to Washington at Yorktown, Virginia. Franklin offers his resignation.

1782　　Opens peace negotiations with British; later joined by other commissioners; keeps journal of negotiations as of May 9.

1783　　Treaty of Paris signed. Arranges publication of American State Constitutions in France; reports on French balloon ascensions.

1784　　Formal ratification of peace treaty; Franklin renews request to resign. Writes Part Two of the *Autobiography*.

1785　　Released from appointment as minister to France (Thomas Jefferson succeeding); leaves Passy with grandsons; visits London and son William; writes "Maritime Observations," "On the Causes and Cure of Smoky Chimneys," and "Description of a New Stove" on the way to Philadelphia. Arrives in September to great acclaim; elected to Supreme Executive Council of Pennsylvania, then as its president.

1786　　Builds addition to house.

1787   Named president of the Pennsylvania Society for Pro-
        moting the Abolition of Slavery. Elected to Federal Con-
        stitutional Convention; moves acceptance of "Great
        Compromise," making representation in House depen-
        dent on population and representation in the Senate
        equal among states. Allows publication of final Conven-
        tion speech.

1788   Writes last will and testament; begins writing Part Three
        of his *Autobiography*. Retires as president of Supreme
        Executive Council of Pennsylvania (end of formal public
        service).

1789   Drafts codicil to will. Writes and signs first protest
        against slavery addressed to Congress. Elected to Rus-
        sian Imperial Academy of Sciences. Sends copies of the
        three parts of his *Autobiography* to friends in France
        and England.

1790   As president of Pennsylvania Abolition Society, peti-
        tions Congress for the abolition of slave trade and slav-
        ery; writes Part Four of his *Autobiography* and his final
        essay, the account of Sidi Mehemet Ibrahim (final
        pseudonym) on the slave trade; final public act in letter
        to Thomas Jefferson on northeast boundary of the
        United States. Dies at age 84 years, three months; bur-
        ied in Christ Church cemetery beside wife Deborah and
        son Francis.

Selected Bibliography

· indicates works excerpted in this Norton Critical Edition.

Amelang, James S. *The Flight of Icarus: Artisan Autobiography in Early Modern Europe*. Stanford: Stanford University Press, 1998.

Anderson, Douglas. *The Radical Enlightenments of Benjamin Franklin*. Baltimore: Johns Hopkins University Press, 1997.

Arch, Stephen Carl. *After Franklin: The Emergence of Autobiography in Post-Revolutionary America, 1780–1830*. Hanover, N.H.: University Press of New England, 2001.

Banes, Ruth A. "The Exemplary Self: Autobiography in Eighteenth-Century America," *Biography* 5, no. 3 (1982): 226–39.

Bercovitch, Sacvan. *The Puritan Origins of the American Self*. New Haven: Yale University Press, 1975.

Bredvold, Louis I. "The Invention of the Ethical Calculus," in *The Seventeenth Century*, ed. Richard Foster Jones et al. Stanford: Stanford University Press, 1951.

Breitwieser, Mitchell. *Cotton Mather and Benjamin Franklin: The Price of Representative Personality*. New York: Cambridge University Press, 1984.

Bruss, Elizabeth W. *Autobiographical Acts: The Changing Situation of a Literary Genre*. Baltimore: Johns Hopkins University Press, 1976.

Bushman, Richard L. *The Refinement of America: Persons, Houses, Cities*. New York: Knopf, 1992.

Buxbaum, Melvin H. *Benjamin Franklin: A Reference Guide*. 2 vols. Boston: G.K. Hall, 1983–1988.

Chaplin, Joyce E. *Benjamin Franklin's Political Arithmetic: A Materialist View of Humanity*. Washington, D.C.: Smithsonian Institute, 2009.

———. *The First Scientific American: Benjamin Franklin and the Pursuit of Genius*. New York: Basic Books, 2006.

Cohen, I. Bernard. *Benjamin Franklin's Science*. Cambridge, Mass.: Harvard University Press, 1990.

———. *Franklin and Newton: An Inquiry into Speculative Newtonian Experimental Science and Franklin's Work in Electricity as an Example Thereof*. Philadelphia: American Philosophical Society, 1956.

· ———, ed. *Benjamin Franklin's Experiments: A New Edition of Franklin's Experiments and Observations on Electricity*. Cambridge, Mass.: Harvard University Press, 1941.

Conner, Paul W. *Poor Richard's Politicks: Benjamin Franklin and His New American Order*. New York: Oxford University Press, 1965.

Darnton, Robert. *The Devil in the Holy Water, or the Art of Slander from Louis XIV to Napoleon*. Philadelphia: University of Pennsylvania Press, 2010.

Dawson, Hugh. "Fathers and Sons: Franklin's 'Memoirs' as Myth and Metaphor," *Early American Literature* 14, no. 3 (1979/80): 269–92.

Delbourgo, James. *A Most Amazing Scene of Wonders: Electricity and Enlightenment in Early America*. Cambridge, Mass.: Harvard University Press, 2006.

Dull, Jonathan R. *A Diplomatic History of the American Revolution*. New Haven: Yale University Press, 1985.

Elias, Norbert. *The Civilizing Process*, trans. Edmund Jephcott. Oxford: Blackwell, 1994.

Elliott, Emory. "New England Puritan Literature: Personal Narrative and History," in *The Cambridge History of American Literature*, vol. 1, *1590–1820*, ed. Sacvan Bercovitch. Cambridge: Cambridge University Press, 1994.

Fiering, Norman S. "Benjamin Franklin and the Way to Virtue." *American Quarterly* 30, no. 2 (1978): 199–223.

Fortune, Brandon Brame, with Deborah J. Warner. *Franklin and His Friends: Portraying the Man of Science in Eighteenth-Century America*. Washington, D.C.: Smithsonian National Portrait Gallery, 1999.

Gilbert, Felix. "The Humanist Concept of the Prince and the Prince of Machiavelli." *Journal of Modern History* 11, no. 4 (1939): 449–83.

Granger, Bruce Ingham. *Benjamin Franklin: An American Man of Letters*. Ithaca, N.Y.: Cornell University Press, 1964.

Green, James N. and Peter Stallybrass. *Benjamin Franklin: Writer and Printer*. Newcastle, Del.: Oak Knoll Press, 2006.

Greenblatt, Stephen J. *Renaissance Self-Fashioning: From More to Shakespeare*. Chicago: University of Chicago Press, 1980.

Houston, Alan. "Benjamin Franklin and the 'Wagon Affair' of 1755." *William and Mary Quarterly*, 3d ser., 66 (2009): 235–86.

Huang, Nian-Sheng. *Benjamin Franklin in American Thought and Culture, 1790–1938*. Philadelphia: American Philosophical Society, 1994.

———. "From the 'Fur Cap' to Poor Richard: The Chinese Connection." *Proceedings of the American Philosophical Society* 150, no. 2 (2006): 205–40.

Hunter, Christopher. "From Print to Print: The First Complete Edition of Benjamin Franklin's *Autobiography*." *The Papers of the Bibliographical Society of America* 101 (2007): 481–505.

Hutson, James H. *Pennsylvania Politics, 1746–1770: The Movement for Royal Government and Its Consequences*. Princeton: Princeton University Press, 1972.

Imbarrato, Susan Clair. *Declarations of Independency in Eighteenth-Century American Autobiography*. Knoxville: University of Tennessee Press, 1998.

Inglis, Fred. *A Short History of Celebrity*. Princeton: Princeton University Press, 2010.

Kammen, Michael G. *A Rope of Sand: The Colonial Agents, British Politics, and the American Revolution*. Ithaca, N.Y.: Cornell University Press, 1968.

• Labaree, Leonard W., et al., eds. *The Papers of Benjamin Franklin*. 40 vols. to date. New Haven: Yale University Press, 1959–.

Lambert, Frank. *"Pedlar in Divinity": George Whitefield and the Transatlantic Revivals, 1737–1770*. Princeton: Princeton University Press, 1994.

• Lawrence, D. H. "Benjamin Franklin," in *Studies in Classic American Literature*. New York: T. Seltzer, 1923.

Lemay, J. A. Leo. "Poe's 'The Business Man': Its Contexts and Satire of Franklin's *Autobiography*." *Poe Studies* 15, no. 2 (1982): 29–37.

———. *The Renaissance Man in the Eighteenth Century*. Los Angeles: William Andrews Clark Memorial Library, 1978.

Lemay, J. A. Leo, and P. M. Zall, eds. *The Autobiography of Benjamin Franklin: A Genetic Text*. Knoxville: University of Tennessee Press, 1981.

• Levin, David. "The Autobiography of Benjamin Franklin: The Puritan Experimenter in Life and Art." *Yale Review* 53 (1964): 258–75.

Lopez, Claude Anne. *Mon Cher Papa: Franklin and the Ladies of Paris*. New Haven: Yale University Press, 1966.

——— and Eugenia W. Herbert. *The Private Franklin: The Man and His Family*. New York: W. W. Norton, 1975.

• Maugham, W. Somerset. "The Classic Books of America." *Saturday Evening Post* 212 (January 6, 1940): 29, 64–66.

Middlekauff, Robert. *Benjamin Franklin and His Enemies*. Berkeley: University of California Press, 1996.

Miller, C. William. *Benjamin Franklin's Philadelphia Printing, 1728–1766: A Descriptive Bibliography*. Philadelphia: American Philosophical Society, 1974.

Mulford, Carla. "Figuring Benjamin Franklin in American Cultural Memory." *New England Quarterly* 71 (1999): 415–43.

Nash, Gary B. "Up from the Bottom in Franklin's Philadelphia." *Past and Present* 77, no. 1 (1977): 57–83.

Olney, James. *Metaphors of Self: The Meaning of Autobiography*. Princeton: Princeton University Press, 1972.

———, ed. *Autobiography: Essays Theoretical and Critical*. Princeton: Princeton University Press, 1980.

Paul, Jay. *Being in the Text: Self-Representation from Wordsworth to Roland Barthes*. Ithaca, N.Y.: Cornell University Press, 1984.

Riskin, Jessica. *Science in the Age of Sensibility: The Sentimental Empiricists of the French Enlightenment*. Chicago: University of Chicago Press, 2002.

Rzepka, Charles J. *The Self as Mind: Vision and Identity in Wordsworth, Coleridge, and Keats*. Cambridge, Mass.: Harvard University Press, 1986.

Sanford, Charles L. "An American Pilgrim's Progress." *American Quarterly* 6, no. 4 (1954): 297–310.

Sayre, Robert F. *The Examined Self: Benjamin Franklin, Henry Adams, Henry James*. Princeton: Princeton University Press, 1964.

Sellers, Charles Coleman. *Benjamin Franklin in Portraiture*. New Haven: Yale University Press, 1962.

Shea, Daniel B. *Spiritual Autobiography in Early America*. Princeton: Princeton University Press, 1968.

• Smyth, Albert H., ed. *The Writings of Benjamin Franklin*. 10 vols. New York: Macmillan, 1905–07.

• Stallybrass, Peter. "Benjamin Franklin: Printed Corrections and Erasable Writing." *Proceedings of the American Philosophical Society* 150, no. 4 (2006): 553–67.

Stourzh, Gerald. *Benjamin Franklin and American Foreign Policy*. Chicago: University of Chicago Press, 1954.

Tise, Larry E., ed. *Benjamin Franklin and Women*. University Park: Pennsylvania State University Press, 2000.

Tourtellot, Arthur Bernon. *Benjamin Franklin: The Shaping of Genius—The Boston Years*. Garden City, N.Y.: Doubleday, 1977.

Van Doren, Carl. *Benjamin Franklin*. New York: Viking Press, 1938.

———, ed. *Benjamin Franklin's Autobiographical Writings*. New York: Viking Press, 1945.

Waldstreicher, David. *Runaway America: Benjamin Franklin, Slavery, and the American Revolution*. New York: Hill and Wang, 2004.

• Warner, Michael. *The Letters of the Republic: Publication and the Public Sphere in Eighteenth-Century America*. Cambridge, Mass.: Harvard University Press, 1990.

• Weber, Max. *The Protestant Ethic and the Spirit of Capitalism*. Trans. Talcott Parsons, with a Foreword by R. H. Tawney. London: G. Allen & Unwin, Ltd., 1930.

Wolf, Edwin, II, and Kevin J. Hayes. *The Library of Benjamin Franklin*. Philadelphia: American Philosophical Society and Library Company of Philadelphia, 2006.

Wright, Louis B. "Franklin's Legacy to the Gilded Age." *Virginia Quarterly Review* 22 (1946): 268–79.

Zall, P[aul] M. "The Manuscript and Early Printed Texts of Franklin's 'Autobiography.'" *Huntington Library Quarterly* 39 (1976): 375–384.

———. *Franklin's Autobiography: A Model Life*. Boston: Twayne Publishers, 1989.

Index